LOOKING FOR TROUBLE

LOOKING FOR TROUBLE

A journalist's life...and then some

Peter Worthington

KEY PORTER·BOOKS

For
Lewis Feuer, whose idea it was . . .
My wife Yvonne, who cracked the whip . . .
John Bassett, who paid for most of the "research"

Copyright © 1984 by Key Porter Books

Canadian Cataloguing in Publication Data
Worthington, Peter, 1927-
   Looking for trouble

Includes index.
ISBN 0-919493-36-X

1. Worthington, Peter, 1927-   2. Journalists—
Ontario—Biography.   3. Foreign correspondents—
Biography.   I. Title.

PN4913.W67A36 1984   070.4′092′4   C84-098583-5

Key Porter Books
70 The Esplanade
Toronto, Ontario
Canada   M5E 1R2

Design: Don Fernley
Typesetting: Q Composition
Printing and Binding: T.H. Best Printing Company Ltd.
Printed and bound in Canada

84 85 86 87   6 5 4 3 2 1

Contents

Foreword

"Who will you be sending to Ishmaelia?" asked Mrs. Stitch.
"I am in consultation with my editors on the subject. We think it
a very promising little war. A microcosm, as you might say, of
world drama. We propose to give it full publicity."

Lord Copper
Scoop, Evelyn Waugh

It was early February 1978 and I was sitting at the video display terminal in my *Sun* office, writing a column about *Soldier of Fortune* magazine and its curious assortment of advertisements for knives, guns and weapons for killing. I had just finished when a message flashed on the screen that I had committed an "error." The computer system was about to "crash" and my story would be killed. I would have to start again from scratch.

I suddenly realized sweat had broken out on my forehead and upper lip. A cold sweat. I wasn't the slightest bit hot. Then I noticed the constriction in my chest—not great pain but a wrenching, squeezing, uncomfortable feeling. I didn't dare move for fear of making the pain worse. I noticed that my left arm was aching up and down, from armpit to fingertips.

"Oh God," I thought. "A heart attack."

I had had a somewhat debatable heart attack three months earlier, on returning from Edmonton where *Sun* publisher Doug Creighton, general manager Don Hunt and I, as editor-in-chief, had held a press conference to announce we were going to start a second paper in that city the following spring.

I had returned to Toronto on the weekend, tired from the awkward two-hour time-zone change. I had made an exotic fish soup for supper and gone to bed early on Sunday, feeling lethargic.

At 1 A.M. I was breathing strangely and my wife Yvonne tried to wake me but couldn't. I appeared to be unconscious, then stopped breathing, eyes wide open and staring. She thought I was dead and phoned the police and ambulance, but just before they arrived I returned to the land of the living. I recall Yvonne's anxious voice calling me from a great distance and our two dogs, Jack Russell terriers named Felix and Lucy, licking my face and wondering what the new game was. I had fallen out of bed.

I didn't argue when the ambulance men insisted that I go to hospital. Yvonne followed in the car and when the ambulance suddenly and inexplicably stopped on Mount Pleasant Road en route to Wellesley Hospital, she thought: "He's dead. They must be trying to revive him. Oh, dear God, don't let him die."

In fact I wasn't dead. True, I wasn't feeling so hot, but the two ambulance attendants were cheerful. "Say," said the driver, "aren't you the guy who runs the *Sun*?"

"Yes."

"Can you decide who'll be Sunshine Boys?"

"I guess so."

"Hey—" he pulled the ambulance over to the side, stopped and wheeled around in his seat, looking back at me on the stretcher "—can you make the two of us Sunshine Boys?"

"Possibly. Can we talk about it later?"

"That's great. We'll give you our names. When do you think you can get our pictures in?"

"Maybe I should get to the hospital first . . ."

"Oh yeah. We'll be in touch. You won't forget, will you?"

"Believe me, I won't forget. Can we hurry?"

"Relax. We've seen plenty of heart attacks, and you haven't had one. Don't worry." And we continued the drive to the hospital.

As it turned out, they never called to have themselves portrayed in the semi-naked, macho pose that was the *Sun*'s popular feature. And they were wrong about the heart attack: I *had* had one, though for a while I tried to blame it on the fish soup.

As a result of further tests, cardiologist Dr. Gary Webb recommended bypass surgery. I reluctantly agreed. Having felt no pain, I was skeptical about the diagnosis. I was in good shape, not overweight, didn't smoke, drank sparingly and had no cholesterol problems. The only negative factor was a high-tension job. Webb had arranged for Dr. Tirone David, an intense, dedicated, brilliant heart surgeon, to perform the operation.

Then came the second attack.

Two thoughts prevailed. One, the attack answered my doubts about the need for the bypass operation. Two, it raised the question of listening to the urging of several friends—none more persistent than Lewis Feuer, the distinguished American sociologist and scholar on Marx, Einstein, Spinoza and assorted radicals—

that I should consider writing a book about the highlights of a career that was personally rewarding, stimulating and sometimes exciting.

I had always shrugged off the suggestion. Unlike many journalists, I never aspired to write the Great Canadian Novel, and I rarely indulged in retrospective writing. My vanity doesn't run in that direction. Besides, journalism is strewn with the wreckage of reporters and editors who are determined, some day, to tell the whole story, but seldom do.

Writing for tomorrow's edition spoils one for writing about yesterday's happenings. I have always looked ahead rather than back. But now, the traumatic reality of two heart attacks and upcoming major surgery forced me to reconsider: perhaps it was time to leave some record of a life other than yellowing newspaper clippings or, worse, assorted stories reduced to microfilm that no one will ever again read.

I had the triple-bypass operation and, through all the intensive care and recuperation, managed to dictate columns and editorials from my hospital bed to my long-suffering assistant, Chris Blizzard. I missed writing the editorial on the day I was operated on, but picked up the tempo a day or two later. I repaired quickly. Three weeks after the operation I played tennis. In four weeks I was playing second base (sort of) for the *Sun* softball team. Three months later I had my first (and last) lesson in hang-gliding. It seemed I had recovered.

But there was still the nagging reality of unfinished business: the book.

I had never started out to be a journalist and was still not quite sure how it had happened. John Bassett, publisher of the now-defunct Toronto *Telegram*, gave me the incredible opportunity to be the paper's main roving reporter for some fifteen years, through forty to fifty crises, wars and revolutions and trips to exotic places that ordinarily one never has a chance to see in person. Opportunities continued for the next decade-plus, in a somewhat different vein, after the *Telegram* died and the Toronto *Sun* rose from its ashes with me undergoing a metamorphosis from reporter and employee to editor and part-owner.

Much of my time was spent covering wars, coups and revolutions: Korea, Lebanon, Iraq, Congo, New Guinea, China-India, Biafra, Israel-Egypt, Czechoslovakia, Vietnam. As well, there was civil unrest and oppression: Algeria, Angola, South Africa, the USSR, and, at home, the Canadian government invoking the Official Secrets Act to get even at critics. Throughout there were always chances for the exotic experience: visiting stone age tribes in central New Guinea; encountering Tibetans in the Chinese Himalayas who were seeing white people for the first time; helping to arrange an escape from Russia.

Journalism provided a chance to meet or see world figures in action—or in decline: Egypt's Gamal Abdel Nasser, Iraq's ill-fated dictator Brigadier Abdel Karim Kassem, King Hussein of Jordan, Prime Minister Nehru of India, the Dalai Lama, the Congo's Colonel Joseph Mobutu, Patrice Lumumba, Ojukwu of Biafra, Dr. Albert Schweitzer, to mention some who appear in subsequent pages.

I encountered villains and heroes, some of whom are remembered, some of whom have disappeared: Lee Harvey Oswald, who gunned down President Jack Kennedy and then was slain by the pathetic Jack Ruby; Igor Gouzenko, who died and was buried incognito, after enduring a life of secrecy in Canada when he revealed a massive Soviet spy ring; master-spy Kim Philby whom I met drunk in a hotel bar during Beirut's crisis in 1958; the revolutionary officer in Baghdad who claimed to have killed a king.

It was a reporter's golden fantasies come to life—at someone else's expense.

I am not the same person today as I was when I started. Nor is the world the same. Only human nature remains constant: cruel and kind, courageous and cowardly, generous yet selfish. I suppose it is testimony to the human spirit that one can remain optimistic, enthusiastic, cheerful about the future. To some, it may seem a contradiction, to others, more folly. But the journey isn't over yet, God willing. I hope there are more experiences to come, changes to be made, battles to be fought. Those interested enough to read on, can judge for themselves.

1

Please do not feed
this dog or boy

FORT OSBORNE BARRACKS
WINNIPEG, CANADA 1930

Heaven on earth is to be a small boy or dog in an army camp. Soldiers, kids, and dogs have an instinctive relationship that is intangible, indefinable, precious. There is intuitive rapport; a shared sense of adventure, irreverence, trust, even mischief. There is considerable truth in the saying that joining the army makes boys into men—and ensures that men will be boys forever.

I was born in an army camp—Fort Osborne Barracks in Winnipeg, 1927, where my father was a captain in Princess Patricia's Canadian Light Infantry (PPCLI), a regiment I was to serve with as a lieutenant in Korea, twenty-five years later. The family stayed in Winnipeg until I was seven and my sister five, then left the city forever, beginning a life of being transferred from one posting to another. Growing up among soldiers may not be the best preparation for a responsible, respectable life of steady job, daily routine, white picket fence, and regular vacations. But it is ideal for filling a childhood with a lifetime of unusual memories.

Fort Osborne Barracks in the between-wars period was on the outskirts of Winnipeg, in both geography and life of the city. The prairie was next door and army brats grew up in the siege mentality that distinguished Canadian military camps in those days and persists to this day. Fort Osborne Barracks was "home" to the men and families of the Princess Pats, a squadron of Lord Strathcona Horse cavalry, a battery of horse artillery, and a detachment of the fledgling RCAF, plus the usual services. Most of the soldiers were veterans of the Great War whose outlook on life had been tempered and molded by the Somme, Vimy Ridge, or Passchendaele. Everyone seemed to have a dog, and kids and dogs and troops were at home with jack rabbits, gophers, partridge, and

1

maneuvers, and the oddity of being a small band of professional soldiers in a country of growing pacifism and disarmament. The army in those days was a family, with the air force acceptable first cousins and the navy, what there was of it, distant cousins, too remote and exotic to be understood. Civilians were the aliens—they and the politicians and bureaucrats they elected who were dismissed by the military with near-contempt as purveyors of "red tape," the bane of all military people who eventually become both the greatest victims and proponents of it.

From the beginning, I knew my father was "different," something special. I never consciously tried to analyze why—just accepted it. He was a stocky man, about five foot seven, with a terrier's grit, a quick temper, and a quicker sense of humor. His eyes, when angry, could melt steel. He had boundless confidence, enthusiasm, a streak of youthful impetuosity, and energy to spare. His humor was the boisterous, pie-in-face variety which, to the day he died in 1967, he considered the ultimate in wit.

Just as Fort Osborne Barracks was the first "home" I knew, so it was also practically the first "home" or family life my father had known. Even as a captain he was something of a legend in the PPCLI. He had no formal education. His father, Henry Worthington, was a doctor, apparently from the Cooperstown, New York, area and related to James Fenimore Cooper, author of *The Deerslayer, The Last of the Mohicans*, and the Leatherstocking Tales. My father's only relative, born and buried in Cooperstown, was a cousin, Mary Graham Bonner, an author of children's stories and baseball books. Dr. Worthington seems to have left Cooperstown and headed West because of some unspecified scandal, the details of which we could never learn. In the West, he teamed up with the Earl of Caithness and John Forbes, both from the Scottish Highlands, all three seeking adventure and sheep-herding in the western states. Dr. Worthington married a widow in California, and their son was named Frederic Franklin, though neither name was ever used to refer to him after he reached his teens. All his adult life he was known as "Worthy." He always claimed that he was born in Scotland, but after his death my mother, my sister, and I came to the reluctant conclusion that he may have actually been born in America. (It is possible, however, that he was born in Scotland while his parents were visiting there.)

First his father, then his mother, died when he was about ten. With no one to look after him, he was sent to live with a half-brother who was an engineer at a gold mine in Nacozaro, Mexico.

John Forbes (Uncle Jack) came out from Britain to assume guardianship of the boy, but by then he was in Mexico. Young "Frederico" didn't much like his half-brother, but didn't have to put up with him for long. Shortly after he arrived at the mine, the notorious bandit Pancho Villa raided it and my father's half-brother was killed before his eyes.

With nowhere to go, the boy became a protégé of an alcoholic remittance man named Grindell, who took him in. An Englishman, Grindell had been to Oxford and had a passion for books which he transferred to Frederico. He taught him to hunt and shoot, became a combination proxy father, brother, teacher, and companion. He instilled in the boy a hunger for learning and reading that lasted all his life. Young though he was, Frederico looked after Grindell when the remittance cheques came in from England and his patron would get drunk for days on end. Frederico worked first as a water boy in the mines, then as a swamper dumping the 300-gallon tubs of slag that had to be hauled out.

Grindell had heard a story about high-grade gold on Tiburon Island in the Gulf of Lower California, and, despite the reputation of the Tiburon Indians for being hostile and cannibalistic, decided to go see for himself. He left young Frederico to tend the adobe hut they shared. Grindell never returned.

According to my father's account of his youth—something he talked about only rarely—his life at the mine ended while he was driving trainloads of ore from the mine down a steep slope and up another slope to be dumped. One particular worker would leap in front of the train on the downward slope, forcing Frederico to apply the brakes to avoid hitting him. The momentum of the train would be lost and it would then have to be cranked up the other side for dumping, thus giving the workers an extra fifteen-minute rest. Frederico would get the blame for not maintaining momentum.

One day, he warned that he'd not slow down next time, but the man didn't believe him and jumped in front of the trolley. My father kept going and killed the man. He left the mine in a hurry, went to the coast at Guaymas, and joined a barquentine heading for the South Pacific as a cabin boy. He was fourteen.

For the next few years, my father sailed the China coast and became a ship's engineer. On April 16, 1906, his ship dropped anchor off Goat Island at San Francisco. The next day Worthy went ashore and while browsing in a bookstore met a lawyer named Scaife. The man was impressed that a sailor would be buying a book by Robert Louis Stevenson. Scaife took a liking to the youth and invited him to dinner with his wife and daughter. That night the earthquake struck. For several days Worthy scoured the streets helping in rescue work, and was fascinated at the looting and anarchy that quickly took over a civilized city. His most vivid memory was of coming across a dead woman in evening dress with her fingers cut off by looters after her rings.

He went to work in a sugar mill outside Salinas for a while, then shipped to sea again. He was on a filthy tramp called the *San Juan* when it put in at Guatemala. Here, he met an Irishman named McGee who had achieved some fame for punching the local *commandante* in the stomach after the man had slapped him in the face. McGee had been given fifty lashes. When news of this reached the British consul, the H.M.S. *Fawn* was sent to San José, where a midshipman delivered an ultimatum: McGee was to be given $1,000 for every lash or the warship would open fire. McGee got $50,000 and the British won Worthy's everlasting respect.

After leaving the *San Juan* in Nicaragua, he spotted a gunboat crew trying to figure out what was wrong with their Gatling gun. Worthy joined in and got it working. The startled officer, Jeb O'Connor, made the newcomer the officer in charge of the gun crew of fifteen Nicaraguans, and Worthy's military career had begun. He became known as the "admiral" of the Nicaraguan navy. He had an almost intuitive understanding of weapons, was an excellent marksman and, more rare, could repair, modify and improve existing weapons.

When Honduras and San Salvador went to war, the Nicaraguans joined in. Worthy never knew what the war was about, but he participated in fierce fighting for the island of Ampala in the Gulf of Honduras. From there he returned to Nicaragua where he took part in a civil war, finally escaping with six Britishers who barricaded themselves on a British ship for sanctuary. The captain was about to use force to throw them off when a Nicaraguan gunboat came alongside and demanded that the renegades be turned over to him. This order infuriated the British captain, who refused, and Worthy and companions were saved, only to be dumped unceremoniously ashore in Panama.

Worthy's travels continued. He went prospecting in Mexico, was captured by Indians, and bought his freedom by showing them how to use an automatic rifle. En route to Scotland to see Uncle Jack, he was doped and mugged in New York and, with no money, had to alter his plans and head back to Central America. There he became involved in gun-running to Cuba, followed by a spell in prison. After that, he went to sea again as a junior engineer, but had to quit the *Ponce de Leon* suddenly in Puerto Rico when he used a wrench to crush the skull of a man who attacked him with a knife. He shipped on another vessel going around the Horn.

While in San Francisco again he heard that Francisco Madero was rallying a rebel army in El Paso, Texas, and heading into Mexico to oppose President Porfirio Diaz. Worthy took off immediately to join Madero and the revolution. He knew Mexico, liked Mexicans, identified with their goals. Ironically, he found himself fighting on the same side as Pancho Villa, who had killed his half-brother. It was 1911 and Worthy was twenty-one.

For the next few years, Worthy alternated between revolutions, wars, and shipping to sea. It was an adventure-splattered life, with no great prospects for either old age or respectability. When war erupted in Europe he was recuperating in San Francisco from an injury—he had kept in touch with the Scaifes, who had befriended him during the earthquake. Worthy determined to go to Scotland to join a Highland regiment. He left for New Orleans, caught a ship to New York, and from there went to Montreal to work his way to Britain. To his amazement, on Peel Street in Montreal he saw a soldier in a Black Watch kilt. Upon learning that there was a Black Watch recruiting office nearby, he promptly enlisted—feeling smug that the King would now pay his fare overseas.

He discovered to his dismay that he had joined, not the Black Watch, but the *Canadian* Black Watch, and that he was in the Canadian, not the British, army. So before he knew anything about what was to be his adopted country, he was off to fight for it. Everything about Canada of that day was suited to Worthy: the openness, the wilderness, the challenge, the rough independence of Canadians, and the courage and unorthodoxy of her soldiers. He knew he had found his country, his future.

One of the few recruits with actual fighting experience, Worthy went to France in 1915 as a private, became a machine-gunner, and quickly adapted to trench warfare. As a corporal he earned the nickname "Nappy," short for Napoleon, because of his manner and size. He had a "good" war, as they say, was twice awarded the Military Medal and, after getting a battlefield commission, twice won the Military Cross. He emerged from the Great War as a captain with MC and bar, MM and bar, of which there were not too many. He had fought at Cambrai, where tanks were first used, and they made a lasting impression on him as *the* weapon of any future war. By then he was in the Motor Machine-Gun Brigade, commanded by one of the war's more extraordinary and unheralded military thinkers, Brigadier-General Raymond Brutinell, who had had the idea for the Motor Machine-Guns (the "Emmy Gees"). They came into their own during the March retreat in 1918, when their concentrated fire power could be quickly moved from place to place. Thus began what was to be a twenty-year campaign to bring tanks into the Canadian army.

As an officer, my father was unorthodox—captive of no dogma. In peace and war his troops idealized his unconventional outlook and his absence of pomposity. Since he didn't suffer fools gladly and wasn't hesitant about speaking his mind, controversy dogged him most of his army life.

In later years a favorite epithet of my father's was "So-and-so is so stupid he is often mistaken for a cavalry officer." But he didn't mean it. In fact, historically the cavalry has always been more open to new ideas in military warfare than other units. In 1938 when tanks were finally accepted into the Canadian army (two of them!), cavalry regiments became the backbone of the Armoured Corps. But that was in the future. By then Worthy was on his way to becoming a general and the "father of the tank" in Canada. He was always "Worthy" to men and officers and was dubbed "Fighting Frank" by the media during World War II. (Until I was in my teens I didn't know my father's first name— just his initials, "F.F." Even my mother called him "Worthy." To have heard her say "Frank" or "Fred" would have been acutely embarrassing.)

My mother's marrying my father was the height of incongruity. Her life had been one of civilized refinement in Toronto. Though it would bother her to say so, hers had been a genteel upbringing, the essence of WASP Toronto. She was of Quaker stock, the youngest of six girls, whose mother was a concert pianist of modest renown. My mother, christened Clara Ellen, was the tomboy of the family, dubbed "Larry" by her father who fondly referred to her as "my only son."

She was a decade younger than my father in years, a lifetime in experience. He had met her while training at Niagara-on-the-Lake, where her family had a cottage. Young men always hung around the Dignum girls, and my father and his best friend, Lieutenant J. K. Lawson (who later died in the defence of Hong Kong in World War II as commanding officer of the doomed

Canadian forces), were just two of many who paid homage to the good-looking bevy of girls.

My mother was intrigued with the "older" Captain Worthington, his colorful background, and his reserve and shyness. Some ten days after meeting her, he proposed to her. Flattered but not very serious, she agreed to an "understanding." Her mother was initially appalled; one of the big complaints she had against my father was that he curled his little finger when he drank tea. My mother, also concerned about this gesture of false gentility that was so contrary to his nature, finally gave my father an etiquette lesson and asked if he'd break the habit. Worthy was apologetic, but explained the finger had been crushed while he was at sea. A Canadian doctor in Peru had experimented and, instead of amputating the finger, had removed the crushed bone and put in a steel bar. The finger was now stiff and useless. When my grandmother heard this, she was so mortified at her earlier criticism that Anglo-Saxon guilt forced her opposition to crumble and she sought atonement by supporting the marriage.

The wedding kept being postponed because my mother had second thoughts, other suitors, and my father kept taking extra army assignments. The final delay was a postponement for three days to fit in with some astrologer's recommendation that my mother's family felt would be foolish to ignore. Clearly, they felt the marriage needed all the help possible.

My mother was especially impressed by my father's insistence, as she put it, "not that I love thee less, my dear, but that I love the army more." He warned her that she would play second fiddle to the job. Somehow she found this an unusual and romantic notion; it seemed a Victorian novel come to life, with virtues of duty before self, of country before family, King before wife. She had been enamored of the adventure stories of Richard Harding Davis, who had turned into books his colorful exploits covering the Boer War, Russo-Japanese War, Great War, and so on. And suddenly here was Worthy, a Richard Harding Davis character come to life and then some—her own personal adventure novel. It was all too exotic. As she was later to say: "I fell in love with the man I married."

Although there was nothing in her background to indicate that she would fit into a somewhat demanding army life, adapt she did. She had a quick, versatile mind and was probably brighter than my father. In a future age she might have carved out a career of her own. As it was, she gave herself to my father's career. They shared everything. She became his confidante and advisor and the only one to whom he'd reveal his innermost dreams, goals, and apprehensions. When I was born she was still more involved with her husband than her child, and the same was true when my sister Robin was born two years later. My father didn't know how to behave toward children, having had no childhood of his own, so we were treated as individuals.

I grew up, *not* as a general's son, but as a captain's kid. When I was born, my father wanted to call me John, my mother Peter, so they agreed on Peter John. The troops also wanted to participate and asked if they could add a name. My parents agreed—Mother somewhat dubiously—and thus my third name became "Vickers," after the machine gun that was a mainstay of British forces in three wars: World Wars I and II and Korean. I could barely walk when I was taken out to the ranges in Winnipeg for my military baptism and put behind a Vickers machine gun to fire a belt at a target. I was unable to see over the top of the barrel, but enjoyed the staccato chatter of that hardy weapon. Though as a kid I was embarrassed by my strange third name and how I got it, we gave my own son, Casey, Vickers as a second name. An honorable part of our history—steady, reliable, true. Not bad qualities to aspire to.

Childhood memories of Fort Osborne Barracks include a huge parade square where squads of soldiers periodically drilled, with sergeants roaring their almost musical instructions and the troops performing in turns and formations with chorus-line precision. At one end of the parade square—the centre of a kid's universe, since so much was always happening there—was the men's canteen, always smoky and noisy and with a vaguely forbidden attraction to toddlers because beer was drunk there. Along one side of the parade square, on the road leading to the main gate and the guardhouse, were the officers' married quarters, with single officers billeted on the other side. The men's barracks was at the end, near the canteen. The married quarters where we lived were sort of framed apartment or tenement houses with balconies looking inward.

Life was rich at Fort Osborne Barracks. When the Depression hit, it didn't change much. No one had anything, but all had security. As a toddler I would do rounds with a Scottie dog named Benny (after Scotland's Mt. Bennaghie, near Peterhead), methodically visiting canteens, cookhouses, barracks, guardhouse, and neighbors. In canteens the men would let me sip their beer and give me gum; at the mess hall I'd snack and chat with the cooks; at the guardhouse on good days, Benny and I would be locked in the cells for a while, where we'd talk to last night's drunk and be fed peanut butter sandwiches. Benny and I became roly-poly and my mother would send us out with a sign around my neck: "Please do not feed this dog or boy." The effect was to get us even more attention, and soldiers would surreptitiously slip us more food.

When soldiers were drilling on the parade square, I'd march on the side with a broomstick-gun, executing the booming instructions of the drill sergeant. I was game for anything and a favorite with the troops, who could always count on a bit of sport with Benny and "Captain Worthy's boy." I grew up thinking that soldiers were cheerful, generous, and entertaining. I still feel that way. Soldiers, regardless of nationality or army, tend to be essentially the same—fighting soldiers, that is, infantry, armour, or artillery.

I can vaguely remember one New Year's Day when, while everyone was sleeping in, I roamed around the house draining the bottles left over from the New Year's Eve party. (I still shudder at the memory of watching a batch of dead flies in a ginger ale bottle swoosh down my throat as I swallowed the dregs.) I then toddled into the street to visit the men's canteen. In the canteen I demanded to sip someone's beer and was told, jokingly, "You wouldn't like that P.J.," whereupon I took the glass and drained it on the spot.

When my mother looked out the window a short time later she was greeted by the sight of her four-year-old son, New Year's hat perched rakishly on his head, weaving drunkenly up the street. She rushed into the bright winter's morn, scooped me in her arms, and demanded that my father get the medical officer. Worthy, made of sterner stuff, suggested I be allowed to sleep it off. I was put to bed, and by the time I awoke I had become a part of Fort Osborne Barracks legend.

And then there was the time I was "kidnapped." Maybe two or three years old, I had the habit of wetting my bed and getting up for a midnight snack. To cure me of the habit, my father filled the refrigerator with pots and pans that would tumble out when opened.

Sure enough, the trap worked and, frightened by the clatter, I crawled under the stove while my father rushed in to catch me—

and couldn't locate me. I was too frightened to come out when called, and panic set in. The Lindbergh kidnapping was still fresh in memories. My parents notified the sentry at the gate. The guardhouse soldiers said they'd seen a suspicious car without lights about the time of my disappearance. The police were called, the Mounties notified, several searches of the apartment failed to find me. I can still recall peering out at the yellow stripes on the breeches of the Mounties as they went over the silver and tried to determine if anything except the kid was missing. I recall one Mountie looking in the oven, and how that intrigued me as a possible future hiding place. It was an early introduction to the fallibility of the police. Finally the troops were turned out. It was perhaps 2 A.M. and the regiment was put on alert with every man in camp patrolling the woods, searching for a body.

Several hours later, when dawn was creeping over the horizon and I was tired, cold, frightened, and needing to go to the bathroom, I weakly called out. No one heard me. I tried again, louder. Still nothing. A third time my mother's sensitive ear picked up the plaintive cry. Relief at finding me alive was mixed with embarrassment, annoyance, and some amusement. The soldiers seemed pleased. My parents were somewhat nonplussed. The regiment was allowed to sleep in, and my father opened the canteen. I became an instant celebrity at Fort Osborne Barracks, and to this day still run into people who participated in the great kidnapping search.

I also remember a birthday party where all the kids were gathered around the party table tucking into ice cream and cake with pennies and nickels hidden in it. It was happy, greedy, noisy. My mother was a Girl Guide leader and had written a take-off play on Little Red Riding Hood. My father had made a papier-mâché wolf's head, complete with flapping jaw and jagged, bloody teeth. Deciding it would be a splendid addition to the birthday party if he performed, he put on the wolf's head, popped up at the window and, complete with blood-curdling roars, snarls, and what he hoped were wolf noises, scratched and clawed to get in. The effect was instantaneous. One look at the apparition and the kids began fleeing the table screaming and, literally, wetting their trousers or knickers as the case might be. The only two unaffected were Robin and me. We kept tucking into our ice cream and cake as well as everyone else's. We knew our father and his tricks.

There was no salvaging the party. The kids were too frightened to go home alone, and parents had to come and collect them, all wondering what sort of family was Captain Worthington's, where birthday parties ended in tears and nightmares about wolves. My father never tired of recalling the panic he caused.

As a youngster, I was game for anything. There was some trait in my make-up that made it impossible for me to turn down a challenge, and the older kids soon learned this. On one occasion I accepted a dare to roll naked in poison ivy, and wound up in hospital swathed head-to-toe in bandages. I tried to explain the situation to my mother, but she had difficulty understanding. For the next ten years I would break out in an all-over itchy rash at the mere suggestion of poison ivy.

As I grew older, the soldiers-boys-dogs syndrome increased and I used to be smuggled in Carden-Lloyd armoured vehicles on army maneuvers, hidden out of sight of umpires. It was cramped, smelly, hot, and wonderful. I'd have peanut butter or bologna sandwiches thrust on me when I got restless. I saw nothing, was bumped around unmercifully, but felt the luckiest kid alive. As reward I'd be allowed to drive a Carden-Lloyd and then was taken to the ranges to shoot with the troops. I could shoot better than many soldiers by the time I was ten (at age eleven I shot my first deer at Camp Borden). My father taught me to fish, to hunt birds' eggs, to survive in the bush—all things he liked doing. For some reason people believe soldiers' kids have strict, regimented lives, that the soldier-father tends to be a martinet. Untrue. Soldiers are like any other parents: some are strict, some are lax. If anything, Robin and I were raised with too little guidance, not enough direction. We grew up as free spirits. I got spanked a lot—and the strap was applied occasionally, but only when I did wrong. There was never a feeling of being unjustly treated. It isn't the nature of the punishment that creates resentment, but the injustice of it. Harsh or lenient, punishment has to be deserved and understood to be accepted as fair.

I suppose Worthy induced in me an unconscious spirit of adventure—*not* to be like him, but to see and do some of the things he had done. I don't recall his ever pressuring me to follow a particular course. He tried to instill in us a feeling of independence and self-sufficiency, and both my sister and I were encouraged to have opinions about whatever was being discussed at the table. My mother would often disagree with my father, and a debate would rage until, often as not, my father would amend his views to incorporate my mother's ideas. In retrospect, it was a "liberated" attitude, but at the time it seemed mere common sense. My father had none of the stereotyped attitudes of his generation, possibly because he was fortunate enough to have escaped a conventional education.

Almost before I could read he encouraged me to learn Kipling's poetry, and I would get a nickel for every poem I memorized. And then another nickel if I taught the poem to my sister. My father never tired of hearing his son recite "Fuzzy Wuzzy," or "Tommy Atkins," or Robert Burns's poems, "Bruce to his Men at Bannockburn" and "Burial of Sir John Moore." To this day I still feel prickles at Kipling's lines.

Worthy's taste in poetry—and mine—is not surprising, given the military background. When I was growing up, uniforms were everywhere. In fact, anyone not in uniform looked strange and out of place. It was always odd to see my father on weekends in civvy clothes. I don't know what age I was before I understood that "civilians" were not some rare and dangerous species, but people much like we were. Professional soldiers in the '30s regarded civilians as representing an attitude that would eventually result in war—an attitude that scorned the military until the nation was in peril. At the last moment, with the enemy at the gate and freedom in jeopardy, the much-reviled military, starved for equipment, depleted in numbers, would once again be called upon to shed its blood to save the country and enjoy momentary adulation and gratitude. Then, the crisis survived, "civilian" thinking was reasserted and the whole ritual of disarmament and scorn for the military would be recycled. This, indeed, seemed the British tradition. Army families of my vintage took Kipling's prophetic poem, "Tommy Atkins," as gospel:

> For it's Tommy this, an' Tommy that,
> an' Chuck 'im out, the brute!
> But it's 'saviour of 'is country,'
> when the guns begin to shoot . . .

I'm not sure things have changed much. Rarely stressed is that soldiers are the ones who have to fight wars and have the most reason to want peace. But they also believe that peace *and* security are the result of being strong and being able as well as willing to defend oneself. We tend to forget, if we ever knew, the admonition of the Chinese military philosopher Sun Tzu 2,500 years ago that the goal of war is peace and a most effective army is the one that wins without fighting. Sadly, it is mostly the Soviets and

Communist countries that regularly study and practise the teach-
ings of Sun Tzu.

Whenever he was depressed at the latest bit of bureaucratic
shortsightedness, my father liked to hear me perform "Gunga
Din," and even more liked to hear Robin, not yet able to read,
attempt the strange, meaningless phrases and like as not break
down in tears when she became confused trying to say: " 'Hi!
Slippy hitheroo! Water, get it! PaneeLao, You squidgy-nosed old
idol, Gunga Din'." He'd roar with amusement while my mother
would shake her head and I'd wonder what it was about my tiny
sister than won the hearts of so many adults.

Meals were the only regular times our family was all together.
My father would express his views on the world, berate all pacifists
who would unilaterally disarm us, and curse the bureaucrats who
deprived the military and guaranteed that Adolf Hitler would
destroy us all unless we woke up. Worthy was a decisive man,
fearless in war or peace and somewhat inclined to overstatement
when discussing politicians, whom he despised in abstract but quite
liked in person. He also loved to invent blood-curdling fairy tales
about the giant High-Heavy, One-Eye the Potato Wife, Henry the
hero, with mayhem, violence, and suspense at every turn. We had
no need of Arthur Ransome, the Grimm brothers, or Hans Christian Andersen as long as we had Worthy's vivid imagination and
boundless enthusiasm.

I grew up in a household in the '30s where, to my child's mind,
the three great villains of mankind were—not necessarily in
this order—Hitler, the Treasury Board, and Prime Minister
Mackenzie King. Hitler was trying to take over the world and
would be defeated only by war; the Treasury Board was robbing
the military of essential funds with which to re-arm and oppose
Hitler; Mackenzie King was a "goddam civilian who would destroy
the military and get our country into a war that we might
not win." Yet damn-fool Canadians kept re-electing him Prime
Minister.

I don't know what effect my father had on my future thinking,
but even at the time I felt fortunate. The values that one has as
an adult are probably implanted during youth. They are not a
matter of choice. They become so ingrained that there is little one
can do about them, even if one wants to. It's too bad every kid
doesn't have the opportunity to grow up among peacetime soldiers. It is a great way to learn human nature and to respect
individuality, decency, generosity, and tolerance.

2

Fat, funny-looking sailor

The biggest problem with being an army brat is having no one place you can call home. Emotional attachments to people and places are frail and transitory. I was in my twenties before the family spent two consecutive Christmases in the same house. I have only a jumbled mosaic of memories with few clear geographical locations and few identifiable individuals. Every year it was a different army camp, city, province, country. It is tempting to theorize that an army kid grows up calling everywhere "home," when in reality he is more likely to grow up calling nowhere home. Fine for creating independence and self-reliance, lousy for developing lasting friends and emotional stability.

My memories of childhood include moving at strange times of the year, going to new schools in mid-term, and becoming the centre of attention for a brief moment, an oddity. The trouble with joining a class in mid-year is that one has to quickly find a place in the hierarchy or pecking order. Recollections of elementary schools are of fighting—which was necessary, I see now, to determine a place in the social order. Fortunately, I grew up stocky and solid and never went through a stringbean stage. I was fairly strong and quite enjoyed fighting, perhaps because I was good at it. It was not so important whether one won or lost, but how one fought. It was not necessary to show skill or courage, but it was essential *not* to show fear or cowardice.

My longest and fondest memories are of Camp Borden, Ontario, where we lived from 1938 to 1940, after returning from England where my father had taken a two-year course on tanks. He came back to Borden to set up the Canadian Armoured Fighting Vehicle School, which was to eventually evolve into the

Canadian Tank Corps. The original twenty-five troops of the CAFV School were "volunteers"—an army euphemism for mavericks and trouble-makers culled from regiments across Canada. The tendency is for regiments, when asked to supply bodies, to send their most expendable, even if it means mild perjury to make them sound like incipient Wellingtons. So the original tank soldiers were a mishmash of individualists who were considered an irritation or pain in the butt to the system. They and my father were well suited.

The war was fifteen months away when we arrived in Camp Borden, which was then a ghost camp of about 100 personnel: the tanks school, an Army Service Corps depot, and a skeleton RCAF base. Six militia regiments designated as "armour" were to be trained at Borden, but my father was given no funds for equipment. However, they were entitled to requisition funds for things like horse nails and saddles, so countless nails were ordered that were diverted into equipment and firing ranges. Model T Fords were converted to tanks, and an anti-tank gun was made out of a sewer pipe mounted on a car axle—which exploded and nearly killed its creators.

Everyone except the politicians knew war was coming. It even infected us army kids, going to a one-room school at the other end of Camp Borden, and we watched belated efforts to prepare. The army was working overtime and every spare moment to learn tanks.

In the late summer of 1938 two British Mark IV light tanks arrived in Borden. I had never seen such excitement—the first tanks ever seen in Canada. Watching them being unloaded, we kids leapt and chanted. We'd never seen such formidable weapons, such dauntless power. Today one stands in the tank park at Camp Borden, puny and pathetic compared to other tanks around it. Still, memory recalls it as lethal and beautiful.

My father was treated to some derision by anticipating a war in which tanks, not infantry, would lead assaults and race across the country, supported by bombers and fighter planes sweeping all in their path. He was regarded as a bit of a nut. But he had read the books on tank tactics by Britain's General Boney Fuller—the same books that Hitler read when he devised his *Blitzkrieg*, or lightning war. In the summer of 1939 a dozen more Mark IV tanks arrived, with a curt message that no more could be supplied. War was clearly coming.

I remember the day Hitler attacked Poland and Britain declared war. To us kids, nurtured on the spectre of war—and not un-pleased at the prospects—it was exciting that the other shoe had finally dropped. Not for a minute did I think we would do any-thing but win. When the British chased the German liner *Bremen* up the English Channel, I told my father: "That'll teach 'em. Now the tide has turned."

I recall clearly how solemn Worthy was. In fact he was down-right apprehensive. I wondered what was wrong with him. "No tide has turned, son," he said. "We might not even win. We may have waited too long. Goddam it, couldn't they see it was com-ing . . ."

I couldn't understand his pessimism, his fatalism. For him it was history repeating itself. For me it seemed opportunity, ad-venture. I wished fervently I was four years older. I was twelve.

With Camp Borden bursting with soldiers training, the summer of 1940 was a kid's paradise. I spent every free moment in the tented lines of the army, begging camp badges, being kidded, listening to stories, running errands. Every couple of weeks I'd come home with a new pet, a dog, a cat, whatever the soldiers would give. I was allowed to keep only one cat and one dog, a fox terrier named Soapy. Both animals were more devoted to my sister, Robin, than to me who teased them. Boys are too rough with small pets.

My father gave a speech at the Military Institute in Toronto and when asked how he thought German tanks would ever get through France's Maginot Line—the supposedly impenetrable wall of steel and concrete fortifications along the frontier France shared with Germany—Worthy impatiently took a pencil and drew a slashing line on the wall map around the Maginot Line and bel-lowed: "Hell, they won't go through; they'll go around!" A news-paper person photographed the map and reported the remarks—and Worthy was in hot water again with Defence Headquarters for speaking out of turn. A severe reprimand was in order when Hitler saved him by attacking France through Holland and Bel-gium and striking behind the Maginot Line.

Extraordinarily, there was still prejudice against tanks and mod-ern warfare. Only recently had Brigadier E. J. Schmidlin, Director of Engineering Services, told the same Military Institute: "The ultimate weapon which wins the war is a bayonet on a rifle carried by an infantryman through the mud . . . no one knows how useful tanks will be . . . The Polish campaign was no true indication of the power of mechanized armies . . . The usefulness of the airplane, though considerably improved since 1918, also remains to be seen."

General Schmidlin didn't believe in vaccinations either, and refused to get one when sent to India. He got smallpox and died. As my father was to scold in later years, "There is something about senior rank in the military that turns brain into bone."

The need for tanks for recruit training was acute. It was learned that some 260 World War I Renault tanks, built in 1917, were sitting in a warehouse in Illinois preserved in grease, never having turned a wheel. They might be available to the Canadians for $3,000 each. My father went to investigate. America was not yet in the war and it was important to preserve the appearance of neutrality, so the matter had to be handled with some sensitivity. My father was dealing, it seems, with a blunt American tank soldier anxious to get into the war himself—one George S. Patton. My father made a deal on the spot and bought the six-ton Renaults, not for $3,000 each as tanks, but for $20 a ton as scrap iron— that is, for $120 each. The sale apparently came up in the House of Commons where the propriety of the deal was discussed, until a message came that there was a trainload of American scrap iron at the Canadian border destined for the Camp Borden Iron Foundry, and where exactly was that? Debate ended, and my father had his tanks—no use in war, but marvellous for training.

Soon the Renaults dominated the Camp Borden scenery and I learned to drive them. The easy informality of the tank family bent rules so that kids could play with the new toys, too. In fact, the very first recruit into the Canadian Tank Corps was one of those kids: Jack Wallace, who later lost a leg in Italy and won the Military Cross, and eventually headed Canada's Civil Defence.

In efforts to teach tank tactics, my father would send teams of Renault tanks into the woods during the deer season to hunt for local farmers poaching. The tanks would pretend that poachers were German Panzers. I remember walking to school one morning and seeing a Renault tank chugging out of the ravine with two pleased young soldiers on the turret, a deer draped over the gun, and two very indignant farmers walking in front of it with their hands on top of their heads in the universal surrender sign. No charges were laid, but since hunting on National Defence property was forbidden, the deer was confiscated and the ranks had venison for supper.

But the kid's paradise of Camp Borden was to end. A year or so into the war, all the army families were moved to Barrie while the men went overseas. My mother, Robin, the dog Soapy, and I lived there for four years, moving to different houses in the town. My father was overseas most of the time, first commanding the 1st Armoured Brigade, later the 4th Armoured Division. Raising the family fell to my mother, as it did to most women left behind in Canada. I look back now with some shame at how little I helped her, how oblivious I was to her burdens and concerns. I was wrapped up in my own life, living each day to the hilt with little care for the future or for responsibilities. Being the place I lived in the longest, Barrie became my adopted home town, and I developed firm, if temporary, friendships. People tend to forget what the war years were like in Canada. Basically, the war was as popular then among kids as the anti-war movement was popular in the late '60s and '70s. Boys were impatient to grow up so that they, too, could go to war. It was the thing to do. We all hated Hitler, mocked Mussolini, and were slightly frightened of Hirohito, who was the symbol for Japan, a country so alien and remote that we had no starting point for comprehension.

Teen-agers didn't feel patriotism so much as they felt the call of adventure. I was desperately afraid the war would end before I was old enough to get into it. At fifteen I ran away from home to join the merchant navy in Montreal. My bid failed, and when I returned home I made a deal with my mother: if I continued in school, the next year she would sign parental consent forms that would enable me to join the *real* navy.

The navy was appealing for several reasons. First, it was far removed from the army in which my father was, by now, a general. My egalitarian feelings were such that I wanted to stay far from his sphere of influence. He was fairly well-known—the country's most colorful and outspoken soldier. I was determined to make my own way, and almost resented his success. Second, the navy accepted younger recruits than the army would. Third, I liked the naval uniform, which seemed glamorous. Fourth, it promised a form of adventure the army didn't—the unfamiliar has its own appeal. Fifth, and perhaps most important, the conventional wisdom was that girls preferred sailors to soldiers and I had a vague idea that once in a naval uniform with bell-bottom trousers and a salty collar, I'd have to fight off the girls who'd find me irresistible. The yearning to get into the service and go to war was almost that primitive. Patriotism was something one didn't talk about—too corny.

I joined the navy in the summer of 1944 at HMCS York in

Toronto, and the first person I met around my own age was Lloyd Bochner, who later became a movie actor. He had joined up a couple of months ahead of me and seemed an old salt by comparison. I longed for the day when I, too, had been in the navy a few months and knew all the ropes.

Bochner was the voice of seaman Jack Marlowe on the wartime CBC radio drama "Fighting Navy," which was receiving critical acclaim across the country at the time. Bochner spotted me one evening trying to iron my navy uniform. In the navy the creases are on the sides and turn inward. I'd never ironed anything before, even with creases on the outside, and was laboriously trying to re-iron creases to turn inward. Bochner, with the patience of an old hand of two months, showed me how to iron the uniform inside out, thus creating creases that turn inward. I thought it the most brilliant bit of information I'd ever heard—and certainly the most useful at that moment. Bochner more or less had the run of HMCS York, with even officers and petty officers occasionally seeking his autograph. I admired him considerably. Another sailor I hero-worshipped was Floyd Curry, later a hockey player with the Montreal Canadiens, who was kind to me at York and used to get me to mop the floor (deck!) of his sports section.

Running the physical training of the landlocked "ship" was Annis Stukus, quarterback of the Toronto Argos and a rawboned Lithuanian in charge of providing noontime entertainment for the crew. One day at morning parade he asked my weight and told me to report to the P.T. office at noon with shorts and sneakers. I did and found I was to participate in a boxing match with another recruit my size. We were both terrified, and slightly reassured that neither of us had done any boxing. While adoring fighting, I hated boxing because every time I got hit on the nose tears would come to my eyes and it looked as if I was crying. In those days men who cried were sissies, and I certainly wasn't anxious to be thought of as one.

I won the fight, and with it got $1 credit at the canteen. It encouraged me to take boxing more seriously, which I did on getting out of the navy and after being shellacked by a real fighter in a bout in England. Stukus and I later became friends when he did sports at the Toronto *Telegram*, and I became a fan when he coached Vancouver's first professional football team to a hilarious but disastrous season of one tie and all the rest losses.

My most exciting moment in the navy was the first time I was allowed out on the streets of Toronto in uniform. I vividly remember standing on the concrete island at Bathurst and Queen Streets, waiting for the streetcar and eagerly stealing glances in a store window to catch sight of myself. Though I could see every-one else in the reflection, I couldn't see myself. I was greatly puzzled. There was the fat lady with the funny hat, then the old guy standing beside me in the windbreaker; then there was this funny, fat-looking sailor, then the lady in the red jacket. But where was I? It was bewildering—until it suddenly dawned that the fat, funny-looking sailor was me! I was shattered. Here I was sure I resembled Gene Kelly, but I turned out to look more like Mickey Rooney.

I remember going to Shea's movie house, hoping that some nice girl would find me irresistible. It was widely believed that girls liked to use movie theatres to pick up servicemen. I hadn't been in the movie ten minutes when a girl sat beside me, began talking—and immediately put her hand on my knee. I was terrified. What to do? I knew I'd muck things up, disgrace the uniform with my innocence. I wondered, fleetingly, if she'd believe it if I told her I was shell-shocked? Battle fatigue? Seen too much misery for my young years? No, of course she wouldn't. Nor would I. My mind raced and I didn't hear a word of the movie as I tried to figure out how the situation should be handled. Her hand didn't move and she offered me popcorn. Too much was happening too fast. I mumbled something about this is where I came in and I've got to go 'cause the admiral is expecting me. I fled in panic.

No sooner was I out the theatre than I settled down and kicked myself and hung around the front of the theatre for the next hour hoping to recognize her when she came out. Now that I had time to think it over, I realized that she had fallen hopelessly in love with me, as I had with her. But no luck. I didn't see her come out, which figures because I'd never had a look at her anyway. I just knew she was lovely. You can tell.

The next shore leave I had I returned to the theatre and took the same seat, hoping for a second chance. But in romance, as in war and politics, second chances rarely come.

My father was back in Canada by this time, commanding at Camp Borden. The tragedy of his life was that he fell victim to army politics and never took his tanks into action. Never had I seen him so shaken. Had he been another type, he would have broken. That he rallied, settled in, and cleaned out the corruption that had taken over at Camp Borden is testimony to his character. It was acknowledged later that Worthy was supposed to have been retired after Camp Borden, but he threw himself into purging the incompetence and straightening the camp out with such fervor that he was sent as General Officer commanding the Pacific area in Vancouver and then to Western command at Edmonton. And all the time his heart was breaking at losing his division and not taking it into action—his *raison d'être* for the past twenty-five years.

The power struggle in the Canadian army centred on General Guy Simonds, representing the young Turks or British-oriented officers aligned with General Montgomery, hero of El Alamein, and General Andrew McNaughton, representing the old guard that wanted to keep the Canadian army united and fighting as a corps as in World War I. My father's loyalty was to McNaughton; thus, when the Simonds faction won and Lieutenant-General Harry Crerar replaced McNaughton as commander of the First Canadian Army, Worthy became a casualty. Command of his division was turned over to another who was more favored by Simonds.

It was hard on the new commander, Major-General George Kitching, who inherited a division loyal to one man. After D-Day, 4th Armoured got badly chewed up at the Falaise Gap, Kitching was demoted and removed from command, and my father wept for his battered children. He didn't blame Kitching personally, and Kitching, a gracious man who later redeemed himself in the military, wrote a letter of apology to my father for what had happened. Ten years later General Simonds told my father that it had been a mistake to remove him and that he should have been allowed to fight with his division. It was small atonement. Losing command of his precious tanks remained the greatest sadness of his life.

I was largely unaware of my father's personal agony when he came back to command Camp Borden. When he was in Toronto, he would occasionally take me out to dinner. It caused raised eyebrows to see a general out chatting and laughing with a very young sailor. When I reported back to HMCS York at 11 P.M., it would invariably cause a flap among the Shore Patrol at the gate when an army staff car with general's flag flying would pull up, a plump, awkward, very young sailor would get out and shake a general's hand, and the pair would briefly embrace and promise to see each other next time. The goggle-eyed Shore Patrol must have wondered at this strange and possibly unnatural relationship between an ordinary seaman and a general. I would never tell them. In those days I was very embarrassed that I had a high-ranking father.

After leaving HMCS York, I went into the Fleet Air Arm as a Telegraphist Air Gunner, and then was sent to Britain for an Observer's course (which I failed because I was having too much fun) and became a sub-lieutenant—possibly the youngest commissioned officer in the Canadian navy, certainly the most inexperienced, and likely the most incompetent. At the end of the war in England, I succeeded in getting tattooed and learned to play creditable poker and to keep a straight face with a full house. My main achievement was once managing to dump my dinner on the lap of the Executive Officer of HMS *St. Vincent* in Portsmouth. I was returned to Canada and was discharged in Vancouver early in 1946, just before my nineteenth birthday. I hadn't heard a shot fired in anger, yet I was considered a veteran, a decade older in experience than other kids my age who were just finishing high school. My appetite for adventure was whetted but I had no idea what I wanted to do. Restless and at loose ends, I joined the parade of veterans taking advantage of a free university education: one year's tuition for every year of service and $60 a month living expenses besides.

I chose the University of British Columbia, but the problem was that I hadn't completed high school and didn't have a junior matriculation certificate from Ontario. So I lied to the registrar of UBC and was allowed to attend classes while a letter was sent to Ontario for my scholastic records. The Ontario Department of Education replied that there was no record of my matriculation. I said there must be some mistake, and UBC wrote again. By the time it was realized that I had not completed high school, I had already passed the first year of UBC and I was allowed to continue on DVA (Veteran's Allowance) as long as I continued to pass.

My only goal in life at that time was to not get mired in a mundane job selling shoes or doing bookkeeping or any indoor job. To supplement the $60 a month from a grateful government, I did a variety of jobs ranging from dishwashing, to selling blood, to posing semi-naked for artists, to logging, construction work, truck-driving, and surveying. During the school year I spent more time training for boxing than I did studying. Vancouver was always a good fight town, and in those days there were amateur fights every week. I got onto the circuit, getting from $10 to $20 a bout. I was in good shape, managed to reach the finals of the Golden Gloves, and won the university light-heavyweight title for a couple of years. As a boxer I had limited talent but a good punch and, since I skipped classes regularly for training, was in better shape than most of those I fought. I discovered I could knock people out with my right hand and for a time went slightly berserk trying for the knockout. I eventually found that it was better to let the other guy wear himself punching me for two rounds, then to rely on superior condition and a harder punch and try for a third-round knockout. My bouts were usually exciting, but not very scientific.

I quit going to classes after my third year, was dropped from DVA credits, and began using money earned in the summer to attend UBC in the winter, continuing a life of sport, indolence, and daydreaming. I still had no particular ambitions. Journalism never entered my mind. The closest I'd come to it was a summer of delivering the *Globe and Mail* in Barrie and winding up at the end of summer owing $30 to the paper. I had tended to spend what revenues I collected on doughnuts and Kik Cola for an expanding group of hangers-on. Wisely, I dropped the route and immediately saved money.

While attending UBC, the job I found most appealing was topographic surveying for the B.C. government, and I became a member of the team that surveyed the Kitimat south of Terrace and the Buckley Valley under Ernie McMinn in 1949, before the aluminum company moved in. About ten of us were on the team; we arrived in early spring and brought enough supplies to last until fall. We were the first whites in the area since the early 1920s and we set up base camp across from the Indian village. From there we made trips up the mountains to build cairns on various prominent features. These could be seen from other ridges, angles could be read, and thus height and contour could be determined.

Our cook had a drinking problem and suddenly headed back to the bright lights of Vancouver, whereupon I persuaded McMinn that I had the potential to be a splendid cook, even though I'd never cooked anything. McMinn agreed and I got the job and extra money and immediately wrote south for a cookbook—any cookbook. Meanwhile I somewhat desperately began searching my memory and relying on intuition for recipes. I became living testimony to the relationship between necessity and invention; by the time the cookbook arrived, I was already baking four loaves of bread a day which tasted terrific if you ate it hot and smothered in honey. My bread stayed with you, too, a solid lump in your stomach. By trial and error I had figured out how to make a cake, mixing dry and wet ingredients separately, then blending. My method of determining the right oven temperature was by the heat on the hand, not by thermometer.

McMinn was the linch-pin of the team. Then around twenty-nine, he was the oldest, most experienced member and had been through World War II in the army. He had developed a cheerful cynicism to go with a slightly vulgar sense of humor and a poet's sensitivity. A curious mixture. McMinn took earthy delight in shocking young members of his crew by catching deer flies with his hands and hurling them into his stew and eating them. It was gross, but the effect on witnesses was worth it. More than one kid was put off his feed. I was very fond of McMinn. Still am.

Meanwhile there were two- and three-week expeditions into the mountains, to work a ridge building cairns, reading angles, and photographing scenery. Kitimat remains a precious, vivid memory, especially in the fall when the humpback salmon began to run, providing our first opportunity for fresh food.

We had no fishing equipment but had found a pitchfork in a barn abandoned for twenty years, which we plundered for wood to build our makeshift cabin. When the tidal tributary to the Kitimat River was low, someone would stand knee-deep upstream with the pitchfork while others would stampede from downstream, driving the salmon toward him. The guy with the fork would try to stab and hoist a fish to the bank. It worked well. We dined on glorious fresh salmon before they had begun to deteriorate during their long journey to upstream spawning grounds.

Later that season the great helicopter pioneer, Carl Agar, joined us to fly us to ridges and peaks so that we could complete the topographic survey, which needed clear weather for readings. Clear days are rare in B.C.'s steep, dense coastal range at any time, and ours had been a particularly wet and cloudy season. No one had ever used helicopters the way Agar did, and until then it was considered too dangerous to use them high in mountains with treacherous upward and downward drafts. But Carl would fly us to ridges, drop us off, and then pick us up a day or several hours later and fly us up to the next ridge. A summer's work could be done in days.

The most poignant memory of Kitimat was an early September morning when the Canada geese were starting their long flight south. We awoke one day to find a family of these handsome birds resting on the tributary in front of our camp, quietly honking and gently swimming before continuing their annual migration. We saw them only as fresh food, not as something wild and beautiful.

Our leader being the best shot, McMinn took aim with his .303 and waited for the heads of two geese to get in line, in the hope of knocking both off with one shot. An ambitious order.

McMinn took aim for what seemed an eternity, then fired. However, he wounded only one of the young ones, the rest took flight—two parents and three other young ones. They circled high and called for the fourth youngster to join them. It tried to take off, churning the water desperately but unable to lift itself out. Again and again it tried. We watched with growing sympathy, hoping it would succeed. The geese in the air circled and honked with growing impatience and puzzlement. What was wrong with their companion?

Finally the two parents swooped down, landed on either side of their wounded offspring, and, moving in tight, tried to take off and lift the wounded bird out of the water. It was perhaps the most forlorn and noble sight I've ever seen. They failed. Again they tried. Then the parents gave up and joined the other three and, in single file, all flew low over their injured kin in the water. Honking their last tribute, they flew off toward the horizon to the south. A final farewell, like World War I fighter pilots paying respects to the fallen. The rest of us, responsible for the small tragedy, watched in some shock, then put out in our boat, chased the bird down, killed it, and had it for supper that night. I think that in our hearts, despite a veneer of casual concern, we wished we hadn't done what we did.

Whenever discussions come up as to Canada's national symbol, I think of this incident. Since then I have been convinced that the Canadian symbol should be the wonderful Canada goose, which embodies such virtues as loyalty, courage, cleverness, faithfulness. Instead, we have chosen as our symbol the beaver, a rodent that works hard, mindlessly cuts down trees, and continuously builds dams, regardless of their worth.

3

No soldiers killed, only 11 Americans

3PPCLI BATTALION NEWSLETTER
KOREA, 1953

After the Korean War started in June 1950, I was kicking around Europe, spending money I had earned surveying in British Columbia and in logging camps. I was living in London, sharing an apartment with my sister and five other working girls, and sleeping in a garret where wildlife artist Keith Shackleton, related to the great Antarctic explorer and navigator *extraordinaire*, worked when he was in town. I was running out of money and had applied to join the Malayan police force, which was gearing up to fight the Communists. I had also written to Ottawa to join the Canadian army, which was fighting in Korea. As far as I was concerned, Korea and Malaya were indistinguishable; both sounded exotic, remote, unknown, and either seemed to offer a chance to do something different. Whoever responded first to my inquiries would win me. In fact, Malaya was over 2,000 miles southwest of Korea: all steamy jungle and rubber plantation as opposed to Korea's mountains and rice-paddy fields, where winters were Siberian.

The Canadian army reacted favorably to my application before the Malayan police did, and since I'd already held a commission briefly, I went to officers' training at Camp Borden, my childhood home, as a second lieutenant. I was on my way to joining the Princess Pats, becoming a paratrooper, and getting my chance to fight in a war. I was ecstatic. What I had been robbed of by my youth in World War II, I'd now get in Korea: a chance to see action.

The Korean War was unusual on several counts. It began at 4 A.M. on a rainy Sunday, June 25, 1950, when some 90,000 North Korean troops crossed the 38th parallel on six general invasion routes and caught by surprise some 60,000 ill-trained South Korean troops manning the front. The 38th parallel, dividing 9 million Russian-dominated Koreans of the industrial north from the 20 million American-assisted Koreans of the agricultural south, was a meaningless administrative line drawn to facilitate the surrender of the Japanese in 1945. Between 1945 and 1950, tensions increased in the "Land of the Morning Calm" as Korea was known historically. The Soviets imposed Moscow-trained Kim Il Sung as premier of North Korea, proclaimed it to be a "people's democracy," and concentrated on building a huge army. By 1950, President Syngman Rhee was an able, authoritarian, impatient leader of South Korea who was not reluctant to use his police to discourage those who disagreed with him and to keep his political opposition quiet. Most of the American troops had gone home by 1950 and South Korean–American diplomatic relations were cool but firm ("I did not care for the methods used by Rhee . . . but we had no choice but to support him," President Harry Truman was to write). Three days after the dawn invasion, the troops of North Korean General Ung Jung Chai, a five-foot-six, 250-pound monstrosity, had entered Seoul, fifty miles south of the 38th parallel. The retreat was on.

Soviet delegate Jacob Malik had boycotted the UN Security Council, thereby forfeiting the Soviet veto, and the General Assembly had voted to support the United States in driving out the invader. American troops were sent into action—and were clobbered.

Eventually, troops from sixteen countries served in Korea. Canada supported the principle of rescuing the South but was reluctant to participate and initially only sent two officers to South Korea as "observers." External Affairs Minister Lester Pearson talked, *not* about sending more troops, but about sending more observers. Canada clearly intended its support to be symbolic. Some six weeks after voting in the UN to support the U.S. action, Prime Minister Louis St. Laurent announced the formation of a "special brigade" of 5,000 men—which the government still did not want to send overseas, partly because it might offend the Soviet Union. The Soviets were still upset over the revelations of a massive espionage ring in Canada and the West, thanks to the disclosures of Soviet Military Intelligence defector Igor Gouzenko in Ottawa.

The government hoped its troops would be an occupation force, not a fighting force, and no speed records were broken to get into the war. The army had withered after 1945 and when recruiting opened up for the Special Korean Force, bizarre problems occurred. Of the first 10,000 volunteers in the first seven months, nearly 30 percent deserted or had to be discharged. During a similar period in World War I, only 7 percent were misfits, and in World War II the figure was 12 percent. A policy of recruit first, examine later, was implemented and resulted in months of snafus and oddities. A seventy-two-year-old man was enlisted as a private, as was a fourteen-year-old boy; somehow a man with one leg was enlisted. In one case a civilian in Ottawa was mistaken for a recruit and herded, protesting, onto a troop train. Weeks later he was found drilling—and still protesting—with the Princess Patricia's Canadian Light Infantry (PPCLI) in Calgary.

Jim Stone, recalled from World War II retirement to command the Special Force Patricias, became a tough, fair soldier, beloved by his men. He took his ill-trained men to Korea a week before Christmas 1950, and refused to let them go into action before he felt they were ready. This created an awkward situation with 8th Army commander General Walton Walker, a tank soldier who'd served with General Patton's legendary Third Army in Europe. A diplomatic confrontation between Ottawa and Washington was brewing when General Walker was killed in a road accident. His successor, General Matthew Ridgway, never raised the matter.

Colonel Stone reported to Ottawa that his troops showed "lack of basic training . . . particularly in caring for weapons and equipment." A typical group of men returned to Canada had such disorders as chronic bronchitis, atrophied leg muscles, cardiac palpitations, perforated eardrums, arthritis, spinal disorders, hernia, and hypertension.

The finest moment of the war for Canadians came when the 700 Pats, misfits finally eliminated, broke the back of a 6,000-man Chinese attack at Kapyong in 1951 and the battalion was awarded a U.S. Presidential Citation. However, it wasn't until five years later in 1956 that the Canadian government finally gave permission for the decoration to be worn.

It was hoped that the war would end quickly but it was not to be. General Douglas MacArthur, an exalted, almost mythical character—aristocratic, autocratic, and inflated with his importance—launched his brilliant and daring amphibious attack at Inchon, near Seoul, and the North Koreans, who had driven the Americans and their Korean allies onto the tip of the 600-mile peninsula, were now in full retreat. The UN forces pushed north across the

38th parallel and, despite warnings of the Chinese, continued pursuit. Pyongyang, capital of the North, was captured in October; one week later the Chinese crossed the Yalu River dividing North Korea from China, and the local "police action" was suddenly and dramatically escalated. There would be no victory by Christmas. The Chinese/North Korean forces recaptured Seoul and, with the troops of sixteen nations fighting, the UN dug in and tried to hold. In the spring of 1951, while advocating bombing of China proper and possibly using nuclear weapons, General MacArthur was fired as Supreme Commander by Harry Truman. ("I fired him because he wouldn't respect the authority of the President . . . I didn't fire him because he was a dumb son of a bitch, although he was, but that's not against the law for generals," Truman recalled later.)

By the end of May 1951, the UN had not only stopped the Chinese but driven them back to the 38th parallel, where ceasefire talks began. The war bogged down into a defensive phase for the UN. Any form of initiative or enterprise was discouraged. The strategy became one *not* of winning but of holding on. The Communist forces would attack, but UN troops could only hold fast and defend themselves, with patrol activity the main aggressive action. It was the most difficult of roles for fighting soldiers and, while politically convenient, was militarily debilitating. The war dragged on for over three years, during which there were three waves of Canadian troops—the first wave being in the fluid war, the second holding recaptured ground, and the third settling into a version of trench warfare, living underground in bunkers, sleeping by day, and patrolling and standing-to by night. It was 1914–18 revisited.

I was in Korea in the final year of the three-year war, when Canada's 25th Brigade was comprised of three battalions: the Princess Patricia's, Royal Canadian Regiment (RCR), and Royal 22nd—the Vandoos—plus artillery and the tanks of the Lord Strathconas and/or Royal Canadian Dragoons. The rest of the 1st Commonwealth Division consisted of a British brigade, an Australian brigade, and New Zealand artillery. With each Commonwealth country contributing more troops and equipment than anticipated, the Commonwealth division became arguably the strongest, most lethal division in military history up to then.

The Canadian infantry was from the Mobile Strike Force, elite airborne units which were rivals and utterly different in character.

The Patricia's had a more rough-and-ready tradition, less pompous and pretentious than the slightly stuffy RCR and more compatible with the Vandoos, who were known as wild, erratic, and effective soldiers whose ranks were interspersed with English-speaking officers. They were an encouraging example of linguistic integration long before Canada's official bilingualism ruined French-English relations. In their way, the Vandoos were proof that the two cultures of Canada could live in harmony. French and English troops generally got on well, despite predictable rivalry (there is nothing like being shot at by others to bring two disparate cultures together). No one much liked the RCR who, though competent, were overly pleased with themselves and did not have much of a reputation as fighting soldiers.

As wars go, the Korean War was relatively "safe" for Canadians. Of nearly one million UN casualties, Canada suffered some 1,500 casualties, of whom 300 were killed. (In the year the war ended, over 2,000 Canadians died in traffic accidents). The U.S. suffered 135,000 casualties, with 30,000 dead. China and North Korea suffered an estimated 1.5 million casualties.

No sooner had the third battalion of the Princess Pats replaced the first battalion in Korea than we were called into action. The Black Watch was attacked and overrun on the most lethal defensive position on the Commonwealth division front, a feature ominously named "the Hook." The Hook was on a hilltop generally exposed to constant fire from the Chinese on a higher feature known as "Pheasant." The Hook had been overrun when the U.S. Marines held it, and was under repeated attack when the British Black Watch moved in.

I was a platoon commander in Dog Company, commanded by gentle, decent Major Shawcross. On a clear, icy-cold November night in 1952 during the static war phase, the Chinese launched a surprise attack on the Hook, overrunning the Black Watch, which called their own artillery down on themselves. Dog Company was ordered to move up to support the Black Watch. After midnight we were formed up at the base of the hill, prepared to counterattack and recapture the hill if necessary.

As my platoon moved into position, the moon glowed bright on the crunchy snow and a chill wind picked up. Understandably, everyone was nervous: counterattacking is perhaps the most unpleasant and costly fighting, since little surprise is possible. It's hard work and requires stamina. After a year's training in Canada, none of us was especially well trained, and while in theory a platoon officer is supposed to know what the thirty to forty men under his command are doing, I could never keep track of mine. From my limited experience in war, there's a hell of a lot of guesswork, luck, and intuition involved. If something succeeds, you invent reasons after to explain why it worked; if things go wrong, there are plenty of volunteers to tell you where and how you erred. Winners write the "official" histories, which is a reason most are unreliable and tend to be, as Napoleon once noted, a set of lies mutually agreed upon. There is more to learn from the losers' accounts of why they lost than from the winners' rationalizations for their triumph.

As it turned out, my platoon's first exposure to possible action was perilously close to a fiasco. We had moved out in a hurry and someone had grabbed a couple of canteens of water to share when necessary. Russ Morrison, the platoon sergeant and more experienced than I, was in charge of the canteens. I noticed in passing that as we got nearer our assembly point beneath the Hook, more and more of my troops were taking sips of water. I put it down to nervous thirst. Personally, although my mouth was dry, I didn't want any fluid.

As we waited, my platoon began to get more bellicose and less cautious. One guy even began to sing a little. I ordered him to keep his goddam mouth shut. Still, I was impressed. It seemed I had a bunch of tigers in the platoon. God help the Chinese if they ever tangled with us. It was then that Morrison worriedly confessed that he'd grabbed, not canteens of water, but canteens of overproof rum, which was rationed an ounce per man per winter night. What we had ready to counterattack, if called upon, was a somewhat drunk platoon. Morrison was amused and appalled, as was I. My men were so relaxed they were now beginning to fall asleep. I really began to get nervous.

Fortunately, we weren't needed. The Black Watch restored control and at dawn Charlie Company of the Pats rooted out what Chinese were left. One of our officers—Lieutenant Don Marvin, if memory is correct—had caught some shrapnel and everyone mildly envied him his wound. Personally, I would have preferred to have been nicked somewhere other than where Marvin was hit: in the rear end. Oddly, Lieutenant Russ Campbell, who'd been through training with me, also got hit in the rear end. I used to wonder how officers managed to get hit in the south end when the enemy was to the north.

Some curious tales emerged from that attack. When the Chinese overran the area, they tried to move out their own dead and our wounded, and had tended to the seriously wounded Black Watch and made them comfortable, filled their pockets full of "peace" propaganda, gave them cigarettes, even food, and shaken hands. It was disconcerting to find those trying to kill us friendly and thoughtful, even if just for propaganda purposes.

As for me, thereafter I kept closer tabs on the platoon's rum supply.

Shortly afterward, the Third Patricias under Lieutenant-Colonel Herb Wood relieved the Black Watch and my platoon was given the dubious honor of occupying the Hook position. It was a dreadful location of collapsed trenches and shell holes everywhere. One trench ran north-south, and was in direct line of Chinese fire from above. We called this the "windy" section, where movement was "safe" only at night. The whole platoon area stank of dead bodies: Chinese buried in the parapets were periodically unearthed by the constant shelling. Most casualties came from shelling, very few from actual fighting. In my view it is hard to be attacked by surprise if patrols are doing their job and the unit is well trained and disciplined. The Princess Pats were never caught by surprise when I was with them, unlike the Royal Canadian Regiment, which was twice overrun during my time. Usually if you encountered excessive enemy activity in the valley at night, you called down massive artillery and disrupted whatever was going on.

Shortly after taking command of the Hook, I led a patrol into the no-man's-land valley that came as close to disaster as I care to be. Pity, because it could so easily have been a small triumph. It was testimony to inexperience. We were to go down through our own barbed wire and minefields and try to encounter a Chinese patrol in the valley. We had Bren guns—light machine guns— Lee Enfield rifles of a type that had been in service since World War I, American carbines, a couple of Sten guns, and grenades. We gathered in one of the underground bunkers and at dusk took our weapons into the freezing night and went hunting for Chinese.

We had been out a couple of hours, I guess, and were lying in wait near a stream and I was about to give orders to move on when there were soft noises in front. We froze and listened. More noises, then there was a murmuring of voices. Chinese! I could feel the hair on my neck prickle and excitement rise. I was reminded of the time I shot my first deer at age eleven in Camp

Borden. There was a feeling of detachment and disbelief that it was actually happening. The enemy was too close for us to use the radio and tell headquarters what was happening. I wondered if I'd get buck fever when the moment came to shoot a human being or if it would be like shooting a deer. I saw a dim shape moving against a hillside. Then another. The Chinese were moving in single file. We had them.

I forget the sequence, but suddenly there was a shout to fire. Nothing happened. I yelled, and began firing my Sten gun. Another Sten gun fired. But no Bren gunfire. No rifle fire either, or carbine. Nothing. Just yelling and cursing. The Chinese hit the ground and their return fire filled the night air. Burp guns, firing much faster than our Stens (unless beer bottle caps were placed behind the springs), fanned the sides. Grenades began going off. Still there was only Sten gunfire from us. When my magazine was empty, I reversed to the other magazine strapped to the first one. Still no supporting fire. My radio operator was radioing in panic about what he thought was happening.

It could only have taken moments, but the Chinese retreated, artillery was called down, and we regrouped and got the hell out of there. I was furious. What had happened? Why had no one fired? My troops were beside themselves. What had happened, it turned out, was that prior to going on patrol they'd taken their weapons from the cold into the warm bunkers, and condensation had formed. When we re-emerged into the cold night, the moisture had frozen, and the moving parts of the firing mechanism wouldn't work. The bolts of the Lee Enfields were frozen shut; so were the siding bars of the Bren guns and the pins in the grenades. Only the imprecisely built Sten guns, each worth about $3, were too loose to freeze. Their shots had frightened off the enemy who, in their return of fire, had hit no one. It was a dramatic lesson and proved again the adage that in war, green troops are in most peril. We never again took weapons from the cold into the warmth and into the cold again without making sure they weren't frozen.

It was Christmas Eve of 1952 and I was by now quite at home on the Hook, conditioned to expect an average of one casualty a day as a result of Chinese shelling. Those in the particularly vulnerable "windy" section were rewarded with an extra shot of rum per day. We were used to the stench of death by now, and when our troops rotated for occasional baths, they carried the stink of the dead in their clothes to the point where others at the shower centre noticed it.

There was speculation that the Chinese might attack on Christmas Eve when, presumably, the Christians would be thinking of home and celebrating. And indeed, that night there was a lot of movement and activity reported in front of our barbed wire. Our patrols came in, we called down flares, artillery, and everyone was more nervous than usual, anticipating an attack. But nothing happened.

Then at first light we were startled to see shapes looming in front of our wire. Some of the men began firing, but the shapes didn't move. They seemed giant figures—the troops called them Manchurians, for some inexplicable reason. We reported the shapes to Battalion headquarters, which reported them to Brigade, which reported them to Division. The Brigade artillery was zeroed in on the Hook, ready to fire the instant it was required.

When the sun came up we saw that the shapes were actually Christmas trees. The Chinese had spent the night putting them up in front of our wire and decorating them with gifts and packages. A huge banner was also stretched along the front, urging us not to fight the Yankees' war.

"Don't let any troops go near them, they may be booby-trapped!" warned Brigade. Too late. Already the men had deserted their positions and were scurrying down the hill like so many crabs through the barbed wire and minefields to get at the gifts.

I was horrified at both my lack of control and their foolhardiness. However, nothing happened. The troops returned laden with the gifts: glass figurines of animals (some of which adorn my mantelpiece to this day), anti-war diaries, packages of tea, safe-conduct passes in case we wanted to surrender, postcards, stamps, propaganda.

Brigade was upset. I was told to order the men to turn all the stuff in and especially warned, "Don't let them read the propaganda!" I issued the instructions and suggested they keep some souvenirs but turn over enough to satisfy the rear-echelon types. Spirits were high, morale good, and I thought it would be a terrific idea if we returned the favor that night by giving gifts in return. I mentioned to the colonel that I wanted to take a patrol over to the Chinese positions and leave gallon cans of "C" ration ham chunks and lima beans, which our troops detested and never ate. After consulting with their intelligence officers, the colonel and the brigadier decided that this verged on fraternizing with the enemy and on no account was it to be done.

I argued that, on the contrary, it would be good for our morale.

"Your men might find it difficult to fight the enemy if they give them gifts," said Colonel Wood.

"Really, sir, to give them ham chunks, which none of our guys like, is a reverse joke on the Chinese. I urge you to reconsider."

"Peter, why do you have such difficulty understanding that when you are told not to do something it means you are not to do it. There are others who know better than you."

"Yessir."

When my platoon decided to disobey orders and take ham chunks anyway that night, I said I didn't want to know—but I added that I thought it important that we go into the Chinese lines to see what was happening. The patrol got the message and that night several gallon cans of ham chunks were left in the Chinese trenches.

On Boxing Day the feeling of satisfaction was still strong, and I mildly wondered if perhaps Brigade and Battalion headquarters were correct in their view that the fighting resolve of our troops might be lessened. It was about 11 A.M. when a couple of Chinese soldiers were seen in the open. The effect on the platoon was instantaneous and electric. The men roused from their bunkers and within moments it was like a shooting gallery, with everyone trying to knock off the two Chinese running and ducking along the hillside. So much for pacifism or reluctance to shoot those from whom you'd just received Christmas gifts and to whom you'd just given a gift of ham chunks!

The big deal in Korea was to try to take a prisoner. Very difficult. The Third PPCLI never captured one. It was said a week's leave in Japan awaited anyone who captured a Chinese.

Every evening our patrols took well-worn trails through the layers of barbed wire and minefields into the no-man's-land valley. The Chinese would also use our trails on their way toward our positions. Both sides would set up ambushes, and firefights and nervous shootings would go on all night. Our orders were that, for safety, ambush patrols had to have at least fourteen men. Anyone who has ever tried to induce fourteen Canadian soldiers to be stealthy knows the virtual impossibility of the task, especially when troops are half-trained, as most Canadians were. Rarely were the Chinese caught in ambushes. In fact, General Allard, by nature an aggressive, enthusiastic soldier more suited to attack than defence, was to wryly note that instead of catching the enemy,

Canadian ambush patrols in Korea tended to be ambushed themselves.

I thought I had a wonderful idea to catch a prisoner. I went to the engineers and asked them to improvise a bear trap that would spring shut when stepped upon, closing with a couple of inches to spare. The idea was to anchor this trap in the ground along one of the trails the Chinese used, cover it so it couldn't be seen, and set up an ambush 100 yards or so away. When a Chinese stepped in the trap, it would slam shut and hold him tight. He'd undoubtedly be screaming that one of the seven devils had him by the ankle, we'd call down mortar fire and move in. The Chinese would retreat while our prisoner would remain.

Colonel Wood was delighted with the idea and would chortle merrily about it in the mess as he fondled his gold watch fob. However, when I told him the trap was near completion, he got upset and conferred with his second in command, Major Charlie McNeil, and then adamantly said we could not do it because it would violate the Geneva Convention.

I was upset, but then thought of digging a pit with sharpened bamboo stakes at the bottom and covering the pit with bamboo matting. We'd locate the pit on a trail well travelled by the Chinese and hope that one would fall in. This was considered far-fetched. I also suggested we put up a flatpole or odd structure in no-man's-land, set up a record player with music, then booby-trap the area with mines and bangalore torpedoes, on the presumption that the Chinese with their insatiable curiosity would find it irresistible to investigate, and be blown up. We would take the wounded as prisoners. Again, no go. I finally gave up and like so many others, relegated my initiative to bitching and grumbling about the brass, and did more or less what was expected of me. I liked the army, but found it limiting and unimaginative.

It was in Korea that I first became aware of the press. We rarely saw any in the forward areas, but the troops were simultaneously delighted to see journalists and mildly scornful of them. That is, they relished publicity but had difficulty relating what they *thought* they said with what eventually appeared in print. Besides, journalists usually misunderstood the situation and were captive of army public relations officers who, by and large, were rejects from the combat units.

In Korea we were occasionally visited by the resident Canadian Press correspondent, Bill Boss, who later became a professor at the University of Ottawa. I had known Boss since I was a boy in

Truro, Nova Scotia, 1942, when my father was training the 4th
Canadian Armoured Division to take it overseas. Boss became a
friend of the family and was trusted implicitly by my father, whose
outspokenness made him quotable and vulnerable to the press.
(Yet journalists rarely betrayed him—except when at the beginning of my journalistic career I once quoted his views as head of
Canada's Civil Defence: "Back it or scrap it." The resulting furore
was terribly embarrassing to him—and to me, since I had difficulty
understanding why, if someone believed something, there'd be
reluctance to say so.)

In Korea, Boss had his own trailer, and was a law unto himself.
Soldiers of all ranks periodically pretended to abhor his craft,
though never within his hearing. When he wrote things they didn't
like, the senior officers of the brigade were inclined to ban him
from entering their zones. On one occasion, orders went out that
only officers were to talk to him. Boss was credited with making
the Patricias Canada's glamor regiment of the Korean War. Other
Canadian units were jealous, and the Pats began to think they
owned Boss, which they didn't. It was not the first case of favorable
coverage being interpreted as uncritical approval, and subsequent
critical coverage being seen as betrayal. When Boss wrote about
the startlingly high VD rate among Canadian troops in Korea, he
was treated as though he'd committed treason. Never having caught
VD, I took a more generous view of his "exposures." Still, I shared
the mixture of apprehension, anticipation, and mild contempt for
the press that was fashionable among the military then, and still
is. Front-line soldiers rarely saw journalists. When they occasionally visited, it seemed they always left as soon as decency permitted.
The few press we saw in Korea seemed to think that Battalion
Headquarters was the "front"; to infantry, it was rest and reha-
bilitation.

However, I paid little attention to journalism—until I became
a minor victim.

First there was a narrow escape. Once, when the battalion was
in reserve, my platoon had the task of reconstructing emergency
fall-back positions on a feature known as Gloucester Hill. This
location had won fame as the position where the British Gloucester
Regiment had made a gallant stand against the Chinese in 1951
and had refused to retreat. They had sacrificed themselves to give
the division time to regroup. The regiment was wiped out—all
members killed or taken prisoner—after savage hand-to-hand
fighting. The commanding officer, Lieutenant-Colonel James

Carne, who was taken prisoner, was awarded the Victoria Cross on behalf of his regiment. (Only four VCs were awarded in Korea, none going to Canadians, while 131 Congressional Medals of Honor were awarded to Americans. As far as "quality" is concerned, the VC is far more respected than the Medal of Honor.)

Canadian soldiers don't like digging trenches for a retreat they are convinced will never happen. After a morning in the bright sun of Korean springtime, the platoon was half-heartedly going through the motions of restoring the old Gloucester trenches. Interest picked up when skeletons and the remnants of war began being unearthed: a buckle, ammunition, a bayonet, a rusted Burp gun and, in one trench, a jumble of Chinese and Gloucester bones, including skulls. Mute testimony to the ferocity of the fighting.

During a field lunch the troops placed some bones upright by an open trench and indulged in a game of bowls, using a skull as a bowling ball. Russ Morrison, the platoon sergeant, and I looked at each other, raised our eyebrows, and pretended not to see. Desecrating the dead it may have been, but it was done entirely without malice. It was soldiers' horseplay, to which it was best to pay no attention. I happened to look down the hill toward the road and who was striding up but Bill Boss accompanied by Lieutenant Bill Beeman, a Brigade liaison officer and a fellow Patricia. Morrison hastily alerted the troops who, in the nick of time, kicked the bones into a trench and threw a groundsheet over the evidence. Boss poked around the position, got monosyllabic answers to his questions, and eventually wrote a story about the fall-back preparations. Over the years I have occasionally wondered how I would have written the story had I been there as a journalist—and shudder at what could have been done with it.

I got into trouble when I was made Intelligence Officer of the battalion after switching from platoon and company duties. I had to color the battle maps, draw in the Chinese positions, and put appropriate identification numbers on where we were told Chinese units were. It was mostly a secretarial job and I could never remember the numbers of the Chinese divisions. I was always puzzled about the purpose it served to know that you were matched against, say, the 43rd Battalion of the 17th Brigade of the 11th Division of the 5th Corps of the 9th Army of the People's Revolutionary Army of the People's Republic of China. To our troops, one Chinese soldier was very much like any other. Besides, when it came to marking up the maps of the company commanders, I often made mistakes in the boundary areas and by the time I realized it, all the maps would be marked and nothing could be done about it. Interestingly, I rarely got a complaint; the markings apparently made little difference to the company commanders, either.

Being Intelligence Officer enabled me to swan all over Korea without being asked any questions, ostensibly doing "intelligence work" that no one knew about and no one ever defined. It was then I realized that life in the army was freest and easiest for those who walked fast and carried a brown envelope. Everyone assumes you are doing something important and rarely ask what. Lounging around, seemingly with nothing to do, causes questions in the army just as it does in newsrooms.

Being IO also entailed writing the battalion newsletter, a monthly report of happenings in the regiment that was sent to retired and former officers of the PPCLI. I used it to vent a lot of frustrations. Anything that happened to irritate, amuse, or interest me I tried to include in the newsletter in such a way that those concerned would know what I was talking about, but strangers would not be quite sure. Subalterns enjoyed getting in licks at senior officers, and it was a wonderful safety valve for the inanities and insanities of army life. Looking back, I think the newsletter was probably the genesis of my entering journalism. Even then it had pitfalls. Once I remarked that a certain lieutenant was so dedicated to duty that he rarely left his bunker, even to the point where he kept a bucket of sand as a form of human kitty litter and slept with his tin helmet on. The inference was that he was a bit nervous. I had assumed he was just dirty and lazy. As it turned out he was scared to death, and one night threatened to shoot me for the innuendo of the newsletter. Suddenly I realized that what was intended as lighthearted mockery had hit a nerve and was a case of the greater the truth, the greater the libel. I was appalled at what I'd done.

Colonel Wood, who later was to write *Strange Battleground*, the official history of Canada's part in the Korean War, knew exactly what was going on with the newsletter and his slightly malicious and mischievous sense of humor delighted in the barbs. But Wood was replaced by Colonel Tony McLaughlin, a Maritimer who had none of the "Patricias" tradition and was more inclined to caution with the newsletter. It made him uneasy.

He joined us when the unit was in reserve, billeted on hills overlooking the Imjin River. One morning at dawn the Teal bridge over the Imjin was attacked and bombed by American planes whose pilots couldn't read maps. As usual. All of us were at first apprehensive at the air attack, not realizing it was the Americans making another error. Initially, we assumed it was the Chinese getting ready to attack. These were the first "enemy" planes we had seen in the war, and we thought they were sealing off our escape. Though it was soon clear what had happened, there was no official confirmation; the planes remained officially "unidentified."

It was newsletter time, so I included a sarcastic item to the effect that "Four unidentified U.S. planes with UN markings bombed and strafed the Teal bridge, but fortunately no soldiers were killed, only 11 Americans." Bill Boss put the item on the CP wires to Canada. It was reprinted in Canadian papers and picked up by Associated Press. In due course an angry response came back demanding to know the writer of the newsletter meant by "no soldiers were killed, only 11 Americans"? Apparently the Americans had filed a protest. Colonel McLaughlin sent me to Brigade Headquarters to explain what I meant by the crack.

"You know how it is," I told the brigade major. "Our troops consider themselves better soldiers than Americans. It wasn't meant for public consumption, it was a joke. Damned journalists."

"Not a very funny joke," said the major. "Especially if you are an American. Well, funny fellow, you can explain your joke to the Americans. See if they are amused. Go to Eighth Army Headquarters in Seoul tomorrow, tell them what you meant, and say you're sorry."

I took a jeep to Seoul, apologized to some bored American brigadier general who didn't know what it was all about, didn't care, and, I felt, had only just learned by my presence that there were Canadians in Korea. He more or less equated us with soldiers from Thailand. He accepted my apology, even though he, too, failed to see the joke.

That was the last newsletter I ever wrote for the PPCLI. But I was made aware of the power of the press and wondered, casually, how one got to write for newspapers. I was to find out in a couple of years.

I was depressed when the war ended.

Like so many of the 27,000 Canadians who rotated through the three-year Korean War, I hadn't gone to Korea for patriotic or ideological reasons, but because it seemed adventurous. I had no particular feelings about saving democracy or halting the Red menace, but there seemed no doubt that it was the right thing to do at the time and that the aggression from the north could not be allowed to succeed. What would I do now? I was unmarried, had no commitments, and had no reason to return to Canada. I had enjoyed the Korean War, but was increasingly frustrated by the army. I didn't like a system where rank is equated with wisdom, and a higher rank is automatically right and has to constantly be deferred to. Opportunities for individual initiative were limited, primarily because Korea was too small a war and senior officers, having too little to do, got too embroiled in routine platoon and company matters. On occasion we had brigadiers and colonels overseeing routine section patrols. (I remember once dressing my troops in pyjamas over their battledress as camouflage on the snow-splattered terrain and incurring raised eyebrows from the colonel, who watched the progress through binoculars and thought the impromptu camouflage somewhat unsoldierly. It also almost got us shot up by the Vandoos, through whose lines our patrol had to return at dawn, since they hadn't been warned about our unusual garb.) Though I was not a very good soldier or officer, I was proud of our troops and our reputation in Korea. We gained superb confidence and were never really tested. Man for man, we felt far superior to the Americans, and never tired of telling one another how, when the U.S. First Cavalry Division was driven off Hill 355 (which they called Little Gibraltar), "they moved so fast their combat cigars looked like tracer bullets." Perhaps it was evidence of basic inferiority or dependence on the Americans that made us believe we were the *real* professionals, they the amateurs. After all, Canadians were volunteers, Americans were conscripts.

Increasingly, I was unenthusiastic about a peacetime military career. After all, for twenty years my father had been a peacetime soldier and suffered all the inevitable frustrations. I couldn't see whiling away my life on garrison duty, participating in annual war games in the Arctic, or serving around the world on UN duty. It never occurred to me to ask my parents for either advice or help— my father was Civil Defence Co-ordinator for Canada and trying to make the country aware of nuclear defences—any more than it would have occurred to them to offer unsolicited advice. Whatever I chose to do would be my choice, my responsibility, and as long as I was content, my parents would be satisfied. (Looking back, I think my sister and I could have benefited from gentle parental prodding from time to time. But it never came. We were on our own.)

Fearing the boredom of a nine-to-five job, I looked for options.

I knew that the French were bogged down in a war in Indochina that none of us knew anything about, and word was that they were anxious to recruit combat-experienced infantry officers on one-year contracts at $1,000 a month. I wrote to the French Embassy in Japan and offered myself, and received a courteous letter to the effect that my information was half right, half wrong. Yes, they were anxious for combat-experienced soldiers from other armies, but no, they weren't paying $1,000 a month for a one-year contract and no, they weren't hiring officers. If I wanted to go to Indochina I'd be welcome, but first I'd have to join the Foreign Legion as a private on a five-year contract and take my chances. It was not what I had in mind. I returned to Canada with no fixed plans.

As it turned out, I left the army and returned to the University of British Columbia to complete my tortured path to a BA degree, begun in the winter of 1946 and interrupted by sports, boxing, pure sloth, and war. I'd finally get that diploma eight years after I started.

4

You'll never make it
as a journalist

GENERAL E.L.M. BURNS
COMMANDER UNEF
JANUARY 1958

In North America, all it takes to be a journalist is the nerve and opportunity. One needn't have any particular skills or training so long as someone is willing to provide the job. In Britain and Australia, shorthand is almost a prerequisite for a journalist. Not in Canada or the United States, where the *inability* to write down exactly what someone says is almost considered an advantage. Prior to the cassette tape recorder, North American journalists liked to think that reporters who knew shorthand would be so intent on getting down precise quotes that they might ignore other important details. This is called making a virtue out of incompetence. It is ironic, but the most recent graduate from secretarial school has more mechanical ability and training to quote someone accurately than the most distinguished North American-trained journalist at the height of a career.

The lack of definable skills and training needed, the absence of any set standards to join the trade, the imprecise nature of the beast, and the exotic, even romantic, reputation of the craft, are perhaps why so many find journalism appealing—and possibly why it is held in such questionable repute by the public. This is not to suggest that there aren't good journalists in North America, or that all British or Australian ones are better. It is just to note that journalism can be a hit-or-miss business.

I consider myself a prime example of one who drifted into journalism accidentally, without any particular skills or calling and who, as a consequence, was far luckier in landing a better job than I had any right to expect.

After returning to Canada from the Korean War, I was posted to the 1st Battalion of the Princess Pats at Calgary and took several courses at the parachuting school at Rivers and Shilo in the Manitoba prairies. I enjoyed jumping out of planes, but the novelty soon wore off and it seemed a rather limiting occupation for peacetime. I figured the army provided too many opportunities for indolence and if I was ever going to shake myself into doing something productive, I'd have to leave the warmth of the military security blanket. I took my discharge and returned to the University of British Columbia to complete my final year. I found that, instead of being a kid keeping up with veterans, I was now a more legitimate veteran in the company of kids. I wanted to get out of the place as soon as possible. In need of money, I tried to exploit my limited experience with the abortive battalion newsletter by joining the university newspaper, *Ubyssey*, and writing sports for it. It seemed a good way to learn the mechanics of journalism.

Others who worked on the *Ubyssey* that year included Pat Carney, who went on to be a top business writer and later a Member of Parliament; Alan Fotheringham, perhaps Canada's most irreverent columnist; future publisher Alexander Ross; TV journalists Peter Sypnowich and Joe Schlesinger. All had varying degrees of impact on the Canadian media and on those of the public who pay attention to the media.

I did occasional university sports stories for the Vancouver *Province*, and on graduation, Ross Munro, a World War II correspondent and then publisher of the Vancouver *Province*, gave me a job as a reporter—not in sports, which was considered too important to turn over to a greenhorn, but in news, which was expendable. At the start of my journalistic career, I waited for an opening in sports that never came. In fact a variety of sports editors never trusted me to report the outcome of athletic encounters, even when I was involved in helping start a newspaper two decades later. In retrospect, I guess that was good luck, too, perhaps for sports-writing as well as for me.

After graduating from UBC I used my veteran's credits from Korea to enroll at Carleton College in Ottawa, which offered a Bachelor of Journalism degree after a one-year course. I took a leave of absence from the Vancouver *Province* to go east, intending to return the following spring. Instead, in the spring of 1956 I was hired as a night reporter by Art Cole, city editor of the Toronto *Telegram*. The pay was $60 a week—better than the $35 a week the *Province* paid.

Working nightside as a reporter for an afternoon paper is the quickest and most painless way to learn journalism. You get every variety of assignment and usually have enough time to write stories without the pressure of deadlines. I did the usual fires, murders, and features, such as finding a talking dog in London, Ontario, which I interviewed with the predictable result that it was smarter than I. Other night reporters, Colin Murray and Bert Petlock on the police desk, helped me get that dog on the Ed Sullivan Show, and for a time I became its agent. It seemed the dog, a dachshund named Heidi, had some sort of ESP rapport with its owner, a very normal, nice thirteen-year-old girl named Barbara Phipps. Every time Barbara concentrated, the dog yelped; so when asked what two plus two was, Barbara concentrated four times and the dog yelped four times and everyone thought it was doing arithmetic. Dr. J. B. Rhine of Duke University's investigated the case and found there was indeed some extrasensory communication. I escorted the dog and the Phippses to New York, where we did a spread on Heidi riding through Central Park in a cab, interviewing Jack Dempsey, Tony Perkins, Lena Horne, and so on. I had to fight off a London radio reporter named Ward Cornell who was trying to steal the talking dog story from me. Cornell eventually became the on-camera host of "Hockey Night in Canada," then was named agent general for Ontario in London, England, then deputy minister of culture and recreation for Ontario. I sometimes wonder if competing for the attentions of the talking dachshund contributed much to his sense of culture.

In the fall of 1956 the Hungarian revolution overlapped with the Suez War. While the Hungarian people rose in one of history's rare examples of a spontaneous uprising, turned on the secret police, and took back their country, Israel, Britain, and France were invading Suez. The Hungarian uprising lasted ten days before Soviet tanks crushed the rebellion; the Suez War lasted sixty hours and had far greater potential for expanded conflict.

With all these exciting things going on, I was trapped in Toronto doing the routine stories of the city—even talking dogs come along only rarely. There was no hint that the Suez crisis would eventually lead to my travelling around the world, trying to anticipate and catch up with various crises—the most stimulating and satisfying job in journalism.

There was always near-paranoia about Colonel Gamal Abdel Nasser, the son of a postman who, in 1952 at age thirty-four, had masterminded the ouster of decadent, dissolute King Farouk and taken over the running of Egypt. Nasser became the symbol for the Arab world and tried to become the leader of a pan-Arab alliance. For some years every insurrection in the Middle East was attributed to Nasser or Communists, with some of the suspicions justified.

The 1956 Suez crisis began with the nationalization of the Suez Canal a week after Britain and the United States reneged on their previous agreement to finance the High Dam at Aswan. British and Americans were angry at Nasser for accepting Soviet armaments after Britain refused to supply what Nasser wanted for his military.

Nasser's declaration made him an even greater folk hero throughout the Arab world. To all Arabs (Nasser was now proclaiming Egyptians to be Arabs, too, which they weren't, but it was politically useful), the Canal in foreign hands was a symbol of subservience, and nationalization of it freed them all. Besides, under the terms of the concession granted by the Khedive Ismail Pasha in 1866, foreign control of the Canal was not due to expire until 1969, and the Egyptians got only a million Egyptian pounds from the Canal while the Anglo-French company got 35 million pounds. Nasser declared that the extra revenues available from nationalization would go toward paying for the Aswan Dam.

British Prime Minister Anthony Eden, by now obsessed with Nasser, wanted him eliminated. Permanently. And the French were closely tied with Israel and even more eager to be rid of Nasser.

Nasser became the man of the moment across the Arab world from the Atlantic to the Persian Gulf. (Two years later Egypt and Syria were to form an unnatural alliance and call themselves the United Arab Republic: the beginning of an Arab empire and an indication of Nasser's charismatic powers at that time.) The Suez Canal gambit was also symbolic and emotional to anti-Nasser elements. Nationalization and the Canal in Egyptian hands constituted a gamble neither the British nor the Israelis were prepared to contemplate. The Israelis feared for their security and economic lifeline; the British needed not only the security of the route but also the income it represented. Egyptians were still regarded by many as "Wogs," incapable of operating the Canal. Perhaps Nasser's greatest triumph was that he dispelled the Wog attitude absolutely and permanently.

Nasser's rhetoric about driving Israel into the sea and his willingness to accept Soviet as well as Western aid and advice increased his bogeyman spectre. Under the hawkish influence of the Israelis and the French, the British government of Anthony Eden agreed to cooperate in a military strike to seize the Canal. Eden, who had dithered too long without power and in the shadow of Churchill, misread the Americans and thought they approved the action, though they never said so.

The Israeli *Blitzkrieg* was brilliant in its success: in one hundred hours Israeli tanks reached the Canal. But rather than being destroyed by defeat, Nasser benefited from it. He was fortunate in that the British and French also invaded. Almost literally, however, as Cyprus-based British paratroopers were floating down on Suez, Eden changed his mind about the invasion and after outrage expressed by the Americans (and opposition from Canada) called off the attack. The French were also forced to quit, and the Israelis withdrew. Turning the confused diplomatic situation into a massive political victory, Nasser immediately claimed that Egypt had defeated the combined forces of Israel, Britain, and France. Anthony Nutting, Britain's Foreign Secretary and Eden's protégé, resigned over the invasion and later recalled that it was Eden's personal obsession with Nasser that made him invade. Curiously, it was Nutting's, not Eden's, political career that was destroyed by this gesture of principle.

Lester Pearson, then Minister of External Affairs, made an impassioned plea at the UN for an emergency force to restore peace and security in the Middle East, eventually agreed to by all parties (winning for Pearson the Nobel Prize for Peace).

It was Canada's most glorious international moment and, for some, the thing that made it fashionable for Canada to be a de facto neutral in world affairs and the quasi-official peace arbiter and do-gooder. Ever since, Canada has been reluctant to stand up firmly for any cause, be it self-determination for Biafra, independence for Afghanistan, Czechoslovakia free of Soviet tanks, Solidarity in Poland, freedom for Grenada, El Salvador, Nicaragua, Cambodia, even Taiwan or Somalia. The only tyranny the Canadian government adamantly and vocally opposes is South Africa.

After the brief war, negotiations began to persuade President Nasser to accept the United Nations Emergency Force (UNEF), comprised of some 5,000 troops rotating among a dozen nations and based around the 1,000-man Canadian contingent. With typical lack of forethought, Canada had at first wanted to send the Queen's Own Rifles to Egypt to patrol the border with Israel, but the inappropriateness of the regimental name drove Nasser into fresh paroxysms of paranoia. Eventually an armoured squadron of scout cars and signallers and administrative troops was sent, while other nations provided the combat arm.

I went to Doug MacFarlane, then managing editor of the *Telegram*, and tried to persuade him that as one who had recently left the army I was a natural choice to go with the Canadians of the UNEF, which was to be stationed along the Gaza strip, a buffer zone established in northern Egypt near the Israeli border. I tried to persuade MacFarlane that because I would know many of the Canadian troops, I'd be able to get inside stuff. (What "inside stuff" I was not sure, except that it sounded valid; no one ever questioned the merits, and it made a good selling point.)

MacFarlane, who had run the Canadian army's popular overseas newspaper *Maple Leaf* while serving as a major in northwest Europe during the war and who had a soft spot for soldiers and ex-soldiers, was skeptical. Not only was he reluctant to trust an overseas assignment to an untried junior reporter (despite his advanced age—thirty—and experience outside journalism), but he was still recovering from the trauma caused by his ace feature reporter, John Maclean, who had tried to stow away aboard the aircraft carrier *Magnificent* taking the first Canadian troops to Suez. MacFarlane was cool to the point of freezing about my proposal.

Maclean, assigned to cover the ship's departure from Halifax, had gotten drunk and hidden somewhere below deck, with a case of cheese sandwiches and a suitcase full of Scotch. He was discovered soon after the *Maggie* had gotten under way, and put ashore with the pilot. Maclean was given another in a series of final warnings by the *Telegram* management that he'd be fired if he ever did anything like this again. The trouble was that Maclean rarely did the same thing twice (except get drunk) and always figured out some totally new and unheard-of antic to indulge in and drive the managing editor crazy.

(On another occasion, while in his cups, Maclean wrote a splendid story about catching Soviet spies in Ottawa's Chateau Laurier hotel, and giving "Boris" the "old one-two" after a typical Russian spy's breakfast of caviar and vodka. The only hitch was that the story was complete invention. Sadly, MacFarlane was forced to fire the wonderful, zany, irrepressible Maclean, who was a functional time bomb. He was a newspaper legend who died of a heart attack—broken heart?—in the late 1970s.)

Not put off by MacFarlane's initial coolness to my proposal, I worked through the Defence Department and arranged for a free military flight to Naples, a U.S. flight on to Cairo, and hopefully a UN transport flight to Gaza, where I would record Christmas with our gallant boys in the Mideast. I hoped eventually to bum my way back home the same way.

I took the proposition to MacFarlane and said I'd make the trip on my holidays and pick up all costs myself. He did some quick arithmetic and somewhat grudgingly concluded that it wasn't a bad deal for the paper. After all, who knocks free coverage?

My $60-a-week salary wouldn't take me very far, and at the last moment MacFarlane in a surge of generosity advanced me $300 to defray *some* costs on the month-long assignment. I had no idea how "foreign correspondents" filed their stories, being barely able to get stories into the *Telegram* when I was in the office, and I didn't dare ask lest I expose my ignorance. But things worked out reasonably well, since I threw myself on the mercy of the army which transmitted stories over their network to Canada and re-layed them on to Toronto. Other stories I mailed via the UN airlift; I took pictures with a camera I had borrowed, guessing at the exposure.

As it turned out, I *did* know quite a few of the officers and men in the 1,000-member Canadian contingent. They, in turn, re-garded me with a mixture of awe and pity, being out in the cruel world where you have to provide your own food, clothing, lodg-ing. They wondered how I'd fallen so low as to become a journalist, and thanked goodness that they hadn't quit the service.

On my way to Gaza my luggage was stolen in Naples, but I forged on, eventually reaching Cairo a week before Christmas. When UN headquarters there said it would take up to a month to be accredited to Gaza, I felt my world collapsing, my venture into foreign corresponding in ruins before it started.

I went to the Palestinian Department, run by one Major Adly El-Shariff, and interrupted him studying maps of Rommel's desert war against the British. He said it would take at least ten days before my visa for Gaza could be authorized. I told him my prob-lem about being there for Christmas, and we settled down to talk about other things. We got on surprisingly well and argued and discussed the army, politics, Israel, Russia, and how encouraging the world would be if only it was as rational as we two were.

It became clear that I knew very little about Middle East policy, and after a while he was urging that I go to Gaza and see for myself. I reminded him that was why I had come to see him.

Suddenly he demanded my passport and called an assistant, who took it away and ten minutes later returned it stamped with a visa to Gaza. I could leave the next morning, on condition that we get together for another discussion on my return.

UN headquarters at first refused to believe that anyone could get a visa so fast: four hours after arriving in Cairo. They checked, and it was true. I felt then, as I have always felt, that in journalism as in war, it's almost better to be lucky than good.

Adly El-Shariff was about my age and we became good friends, and though we only occasionally encountered each other in subsequent years, it was always pleasant. He was a 100 percent Egyptian nationalist, and when I first met him he was more pro-Soviet than pro-West, though by no stretch of imagination could he be considered Communist. Once I got him to write an article for the *Telegram* putting forth the Egyptian point of view. The *Tely* editors were aghast at the thought of gratuitously printing an Egyptian point of view in the ardently pro-Israel *Telegram*, so it never ran. Moderate by yesterday's standards, his viewpoint is still reasonable today. Shariff thought the Soviet Union was winning in Egypt and the Arab world. "Look," he said, "you can buy books from all over the world here in Cairo. Our people hunger for knowledge. So we go into a store and we see a 600-page book on Russia and the Communist system on sale for 12 piastres (36¢), and a book on America and the democratic system on sale for 3 pounds ($9). Which do we buy? We buy the Russian one, of course—the same one you'd buy if you were poor and hungry and eager to learn. So we wind up buying Russian propaganda—and that's surely what both books are."

(When I last heard of Adly El-Shariff, he was a general commanding tanks in the 1973 Arab-Israeli war, had crossed the Suez Canal into the Sinai, participated in restoring Egyptian honor, and helped Egypt make initiatives that led to the Camp David Agreement.)

The next day I bummed a ride on a Canadian supply truck leaving Cairo at dawn and driving all day to the Canadian camp at Rafah, between Gaza and the border with Israel. It was a remarkable drive. Egyptian forces had been humiliated, and the road from the Canal to Gaza was still strewn with the debris of battle. The desert winds still unearthed boots and shoes, which, extraordinary as it may seem, are the common remnant of any disaster, be it a riot in the streets, a massacre, or a military rout. After quiet has descended on any crisis anywhere, scores of discarded shoes remain on the scene as a silent memorial of panic. So it was with the Sinai. I found it extraordinary that a defeated army would not clean up the evidence of its shame. Yet it seemed to have occurred to no Egyptian to do so, and the chewed-up tarmac road was littered with burned-out tanks, trucks, and houses blown apart by the Israelis. Even telegraph poles were still down.

In Gaza, where UNRWA (the United Nations Relief and Work Agency) was in charge and General E. L. M. Burns maintained his UNEF headquarters, there was sullen activity. A couple of hundred thousand Palestinian refugees were clustered there; everyone was on the dole, and self-respect took the form of re-senting those who were trying to help. People lived in makeshift huts that were better than tents, but water was from a communal pump, and there were communal feeding areas and a few stores. At the clinic, women having babies were given three days before having to go again into fields to scratch out a living.

UNEF in Gaza was the UN's first major military effort since the Korean "police action." Ostensibly, the mission was one of "peace-keeping," and that term has stuck to subsequent UN operations in the Congo, Cyprus, Kashmir, wherever. It is a gross misnomer. The UN has *no* mandate to either keep or impose peace: it is pure bluff and gamble. That they've gotten away with it for so long is sheer luck and the good management of troops on the ground, and no thanks to expedient bureaucratic decisions in New York. The formation of UNEF established the Canadian military as the backbone of this and future UN military operations. The Cana-dians kept UNEF oiled and functioning, with precious little help and often lots of obstacles from civilian authority.

The Canadian troops had adjusted to the Sinai desert with speed, ease, and professionalism. They had set up projects, were assisting local Bedouin, had even managed to catch VD in an environment that looks askance at that sort of activity. Invariably on UN peace-keeping assignments, Canadians get involved with locals by raising money among troops for orphans or kids or social projects—very sentimental and no doubt well meant and useful in establishing amiable relations. In Gaza, various Christmas projects were launched for local kids in attempts to show the Bedouin Christian charity. These nomadic Arabs hated the Egyptians and saw UNEF as something to pillage. The Scandinavians and Canadians were prime targets, whereas the Indonesians were mostly left alone by pilfer-ing Bedouin. When they caught local thieves the Indonesians tended to kill and bury them and say nothing. The Finns were rough to steal from, too: they shot first, asked questions later. Senior UN officials used to ponder why some units got raided and others didn't. It seemed never to occur to them that unmarked graves might be the reason.

A padre-initiated drive to raise money among the Canadians to help impoverished refugees met with limited success. When asked what he thought each soldier should be asked to give, a Military Police sergeant said: "I don't understand why we bother giving anything. They come in every night and take what they want. They think our camp is their supermarket." As if to support his observation, one of the officers had his tent and belongings stolen from around him while he slept.

General Burns (nicknamed "Tommy" after the Canadian-born heavyweight boxing champion of that name) was an ideal commander and possessed the diplomacy to bring together Yugoslavs, Indians, Brazilians, Indonesians, Swedes, Norwegians, Finns, and the galaxy of UN nationalities. It was widely felt among UNEF troops that Burns deserved a Nobel Peace Prize, for without his moderating influence the whole operation might have collapsed in the early days, especially when the Egyptians were so wary and suspicious.

Burns even pretended to take seriously the statue Nasser had erected in Gaza marking the triumph over the combined forces of Britain, France, and Israel. The statue was an Egyptian soldier (carrying a Swedish Sten gun) in heroic pose and pointing toward the Israeli border, with the inscription EGYPT WILL DESTROY HER ENEMIES. Irreverent Canadian soldiers expressed amusement at the top of their voices. Canadians tended to be contemptuous of the Egyptian military, and admired the professionalism of the Israelis, who in their four days in Egypt had literally destroyed everything in their path.

The one battle that Nasser won was the propaganda one. With that victory he won the war. The 250,000 Palestinian refugees confined to Gaza amid depressing conditions and barely sufficient food and no prospects of a meaningful future, and 100,000 local residents of Gaza, seemed to believe Egyptian propaganda implicitly. The flight of the Egyptian army before the advancing Israelis was explained as the brave soldiers racing back to defend the Canal. And their shedding of boots was simply to enable them to run faster to prove their loyalty. Funny to the Canadians, heroic to the Egyptians. One should never underestimate the power of propaganda, despite its apparent nonsense. As my Russian guide in Moscow was to point out some years later: "Repeat nonsense five times and people laugh; repeat it fifty times and they get angry; repeat it five hundred times and they are ready to die for it." Coca-Cola recognizes this truth but Western governments don't.

Schools in the refugee camps, paid for by the UN (and therefore by the United States, which still carries the financial load of the world body), were centres for anti-West, socialist-Marxist ideology, the fruits of which were to mature in 1970s in the form of a more militant PLO and various mutations of ideological terrorism. The soldiers, being straightforward, simple souls, saw this more clearly than politicians.

Still, UNEF was a bluff that worked. Mutually useful, it kept the peace but was also a wall behind which Nasser rebuilt his military until ten years later in 1967, feeling secure and strong, he ordered UNEF out of his country. And almost within days, Israel attacked.

It was at Gaza that I encountered a flock of foul-ups with the UN administration and wrote an article for *Saturday Night* magazine that landed me in trouble with General Burns and the UN administration. I described the scuttlebutt of UNEF, noting that the general had designed his own white uniform with gold braid that troops thought made him resemble a Good Humor ice cream vendor or the doorman of a posh New York hotel. Troops were scathing toward the UN administrative skills. For example, when four relatively inexpensive walkie-talkies were ordered for use in camp patrols, the UN procurement officers requisitioned four huge radio transmitters worth thousands of dollars. Canadians used them every night to contact North American ham radio operators, who would patch in phone calls to relatives and loved ones. Free long-distance calls every night.

I described how, when buying white paint for UN vehicles, someone had decided to economize and bought cheap paint to which sand stuck, or which washed off in the first rainstorm, leaving puddles of white paint beneath the vehicles. Another time, when 2,000 two-ounce bottles of cough syrup to give out to individual soldiers had been ordered, the UN sent by mistake 2,000 *gallons*, which troops began distilling into home brew. When filling an order for something called "rat-trap springs" for vehicles, the UN instead sent rat traps. When nails were ordered from New York the query came back: "What color nails?"

Most gruesome of all, when a Canadian soldier was blown up

by a mine left over from the Suez War, the UN purchased cheap $20 Egyptian coffins instead of expensive hermetically sealed coffins from North America. At the funeral in the cemetery at Ismailia, one of the six Canadians bearing the coffin—the shortest man at the back—noticed that the contents of the coffin were leaking down his side, onto his shoulder. He hoisted his corner higher, thus tipping the slurping contents down the front end. The front men then raised their corners higher, and soon the funeral became a Monty Python parody, like carrying a bowl of soup. These and other incidents both amused and irritated the troops, and made the UN seem incompetent—which it was.

I didn't write about this last incident because the victim in question could have been easily identified and the story would have caused unnecessary anguish among his kin in Canada. Instead, I wrote about a Brazilian soldier who had drowned and whose body was flown home in one of those cheap Egyptian coffins in an RCAF Hercules transport. Trying to avoid turbulence in a mid-Atlantic storm the aircraft went up to 20,000 feet and the gas inside the coffin caused the lid to blow off. The resulting stench made the crew so ill that the plane had to descend and open windows for the rest of the trip. In future, Canadians handled their own coffin requirements and ignored the UN.

In a more-in-pain-than-anger letter to me, General Burns recalled his friendship and admiration for my father, under whom he'd served in the war as a brigade commander. He lectured me that if I reported this way I'd never make it as a journalist. He said he had written his "old friend" John Bassett about me. Bassett, publisher of the *Tely*, had served under Burns in Italy during the war, and the two enjoyed a special relationship.

I got General Burns's letter when I was back in Toronto and after I had mailed him photos of himself and UN Secretary-General Dag Hammarskjöld, who had been visiting UNEF. Uncertain how to handle the situation, I decided on direct action, went to publisher Bassett, and said I thought his old commander would be writing him complaining about my coverage.

"Yeah, Tommy Burns wrote me about you," bellowed Bassett. "So what?"

"So I think he wants you to fire me," I said.

Bassett roared with laughter. "That's right. But listen, the day your stories don't get people like Tommy Burns upset is the day you aren't doing your job properly for the *Telegram*! Where do you wanna go next?"

Needless to say, after such an endorsement I'd have walked through fire for Bassett, arguably the most dynamic publisher in journalism. He had been general manager of the *Telegram*, had bought in when it was on the verge of collapse in 1952, and was leading the paper in a slow, ferocious, uphill battle against the rival Toronto *Star*. Bassett was one publisher who was more interested in the story than the accounts book. He had all kinds of flaws, foibles, and prejudices, most of them larger than life, but he was a publisher like no other in his day and inspired loyalty and enthusiasm among staff—though not uncritical or blind loyalty. He was a working journalist's publisher, a reporter's publisher, if not a deskman's. When hot on a story, it was damn the expense and to hell with the accountants who said he couldn't afford it.

My first exposure to the vagaries of the Middle East influenced me more greatly than I realized. While one had to be impressed with the Israelis, I found myself unable to shake the feeling that the Arabs had been badly done by—not so much by Israelis, but by the rest of the world. I could see no interest on the part of anyone to solve the refugee problem, other than talk about it. Everyone seemed anxious to exploit it, with very few thinking of the long-term future of the displaced Palestinians. A certain responsibility lay with Israel and Western countries, and the Soviet Union was agitating the brew; thus it meant that ideological battle lines were drawn with the innocent Palestinian refugees helpless in the middle. It was clear the status quo would continue indefinitely.

I didn't know it at the time, but I was on my way as a foreign correspondent of sorts—fifteen years of specializing in civil wars, revolutions, crises, and uprisings, to be followed by eleven years of saving democracy every day except Saturday by determining editorial policy on the upstart Toronto *Sun*.

5

Don't step on a bikini, boys, watch for rebels!

U.S. MARINE SERGEANT
LEBANON, 1958

After what has happened to Lebanon in the last decade of war, terror, murder, hate, and fear, it seems extraordinary that it wasn't taken very seriously twenty-five years ago when the first hints of future violence erupted. In those days Lebanon was regarded as a pacifist state that had not even gone to war against Israel, as had other Arab states. This caused no resentment because Lebanese were not considered warriors, in the same way that at one time Jews were not considered suited for soldiering or farming.

In 1958 Beirut was still the Paris of the Near East, easygoing, soft, available, a city of merchants, not warriors; pragmatists, not ideologues. It was physically beautiful, with a palm-splattered waterfront where yachts anchored, the affluent water-skied, beautiful women adorned the beaches in the only bikinis in the Arab world. A city of lavish hotels, divine food, a cosmopolitan attitude, with skiing an hour's drive from sun-drenched beaches; a city where anything could be bought for a price, where business flourished and common sense reigned.

Lebanon had the greatest per-capita income in the Arab world, and the lowest taxes. The population of the country was almost equally divided between Christian and Moslem, with subdivisions on each side—the Maronite Christians having a historic monopoly on wealth and influence. It had avoided wars with Israel and had made itself into the meeting and bartering place of that part of the world. It was the most civilized of the Arab countries. Life was good.

When Lebanon got its independence from France at the end of World War II without a shot being fired, some considered it fortunate. Others felt that having had freedom granted on a plat-

56

ter, without having to fight for it, Lebanon had little patriotism, little soul. Those who feel that tears and blood bring nationhood must be satisfied with the 1970s and '80s, when bloodshed, pain, and misery have been plentiful.

In 1958 the president of Lebanon was Camille Chamoun, a Maronite Catholic, as all Lebanon's presidents had been until the troubles of the mid-'70s. Chamoun was urbane, suave, even slippery, and more French than Arab. Known as the "Silver Fox of Lebanon," he had escaped periodic assassination attempts. It was believed that he was trying to extend his six-year term as president into another six years, in defiance of the constitution, and to make Lebanon into a sort of Christian Israel. Moslems, ever suspicious, and with growing confidence and strength, campaigned violently against him.

When rebel factions took to fighting the government with gestures of early terrorism, with bombs going off *not* to kill people but to register disapproval of the government, Chamoun appealed to America and Britain to send troops to keep the peace; that is, to keep him in power. He invoked the spectre of Nasser plotting, of Moscow plotting, of rebels plotting. All was true, all was overstated and exaggerated. London and Washington, inclined to hysteria in their respective ways about Nasser and/or communism, were only too willing to believe the worst of these twin menaces to stability.

Chamoun claimed that rebel activity was being fed by arms from Nasser and Communists through Syria. London and Washington told him to take Lebanon's case to the United Nations before appealing directly to them for help. As a result UNOGIL (United Nations Observer Group in Lebanon) was formed, which sent 170 military observers to watch the border area and report on illegal shipments of arms and on agitation.

As it turned out, Lebanon controlled barely 35 miles of the 250-mile border with Syria and, as usual with UN observers, they saw nothing. In fact, most of the mountainous border area was controlled by the Druze Moslems of Kamal Jumblatt, the colorful Druze chieftain whose grandfather, Said Bey Jumblatt, had led the Druze against the Maronites in their first war between 1820 and 1840. Kamal's assassination in 1977 touched off massive reprisal massacres by the black-robed, mustachioed, bandoleer-toting Druze warriors. Kamal's son Walid carried on the family tradition of warfare into the 1980s.

As the mixed brew of rebellion simmered in Beirut, an army

coup in Iraq killed young King Faisal II and the royal family and, suspecting Nasser and Communists again, the West panicked. President Eisenhower dispatched the Sixth Fleet and 10,000 Marines and soldiers to keep peace in Beirut, while the British sent paratroopers to Jordan to prop up King Hussein, cousin of the murdered king.

Although Christians and Moslems were fighting each other in Lebanon, rather like Catholics and Protestants in Northern Ireland, the Moslem forces were subdivided into several rebel groups. Pro-Nasserite Saeb Salam (a future premier) controlled the Beirut rebels; Rashid Karami was based in Tripoli (where his family still holds power) and specialized in shooting at U.S. Navy planes; Kamal Jumblatt lived in a mountain fortress and was dubbed the Fidel Castro of Lebanon. And then there was General Fuad Chehab, a slow, methodical, gentle, and modest man who was the somewhat ponderous head of the Lebanese army. General Chehab was meticulous about keeping his troops from taking sides. While one rebel group fired on another and all fired on the government, the Lebanese army maintained scrupulous neutrality and ate watermelons, drank soda pop, and ogled girls while protected by sandbag fortifications. Even during the civil war Beirut shut down every afternoon for a traditional siesta, with shooting beginning again in the evening. Civilized. Leisurely. Bewildering.

All factions, except the shy Chehab, held ongoing news conferences. The world's press, which had descended on Beirut to be in on the kill, had an exciting and confusing time racing around from one group to another, all under the watchful eyes of the docile Lebanese army. Journalists compiled colorful, puzzled stories about possible Soviet intervention, the likelihood of World War III erupting at any moment, the possibility of Israel launching a pre-emptive attack, the extent of Nasser's devious plotting, speculation on the CIA's involvement, and so on. In those days the Western press was uncritically pro-Israeli and the White House and Pentagon still had credibility.

Lame duck President Eisenhower, with two years of office remaining, was still mired in his policy of massive retaliation (including nuclear) against any Soviet aggression, no matter how minor. He made it clear that the Marines were in Lebanon only at the invitation of the elected government and only to restore order and keep the peace.

Since I was the last *Telegram* staffer to have been to the Middle

East, I was deemed to be the paper's Arab specialist of the moment. Thus I flew to Beirut complete with a new Cable and Wireless card for sending stories collect, and only a faint idea of what a foreign correspondent was supposed to do. I had a pretty good idea what a soldier might do in a civil war because of my experience as a paratroop officer with the Princess Pats in Korea—but I wasn't sure that would help in reporting battle-torn Beirut.

After the plane landed at the Beirut airport late one July night in 1958, there was discussion among passengers and airport officials as to whether we should risk driving into town because of sniping on the road. A bus had been shot up an hour earlier. Taxi drivers charged extra for those willing to make the dash. Eventually a bus driver was persuaded to make the run, not because he was paid extra, was dedicated, or especially brave, but because he had a date in town and wanted to keep it. The ride was uneventful, and the driver kept all lights on inside the bus to show any would-be snipers that we were foreigners and not part of the internal quarrel.

Instead of the gutted buildings and wreckage of war that Beirut has become, the relatively civilized city was conducting business as usual and seemed embarrassed that its crisis was occurring during the height of the tourist season. Everyone had a favorite villain; Christians blamed Moslems, and vice-versa; left and right blamed each other; the U.S. blamed communism; the USSR said it was all an American-sponsored imperialist plot to take over Lebanon; Israel blamed Nasser. All were a little bit right and an awful lot wrong. Still, the Lebanese army was content to let warring groups shoot each other so long as they avoided innocent civilians. Occasionally, soldiers would shoot up streets just to let the other side, wherever it was, know that the Lebanese army was eternally vigilant.

John Foster Dulles was American Secretary of State and his brother Allen headed the CIA. Both saw Nasser as an unmitigated evil force behind every agitation—along with Moscow, which might even be pulling the strings for puppet Nasser, now that the USSR was taking over the building of the High Dam at Aswan from the Americans. Any form of Arab nationalism or independence movement was assumed to be Nasser-provoked. And overreaction was a State Department specialty.

It was my first real crisis as a journalist: if I fouled up this assignment, it would end a budding overseas career. I felt like a fraud because I hadn't a clue how one person covered a crisis involving several countries, including the superpowers. So I decided to follow the journalistic herd and hoped to improvise as events unfolded.

I registered in the Palm Beach Hotel, which had use of the Excelsior Hotel's swimming pool across the street, where journalists would while away the mornings getting a tan. Then they'd be off to the elegant St. Georges Hotel, which was the centre of intrigue and information (few intrigue better than Lebanese) for an afternoon of gossip, assessing rumors, water-skiing, and admiring the elegance of Beirut's bikinis. At night there'd be gunfire and occasional explosions, but in daytime very little happened except soldiers in jeeps hurtling through the streets.

I looked up Joe Alex Morris of the New York *Herald Tribune* who lived in Beirut and whose copy ran in the *Telegram*. He graciously took me in hand and we travelled Beirut and Lebanon together and became good friends, covering subsequent Middle East crises together.

Everyone took the 1958 civil war in Beirut seriously, but not too seriously. This included the Lebanese themselves, and I personally recall being advised not to go down a certain street during the next half-hour when a bomb was set to go off. I didn't, the bomb did, and no one was hurt. The incident was so routine, it was hardly worth reporting.

No one who witnessed it will easily forget the day the U.S. Marines landed at one of the more fashionable beaches just outside Beirut. Landing craft from the Sixth Fleet rushed toward shore and the local citizenry, young men and women in bikinis sunning and flirting, looked up to see the ramps of the landing craft go down and Marines, loaded for bear, storm ashore, guns at the ready. The Marines raced up the beach, carefully stepping over the sunbathers, and took up defensive positions straddling the road and around the beach. "Don't step on a bikini, boys, watch for rebels," yelled a sergeant. Bathers were more puzzled than frightened. Few could understand what was happening or why. The Marines, slightly embarrassed, were resolutely determined not to be sidetracked by mischievous propaganda, and sergeants roared at their men not to stare at the scantily clad bathers.

It is a tribute to Lebanese pragmatism or adaptability, I suppose, that within minutes of landing the Marines were being pestered by kids and vendors trying to sell them pop, chewing gum, postcards, their sisters. Throughout their stay in Lebanon, the Marines

couldn't make a move without hordes of Lebanese kids and huck-
sters trying to separate them from their money. The first Marine
casualty was a guy who was accidentally shot by a sentry while
returning from a midnight assignation. The second was a Marine
shot by a jealous Lebanese who resented the shifting affections of
his girlfriend or wife. Discipline was tenuous.

I fell in with two American life insurance agents, Stan McCabe
and Ken Shaker, who'd flown in from West Germany and were
doing a booming business selling life insurance to the Marines.
Despite its ghoulish overtones it wasn't a bad buy for the young
Marines, most of whom were eager to take out the insurance
because it flattered their macho egos and made them feel brave
and responsible. In fact, the greatest threat to life came from their
accidentally shooting one another. But in crises you never know.

The press got on to the two Yanks, who were depicted as being
on a death watch. Orders were given that the insurance hustlers—
both veterans of World War II or Korea—were not to be allowed
in the Marine area. Reluctantly the pair returned to Germany. I
felt they got a bum rap, but whoever said war or politics or the
insurance business was fair?

It was such a looking-glass war that the main rebel leader in
Beirut, Saeb Salam, would hold press conferences in his redoubt,
which was guarded by a Pancho Villa assortment of unshaven
ruffians, all of whom resembled Yasser Arafat, blended with
beardless kids, some in their pre-teens, bedecked in bandoleers
of ammunition and toting weapons they could barely lift. These
press conferences were jolly affairs with much kidding and raucous humor. I recall one during which suddenly the electricity
went dead. Saeb Salam was furious, got on the phone, and gave
the local hydro people hell for cutting off his power. Within moments it was restored. He complained that periodically they cut
off his water, too, and he would scold until it was restored. The
Warsaw Ghetto or the Siege of Leningrad it wasn't. Every day
Salam's daughter would go through Lebanese army lines to the
American University of Beirut and return to the barricades at
night. Any taxi driver would take you through the lines and barricades to see Salam. It didn't seem real at the time, and probably
wasn't. But it was fun and useful to journalists who interviewed
him and pretended world peace hinged on Lebanon. Salam was
always quick with a colorful ultimatum to Eisenhower which the
press dutifully regurgitated.

The other rebel leaders were outside the city, most of them

friendly, all of them exotic; but Rashid Karami and Kamal Jumblatt were deprived of the publicity accruing to Salam, who was more accessible to the press and more conscious of how to use it to advantage. This publicity knack helped Salam to become prime minister—a post most of the various rebel leaders were eventually to hold from time to time, with little effect.

When elections were held in hopes of stopping the fighting, the army's nonpolitical General Chehab, who had refused to let his troops attack anyone (how things were to change in Beirut!), found himself everyone's hero and was easily elected president of Lebanon. Joe Morris and I got the first interview with him—an unusual meeting where outgoing President Chamoun introduced him to us and translated for him. It was quite a contrast. Chamoun the personification of polished elegance in a white suit and fluent in English and French (but not Arabic), Chehab in an open-necked army shirt, with three rows of medal ribbons. Dubbed "Hamlet" for his penchant for soul-searching and indecision ("will I or won't I shoot?"), Chehab loathed the limelight and politics. When the deputies argued over who should be his premier, Chehab resigned and said he'd prefer to spend his time on the Riviera.

His reluctance to accept high office made him even more desirable. He became Lebanon's indispensable man. Ninety of the country's ninety-nine deputies once marched on his house and in a dramatic ceremony burned his resignation on a silver tray and insisted that he stay as president for the sake of Lebanon. He agreed on condition the deputies behave themselves. Relief was such that when he agreed to stay on, the deputies pulled out pistols—one even carried a submachine gun under his jacket—and fired them joyously into the air.

It was in Lebanon that I saw my first hanging, and the memory has never faded. Ibrahim Nabulsi was twenty-one and had been convicted of kidnapping and murdering three men two months earlier. He was a dashing figure in the young Lebanese activist set, and the authorities were anxious to restore law and order after a season of anarchy and indiscriminate shootings and killings. Nabulsi was a high-profile, mouthy kid who admired Nasser, but to the end it was very questionable whether he ever killed anyone. Clearly, a large segment of the youth of Beirut considered him innocent. Throughout his trial he had vigorously proclaimed his innocence.

It was about 5 A.M. in front of the Justice Building, where overnight a scaffold had been built. There were fears of incidents.

The streets and rooftops were packed with people. The condemned youth's family were on benches in front of the scaffold. Good-looking and of slight build, Nabulsi was dressed in a sweater and pinstripe pants. The crowd began their peculiar Arab yodelling when he appeared. He smiled at his family—mother and brother— and a white poncho was slipped over his head, his hands tied behind his back. At one point he seemed anxious to slip his head into the noose and get it over with. The call to prayers could be heard from minarets of mosques around the city.

His family and friends were weeping copiously and sobbing loudly and dramatically when he mounted the scaffold platform to give his final speech, which traditionally would last until he was ready to die. Tears streamed down his otherwise calm face and he began to exhort Allah to see that justice was done and to show mercy, and he again proclaimed his innocence. The crowd was getting increasingly restless and soldiers scattered everywhere were nervous and uneasily fingering their weapons. Suddenly the trapdoor was sprung, cutting off Nabulsi in mid-sentence. His last coherent words were a strangled "*Allah akhbar . . .*" God is everywhere.

The trouble was that his body didn't disappear and his neck didn't break. Instead, he dropped perhaps two or three feet, visible from the shoulders up. He was squirming and strangling to death at the end of the taut, twisting rope. His body shuddered spasmodically as his feet kicked out beneath him. His neck was stretched, his face bloated and purple, his eyes bulging, his tongue protruding. It was ghastly, and the crowd reacted with yells, tears, and anger. Nabulsi's brother broke from his seat, dashed under the scaffold, and began tugging at the legs, clearly hoping to break his brother's neck and put him out of his misery. Pandemonium was close to erupting when the police and army moved in to clear the square. I was in a doorway, feeling a sense of unreality, frightened, angry, and somehow humiliated by what had gone on. I wanted to escape. I looked back and the youth was now dead, his body twisting gently from the scaffold.

The whole scene had taken perhaps twelve minutes, yet it had seemed an eternity. After quickly clearing the area the police found a suspicious package in a doorway which turned out to be a bomb. It was defective and hadn't exploded—typical for Lebanon of that era. I returned to the Palm Beach Hotel for an uneasy breakfast with Joe Morris. Two hours later we went back to the hanging area and there was no sign that anything had taken place. The scaffold was gone, fruit stalls were up, and the hubbub of the city had returned. The main topic of conversation in the square centred on new bylaws being introduced to outlaw horn-honking, and drivers were furious at this intrusion into their lives. How could anyone drive safely without honking his horn? That restriction was considered a greater threat to civil rights than shooting at someone.

On the very day he was hanged, Ibrahim Nabulsi was forgotten as if he'd never existed. So much for martyrdom. Subsequently, it was acknowledged that although he was probably not involved in the murders, his death was necessary to show others that such behavior would no longer be tolerated. Nabulsi's hanging was a symbolic gesture to warn future trouble-makers and agitators that civilization was returning. A scapegoat and early martyr to Lebanese violence; more victim than villain.

In a couple of months, contrary to Moscow's dire predictions, the U.S. Marines were gone from Lebanon. Within a year Rashid Karami was premier under President Chehab. Saeb Salam, the indignant voice of Beirut's downtrodden poor who periodically threatened the U.S. Marines with mayhem, was leader of the op-position in the legislature. The bearded Druze leader Kamal Jum-blatt was writing a book explaining the crisis and trying to get a government subsidy to start a cement factory. In Lebanon, busi-ness came first. But the seeds of future trouble had already been sown. The PLO would find a shaky ship of state in Lebanon, easy to exploit and undermine when the time came. Only Saeb Salam, his old rival Camille Chamoun and Rashid Karami still survive. Salam is still active in politics, Chamoun is retired. Karami was named premier in 1984, the tenth time in thirty years.

I had one regret about Beirut. I had been approved to receive a Canada Council grant to attend the American University of Beirut to study Arab affairs, and was torn whether or not I should do it. Also, I was enthralled with the adventures of the famed Arabist St. John Philby, whose exploits in Arabia were legendary. I made a point of looking up his son who was correspondent for the London *Observer* in Beirut—Kim Philby. I met Philby in the bar of the Palm Beach, tried to talk with him about Arabs, his father, and his views. But he was drunk and I got nothing out of him but slurred, incoherent sentences. The few other times I saw him around the bar, I paid little heed. He seemed perpetually into the sauce and I was disgusted. I assumed he was simply another victim of a too-famous father.

It wasn't until later that I realized who Philby was. I had missed the whole Burgess/Maclean spy caper and their escape to Moscow because I was in Korea at the time and such details meant very little. When Philby became famous in 1962 by also defecting to Moscow and being revealed as a master Soviet spy inside British Intelligence, I had no memories or anecdotes of him to write about. (I once phoned Donald Maclean when I later lived in Moscow and was told politely, firmly, irrevocably, to kindly "piss off.")

I finally decided against studying Arab affairs at the American University of Beirut, and opted instead to learn practical international politics via journalism—by being there and seeing the world as it is, and not as textbooks say it should be.

I had gone to Beirut expecting to find strong Soviet (or at least communist) and Nasserite subversion and influence. Not so. Oh, it was there, but the threat as seen in diplomatic reporting was not reflected in reality. You couldn't report from the scene without being impressed by the reality that there was *no* way the various rival Lebanese factions could be controlled or easily manipulated by outside elements. Not by the USSR, not by the United States, not by Nasser. The Salams, Karamis, Jumblatts had their own priorities.

By the same token, it was abundantly clear that the United States did *not* intend to take over Lebanon and wanted to get its troops out of this no-win situation as soon as possible. They really thought they were there to impose order—which they did—and then get out. In that sense it was an American triumph. The mere presence of Marines and paratroops discouraged rebellious behavior. Fortunately, the bluff worked.

It would be tempting to say that a lot of Lebanon's future troubles had their roots in that crisis, but it is not quite true. There was no hint of trouble from the PLO, or from Israel. That came later.

Lebanon was a useful lesson, if one cared to learn it, that there is rarely clearly defined right and wrong in international disputes; both sides are right, both wrong, though one side is usually more right or more wrong than the other—and not necessarily the side that has the most publicity. Lebanon served to create a sense of skepticism in me concerning foreign affairs.

6

Great heavens, what a place to hear from a Canadian!

MILTON GREGG
UN REPRESENTATIVE, BAGHDAD
JULY 24, 1958

Competition keeps journalists sharp, even though competition run amok can result in too much sensationalism and the temptation to make stories seem more exclusive than they are.

Competition or rivalry, of course, is not the same on foreign assignments as it is in domestic reporting. In covering foreign crises the agencies—Associated Press, United Press International, Reuters, Agence France Presse—as well as the television networks like to be first with a breaking story. Considerable importance is placed on being a few seconds or minutes ahead of the competition, though to the public it makes little difference. As far as news agencies are concerned, the first bulletin on a big story makes the first edition or goes on the air first, and the agency gets credit. Its staff in the hot spot get *herograms* from head office and everyone walks a bit taller and feels superior for about ten minutes.

For individual journalists representing the "specials" or individual newspapers, it is hard to get a beat on a big story or a sensational news break or interview. The big prestige media outlets like *Time* magazine, *Newsweek*, the New York *Times*, the London *Times*, or the television networks have an automatic jump on the pack because doors open to them that remain closed to others. Or big names on special assignments get special treatment that others don't. Henry Kissinger on assignment for the Sacramento *Union* would get interviews denied even the *Times*.

One way for the "specials" or one-man teams to compete with the biggies is to get there first. Usually when there is a coup or revolution, the borders are closed and it is hard to get on-the-spot, firsthand accounts of exactly what happened. Whoever gets in first gets a certain amount of kudos as well as a good story ahead of competitors.

A considerable logistical problem develops when big stories overlap, which is what happened when the U.S. Marines were in Lebanon to quell the civil war in 1958 and British paratroops were invited into Jordan by King Hussein, who feared an Egyptian plot to overthrow him. Over in Iraq, the British-trained army staged a surprise coup and killed young King Faisal II (Hussein's cousin) and his family, as well as the premier, Nuri as-Said.

All these crises were big news with unknown ramifications for Western powers. There was growing urgency among the world's press to get to Iraq and report from the scene, simply because it was glamorous. Iraq's borders with Syria, Jordan, and Iran were sealed, little information was seeping out, and journalists, like the South American piranha, circled on the outside waiting for the new regime to relax so that they could get in and pick the bones of an intriguing tale of regicide and revolution.

The revolution occurred in the pre-dawn hours of a hot, dry July 14, 1958, when two Iraqi armoured units, the 19th and 20th Armoured Brigades, were secretly passing through Baghdad en route to the Jordanian border. The 19th Brigade was commanded by a sullen, brooding, pro-Nasser nationalist, Colonel Abdul Salam Mohamed Aref, while the 20th Brigade was commanded by his superior, Sandhurst-trained, soft-spoken, and respected Brigadier Abdul Karim Kassem. Troops of the 19th Brigade occupied such strategic spots as the radio station, railway station, and airport in Baghdad, and the prisoners they released from the jail at Baaqubah formed the nerve centre of a mob that stormed through the city. The 20th Brigade surrounded the temporary palace of King Faisal at Qasr al-Rihab (a permanent palace was under construction) and apparently an ultimatum was delivered to the king to resign or be killed. The king and his eighty-two-year-old prime minister, the wily, autocratic, Communist-hating Nuri as-Said, who had been premier of Iraq a dozen separate times, were to have flown to Istanbul that day for meetings on the Baghdad Pact, a mutual defence alliance among Iraq, Turkey, Britain, Pakistan, and Iran. The whole royal family was at the palace and details of what happened are unclear to this day. One report has it that Crown Prince Abdul-Illah, Faisal's uncle, refused to surrender. In any event, the whole family, including children, was massacred.

Across the river, crafty old Nuri as-Said escaped in a *bellum*, or river boat, and apparently spent the day and night seeking sanctuary from friends, all of whom were too frightened to help him. Eventually he disguised himself as a woman but was reportedly caught when a child noticed pyjamas beneath his gown. Instantly recognized, he was torn apart and dismembered, his armless, legless, headless torso dragged through the streets of Baghdad behind a truck and eventually strung up on a lamppost. The same fate befell the mutilated corpse of Abdul-Illah; both men were hated symbols to the anti-West nationalists, the pro-Communists, the Nasserites. Rampaging mobs raided the posh, newly built Baghdad Hotel and kidnapped and killed several guests. Others were trampled to death in the street. The coup was brief, bloody, successful.

A revolutionary military regime was installed under the command of the obscure Brigadier Kassem, a handsome, ascetic bachelor who neither drank nor smoked and was ardently religious. Kassem was an oddity. He preferred to eat his lunch from a mess tin like a private soldier in the field, and owned six dogs, all named "Lassie." A stickler for discipline, when he called his dog, he would be bowled over by six of them answering their collective name. It invoked bizarre imagery.

Kassem was a purist; he reminds me of Colonel Khadafy of Libya, except that Kassem had a humane, generous streak that ultimately killed him. Nor was Kassem quite the egomaniac Khadafy turned out to be. Still, in those pre-Khadafy days, Kassem made everyone uneasy.

I was in Beirut trying to make sense of the Lebanese civil war and not having much luck, although I was intrigued by the various rebel groups, all of whom were like colorful extras in a John Ford movie. The rest of the press were poised for possible violence during Lebanese elections, so I cabled the *Telegram* that I should try to get to Baghdad before others did. I received a cable agreeing with my idea and ending: "Okay you go Baghdad unless there is trouble Lebanese elections." That put the onus squarely on me. If I went to Iraq and there *was* trouble in Lebanon, I'd be blamed for missing the story. If not, they'd take credit. Thereafter when communicating with the office I'd always put the ball in their court: "Unless hear otherwise, intend to do so-and-so. . . ." Rarely did the office ever respond, and if they did they missed my deadline. So if things went wrong, technically it was their fault for not letting me "hear otherwise."

There were no flights into Baghdad, no trains, buses, or conventional way in. Iraqi embassies were wary about issuing visas because they had no idea what was happening. Ken Ames of the London *Daily Mail*, Gunnar Neilsen of Sweden's *Stokholm Expressen*, and I went to Damascus and tried to hire a taxi to drive us to Baghdad, on the other side of the desert, 500 miles as the vulture flies. We finally found a driver with a modern De Soto who said that for $400 he'd make the trip.

"Do you know the road?" we asked.

"No road. Just desert. But trails. I know the trails."

The driver seemed confident, so we made a deal. At the hotel we ordered box lunches and several large thermoses of ice water, then started out. Quickly the road ended and we headed into the desert—dubbed the Whispering Desert because of the hot winds and the noise the sand made while shifting. We had started out in late afternoon in order to avoid the worst of the sun and heat, and drove all night. It was perhaps the worst drive of my life. After a while even the trails seemed to disappear. The heat was dry, like an oven, and almost unbearable. If we rolled down the car windows, sand came in like spray over a dinghy.

After a few hours we stopped for a rest and a drink, and to our dismay found that our "iced water" was sickly sweet lemonade. The hotel had figured lemonade was tastier. We were upset, but the driver assured us that around midnight we should reach a mid-desert staging post or station where there was fresh water.

"You know the place?" we asked.

"I know where it is supposed to be."

"When were you last there?"

"I've never been there. My brother tells me it is there."

"If you've never been there before, which way do you usually take when you drive to Baghdad?"

"I've never driven to Baghdad. This is the first time."

"But you told us you know the way!"

"I do. My brother told me. You drive east. But I've never driven it myself. *Malesh.* Never mind. God willing, we'll make it."

We looked at one another and shrugged. What the hell . . .

We drove all night, wandering across the moonlit desert, which in other circumstances would have been beautiful. Everything seemed pale blue under a huge silver moon. Occasionally we'd get stuck in sand drifts and have to get out and shove and dig with our hands. Eyes, nostrils, throat were clogged with sand. I had vague ideas of being lost and disappearing in the desert. It seemed an exotic way to go—if one had to go.

Oddly, deep into the night we came across a way-station with a couple of trucks around it and shrouded bodies sleeping. We roused the attendant, got water, Pepsi-Cola, gasoline, and continued our eastern drive. Dawn came and the desert, marked by faint tracks of other vehicles, was again beautiful in a different way. We got lost, but kept driving into the sun, and eventually came across the oil pipeline, which we followed until we reached the Iraqi border. A tarmac road began there and we located an army post.

Soldiers promptly ordered us into a cell while it was decided what to do with us. A couple of young German hitch-hikers who were also there said they'd been in custody for five days. They asked if we could help, but obviously we couldn't. If we got out, we promised to tell the German Embassy in Baghdad.

After an hour or so, an officer said it was all right for us to continue. He was suspicious but cordial, and clearly uncertain about what to do. He seemed to understand that "journalists" were not like other people and should not be treated casually or cruelly. It was late afternoon when we finally drove off.

As we got closer to Baghdad, towns and villages increased. So did suspicions and hostility. When we stopped for a roadside Pepsi, people instantly gathered and asked menacingly if we were Americans. Our driver was clearly nervous. "Rooshi," he told the gathering mob. "No Americans—Rooshi," he repeated more loudly and the people grinned and poked at us. It was interesting that hostility was directed against Western countries and not against the Soviet Union, which was largely unknown and therefore not suspect.

We began to wonder if the De Soto would make it. A tire was losing air, the rear springs or shock absorbers were broken, and the engine was knocking ominously. When we finally limped past the city limits our modern car seemed to have aged a dozen years. We drove to the Baghdad Hotel, the city's best, which during the height of the revolution had been raided by soldiers.

We reached our destination some twenty-six hours after leaving Damascus—the first foreign journalists to get into Baghdad after the revolution.

The city was a mixture of old and new; Arabian Nights atmosphere of bazaars blended with modern buildings. Wide streets and narrow lanes; paved, well-lighted arterial roads and potholed, unpaved back roads one street behind. Running water next to sump holes. Poverty beside luxury. Business suits and *djellabahs*. The story of modern Arabia. Iraqis are a volatile, quick-tempered, emotional people, erratic and unpredictable. Foreigners in Baghdad were nervous and justifiably so, since paranoia and xenophobia seemed national characteristics.

The first thing I did was phone Milton Gregg, who was head of the United Nations mission in Baghdad. Gregg had been Minister of Labor in the St. Laurent Liberal government, but lost his seat in the 1957 election that saw John Diefenbaker win his Conservative party the greatest electoral victory in Canada's history (208 of 265 seats in the House of Commons). Milton Gregg then got a job with the UN and went to Baghdad as its technical assistance representative. There was considerable anxiety in Canada over the fate of Gregg and his wife, since nothing had been heard from them since the revolution.

I got him on the phone and identified myself.

"Great heavens," he said. "What a place to hear from a Canadian!"

I told him of the concern in Canada for his welfare and he laughed. He was having a marvellous time, truth be known, and he suggested I come over immediately for a drink and something to eat. I did.

Gregg had quite a story. He agreed to my doing an as-told-to story for the *Telegram* (that is, I wrote the story under his byline, based on what he told me). It was the first eyewitness story of the overthrow. One could not have chosen a better person to be in a ticklish situation than this man. Small, wiry, with a vaguely Semitic face that enabled him to pass for an Arab, Milton Gregg was a genuine hero of World War I. He had won the Victoria Cross and was incapable of panic. On the day of the revolution, all foreigners were warned to stay at home and inside, but Gregg dressed as an Arab, wore a *kaffiyeh*, and walked through Baghdad to the UN office, where he raised the flag and opened for business.

When he saw that Kassem was clearly in charge and that there was no reversing the revolution, he tried to contact New York to give his assessment and to receive instructions. Unable to get through, Gregg took it upon himself to telephone Kassem and personally accord UN recognition to the new regime—the first international organization to recognize it. Thereafter there was a special relationship between Kassem and the UN office in Baghdad, and Iraqi troops were always on hand to ensure that no UN property was threatened.

Since we were the first foreign journalists into Baghdad, the new regime was anxious for publicity. Ames, Neilsen, and I were given a conducted tour through the royal palace, which was a shambles. It was surrounded with armoured cars and tanks, there were shell holes in the walls, and crowds were lined up outside staring at it during daylight hours. Outside was a pile of furniture flung from windows; inside, floors were littered with rubble, thousands of colored slides, and literally hundreds of photos of Crown Prince Abdul-Illah taken by the Canadian portrait photographer Youssuf Karsh. While being shown around I scooped some of the scattered slides of the royal family into my pocket.

We ran into an officer who claimed to have killed the king (a lot were claiming this distinction). Captain Monther Salim was proud of his feat and declared his company "had the honor of leading the attack on the palace." He said that there had been no intention to kill Faisal. "He was a nice young man, and we wanted to let him resign and leave the country. The Crown Prince, Abdul-Illah, was too proud and bad, and we would never let him escape with his life. We had a resignation all printed up for the king to sign. But Abdul-Illah ordered the king not to sign, so both had to die. Blame the Crown Prince, not us . . ." All over Baghdad there was some regret that Faisal had to die. If not actually popular, the young king was tolerated and not despised as were his uncle and Nuri as-Said.

Captain Salim said everyone was taken outside the palace and clustered under a tree. Without being explicit, as if he himself was not sure, he said that a soldier in a tank inexplicably fired his machinegun. Before anyone realized what was happening, everyone had opened fire and the Iraqi royal family was suddenly dead, king, crown prince, grandmother, Princess Abdya, the two small children of Abdul-Illah. In one burst of gunfire the Hashimite dynasty was ended in Iraq. The kingdom that had been formed by Britain after World War I, and British influence, which had begun with the legendary Lawrence of Arabia, were finally terminated in blood.

Salim admitted he felt badly about the king and the children, and their bodies were rolled up in rugs to protect them from being mutilated by the mobs, which soon broke in to the palace grounds and began the sort of vandalism peculiar to revolutionary mobs. In the king's bedroom were a couple of blown safes, which the soldier said contained bars of gold, 300 gold watches to be given as gifts, the crown jewels, and American money. To one side was an exercise bike. The king's army tunic was on the floor and Captain Salim hoisted it on the end of his swagger stick and twirled it around for a photograph, then flipped it on a heap of rubble—symbolic of what he'd done to the royal family.

There were some tragi-comic aspects of the brief, passionate uprising. Britain was the foreign target of the revolution, and when the crowds burst into the British Embassy grounds and swarmed toward the main entrance, the staff retreated indoors. However, military attaché Colonel Ludovik Graham was apparently of the old school and the thought of the "Wogs" desecrating Her Majesty's property so incensed him that he seized his swagger stick and marched resolutely outside to confront the mob. The horde paused as he strode toward them, slapping his swagger stick impatiently against his thigh and demanding in his Sandhurst voice that they disperse immediately or by God he'd know the reason why. Without further ado someone shot him between the eyes. In the movies such grand gestures always succeed, but in real life they are more often fatal for the actors. The army soon arrived to clear the mob back to the streets where they belonged.

Journalists were starting to arrive, all with the same goal as ours: to get a story and to get out and file it, free of censorship. Kassem decided to hold a press conference—more an audience—and it was the first chance to size him up. He, and most Iraqis, expressed interest in and admiration for Nasser, whom the West blamed for the revolution. But Kassem made it clear that no one in Iraq was beholden to Nasser. Iraq did not intend to be dominated by Egypt. Or Russia. Or by any nation. His Iraq, said Kassem, was a revolutionary Iraq in which Iraqis would be in charge of their own house, friendly with all, subservient to no one. He exuded a naïveté that was never to leave him.

At Kassem's side was his friend and comrade in revolution, Colonel Abdul Salam Aref, a shrewder man than Kassem and the one who was probably the brains behind the plot. Aref was trusted by Kassem, but was adamantly pro-Nasser and anti-Communist. A year or so later Kassem caught Aref plotting against him: an assassination attempt against Kassem failed, and he was only shot in the shoulder. Aref was put on trial—on television—and sentenced to death. Baghdad erupted with the delirious joy of vengeance. Aref and Nasser were hanged in effigy; dead dogs were strung up around Baghdad with Aref's and Nasser's names on them.

Then Kassem, showing unusual mercy for a Middle East despot, intervened to save the life of his old comrade. A mistake, for a couple of years later Aref killed Kassem and took over—only to be assassinated himself. Why anyone would choose to lead a revolution in the Arab world defies comprehension. It is a virtual death warrant, especially in Iraq.

Few of the correspondents understood Kassem or could agree on whether he was good or bad, a fool or shrewd. I tended to trust my gut feeling. I returned to Baghdad on the first anniversary of Kassem's rule and had a three-hour meeting with him. The big question was whether he was pro-West or in the Soviet orbit. All the rhetoric of the system and the press was directed against the West; paranoia was rampant. But was it real or for show? No one was sure. I was able to see Kassem because I had befriended his foreign minister, the distinctly sensible Western-educated Hasem Jawad, who recommended that Kassem see me. The American and British ambassadors were anxious for a journalistic assessment, and I was debriefed by them later. The meeting with Kassem—by now known in his press as Sole Leader—showed a figure beyond criticism or comment. He was erratic enough to have even his closest advisors uneasy.

At the time treason trials were being conducted on TV, and it was by far the most popular and grisly performance I've seen: the Iraqi version of bread and circuses. The judge was a hanging judge, Fadhil Mahdawi of the People's Court. He was also Kassem's nephew. He and the prosecutor, Colonel Majed Amin, would joke back and forth about the witnesses and the accused, and laughingly sentence most to die. The judge was disgusting, and educated Iraqis were ashamed, while the street loved him. All day on TV, judge and prosecutor would play to each other in mocking, ridiculing, parodying the testimony—and when bored or satiated, sentence the victims to be hanged. The Iraqis are a violent people with barbaric passions never far from the surface.

In a country of sinister figures, none was more sinister than Kassem's aide and bodyguard Brigadier Wasfi Tahir and his enormously fat younger brother, Colonel Lufti Tahir. Wasfi, seldom without a Sten gun, was always lurking at Kassem's side—as he once had been at Premier Nuri as-Said's side when he was his aide. Wasfi was a member of the Central Committee of the Iraqi Communist Party, as was his brother, who was the chief censor for Iraq and a gross, stupid, stubborn man. In the early days, Kassem referred to Wasfi Tahir as "my drawn sword" and seemed to rely on him, giving substance to the apprehension that he was pro-Communist. Later, Kassem backed off the Tahir brothers and vigorously denounced communism, which he felt was intruding into Iraqi affairs even more than Nasser and the Americans. Shortly after that there was an assassination attempt that failed. But all that was in the future.

My interview with Kassem in 1959 was done through an interpreter, whom Kassem didn't need: often he'd answer ahead of the translator. The conference room in which we met was decorated with seventeen photos and portraits of Kassem. I recalled an exhibition at the art gallery in Baghdad where the main "art" was Kassem himself: sculptures of him, portraits of him, photos of him, poems about him. When writing about the exhibition being opened by Kassem, Douglas Brown of the *Telegraph* got around the censorship problem by noting that Kassem had praised the artists for the "versatility and variety" of their subjects. The sarcasm not only escaped the censor but also eluded Brown's editors in London who didn't understand tongue-in-cheek.

Kassem expressed gratitude to the Soviets for their support, but he was too good a Moslem to be enamored with the ideology of godless communism. While expressing friendship for the United States and Americans he felt that "elements" there such as the CIA and the military and the Jewish-controlled press were not to be trusted. I asked him if he feared death and he looked genuinely amused. "No. If I am to die, then I am to die and nothing I do will change that. Being afraid of death is worse than death itself." He grinned and shrugged.

The official photographer who took our picture at the interview was so nervous that he couldn't focus properly and his hands shook so that the shot was ruined. Clearly, he was no fatalist about death. Kassem laughed, and I wondered what the photographer knew that made him so uneasy. The resulting interview ran for five straight days in Baghdad's English-language newspaper. It was noted that Sole Leader was far too clever for the "devious" Canadian "so-called journalist" and had skillfully avoided all the traps I was supposedly setting. It was clear to the newspaper that I was a CIA lackey.

As our interview neared its close, Kassem asked if I'd like an autographed photograph of himself. I said of course. A collection of photos of various sizes was brought in, plus reprints of his speeches and a photo of Iraq's new coat of arms. Kassem began signing photos like mad. I wondered what on earth was happening. He gave me nineteen autographed photos, then began signing his speeches, printed in various languages. When finally done, he smiled his crooked-tooth smile. I was appropriately grateful. Since he clearly enjoyed signing his name, I decided to gild the lily and asked if he'd sign the photo of the constitution, too.

Kassem exploded in anger. "Under no circumstances. This is our constitution. It belongs to the people, not to any one man. I will not sign it. You should know better than to ask. It is the property of the people of Iraq!"

"Of course, Your Excellency, foolish of me to be so ignorant."

Kassem grinned. "Can I drive you back to your hotel?"

"Thank you, I'd be most grateful."

Kassem explained why his photo was everywhere: "It is my way of sharing myself with the people. I am theirs, their servant, and photographs are a way for them to have a part of me."

Kassem and I got into his Chevy station wagon while he shooed away a soldier with a submachine gun. He sent his armed guard to a couple of Land Rovers to follow behind. Only Wasfi Tahir got in the rear seat, his small, humorless eyes darting everywhere, and we drove into the Baghdad streets jammed with people. We were quickly surrounded, the bodyguards in the Land Rovers cut off. People cheered, waved, hysteria began mounting. Wasfi Tahir looked most uncomfortable while Kassem smiled his snaggle-toothed smile, waved, and saluted the mob, which was now running beside the station wagon. He'd have been ridiculously easy to kill. And Tahir knew it.

At the hotel I got out and we wished each other good luck. By this time the Land Rovers had caught up and the armed entourage sped off while the hotel staff gaped with stunned incomprehension. The hotel service as far as I was concerned improved enormously after that, breaking down only when I offered to give them an autographed photo of Sole Leader in return for a free room. They weren't *that* patriotic.

Baghdad, situated at the junction of the Tigris and Euphrates rivers, is an oasis amid the barrens. One can see why many think it was the biblical Garden of Eden. Under Kassem, the country had cut ties with the past and was on a different course. Within a year an enormous monument to Iraq's "Revolting Arab" was being constructed, while much-needed housing was still being neglected. Productivity had plunged 50 percent in a year, wages increased by 30 percent, and Iraq would soon have to be bailed out—if not by the West, then by the USSR. Kassem increasingly tried to pull back from the Soviets and hold his own ideologues at bay, but got deeper into political and economic quicksand.

Tragedy was in the air and I wrote from Baghdad: "The first martyr of 'new' Iraq will probably be Kassem. He seems destined to be killed . . . the real horror story of Baghdad has still to be written."

That was in 1959. Six months later Kassem was shot and wounded; three years after that he was killed. His "friend" Abdul Salam Aref, whom he had saved from execution, became the new Sole Leader. I wrote at the time that Aref "is now on a trail that could lead to his eventual assassination."

That prophecy took five years to be fulfilled. In 1968 he was deposed. As it turns out, predicting disaster for Arab leaders is a pretty safe bet. Still, there is no shortage of contenders for the top job, no matter how temporary. . . .

As soon as I had filed the story of Baghdad ("Tely Man First to Arrive in Iraq—Taxi Trip Over Desert Cooked Eggs" shouted the *Telegram* headline), I hustled off to Amman, Jordan, where British paratroopers were keeping an uneasy lid on a potentially explosive situation. Despite fear of a Nasser plot to overthrow the king, everything seemed calm in Jordan, but I succumbed to the prevailing myth and wrote what was to be the first of innumerable stories on how precarious Hussein's hold on the country was, and how he would be toppled at any moment. As it turned out, King Hussein was one of the world's most durable monarchs and had one of the most stable Arab governments this side of Tunisia and Morocco.

Jordan was tense, and made even more tense because nothing much was happening, and the journalists were tired of writing daily stories about how Amman was a city of fear and the kingdom tottering . . . again. There is only so much mileage to be gained from cities shrouded in fear and tottering on brinks. I arrived fresh from the civil war in Beirut, agitations in Damascus (where we had hired the taxi to Baghdad), and the revolution in Baghdad. I checked in at the Amman Club Hotel where British journalists stayed. American journalists and big shots preferred the newer, more elegant, and expensive Philadelphia Hotel. I arrived at lunchtime and got a bored briefing from my colleagues, who burst into guffaws when I asked about prospects for interviewing King Hussein.

"You can leave your name at the palace with his minister of protocol," I was told. "But it's a waste of time. Hussein's not seen anyone since the crisis began. We've all been trying. Cheeky bugger to ignore us!"

I said I'd go and leave my name. The others shrugged. They had done the same thing weeks ago, when the crisis started. No luck.

After lunch I took a taxi. "To the king's palace," I said grandly, wondering how often the occasion arose to tell a taxi driver that. An Arab legionnaire with a Lee Enfield rifle at the gate leading into the grounds of the palace shook his head in puzzlement when I asked for the king or the chief of protocol. He phoned the palace, a rapid conversation ensued, after which he suddenly showed more respect and motioned that I proceed up the winding road. At the palace I muttered something about being there to see the king and was ushered unquestioned into an anteroom with four other Europeans in business suits. I was in khaki pants and a sports shirt. When I asked to see the chief of protocol, I was gestured to sit down and be patient. The other foreigners and I chatted briefly in English. They turned out to be German businessmen.

Without warning, an aide came and led us down a corridor into a spacious living room filled with soft chairs, paintings, deep rugs. Waiting for us was King Hussein. We all shook hands, sat down, and were served Coca-Cola or coffee. There was some polite chit-chat until I broke the ice and asked about the present situation. What was Nasser up to? Were there fears of an overthrow? Who was to blame? What about Palestinian refugees? Was the Arab Legion strong? The king responded cordially, fairly frankly, and seemed a little surprised. He blamed Israel for the unrest; yes, Nasser was up to no good since he wanted to create a pan-Arabic empire with himself at the head; the refugees were a great burden on Jordan and Israel could not be forgiven. While he was grateful to Britain for sending paratroopers to help encourage stability, that country was still not to be trusted. Nor was the United States because it was dominated by Israel—though he appreciated American aid. And no, he didn't trust Russia. Communism was not for Arabs and was not compatible with the Moslem religion.

I asked about the firing of Glubb Pasha as commander of his Arab Legion. Hussein admitted that perhaps he'd been over-hasty and that it was a mistake to have gotten rid of him. He said he'd been impetuous and had gotten bad advice from jealous people who feared Glubb was working for Britain rather than Jordan.

Lieutenant-General John Bagot Glubb had served the Arab Legion since 1939 and had made it into the most professional Arab army in the Middle East, and the only Arab army that held the Israelis in the 1948 war. A soldier, not a diplomat, Glubb was inclined to be abrupt and patronizing to the youthful king he served. So it didn't take much to feed Hussein's suspicions—which those who favored Nasser and a republic for Jordan did. In the spring of 1956 he gave Glubb Pasha and his senior officers twenty-four hours to leave the country forever. It was a cruel way to treat Glubb, who had served Jordan and the Hashimites so loyally, but when I met him a few years later, and in subsequent exchanges of letters, Glubb Pasha showed not a trace of bitterness or resentment. He understood completely a young man's intolerance and an old man's impatience.

Almost as if he were atoning for past paranoia, King Hussein made a point of stressing how much he admired and appreciated Glubb Pasha's loyalty to and love for Jordan. But no, he didn't think Glubb could or should come back, because history moved on and his Arab Legion was already well trained and no longer needed foreigners in command, no matter how devoted or loyal these foreigners might be. Later, when I got to know Glubb, I related the anecdote and he agreed with Hussein's view.

Though only twenty-two, Hussein had already seen more harshness than many far more experienced than he. His courage, even then, was legendary and he had the absolute devotion of the Bedouin troops of his Arab Legion. He had great self-possession. After all, he had witnessed the assassination of his grandfather, King Abdullah, in the mosque in Jerusalem in 1951. His father, Talal, briefly inherited the throne. Unlike his boisterous, gregarious father, King Talal was a serious, gentle, conscientious schizophrenic. Though a good king when rational, Talal willingly gave up the throne in favor of his son in 1952 and entered permanent compassionate confinement in Turkey.

At the group interview King Hussein wondered why I, a German, was so curious about such things, and what sort of business did we have in mind? I said I didn't understand what he was talking about. It then began to unravel. Everyone (except the German businessmen) thought I was a member of their trade delegation and I had mistakenly been included in the audience. Hussein burst into laughter at the error, while his sullen young brother, Prince Mohammed, aged seventeen, glowered and nervously toyed with the submachine gun he always carried. Mohammed was believed by the foreign press to be as mad as a hatter, and it was said that on impulse he would occasionally fire his weapon in the palace just for the hell of it. Everyone was uneasy around Prince Mohammed.

Hussein let me stay for the audience, after which the Germans gave me a lift back to the hotel. I entered the bar and asked where I got accreditation to file a story. It was about three o'clock and I had been in Jordan perhaps four hours. "You can't have much of a story to file," said one.

"Get your name on the list?" said another.

"No," I said, "I got an interview with the king. Not bad. Got to write and file it now."

There was cursing and a clatter as all abandoned their beers and raced for taxis to dash to the palace and try their luck. They all got their names on the list again, but no interview. I filed my story fairly straight, and for the rest of the crisis was treated with a mixture of envy and respect. Everyone knew it was the blind luck of a beginner, but everyone was also experienced enough to know that you don't knock luck.

Experiences in Lebanon, Iraq, and Jordan collided with the conventional wisdom at the time that Arabs were receptive to the blandishments of the Kremlin. Arabs, like most of the Third World, try to use or manipulate whoever is willing to be manipulated. Usually the West panics more quickly than the Kremlin, hence it is more susceptible to blackmail. But more than most people, Arabs as individuals make poor socialists and practise free enterprise wherever they can. Any foreign power that thinks it can control or dominate them is doomed to disappointment. They make poor puppets and invariably turn on their puppet-masters.

I suspect one could devise a law or a truism to the effect that the people with the fewest material goods are often those with the richest spiritual values. One counterbalances the other. By the same token, people with the least wealth are often the most generous and hospitable—and this seems especially true of Arab countries, Africa, and Asia. I have difficulty recalling any examples of discourtesy or unpleasantness in Arab countries. Even when they periodically were bent on killing Europeans, it was never a *personal* thing. Nor was it racial.

7

192 glasses of milk for a dime

TORONTO *TELEGRAM*
28 AUGUST 1959

It's one of the prevailing myths of our system, perpetrated by those in the business, that the press has its finger on the pulse of the people. That is, newspaper people—now expanded to include everyone in what collectively is known as the "media"—like to think they instinctively know what the public thinks, feels, wants, and what is best for them. This, of course, is rubbish. Media people are incipient elitists and it's mere accident or coincidence when they are in tune with the public mood. Usually they are out of touch with the masses but don't know it, nor do the masses, who also tend to believe the propaganda that the press is in touch with popular opinion.

The impotence of newspapers can be seen at elections, when editorial pages solemnly tell people whom they must vote for, else doom will befall the nation. Mercifully, the people usually blithely ignore the advice and vote for whoever wins—often at their peril, according to editorial wisdom. When Ronald Reagan was running for president in 1980, most in the media were against him, depicting him as something of a dangerous joke—a semi-senile, grade B movie actor who was probably a mad bomber. The American people, brainwashed by the media, were reluctant to admit they were voting for him, even though on TV Reagan seemed mild, unfailingly courteous, and not nearly as wild-eyed and erratic as Jimmy Carter who, like Britain's erstwhile Labor leader Michael Foot, had the appearance of The Man Who Had Just Seen the Most Awful Thing in the World. On election day forty-three out of fifty states went for Reagan, much to the media's consternation.

In three general elections in Canada (1974, 1979, 1980) the Toronto *Star* editorially urged voters to go Conservative, Socialist,

Liberal. Small wonder the public ignores newspaper advice. Politicians especially are captive of the myth that newspapers know what the public wants, but that's only because politicians are dependent on the press and are usually in more of a quandary than even the media.

Newspapers are always trying to tap into what will make the public buy their product. If it were certain that, say, putting headlines upside down would sell, all newspapers ranging from the New York *Times* to the North Bay *Nugget* would do it and rationalize that it was for esthetic purposes, or in the national interest, or a decision of principle.

Even newspapers that advertise themselves as community-oriented do so primarily because they think it is good for business. Where possible, newspapers try to tie promotion stunts into something that will be of value to the community. Such schemes are more productive than straight appeals to greed, like bingo games, or spot the missing football in the photo, or prize crosswords.

It was the double threat of community appeal and commercial rewards that persuaded the Toronto *Telegram* in 1959 to sponsor a Milk Ship to deliver surplus Canadian milk powder to undernourished children around the world. The scheme was a brainchild of CARE, the international relief organization, which got the Canadian government to donate up to 10 million pounds of surplus powdered milk on condition that someone else paid to transport it to malnourished children. Enter the *Telegram*.

Paul Courian, the director of CARE-Canada, convinced the paper that if we sponsored a campaign in which readers gave money to rent a ship, we'd feed the hungry children, Canadian donors would feel good, the *Telegram*'s circulation would soar, and the rival Toronto *Star* would be beside itself with envy.

The latter prospect particularly appealed to the swashbuckling John Bassett. CARE figured that every dime donated would deliver 192 glasses of milk to needy kids in Italy, Greece, Turkey, and Egypt—the destinations of our Milk Ship. So $1 meant 1,920 glasses of milk and $10 was 19,200 glasses. It sounded good.

One day I was called in to the office of Art Cole, the giant of a city editor who was as gentle as a lamb but disguised this fact so well during working hours that every reporter was terrified of him.

"Pete, you've been around lots and have seen hungry kids." It was a statement more than a question. Cole glared as if daring me to disagree.

"I guess so, Art. Why?" Reporters are naturally wary when city editors ask seemingly innocent questions.

"I mean you've seen *really* starving kids in those refugee camps, haven't you? Jesus, you've written enough about the plight of those goddam Arabs" (the *Tely's* notoriously pro-Zionist attitude tended to rub off on editors).

"Yeah. Maybe. So what?"

"Good. We've got this promotion about milk. I want you to write a feature a day for the next three months about milk and starving kids so we can raise money. You'll work with the Promotion Department. See Baz Mason or Cliff Daniels. Your baby exclusively." He beamed one of those city editor smiles that tells reporters they've been had.

So I got the assignment and for the next three months tried to nurse tears and dimes out of schoolkids and corporate bucks from advertisers who thought donating would improve their image. We were serious about getting the most for our money and tried to rent the cheapest cargo vessel possible. I recycled old stories about refugee camps and wars and tried to relate everything to milk, which meant a lot of poetic licence and outright invention. From the start it was a remarkably successful promotion, and by the end of the summer we had close to $100,000 and were plotting successors to the Milk Ship—Son of Milk Ship, Milk Ship II, More Milk Ship. That sort of thing. Any tearful letter about milk meant instant publicity in the *Tely* for the sender.

Meanwhile circulation grew rapidly. Phone canvassers were issued a special screed to read to prospective customers: "Hello Mrs. So-and-so, I'm calling on behalf of needy children of the world. Can you hear me all right? Good. As you know, Mrs. So-and-so, there are thousands of children throughout the world who have never tasted a glass of milk. Recognizing this need, the Toronto *Telegram* newspaper in cooperation with CARE of Canada plans to launch a shipload of milk from Toronto to the hungry children of the world. I feel certain, Mrs. So-and-so, that knowing how important this cause is, *you* will allow us to deliver the *Tely* to you for just ten weeks. A cash donation will be made in your name and you will receive a personal letter of thanks from Canada's food crusade. Will that be all right? Good. And for your order the children will receive over 600 glasses of milk as your personal gift—will that be all right?"

So the pitch went.

By the time the *Star* realized we were on to a good thing, the

Tely alone had raised nearly $9,000 for the Milk Ship through 25¢ per new subscription, and some 36,000 new *Tely* subscribers were anxious to get starving kids drinking surplus Canadian milk.

The lowest bidder to be the Tely Milk Ship was the *Star of Assuan*, an Egyptian ship that presented a bit of an ideological problem, since Bassett and the *Telegram* thought Israel could do no wrong. Our main readership was supposedly Toronto's large Jewish population—another myth, because Jewish readers, sure of the *Telegram*'s loyalty to Israel, preferred to read the *Star* and get angry at the occasional critical articles.

However, we rationalized that giving the milk contract to an Egyptian vessel to help Egyptian kids showed nonpartisan humanitarianism and a desire for world understanding and all that— so long as Israel was more equal than her neighbors.

We didn't stress the *Star of Assuan* bit, and on photos meticulously painted *Tely Milk Ship* over the ship's name. The ship was loaded with appropriate fanfare and speeches from every dignitary we could muster. The wife of the editor was one of several passengers making the trip as a holiday. I had parlayed the daily articles about milk into a trip to each port, to write about the reception and the joy of starving kids getting the milk. But I went by plane, not by slow Milk Ship.

Memory fades, but the trip was clearly a disaster from beginning to end. In a dreadful way it was even funny, but a public relations calamity nonetheless. Journalistically it paid off, because I got an interview with Nasser, used CARE connections in India to meet the Dalai Lama, interviewed Prime Minister Nehru of India, and got into Laos, which was at war with itself, went on to Taiwan, which was in the throes of being shelled from mainland China on odd days of the month (or was it even days?), and interviewed Generalissimo and Madame Chiang Kai-shek.

Meanwhile, at dockside in Naples there was no hint of a growing controversy at home between the *Tely* and the *Star*. Naples was something out of *Bicycle Thief*: poor, run-down, unspeakably depressing, still showing the after-effects of the war. It was a grey, overcast day with rain in the air. You just knew the rains would hit during the ceremonies when the Canadian powdered milk was being ceremoniously handed over to Italian orphans. A makeshift stand had been set up with a billowing canopy overhead, a ragtag band in front of the stand, and a few press and stragglers to one side. As the ceremonies began, so did the rain. The band was struggling with "O Canada" when the bottom fell out of the sky.

After a few gallant moments the band dissolved and fled in various directions, with a few more resolute members still struggling with the anthem.

The Canadian chargé d'affaires, Norman Berlis, floundered through an appropriate speech over the loudspeaker, though no one was listening. Dignitaries sat smiling tightly in the stand beneath the canopy. I was outside, huddled by a shack, when an unshaven Italian workman suddenly grinned at me and motioned with his eyes to the canopy over the dignitaries. It was rapidly filling with water and stretched tight like a pregnant tummy. Clearly, it was about to burst. Should I warn them or shouldn't I? I looked at the workman, who looked imploringly at me to do nothing. I made my decision, winked at him, and shrugged. Let nature take its course. He gave me the international forefinger-to-thumb sign of approval and we settled back to anticipate the inevitable.

We didn't have long to wait. Suddenly the canopy split down the middle and gallons of water flooded over the heads of the guests. The speech ended amid screams and squeals, and women's hairdos disintegrated as everyone scampered for cars. We adjourned to the Casa Materna orphanage, where the director gave a symbolic speech about the necessity of rain for crops, and his orphans performed what they considered a typically Canadian song about Ten Little Indians.

Worse was to come. A Communist newspaper noted that white paint had gotten mixed up with powdered milk from Canada, and half a dozen orphans had perished from drinking it. Canada was accused—falsely, as it turned out—of mixing white paint powder with milk powder. The Communists speculated as to whether the Milk Ship might be a capitalistic imperialist plot to destroy Italian orphans. By the time it was discovered that it was not *our* white paint and milk, the damage had been done. Oh well, three countries to go.

In the Greek port of Piraeus we had arranged for Queen Frederika to do the honors, but the ship was behind schedule and she left before it arrived. It was just as well, in view of the anti-royalty sentiment: it was felt our milk would be better untainted, so to speak. Instead, we recruited Mrs. Roland Michener to do the honors, along with Canadian Ambassador E. D. McGeer who, in turn, quoted Prime Minister Diefenbaker as supporting the Milk Ship and being constantly concerned for Greek children. Mrs. Michener was a good sport but when we tried to pose a symbolic picture of her giving Greek orphans a drink, they'd have no part of it. It tasted too awful. Finally, a batch of milk was prepared and laced with sugar so that the kids would drink it without grimacing. Mrs. Michener took a taste and while the photo of the kids came out okay, she had made such a grimace at the sickly sweetness that the picture was unusable. It looked as if she found the kids repugnant. Meanwhile the local press was feuding with the royal family and the Milk Ship became an inadvertent casualty.

In Turkey we landed in another feud: CARE was working with the Red Crescent Society *and* with the government welfare people, who were in competition with each other. The Canadian Ambassador, Benjamin Rogers, and the CARE director for Turkey, Chris Fallon, had to arrange separate, semi-secret ceremonies to avoid offending either group. CARE was anxious for us to get out of town as quickly and quietly as possible, before a political incident occurred.

In Alexandria, Egypt, officials were grateful for the milk, but pointed out that it wasn't customary for Egyptian kids to drink milk. We arranged for the milk powder to be given to a bakery, which would add it to buns so that children would get nutrition that way. A ceremony was arranged in Alexandria involving then-Ambassador Arnold Smith, perhaps our most effective diplomat and one whom Nasser credited with smoothing relations between Britain and Egypt, which was still smarting over the Suez War and claiming victory over the combined forces of Israel, Britain, and France. Smith had invited an array of Egyptian VIPs whom he wanted to impress with Canada's friendly neutrality.

The embassy had put the wrong date on the invitation, and dignitaries who made the drive from Cairo to Alexandria arrived a day early. Ambassador Smith labored mightily to undo the insult, which some Egyptians seemed to think was a deliberate snub. No ship, lots of indignation. We endured a makeshift ceremony, which wasn't the same somehow, and the whole exercise was rescheduled for the following day. The second reception played to a mostly empty house and was not the greatest success. None of this, of course, appeared in my writings at the time, just halellujahs for the *Telegram* and its readers.

Meanwhile, in Toronto, something of a newspaper war was erupting over CARE, surplus milk, and the *Tely*. The powerful *Star* was apparently alarmed at the 36,000 jump in *Tely* circulation, thanks to the paper's gimmick of giving 25¢ of every new subscription to the Milk Ship. The *Star* contacted Paul Courian and threatened to expose the circulation gimmick if CARE didn't abandon the *Tely* campaign. The *Tely* responded with an editorial attacking the *Star* and recounting how editorial writer Mark Harrison (later editor of the Montreal *Gazette*) had threatened Courian and how CARE's board of directors met and sided with the *Tely*.

"The *Star* is a bully," the Tely editorialized, "but happily in this instance those responsible for the direction of CARE are men of character and integrity and the *Telegram* is big enough to defend itself." The *Tely* accused the *Star* of intruding bully tactics into the realm of social welfare and foreign aid, and said: "The *Star*, smarting under its own circulation losses and the *Telegram*'s gains, attempts to frighten CARE and this newspaper . . . in vain."

The controversy was the last thing CARE or Courian anticipated, and eventually they backed off and tried to keep a foot in both camps. This won the enmity of Bassett, who recognized a faint heart when he saw one. In those days the *Tely* and John Bassett were unforgiving of those who played footsie with the *Star* or who were timid about doing battle.

All this trouble erupted after I had flown to Naples to meet the Milk Ship when it was apparent that this was an unexpectedly successful public relations effort. I knew nothing about the chaos at home. The two papers were probably the most competitive in North America at the time and everything from smashing cameras, pushing reporters into lakes, kidnapping news sources, and stealing each other's property was considered routine rivalry.

Cliff Daniels, the mastermind of the Milk Ship, nervous at the best of times, was now distraught with indecision and, in fact, soon after committed suicide—coincidence, no doubt, but still a sad and drastic solution to personal problems.

Meanwhile, I reverted to honest journalism and was busy trying to parlay the *Telegram*'s humanitarianism and well-known love of children into an interview with Gamal Abdel Nasser, who was always difficult to see.

Ambassador Smith found the Milk Ship diplomatically useful, too, and was using it as evidence that Canada was not totally committed to the Israeli side. Why else would we seek to help Egyptian kiddies with milk powder? Speaking on my behalf with the Egyptian government, he said it would be taken as a friendly gesture to Canada if President Nasser would grant me an interview.

Though President Nasser had lost the 1956 war, he had won the peace and wasn't one to forgive or forget easily. Tension, suspicions, paranoia toward Britain and her allies lingered. At the time of the ill-fated Milk Ship's arrival in Egypt, British news outlets were obsessed with the story of a young British lieutenant named Anthony Moorehouse who had been kidnapped at the height of the Suez invasion, locked in a large box, and put in the closet of a house in Suez, where he had suffocated.

The furore in 1959 was because the Egyptians were planning to make a museum out of the death house and turn it into a shrine to Egyptian bravery. Fleet Street was furious at plans to glorify the infamous deed, and their jingoistic ire was jeopardizing the restoration of diplomatic relations between Britain and Egypt. Egyptians were so defensive that Saad Affra, the commander of guerrillas who had captured Moorehouse (and was now Director-General of Information for Egypt), wryly told me that he thought the museum a good idea ("after all, it was our victory!") and blamed "one lazy British soldier" for the death of Moorehouse.

He said that during the house-to-house search by British troops, Moorehouse's Egyptian captors had left him locked in the box that was to become his coffin, and then hidden across the street to watch what would happen. A British Tommy had paused at the house, shrugged, put a chalk mark on it to indicate it had been searched, and had passed on. Three days later when the Egyptians could safely enter the house, Moorehouse was dead. Had the troops checked, they'd have found him.

Ambassador Smith, busy negotiating the restoration of diplomatic relations, was angry with the press for what he considered irresponsible sensationalism, which he feared might prevent my getting an interview with Nasser as well as hurt chances for British-Egyptian reconciliation. Up to then Nasser had been favorably inclined to grant an interview, thanks to the gesture of the Milk Ship.

I waited and waited, made applications, and was repeatedly told to stand by. There was one uneasy moment when the Director of Information looked into files and noted that the *Telegram* had once before interviewed Nasser. It was news to me, and before my time.

"Are you sure it wasn't the *Star*?" I said.

"No. *Telegram*. A Mr. Slonim."

My heart sank. Reuben Slonim, a Toronto rabbi, covered Israel for us, making several trips a year and writing what I considered exclusively pro-Israel reports. I hadn't realized he'd once seen Nasser. "Oh," I said, "Yes. Slonim. Hmmm."

The Egyptian looked at me reproachfully. "He never told us he was a rabbi."

I suddenly wished I was blond and blue-eyed.

If Nasser agreed to see me, it would be his first meeting with a Western journalist in recent times. And it would be for several overlapping reasons: partly because Canada was seen as friendly and had opposed the 1956 war; partly because Lester Pearson was instrumental in creating the United Nations Emergency Force; partly because Nasser had great respect and affection for Ambassador Smith; partly because it suited Nasser's purpose to be interviewed at this time.

I had undergone a pre-interview by Mohammed Heikal, Nasser's best friend and advisor, and then editor of the influential *Al Ahram.* (Heikal was subsequently arrested and fired by President Sadat and later resurrected by Mubarak—the fate of being close to power in the volatile Middle East.)

Heikal was a swarthy, handsome man who exuded arrogance and boredom. He gave the impression of believing what was expedient for him to believe, but had the ability not to be deceived by those who reflected the same qualities of opportunism that he embodied. He was a useful screen for Nasser. He was intelligent and we got on reasonably well. I think he trusted me, even though he must have considered me somewhat naïve.

While waiting for the interview to come through, I stayed at the Cosmopolitan in Cairo, a somewhat seedy hotel left over from another era. It was near the post office and cable office and was where British journalists who wanted to save on expense accounts usually stayed. At the time Jimmy Cameron of the *Observer* was there, tippling in the evenings and bemoaning the fact that while he had done so much to help Nasser in the past, he couldn't get an interview with him in the present. Cameron regaled whatever audience he had in the bar with tales of his carnivorous pet rabbit in England. The rabbit was a meat-eater and so big and mean that his dog was terrified of it and would be literally kicked away from its fireside spot by the rabbit, which also liked that place. The rabbit could easily climb the stairs, but couldn't get down them, and would sit on the landing thumping angrily until it was carried down. I don't know whether this story is true or apocryphal, but it was delightful and I have never tired of recalling it. If it isn't true, it should be.

Cameron gloomily predicted that if Nasser wouldn't see him, he certainly wouldn't see me. And yet I kept getting encouragement from the Egyptians to hang on. Days went by. Unless some-thing happened soon, I'd have to leave, because I wanted to catch President Eisenhower's visit to India.

It was during one of the bar conversations that I learned that Queen Dina, the exiled wife of King Hussein of Jordan, lived in Cairo. She was a Cambridge-educated beauty who had once cap-tured the young king's heart. But when Egypt and Jordan feuded, so did the young king and queen and the marriage crumbled. She had returned home to Cairo, while Hussein kept their four-year-old daughter, Princess Alia. It sounded like a possible story, so I phoned Queen Dina and found her not only willing to see me but eager to talk.

I took a taxi to an address in the suburbs and was escorted into an opulent setting—gorgeous furniture and appointments. It was rather like a British palace: not much for relaxing in, but chairs for sitting carefully on and china so delicate one was afraid to hold it for fear it might break.

Queen Dina was beautiful, gracious, and shy. And desperate, otherwise she would have never seen a rather bumbling stranger like me. She was not divorced but merely separated, and was distraught because the king refused to allow her back to Jordan to visit her daughter. She had gone to Cairo in 1956, ostensibly for a short visit, but Hussein had turned it into virtual exile.

Though born in Egypt she considered herself Jordanian and wanted her daughter to be Jordanian. On a small table were silver-framed photographs of Hussein, his grandfather King Abdullah, young King Faisal of Iraq, and the Crown Prince Abdul-Illah. All but Hussein had died violently from assassins' bullets.

While we shyly drank hot chocolate from gold-plated cups, her composure cracked under the strain of keeping emotions to her-self, and her anguish and unhappiness flooded out. I am not good with weeping women at the best of times, but when queens start to weep I am utterly at a loss. I found myself sitting on the settee beside her murmuring things like, "There, there, Your Majesty, be brave . . ." and patting her shoulder. She'd dab her eyes and continue her tale of woe.

The essence of her story was that she realized the problems Hussein faced and why they had to separate. She loved him still and was ready to sacrifice herself for his good. But she loved her daughter dearly and missed her mightily. All she wanted was the chance to see Alia once a year, perhaps a rendezvous in Turkey or Cyprus or Lebanon. Anywhere. But no. The king, who'd promised this when they separated, had reneged and wouldn't cooperate. Why? she asked herself. Was it his advisors, who had never liked her? His mother? Brother? Who? What could she do? What could I do?

With tears flowing and emotions strained, she asked if there was any way I could help persuade the Canadian ambassador and the British to intercede with Hussein to permit her to see her daughter. I was upset on her behalf, but somewhat out of my depth; what had started out as a routine interview with exotic royalty had dissolved into a domestic crisis. Unused to queens begging for my help, I promised to do whatever I could. At that moment I would have done anything to help. I suppose I was infatuated, and in another era I'd likely have been down on one knee pledging everlasting fealty. As we talked about a variety of subjects, it quickly became apparent that her difficulties with Hussein were probably because of intellect: she had too much, he too little.

Her dilemma was that she had no official standing and there were no sources she could turn to for help. ("As a queen I cannot go up to some minor embassy official and throw myself on his mercy.") I vowed to try to persuade Ambassador Smith to take up her case. I was imbued with the zeal of a true believer, a recent convert. This, surely, was my true calling—helping fair queens in trouble, not delivering powdered milk to Egyptian kids who didn't like it anyway!

I had an emergency meeting with Ambassador Smith and told him the sorry tale. It is a measure of the man that he, too, was touched, although more realistic than I. There wasn't much he could do; however, he arranged a luncheon at which I'd have a chance to talk with Colin Crowe, the British representative in Cairo and the central figure in the restoration of diplomatic relations.

I called Dina—she was Dina now—and we had more hot chocolate in gold cups, more tears, more sympathy, and more mutual lamenting about the unfairness of life.

While all this was going on, I kept trying to see Nasser. And kept being told all was well, but be patient.

The lunch with Arnold Smith and Colin Crowe was inconclusive. I presented the story as dramatically as I could, and hoped for some accommodation for ex-queen and daughter. Crowe was in touch with Jordan and said he'd bring the matter up, but didn't sound hopeful. He explained that no matter how cordial relations might be with Hussein, it was rarely advisable to interfere in royal marriages in Arab kingdoms. However, if the opportunity occurred to bring the matter up with the monarch, he would.

During lunch I was offered what I thought were string beans. They turned out to be peppers so hot that I couldn't speak and could barely breathe. My eyes filled with tears, sweat burst on my upper lip, and I was in silent agony. I'm sure everyone thought I was heartbroken over Colin Crowe's discouraging prognostication for helping Queen Dina. I felt myself being stared at, but was unable to speak and could only stare back through pleading, tear-filled eyes. When I took a swig of water, the fire simply spread. I gestured and gagged and all activity around the table ceased. Migod, I thought, Ambassador Smith must think this fool journalist has gotten himself so emotionally involved with this ex-queen that he's speechless with desire. Whatta woman . . . !

At that moment Colin Crowe suddenly doubled over, clapped a napkin to his mouth, and started gagging. His eyes streamed tears and he was a mirror image of my agony. Was he so moved by Queen Dina's plight that he couldn't contain himself either?

"Good God, Arnold, those aren't beans!" gasped Crowe. "What in God's name are you doing to us!"

The crisis passed, and Arnold Smith promised to do what he could for Dina, said he'd try to get in touch with her, and promised to be more careful in the future with peppers.

Over yet more hot chocolate, I told Dina what had happened, gave her Ambassador Smith's phone number, but never learned if anything was done. She remarried a few years later and, I suspect, wrote off her daughter as a casualty of Arab politics.

I had already stayed too long in Egypt and had decided to give up on Nasser. In fact I was boarding the night plane to India when security police came into the aircraft and took me off, claiming that the president wanted to see me the next day.

From then on it was red carpet. Nasser still lived in the same house he had had before the revolution, and while comfortable, it was extremely modest. I found him bigger than I expected, with a friendly, self-deprecatory sense of humor. He radiated strength and candor as well as charm, and it was difficult not to fall under his spell. I was impressed and found surprisingly little wariness in him.

I asked him about the Moorehouse case and he seemed genuinely distressed about the incident. He blamed General Stockwell, who had commanded the British invasion forces, for the death.

Nasser said he'd sent a message to General Stockwell offering to send an emissary to Suez to negotiate the release of Moorehouse. Stockwell had refused. "This unfortunate boy needn't have died," said Nasser. "General Stockwell is as much to blame as anyone else."

Nasser said he had only learned of the plan to make the house into a museum by reading the British papers, but it was now impossible to revoke the plans. "When foreign interests try to pressure us, we have no alternative but to take contrary actions. I felt sorry about Moorehouse at the time; I feel sorry now that our hopes for renewed relations have gotten off to such a bad start."

We chatted alone in his study for some three hours. He joked, saying that he liked reading the British papers more than his own because he knew in advance what his papers would say. He said he learned more from criticism than praise, and the problem was to balance the uncritical praise of Egyptian papers with the totally critical abuse of the British press. He told me he used to keep scrapbooks of anti-Nasser cartoons in the British press, "but there are now too many to keep up with!" He professed mock astonishment that "for some reason Egyptian papers never run anti-Nasser cartoons."

He seemed genuinely paranoid about Israel, and repeatedly said it wouldn't surprise him if someone were to burst in and announce that Israel had invaded again. When I mentioned Israel's apprehensions about threats of being driven into the sea and so forth, he laughed and said it was Arab rhetoric and, of all people, Israelis should know they were mere words.

"Look at my desk," he said. "Go on. Look at that pile of papers and books. See what they are? Yes, not strategies and battle plans, but economic reports. Is this the desk of someone plotting war against Israel? Our war is with the economy. Too many people, not enough arable land. We don't want war, we can't afford war. If I were planning war, I'd not be so concerned about improving our economy."

Yet he exuded a strong feeling that he'd fight again, even knowing that Egypt would lose. "We won't lose forever. After all, it was you British who proved that you can lose all battles except the last one and thus win the war. But I want peace, not war."

I mentioned Queen Dina, but he merely shrugged and said that Hussein viewed him as an enemy and that he had no influence over barbarians. Or words to that effect. It was a good interview.

Back at the Cosmopolitan Hotel, I wrote the interview with Nasser and a separate story about his reaction to the Moorehouse/museum affair, which was the hot news, and planned to cable the stories from India, where there was no censorship and cable rates were cheaper. In the bar prior to leaving I met Tony Brown, later a best-selling author (*Bodyguard of Lies*) but then correspondent for the *Daily Mail*. I told Tony I had lucked into an interview with Nasser, and was sorry I couldn't give him details.

"Look," said Brown, always good with words, "you're going to India. Tell me what he said and I promise not to use it until the weekend—after you've filed. It'd be a big help to me. I'm in a spot of trouble with the paper, and it'd be good publicity for you and your paper. I'll give credit. How about it?"

"I can't risk it," I said. "It's cost my paper a lot of money and I can't chance losing it."

"C'mon. What are friends for? You can trust me."

"Well . . ."

"Thanks, that's awfully decent of you."

So I gave Tony the carbon of my story on Nasser and Moorehouse, much against normal instincts, on condition that he not file for twenty-four hours. I was uneasy, but in foreign reporting you build alliances, trust competitors, and share material you would never contemplate doing at home, where rivalries are more personal and cutthroat.

I arrived in New Delhi the next day and learned that my story on President Nasser's reaction to the "unfortunate" Moorehouse had been published on Fleet Street and was recycled on the BBC news. There was speculation that by granting such an interview Nasser might be amending or moderating his policies toward Britain. The Foreign Office was presumably carefully analyzing his words.

I felt like a fool for being so trusting of a journalistic colleague, even though it had no effect on the coverage in the *Telegram*. I have not seen Tony Brown since. The curious thing is that if I had it to do again with someone else, I'd probably still give the story on the promise not to use it. Most journalists are reliable, but sometimes the temptation for a beat is irresistible.

8

Hurtling headlong into the thirteenth century

LAOS, 1959

The trouble with encountering living legends, or those in the process of being granted sainthood by the media, is that if you are unaware of their exalted status they can seem enormous bores.

I was flying from New Delhi to Bangkok in 1959, en route to Laos after covering the visit of President Eisenhower to India and trying to track down the Dalai Lama who had escaped from Tibet. My seat companion had initially been friendly and garrulous, as many travelling Americans seem to be, but he'd become tiresome, the most egotistical yakker I had ever encountered. I intended to spend the night in Bangkok and catch a plane the next day to Vientiane, the administrative capital of Laos. The year before, Laos had been fighting against alleged Communist insurgents, the Pathet Lao, and again was embroiled in fighting in remote spots. I was going to Laos to determine whether or not recent reports of fighting there were real or phony. It wasn't that readers of the *Telegram* were panting to know more about Laos but that I was keen to make this exotic side trip en route home on a round-the-world ticket.

When I interrupted my seat-mate's bragging monologue and said I'd been covering Eisenhower in India, he interrupted me to tell of meeting Ike and of the banquet the president had thrown for him. I smiled weakly and wondered at the guy's gall. He asked if I was based in Thailand. I replied, rather aloofly, that I was heading for Laos. Instead of asking me what was going on there, he upstaged me with descriptions of the country and asked if I knew his friend Prince Souvanna Phouma? No I didn't, I said, somewhat resentful that he was able to top anything I had to offer. He described how his "home" was in Laos and how he had just been travelling through the United States, where he had been given the freedom of cities, banquets, honors, interviews, and acclaim everywhere he went. He said he ran a hospital in Laos near the dreaded Chinese border. In those days it was always *Red China*—the real China that America recognized being the 10 million or so on Taiwan, or Formosa, as it was then called.

I forget precise details of our seemingly endless flight, but the man was so boastful, talked so much about the money he was collecting, books he had written, TV shows he had been on, adulation he had received from every variety of celebrity, big shots who lined up to meet him, that I knew I was in the company of a pathological liar and con artist. Finally I was almost too embarrassed for him to look at him, and it was a relief when we landed in Bangkok. I had long ago closed my ears to his dogmatic opinions and judgments that brooked no contradiction, dispute, or debate. An authoritarian pain in the ass.

As the plane taxied to the terminal, we could see a crowd of assorted dignitaries and limousines by the entrance. When the aircraft stopped, a red carpet was rolled out. "Must be a VIP aboard," I said to my companion.

"Yes, it's probably for me," he said, with insufferable poise and conceit.

"God," I thought, "What an ego!" I managed to refrain from a nasty put-down.

Well, the American ambassador and various American aid and Thai officials *were* there for my seat companion. As he walked down the ramp, there was a ragged cheer and the wives of diplomats rushed out to tearfully embrace the thin young man. The big shots, faces wreathed in smiles, shook his hand, hugged him, and were so filled with respect and affection that I just stood there staring in the sunlight and heat of Bangkok's mid-afternoon.

The man paused in his greetings, grinned boyishly, and asked the diplomats if I, his new "friend" and travelling companion, could get a lift with them to the hotel since we were both going to Laos the next day. Americans, being Americans, eagerly and without question took me to their collective bosom. I was speechless and still hadn't the faintest idea who this person was, or what his peculiar hold on the affections of the mighty was. All of a sudden he didn't seem quite so insufferable.

I asked a Pan Am stewardess who was sopping up the ceremony, adulation in her eyes, who the man was. She looked surprised. "Why that's Tom Dooley," she said. "Isn't he wonderful!"

"Oh," I said, "of course," and wondered frantically who on earth Tom Dooley was. I was afraid to ask again, suddenly realizing that, whoever he was, I should know. How to find out without revealing ignorance? The stewardess remarked that it must have been a great thrill for me to have had him to myself on the flight, since he was the most popular man in the world at the moment. He was on his way back to his jungle hospital in Laos, she said, after a wonderful fund-raising tour of America to publicize his work. He had met, she said, all the movie stars, and even the president. She said something about his being terribly brave and everyone admiring him so much. Wasn't it awful about his cancer and wonderful that he was helping lepers and didn't he have the most boyish smile?

I had never heard of Tom Dooley. I had been travelling for the past six months or so and was out of touch. His name was in headlines across the United States as it rallied to his cause and donations flooded in to help him in his work. He had captured the imagination of the nation, where such things are prone to happen.

On the drive to the hotel I was suddenly very respectful, and fished for more information. "Perhaps you'd like to interview me?" he said. "I'm news these days, and your paper will be very interested. In fact, you'd probably get in trouble if they knew you were with me and you didn't interview me. I get contributions from Toronto. Perhaps your paper would like to become involved in fund-raising for me?"

He said that he was very tired, that his cancerous shoulder was aching, and that he needed an hour's rest. If I'd drop around later we'd have our interview. But it would have to be quick. The American Embassy was having a banquet in his honor that night.

An hour later I knocked on his door. Dooley was in a bathrobe, looking even thinner and paler than before. His jaw had that bony outline that indicates excessive frailty. We drank tea and ate cookies and I began to ask him about his work, his hospital, and so forth. Within minutes he interrupted. "You don't know anything about me, do you?" he said abruptly, more in surprise than annoyance.

"Well, I've not been home lately."

"I've been written about everywhere," Dooley countered, somewhat miffed.

"Well, frankly, I haven't been reading papers lately, either. Can't you tell me?"

"Look, I haven't time to brief you. My life's on borrowed time these days. Take these and read them and then come back and we'll talk. My time is too precious to waste." With that he fished into his briefcase and handed me a press-release package of newspaper and magazine clippings and photostats about himself. Mortified beyond words, I took them to my hotel room to study, feeling like a kid boning for an exam—which I guess I was.

Dooley was an intensely religious Catholic who, after discharge from the navy in 1956, opened a remotely located hospital in Northern Laos and helped form a nonprofit agency called MEDICO (Medical International Co-operation Organization), which had a philosophy of not interfering with local cultures or people's customs, but of trying to upgrade medical standards. A medical doctor, Dooley was occasionally accused of practising nineteenth-century medicine and of offering little more than a glorified first-aid service.

Dooley welcomed such criticism and the chance to debate. He responded by saying that where he practised medicine in Laos it was like the thirteenth century, so if he brought nineteenth-century medicine to the area, it represented a massive leap forward of six centuries. He was right, of course. He was also a determined anti-Communist and told horror tales of what Communist insurgents from China were doing to the countryside. His anti-communism was not an intellectual thing, it was based on what he'd seen of the ideology in practice.

Dooley had "interned" at the jungle hospital of Dr. Albert Schweitzer at Lambaréné in West Africa, and had written bestsellers with faintly religious and distinctly anti-Communist overtones which raised considerable money for his medical missionary work. His work was largely unnoticed, or ignored, until he was struck with cancer. Instead of capitulating, he fought back, using his disease as an instrument to raise more money for his hospital and his work. Articulate and resourceful with boundless energy, he wrote openly about his illness, returned to the United States long enough to get treatment, then went back to his work in the field as soon as possible. The cancer was terminal, and Dooley frankly admitted that his was a race against time and against death; the normal channels or normal courtesies were thus not available to him. His legacy, his memorial, would be his hospital at Muong Sing near the Chinese border, in the heart of the Communist area. Overnight, he became a gallant, heroic figure to middle-class America, personifying all the decent, God-loving, traditional virtues of American humanitarianism and courage. He was shame-less in extorting money from people, all of it going to bring medicine to Northern Laos, where no other white person had been, much less called home. There, he was a deity.

Dooley's crusade was not always appreciated. He was pushy, insensitive, filled with himself, and perhaps a bit of a bully and showoff. These negative traits were overshadowed by what he was and what he was trying to do. Pain and sickness failed to slow him down. He had no time for small talk, no time for a soft approach. Everything was hard sell. Go-go-go. One could feel enormous sympathy for him, and respect and admiration for his courage and drive, yet still not like him very much. His very intensity made him uncomfortable to be with. Fanatics—or saints, I suppose—can have that effect.

I subsequently interviewed Dooley, wrote a story and sent it to the *Telegram*, which, strangely, had not paid much attention to the Dooley-mania in the United States. I suspect the editor con-fused Tom Dooley with a song (no connection), so he didn't run my piece about the doctor's work in Laos. It was hard enough, in any event, to convince the desk that Laos was a real place and that it was a legitimate place for a reporter to be. A while later the *Tely* did get into Dooley-mania, but by then I was somewhere else. (That is a continuing problem working in foreign countries for a newspaper that is really more interested in city council and three-alarm fires than it is in international affairs. If the city editor hasn't heard of it, it doesn't exist.)

I flew to Vientiane, the steaming, sleepy administrative capital, with Dr. Dooley. The reception there was more modest but more intimate than in Bangkok: he was among his *real* friends now, the ones who dealt most closely with him. He had been given a motor scooter in Bangkok by local Americans, and it was flown in with us. He drove it in from the airport, gingerly nursing his cancerous shoulder. He stayed at the embassy. I checked into the Constel-lation Hotel, which was a holdover from French colonial days and mindful of something out of Somerset Maugham.

The Constellation was French tropical-style and had no front wall. The lounge and bar opened directly on to the street with the dining tables to the rear, and huge wooden fans slowly churn-ing the steambath air. Very picturesque and Humphrey Bogartish. The rooms had plaster walls with a toilet and a washbasin against one wall and a shower head over the basin. No partitions. The water came from tanks on the roof to catch rain, and was heated by the sun. You took a shower, the water ran into a sloped drain in the middle of the room, and the heat dried the floor almost immediately. All the hotel walls were literally covered with lizards that snapped up flies and mosquitoes with impressive speed and accuracy. You grew strangely fond of them. I thought the accommodations wonderful.

By any objective standards the country itself was hurtling into the thirteenth century. The landlocked kingdom was bordered by two virulent Communist states, China and North Vietnam, with pro-American Thailand and neutral Cambodia on its southern flank. It was incongruous that a remote country of startlingly kind, relaxed people would become the muddled battleground of whether American dollars could thwart communism and subversion.

Leaders in underdeveloped countries were becoming aware that the bogey of communism had an almost magical power to attract American money, aid, arms, and handouts with no strings attached. This syndrome was eventually used to advantage by left-wing ideologues, who correctly noted the enormous profits to be made in the form of payoffs and handouts to all who claimed to be opposing communism. While there was some attempt to cut down on these lavish and poorly researched aid programs at the risk of being branded pinkos or Commie-sympathizers, the prevailing American solution to the Communist threat, real and imagined (for it was both), was to throw money at it. That philosophy applied not only to communism but to virtually all problems, and won considerable resentment and contempt for the United States in the Third World.

Laos was a living example of American foreign aid gone crazy. Before it became an East-West battleground, Laotians were among the world's most tranquil people. Eventually, like the erstwhile friendly and gentle Cambodians, they became the personification of human savagery and barbarism, thanks to twentieth century values and ideology.

Until Laos was allegedly invaded from North Vietnam, news editors and political commentators in the West were not certain whether "Laos" was a tropical disease, an oriental food, an insect similar to a flea, or a piece of exotic geography. The 25,000-member Laotian army was presumably fighting somewhere for king and country—the trouble was no one knew where. It was before the Vietnam War. Camouflage warfare was not yet a household word. The "enemy" in Laos was invisible, not imaginary, but the Western world was reluctant to believe what it couldn't see. Especially the media.

About all I knew of Laos was that it had been part of the French colonial empire in Indochina (Laos, Vietnam, Cambodia) and that its traditional name was "Land of a Million Elephants and a White Parasol." How could a place which called itself that be taken seriously?

The supposed crisis the year before had evaporated into exaggeration and falsification to get more aid. The world's press, which had staged its own invasion of Laos and been foiled in obtaining eyewitness coverage, was more skeptical this time around. The UN had sent an investigating team (comprised of Japan, Italy, Argentina, and Tunisia) which had discovered nothing. Then, as now, the UN found it more convenient to see nothing than to decide something.

The Pathet Lao were supported (sponsored?) by North Vietnam, which was still cocky after defeating the famed French Foreign Legion at Dien Bien Phu and winning independence for Indochina. At that point the world didn't realize the scope of Ho Chi Minh's ambitions. The media and intellectuals were convinced the Laotians were fighting a fabricated war in order to get more American aid. At the time Laos was the greatest per-capita recipient of American dollars in the world. Some $250 million had been plowed into the country in five years—about $160 million on the military, indicating where America's main concern lay. Present "aid" was $40 million a year for "defence," $1.5 million technical. Corruption and mismanagement prospered. It seems that aid coming into Laos at the official rate of exchange (35 kip per dollar) was being sold on the black market at 150 kip to the dollar, meaning a lot of money was being made. Then the currency was revalued at 80 kip per dollar, which cut illicit profits in half.

When the United States tried to tighten its aid program, a lot of personnel were suddenly transferred or eased out. Tougher spending regulations were implemented. A Laotian civil servant grumbled: "America must really be in trouble if it has to account for the money it spends."

Laos was a frustrating place for Americans in the 1950s. It had a population of between 1.5 million and 5 million people. No one was sure: there had never been a census. There still hasn't been one. The U.S. Information Service had done a survey whose results were discouraging. It found that 88 percent of the villagers questioned had never heard of the United States. Some 90 percent thought the world was flat and inhabited mostly by Laotian people, with a few Chinese and fewer whites scattered around the edges. Most were unaware that they were ruled by a king. Most seemed to think a prime minister was a choice serving of missionary.

Opium was the main product of the country (cheapest in the world) and poppies were a respectable crop. Vientiane, with a population of 50,000 people, had some 400 opium dens, which were the Laotian version of coffee houses (civil servants had their opium breaks for a quick puff). Still, the country was easygoing and seemed relatively content with itself—if only it weren't being hassled by Commies and protected by Americans!

There were few telephones in the country, communications were impossible, and mail took a month to be delivered. It took longer to drive a car across Laos than it did to drive across North America. It took only a few minutes for a jet to fly across the country.

What really distinguished Laos for a Western foreigner was that it had the greatest percentage of Mercedes Benz cars in the world: 800 or so in a car population of 4,000 . . . and barely fifteen miles of paved road in the whole country! The Mercedes was a status symbol. Those with cars would drive 100 yards from residence to office, just to flaunt their importance.

Under terms of the Geneva Agreement, Americans were not supposed to be militarily involved; that was a French mandate. But the French were no longer interested and wanted the Americans to inherit their mantle, so the U.S. supplied and trained the Laotian military surreptitiously on behalf of the French. While in Laos, American military personnel dropped their rank, called one another "mister," and wore sport shirts instead of uniforms. It fooled no one but puzzled the Laotians.

The White Parasol, symbol of royalty, was replaced by a popular symbol: mirror-faced sunglasses, which were worn day and night, cloud or sunshine, by nattily dressed Laotian army officers who resembled miniature airline pilots. Neither the Americans nor the Laotians understood one another's thinking, but each was mildly amused by the other. Strangely, they got on rather well.

Of course, on a more thoughtful level, there was nothing amusing about what was happening to Laos and its people. Instead of being allowed to live their traditional lives, they were becoming pawns of atomic age, cold-war politics and would never be able to go back. It was not the *fault* of the United States, but instead its *reaction* to Ho Chi Minh's army which was pushing at the Laotian walls to see if they would collapse. They didn't, but they certainly trembled.

King Sisavong Vong had died the year before and his body was resting submerged in a hollowed tree trunk-turned-coffin filled with honey, as was the tradition. After another year there would be a burial ceremony. It was difficult for anyone to fully comprehend Laotian customs and politics, such as they were. Not even Laotians were sure. The ceremonial capital was Luong Prabang, in the middle of the country, and the administrative capital of Vientiane was near the Thai border, where most of the foreigners, commerce, and graft were. It at least localized the blight.

There were four main factions vying for control, all living in a sort of peaceful coexistence for the time being. Souvanna Phouma, a neutralist leader, Prince Souhanouvong, the Communist Pathet Lao leader, Phoumi Nosavan, the pro-American right-wing prime minister, and Captain Kong Le, a thirty-two-year-old paratrooper. But only Kong Le, despite his pocket-sized cuteness, was taken seriously—and the Pathet Lao, which had Hanoi's support. Everyone knew, though they didn't dare mention it, that the Communists would eventually win.

When Captain Kong Le engineered a coup, he was suspected of harboring Communist sympathies until it dawned on the Americans that he was honest, able, naïve, and determined to root out corruption. For a while he seemed the best thing that could have happened to the country. He didn't last.

While I scurried around absorbing atmosphere and listening to exotic tales of subversion and corruption, Dooley was preparing to go to his border hospital for Christmas. He was actively disliked by many American officials who, while recognizing his talents, still resented him. To get what he wanted, Dooley had no compunctions about threatening to contact such-and-such a senator or calling the White House direct, playing to the media and threatening blackmail, using tricks, flattery, and cajolery. He dominated Vientiane's foreign community and at private dinners would solicit contributions. Anything to get equipment, drugs, money, publicity. His cause was sacred, the only thing keeping him alive and holding back his cancer.

I saw him when he'd come by the Constellation Hotel for an occasional drink and a chat with the few journalists who might be there, although the only other journalist there at the time was Jim Lucas, who had won a Pulitzer Prize for coverage in the Korean War, and who was killed a couple of years later in Indochina. He and I became friends. As the only English-speaking newsmen in Laos, we would sit at the open-street bar in the evenings and relive the mutually shared experiences of the Korean War, in which I'd been a soldier while he was writing his way to a Pulitzer Prize. We would agree how irritating Tom Dooley could be and how no newspaper would ever dare print the truth about what he was really like.

One morning there was a squeal of Moped brakes outside the hotel and Dooley rushed in—he always rushed—and plopped himself down at my breakfast table.

"A great Christmas story for your newspaper," he said with enthusiasm. "Why don't you come with me to my jungle hospital on Christmas Day? You'll get a wonderful sentimental story for Canada which you can easily sell in the States."

"Terrific," I said. "How do we do it?"

"Leave it to me. We'll fly up by Dakota. You're sure you're on?"

"Absolutely. How'll I get back?"

"Oh, we'll figure out something. There are always supplies being flown in. I'll be in touch."

I told Jim Lucas about the deal and he was wary. "Dunno," he said. "I'd be careful with Dooley. The son of a bitch never tells you everything. He's got some scheme cooking."

"Well, it can't hurt," I said. "It's still a good story."

For a couple of days things proceeded normally, then Dooley came to me and said the owners of the Dakota wanted $2,000 in advance. "So?" I said, puzzled.

"So you'd better pay them," said Dooley.

"Me?"

"Yes. You rent the plane, we fly up with supplies, you get the story of my hospital at Christmas. It's a natural for *Life* magazine."

"Jeez, I don't have that sort of money. I'm prepared to give my time for the story; maybe pay my fare—but that's all."

"The understanding was that you'd rent the plane and get the exclusive story."

"You should have mentioned it earlier. I haven't got enough money and the paper wouldn't go for it anyway."

"I've already contracted the Dakota in your name!"

"Then uncontract it."

"Then someone else gets the story. I don't think you've got much idea of what makes news. This is great human interest."

And so it was. I didn't go to Muong Sing and Dooley was probably right, I did miss a lifetime experience. Lucas thought it amusing. "I told you he was devious. Lucky he told you first and didn't give you the bill at the end. He's done that before, too."

Tom Dooley died two years later, the day after his thirty-fourth birthday. Nearly twenty years later, campaigns were under way in the Catholic Church to have him declared a saint. The Vatican, while willing, was curious to know what miracles he had performed in order to qualify for official sainthood.

His "miracle," and it was virtually that, was *not* that he became obsessed with, or committed to, helping the people in a remote corner of the world, but that by dint of his personality and his relentless, singleminded drive, energy, and force of will, he made his cause a worldwide issue and inspired North America to help the sick and deprived of Northern Laos. If not a saint, he was certainly an exceptional human being who worked courageously and tirelessly and deserved some form of immortality.

Detractors today claim that he worked for the CIA. Unlikely. No question he provided information to the Americans, no question he was anti-Communist, as all decent, humane, intelligent people *must* be who have seen at first hand how communism is imposed on defenceless, ignorant people. And no doubt he did what he could to thwart its spread. Tom Dooley was an American patriot, had a sense of values, and was not knee-jerk anti-CIA. He would help them, sure, but he was probably not a CIA agent or he could not have given so much of himself to his hospital and Laotian tribespeople.

Dooley had to celebrate Christmas at his hospital in Northern Laos without me on hand to record it. I had run into a Canadian team surveying the Mekong River as part of an aid program to Laos. Sent to investigate the river for hydro, irrigation, and dam possibilities, they encountered frustrations from the start and were frankly bewildered at the customs. But before they left they had adapted and flourished in the environment, as Canadians so often do.

When they first met the Minister of Public Works, Phoui Sananikone, with whom they would have to deal, one of the Canadians asked a routine question about the army. The politician loftily said that was not his department and the only one who could give an adequate answer was the Minister of Defence. Fair enough, until the Canadian learned that the Minister of Public Works was also the Minister of Defence. Not only that, he held four other posts, including Prime Minister! At the time he was being mildly criticized for refusing to sign a contract to have a school built because a relative had not gotten the contract. He was replaced by an army coup.

The Christmas Eve I spent with the Canadians turned out to be a typical Canadian Christmas away from home. They had set up a camp some miles out of Vientiane and I took a taxi in the evening to celebrate the season with them. Put half a dozen young, lonely, aggressive Canadians together with unlimited booze, and a party will inevitably evolve into near-chaos. As liquor flowed and the night wore on, arguments, shouts, and eventually fights broke out. At the height of the evening everything but peace and good-will was evident. I found myself having to defend the policies of the Toronto *Star*, of all things. Someone wanted to fight over the merits of the Toronto Maple Leafs versus the Montreal Canadiens. If I disagreed that all politicians were crooks, I risked getting into a punching match, and when I said it was rubbish to suppose newspaper advertisers tell reporters what to write, I was on the brink of blows. When Canadian males are drinking and getting sentimental, there comes a point when you have to decide whether you are willing to fight to prove a point (the winner is right!) or abandon the battleground. On this occasion I chose the latter and left the party. I started to walk the five miles or so back to Vientiane.

It was one of those unreal Southeast Asian nights: still, soft, steamy, with the stars bright above and the tarmac road straight and flawless past swamps and occasional houses on stilts in fields of water. I thought the thoughts one might expect in such an exotic location at Christmastime. A mile or so from town, I passed a settlement on stilts, and my presence in the post-midnight hours set off a howling of dogs. About a dozen gathered around me on the road and began barking themselves into hysteria. Then some began darting in and out to nip at me. I didn't dare run or show panic for fear of inciting them to greater daring. However, they were getting bolder and it seemed inevitable that they'd rush me. The thought occurred that it would be most ironic and quixotic to expire on Christmas Day because of a pack of Laotian dogs. The only trouble was that no one would ever know of it.

The dogs were all around me now and one, bolder than the rest, lunged in to nip at my ankles. I reached down quickly in the dark and grabbed it by a foreleg. As it snapped and thrashed, I whirled it over my head, smashed it on the road, and flung it into the ditch. The dog's snarls turned to screams, and all the other dogs piled on the injured one.

In the pandemonium of noise, screams, and snarling I took off and ran toward Vientiane. The dogs paid no heed, their blood up over the injured animal. I finally reached the city, now sober but exhilarated to be in something resembling civilization. I fell into bed and slept in my clothes. I was awakened by street noises, like Ebenezer Scrooge on Christmas morn, and looked out to see every store open and bustling with people shopping and visiting. Strange Christmas decorations looking charming but not very Christmasy adorned the open-face stores. Laotians clearly were enjoying the Anglo-Saxon tradition, though they didn't understand anything about it.

A day or so later I went with one of the men on the survey crew—Doug Scott from Oshawa, Ontario, if memory serves—to see if the rumor was true that Laos was the opium capital of the world. The French concierge at the hotel said we should try a certain location. Scott recalled what a great party it had been at Christmas—so great that he was only now getting over it. Just like home. Canadians tend to judge the success of a party by how drunk one gets or how many fights break out. Some things never change.

When we approached the bamboo shack, an old Chinese welcomed us and offered us tea. We explained we wanted to try opium. The old man took us into a room and had us lie on mats with concrete blocks as pillows. Giving each of us a pipe with a small bowl, he dipped a long needle into a brown fluid, heated it over a flame until it turned sticky, then dipped more and kept heating until he had a small dark nugget.

He put two wads in the bowls of our pipes, and told us to hold them over the flame and inhale deeply. Before doing so, I recall looking at the wall and there, side by side, were faded colored pictures of Mao Tse-tung and of Chiang Kai-shek. It was an opium den for any ideology.

I took a tentative suck at the pipe and the old Chinese cackled and gestured that I should inhale deeply. I did and my lungs filled with acrid smoke. I felt nauseated but little else. Disappointing.

Later, when we went to pay, the Chinese would accept no money. Scott asked what a bottle would cost. The old Chinese indicated $20. When Scott handed over $20, the Chinese cackled and refused payment, saying it was a gift to prove eternal friendship. Or something. It was the first and last time I tried drugs. I survived. Laos didn't.

9

Africans are children and cannot govern themselves

DR. ALBERT SCHWEITZER
LAMBARÉNÉ, GABON
OCTOBER 1960

Perhaps it comes with the territory, but most journalists are skeptical (if not downright cynical) of do-gooders and professional humanitarians. Among themselves, that is. There are official saints or humanitarians of such stature that it is risky to tamper with them. Those in the media do not usually like to mess with public icons. For example, few of the Canadian establishment or media find it productive to recall that Dr. Norman Bethune was unpleasant and lazy, an alcoholic and a libertine. Instead he has become an official, if late-blooming, Canadian idol, mainly because he is a genuine Chinese Communist hero who worked for Mao Tse-tung's revolutionary army in 1939 (and died of blood poisoning in a year) and whose legend in recent times has helped sell Canadian wheat to the Chinese. He's a questionable choice as "humanitarian" because he was a fighter for communism and contributed nothing to the Chinese people in the way that, say, Dr. Robert McClure did when he worked among the peasants, ignoring the civil war often at considerable risk to himself and introducing the bicycle doctor concept to China. McClure was of far greater stature than Bethune.

Humanitarians come in many different guises. I have remarked on Dr. Tom Dooley, whose jungle hospital in Laos was an incredible achievement, even though he, personally, was a driven and not particularly pleasant man. Dooley had apprenticed at the jungle hospital of this century's most renowned guru of all do-gooders: Dr. Albert Schweitzer, fifty years Dooley's senior and an unusual, temperamental man in his own right.

While covering stories in Africa in the early '60s, I decided to visit the legendary Dr. Schweitzer in Gabon (formerly French

108

Equatorial Africa). Even before he was awarded the Nobel Peace Prize in 1952, he was granted virtual sainthood by his legions of admirers and disciples around the world.

Schweitzer was not easy to visit. His hospital was on the Ogowe River, upstream from the island town of Lambaréné, which took about three days of catching planes to reach. Schweitzer, at age thirty-eight, had abandoned a distinguished career that included doctorates in theology, medicine, music, philosophy, to become a medical missionary and start his African hospital. That was in 1913. His wife Helene died there in 1957; he died in 1965 at age ninety. Their graves are side by side, a few yards from their modest bungalow overlooking the river. He gave his life and talents to the sick of Africa and, in the process, history passed him by and controversy dogged his work. Ironically, as his fame grew, his achievements diminished.

When I arrived at Dr. Schweitzer's doorstep he was eighty-five and, despite (because of?) his fame, had the reputation of being testy and unpredictable.

"For God's sake, don't land on him unexpectedly," warned Donald Wise, the brilliant, colorful ex-soldier/correspondent for the London *Daily Mirror* who was perhaps the most knowledgeable and mischievous journalist in the world. "If he decides he doesn't want to see you, he's quite capable of standing on the wharf and pushing your boat away with his foot. There's no predicting the old goat—even when he invites you."

I had sent a cable to Dr. Schweitzer saying how much I personally admired him and how all Canada was eager to read about his quiet heroism on behalf of humanity in the rain forests of Africa. In this business you get accustomed to using hyperbole to make a point. Dr. Schweitzer's hospital was an hour's dugout canoe ride upriver from Lambaréné and it sounded exotic and adventurous. (By the time I received a wire from Dr. Schweitzer inviting me to stay at his hospital I was in Rhodesia, irritating the government of Sir Roy Welensky by deploring how the white militia were using the black townships for weekend search-and-seize exercises in preparation for the inevitable trouble ahead. One who witnessed riots and demonstrations in Salisbury's Harare township at the time was a young man who was a product of Catholic schools: Robert Mugabe, later to be radicalized to African Marxism. He would eventually use terrorism, propaganda, liberal humanitarianism, and a misguided clergy in the West to defeat the white, paternalistic government. In 1980 Mugabe became Prime

Minister of the country, which, like a butterfly reverting to a caterpillar, changed its name from Rhodesia to Zimbabwe. Those able to rationalize murder, atrocities, and terror in the name of "liberation" endorsed Mugabe's Chinese-backed, Shona-speaking ZANU organization and Joshua Nkomo's Soviet-supported Matabele ZAPU, which together formed the Patriotic Front. I was pleased to leave Rhodesia, which seemed a hopeless cause even then.)

Strangely, not too many of the journalists based in Africa had visited Schweitzer's hospital, perhaps because few could afford the time and their publications were more concerned with breaking news than with feature stories. It was a time when all Africa was on a determined march into the twentieth century and independence—and often into chaos.

Lambaréné was reminiscent of a Hemingway novel with a touch of Joseph Conrad: colorful, remote and filled with exotic characters. The Air France hotel was the centre of civilization and, as was customary with Air France hotels, served excellent French cuisine in a comfortable, informal atmosphere. The hotel was accustomed to pilgrims passing through en route to a spiritual rendezvous with the Schweitzer hospital and sold Schweitzer's books.

Lambaréné was a community of some 5,000 blacks and 60 whites. The town stretched along the riverfront for about a mile, with makeshift stores and stalls where a popular item was a sport shirt bearing the picture of President Leon Mba. Everyone seemed to wear those shirts with portraits of African leaders on them—a walking Gallup poll. It was steambath hot, and any exertion caused one to perspire in torrents. The town teemed with humanity, and pedestrians walked along jumping over mud puddles from daily rain showers and dodging people on bikes. At the end of the village there was a rickety landing where a visitor bartered for a dugout canoe with an outboard motor to take him upriver to the hospital. Or one could wait for the daily canoe from the hospital, paddled by a couple of lepers. I chose the lepers.

Before I left the hotel, the elegant Frenchwoman in charge warned that I should wear a hat because the doctor was convinced that sensible white men did not venture into the African sun without one. The doctor himself wore a pith helmet—the first I'd seen in modern Africa, as it turned out. It's mostly in movies about Africa or the desert that pith helmets are worn. I bought a hat in the village, along with a President Mba shirt, which was later stolen at Schweitzer's hospital. I also bought one of

Schweitzer's books, on the advice of the hotel manageress, who warned that the doctor looked favorably on visitors who brought copies for him to autograph. It wasn't necessary to have read them, though he was known to occasionally question visitors on the contents.

I located the canoe, negotiated a price with a man whose head was infected with the ugly white blotches of leprosy, and was paddled up the river for an hour or so. My paddler told me not to worry because he didn't think any hippos would surface and tip us. I started worrying immediately. The Ogowe was a wide, slow, muddy river that seemed the essence of Africa. The enormous trees of the rain forest pushed to the very banks; one could hear the moist jungle sounds and a soggy heat rolled over the water from the shore. The atmosphere was serene and intriguing.

As we approached the hospital I could see the solid, stooped, white-maned form of what must be Dr. Schweitzer waiting, apparently eager to meet some new blood. At least I was not going to get his saintly foot shoving me off. "Dr. Schweitzer, I presume," I said banally as I bounded up the shore to shake hands, like some latter-day Stanley. He flashed a wintry smile beneath his stained walrus mustache and muttered something about every visitor saying that. He was shorter than I expected, a dumpy, slouched figure who shuffled along, speaking German or French and scolding whatever got in his way. Nurse Mathilde Kottman, who came out to the hospital in 1924 for a year and never left, translated whatever he said into English.

Superficially, the hospital was mindful of a slum, with an open concrete sewer through the main area. Goats browsed through garbage; a variety of animals wandered about freely. There was a prevailing stench of raw sewage. Sanitation was not a high priority. Dr. Schweitzer seemed uninterested in showing me around, just eager to have an outsider to talk with, to lecture.

Nurse Kottman was my main guide. My quarters were in a special section, rather like army huts with latticed walls to catch any air. Light was by kerosene lamp—not too bright, so as not to attract insects to their death. "Be sure to lock everything," explained Nurse Kottman who, despite her compassion, was under no illusions about her wards. "Things get stolen quickly here."

The week I spent there was an education. The success of Schweitzer's hospital was due to the fact that, where possible, patients were confined in tribal groups, not according to their diseases. This meant that chances for contagion were higher, but patients were more content and willing to undergo treatment. Dr. Schweitzer also permitted kinfolk to live with patients so that each ward was like a tribal gathering. Patients far preferred his hospital to the more modern French one in Lambaréné which had far better facilities and greater sanitation. In fact, World Health officials complained that Schweitzer was actually holding up medical progress in the area. And at one time the French planned to shut down his hospital until the local tribes objected vehemently and wouldn't use the new facilities.

Africans preferred Schweitzer's old-fashioned medicine to modern techniques. Medical standards in the area were lower than elsewhere. Dr. Schweitzer ran his hospital pretty much as he had run it forty years earlier. He worked on the theory that if he built something, he could repair it. So he personally poured concrete, did construction work, repaired the generator for the operating table. He was loath to delegate authority.

When I saw it, Dr. Schweitzer's hospital was near anarchy, and virtually out of control. A melancholy place. He did not hold much with psychiatry and his mental ward was a square block of loosely linked logs, a small room on each side. Patients got bottles of palm wine, provided by relatives, and were drunk most of the time. A constant babble and shouting emerged from this block, situated well apart from the rest of the hospital. Apart from the unsanitary presence of goats, deer, chickens, and stray animals, stealing was rampant and prostitution endemic. I found it hard to move anywhere without being propositioned. Females were almost queued up outside my quarters to beg money or clothes or to sell themselves. Anything for a bit of money.

By objective criteria, the hospital was a frustrated, unhappy place. The staff of five doctors, eight nurses, and four administrators felt unfulfilled. Most had come filled with high expectations, altruism, idealism. They planned to work for him for a year or two, learn from him, and get experience and credentials for other jobs. Being able to say you had apprenticed under the great Dr. Schweitzer was prestigious and guaranteed a medical job anywhere in the world, so he was fortunate in having doctors who were far better than might be expected in the jungle. Japan's Dr. Takahashi was said to be brilliant and versed in the latest leprosy techniques and theories, and Dr. Adler, a Swiss surgeon, was far too good for most of the ailments he was called upon to deal with, and he was increasingly frustrated at the deliberately primitive conditions. There was often bitterness and resentment because

Dr. Schweitzer's stubbornness prevented the staff from practising the sort of modern medicine they knew and wanted for their patients. As a group they were disillusioned, though loyal to him personally.

The whole hospital had an unreal quality. Schweitzer would allow no electric lights except in his operating room because they would unnecessarily attract insects. Meals were perfunctory affairs, but the evening meal was special. We'd sit at a long table, all paying homage to Dr. Schweitzer, who'd launch into philosophical monologues or ramblings. Everyone felt, perhaps subconsciously, that he wouldn't be around much longer and these sessions were something to treasure. When he spoke, few dared challenge or dispute his categorical statements. He had a temper that few cared to arouse. After the evening meal he'd play the piano for the assembled staff, and it was a unique privilege to hear one of the great musicians of the civilized world perform. On such occasions you understood why he was renowned, half a century earlier, as one of the great interpreters of Bach, able to draw thousands to his concerts throughout Europe.

After dinner he'd retire to his rooms and summon me, the outsider, to join him with Nurse Kottman to talk for a couple of hours. His quarters were a hodgepodge—bedroom, sitting room, and study all combined. In one corner was a special humidity-proof piano that he was wont to play at strange nighttime hours. A couple of packing crates served as a makeshift closet. Books and papers were everywhere, most of them old. Letters and correspondence bearing stamps from all over the world littered the premises. A huge ball of string was in one corner. It was almost as if he'd never unpacked when he arrived here forty-seven years before, and had just let things pile up.

"Normally, Africans are indifferent to any life except the welfare of fellow tribesmen," he would say. "I try to encourage natives here to extend tribal feelings to all forms of life. It is something all people must do if we are to escape the horror of war and our nuclear age."

I would try to steer our conversation toward independence for Africans, self-determination, and the nationalism that was sweeping the Third World—especially Africa. I had recently discovered the continent and it fascinated me. The politics of Africa especially intrigued me, but Schweitzer was bored by Africa and Africans. "They are children," he'd say to me. "They are not ready to govern themselves. They are the unchanging aspect of Africa."

He had greater global and philosophical questions on his mind. Especially the nuclear issue. Nuclear disarmament and world peace, on the other hand, were far beyond me, too academic, too remote. There was nothing any of us could do to influence nuclear war. Dr. Schweitzer was undeterred: "Look, Africa is the same as ever. People are people and don't change. Ours is no longer a world of humanity. It is a world of inhumanity. Unless we change, we are lost. My philosophy seems the only answer: reverence for life, the projection of love of human life to all forms of life. The Christian spirit must be broadened to include respect for all things living—fish, insects, birds, animals, people. Never kill for pleasure, only for food. Never kill a fly because it is a fly, but only because it bites you. Why cannot the world understand?"

And so on. Every conversation revolved around this theme and the folly of nuclear arms, the "madness" of America, and the USSR. He was interested in names like J. Robert Oppenheimer, Linus Pauling, Bertrand Russell. He seemed desperately sad, weary, resigned.

His views on Africa appeared dangerously paternalistic and out of touch. He did not appreciate the independence movement. I would argue halfheartedly that all people had a right to self-determination and to make their own mistakes. "You would not let children play with matches unsupervised," Schweitzer would reply. "Nor should Africans play with their own destiny or independence, unsupervised. It is negligent to give in to their desires and let them govern themselves. I repeat, Africans are children and cannot govern themselves properly. Someday, maybe, but not now."

I would put up token protest, but he would draw on forty years' experience in Africa and tolerate no dispute. Then he would go into an alcove and play on his piano, and it was impossible to remain immune to the music that wafted into the jungle night from this astonishing old man—a true Renaissance figure who was perhaps the world's most revered humanitarian. Despite his genius, he was still a man, a man with human frailties. His tragedy was that his time had passed and he didn't know it; those around him did, but didn't dare mention it.

When I left Lambaréné he seemed a trifle wistful at losing a companion for conversations. I suspect he was terribly lonely. For several years we exchanged letters, mostly through his faithful, relentlessly loyal nurse who could see his frailties but worshipped him in spite of them. When I wrote my articles in the *Telegram*, trying to be fair and put Schweitzer and his hospital in perspective, I got more hostile mail than I ever received before or since. I was accused of distorting his views, of taking them out of context, of even inventing them. One analogy that intrigued me was the one that compared me to a gnat trying to bring down an elephant with bites. It is always risky to tamper with saints, legends, or myths—but it is more dangerous to make gods out of mere mortals. Humans don't wear well on pedestals, even mortals like Albert Schweitzer—or, for that matter, Tom Dooley. I sent Dr. Schweitzer copies of my articles and got a courteous, noncommittal reply from Nurse Kottman, who seemed to accept them in the spirit in which they were written. I suspect she never showed them to him.

In the fall of 1965, Dr. Schweitzer died and was buried under a simple wooden cross. He had lived too long, his impact diminished by those who saw him only as a crusty old man holding up progress. But in some ways he was far ahead of his time: obsessively concerned about nuclear weapons, which he could not have fully understood; yet he realized more than most of us that they were the potential that could spell the end of mankind.

It was a couple of years after, in the summer of 1962, while covering a massive earthquake in Iran that killed 10,000 to 30,000 people (one could never be sure of numbers living in the remote "uncounted" areas), that I encountered another, more modern humanitarian who was regarded as "saintly" by impoverished peasants of central Iran.

I had heard in Tehran of a Canadian woman doctor who had married into minor Iranian nobility and was setting up medical clinics in an area of the country where there was no running water, no medicine, few facilities of any sort. When the *Telegram* cabled that the parents of Gloria Pierce Bahktiar were worried about her fate in the earthquake (which had occurred a thousand miles away), and asked me to find out what I could, I checked with the Canadian Embassy. Ralph Branscombe, the chargé d'affaires, said he had "heard something" about a Canadian woman doctor working somewhere in Iran, but that was all. It sounded like a potentially strong human interest story: a combination Dr. Livingstone-Dr. Schweitzer, with perhaps a dash of Dr. Dooley.

While making inquiries, I encountered a young American-educated businessman, Turaj Shahrokhinshah, who was a friend of the woman's husband and knew they were living in Agili, in central western Iran. We couldn't find Agili on any maps. Turaj, like so many Iranians, was generous and kind to an astonishing degree; he "thought" he knew how to find the place and said he'd come with me.

Turaj and I flew to Abadan, in the south of Iran, took a five-hour taxi ride north through the Whispering Desert, and then transferred to jeep-truck for two hours of ricocheting over roads that were more like goat trails. We arrived, unexpected, at the Bahktiar estate, which turned out to be a modest villa in perhaps the hottest place I'd ever been. The temperature in the evening was over 100 degrees, and reached 130 in the daytime—a dry heat as opposed to humid heat, a real sun's anvil.

In Agili I learned Gloria Pierce Bahktiar's story. She was born in Winnipeg and her family later moved to Toronto. She received her medical degree from the University of Toronto in 1959, and then went to work in the Santa Barbara Cottage Hospital in California. While there she met Abol Bahktiar, a cousin of ex-Queen Soraya (who'd been divorced by the shah because she had borne him only daughters). Abol, a graduate chemist from the University of California, had been in America fifteen years. He was the *khan*, or chieftain, of the influential Bahktiar clan, and he controlled vast desert holdings in the Agili area of Iran, where 10,000 illiterate, impoverished people lived in twenty-two villages while 50,000 nomadic people roamed the area, tending sheep and scratching out a living. Abol felt obliged to return home, take over his fiefdom, and try to use his fifteen years in civilization to raise the standards and the lot of his people. He and Gloria fell in love, married, and she returned to Iran with him.

She was twenty-seven when she flew to Iran—and in that one flight she went from the twentieth century back to biblical times. In the Agili area there were no civilized amenities, no schools, medicine, hygiene—only tradition and superstition. The peasants had never seen a doctor, only shamans. They had never had a pill, never had an inoculation or vaccination, never seen soap, much less used it. They were as backward, poor, and unhealthy as it is possible to be. It was a traumatic change for Gloria Pierce Bahktiar, but the enormity of the plight of the people prevented her from feeling sorry for herself, and she resolved to do what she could to help.

It was difficult not to be awed by what Abol and Dr. Gloria were doing. They were not motivated by any missionary fervor or do-good instincts, just a sense of duty mixed with compassion. Abol, using his Western education to enormous advantage, was building an irrigation dam on a sludgy river that poked through the region. In an effort to introduce some semblance of modern agricultural methods he scoured the area from pre-dawn darkness to nightfall trying to mobilize the peasants to improve their lives.

At first Gloria felt helpless when confronted with the health problems. Trachoma was endemic, everyone had degrees of pneumonia, worms, anemia, malnutrition, parasitic infections, unknown fungus infections. The infant mortality rate was beyond measuring. She set up clinics in the villages, taught the more intelligent villagers primitive first aid techniques, and did daily rounds. She spent about $150 a month on medical drugs. She used a fishing tackle box instead of a black bag, sterilized needles in a pressure cooker, baked other instruments in an oven. Her only disinfectant was alcohol. Like Dr. Dooley, she was trying to upgrade standards rather than bring the twentieth century to Agili.

The people came to think of the needle as a miraculous cure-all. Every time they felt sick they asked for a needle. They equated their feeling better not with what was injected into them but with the needle going in. Dr. Gloria considered her greatest single feat was introducing soap to the area and persuading mothers to wash. The disease rate plummeted. Turaj called Gloria "The Canadian Dr. Livingstone-Schweitzer." She admitted to feeling lonely sometimes and having moments of despair and frustration. But then she thought of what it was like before she was there and found the strength to continue. Her letters to the relief agency CARE, to various governments, to the Ford and Rockeller foundations, and to other sources of funds were all met with sympathy—but no help.

I admit to some skepticism about the *achievements* or effects of professional humanitarians, if not their sincerity. After seeing them and missionaries in various places, I am forced to wonder whether they are motivated to genuinely help the helpless, or to satisfy their own egos. It's a version of the old question: does the giver or the given benefit most from the gift?

In the process of dispensing good works, "humanitarians" can inflict irreparable damage on the existing cultures and creeds by superimposing their own prejudices on customs and traditions that have worked for the people in question since the age of stone axes and cave drawings. I didn't much like Dr. Dooley, but recognized his value; I *did* like Dr. Schweitzer, but wasn't too impressed with his *recent* work; I admired Dr. Gloria in every way, perhaps because she was a humanitarian by accident, by necessity, rather than by vocation or choice.

All three doctors, for varying reasons, tried to help people in desperate need, and all had limited success. Schweitzer at the end of his life was not helping the people of his area much. The effects of Dooley's dedication today are negligible; that area of Laos has now reverted to the thirteenth century. Dr. Gloria's work, while more modest and less publicized, may, ironically, have the most lasting effect, since the habits of soap and cleanliness she introduced may outlast modern medicine and survive even in an Iran gripped by the raging theocracy of the Ayatollah Khomeini.

10

Where tape recorders
eat human souls

SATURDAY NIGHT
DECEMBER 24, 1960

Although the Congo gained independence from Belgium in 1960 and has since renamed itself Zaire, it still stands as a symbol of self-determination gone crazy. It was the first case of genuine African anarchy, which so many predicted would be the inevitable result of black Africa getting freedom after a lifetime of colonial rule, but which—until the Congo—hadn't materialized.

Situated in the steamy west-central part of Africa, with Angola and South Africa to the south and the smaller, poorer French Congo to the north, the very name "Belgian Congo" evoked romantic images: of Stanley navigating the exotic, lethal Congo river; of unknown, priceless resources; of rain forests, elephants, gorillas, Tarzan; of exotic tribes and curious customs; of diamonds, pygmies, cannibals, and God knows what. The Congo's history is one of the most disreputable in black Africa. Journalist-turned-explorer Henry Stanley explored the mighty Congo River, which bisects the northern half, in 1874, after he had "found" Dr. David Livingstone and was hired to claim the Congo "Free State" for King Léopold II of Belgium. The whole country, some seventy-five times the size of Belgium, became King Léopold's personal property and he amassed a huge fortune from rubber and ivory. The country was exploited so ruthlessly that missionaries (the only Europeans with access) came back with horror tales of amputated hands as reprisals and villages in which every human being had been killed for rebelling against forced labor. It was, in fact, a slave state and by the early part of the twentieth century, the population had been reduced by some two million through massacres. Public dismay was such that the Belgian government took control. To atone for the terror done in the name of King Léopold, a form of welfare state was implemented that with its housing, schools, and social services, was the most progressive in Africa at the time. Until the 1950s it was a case of "houses instead of votes" on the theory that, if given economic benefits and decent treatment, Africans wouldn't demand self-rule. Thus, Africans could become bishops and schoolteachers, but not lawyers or politicians.

The Congo was run more as a Belgian business venture than as a colony. The discovery of copper and uranium made the Belgian Congo the second richest (next to South Africa) state in Africa. In contrast to Northern Rhodesia, into which stretched the Katanga copper belt, the Belgians taught blacks how to run machinery, cranes, equipment, and perform most of the other skilled and semi-skilled jobs. Blacks became foremen and held minor management positions. Over in Northern Rhodesia, white settlers had unions that kept blacks out and didn't train the locals. Because black labor was cheaper, Katanga became more profitable than its "white" neighbor.

To many, the "Congo solution" was the answer to African nationalism. But in 1959 a recession, a drop in copper prices, plus a rising tide of nationalist feelings resulted in riots during which police fired indiscriminately into demonstrators, killing up to 200. After four days of rioting, smashing stores, and burning in the Congolese capital of Léopoldville, paratroops were flown in from Belgium to restore uneasy order.

King Baudouin I, great-grandson of King Léopold, announced reforms that "without imprudent haste" were designed to satisfy the fourteen million blacks who shared the country with a handful of whites. The King gave impetus to the political bandwagon for independence that was already in motion. There would be no more color discrimination; universal suffrage would be granted; a legislative council set up, and democracy initiated. But all came too late. The near-century that Belgium had ruled and plundered the Congo with authoritarianism ranging from savage to harsh to paternalistic, before succumbing to world pressure to grant independence, made violence inevitable.

In the summer of 1960 the Belgians gave the Congo independence with almost malicious haste, as if knowing there was not the expertise or knowledge available for self-government. Belgium seemed to be gambling that the Congolese would have to beg the Belgians to stay and help administer the country. That would leave the Congolese with symbolic political control, but give the Belgians commercial, practical, and *real* economic control.

If that, indeed, was the intent or hope, it didn't work. The Congo would never return to the past. Nor would any African country. Independence might not mean improvement, democracy, or a better life—in fact, in practical terms it might even be worse. The Congo became living evidence that the abstract concept of freedom is more important than the pragmatic reality of a full belly. The *appearance* of liberty and independence is always more important than the actuality. Like socialism, which pretends to act in the people's name but more often is state capitalism, the propaganda dispensed is more significant than the truth.

Upon independence, the Congo went mad—the inmates took over the asylum, so to speak. Four days after Independence Day ceremonies on June 30, 1960, the Congolese army mutinied and turned on its Belgian officers and noncommissioned officers, then on the 2,500 Protestant and 7,500 Catholic missionaries living and working in the country. The Belgians had no stomach for holding firm, and in a craven display the officers fled, the white population evacuated. Where once there had been 180,000 whites in the Congo, in short order there were only 20,000. Priests were killed, nuns were raped—atrocities that guaranteed the outrage of the world and the flocking of journalists to the Congo to find raped nuns and document their nightmare. In those days—as now—few things had the journalistic appeal of a raped nun. In a way, that image became the symbol of the Congo. During the first couple of years of independence, most background stories of the Congo mentioned raped nuns; the truth is that the number of nuns who suffered that outrage was relatively small. Still, the image became the reality and soon only some 2,500 missionaries (2,000 Catholic, 500 Protestants) remained to serve the estimated 8 million Christians in a population of 14 million. Paganism made a comeback, and soon reports of cannibalism were being revived—which pleased attendant journalists immensely.

I spent a good portion of 1960 and 1961 in the Congo and, to be honest, it stands out as one of the less charming interludes of my journalistic experiences. When one thinks of it, it is a rare privilege to see anarchy in action. Tyranny, despotism, cruelty, yes—but rarely real-live anarchy where no one is in control. And in 1960, if the Congo was a country out of control, the capital city of Léopoldville (since renamed Kinshasa) was a city without order, direction, authority, or reason. And yet it worked. Sort of. When the Congo became independent, there was not a single Congolese university graduate available to help govern the country. The educated elite consisted of fifteen university students, most of them studying in Belgium. They came home to comprise the civil service and run the new regime.

In fact, one of the first things these student princes did upon getting ministries was to get girlfriends (political power is a strong aphrodisiac, it seems, regardless of country or system) and the barometers of who was in power focused on three Belgian girls who were "protégées" of politicians. They could be seen every night in Léopoldville's Afro-Negro Club in their skin-tight pedal-pushers and escorted first by supporters of Prime Minister Patrice Lumumba, then by bigshots of Joseph Kasavubu, then with Joseph Mobutu's student princes. They avoided whites, sneered at rapacious journalists, and couldn't afford to make mistakes. Whoever their escorts might be, they were the current power.

The outstanding Congolese figure prior to independence was Kasavubu, a bulbous, gracious, gentle man who had little of the fire of revolutionary in him, but was respected and revered, even loved. After independence he was overshadowed by firebrands and militants. He became irrelevant, bypassed by events. A long-time nationalist, Kasavubu had dreams of re-establishing the Bacongo empire, which had existed in the late 1400s when the Portuguese first arrived, a decade before the discovery of America in 1492. This dream he shared with Youlou Fulbert, the defrocked priest who ruled the neighboring Republic of Congo. By 1960 Kasavubu, the hero of the past and the first elected black mayor of one of the townships, had been named president—and was politically redundant. He became an historic oddity.

Patrice Lumumba, an impassioned orator considered to be in the Soviet orbit, was deemed a dangerous, opportunistic, semi-educated, lecherous demagogue who was anti-West to the extent that he was pro-Lumumba. Resentment dominated his thinking, and he was by far the Congo's most charismatic figure.

The Favorite Son of the Kremlin was Antoine Gizenga, a studious womanizer whose base was in the Stanleyville area and whose soldiers, or rabble in arms, periodically ran amok and created havoc. A supporter of Lumumba, Gizenga tried to increase his hold when Lumumba fell. Over in what was invariably described as "mineral rich" Katanga, on the southeastern edge of the Congo, was Moise Tshombe, perhaps the most able and intelligent of the Congolese leaders, the pet of Belgian interests, and a pro-West free enterpriser. He wanted to run the whole of the Congo or, failing that, set up an independent Katanga on the basis of self-determination for the tribes who lived there. He disliked and disparaged the rest of the Congo as "barbarians." And there were other minor factions led by strong-willed, ambitious men with garbled names that meant nothing to the West.

When the Belgians bolted the Congo, the UN quickly sent experts, advisors, and some 20,000 troops from thirty countries on peacekeeping duties. The UN could not afford to let this experiment in independence fail. If the Congo *did* fail, it would have dramatic symbolic meaning for both whites and blacks: it would justify the apprehensions of the former, destroy the hopes of the latter.

The military was about the only thing that worked for the UN; administratively, the Congo was a UN disaster. First, UN Secretary General Dag Hammarskjöld sent as his representative American black (and Nobel Peace Prize winner) Ralph Bunche, who turned out to be too idealistic, naïve, and unacceptable to Africans—partly because, while technically a black, he didn't look "black" and, worse, didn't *think* black. He was succeeded by India's Rajeshwar Dayal, a devious, ideological manipulator who was both anti-white and anti-West. When he failed, the Sudan's nasty-tempered Mekki Abbas took over, quickly cracked under the pressure, and became a psychological basket case, indulging in public rows with anyone who disagreed with him, or to whom he took exception. Finally a colorless, mild-mannered Swede, Dr. Sture Linner, got the hot seat and proved to be by far the most restrained, unassuming, fair, and effective administrator.

Dr. Linner's opposite number heading the military operations was an ineffectual Swedish general, Carl Von Horne, who wore fourteen medal ribbons and had never heard a shot fired in anger. (In fact the last Swedish war against Russia was in 1790!) Von Horne was a bluff fellow who was as close to being useless as a general can be; the real UN military power was Brigadier I. J. Rikhye, who adored publicity and had no trouble making decisions. He eventually headed UN forces in Egypt. When I interviewed Von Horne, he joked that his twelve-year-old child was worried about his being in cannibal country, but reassured because "before they can eat my daddy, they'll have to eat his colonel first." Von Horne decorated his walls with assorted spears, shields, and implements of violence. He liked to recall that the first six casualties among the Tunisian forces were one soldier eaten by a crocodile, one killed with a poison arrow, one by blunderbuss, one crushed by a gorilla, and two misssing, presumed eaten by cannibals. Apparently it was true.

Canadians, the backbone of the UN forces in the Congo, as elsewhere, provided the vital communications link. In Léopoldville they were quartered in a former Belgian children's boarding school, and the barracks for the troops were decorated with paintings and wall murals of Mickey Mouse, Bambi, Sleeping Beauty, Snow White, Grumpy, Doc, Dopey and the gang, and other characters from children's tales. It was a strange juxtaposition. The Canadians quickly fitted into the climate of anarchy, and almost immediately some soldiers combined to occupy a deserted house and open a makeshift brothel. Others got into the black market trade. Soon the medical officer was giving lectures about the hitherto-unknown strains of venereal disease that were being discovered. Once again, Canadian soldiers were proving to be among the least discriminatory or selective in the world, especially when it came to sex. The call of overactive hormones was rarely resisted.

It was an odd sensation catching the night flight from Brussels to Léopoldville, since the Belgian press made a habit of interviewing people heading to the Congo—a place people were trying to get out of, not into. My flying companion was Serge Fliegers of the Hearst newspapers and one of the legends of journalism at the time. Fliegers was totally, unrepentantly, and perhaps even congenitally mischievous and irresponsible. That is, he had a completely different concept of journalism than I did. He wrote the stories he thought his editors wanted and his readers expected. His coverage of the Congo were not reports, features, or news stories. They were adventures, entertainment, excitement: Serge Fliegers donning a German uniform to sneak into an area, Serge Fliegers under fire and commandeering a machinegun to fight back, Serge Fliegers on the trail of Russian spies broadcasting secret messages from various Iron Curtain embassies.

He was awful, yet engaging. I was both hypnotized and appalled by him. I remember when he left the Congo his editors wanted him to visit the newly independent countries of West Africa and write features on each: Ghana, Guinea, Ivory Coast, and so on. Serge kept procrastinating. The deadline approached and finally he took a flight that stopped for a few hours or overnight in each country, so that he could legitimately say he had been there. He used these datelines to create stories. I wondered at his nerve.

I saw Serge a year later and asked about the series. He bellowed with laughter. Yes, he said, he'd done the assignment, spent a few hours in each country, then rewritten relevant chapters in John Gunther's excellent book *Inside Africa*, rejigging Gunther's anecdotes, and got his series. Were his editors satisfied?

"Satisfied?" said Serge. "They were delighted. So delighted that they have submitted the series for an award. They now want me to go to South America and do the same thing. Has John Gunther been there yet . . . ?"

The UN had press conferences every day in their headquarters in the Apartment Royale. Of course, these were next to useless for the journalists because, like everyone else, the UN hadn't a clue what was going on. But they were marginally useful to the UN for getting information from the journalists.

All the rival Congolese factions gave out their own accreditation and one had to be careful when stopped by troops to show the identification that the soldiers would accept; otherwise there might be trouble. For example, in Stanleyville, a thousand miles up the Congo River from Léopoldville, troops loyal to Marxist Gizenga had seized, humiliated, and beaten up eight Canadian UN soldiers in honour of a visit by Prime Minister Patrice Lumumba. They had arrived by aircraft and had no sooner been billeted in the hotel adapted as UN headquarters than Congolese troops burst in. The Congolese were headed by a Commandant Kabongo who, just the day before, had given the commander of the Canadians, Captain Jean Pariseau of Edmonton, permission for the eight to open communications. "You are hiding Belgian paratroopers!" Kabongo shouted.

"You remember I visited you yesterday about troops coming in!" Pariseau said to the Congolese. Kabongo pretended not to recognize him. The Canadians were herded into the street where crowds were being worked into a frenzy. Ethiopian troops on UN duty watched nervously and took photographs. "Don't worry," Kabongo whispered to a UN official. "We won't kill them—this is only for political appeasement."

The Canadians were taken to a compound, forced to strip and, while the crowd watched and jeered from behind barbed wire, were beaten, abused, jabbed with bayonets, hit with rifle butts. Some Congolese troops took haymaker swings at them, stopping just short of hitting, and screamed horribly to give the crowd the impression of a beating. Throughout, Pariseau warned his men not to make a fuss or else it might go worse.

Eventually they were freed. Two of the nine had to be evacuated because of injuries. I flew to Stanleyville, hoping to get more details on the story, which was being downplayed by the UN in Léopoldville. I was startled and delighted to find Johnny Pariseau, who had been a brother officer in the PPCLI. We had a small reunion. The Ethiopians had rescued the Canadians. I sent the photos they'd taken back to the *Telegram* and they made a nice spread. Pariseau was a solid officer, incapable of panicking, and his coolness saved a dicey situation.

Stanleyville was quiet at the moment, largely because Pariseau had the poise and the sense to make contact with the Congolese commander *after* the incident to his troops, invite him to dinner, and explain that there were no hard feelings. He established a rapport and accepted the Congolese explanation that what had happened was a ghastly mistake and some unknown person's fault, and thus reversed an otherwise awkward situation. In the process Pariseau made it clear that if ever anything similar happened again, his troops would fight and the Congolese would be answerable to the Canadian army. A bluff, but effective.

The Canadian military was always handling ticklish situations with resourcefulness, initiative, and an aplomb that professional diplomats could well learn from—if they had a mind to abandon arrogance and snobbery.

Léopoldville, on the other hand, was out of control and working only through force of habit. Curiously, while streets went uncleaned and lawns untended, the statute of King Léopold was, for the first year of independence, meticulously cleaned, the grounds around it manicured, the flowers kept fresh, and grass cut. It stood out like a rose bush in an onion patch. Investigation showed that the old Congolese who had tended the statue for the Belgians had never been told not to continue his work and so, for a year without pay, he had faithfully performed his gardening duties. Finally Congolese patriots told him to desist, and the grounds around the statue deteriorated like the rest of the city.

With no one in control, it was inevitable that a strongman would eventually take charge. That person turned out to be Colonel Joseph Mobutu who, prior to independence, had been an orderly room sergeant in the Belgian Force Publique and later became a journalist. On a memorable summer evening we were all in the bar of the Memling Hotel when word came around 10 P.M. that Colonel Mobutu was coming to the bar of the Stanley Hotel to make an announcement. No one took Mobutu very seriously, but we all drifted over. It turned out to be an extraordinary scene.

The room was cluttered with those small round tables one used to see in beer halls. In came Mobutu—a boyish twenty-nine-year-old colonel who seemed unsure, hesitant, modest. He stood on a table and announced that he and the army were taking over the government of the Congo, banning all political activity and suspending Parliament. In effect, he was now the sole authority of the Congo. Any questions?

Journalists looked at one another. "When does this go into effect?" someone facetiously asked.

Mobutu whispered a moment with an escort, as if he hadn't thought of that yet, then replied: "As of eight o'clock tomorrow morning."

He got off the table and walked into the night.

No one was sure how to treat the story. Disregard it? Serious? A nut? What? It was decided that Mobutu had to be taken seriously. Journalists raced to get to the all-night telegraph office in Brazzaville in the French Congo across the two-mile-wide Congo River, which was fast-flowing and dangerous, especially at night when fishing boats, or dugout canoes with outboard motors attached, had to be hired.

In my ignorance, I took Mobutu at face value—although it was the first and up to now *only* coup that I've ever heard of that gave a ten-hour advance warning. Yet at eight o'clock in the morning we went to the Parliament buildings, to find them ringed with troops and in essence closed down. Politicians were also denied use of cable facilities. Mobutu, it seemed, had the army with him. And in Africa, as elsewhere, he who controls the army bosses the country.

It was that day, incidentally, that a Ghanaian officer with the UN force, the best field troops in the Congo and more British than African, said contemptuously that the troops were guarding the tree by the windows of the legislature building so "members could not swing into their seats." The gibe reflected the tension between Ghanaian troops and Congolese. Many Congolese refused to believe that the Ghanaians were African, and thought them American blacks because they were too disciplined, too Western-oriented, too professional. Besides, they spoke English and not French or any African dialect that was familiar to the Congolese. Had it not been for Ghanaian soldiers and Nigerian police in those early days, nothing would have functioned in the Congo.

While the Ghanaian troops may not have been overly impressed with the Congolese, the Ghanaian government and its leader,

Kwame (Redeemer) Nkrumah, were almost blatantly supporting Mobutu. The Ghanaian chargé d'affaires was Nathaniel Wellbeck, who would hold meetings in his office or residence with dissident Congolese factions and try to coordinate them into supporting Lumumba and Soviet policies. Despite his charisma and left-wing support, the longer Lumumba was around, the more disruptive and unsettling his influence.

At the outset, Mobutu had very little support from anyone. It was even said that he was an instrument of the CIA. While controversy raged over whether he was a strongman or a puppet, he quietly increased his grip. Most journalists who had initially dismissed Mobutu as a temporary aberration began to change their opinion after he moved quickly and decisively to expel the Soviet Embassy and all its staff from the Congo for indulging in espionage. This was the first time I'd ever seen a Soviet Embassy driven from a country with its tail metaphorically between its legs.

It was a hot, sunny Saturday morning and the memory of smoke from burning files in the embassy back yard and of carloads of tight-lipped Soviets leaving the Congo is still strong. I wrote at the time that, downgrade Mobutu as we might, the Soviets took him seriously and he was one of the few world leaders who ever got rid of the centre of Soviet subversion in his country with the stroke of a pen. And he expelled them the first weekend after seizing power! Of course the Soviet Embassy was up to its eyeballs in clandestine activities, trying to bribe, persuade, corrupt, cajole, seduce the Congolese into supporting them.

Lumumba, still officially the Prime Minister, was under loose house arrest in a posh villa a few minutes from the centre of town. He was still favored among many soldiers, possibly because after he got the top job he had promoted every member of the 27,000-man Congolese National Army by one rank, thus making it the largest (only?) army in the world without any privates. Still, his credentials were frail since his supporters had won only 29 of some 120 seats in the elections. Some 20 parties held seats, thereby ensuring that whoever was elected would always be massively outnumbered by the combined opposition. Democratically, there was more hope for political stability in a volatile country like Italy than in the Congo.

In the afternoons Lumumba, a strikingly handsome man with gentle eyes and a small goatee, would hold impromptu press conferences outside his villa-prison while uneasy Congolese troops, ostensibly guarding him, shuffled nervously, obviously influenced by his aura. Ghanaian troops, on the other hand, there to protect Lumumba if necessary, would stand impassively, immune to his magic. They were more sophisticated.

Lumumba was most impressive: tall, well-built, arrogant, brave, intelligent, ambitious. He was Moscow-trained, but no one was sure whose side he was on. In retrospect, I think he was a mixture of patriot, nationalist, and opportunist. He used to leave his villa-prison at nights, and appear in the poor African districts of Léopoldville where the bulk of his support was. It was widely believed among Congolese that Lumumba used magic to turn himself into a bird and fly out at night. His supporters encouraged the myth that he had supernatural powers. Lumumba vowed vengeance on Mobutu who, curiously, didn't seem either concerned or perturbed when the press confronted him with the latest Lumumbaism. Mobutu was more accessible in those days than he was to become after he Africanized his name to President Mobutu Sese Seko and adopted the trappings of a cane and a leopard cap and a megalomaniacal cruelty. In those days Mobutu seemed genuinely gentle and sincere when he said he wished no harm to Lumumba. He was generous and tolerant to an unusual degree. Lumumba, on the other hand, grew increasingly erratic and anti-Western and would even launch into diatribes against Canada as an imperialistic power.

No one, in the press or not, had ever witnessed anything quite like the Congo before—lots of them since, none up to then. It was the first of the trend. With Lumumba constantly escaping from house arrest, there was always the chance of violence. He was a rabble rouser. I remember one afternoon when word came down to the Memling that a mutiny was under way at that very moment in the army's Camp Léopold. Serge Fliegers and I were with the Canadian public relations officer who was an old friend from army days. He was a *laissez passer* through Congolese troops, and we took his jeep through all checkpoints into the army camp. We found the place in an uproar.

Lumumba had apparently paid a surprise visit to the camp with the head of the army, General Victor Lundula, who had been a sergeant-major in the Belgian Force Publique. Unknown to Lumumba, the Congolese soldiers were mostly of the Baluba tribes from Kasai province, where Lumumba's troops had waged terrible violence, killing women and children in the most frightful way. Determined to avenge these massacres, the Baluba soldiers had turned on Lumumba and Lundula and chased them into the

Ghanaian officers' mess where they sought refuge. The two-storey stucco building was surrounded and under seige by Mobutu's troops. The mutinous Congolese were clawing, punching, and fighting their way into the mess, while only a thin line of Ghanaian soldiers was holding them back, behaving as coolly and professionally as a regiment of Guards. We managed to get through the berserk Congolese and inside the mess, gaining a measure of security behind the steady Ghanaians. Upstairs, Lumumba was in a room with Ghanaian officers who were trying to persuade him to leave. Lumumba was composed and defiant, but Lundula's nerve had broken and he was crouched in a closet weeping and gibbering that he didn't want to die.

Serge and I were the only journalists there and, as it happened, he was the only one who was fluent in French and English. He was seconded as an interpreter for the Ghanaians. A French-speaking UN official was telling the Ghanaian officer that something had to be done quickly to get Lumumba out of there, or else the Congolese troops would eventually kill them all. The Ghanaian turned to Fliegers: "What did he say?"

"He said to hell with Lumumba—give the son of a bitch to the Congolese and let them string him up." Serge despised Lumumba and anything that smacked of the left.

"Oh, I'm not sure we should do that," said the aghast Ghanaian.

"Well, *he* says you should turn Lumumba over to the Congolese. Let them solve it," reiterated Fliegers as the UN fellow looked on, puzzled at the apparent indecision. He nodded briskly when Fliegers was supposedly translating his words, not realizing he was trying to get Lumumba killed. He couldn't understand the Ghanaian's apparent reluctance to save Lumumba's life.

Meanwhile, the British-style Ghanaian troops were retreating slowly up the stairs, the mob of sweating, screaming, sobbing Congolese soldiers getting closer, more hysterical, more aggressive. I was filled with admiration and unease watching these Ghanaians get punched, hit, cursed, without the slightest panic or sign of their breaking. They were commanded by a young British captain, Richard Hudson, who stood with his troops and impassively took the blows of the Congolese. He was inspirational to the Ghanaians.

Eventually Lumumba was persuaded to leave and was driven away in a guarded jeep, while Congolese troops screamed and punched him, blaming him for the massacre of their families. General Lundula reportedly was smuggled out of the camp hidden in a garbage truck, and vanished with barely a trace from the

Congo scene. The whole episode made a lively story for me, but nothing compared to the one it made for Fliegers. I still shudder at what would have happened if his alleged translation had been accepted at face value. I didn't include him in my stories to the *Tely*, since it hardly seemed relevant and in those days newspapers didn't appreciate stories about other journalists.

Perhaps it wouldn't have mattered. Barely a year later Mobutu decided that Lumumba must die and he was flown to Katanga and killed. Mystery still surrounds his death. While trying to trace the story of his death, I met a South African who claimed to have piloted the plane Lumumba was flown in to Elisabethville (now Lubumbashi). The South African and Swedish UN troops who witnessed the transfer told a horror tale of Lumumba's being so tortured in the rear of the Dakota that the South African pilot, no fan of Lumumba, took evasive action so that the Congolese guards lost their balance and could not go on with the torture. Earlier, Lumumba, his Minister of Sports, Maurice Mpolo, and Senate President Joseph Okita had been flown by light plane to Luluaburg in Kasai province in order to get his mischief-making out of Léopoldville. They were transferred to a DC4 under guard of Baluba soldiers and flown to Elisabethville, and it was during this flight that the tortures began. Lumumba's goatee was pulled out, hair by hair, and the Balubas took turns bashing him around.

At Elisabethville, the prisoners were transferred to a truck, now more dead than alive, and by the time they reached the prison, the soldiers of Moise Tshombe, ruler of Katanga, had finished the job. Lumumba and Mpolo were dead—battered to death—and Okita, barely alive, was dispatched with a rifle butt to the temple. Their deaths were unplanned, and Tshombe and his Belgian advisors had the three bodies disposed of in an acid bath at the smelters of Union Minière. A story was circulated that Lumumba had escaped and was later killed. His body has never been found.

Today Lumumba is immortalized as a martyr of independence, and in Moscow the Patrice Lumumba University has been established in his honor. Fittingly, Third World students go there for a mediocre education and expert training in subversion and Marxism. It is the KGB's main institution for espionage and indoctrination, and it was there that the Marxist leaders of Ethiopia, for one, got their training in the '60s.

Mobutu was obviously reluctant to kill Lumumba, but was virtually forced to do something. I remember that once a few of us journalists gathered at Lumumba's residence when Mobutu came to debate Lumumba, hoping for some sort of reconciliation. Mobutu asked Lumumba to speak his mind and then, during the resulting half-hour tirade, he took out his newspaper and started to read it.

"Why do you try to arrest me and block Parliament?" asked Lumumba.

"Why do you send people to try to assassinate me? responded Mobutu.

And so it went until Mobutu impatiently shook his head and left. The Ghanaian officer on duty, Captain Jonathan Peel, wearily remarked: "Typical of the Congo—no agreement and less understanding."

Throughout most of the Congo crisis, white mercenaries figured prominently. They were the most feared and they constituted the only semblance of a cohesive fighting force in the whole Congo. Their motives were mixed and suspect, but most were in it for pure gain, either in wages or pillage; some for adventure, a few out of conviction. The mercenaries were led by Colonel "Mad Mike" Hoare, also a legend in his own right. It was in the Congo that he gained his reputation—one that had considerable lustre until he led an abortive, ill-planned coup attempt on the Seychelles which convinced some that he was suffering from precocious senility.

Allegations were that the Belgians were recruiting mercenaries, which Belgium hotly denied. In 1961, when I was in Belgium en route to Africa, I decided to find out if the government was indeed involved in hiring mercenaries for Katanga. I went to what was supposedly a Katanga administrative office and said I wanted to volunteer for the mercenaries. I showed my old Canadian army identification card and presented myself as a former paratroop officer with combat experience in Korea. Much to my surprise, I was shepherded quickly through interviews with burly crew-cut civilians all wearing Belgian army para wings in their lapels. I was told that if I signed up and was accepted, I'd get $600 a month and that I'd be expected to serve for at least a year. If I wanted, I could leave that night for Katanga. Ordinary recruits signed contracts for $300 a month—not bad pay at the time, when I was earning $90 a week at the *Tely*. The Belgians were trying to "internationalize" the mercenaries into a sort of foreign legion for Africa, and recruited a total of nearly 5,000 members.

I debated briefly whether I should follow through and concluded that the *Tely* wouldn't look kindly on such a venture (to say nothing of my wife, Helen, who lamented the fact that our family life was constantly being disrupted by my hustling off into the unknown on a moment's notice). Besides, my French wasn't good enough, although they assured me that it would improve instantly if I signed. However, I now had conclusive evidence of Belgian government collusion with mercenaries, and filed a story to that effect.

As a matter of fact, I have mixed feelings about mercenaries; one could argue that they have a unique code of honor. While any citizen should be prepared to give his life for his country, a mercenary is essentially prepared to give his life on his word. He swears allegiance to a particular cause, and his word is all that binds him. Money, gain, adventure are factored in the equation, but in the final analysis he is prepared to die because of his handshake. There are various kinds of mercenaries, of course, and not all are imbued with honor or a code of behavior. Despite the prejudice against those who fight for money, one should remember that the Swiss Guards around the Pope are pure mercenaries, as are the Gurkhas, who rent their services to Britain and India and are considered by many to be the finest fighting soldiers in the world.

Endless anecdotes emerged from the Congo, most of them true. It was still in many ways in the dark ages. I was once stopped at a checkpoint by Congolese troops and accused of being a Belgian paratrooper because I had a tattoo on my left forearm.

"But it is a ship," I said. "Paratroopers never have ships on themselves. Only Canadians sailors do." Unconvinced, the soldiers held a meeting about it, and finally decided to give me the benefit of the doubt. I was relieved until the sergeant wanted me to exchange my tattoo for the tribal scars on his face.

At first I thought he was kidding. He insisted I trade my tattoo for his scars.

"How do I do that?" I asked.

"I don't know," he said. "You're the white man—you figure it out."

One incident that always delighted me involved a Japanese correspondent in Brazzaville, capital of the French Congo across the river from Léopoldville. A group of us—Donald Wise, Peter Younghusband, and Dennis Eisenberg, if I remember correctly—had gone over to exchange money at the black market rate and to have a French cuisine lunch, which was better than the fare offered in Léopoldville. We encountered a Japanese journalist who'd recently arrived from Japan and could barely speak English. We discussed in stilted, courteous pidgin English the political situation. Finally he remarked: "Of course situation here very bad, very dangerous, but if you don't know how dangerous it seem very safe, very ordinary, yes, you agree?"

It seemed an odd thing to say and we quickly discovered that the chap had spent four days filing stories about violence and anarchy from the French Congo, under the mistaken belief that he was in the Belgian Congo. To a Japanese one Congo is very much like another, I guess. I found it a charming thought, and typical journalism. I've often wondered what impression his readers in Japan must have had. Probably it didn't matter. The incident brought to mind—as so many things in foreign reporting did— Evelyn Waugh's great comic novel *Scoop*, which is more journalism *verité* than the satire it was meant to be.

Don Gordon, covering the Congo for the Canadian Broadcasting Corporation, ran into some trouble when natives were convinced that his tape recorder was "eating human souls." On another occasion Congolese police invaded the Memling Hotel dining room, in the process roughing up foreigners without proper identification passes. Donald Wise of the London *Daily Mail* tore the menu in half and signed "Julius Caesar" over the item "Escargots de Bourgogne," which satisfied the Congolese, who were illiterate anyway. A BBC correspondent told the story of coming back to the hotel after midnight from an embassy function and the Congolese concierge at the Memling asked him, as he did every night to every foreigner, if he wanted a woman sent up to his room. Instead of the usual impatient rejection, this time the BBC chap said "Yes, I'd like a blonde, blue-eyed, beautiful Swedish girl sent up immediately, please."

The Congolese's eyes widened, he grinned, nodded, and disappeared. The Englishman thought no more of the matter until an hour later he was roused from sleep by the concierge who was at his door with a squat Congolese woman with her black hair a mass of braided rattails, her skin the color of purple ink.

"Here is your woman, boss," the boy said.

"What do you mean?" he shouted. "I said blue-eyed, blonde, and Swedish. She isn't any of these!"

"Yes, boss, but she is the closest we could find."

The BBC man slammed the door.

The Congo was a mass of contradictions and frustrations, a curious mixture of everything that makes Africa, well, Africa. It was simultaneously hopeful and depressing. Those who didn't think black Africans were capable of ruling themselves sensibly found abundant evidence to support their prejudices; those who felt the Congo could lead the way for the rest of Africa could also find evidence for optimism. That it satisfied neither its supporters nor its detractors in the long run is again typical—not just of the Congo, but of Africa.

While lethal to Africans, the Congo was relatively safe for whites. I was with Leonard Parkin of the BBC when we were given an explanation of why Congolese were reluctant to do anything to whites. "Because all the white people are counted," was the reply. "No one ever counts the blacks." At the time the Congo was terribly anti-Belgian, but not anti-white. In fact, I cannot recall an experience in any part of Africa where I encountered much in the way of anti-white sentiments. African racism is confined to tribalism, and to those who do them harm. I found the lack of hostility to whites, per se, one of the more wholesome and encouraging aspects of that turbulent continent, be it in the Congo, Nigeria, Ghana, Rhodesia (Zimbabwe), East Africa, even Angola. One has the sublime luxury of occasionally getting angry at blacks as individuals and not having it interpreted as a reaction to color— and of having blacks get angry at you without the color aspect intruding. It is healthy and reassuring.

The hopes and dreams, the backwardness, the striving of the Congo are perhaps best depicted in the story of Victorien Nzamwita who, in honor of the first anniversary of independence, became the first Congolese citizen to fly a plane. He was the Wright brothers, Lindbergh, Chuck Yeager, and cosmonaut Yuri Gagarin rolled into one when he soloed in a Piper Cub.

As Léopoldville's *Courier d'Afrique* put it: "At 8 o'clock on the morning of May 8, 1961, the first Congolese pilot took to the air, flying a Piper Cub." It was deemed a "magnificent success" and Pilot Nzamwita was promptly given the title First Pilot and made Minister of Civil Aviation. It was noted that he had soloed after only fourteen hours of instruction, while the first pilot to solo from Katanga took thirty-two hours—suggesting that the Congolese were twice as quick and intelligent as the Katangese.

In a question-and-answer interview with *Courier d'Afrique*, First Pilot Nzamwita said: "To venture into the sky and explore the heavens and continents is a dream I've had since childhood. In

1958 I asked permission to learn to fly, but [Belgian] authorities refused because of my race; they told me a black man would never be able to fly a plane."

I tried to get an interview with the hero of the hour, but was told he was too busy organizing aviation matters to waste time on a journalist. Celebrities are the same everywhere.

11

By day, doctors—by night, assassins

DR. JEAN SALASC
MUSTAPHA HOSPITAL
ALGIERS, APRIL 28, 1961

The Casbah in Algiers during the height of the troubles in 1962 was probably the most dangerous place in the world for foreigners. In fact, Algiers itself in those days is probably still unmatched as a place of indiscriminate, sudden murder. What began as a straightforward anti-colonial war for self-determination and independence deteriorated into a virtual racial/religious war of terror and assassination, and skin color alone was sufficient reason to kill.

Pointless violence as a means of political expression has steadily increased everywhere through the 1960s and '70s and into the '80s with no sign of abating. Acts of terrorism or violence that would be considered bizarre and senseless back in the days of Algerian independence (car bombs on crowded streets, Kamikaze trucks loaded with explosives driven like land bombs into soldiers' barracks, hijacked planes, genocidal slaughters on the scale seen in Cambodia and Uganda) are now so routine that unless done on a grand scale, they are hardly news. Algeria in the early '60s was a freak, ahead of its time in violence, so to speak.

Four times the size of France, Algeria was always considered something special, even among France's African colonies. Prior to 1830 when the French army moved in, Algeria was the domain, the sanctuary, of pirates and brigands. Until it won independence in 1962 it was never a real country with a distinct identity. The Turks occupied it in the sixteenth century; then various pirate kings controlled enclaves, the most infamous being the Dey who plundered the Mediterranean and discovered the profit in selling white slaves to blacks and Arabs who could afford them.

France moved in on a pretext and, after a forty-year war with

137

Arabs and Berbers, extended its power to Tunisia and Morocco. There was never a king or ruler of Algeria—just a mishmash of some 250 Arab tribes or groups, ranging from city- to mountain- to desert-dwellers, who shared only one thing: the Islamic religion.

Algeria was not a colony but officially a part of Metropolitan France, with all inhabitants, European or native, having full rights as citizens of France. Frenchmen—peasant and entrepreneur alike—moved to Algeria in search of a better life. Maltese, Italians, Spaniards moved there for the same reason. While there was theoretical equality for Moslem and Christian, Arab and European, in practical terms there was none. Socially, culturally, and economically, they remained poles apart, a divided society—and each group subdivided. As France improved the existing conditions and amenities, the Algerians profited most. The Algerian population soared from 1.5 million in 1900 to 10 million by 1960 as health and living conditions lowered the infant mortality rate.

On V-E day in 1945 there were riots and the beginnings of Arab or, rather, Algerian nationalism and hundreds, possibly even thousands, were killed; but *real* trouble didn't erupt until the mid '50s as France's other colonies, notably in Indochina, challenged Paris and won. Though communism was banned in most Arab countries and there was no Soviet diplomatic representation in any Arab country through most of that decade, the Communist party and its publications were available in Algeria because it was a part of France. Rebellion or partisan war—liberation war—erupted in 1954, catching France and Algerians by surprise. Although France minimized its importance, insisting that most Algerians were docile and loyal, it was a humiliating blow. It is perhaps significant that only 3 percent of Algerian Moslems were conscripted into the French military, the remaining 97 percent being considered politically and ideologically unreliable.

The various Algerian nationalist movements became dominated by the FLN (*Front de libération nationale*), many of whose leaders lived in France or commuted to France and who had the support of the French Socialist and Communist left. The French army, and notably the Foreign Legion headquartered at Sidi-bel-Abbes in Algeria, returned from humiliating defeat by Ho Chi Minh at Dien Bien Phu in 1954, determined to make short work of Arab insurgents. The French have never been overloaded with scruples when it comes to inflicting punishment, extracting confessions, or dealing with subversives, and Algeria turned into a particularly nasty campaign.

As the Algerian nationalists gained strength, terror expanded, the war and costs increased, a succession of French governments fell, coalitions emerged, then fell, and individual politicians saw their careers shattered. The army remained basically firmer than the politicians, who would have done anything to escape the quicksand of Algeria. In the midst of this, in 1958, Charles de Gaulle emerged from postwar retirement to take over the reins of France as a desperate nation turned to him as the *only* possible solution. On assuming the presidency, de Gaulle vowed to keep Algeria French. The army figuratively tossed its kepi into the air and cried "Bravo." The hero of France's wartime Resistance was back.

De Gaulle, however, turned pragmatist, reversed himself, and declared that Algeria would get its independence. That decision brought a series of crises. The European of Algeria, the *pied noir* (literally "black foot" or pioneer) whose ancestors often went back four generations, was an unique individual. He was not at home in mainland France; he was not an Arab; he was a special type who thought of himself as virile, generous, appreciative of physical beauty, a person of sunlight and beaches and hard work and dirty fingernails. He viewed the European French, the *francoui*, as soft, petty, mean, intellectual, a creature of shaded rooms and perfume, of pencil mustaches and white shoes. The *pied noir* wanted to establish his own independence in Algeria, to break away from France and keep the Arabs in their place. But he lacked the numbers, the know-how, the wit.

Meanwhile, a combination of the extremist *pied noir*, the nationalist officer class of the army, the anti-Communist right, and the ultra-patriotic Frenchman vowed to challenge de Gaulle. From this alliance of differences emerged the OAS (Secret Army Organization), which was determined to fight against Algerian independence using the same techniques and methods that the Algerian nationalists applied in their fight for independence. The OAS waged a terrorist campaign that was up to then unparalleled. People were executed on the streets of Algiers and Oran simply because of their race. As the OAS gained power and de Gaulle grew increasingly desperate and determined, five respected army generals rebelled and a famed Foreign Legion regiment committed the unthinkable heresy: it mutinied.

The shock reverberated around the world. There was a 50-50 chance that the army would stage a coup and take over the government in Paris. French conscripts were turned out to defend Paris against possible invasion by the elite, the paras and the Legion and the regulars of the French army, commanded by the most distinguished generals in the service of France. It never happened, but it was close.

As well as the main factions in Algiers—the FLN, OAS, and army—there were the *barbouse*, the "red beards" of the French secret police. They were a mysterious, clandestine body of thugs and brutes who used terrorist tactics to fight terrorists. They assassinated those whom authorities could not touch. Along with daily killings, there were reprisal killings, with OAS, FLN, or *barbouse* killings with bodies mutilated, ears, nose, and testicles cut off, the corpses strung up on telephone poles or tied and dumped from cars in front of police stations as warnings to the concerned parties.

In a way, the ultimate horror of Algiers was how normal this violence came to be for the people who lived there. Shops would open, commerce and life would continue; instead of cops and robbers, kids would play OAS and FLN in the streets. The human animal can adjust to any obscenity and live amid the most appalling conditions. It is both his strength and his weakness. Most resilient and toughest of all are children, who can survive anything.

Algiers begged the question why the whites were so bitter, so stubborn, so determined to fight the Moslems. The 9 to 1 ratio of Moslems to Europeans in Algeria was not that great (it was 55-to-45 percent in favor of Europeans in Algiers itself, 50-50 in Oran). What had started as a political campaign deteriorated into race war. The Algerian *pied noir* had no special affection for France and, indeed, rightly felt that he and his kind were ignored, forgotten, misused by France. So why the determination to remain part of Metropolitan France?

The reason was economics. Algeria was one of the few places in Africa where there were poor whites, or lower-class whites doing menial jobs. They would have to compete economically with the indigenous people if there was genuine equality, or if the Moslem majority had control. The Algerian Europeans were *not* fighting a race war because of color but because the majority of Moslems could do their low-skilled jobs as well as they—driving cabs, working in hotels, stores, delivering mail, and so on. And the Europeans of Algeria were right: their future was in jeopardy, as history has proved. But they fought harder than any whites in the rest of Africa to maintain the status quo after the decision had been made to abandon them.

In the spring of 1961 when the first army crisis occurred and it seemed as if French tanks might occupy Paris, I was in Miami trying to make sense of the Bay of Pigs. It seemed for a while that exiles had invaded Cuba. It sounds bizarre now, but a public relations firm was actually accrediting journalists to join the invaders when the beachhead was secure, and to be there when the island was liberated from Castro. I was surprised to meet Joe Morris, whom I'd last seen in the Middle East when he was with the New York *Herald Tribune*. Now he was with *Newsweek*. We gratefully teamed up, each of us relieved to find a kindred soul in a new crisis centre. For the first day the myth was vigorously perpetrated that the United States was in no way involved in the invasion, which might or might not work. Morris and I found a couple of vacated private houses stacked to the ceiling with every imaginable type of equipment (excluding weapons) destined for the invading force. Though depicted as being war surplus, it was modern and new and clearly from some working military base. I wrote a couple of stories to this effect, noting that, despite denials, there certainly seemed some official U.S. involvement—and who in the deuce had the foresight and expertise, not to mention the inclination to issue identity cards, complete with instant photos, for journalists? Morris and I were in the process of trying to hire a boat to perhaps go to Cuba when I got a message from the *Telegram* to forget about the Bay of Pigs and head to Paris, where it seemed the French army had mutinied against de Gaulle and there might be tank-fighting in the streets.

It seemed strange to abandon one crisis for another, but I knew that if I objected, someone else would go—and I was afraid, if that happened, the office would realize that anyone can cover crises. So I bade farewell to a startled Joe Morris and caught the next plane to Paris. Morris could not figure out what sort of a newspaper the *Telegram* was that had only one correspondent who was expected to be everywhere at once.

Paris was uneasy, but in no real danger of military coup. There were demonstrations in the streets, but the Garde Mobile and the blue-caped riot police—the two main instruments of unruly crowd control—effectively broke up demonstrations by wading in with batons flailing, leaving the bleeding and the battered in their wake as they scattered the marchers.

I teamed up with Bernie Kaplan, who lived in Paris and did occasional work for the Montreal *Star* and a variety of papers and radio stations. Kaplan had a fey sense of humor and was kind to a fault. More important, he had good instincts and accurate judgment. He gave me an instant comprehensive fill-in of the type that is so valuable to journalists. I then went to see Jacques Soustelle, once de Gaulle's aide and onetime governor general of Algeria before falling out with the Great Man. Soustelle, bitter and pessimistic, felt betrayed, as did so many erstwhile Gaullists. But the "real" story was in Algiers, where the Foreign Legion had mutinied against de Gaulle.

I caught a special journalists' flight to Algiers and booked in at the Aletti Hotel, headquarters of the world press. Algiers in turmoil was very much like the Algiers of peace. It camouflaged its horror. It was a European city, not an Arab or North African one. Apart from the Casbah, or Arab quarter, it was cosmopolitan France. The stores on Rue d'Isly were elegant, the women trim and beautiful. The restaurants were as fine as any in the world. Streets were tree-lined and the city circled the harbor. It seemed tranquil, civilized, beautiful. But instead of occasional backfires of cars, in Algiers it was more likely to be the pistol shot of another *attentat*—assassination. People paid about the same attention to both.

The style of murder in Algeria was a bullet in the head. Ordinary people were targets. As an assassin passed a person, he'd pull a pistol, shoot for the ear or the back of the head, then disappear up an alley. Or an assassin would emerge from an alley, shoot someone in the ear, and be gone. Every day the newspapers carried a list of the previous day's assassinations. People read the *attentats* the way others read birth, death, and marriage announcements. There would be forty or so a day, most of them in the bustling centre of town.

Both OAS and FLN assassins specialized in indiscriminate murder, based only on race or, if they knew it, religion. But since de Gaulle had sided with the Moslems, they were under some restraint, while OAS imagination ran from the macabre to the obscene.

The bloody anarchy continued through 1961 and 1962 and beyond. It seemed endless. By 1962, when I was there again, virtually all the moderate Europeans had left Algeria. The only ones who remained were the activists, the fanatics, and the working poor. In the 2,500 bed Mustapha Hospital—largest in North

Africa, with twenty-eight operating theatres—where most of the gunshot victims were treated, doctors boasted that they were becoming the finest neurosurgeons in the world, treating in any one month the number of head wounds that a surgeon elsewhere would encounter in a lifetime. I spent a fair amount of time among doctors there, along with Ken MacLeish of *Life* magazine (who spent hours in the operating room, where blood and gore actually swished around the feet after a few hours of treating one gunshot victim after another). At all hours the emergency section of the hospital was a scene of frenzy. Buckets with the ends of amputated legs and arms would line the corridors, awaiting disposal, and the wards were so crowded and beds in such short supply that corpses were placed *under* the beds they died in while new patients would be put *in* the beds. Most victims were so badly wounded they were not aware of the garish spectacle.

Most of the doctors hated de Gaulle with a passion, especially the younger ones. Appalling as it sounds, it was the younger ones who boasted that when they were off duty at night, they became OAS assassins prowling for victims. By day they reverted to being dedicated doctors, working overtime to save the victims of attacks—possibly even their own attacks. "As a terrorist I might shoot someone at night, when I'm off duty, but when I put on my surgeon's gown in the morning it is impossible for me to deliberately kill anyone," said Dr. Jean Salasc, one of the more outspoken doctors. They saw no contradiction in these roles; one was politics, the other was humanitarianism. Real-life Jekylls and Hydes.

There was no law, no attempt to catch murderers. Many used the OAS to settle old scores. The police kept to themselves, tried to protect their own. The conscript soldiers from France, whose loyalty was suspect, maintained a neutrality similar to that of the Lebanese army in the 1958 Beirut civil war. One day only postmen might be assassinated, causing a general strike; next day only pharmacists might be shot; then café-owners, then schoolteachers. Next day, who knew? Every day brought a fresh horror.

The one place where Moslems were safe was the Casbah, a collection of some 80,000 inhabitants in the oldest part of Algiers, a maze of twisting streets and a world of alleys and flat rooftops on a hillside where the Europeans and the army had limited access and no control. Stationed in a garrison atop the hill overlooking those rooftops were the Zouaves, France's racially mixed units of Europeans and Moslems who were rough and unsophisticated.

Rebellious Moslems resented their fellow Moslems serving in the French army, and the Zouave Moslem troops were heavy-handed and unforgiving in how they controlled the Casbah.

The French troops had their automatic weapons chained to their bodies so that if they were shot, their weapons could not be stolen. They went on regular patrols in single file of ten through the Casbah, and for a time foreign journalists could go with them. Several times I went, and it proved to be an education of another sort. It was like a guided tour of a Hollywood set, only this time for real, visiting the brothels that Humphrey Bogart would have blanched at, chatting up madams, wondering at the bleached, battle-worn girls who charged $1 to $1.50 per session, tips included, and checking various meeting places to see if anything unusual was afoot. But these tours ended in 1962, just prior to independence, when violence reached a peak and Moslems began responding to the OAS's escalated campaign of terror with terror of their own, even killing the Zouaves.

I recall once coming out at the bottom of the Casbah on the Place du Gouvernement, which separated the Casbah from the European area and which was a teeming mass of commuters and workers at evening rush hour. I was approached by a man who whispered that my friends and I should get out of the area quickly. You were always being told such things. Sometimes you paid no attention, sometimes you listened. This time Robin Stafford of the *Daily Express* and I paid heed, and got out. Our companion, a French photographer named Jean Poggi, didn't, and stayed for a few more pictures. Twenty minutes later Poggi was dead from a 9 mm bullet in the forehead.

Another time I went to the square to buy Paris newspapers just as OAS mortars fired from the European working-class district of Bab-el-Oued to coincide with rush hour. Five or six bombs whistled down in rapid succession and all hell broke loose. There was pandemonium—screams, panic to escape, thirty dead, and an unknown number wounded, almost all of them Moslem. The Place du Gouvernement became known as the *Abattoir*, a place to avoid. Even the Zouaves abandoned the practice of giving escorted tours to journalists.

The day after the OAS bombing of the *Abattoir*, the FLN took vengeance. All along the waterfront Moslem assassins shot Europeans. I saw a man reading a newspaper suddenly shot in the head. In his pocket were discharge papers from the French army and permission to catch the boat home to France. Further on was another corpse. A Moslem quietly came up and suggested I go another route: "I tell you because you are not French and I am your friend." Such warnings were disregarded at the recipient's peril. I returned to the hotel by another route—and encountered another corpse. The talk of the Aletti that day was the vengeance being wreaked all over Algiers by Moslems. It was the worst kind of war. Usually the FLN were choosy about whom they killed, but this day all Europeans were vulnerable.

Early in March a cruise ship stopped at Algiers and tourists were given the afternoon to stroll through downtown, usually safe enough because no one was after tourists, who were easily identifiable. An elderly British couple managed what was believed to be impossible: they climbed over barbed wire to get into the Casbah, strolled unguarded and unescorted through the heart of it, and emerged unscathed at the other end. Not only unscathed, they had a wonderful time. A patrol of Zouave troops crossing the *Abattoir* could not believe its eyes. Nor could journalists. Word spread quickly and there was an impromptu press conference at a sidewalk café.

The elderly pair were inappropriately dressed in matching tweed suits, he with a Sherlock Holmes cap and muttonchop whiskers, she with an umbrella, sensible shoes, and a hat like a pancake with a feather in it. Neither seemed bothered by the sun. Nor did either seem aware of what they had done. I wrote about the incident, which at the time seemed a small miracle.

The couple ordered tea and crumpets at the café and got coffee and croissants instead. A journalist suggested that they had drifted off the beaten tourist track.

"We've had the most marvellous time," said the tweedy lady. "Tiring but absolutely delightful. Charming people. And those funny twisting streets and those funny brown and black people in nightgowns and sheets . . ."

Her husband was distressed that the alleys and streets were too dark for their photos to turn out.

Newsmen were incredulous that they had managed to take photos—perhaps the most hazardous journalistic job in Algiers, and certainly taboo in the Casbah. Photographing in the Casbah provoked riots.

"Of course we took photos," said Mr. Tweed Suit. "One has to have souvenirs. Besides, everyone was jolly nice. Such friendly people, all standing about laughing and smiling at us. A pleasure. They gave us little green flags." And his wife dived in her purse

and produced a small FLN flag. They had been protected by their
innocence to the apparent delight of the Arabs, who appreciate
incongruity as much as anyone.

The pair went back to their ship with a polite but pointed comment that "you journalist chaps do tend to exaggerate things—
Algiers is not nearly as unpleasant as the newspapers claim." Their
story went the rounds of the Aletti Hotel and somehow made
everyone feel better.

A more unwholesome incident occurred on the rue Isly, the
fashionable main street of Algiers that was witness to daily violence. Just before leaving a bus, someone rolled a grenade along
the floor. Panic erupted, but the grenade turned out to be faulty
and didn't explode. Suddenly there was a commotion outside the
bus and someone shouted to "stop that boy." Immediately a cry
went up inside the bus. "That's him!" shouted a passenger and
quickly everyone got out and gave chase to a lad of ten or twelve.
He was caught and the crowd began kicking and punching him.
It looked as if a lynching was about to occur.

The person who had given the original alarm came up and was
appalled. "My God, you'll kill him, he's only a thief."

"Thief? What about the grenade?"

"What grenade? I saw him snatch a woman's purse."

A case of mistaken identity. The boy was released, and fled.

Every night I had to go about half a mile up the street to file
copy at the post office for transmission to Canada. (The British
journalists phoned their stories, others filed to their European
bureaus. Only I had to contact North America direct.) I'd usually
go at 10 P.M., after dinner, and it was somewhat uncomfortable
because streets were deserted except for armoured cars or patrols
of soldiers, or marauding OAS assassins. The dilemma was always
whether to walk close to the wall and risk being ambushed from
an alley, or to go in the middle of the road and risk being shot
at. I usually chose the latter on the theory that openness demonstrated innocence.

Occasionally I'd get trapped in a firefight as nervous French
soldiers fired at shadows. One night was particularly noisy, and
as I dashed door-to-door down the street, hoping to dodge stray
bullets, the Aletti Hotel press corps gathered in the recessed hall-
way of the hotel betting on whether or not I'd make it. I tried to
time my dashes between bursts of machinegun fire, and made it
to the cheers of my colleagues. Those who won bets bought me
a beer.

I seemed to encounter so many assassinations in Algiers that Bob Nielsen of the Toronto *Star's* London bureau began calling me "death's head" which, while amusing, bothered me more than it should have.

Even in the most unpleasant situations journalists usually feel some security being with one side or the other. Not in Algiers. There it was every man for himself with no protection anywhere. Only the Aletti offered a tenuous sanctuary. When de Gaulle was negotiating a ceasefire with the FLN in 1962, the OAS stepped up their terrorism and virtually ruled the city. They zeroed in on the foreign press—especially Italian, who were particularly critical of their exploits and had an avid audience among the Italian expatriates in Algiers. One day the OAS, dressed in army uniforms, invaded the Aletti, filled the lobby, and held everyone at gunpoint. Earlier, they had kidnapped an Italian journalist, Giovani Giovannini of *La Stampa*, and held a kangaroo court that found him and all Italian journalists guilty of maligning the OAS. Through Giovannini, all Italians were told to leave Algiers or be killed. Now the raid on the Aletti reinforced the ultimatum. They personally gave eleven Italian journalists twenty-four hours to get out of the country.

To get money the OAS would rob stores—facetiously called "OAS taxes"—often with the complicity of store owners. I was once in a bank when the OAS robbed it, and it was done so quietly and routinely that one hardly knew it was happening. The OAS apologized for disturbing the customers and walked out with their money. "Just the OAS tax collectors," remarked a customer.

One day the same bank was robbed twice, apparently by mistake. The money was collected in the first robbery at 10 A.M., and the manager was furious when the second one occurred at noon. The sheepish robbers, sent away with a scolding and no money, were told severely to get their orders straight. Insurance rates against bank robberies were prohibitive in Algiers.

For a long time there were doubts as to whether the French army would fire on Frenchmen if called upon to do so. As a consequence, there was a deliberate policy not to put the army into situations in which they might have to make that choice. The famed First Parachute Regiment of the Foreign Legion had mutinied against de Gaulle and been disbanded. Would the largely conscript 400,000-man army in Algeria obey controversial orders? No one was sure. Those who wondered didn't know the French very well. Historically, Frenchmen have never suffered qualms about either killing or betraying other Frenchman. In Vichy France during the war, Frenchmen outdid the Gestapo in their zeal to root out anti-Nazi Frenchmen.

And in Algiers when a peaceful march of thousands was staged through the heart of the city, a French soldier panicked and allegedly fired into the air to warn the marchers. He was the fuse that touched off a horrible bloodbath. From three directions the army fired into the marchers, who were singing the "Marseillaise," and within moments there were hundreds of casualties. The thing I remember most vividly is shoes filling the streets and groans filling the air. I remember, too, an old man who'd been leaning back on a chair against the wall of his store: the whole top of his scalp was plastered against the wall where the machinegun ripped his head apart. Another man was impaled by a jagged icicle of plate glass from a store window.

After the bodies were taken to the morgue and only the blood remained on the street, bunches of flowers appeared as if by magic by each pool of blood. Even the army was shocked by its deed. It announced that someone from the crowd had fired on them first. No one had.

When the First Regiment of the Legion mutinied in 1961 and was confined to barracks at its headquarters at Zeralda outside Algiers, the area was kept in isolation as a sort of quarantine. Henry Kahn of the British *Daily Herald* and I found a taxi driver who knew of a back way in. We were dropped off on a side road and told to take a trail into the woods, across fields, and along a creek bed, where we would come upon an asphalt road that passed the legionnaires' camp.

Henry was in his mid-fifties, fat, ponderous, and a bit of a bore, but he was an experienced journalist and eager for a story. We followed the route for perhaps three miles without seeing a sign of life. Then we came to the tarmac road in a pine forest. Soon we reached the high walls of the Foreign Legion stockade. The occasional sentry glared down at us from a watch tower as we strolled nervously along, trying to look inoffensive. Suddenly out of the main gate, about half a mile away, a jeep roared out and headed toward us. We continued walking. The jeep picked up speed. It suddenly occurred to us that it wasn't going to stop. It headed straight for us. I yelled at Henry and we both leapt for the ditch. I was younger and faster and sprawled safely in the ditch. But the fender of the jeep nicked Henry, sending him flying and smashing his glasses.

We got up and Henry waved and ran toward the jeep which

had turned around and was just sitting there, again pointing at us. A sergeant was driving. "English!" shouted Henry. "We are not French. We are English. English friends . . ."

It had the same tranquillizing effect on the sergeant that oil has on a fire. "Fucking English," he screamed with a heavy German accent, gunned his engine, and raced at Henry who, almost too late, again leapt for the ditch—and again was clipped and sent flying. By now the legionnaire was weeping and screaming obscenities about England, and I realized he must be one of the 50 percent of the Legion who were Germans—probably a survivor of El Alamein or the desert war. I briefly considered yelling that I was not "fucking English" but "fucking Canadian," thereby dissociating myself from Henry. But I felt that would be uncomradely, so, mentally cursing Henry, I accepted the label of also being English. I hoped the guy wouldn't think of using his automatic weapon.

After the jeep made a couple of passes, another truck of legionnaires came out and an officer took us into custody. The camp was a mess. The legionnaires had destroyed most of the facilities, tearing out washbasins, plumbing, electrical fixtures, furniture. The regiment was being disbanded: the ultimate disgrace for a gallant unit that had fought long and hard for France at Dien Bien Phu and had fought thanklessly in lonely desert outposts in the Algerian war.

"We have died for France, and we obey our officers," said one of the few British-born legionnaires. Feelings were tense and some men were due for court-martial. For most, the Legion was their home, their country, their mother, their friend, their everything. The Legion's loyalty was to itself. In those days only Frenchmen could be officers, and the bulk of the remainder were ex-German soldiers—the noncommissioned officers of the Legion. Some were Nazis on the run, maybe 10 percent were Italian. Their loyalties were misguided, but they didn't resist the French army when their own officers failed them. At the time the OAS was being led by four French generals who were eventually court-martialled: Maurice Challe, Raoul Salan, André Zeller, Edmond Johuad. The revolt of the generals and the Foreign Legion was the price of independence, which almost caused a civil war and has since been forgotten almost completely.

In some ways Algiers was the perfect journalistic story. It could be covered at several levels: as a running color story with enough violence, imagination, and mayhem to satisfy any tabloid or Fleet

Street popular press (or, for that matter, the Toronto *Telegram*). Or it could be covered as a sociological and psychological study. Or a political, ideological story. Or, simply, as a war of liberation from colonialism. It had everything.

For the adventurous newsmen, the OAS, or mischief-makers, would always cooperate. While you were having dinner at a small restaurant or bistro, or sitting at a bar, there was always the likelihood that someone would slip you a note, ostensibly from the OAS, giving you twenty-four hours to get out of town. Or warning you that continued aggressive coverage would mean you were next on the OAS hit list. There was no sure way of knowing whether death threats were genuine or a prank but, regardless, it would be included in the next story home to appear in a headline, giving the impression that the reporter was so hard-hitting that the "enemy" felt he must be stopped. I was as guilty as any of exploiting this.

Journalists reacted differently to the pressure, and the Brits were usually replaced every two or three weeks, Algeria being considered an emotionally hazardous assignment. One reporter who was exceedingly nervous wrote himself four threatening notes from the OAS in an effort to get recalled by his paper. He had them delivered to his hotel and when he collected his mail he found *five* threatening notes. He caught the first plane out, without waiting for permission from his editor.

I found Algiers both frightening and intriguing, depressing and stimulating. My sympathies were heavily on the side of the Moslems and FLN who did not need to resort to guerrilla warfare once they had the political momentum. They had right, or justice, on their side. The greatest fear was to be shot by accident—by either side. I could imagine someone saying, as my gunshot corpse lay sprawled on the street, "Mon Dieu, if I had known he was a journalist I would never have killed him!" Somehow it never seems as bad being a victim on purpose. It's the accidental death that is worrying.

Eventually, the "neutral" conscript army in Algiers was called upon to prove its loyalty to de Gaulle and France. As atrocities escalated and a tenuous ceasefire was arranged between de Gaulle and the FLN, the decision was made to clean out the European working-poor district of Bab-el-Oued, where some 40,000 to 50,000 *pieds noirs* lived and where the OAS were regarded as heroes and saviors. With armoured cars and infantry moving in, supported by propeller-driven fighter planes swooping over the flat-topped apartment buildings of Bab-el-Oued, the take-over began. It was World War II street fighting: very exciting and quite unreal. The question of whether French conscripts would fire on French citizens was resoundingly answered. It was strange. Journalists would wander into the fighting zone, get a feeling for the battle, maybe endure a firefight, then, when they'd had enough, get out of the area by dashing house-to-house, doorway-to-doorway. Back in the relative serenity of the Aletti bar, they'd have a drink, compare anecdotes, and file their stories.

I went into the area the first time with Dennis Eisenberg of the *Daily Herald*, Peter Stephens of the *Daily Mirror*, and Robin Stafford of the *Daily Express*. We strolled nervously along deserted streets toward the sound of gunfire: armoured cars and planes firing and being fired upon from balconies and roofs. We raced up an alley when an armoured car at one end opened up with a .30 calibre machinegun and sprayed the street around our scrambling forms. We turned the corner and were resting when French troops behind a garden wall began shooting. The four of us jumped into a doorway and began shouting that we were innocents. The troops exchanged shots with others down the street. We were caught in the cross-fire. The soldiers evidently mistook us for locals and started firing at our alcove. Chips flew off the corner of the window as we sucked our bodies thin and tried not to expose any parts.

Stephens and I were calmer than Stafford and Eisenberg, perhaps because both of us were lean and no part of our anatomy protruded beyond the edge of the doorway. Stafford and Eisenberg, however, both with protruding tummies that indicated countless expense-account meals courtesy of their employers, had more difficulty keeping their silhouettes from projecting. Only by great effort could they suck their stomachs up temporarily into their chests. Every so often they'd have to gasp for another breath, allowing their stomachs to sag into profile beyond the doorway, thus attracting pot shots. Eisenberg summed up the dilemma succinctly when, through sweat and strain, he gasped: "Christ, I don't like this a bloody bit—even if it does mean tomorrow's 'splash'!" (A "splash" is a front-page spread—something most Fleet Street journalists, all incurable egoists, would kill, lie, distort, and occassionally die for. Some more than others, but few more than Stafford or Eisenberg.)

Drama was added to our particular plight by a man apparently dozing in a doorway across the street from us, a cigarette dangling casually from his lips. We yelled at him to get the hell out of there before realizing that he was dead—shot through the head.

During a lull in the firing, a French soldier jumped up and waved for us to cross the street. I was suspicious, darted out and jumped back—just as a burst of machinegun fire chewed the wall behind me. After considerable yelling and undignified hollering about *journalistes*, we were waved at again and this time allowed to cross and flee the area. We went without further delay to the hotel, where we congratulated ourselves on surviving and tried to bedazzle our colleagues, who all had similar tales. Then the Brits went to file. I was beset with inexplicable despondency, and felt compelled to wander back into the heart of the Bab-el-Oued battle zone for another "fix" of fear. For danger *is* a narcotic, and surviving a dangerous situation unleashes such a surge of euphoria that it acts like a drug. One sometimes feels, after enduring stark terror, the need to go back for more.

It was on one of the repeat performances that I ran into Stanley Burke, then the Canadian Broadcasting Corporation's Paris correspondent who was covering Algeria for the People's Network. Burke, a naval officer during the war, impressed other journalists with a certain naïveté, intensity, and sense of absolute fearlessness that was disquieting and rather frightening. In Bab-el-Oued it was best to blend with the local citizenry and not be too obviously a journalist or outsider. A tape recorder slung over the shoulder was a dead give-away. When Burke bundled his beneath his raincoat, he drew outraged howls from other journalists, who didn't want him near them, since anyone hiding something beneath a coat was suspect of hiding a gun and likely to be shot on the spot. Burke shrugged and thought everyone was overreacting.

In Bab-el-Oued he and I crouched behind a pillar during an intense firefight, with planes diving overhead and civilians rushing about in panic and anger. Burke turned on his portable recorder and began describing the battle in measured tones. Occasionally his voice would be drowned out as the armoured cars opened fire and the planes dived. Still, his carefully modulated voice droned on with running commentary. A citizen appeared and grabbed his mike. "If it comes to a choice between surrender and the coffin, we Algerians choose the coffin," the man said with colorful indignation. (As it turned out, most Algerians eventually chose evacuation to France!)

When we got back to the hotel I found a neat round bullet hole burned through the sleeve of my coat. Burke played his three-minute recording for other journalists and won the highest accolade possible: his peers wanted taped copies for themselves. He broadcast it to Canada—the full drama of the Algerian war in three minutes—and confidently waited for the herograms from his grateful employers. Instead, he was told that a ten-second portion of gunfire had been played on the news but that the rest had not been used because there was too much noise and interference and the tape was running slowly.

The successful attack on Bab-el-Oued seemed to tear the heart out of the European resistance. Even the OAS was reeling. Contrary to their hopes, the French army had sided with de Gaulle and democratic authority, and the rebellion seemed doomed. It also persuaded the Moslems and Algerian nationalists that de Gaulle was serious about their independence and that, for the first time in its history, Algeria was about to become a country.

12

Shaking hands is unnatural for blacks

J. J. HURLEY
CANADIAN AMBASSADOR TO SOUTH AFRICA
JUNE 1961

In 1961, Canada's Prime Minister John Diefenbaker played his most dramatic role in foreign affairs when he made a proposal at the Commonwealth First Ministers' Conference in London that forced South Africa to quit the Commonwealth.

Britain and New Zealand wanted South Africa, which had recently proclaimed itself a republic, to remain within the Commonwealth club without any discussion. Over their objections, Diefenbaker proposed that the conference's communiqué should declare that racial equality is a basic principle of the Commonwealth. Because South Africa could not agree to such a resolution, it withdrew its application for membership and Canada, rightly, was universally regarded as the one that had expelled South Africa from the Commonwealth.

Diefenbaker was an instant hero in Canada and the nonwhite Commonwealth, notably Ghana and Nigeria, both of which had been most vehement in their opposition to South Africa's continued membership after that country had declared itself a republic. The year before, the 3 million whites of South Africa (1.8 million Afrikaaners, 1.2 million British stock), of a population of 15 million, had decided by a 73,000 vote majority in a referendum to dump the monarchy and become a republic. There had been considerable anxiety over the referendum because, while the Afrikaaners resented paying symbolic homage to the British monarch and wanted republican status, most whites and the government didn't want to jeopardize South Africa's Commonwealth status. Prime Minister Hendrik Verwoerd had repeatedly assured the country that when South Africa's application for Commonwealth membership was resubmitted, it would be rubber-stamped

154

by the "white" Commonwealth countries of Britain, Canada, Australia, and New Zealand. Some doubts had been expressed about Canada, but Verwoerd was adamant. I was there at the time and was flabbergasted to hear and read his assurances that "like South Africa, Canada is a white country" and would vote along racial lines.

I tried to impress on everyone I met that very few of my countrymen had any tolerance for apartheid and that most detested South Africa's racial policies, though few understood them. Even among the South African liberals who favored integration and equality, there were doubts that Canada would side with India, Ghana, the nonwhite Commonwealth.

I couldn't believe Verwoerd was serious, but it was my first visit to South Africa and I wasn't yet conditioned to the reality that the whites simply do not see the blacks in terms of being like themselves. Even the unprejudiced tend to turn a blind eye to the blacks. Intellectually, they may feel one way; emotionally, quite another. In those days, at any rate.

A year later I was back in South Africa for independence ceremonies after the regime had been forced to quit the Commonwealth. I had never before (nor have I since) witnessed such an outpouring of hate and a feeling of betrayal toward Canada as there was in South Africa then. Prime Minister Verwoerd denounced the country on the radio and in the press, and there was apprehension in the air about what the future might hold. South Africa was now truly isolated in the world—rich and resolute, but still vulnerable and alone. There was bewilderment, too, at Canada. What had gone wrong? How could South Africa have so misunderstood? Verwoerd's denunciations were made as much in hurt as in anger. His constant assurances that Canada would support South Africa now made him look bad too. He hadn't wittingly been lying to South African whites to persuade them to support the republic idea.

Adding fuel to resentment in South Africa were news reports from Canada of the pride and approval of ordinary Canadians in Diefenbaker's actions, even with the pious nonsense Dief uttered that someday South Africa would rejoin the Commonwealth and that "there would always be a light in the window."

The contrast between the Congo and South Africa couldn't have been more pronounced. As a Canadian, I found almost everything about South Africa society offensive. All my egalitarian instincts rebelled. From the moment I wandered into the wrong washroom at the airport, I was mortified that people were being treated so differently because of race. Most people experience these attitudes at first exposure to South Africa, but after a while you, too, begin to adopt the prevailing attitude. Not that you agree with it, but you don't fight it. I found most contacts with black South Africans difficult and meaningless. The nonmilitant blacks you could meet tended to say what was expected of them, like tape recorders, and accepted their fate without rancour or comment. I was surprised, too, in this much-maligned regime, to find the press so critical of its government and to find it easy to meet dissidents, or those liberal, self-styled "progressives" who actively fought apartheid. A few years later I was to see dissidents in the USSR who would give their lives to have the freedom of expression that South African dissidents, black or white, had.

I found that most South Africans, even the anti-apartheid ones—a courageous, determined core—deplored the outside world's lack of understanding of South Africa's unique circumstances and special problems. South Africans are not an endearing people, though they are tough and talented, efficient and energetic, rich and resourceful.

No matter how offended I was, I still didn't see much hope for blacks or "coloreds" (mixed bloods) unless liberalization came from the whites themselves. At the time there were roughly 10 million blacks in South Africa, 1.5 million coloreds, 500,000 Asians, and 3 million whites, split roughly 60-40 in favor of Afrikaaners over English. With the odds only 4 to 1 against the white population, there was *no* chance in the foreseeable future of blacks winning in South Africa. One South African white is more than able to cope with four blacks or coloreds, especially when the one has all the guns, police, money, organization, power.

The ratio in Southern Rhodesia was more marginal, where the white population was outnumbered 12 to 1 and the whites were far more liberal and accommodating than South Africans. In the Federation of Rhodesia and Nyasaland (now Zambia, Zimbabwe, and Malawi), the odds were 35 to 1, blacks over whites. Far more tenuous for the whites.

I had to interrupt the South African assignment to go north to Salisbury, capital of Southern Rhodesia where, for the first time in memory, violence was erupting in the black townships. The nationalist or independence movement was beginning to stir there, as it had stirred all over colonial Africa. Joshua Nkomo was agitating; so was Takawiri, whom I met in secret session at the back of a store in Harare township. And somewhere in the township, active but unknown to any save possibly Rhodesian security forces, was Robert Mugabe, just starting his long march through the ranks of white collar terrorism that would take him to the prime minister's office in twenty years.

I returned to South Africa for the official Independence Day ceremonies. I wrote that South Africa was a republic conceived in anguish and carried out in apathy. It was a *sjambok* republic—named in honor of the rhinoceros-hide whip associated with the country's history. Always rather cheerless, South Africa was now harder, more resolute. Afrikaaners were solidly in control, the Nationalist government of Verwoerd unmovable. Liberals or moderates who favored easing or abandoning apartheid were in retreat and without influence at home. In the rest of the world voices were raised denouncing South Africa. It had officially become the world pariah—a condition that would intensify until any who attempted to defend or understand the mentality of the country were deemed racist, too.

At best South Africans—especially those of Boer extraction—are not a lighthearted people, not impetuous, not filled with gaiety. In fact, an impartial observer might regard them as downright dour. By comparison, Russian commissars are frivolous.

And so it was fitting that on a gloomy Saturday, in the capital of Pretoria, South Africa celebrated its independence in a sullen rain. A parade included all the ambassadors and diplomats, and apart from ritualistic applause at appropriate moments, most emotion was reserved for the Canadian High Commissioner turned Ambassador, J. J. Hurley, whose limousine with the Canadian flag—the Red Ensign—was booed and jeered by the crowd as it passed. I dog-trotted beside his car, bounding over puddles and picking up the abuse: "Canadian hypocrites . . . *kaffir* lovers . . . Judas . . . two-faced . . . traitors . . . what about your Indians?" and similar epithets.

The morose hostility there contrasted with the pride and pleasure in Canada, where Diefenbaker was relishing his new prestige and calling the London conference that dumped South Africa the "most momentous in all history" and his own role the "watershed of history."

I decided to see Ambassador Hurley and obtain an on-the-record interview to explain the complex situation to Canadians. I had heard that he was very popular with the South African government and quite influential within it. I was curious to learn what his reactions were. Two South Africans, Maureen Chilwell and Peter Younghusband, then of the London *Daily Mail* went with me and after some chitchat with the ambassador, Chilwell and Younghusband began to take exception to some of his views. A heated discussion evolved.

As Hurley began to lose his temper at my two companions, he ventured deeper into waters he would never wittingly enter with the press in attendance. For the most part I listened and as the conversation progressed, it became clear why the South African government was getting such a wrong assessment of the Canadian reaction to apartheid. The Canadian ambassador himself was favorably inclined toward South Africa's apartheid policies, to the point that he thought them enlightened. But his view, sincere as it may have been, was utterly out of touch with public opinion in Canada and, what's worse, out of kilter with government policy. He could be classified by the ethics of the day as an out-and-out racist.

J. J. Hurley was not an evil man. He was, instead, quite old-fashioned, immune to the changes gathering momentum throughout Africa, particularly southern Africa. He had been a distinguished soldier in two world wars. In World War II he had been commanding officer of the Royal Hamilton Light Infantry and had taken a demotion in order to go overseas. He had been captured at Dieppe and spent three years in a POW camp. After the war he had joined External Affairs and served as High Commissioner in Ceylon. South Africa was to be his last posting prior to retirement. He was an uncomplicated man who happened to be in the wrong job at the wrong time in the wrong country. Perhaps it was not his fault, but it was someone's for his being there.

He argued that South Africa could properly be classified as a police state, but if so, it should be remembered that a police state was necessary to introduce certain progressive policies in a country of such backward people, incapable of comprehending modern technology and twentieth century concepts.

"Think if Canada were in South Africa's position," he said in a manner one would use to address stubborn children who refused to understand. "Suppose we had ten million Indians, five million Eskimos, three million Dukhobors—and three million whites. Our attitude toward apartheid might be quite different. Can't you see that?"

"Yes, but that wouldn't make it right."

"I'm not saying that the Nationalist government is perfect or that apartheid is perfect. But neither is it all bad, either, and to be fair one should admit the good things."

"What are the good things?"

"Look, the Nationalist government has greatly advanced education, jobs, and housing for the Bantu. South African blacks are the best-off blacks in Africa. Most blacks are content; the trouble that occurs is mostly the work of a few agitators. And of foreign journalists who come here and don't understand, who make no attempt to understand and report only bad things they think people back home want to hear. They ignore the good things. Verwoerd is not a warm man who attracts affection. But he does attract respect. Verwoerd is genuinely trying to help the Bantu, to assist blacks. He may well be ahead of his time. A man of the future. I consider him one of the cleverest men in Africa."

I tried discreetly to scribble notes, not appearing too intent. Younghusband and Chilwell were beside themselves. They'd never met an ambassador quite like this one. All pretence at objective journalism was abandoned and Peter was fighting back vigorously. Maureen, who opposed the Nationalist government more than she opposed apartheid, was firing at J. J. Hurley with both barrels. I was silently begging them to stop, to pull back, because he had already revealed more than he intended. I had had enough. He had effectively hanged himself. In front of witnesses yet.

"Why can't you understand that the ideals and outlook of blacks are different from ours? Most Africans don't worry about politics or apartheid unless they are roused by agitators, Communists, and *tsotsi* [toughs and hooligans]."

"What about Sharpesville—how many died there?"

"My point exactly. Agitators. And who suffered most? The blacks. Look, I play golf with the Administrator of Bantu Affairs and you could not wish for a more pleasant man. He explained to me that the Africans have different customs. Take shaking hands. That is a European custom, not an African one. You don't go out of your way to shake hands with blacks because they don't understand the gesture. Shaking hands is unnatural for blacks. It's like our Indians: the traditional greeting is not a handshake but to raise the hand in greeting. The Administrator and I joke about it."

"Good God!" said Younghusband. "I was born here. I *am* South African. And you are lecturing me about my country—and lecturing rubbish at that."

Hurley ignored him and went on: "Frankly, I don't blame South Africa for being upset with Canada at the London conference. You must remember that Mr. Diefenbaker is an idealist and a religious man and his Bill of Rights made him go along with the expulsion of South Africa from the Commonwealth. It was a wrong decision."

"But most Canadians support the decision."

"The majority is not always right. If the majority favored the move, the majority was wrong. The majority in Britain once favored appeasement of Hitler. And that was wrong, as history proved."

He said "apartheid" invoked unfortunate images, and instead of separation or segregation, a more apt description would be "equalism—but that's a hard word for Afrikaaners to pronounce." He added: "Remember, 'apartheid' means equal with whites, but separate, and preserving their cultural differences. And, as I said earlier, a police state may be necessary to implement necessary things for the greatest good to the greatest number. To help them in spite of themselves . . ."

By now Maureen and Peter were incoherent with anger and I just wanted to escape with my bombshell story. I got up and made apologies and thanked Hurley for being so candid. Chillwell and Younghusband fumed silently.

Hurley realized that he'd gone too far. "Our conversation was off the record, of course."

"On the contrary, sir, I made it clear from the start that it was on the record."

"My understanding was that it was background only."

"No, it was to give Canadians an idea of what the reality of South Africa was. To educate them."

"Please. I am asking you. It was meant to be off the record. You know how it will be interpreted. What purpose can it serve?"

"It may educate Canadians."

"Do you want to destroy me? I am due to retire this year. Whatever you write will be misunderstood. What I said was off the record . . ."

I felt shame for him, embarrassment, and even pity. I agonized over the decision: should I write the story, which, if used the way it should be used, would destroy him? Yes, Hurley was a throwback to the past, reflecting ideas that had no place in modern diplomacy. But was it fair? If I wrote the story that had been goaded out of him, it would change nothing. What had been done was done. South Africa was out of the Commonwealth, Canada looked good, Canadians were pleased. Only South Africa felt betrayed for some inexplicable (and now explicable!) reason.

Hurley could do no further harm. He was approaching his mid-sixties and about to retire. Was it fair to write a story that might be a one-day sensation and leave in its wake a shattered man with his hitherto honorable career in shreds? I kept seeing the headline of how the story might be used, *should* be used if the paper had any news sense: "Canada's Racist Ambassador."

To my discredit, perhaps, as a journalist, I decided not to file the story. I saw no real purpose. If the Commonwealth decision had still been pending, if South Africa had not already left the Commonwealth and declared itself a republic, and if J. J. Hurley had not been about to retire to obscurity but to be transferred to another diplomatic post, then I would have filed it. However, I let concern for the old dinosaur overrule news judgment.

Ever since, I have pondered the ethics of the decision and, usually, I rule against myself. The few journalists to whom I've told the story for the most part think I should have run it. Yet I didn't. I decided then I'd file it away for memoirs.

Peter Younghusband didn't file the story either. If he had, I would have had to. His reasons were different: "An old Canadian diplomat who is an obsolete leftover from colonial racism is hardly news on Fleet Street." Maureen was not a journalist, but a friend, and was thus spared the necessity of making a decision.

Two years later, when J. J. Hurley was retired in Brantford, Ontario, he suffered a heart attack and died. He was sixty-five and his modest obituary in the *Globe and Mail* gave no hint of the controversy that would have clouded his final days, had I written the story. I still suspect I betrayed my role as journalist, but it no longer seems as important as it once did.

13

We like neither your profession nor your nationality

PORTUGUESE SECRET POLICE (PIDE)
LUANDA, ANGOLA
MAY 25, 1961

In 1961 I had the privilege of being witness to a turning point of history: I was the only Western journalist in Angola at the beginning of the terrorist uprising and Portuguese repressions, which, in fact, marked the beginning of a fourteen-year civil war. The war would end in the dismantling of Portugal's overseas empire, which was supposed to last forever. António de Oliveira Salazar was president and dictator of Portugal and had been in power twenty-nine years, longer than any other ruler of Europe. He was beginning to experience cautious political opposition at home and overseas, and could not afford a black challenge, too. Therefore he sent troop ships of Portuguese soldiers to Angola to beef up existing forces and combat the terrorism that was out of hand in the northern regions near the Congolese border. In order to avoid unwanted publicity, all foreign journalists had been expelled from Angola. The international press, sensing a new crisis, were clamoring to get in but were denied visas.

That spring terrorists, supported from the Congo, began turning on isolated Portuguese communities. Their atrocities were literally blood-curdling. Five hundred years of harsh Portuguese domination finally erupted in violence and massacres, which were largely unreported and unconfirmed until refugees and survivors began coming out. They were as savage as have ever occurred anywhere. Some 1,000 Portuguese settlers were reported killed in a three-month period—ten times the number of whites killed by the Mau Mau in Kenya in three years of war. In return, the Portuguese military had killed an estimated 30,000 blacks—not terrorists, but people from the villages, on the assumption that all were guilty and massive retaliation would discourage repetition.

Although Angola and Mozambique had become Portuguese territories in the sixteenth century when Portugal dominated the world through its navy and explorers, it was only in the last century or so that they became fully colonized. The great influx of Portuguese began after Brazil achieved independence from Portugal. Around 1907, Portugal actually took the first steps toward giving Mozambique the beginnings of self-government, but back in the mother country, rudimentary democracy was floundering in anarchy, strikes, assassinations, rebellion. Experiments in democracy were abruptly terminated by a military coup in 1926.

At the time of the coup, Salazar was thirty-two. He had studied for the priesthood, had been elected to Parliament in 1921, and had quickly concluded that parliamentary democracy was "futile" for Portugal. He declared himself to be "profoundly anti-parliamentary." After the coup, Salazar was appointed finance minister, but resigned when the colonels refused to implement the restrictive economic policies he advocated. Two years later, deteriorating conditions forced them to reconsider. They appealed to Salazar for help and he responded by cutting government spending to the bone, reducing wages to near-subsistence levels, and raising taxes—a sort of primitive Margaret Thatcher, some might say.

In 1932 Salazar became premier, an unobtrusive dictator who held firm for thirty-six years. When he was incapacitated by a stroke in 1968, Marcello Caetano replaced him and followed the same policies, while those around the ailing dictator pretended to him that he was still running the show. For two years the charade was maintained, until Salazar's heart gave out in 1970.

Though Salazar could never be confused with a liberal reformer, he was a *nationalist* reformer, determined to make his country prosper. He did bring stability verging on rigidity to Portugal, but, like so many reformers when they get power, he became even more autocratic and oppressive than the military junta he replaced. Most tyrants take power on the promise of making things better. Usually they make things worse. One could mention Russia going from bad under the tsars to monstrous after the commissars took over. Latin America today is an example of pernicious authoritarianism being replaced by dictatorial brutality. China is debatable, but China is not like other countries. Nor is India. As the totalitarian argues, where there are massive, illiterate populations, some form of authoritarian government may be more effective in bringing the greatest welfare to the greatest number, even if it means compromising on abstracts of freedom and individual choice which are important to people born in liberty. The democrat rejects this argument.

The Portuguese used their 500-year presence in Angola as justification for doing as they wished. They were as wedded to the idea of Angola being theirs indefinitely as South Africa was irrevocably wedded to the concept of retaining white control. With no democracy in Portugal, Salazar had no incentive to encourage democracy or liberalism in the African colonies-cum-provinces. The Portuguese maintained a work force that was little more than serfdom. People were regularly deported to work and often disappeared in the plantations of Saõ Tomé and other African holdings. Though not called "slaves," this is what the *contradados*, or "contract workers" were, and this labor force was investigated by such bodies as the prestigious Anti-Slavery Society of Britain and the International Labor Organization. By 1960, half the labor force in Angola—some half-million blacks—were *contradados*, many of whom were accused of committing petty crimes. Local chiefs were required to supply a quota of *contradados*, which put them firmly on the side of the oppressors against the oppressed.

On the other hand *voluntarios* were what their name implied. They also went to plantations but had a somewhat better time of it than the *contradados*. For most Angolan blacks, life was far harsher and more precarious than for blacks in South Africa, although the Portuguese were motivated by economics rather than by racial prejudice and had no color bar as such; discrimination was on the basis of equality, not color.

The Portuguese practised cruelty that was unknown even to South Africa. They used a *palmatoria*, a sort of Ping-Pong paddle with holes in it, to punish people for minor offences. A sharp blow with the *palmatoria* caused the skin to pop through the holes in the bat and break out in a network of blisters that were extremely painful. People were smacked on the palms of their hands or soles of their feet; while it caused pain and left scars, it did no permanent damage.

Without the revenue from Angola and Mozambique, Portugal, one of Europe's most threadbare economies, would have been even more impoverished. Mozambique, on the more healthy southeast coast of Africa, was more sophisticated, cultivated, and developed than Angola on the west side. The climate was better and Lourenço Marques (renamed Maputo) was considered one of the great cosmopolitan playground cities of Africa—for whites, not blacks. It was where South Africans and Rhodesians came to let their hair down and to enjoy a slightly decadent continental atmosphere of bars, girls, and luxurious surroundings, away from the staid, regimented routine of Johannesburg and Salisbury.

Both Angola and Mozambique bordered South Africa, and between them lay the East African Federation of Northern and Southern Rhodesia and Nyasaland (now Zambia, Zimbabwe, and Malawi). The solidly white-controlled southern tip of Africa was a bastion of western civilization—or so was seen by those who lived there. However, policies in the three main white regimes differed. Of the three, the British-dominated Rhodesian federation was the softest, the most liberal, most accommodating for blacks to live in. They encountered little physical oppression or mistreatment, for Rhodesia was paternalistic, colonial, an Outpost-of-the-Empire sort of place, exuding an insufferable superiority that can be harder for its victims to stomach than outright hostility. There was also education, some opportunity, laws, and decency.

South Africa's apartheid policy is well known, and that country was the most adamantly discriminatory of the white-dominated nations of southern Africa. It displayed no flexibility, no tolerance, very little hypocrisy, and a massive capacity for error and insensitivity. As far as most South Africans were concerned, Southern Rhodesia was dominated by bleeding hearts. To those same South Africans, the Portuguese were of sterner stuff and had the right idea, even though they were only marginally white and not quite civilized themselves.

While Angola and Mozambique under the Portuguese are often equated with South Africa as harsh, racist regimes, the comparison is neither fair nor accurate. Angola was harsher on blacks, but not as racist. To the Portuguese, a drop of white blood meant a person was white (in the United States at the time, any black blood meant a person was "Negro"). In South Africa, racism was based more on looks; those who looked white were more likely to be considered white. In South Africa today, Japanese are considered white, primarily because South Africa wants Japanese business. Money and commerce, it seems, make even racists color blind.

The Portuguese relationship with its Africans was distinct and different—and far more sinister. While the ratio of blacks and coloreds to whites was 4 to 1 in South Africa and 35 to 1 in the federation of the two Rhodesias and Nyasaland (12 to 1 in Southern Rhodesia), in Angola the ratio was almost 45 to 1; that is, 4.5 million blacks to 100,000-plus whites. The Portuguese discriminated on the basis of equality, not color. And they let only a trickle of blacks achieve the status of *assimilado* and equality with whites.

Blacks regarded as *assimilados*, or given white status, were those who could read, write, and speak Portuguese; whose income was at least $75 a month; who joined the Catholic Church and gave up association with backward Africans; who had done military service; who adopted European ways and ate with a knife and fork. Statistically, given those requirements, the chance of an Angolan black ever gaining full equality was roughly equivalent to the chances of winning with a lottery ticket. After 500 years of control in Angola, Portugal had given equality to only 30,000 of some 4.5 million blacks—less than 1 percent of the population.

That so few managed to qualify over so many centuries (Luanda was the oldest European settlement in black Africa) indicates the restrictive nature of the policies. Portugal thus seductively enticed the best, most talented, ambitious, and able blacks into European or privileged status. Inevitably, what *assimilados* there were became more Portuguese than the Portuguese, self-interest and human nature being what it is. And the policy of equal standards kept African nationalism at bay and the majority of blacks without aggressive, intelligent, charismatic leadership.

I was in the Congo when the first news of Angolan atrocities began surfacing through the accounts of refugees. I was especially persuaded by a missionary who had fled to Léopoldville from northern Angola. For eleven years Edna Stapleton of Watford, England, had run the mission hospital at Bembe. One dawn the whole area was attacked without warning by local blacks who bypassed her hospital and the Baptist mission and slaughtered every white on every farm in the district. Later, wounded rebels came to the hospital for treatment. She warned them she'd have to report to the authorities, and they understood this. Miss Stapleton was a good person who told a harrowing tale of the wounded rebels appearing at the hospital with their trousers inside out, which was how they identified comrades in the dark.

To the Portuguese, the fact that Protestant missionaries were not molested constituted evidence of complicity and collusion. Treating wounded blacks reinforced suspicions. More proof was seen in the fact that many of the rebels had been educated by Protestant missionaries. On the other hand, Catholic missionaries, who tended to be regarded as hand-in-glove with the Portuguese authorities, were attacked.

There were some grounds for Portuguese suspicions because even then missionaries were becoming involved in political and ideological actions—good intentions, questionable acts. The World Council of Churches, which was to blossom into an important source of propaganda and financial supporter of Third World terrorism and increasingly become an apologist for Marxist subversion (not to mention a de facto supporter of Soviet foreign policy), was even then active in secular and subversive politics. In 1961, the church was largely innocent in Angolan terrorism; not so a decade later. As usual with missionaries (Protestants mostly), discretion triumphed over valor and many fled to the Congo until the emergency eased.

Angola was clearly a potentially big story with repercussions for the whole of Africa, white and black. I was anxious to get there and see and feel the atmosphere for myself. But how? All journalists had been methodically kicked out. In the Congo I was so near, yet so far.

The leader of the main Angolan rebel faction at the time was Holden Roberto (an assumed name). This gentle, shy, soft-spoken leader of the UPA (Union of the Populations of Angola) was eventually to lead the FNLA (National Front for the Liberation of Angola), an anti-Communist organization that was the eventual loser in Angola to the Marxist MPLA (Popular Movement for the Liberation of Angola). The headquarters of the Angolan rebels in Léopoldville was a brightly painted orange and green stucco house in the African quarter. It was without electric lights but had a generator powering an electric mimeograph machine, which was in constant use pouring out revolutionary tracts. Roberto, who was the brother-in-law of the Congo's President Mobutu, and was handsome and something of a dandy, seemed a living contradiction to the blood being spilled so savagely. He discussed violence with sadness but determination. According to him, his movement had 50,000 fighters under arms, many of them deserters from the Portuguese army (which was mostly black).

While independence was the goal for Angola and Mozambique, Roberto stressed that the people were not yet ready for full independence; what was wanted was a change of government in Portugal and a more enlightened policy of education and preparation for eventual freedom. This reasonable, moderate view was—still is—unusual among African revolutionaries and terrorists. It was not difficult to sympathize with the aims, as stated, of Angolan blacks.

When I met Holden Roberto at his headquarters, I was only vaguely aware that troubles were erupting in neighboring Angola, which was clearly being influenced by events in the Congo. At the time, journalists who showed any interest in Angola were being "adopted" by Roberto and his UPA, and mock ceremonies would be held to indoctrinate any into the liberation movement. Tongue-in-cheek, Roberto pinned a UPA button on me and announced: "You are now an honorary member of UPA. Would you like to join us on our next raid into Angola?"

Although no entry visas were being issued, I had a secret weapon: a valid visa. A couple of months earlier, the Portuguese cruise ship, *Santa Maria*, with some 600 passengers on board, had been hijacked in the Atlantic by anti-Salazar Portuguese, led by a sixty-six-year-old buccaneer, Captain Henrique Galvao, acting as the proxy for General Humberto Delgado. This act of modern piracy for political purposes captured the imagination of the world, and for twelve days the *Santa Maria* eluded the British, American, and Portuguese navies. The Western media raced from port to port hoping to catch the ship. At one point when it seemed that the *Santa Maria* was heading for Angola to team up with anti-Salazar elements, I happened to be in Morocco trying to trace the illegal escape route that Jews were using to get to Israel via Gibraltar. I went to the Portuguese Embassy in Rabat and persuaded them to give me a visa so that I could be in Luanda when the pirate ship docked. The Portuguese consul, outraged over the piracy and anxious to have it exposed, took it upon himself to issue me a visa without consulting Lisbon. When the *Santa Maria* went to Recife in Brazil instead of Angola, I didn't use the visa. (Pirate Captain Galvao held a press conference on board the ship in Recife and declared: "We wanted to, and we succeeded, in proving Dictator Salazar is not invulnerable . . . we made him ridiculous before the whole free and Christian world.")

After the conversation with Roberto, I sent my usual wire to the *Tely* when I wanted to move fast: "Unless hear otherwise plan to go to Angola . . ." and boarded the Lisbon-Luanda plane when it landed in Léopoldville to off-load passengers. I was the only one to board the aircraft.

It was a Sunday and life in Luanda had slowed to a halt. I was regarded with some curiosity, but the visa was obviously real, so the soldiers and immigration people shrugged and felt that someone in authority wanted me there. Luanda is, or was, unbelievably pretty and picturesque. Not beautiful, because that's too grandiose.

It was more quaint, like an African Grandma Moses painting. Looking down on the city, one saw a deceptively tranquil sea of pink-, green-, blue-painted houses against a background of azure sea and impossibly blue skies. But the serenity and prettiness were less than skin deep: Luanda and Angola were unpleasant, dangerous, and explosive.

The city was filled with refugees who told horror stories, all of which were similar, all of which had a special twist or obscenity. The imagination of the terrorists knew no restraints. These refugees were not fanatics or cruel people, they were farmers, workers, lumber people. Tough, hard people, but not bad people. There was an anger and hurt in them that was palpable. The atrocities defied description—violence committed by Holden Roberto's rebels mixed with Marxists from the Soviet-backed (even then) MPLA. In one logging mill the white victims had been sawed in half lengthwise, each watching the one before him being sliced. Husbands were forced to watch their wives being raped. Babies were stuffed back into their mothers' wombs. Men were forced to eat the flesh of their children and wives. A mother was forced to eat the flesh of her child. Ritualistic ceremonies of eating the organs of the dead and Mau Mau-like obscenities were committed. Bodies were fed to pigs. There was no obscenity too vile for the terrorists to commit.

The nightmarish scenes that greeted the avenging Portuguese troops when they reclaimed these massacred districts resulted in savage reprisals. Misery was inflicted on the innocent and the guilty alike. Without proof or information, the army would overrun villages and in some cases all males were shot through the wrists, making their hands useless flippers. Villages were put to the torch. Napalm became the weapon of mass reprisal, and since the dry season was just beginning, vast areas became charred desert, with crops and wildlife destroyed and hunger and deprivation an inevitable consequence. Instead of intimidating black Angolans, the Portuguese military action had the effect of uniting the country against Lisbon and, curiously, weakening Salazar's hold on the Portuguese.

The rebels fought hard. Their leaders had persuaded them that they could be made invisible or immune to injury. They believed that red dye made them bullet-proof; after painting them, the leaders had fired blanks at them to prove their invulnerability. In subsequent attacks the rebels fought with a ferocity and disregard for their lives that amazed and alarmed the Portuguese.

Although the rebellion didn't reach Luanda, reprisals did. One white refugee thought he recognized an African as a terrorist who had bayoneted his child. He chased the wretched fellow. Others joined in and caught the black on the main street, literally tearing him to pieces like an overcooked chicken. Rather than attracting a crowd, the man's screams cleared the streets and everyone vanished except the gang of whites committing the atrocity.

On another occasion white farmers took a suspected terrorist to the top of the highest building—six stories—and threw him off. Another time, a black was dangled over the edge of the same building until the person holding him got tired and let go. The screaming man crashed through the striped awning of a sidewalk café to the pavement. A policeman sat at a nearby table, calmly taking notes. For a while any reprisal was tolerated and served as a safety valve for angry whites who might otherwise have turned against the Salazar government, which even then was entering its death throes although it wasn't realized at the time. The culmination of dictatorial repression would result in a coup in Portugal in late 1974 and the end of the last European empire.

The Portuguese blamed everyone except themselves and their own policies for the rebellion and uprisings. Frightened, they were by no means intimidated or cowed. Some 25,000 Portuguese troops—tough paratroopers, whose camouflage uniforms had earned them the nickname "leopard men"—were idolized and looked upon as saviors and heroes in Luanda. The liberal policies of Protestant missionaries, American and British support of self-determination and independence, plus rampant Communist subversion and agitation were variously blamed for the unrest.

The United States was also a prime target because it voted in the UN to have the situation in Angola investigated. Lisbon refused to permit UN investigators into the country. The week I was in Luanda, the American consul's car was thrown off the waterfront promenade. Another American had his car heaved into the sea and only escaped following it in when a quick-thinking friend persuaded the crowd that only the car was American; its owner was South African. He got apologies and handshakes instead of tar and feathers.

All this I absorbed in Luanda while avoiding reporting to officials and trying to meet select people who could be trusted. Being the only foreign journalist in Luanda, I was subject to constant interest by PIDE, the omnipresent Portuguese secret police, who were hated and feared by Europeans and blacks alike. I was constantly reminded at the hotel that I should check in with the foreign press office—which I swore I'd do, then didn't.

I went to see the sinister head of information services, Colonel Francesco Lucena, who was a dark, hawklike man with slicked-back hair and the flashing eyes of a Hollywood movie villain. He was in a perpetually bad mood, not so much because he had difficulty selling the virtues of his regime to the outside world, but because he was suffering from acute gout. His foot was wrapped in a bandage and propped on a stool.

He, too, was curious as to why I'd been allowed in, but evidently assumed that someone in Lisbon had approved of me as a "reliable" or "objective" journalist (that is, someone who was friendly to the regime and would regurgitate the official line). Colonel Lucena was frank. He boasted that Portugal would never surrender and would uphold the values of Western civilization even though Western civilization was craven and collapsing. "We Portuguese are not Belgians to run at the hint of trouble," he almost snarled. "And Angola is not the Congo. We shall not be frightened into fleeing. The rebels know this. For every atrocity we suffer, they shall suffer tenfold." He sounded like something from a Grade B movie.

Once started on a diatribe, Colonel Lucena was hard to deflect. Not much information was forthcoming, but lots of emotion and rhetoric with an intensity that was depressing and scary. His attitude was fairly representative of Portuguese opinion.

"Their atrocities prove the rebels, filthy people, are animals, so it is appropriate that we kill them like beasts," he went on. "They butcher whites and feed corpses to swine; they torture babies before the eyes of mothers, then kill both. They foul and disgrace the corpses." The UN, United States, Canada, Ghana, Liberia, USSR, Protestant missionaries, Communists, humanitarians all were involved in the plot against innocent Portugal and virginal Angola. I was glad when I escaped his outburst of undiluted meanness.

Most of the time I was followed in Luanda, not threateningly, just routinely. At night I'd get a couple of phone calls at ridiculous hours and as soon as I'd answer, the caller would hang up. I assumed that it was the police checking to see if I was out at clandestine meetings. I was into my fourth day when I was picked off the street and taken to the PIDE headquarters where my passport was confiscated. I was put in a windowless room without explanation for the rest of the day and told that I was in Angola improperly and was to be expelled.

"Why?" I said, not surprised, but appropriately indignant. "I have done nothing wrong."

A scrupulously polite man in a patterned sport shirt who was called "colonel" by his staff replied with menacing lack of concern, as if talking to a child: "Because you should not be in Angola. We do not want you in Angola, and we are going to get you out of Angola."

Feeling that one should squirm a bit before capitulating, I halfheartedly said something about this not being democratic and asked what was my offence.

"Your 'offence,' good sir, is your nationality and your profession. We like neither your profession nor your nationality." Angolan whites, like South Africans, were resentful of Diefenbaker's stand on human and African rights.

I said something about wanting to call the British Embassy, since there was no Canadian diplomatic representation in Angola.

"No," said the man. "There is no need for you to call anyone."

I "demanded" the right to call. He smiled sweetly and replied that I could demand anything I wanted, but it would be ignored. "This is our country, we are in charge, and no one has any 'rights' we don't want them to have. Do you understand?" I did.

I was kept in the room for the rest of the daylight hours and then taken back to my hotel in the evening with the admonition: "Please be sure not to miss your plane tomorrow, else you may stay in Angola even longer than you, as a journalist, may wish . . ."

A car picked me up in the morning and took me to the airport, where I saw Colonel Lucena. He gazed distastefully past me, no sign of recognition crossing his face. Was he there just to make sure I was leaving, or was it coincidence? I was put on a plane to Lourenço Marques. In Mozambique I was intercepted at the airport and expelled to South Africa, equally unenthusiastic about Canada in those days. In fact, the only ones pleased over the incident were me, because of my story, and the *Telegram*, which ran a banner headline about "Tely man expelled from Portuguese police state." The *Tely* always liked to have its correspondents seeming to be in dire circumstances.

Even at the time there was very little, except its physical appearance, that I liked about Angola. The tension was heavy, the whites adamant and unpleasant, the blacks bitter and sullen. One could feel it as a lost cause, partly because the Portuguese were also opposed to the dictatorship at home.

While scapegoats are always popular, even necessary for a government, the Portuguese accusations against the Soviet Union and Communists were not entirely unjustified. It is now known that the Soviets have been clandestinely involved in Angola since the early '60s, when MPLA members were trained in the USSR and Cuba and arms and cash were available through Tanganyika (now Tanzania). The Soviets cooled toward the MPLA in the early '70s when that body seemed loath to wage guerrilla war. Support revived after the 1974 coup in Portugal replaced the Salazar regime with a hodgepodge of liberals, Socialists, and Communists.

When it looked as if the Soviet-backed MPLA faction was not popular enough to win in Angola against UNITA (National Union for the Total Independence of Angola) and the FNLA, some 20,000 Cuban troops were secretly (at first) dispatched to Angola in 1975 to prop up Agostinho Neto as president. South Africa was helping FNLA and UNITA with the tacit agreement of black non-Communist neighbors and the quiet approval of the United States; however, demoralized and indecisive after defeat in Vietnam, the United States lost its nerve and cancelled its support. The South African military then retreated, although poised on the outskirts of Luanda and on the verge of conquering the MPLA. Ever since, a guerrilla war has been waged by Jonas Savimba's UNITA forces, which today dominate the Angolan countryside. MPLA increasingly is reduced to concentrating only on major cities.

President Neto went to Moscow for routine treatment of illness and managed to die on the operating table under puzzling circumstances that provoked suspicions of murder. He apparently turned out to be more Angolan nationalist than Marxist, and by questioning some Moscow directives he had outlived his usefulness to the Kremlin. Conveniently, he died on cue.

Ironically, South Africa still aids UNITA, but it is a marriage of convenience against a common Marxist foe. Once the alien Cuban army has been ousted and communism defeated, a UNITA-ruled Angola will likely find itself opposing the creed that keeps South Africa white and powerful.

14

No tabaccy . . . no hallelujahs

DANI TRIBESMAN
DUTCH NEW GUINEA, 1962

When people ask a journalist—as they invariably do—what his (or her) most exciting or interesting or dangerous assignment was, the journalist is hard pressed to answer. Each story is different, each similar in certain ways. Yet some experiences remain more precious, more memorable than others.

Perhaps the memory I treasure most was trying to cover the invasion of Dutch New Guinea by Indonesia in 1962, and the chance to visit the Stone Age culture in the mysterious Shangri-la-like Baliem Valley in the heart of the territory. Dutch New Guinea is now called West Irian, since the Indonesians won or were given control by the UN in 1963. New Guinea, the huge dinosaur-shaped island that geographically was once part of Australia and drifted loose unknown millions of years ago, leaving a big bite out of that continent, is politically divided down the centre. The eastern or Australian half is now independent Papua and one of the few "free" Third World countries, with a population of 3.3 million primitive people who still think airplanes are messengers of God. The 700,000 Papuans of the western half are not so lucky. When the UN ordered the Netherlands to turn over the territory to Indonesia, the natives lost their "free" colonial status and became "unfree" vassals, dominated by an alien Indonesian culture and military control verging on oppression.

In the Baliem Valley aboriginal tribes had only recently been discovered, and Dutch administrators and various Christian missionaries had moved in to begin the questionable process of civilizing the 50,000 or so Dani people, divided into perhaps a hundred tribes (and ten war confederacies). The goal was to bring them from the Stone Age to the atomic age.

174

To begin with, it was odd that the *Telegram*, despite its penchant for sending me to strange, remote places, would get excited about Dutch New Guinea. It was far away and world peace did not hinge on the outcome. But it proved once again that the media thrives on the exotic. Since this was a "new" crisis, editors everywhere were hopeful that it could be generated into a major crisis and sell lots of papers. I was dispatched to make the most of it.

Few will remember what it was all about, but Sukarno, the playboy dictator of Indonesia with no first, last, or middle name, only "Sukarno"—which in Indonesia was like being called "Charlie"— was trying to divert the attention of his people from the shambles he was making of independence. Indonesia itself was in economic and social chaos, whereas under the Dutch it had been the essence of prosperity. Sukarno was rallying his people against the so-called imperialistic colonizers, in this case the Dutch, and trying to juggle aid from the United States, the USSR, and any other state that could be conned into giving it. With his policy of "guided democracy," a euphemism for benign dictatorship, Sukarno fooled mostly Westerners into thinking he wasn't stage-managing a nasty little tyranny. He effectively turned the economic gold mine of the Dutch East Indies into a failure.

Charismatic and demagogic, Sukarno was also irresponsible and opportunistic. He managed the not-inconsequential feat of "allowing" the Soviets to equip his air force, the Americans to equip his army, and any who would contribute to build up his navy. An American military attaché once told me deadpan that if "we aren't careful Sukarno won't accept our military aid and then will become totally dependent on the Russians." There is a certain irony as well as immorality in the practice of appeasing petty despots so that they will accept your military aid instead of your enemies', thereby becoming dependent on your largesse instead of theirs.

It sounded as goofy then as it sounds now, but that's the way the modern world works. Perhaps the Americans were right because they seemed to win when the Communist Party of Indonesia overplayed its hand, overestimated its strength, and prematurely tried to take over in 1965, touching off one of the major bloodbaths of our times. The Indonesian army massacred every opponent who might be a Communist, Socialist, or liberal do-gooder. The toll reached about 150,000 although some say it was closer to 500,000. No one really knows. General Suharto replaced Sukarno—the same Suharto who was in command of Indonesian invasion forces in Dutch New Guinea in 1962.

Of course, there were neither historic nor economic reasons for Indonesia's coveting Dutch New Guinea, the world' second largest island—only political reasons. New Guinea's dinosaur shape is appropriate: it is probably the most inhospitable terrain on earth, with no roads, no resources, no prospects, but lots of pythons, crocodiles, mountains, and swamp. It was "home" to the Papuans, who were among the world's most primitive people. While many of them still longed to go back to head-hunting, the Dutch were leisurely nursing them toward self-determination. In fact, the Papuans and 20,000 Dutch got on famously, and both groups dreaded and despised the Indonesians, who falsely claimed the island as part of the Indonesian archipelago. It wasn't, having once been part of mainland Australia—which likes to pretend it is not an island but a continent.

In 1962, the UN was siding with the Indonesians because even then the Third World was never wrong and forever had to be appeased. Britain, the United States, Canada, and Western allies were aligned against the Dutch, who would have saved money by letting Indonesia take over the western half of the island (it cost them $30 million a year to administer). But they refused to be driven out in order to let Sukarno boast of his triumph; had he asked or requested the Dutch to leave, they'd have been gone as soon as decency permitted and as soon as they could conveniently betray their oath to support Papuan independence.

Australia supported the Dutch because it feared its part of New Guinea would be next on Sukarno's dance card—and it probably would have been except for the abortive Communist coup that put the pro-West Suharto in command. He was a bit rougher than the womanizing Sukarno and also more responsible and intelligent. Tension had built to the flashpoint in 1962 and Dutch Marines were calmly preparing to defend against Sukarno's invasion fleet, while in Djakarta and at the UN, bellicose anti-colonial pronouncements were uncritically swallowed by otherwise allies of the Netherlands. Delegations of Papuans were ignored or bribed by the Indonesians.

As it happened, Dutch New Guinea had recently been in the news because Michael Rockefeller, son of then-New York Governor Nelson Rockefeller, had disappeared while on an expedition in New Guinea and was presumed eaten by crocodiles—or Papuans.

So there I was, flying into Hollandia over masses of islands where, extraordinarily, there were said to be Japanese soldiers still hiding out seventeen years after the end of World War II. On one island, near the military headquarters of Biak, there were reports of two Japanese soldiers who periodically raided fisherfolk. Foodstuffs were left on the island for them since they were in bad shape and could not be coaxed into surrendering. Otherwise they did no harm. (Some ten years after the war, twelve Japanese who'd been living within walking distance of Hollandia were carried out by natives who were worried about their deteriorating health.)

Hollandia has one of the hottest, most humid, most uncomfortable climates on earth. It is a living stream bath. In 1962 the beaches and shoreline were still splattered with the rustling hulks of landing barges and tanks from the war. Palm trees grew out of some of them. There was a strange, ghostly feeling about the place—as if time had stood still.

I arrived on a weekend and was billeted at the transit quarters for Dutch officials high on a hill that hopefully caught any stray breezes. There were a handful of other journalists there on death-watch, mostly Australians. They were all going on a cruise to some of the islands for the weekend. Dutch authorities were nothing if not generous and anxious to entertain their exotic visitors. Every journalist had signed up for the tour. I was the only Canadian in the group, as usual, and arrangements were hastily adjusted so that I could join the cruise. All were excited as schoolkids about the excursion, which would involve lots of swimming, snorkelling, beach parties, seafood barbecues, and cold Dutch beer. Anticipation was heightened because there is nothing, but nothing, to do in Hollandia, the farthest outpost of the Dutch empire.

Since I had just arrived and had no feel for the place, I decided to forgo the excursion and instead to poke around Hollandia and write some color pieces: city of fear, nervous tension rising, armed camp, and all that. The next day I was regretting my choice, because while Hollandia was a pretty town of 20,000 inhabitants scattered over five hills, it was as drowsy and dull as a Scottish village. Having walked all over it, I was bored to tears and wondered how long I'd have to stay before moving on to Kenya, where I hoped to interview Jomo Kenyatta.

It was around 10 P.M. when Claude Belloni, the nervous, fussy Dutch information officer, burst into my room and announced that I should come with him immediately because the invasion had started. I pulled on trousers and we drove at breakneck speed toward the telegraph office in town. It seems that at Etna Bay

near the garrison town of Kaimana on the southwest coast, the
Dutch navy had intercepted the first wave of Indonesian torpedo
boats bringing troops ashore, with other landing craft behind.
Fighting was under way as we spoke. The Dutch had sunk two
torpedo boats, chased the invasion fleet away, and killed and captured some seventy Indonesian assault troops.

I was the only journalist in the world, foreign or otherwise, in
Dutch New Guinea at that moment who could get the news to the
outside. I set up my typewriter, the Telex lines were opened, and
I waited while Belloni paraded to me every official he could mus-
ter. I cross-examined the senior naval staff officer, Captain R. M.
Elbers, got a quote from the over-all commander, Rear Admiral
Liendert Reeser, got a pyjama-clad reaction from Governor Pietr
Platell.

"No, there's no question that it was an invasion," said the admiral. "They intended to land, raise the Indonesian flag, take over
the small garrison at Kaimana, and take fake photographs of
cheering Papuans, then disappear in the jungle while we committed thousands of troops to search for them. And all the time
Djakarta would make propaganda about the invasion. Of course,
the poor Indonesian troops would be sacrificed. But for Sukarno,
propaganda is all that matters."

In record time I had the story on the wire. It was 7 A.M. in
Toronto and mine was not only the *first* word of the invasion
("The battle for Dutch New Guinea has begun," I led off. "The
Dutch navy tonight intercepted an 'unknown number' of Indo-
nesian motor torpedo boats . . ."), it was the *only* story on the wires.

There was considerable nervousness at the *Tely*. "Do you suppose Worthington's into the coconut brandy?" asked the news
editor.

"Naw, he's not much of a drinker," said city editor Art Cole.

"Odd that the agency stringers have nothing—not AP, UPI, or
Reuters," said Charles Nichols, overseer of the news operation.
"Maybe he's overreacting."

It's one of the paradoxes of journalism that when newspapers
send their own staff to big stories, they prefer that their high-
priced help echo the general line of the low-paid news agencies.
That is, if their man's assessments or his facts differ from the
agency stories, the tendency is to assume their man is wrong.
Newspapers find it comfortable and safe to run with the herd.
Thus we have "pack journalism"—the hallmark of Fleet Street

especially. A story such as mine, which no one else was carrying, well, posed a dilemma that editors prefer to avoid.

"He's our man, he's done this sort of story before, and I think we've gotta go with him," said Doug MacFarlane, editor-in-chief.

So with more nervousness than any of them wanted, they blasted with a front page splash: "Dutch Repulse Invading Fleet" with the usual tag about "Tely Man" being on the spot.

Meanwhile, other papers put in calls to The Hague. My story was confirmed, and by the next edition every paper in the world had the story. It seems I had scooped the world, although I didn't realize it at the time. By evening all the journalists were back from their interrupted cruise, all composing responses to irate queries from their home offices about why they had missed the big story. I got a lot of dirty looks and clucked sympathetically and happily. Better me than them.

As it turned out, the "invasion" wasn't full-scale (that came later, after most of the press had departed) but a raid, probably for the purposes the admiral suggested. The next day we were allowed to interview the Indonesian prisoners ("not 'prisoners of war,' because officially there is no war," we were told). They were crim-inally young and frightened-looking children. Indonesians fared rather badly on these probes because the Papuans, recalling World War II, had a habit of appearing at Dutch administrative posts with little bags full of ears, hoping for a shilling per set. (During the Pacific war against Japan, Australians and Allied forces paid threepence, or a shilling, or whatever, for every set of Japanese ears the locals brought in.)

Flush after my small coup, I ran into a person passing through Hollandia who'd long been an idol of mine, Heinrich Harrer, author of *Seven Years in Tibet*, who was leading an expedition into the heart of New Guinea to climb the Carstenz range, highest peaks between the Himalayas and the Rockies.

Harrer was a former Australian ski champion and a legendary figure who had been interned in Calcutta at the outbreak of World War II. He had escaped and literally walked north, crossing the Himalayas on foot into Tibet, a feat of epic proportions that, had not Harrer done it, would have been deemed impossible for a lone man. He stayed in Tibet throughout the war and was tutor to the Dalai Lama, whom I later met at Dharmsala in India, where he had fled the Chinese. When I interviewed him, he seemed a lonely, attractive young man ravenous for company after being perpetually treated as a man-god. He remembered his tutor with affection and nostalgia.

Harrer and I immediately hit it off. He said he was flying into the Baliem Valley, which runs the wrong way in the mountains and had only been discovered a few years before. Did I want to climb mountains with him? Did I! Of course I did, but how could I? My nerve failed at doing a complete disappearing act from the paper to climb a mountain. I doubted the *Tely* would appreciate it. And I was certain my wife Helen wouldn't. From the start she hadn't appreciated my opportunities to visit crisis spots and revolutions. She was a journalist, too, and I had mistakenly supposed that she would understand that I could not say no to an assignment, even if I wanted to. While I tried to balance being at home with being on the road, it sometimes seemed as though I was always away somewhere.

I feel more sympathetic toward her point of view now than I did then, but just as my father had once warned my mother that the army took precedence over wife and family with him, so I guess I was implicitly saying that my job had priority over my family life. The marriage was on shaky ground, but I was determined that Helen, not I, would be the one to call it quits. Meanwhile, I answered the bell whenever assignments rang, never quite sure whether she'd be waiting for me when I returned. (I wonder now why our marriage lasted as long as it did.)

I went with Harrer to the Baliem Valley, unable to pass up an opportunity that rarely occurs in anyone's lifetime: to go back in time and see, meet, and experience firsthand, a genuine Stone Age culture. In such an environment, one's senses are constantly tuned to absorb every experience possible. What I found startling and depressing was the speed with which the missionaries had moved in. They must have some ecclesiastical radar that guides them to targets for conversion or Christian enlightenment.

First seen by white man in 1938, the Baliem Valley was forgotten and briefly rediscovered when a U.S. transport plane loaded with WACs crashed during the last days of World War II, killing twenty-three of twenty-six on board. They were rescued, and only then was it realized that this was a hitherto-unknown valley, some thirty-five by ten miles large at an altitude of 5,000 feet, and sandwiched between 15,000-foot peaks. It was everything the rest of New Guinea was not: temperate, fresh, with rolling plains, bubbling rivers. Little swamp or jungle. It was immediately dubbed Shangri-la, and then forgotten again. In the mid-1950s the Dutch set up an administrative post there, anthropologists pounced at the chance to study an aboriginal culture, and missionaries descended like avenging angels.

The people were so primitive that the twentieth century had no effect on them. It was a world of Alley Oop without clothes. Women wore a string across their loins and carried a net bag for odds and ends; the men were stark naked except for garish wicker penis sheaths, some of them three feet long and decorated. Until you got used to them, they made an astonishing impression. Bones through noses, white plumed heron and bird-of-paradise feathers, black pig grease, and white streaks painted on the body made the Dani very exotic sights indeed. They were not negroid but had almost Semitic features. They were short and wiry, had ferocious scowls, and grinned easily.

The Dani had stone axes and flint knives and had not yet invented pottery. They heated water by putting rocks heated in a fire into wicker baskets of water. The wheel was unknown and arrows were not feathered, wobbled in flight, and rarely hit their target; whenever an arrow killed a victim, it was assumed to have magical powers and was stuck over the door of the owner's hut to impart its magical powers to others. The Dani had no music, no art, no written language. Theirs was a culture based purely and simply on war and revenge. It was their religion, their creed, their purpose for living. And it was "war" that the Dutch and the church wanted to eradicate, and "war" that the anthropologists were determined to witness and record for posterity and sociological research.

The Dutch had a program of exchanging stone axes for steel hatchets—a leap forward of some 5,000 years. They outlawed war and this caused considerable unhappiness and disruption of life. When villages were told they could no longer go to war against each other, individual tribes put an imaginary line down the centre of their villages and one side fought against the other side. It was the only way for them to maintain their status.

And scores had to be settled. Recently there had been a massacre of six people in one village, and everyone knew that there would have to be revenge, even if it took ten years. Six people from the offending village would have to be killed. One man went on a rampage to kill those whom he considered "unnecessary." In the space of a few weeks he killed thirty-five people, mostly the very young and the very old. He viewed it as an act of service to the community. He was caught and could not understand why he was

sentenced to two years in jail in Hollandia. It was freely acknowledged that when he returned to the valley he would be killed by
fellow Dani—with thirty-five arrows shot into his body, one for
every victim. It was their justice.

If the whites were a source of interest and wonder to the Dani,
the reverse was also true. It was decided that the main chiefs of
the Dani people would be flown to Hollandia to meet the governor.
They would be fêted, given the royal tour, so to speak, and exposed to the wonders of civilization. However, the visit was a bust.
After being briefed about the importance of the governor, one
of the chiefs asked how many wives he had.

"One," said the startled Dutch official.

"Humph," said the Dani chief. "How many pigs then?"

"None; the governor doesn't need pigs."

"Hmmm. One wife and no pigs. He can't be such a big chief!"

What *really* impressed the Dani chiefs in Hollandia was a hard-
ware store whose window was filled with axes and knives. They
gathered in front to stare. "Now here is a man who must be
important," they said. "Only a very big man would have so many
axes."

Also, they were dazzled by the size of the ocean—and flabbergasted to learn that it is salty. They insisted on collecting salt water
in bottles to take home, salt being a sought-after commodity. The
visit did not have quite the effect the Dutch had anticipated.

Another mark of status among the Dani was self-mutilation. At
significant moments in their lives, women would lop off a knuckle.
A child dies—off comes the joint of a finger. A husband is killed—
off comes another knuckle. It was not unusual to see an old lady
squatting by a trail waving a pair of knuckle-less fists at passers-
by: great status indicating great suffering and prestige.

The operation itself was primitive. A woman (men were too
smart to go in for such nonsense) wishing to display her grief
would have the funny bone of her elbow sharply hit on a rock by
the medicine man; then, when mild numbness wracked the arm,
the "doctor" would put a honed edge of a stone axe on the joint
and, with the smack with another rock, lop off the tip of the finger.
So with fourteen joints per hand, there was room in a lifetime for
twenty-eight tragic or memorable events to be recorded.

It was from the administrative post of Wamena—a collection of
tin shacks around an air strip—that Heinrich Harrer was going
to lead his expedition into the Carstenz range, using the Dani as
porters. Seashells were their currency and were rare, because they

came from the coast or were left over from primordial times. Harrer had a large supply of them from California; they would contribute to inflation. One could leave cameras and equipment and money around, but Harrer's crates of shells had to be constantly guarded.

Throughout this period my Anglo-Saxon conscience was tormented with desire to go on the expedition into the mountains, yet I was unable to make the leap from "duty" to self-indulgence. Harrer was in the enviable position of using income from his last book to pay for the present expedition, which would produce the next book. I was not so lucky, and was only as valuable to the *Telegram* as my last published story.

The Dutch authorities in the Baliem Valley were conscientious, sensible, realistic people with a sense of humour and proportion. Karel Schneider, the district officer, was a tall, handsome man who lived there in splendid isolation with his wife and a couple of beautiful blond kids—who made a startling contrast playing with naked Dani kids, with their puckered-up, wise, and little old faces. Schneider commanded forty Papuan police brought in from the coast, and they were the law, the judge, the jury, the lords of the valley.

There were twelve missionary stations in the valley: seven Roman Catholic missions, four Christian and Missionary Alliance (CAMA) evangelical stations, and one Dutch Reformed Church mission. For all their efforts, none of the missionaries could claim a single convert. The Roman Catholic church was beautifully made of wicker matting and filled every Sunday with naked Dani eager to sing and chant. But none were believers. For them it was entertainment, something to do, fun. Father van der Stap was still ruefully chuckling over a recent incident that occurred when the weekly ration of tobacco for the Dani ran out, and the local headman refused to let his village come to church. "No tabaccy . . . no hallelujahs," he said solemnly. The priest claimed to have 20,000 parishioners, "but none are Christians yet. It will be years before they are ready to understand the power of God."

In one of the villages I entered the headman's hut, which was smoky and cramped, maybe three feet high and eight feet in diameter, with an upper platform on which the family slept in communal fashion. Hanging on the greasy, smoke-blackened walls were a string of intestines, a couple of pig jawbones, and an arrow that had killed someone and now symbolically protected the home. The chief reached up, grabbed a four-inch boar's tusk, and put it through his nose. I asked what he thought of our religion and he seemed confused and wondered, "How many gods do you Christians have?" I gave the conventional answer. If there was only one God, he wondered, why was there such competition among missionaries to woo followers? It seemed a valid question, and clearly the Dutch district official was delighted with it. Karel Schneider had no great affection for missionaries and took a jaundiced view of the concept of "converting the heathen."

Without any qualifications I found that the most disquieting and disruptive element in this Stone Age environment was twentieth-century religion. While there was no nonsense like trying to put trousers on the Dani men to replace their ornate and exaggerated penis sheaths or brassières or skirts on the women, there was an overwhelming feeling that Christianity had no place in this culture. It could only bring harm, division. The Dani seemed unaffected by the competition for their souls, though they slightly favored the Catholics, whose rituals and ceremonies they quite enjoyed though they found them incomprehensible.

The Evangelists also claimed no converts and would hold meetings with Dani and treat them to an old-fashioned fire-and-brimstone harangue. "But surely they wouldn't understand what you are talking about?" I asked Jerry and Darleen Rose of CAMA, who had a modern two-storey, Midwestern farmhouse and ate corn flakes—imported from the outside world—for breakfast every morning. Their naked Dani servants served meals, made beds, swept floors. The Roses had a good life, minus the companionship of their own kind. But the Lord's work evidently provided ample satisfaction.

"No, they don't understand what we say," said Darleen. "But we know that if we keep preaching, some will eventually be filled with the spirit of the Lord."

Husband Jerry added: "We do not believe in lowering God's message to their level, but hope the spirit of God will enter their souls and enable them to understand. So we continue to preach God's message without diluting it. Some day they will have faith."

Darleen claimed that some of the young people were already coming to understand and to believe. I had difficulty understanding, and ever since have wondered how a Stone Age tribesman can possibly comprehend the abstract imagery of God being the Father, the Son, and the Holy Ghost all wrapped up in one entity, and appreciate that a sip of wine is His blood and a morsel of bread His flesh. The Evangelists were determined to make headway in the Baliem Valley, despite the apparent futility and perhaps immorality of interfering with a working culture. They stopped Dani on paths, by streams, wherever, to preach fundamentalist gospel at them. As it was, the Dani exploited them, took what they could get away with, and considered them all mad.

The evangelical people bothered me most. Clearly, they had a lot of money, and in the midst of a very primitive society these missionaries lived bizarrely modern lives. I had breakfast at Jerry and Darleen Rose's farm and it was an unreal experience. It seemed a great luxury to have electric lights supplied by a windmill, a refrigerator, and milk cows grazing outside—all protected by an electric fence, which the Roses said was to keep their cattle in, but was more likely to keep the Dani out. The milk cows grazed serenely and were something never before seen in the Baliem Valley. The CAMA plane had flown them in.

Breakfast was served by a Dani servant, bone in his nose, penis sheath at the ready, naked as a jaybird. Afterward he put the food back into the refrigerator, washed the dishes, and became nanny for the Rose's two young children, who were thoroughly adjusted to the astonishing spectacle. All the missionaries lived like kings— or gods—yet they were irrelevant because the Dani people could not relate to them.

I was struck by the arrogance of a formal religion that feels compelled to impose an alien culture and creed on people whose lives were orderly and contented until they were told it was all wrong. The Dutch civil servants were far more concerned for the ultimate welfare of the Dani people than I felt the representatives of the professional religions were.

Yet while the administrators in the Baliem Valley were caring of Dani ways, their bosses in The Hague were not so understanding. The visit of the Peabody anthropologists, of which Michael Rockefeller had been a member (Rockefeller Foundation money was involved), had caused considerable disruption in the valley. The Hague had given the Peabody group permission to start a war and to film it—for scientific purposes, of course. Two villages were paid off in seashells (which immediately caused inflation and upset the economy) to fight each other.

It was an extraordinary movie, a genuine Stone Age war. The two sides lined up on opposite hillsides and huffed and puffed and stamped and shouted at each other, waved unwieldy fifteen-foot spears, fired unfeathered arrows, and went through a menacing ritual. Then about two hundred actually attacked and fought for a few minutes without much sense or direction. At the end there were about twenty casualties, perhaps five or six of them fatal. The families of the dead got extra seashells.

Karel Schneider was furious: his peacemaking work was undermined by his government. Afterward, chiefs of other villages would formally request that they be allowed to go to war, too, "and you don't even have to pay us!" By then the Peabody anthropologists had moved on. The movie of the prehistoric war is still occasionally shown on public educational television.

Heinrich Harrer went to climb his mountain without me, and we corresponded for several years. Then I lost track of him. I've often thought about the Baliem Valley and the wonderful Dani people, so warlike yet so kind, gentle, generous, always willing to take you into their smoke-filled huts. When the Dutch finally abandoned New Guinea, it meant that not only the Dani tribes of the Baliem Valley but the 700,000 Papuans along the coast were doomed to servility under the Indonesians. More victims of UN cowardice and expediency. The Dutch had been taking New Guinea gently toward self-determination and independence, but the Dutch were the wrong color, they were not Third World. The UN overruled the Dutch, it ignored the pleadings of the Papuans who feared, mistrusted, and disliked the Indonesians and knew they would never be allowed their freedom if they were delivered in bondage.

None stood beside the Dutch and for what was right. Not even countries like Britain, the United States, Canada, which should have known better, which should have had the courage to do the decent thing. But they didn't. They joined the herd. And so a people were lost, and have hardly been heard from since. What happened there did much to color my future attitudes on both missionaries and the UN. Not much has happened since to encourage a reappraisal.

Lord knows what has happened in the remote Baliem Valley. Are the missionaries still there? Have the Dani reverted to prehistory? Have Indonesians moved in? I don't know. I have never met anyone else who has been there.

15

My dear chap, these are the Himalayas . . . not an English garden

GENERAL PATHANI
NORTH EAST FRONTIER AGENCY
INDIA, 1962

The world was caught by surprise in the fall of 1962 when the long-standing dispute over the border between Tibet and India looked as if it might flare into a war between India and China. There was no excuse for the surprise. Tension had always existed over the legitimacy of the McMahon line (named in 1914 after the British negotiator Sir Henry McMahon) separating India and Tibet. Even then, China's crumbling Manchu dynasty, against whose authority Tibet was rebelling, had refused to accept the demarcation line and insisted that Tibet was rightfully subservient to China. And ever since the Communist regime of Mao Tse-tung had won power in 1948 and unleashed its People's Revolutionary Army to crush Tibetan independence, Peking had been making noises about renegotiating disputed frontiers—both along India's North East Frontier Agency (NEFA) and farther west in the remote area of Ladakh (Little Tibet), a large portion of which China traditionally claimed as its own. (China has also disputed its frontier with the USSR, and this has resulted in sporadic fighting over the years.)

Jawaharlal Nehru, India's first prime minister, was a gentle man with a stubborn streak, a convenient hypocrite who was possessed of an overwhelming reluctance to believe ill of any left-wing cause. Refusing to consider China's arguments as either serious or valid, he rejected Peking's efforts to negotiate the border, this despite a peace agreement (Pancha Shila) that India and China signed in 1954 pledging eternal peaceful co-existence and damnation to foreign imperialists. Instead, some time between 1954 and 1959, Nehru had secretly sent administrators and troops to occupy hitherto-uninhabited areas of NEFA and Ladakh—notably the

centre of Towang in NEFA, previously celebrated for being the
religious centre of Buddhist lamas.

When China launched another purge of Tibetans in 1959, aimed
at deposing the Dalai Lama and replacing the archaic religious
fervor of Tibetans with Marxist revolutionary ardor, the Dalai
Lama and some 13,000 followers took flight for the Indian border.
It was a pursuit the world followed mostly through the breathless
dispatches of Fleet Street jouralists, who resorted to such antics
as hiring planes to fly over the general Himalayan area and writing
stories of what they imagined it would be like for the twenty-five-
year-old Dalai Lama trying to keep a step ahead of the pursuing
Chinese.

The Dalai Lama escaped when the Chinese army unexpectedly
encountered Indian army posts along the McMahon line frontier
of NEFA. They were surprised, annoyed, and felt betrayed by
Nehru. Why was India violating tradition by occupying hitherto
neglected regions?

That was the year President Eisenhower paid a formal visit to
India and I went there to cover the event. I also took the opportunity to fly to Bombay, where I had a brief audience with the
Dalai Lama. Because he was required by his Indian hosts *not* to
make any statements to the press that the Chinese might construe
as provocative, I was not allowed to speak to him; so the story I
wrote had to create the *impression* that we were intimates, which
was somewhat frustrating and meant some poetic licence, leaving
a lot to the reader's imagination. I went to see him a couple of
years later in Dharmasala, when the pressure was off and he could
talk. It was an emotional and engaging experience. I felt very
sorry for the man-god without a job. His seemed a lonely life,
with no one to joke or relax with. He was always on stage and
being worshipped by followers who were convinced—as he presumably was, too—that he was the reincarnation of Buddha, supposedly born the precise moment that his predecessor died in
1933. For several years after the death Lamas scoured Tibet
searching for the child whose birth would roughly coincide with
the death and thus be eligible as the reincarnated god.

By 1962 the situation between India and China seemed about
to explode, and expert Western opinion was that the highly
professional Indian army, modelled after the British military, would
be a tough opponent for the Chinese. No Korea here. I went to
India for the *Telegram* in case fighting broke out. I interviewed
Nehru and he seemed genuinely puzzled and hurt by China's

bellicose posturing. He could not see that his proclaimed policy of nonalignment and nonviolence was already in shreds. While sanctimoniously preaching peace and pacifism like a latter-day Gandhi, he had unleashed his army to seize the Portuguese enclave of Goa and occupy hitherto-empty and disputed regions of the north. Nehru was as chauvinistic and nationalist as anyone. "When China feels strong, it tries to expand and increase its territory," he said by way of explaining China's actions. "When weak, it shrinks and loses territory. Right now it feels strong and is in an imperialistic phase." Not a very convincing argument, but the best he could come up with.

Clearly, Indian sentiment was on the side of the Tibetans, although by seeking refuge in India the Dalai Lama had embarrassed the Nehru government, which preached nonviolence but didn't hesitate to use force when it served its purpose.

The bulk of the world's press was poised in New Delhi, where the political story was, and where communications were straightforward. But the action—if there was to be any—would be in the province of Assam, immediately south of NEFA. It was there that the Chinese hordes would pour in, *if* they attacked, and *if* the Indian army failed to hold.

I headed immediately for Tejpur in Assam, the nearest large town to the frontier in the heart of the tea-growing district. Tejpur was something out of India's colonial past, a centre where the British tea-growers congregated, socialized, and did business— the administrative headquarters for the region. It was typically Indian and colorful, jammed with people, open store-fronts, unpaved roads, cattle wandering arrogantly and unmolested, wagons bumping along heedless of beggars, the blind, the deformed, the cripples, the holy men; a bustle of commerce, perpetual street noises, and the shrill babble of humanity.

I went to the Station Club, which rented out a few rooms, mostly to tea-planters or local Europeans unable to get home for the night. At the moment it was taken over by Fleet Street journalists who like to travel together, not so much because they enjoy one another's company or feel more secure in numbers of their own kind, but because they feel if they lose sight of a colleague and competitor, they may miss a story and get a rocket from home. Nothing worries a British journalist more than the possibility of a rival's getting an exclusive story, real or imagined. Mostly the Fleet Street's popular press write variations of the same story with a different slant—the *Daily Express* taking an up-the-Empire, phooeyon-Wogs approach; the *Mirror*, an anti-Communist, socialism-will-save-us approach; the *Daily Mail* somewhere in between; the *Herald* (before it blossomed into the bosomy *Sun*) a less radical, left-of-centre working person's paper, which, in the early days of the Russian Revolution, was partly financed by Moscow. And, of course, there was the London *Times*, aloof from the hubbub of popular journalism, stuffy and responsible and usually a day or two behind the breaking news but not caring. The *Telegraph* was the most conservative and balanced, albeit slightly dull and ponderous. And, of course, the *Guardian*, perhaps the most sanctimonious and self-righteous of the British press, so certain that its do-good, lib-left bias was absolute truth that it verged on intellectual corruption.

While the penny-dreadfuls chirped and maneuvered for angles, the *Times* consorted with generals and administrators and tried to do interpretive behind-the-scenes stories, quoting officials at length and analyzing their utterings. The *Guardian*, rich in snob appeal, ground its left-wing axes in the name of objectivity and greater truth and was the butt of ridicule among the dirty-fingernail press. In various travels I have found little to admire in the *Guardian* or in those who work for it.

I got the last bed at the Tejpur Station Club, and was warned that I would soon have to move because it was expected that locals would be coming in by mid-week. Outside the Station Club was an enormous tree, which during daylight hours was literally festooned with bats the size of small dogs, all hanging upside down and sleeping in the branches a hundred feet above the ground. At twilight it was remarkable to see this tree suddenly seem to shed its leaves as thousands of these large creatures, as if with a single mind, suddenly let go and flew off on their nocturnal activities.

As the crisis with China intensified daily, British tea-planters began moving into Tejpur from the countryside just in case there *was* an invasion. Other families began moving out. Locals took over the Station Club and journalists had to find other lodgings. I moved to the outskirts of town and took up residence in the home of missionaries at the Baptist hospital. The Europeans, or in this case Americans, had evacuated for the duration of the crisis and were glad to have Westerners occupying their homes while they were gone. Mattresses were laid on the floor and I shared accommodation with the *Time* magazine group. Edward Behr, who had once been a captain in the Garhwal Rifles of the Indian army, hoped to use these credentials to get special permission to visit the front. Larry Burrows, the great photographer with *Life* magazine—perhaps the best action photographer in the world at that time—shared our space.

I was trying to parlay my credentials as a former paratroop officer with the Canadian army in Korea into getting special treatment by the Indian army. Every day I'd tag along with Behr and go to nearby army headquarters where General Kaul, handsome and debonair, allegedly a ladies' man, was in charge of planning the defence of NEFA. On his strategy India's fate rested. We would press him for permission to go to the "front." Behr had an advantage over me, having served in the Indian army, but I had an advantage in having actually fought the Chinese. Remarkably, neither General Kaul nor the Indian army was much impressed by either of us, and our efforts to exploit our limited credentials infuriated our colleagues. From the Indians we got vague promises that they'd see what they could do, which was nothing, while other journalists seemed convinced that we were on the verge of gaining an advantage over them.

Meanwhile, panic was never far from the surface in Tejpur in particular and Assam in general. Rumours of an imminent Chinese attack were rampant and, as usual, the most susceptible to fear and panic were the missionaries, Protestant more so than Catholic. In virtually any crisis that I can recall, the faith and the dedication of Roman Catholic missionaries seems to sustain them more than does the faith of Protestants. In Assam the Protestant missionaries—mostly Baptists—were heading south, abandoning their parishioners to an uncertain fate if the rumors turned out to be true. Even the Baptist missionary doctor fled before a shot was fired, leaving patients to fend for themselves under the care of an Indian servant. While some of us journalists had relatively comfortable quarters as a result of the missionaries' flight, there was still disgust at the lack of moral commitment that would permit them to think of themselves first and their parishioners and their faith second.

It often seems that the more primitive and remote the missionary posting, the more questionable the Christian ethic. In Assam—as in New Guinea and Africa—the prevailing Christian creed seemed to be to destroy or undermine the existing culture and its spiritual core—then run for cover at the first hint of danger.

An exception to the rule was the Reverend Francis Wild, a Church of England missionary who had lived in Assam for thirty-

five years and would no more think of leaving in face of a Chinese
threat than he would, well, have considered denouncing the Queen.
British to the core, and made of sterner stuff than most missionaries, even in Assam, which was replete with characters, the Reverend Wild was considered something of an eccentric.

He lived in a rambling, overgrown house on the outskirts of
Tejpur and Derek Lambert of the *Daily Express* and I went to see
him one Sunday evening. It was like stepping through a time warp
into another era. His large living room, like an old-fashioned
summer cottage, was filled with bric-a-brac. The most modern
thing in sight were World War II posters of Winston Churchill
admonishing the world to hold firm in the face of Naziism. Wild
cheerfully acknowledged that he intended to die in Assam, be it
in two days, two months, two years, or twenty years, and it didn't
much matter to him whether it was from old age, disease, auto-
mobile, sacred cow gone berserk, or the rampaging Chinese army.

"The difference will be only a few years, so what does it matter
anyway?" he would say.

Wild was irrepressibly cheerful and would shrug when asked
about political matters like the war. "I know the Chinese and I
knew when they occupied Tibet that they'd come down here some
day. If it had worried me unduly, I would have left then. But it
didn't worry me then, and it doesn't worry me now. Besides, how
could I ever move everything I have here? Impossible. So I shall
stay."

In deference to his decision to remain, the Indian army had
rigged a special telephone line for him in case he needed to call
for help. Wild was loved and respected, even though the Indians
chuckled at his eccentricities. He wore knee-length blue shorts,
an open shirt, and a pith helmet. He usually travelled everywhere
by bicycle and explained that it took a little longer, but what was
the hurry? Lately he had given up the bicycle because there were
leopards in the area that seemed inclined to attack bike-riders.
While the Chinese army didn't intimidate him, he was not one to
tempt fate with leopards. He seemed apologetic over this un-
characteristic caution. The army had loaned him a Land Rover
and though he didn't drive it very well, he quite enjoyed the sport
of dodging pedestrians.

What Francis Wild was concerned with, far more than a possible
Chinese invasion or the unseemly evacuation of whites and his
fellow missionaries (he seemed mortified over what he saw as a
dereliction of moral duty to lead and provide an example to

parishioners, but didn't want to discuss it), was a game he had invented. It was a form of indoor tennis that could be played in any living room. He claimed to have a patent pending and we "gentlemen of the press" could perhaps help him to get his game circulated throughout the world.

Lambert and I were a bit nonplussed. We were more interested in local color and his views of India from the vantage of thirty-five years' residence. Did he know Gandhi, for instance?

"Gandhi? Gandhi's shot. Shot by one of his own. Misunderstood anyway. Now my game is the answer—anyone can play it, anytime, anywhere. It really keeps the blood circulating."

Would the people of Assam fight if the Chinese army invaded?

"Indians are always fighting. They preach peace but kill one another in various ways, from starvation to religious riots. What would really help them would be my indoor tennis . . ."

At first we thought he wanted to make money from his game. But no. He had no interest in money. He wanted to make the world fit, to give pleasure, to entertain. He insisted we try out the game. I was doubtful and wondered how we could possibly play in his cluttered living room without wrecking everything.

Wild cackled with glee. "You see! You see! That is precisely it! You *can* play in here with complete safety, get exercise, and cause no harm. That is the joy of my indoor tennis!"

He cleared a small space, stretched a net across part of the room, and then produced big rackets and a Ping-Pong ball. I forget the precise rules but we lashed, slashed, and lunged at the little ball, which zipped around and when it hit something, did no damage.

Prior to playing, Wild turned on an old-fashioned gramophone—one of the His Master's Voice variety, with a huge trumpet curling out. Like everything else, the records were antiques. He played records of Churchill's wartime speeches. There, in the twilight softness of an Assam evening, with rain beating on the tin roof, the missionary, two journalists, and his house servant bashed and chased a Ping-Pong ball around the living room while Churchill's voice echoed loudly that never in the history of human endeavour had so much been owed by so many to so few. On one wall overlooking our living room playing field was a framed bit of embroidery proclaiming "Jesus is the invisible and silent listener."

We finally stopped, exhausted, and had dinner. Wild was exhilarated. "You see, even you journalist chappies are weary. This game would make you splendidly fit. You could play in hotel rooms as you travel. Do you a world of good."

A delightful man, gentle, serene, but not your typical missionary. He didn't believe in rice-bowl religion—winning converts by feeding them or, in effect, bribing them to become Christians. He believed in education more than prayers, in personal example more than spoken words. He sought to help people and devoted himself to teaching Indians of any age, giving them knowledge, confidence. He didn't much worry about their souls and, in the process, won their hearts. Would that more missionaries were like the Reverend Wild.

The British tea-planters, being of more hardy stock than the missionaries, for the most part stuck it out. Word was that in a feat of precautionary zeal the Bank of India branch in Tejpur had filled a safe with gold and precious holdings and dropped it in the middle of a nearby lake for safekeeping. Small boats made furtive fishing expeditions to see if they could locate the safe, which probably didn't exist but certainly was a subject of considerable debate and constant fishing expeditions.

As more and more journalists descended on Tejpur and the crisis dragged on, the Indian army decided to take a select number of correspondents into NEFA, as close as they dared to the Tibetan border, where their troops were dug in, waiting to repel attack. The trip would take several days and we were to travel by Land Rovers. The day before departure a meeting was held among the British journalists who agreed that none of them would file stories in advance, thus giving all an equal break and a chance to relax without watching competitors.

Not being British, I wasn't invited to the meeting and, in fact, knew nothing about it. However, unknown to my Fleet Street pals, I was stringing for the *Daily Herald*. While the Brits were having their meeting and agreeing not to double-cross one another, I was busy filing an advance story to London about the war in the clouds. As it turned out, the *Herald* splashed all over page one my fabricated advance story about what it was like in the battle zone on the rim of the world. I wrote under the byline "John Steele" (their choice, not mine) and on our return to Tejpur there was a mild uproar among the Fleet Street types as to which one of them was John Steele and how come the *Herald*, which had no one in India, beat them all to the story? I kept silent and hoped it would blow over, which it did.

The Indians were frantically trying to improve an inadequate primitive road north through NEFA. Tibetan refugees and local Khampa tribespeople, the same stock as Tibetans, had been recruited to work. Dressed in colorful local costumes of mukluk-style leggings, red ponchos, and rawhide cowboy hats, they resembled oriental cowboys as they drove bulldozers or dug into the side of the mountain. Invariably they'd wave, grin, chat if they could, while the Indian army engineers remained sullenly aloof and reserved. The deeper into NEFA, the steeper became the road and the more forlorn the surroundings. Giant elephant leeches were said to infest the forest and elephants themselves were used to lug logs around for the roadbuilding. The Tibetans were proud of "their" road, which they boasted was the highest in the world, and resented its being used in the rain because it spoiled its appearance and left ruts.

The two-day trip to Se la—the 14,000-foot pass leading to the Tibetan border where the Indian army had assumed defensive positions—took two days. We spent the night at an Indian army camp halfway through NEFA where there was a lovely, gushing mountain river that could not safely be used because of something called the dum-dum fly, which breeds in running water, gets into the human body, and can prove fatal. Besides, the Indian army used the river as a latrine.

With Indian troops such as Jats, Dogras, Sikhs, Gurkhas, and paratroops around, it was impossible not to notice how British they were—brown Tommies, with all the mannerisms and quirks that make British-trained soldiers unique. Many officers were Sandhurst-trained, all of them Sandhurst-imitating. Senior officers were mostly veterans of Burma and the Eighth Army of World War II. All wore sweaters with rank badges on them, as Brits in the field do, and all tended toward military mustaches, swagger sticks, and, more recently, the large walking sticks that British officers had adopted during the Korean War. Noncommissioned officers had the bristling mustaches and the clipped manner of their British teachers. The Indian army was British to the point of taking morning and afternoon tea. The former took a bit of getting used to. We slept on the floor of what had once been a schoolhouse and as dawn touched the surrounding mountain peaks, a bugler sounded reveille and a pair of soldiers entered carrying a shiny new garbage pail of hot, sweetened tea, which they ladled into our mugs for a pre-breakfast wake-up. Very civilized, veddy British, even if a shiny garbage pail seemed an unusual teapot.

Basically, the visit by journalists was a propaganda exercise—or news-managing, to put it more politely—by the Indians to persuade the media of the justice of their cause. We diverted briefly at Towang to visit the High Lama and his gompa, or temple. Amid the stunning scenery and surroundings it was hard to concentrate on this gentle old (sixty-six) Abbot Phontso's tales of Chinese barbarism and his determination to resist regardless of what might happen. Giant prayer wheels spun good thoughts into the winds, and a huge thirty-foot prayer flag flapped in the constant breeze beside the temple, which resembled an inverted teapot. Lamas in wine-colored robes quietly played skin drums and it was Everyman's vision of Kipling and Kim. In spite of the High Lama's clearly rehearsed exhortations, his sincerity and genuineness were impressive.

The higher we got and the closer we came to the "front," the more confident the Indian officers became—and the more forlorn their troops appeared.

When our strange convoy reached Se la ("la" translates as "pass"), we really were in the clouds and there was a permanent chill in the air. Some of the correspondents were woozy from the altitude. I was wearing a short-sleeved shirt and a scarf, while the Sikhs of the Indian army were bundled to the eyeballs and huddled over small fires or clustered in trenches with blankets around themselves. Others had balaclava helmets pulled down, trying to keep warm. I have rarely seen such dejected troops, for so little apparent reason. What would they do when it got *really* cold? The weather reminded me of a soggy spring day in the B.C. coast range where I'd done a lot of surveying a dozen years earlier. We had a lunch of potato curry in the field with the senior officers of the division. When I found out that the troops were vegetarians, that explained to me why they seemed so rundown and lethargic. At high altitudes, apart from acclimatizing, which they hadn't had time to do, having proper nourishment is vital. Potato curry and vegetarian fare are not high-energy foods. Their Chinese opponents on the next ridge north (or behind their lines in the valleys, as it turned out a couple of days later) were eating snakes, lizards, and every other bit of protein available and were exceedingly fit. At the time I didn't see how dangerous the vegetarian diet might be, and was only puzzled at what I considered inappropriate and inadequate rations.

Looking from Se la north, one could see into Tibet—or what used to be Tibet, before the Chinese army moved in in 1950 and tried to tame the three million inhabitants of the Roof of the World. What happened in Tibet is one of the outrages of the twentieth century—not so much for what China attempted to do with its cultural genocide and physical and religious oppression, but that it was allowed to do so for so long with so little interest from the rest of the world. True, Tibet is remote and difficult for the media to cover and report on, but that's no excuse for ignoring it. Instead, it should be a challenge. The truth was always known from those who escaped, but as is often the case with lost causes, truth, justice, and decency were spurned.

We saw examples of it in Indochina *after* Communist liberation when the media watchdogs of Western democracies turned into lapdogs and chose not to see what was happening in Cambodia and Vietnam with massacres and "re-education camps" in remote areas that were in reality extermination centres. Were it not for the Boat People in 1978, the story might never have been told.

China's repressive policies in Tibet, which started in 1950, escalated in 1959 and steadily intensified through the '60s and '70s until, after Mao's death, moderation replaced extremism and the velvet glove replaced the iron fist. In Tibet, religion and culture have proved stronger and more resilient than unbridled totalitarian arms and reprisals. So far. The contest continues (does it ever really end?) but the tactics have changed. Neither the Chinese nor the Tibetans are likely to give up.

Our vegetarian field luncheon at Se la provided the only chance to mix and talk informally with senior officers of the division (in deference to security, we had agreed not to quote or photograph officers above the rank of lieutenant-colonel). The road bothered me: it was the single lifeline poking through NEFA on which the whole Indian defence strategy was based. I asked the commander of the division, General Pathani, what sort of Chinese activity was going on in the area and what he was doing about patrols and so on, in case the Chinese might try flanking movements.

The general looked at me with great patience and with what I interpreted as condescension—something the military (especially British-style military) likes to employ with the media and other inferiors. As assembled officers and fellow correspondents watched he replied: "My dear chap, you talk of patrols and flanking movements. Look about you. May I remind you that these are the Himalayas. You don't walk through the Himalayas as if they were a paved highway or an English garden!" The officers chuckled, and I blurted something about its seeming reasonable to send patrols out in case the Chinese might try the unexpected.

The general was indulgent: "Please, you let us worry about tactical measures. We are the soldiers, the Himalayas are ours, and we understand them. Please accept that we are doing all that is necessary. Any other questions? No? Perhaps we should move along . . ."

Thus ended my encounter with the general.

I was irritated and embarrassed. I recalled that in Korea we had assumed the Chinese could, or couldn't do certain things— and we had usually been wrong. Finally, we automatically assumed the Chinese troops could do *anything*, and were constantly prepared for the unexpected. That attitude helped make the Commonwealth Division in Korea one of the most formidable in contemporary history. However, I didn't have the nerve, or *chutzpah*, to lecture a general on the dangers of underestimating the Chinese. Prime ministers or politicians, maybe, but not professional soldiers!

We spent a day at the "front," then started the tortured drive back to Tejpur where everyone filed color stories and made arrangements to fly back to Delhi and relative civilization as soon as possible. That night the Chinese attacked, and immediately the whole defence of NEFA collapsed. The Chinese army poured south. India was rocked. The Western world was shocked. It was almost beyond comprehension. Second-guessing quickly took over, but at the time it seemed inconceivable that the vaunted Indian army could be such a fragile reed.

Even the Chinese were nonplussed. They, like everyone else, had accepted the prevailing mythology about the professionalism of the Indian army. Peking clearly didn't quite know what to do with its *Blitzkrieg* success. Instead of a timetable of several days to conquer NEFA, China had done it instantly.

It seems that while we journalists were standing on the mountain border overlooking Tibet, the Chinese army was already behind us, infiltrating through those Himalayan passes as if, to paraphrase the Indian general, they were "a paved road or an English garden." Simultaneously with their frontal attack, the Chinese attacked from behind the Indian positions. They cut off the road, occupied the main town of Towang, and swept onward to halt on the fringes of the plains of Assam. It was a military triumph of awesome proportions considering the terrain. NEFA turned out to be the Maginot line with an Asian slant. The Chinese simply went around the obstacles. I, of course, thought of my brief conversation with the general, and recalled in the *Telegram* his words—without naming him, as per the agreement. As far as I knew, he was by now killed or a prisoner.

It was the same story in Ladakh, where the Chinese now occupied the 50,000 square miles they claimed as historically theirs. Forgotten now were earlier Chinese offers that both sides withdraw twelve miles from their positions, leaving a buffer zone, and India's counterproposal that both sides should withdraw to previous positions, restoring the status quo. The Chinese held all the cards—too many cards, in fact, for now there was nothing to negotiate and *if* China was not intent on a full-scale invasion, it would mean a unilateral withdrawal and imposed truce or peace terms. Indian humiliation was complete.

The totality of the Chinese victory and the completeness of the Indian army's collapse do not mean that some Indian units did not fight valiantly. There were isolated examples of Indian heroism, such as the platoon of Sikhs at Bumla Pass in NEFA. Thirty-five men held off attacking Chinese for twelve hours until, ammunition exhausted, mortarman and champion wrestler Bahan Singh, rather than retreat, leapt from the trench and charged the advancing enemy empty-handed. What was left of the platoon followed his example and charged with him. The Chinese, startled at such lunacy, suspected a trick and retreated. I spoke to Sepoy Singh later and he provided the colorful quote: "My God, sir, my blood won't sleep until I get a chance to fight them again."

The effortless victory posed a dilemma: what would the Chinese do next? Their schedule had been disrupted by their successes. Would they attack Assam? Try to conquer all of India? Incorporate NEFA into China, as they had Tibet? What?

Indian propaganda was in high gear, humiliated but unbowed. The country was united by necessity, and government admonitions that they were prepared to fight to the last sepoy were popular morale-builders. The Indian Communist Party was in disarray and disfavor and keeping a subdued profile. Indians were encouraged to donate gold and jewels to the war effort, and perhaps the most poignant sight in India occurred at Nehru's New Delhi residence every dawn. People—the poor and bedraggled, the affluent and powerful, the ordinary and working class—would stream in to dump jewels, coins, rings, whatever they had, in a large pile on Nehru's lawn while he and daughter Indira and others of his family would mix and chat with them. It was a wonder of humility, love, patriotism and democracy. Nehru *really* did belong to the masses.

What I remember most from my pre-invasion interview with the Indian Prime Minister was a large rat scurrying unnoticed (except by me) from corner to corner in his office. My questions were basic and easy, but Nehru seemed to relish the opportunity to ruminate. Almost detached from the present, as if in another world, he pondered the "whys" of China's actions. He recalled India's solidarity with China at the 1954 Bandung Conference and mentioned how loyal he'd always been to the concept of China's independence and autonomy. He was deeply hurt by what he saw as China's aggression and humiliated and frightened by India's failures. Already the suave, polished General Kaul had been fired—the fate of most unsuccessful commanders.

"I suppose we shall now have to spend more on our military," Nehru said more to himself than to me. "We shall have to become like other countries, maintaining a large military force. It is a great pity. Why would they do it to us? It escapes me. We are not their enemies. Why do they behave like this? Who knows what goes on in the Chinese mind?"

Comments to me in that earlier interview applied to the present situation. "What is happening is a Chinese trait rather than a Communist one. The problem is now to figure out what territory China feels is hers."

I felt sorry for Nehru. I recall his being startled out of his monologue by division bells ringing, which signalled a vote in the House. He told me to wait while he went to vote and I said something about hoping his side would win. He allowed himself a gentle smile: "My side *always* wins the vote." He straightened his wedge cap and scurried off. I sat drinking tea and nibbling a digestive cookie. The rat appeared in the corner and we eyed one another warily.

Nehru never fully recovered from the shock of China's invasion, and some eighteen months later he died at age seventy-five. Although India had tended to side with China against the USSR prior to border disputes with Peking and had shifted back toward the West after Nehru's disillusionment, it now shifted further into the Soviet orbit. Little has happened since to change the direction.

In November 1962, after occupying NEFA for eighteen days, the Chinese were not sure how to exploit their unexpected military successes and unilaterally withdrew to their original positions. They hinted that unless India observed a neutralized buffer zone, the army would return. India got the message. In Ladakh, on the other hand, the Chinese kept their conquered territory and the border road that they had secretly built. Thus ended Nehru's experiment in nonalignment.

China's withdrawal turned the military exercise into a diplomatic triumph. Whoever said that military force proves little? In fact, it proves everything. Without military strength and resolve, diplomacy is bankrupt and relies only on good will and trust—with maybe a touch of deceit. Fine for friendly, democratic countries; fatal in dealing with bullies, be they in international arenas or beerhalls or schoolyards.

Bob Nielsen, the Toronto *Star's* London correspondent, was in New Delhi and we cooperated as much as rivals can. He was fairly left-leaning at that time, having studied under John Kenneth Galbraith while on a Nieman Fellowship. (Galbraith was then U.S. ambassador to India.) Nielsen has a nice sense of humour and we later went through a portion of the continuing Algerian bloodbath together and consequently felt the sort of bond that is common among overseas reporters. In later years Nielsen was to shift from left-wing to common-sense centre. He thus became odd man out with his Toronto *Star* employers, who gave him early retirement.

In New Delhi, Nielsen and I went to see the Canadian High Commissioner, Chester Ronning, who was decent, cordial, and very generous with his time. He was also remarkably frank. At the time I didn't completely understand the full ideological thrust of Ronning, who was generally regarded as left-wing radical in his views. As opposed to most of the Western diplomatic community, which professed to think that China was war-mongering and on an imperialist kick, Ronning was quite pro-Chinese and tried to understand Peking's actions and put them into perspective. From this viewpoint he may have seemed anti-Indian, but in fact made more sense than most.

From my basically uninformed position, his analysis of the crisis was plausible and convincing. Without quoting him (a condition of background briefings), I incorporated his assessments into my stories. In fact, the Chinese *did* have a case, and China's subsequent actions underscored its sincerity. Peking was *not* land-grabbing but trying to rectify history—*its* history. I was later to vigorously disagree with Ronning's view of the world as it pertained to Vietnam, China, and the United States in the '60s and '70s, but in the border war between Indian and China, he was perhaps the best informed and most enlightened of all Western diplomats. He was, in fact, the local oracle in the matter of trying to comprehend "why" the Chinese had invaded.

The Indian-Chinese border war never got the massive publicity it deserved—not because it wasn't important, exciting, or newsworthy, but because it was overshadowed by another crisis that captured the spotlight. In the middle of the war the Cuban missile crisis erupted, when President Kennedy went head-on against Nikita Khrushchev because the Soviet Union was secretly installing missiles in Cuba. The threat of a nuclear showdown captured all the headlines. By comparison, the events on the other side of the globe were minor parochial irritations—and being immersed in *them*, I missed most of the tension and drama of the missile crisis.

I didn't enjoy India. Too many people, too much religion, too much rigid tradition, and an immovable caste system. And too much self-righteous hypocrisy. It was hard to see any hope for an impoverished subcontinent where people starved while sacred cows strolled the streets and monkeys could eat with impunity the grain that humans desperately needed. While most of my journalistic experiences have involved various forms of tyranny and despotism, India has always struck me as being one example of a country in which a benign despotism might better serve the majority of the people than a democracy in which a million people a year are allowed to starve to death. Just flying over the land reveals human habitation as a blight, a cancer on the surface of the earth. And a stroll through the heart of, say, Calcutta reveals the full hopelessness, not to say helplessness, of the country. By comparison, Africa seems a beacon of human hope.

16

Shoot first—pray later

FATHER HOA
MEKONG DELTA, VIETNAM
DECEMBER 1962

In his autobiography, *Chronicles of Wasted Time*, Malcolm Muggeridge described how a year of working as the Manchester *Guardian* correspondent in Moscow cured him of his left-wing, pro-Soviet tendencies.

He went to Moscow in the early 1930s with impeccable leftist credentials: as well as representing the then-pro-Soviet *Guardian*, he was the nephew of Sidney and Beatrice Webb, the most famous fellow travellers of their time. He was welcomed by the Soviets and given those special perks and privileges which are available to favored journalists and "guests" of the Soviet state.

However, Muggeridge was not the usual foreign visitor to the USSR, nor was he a typical journalist (unlike, say, U.S. Ambassador Joe Davies, who went to Moscow in 1936, vaguely right of centre politically, and left in 1938 believing that the purge trials were genuine and that Stalin was grossly misunderstood). Muggeridge increasingly fell into disfavor with his newspaper, the British "intellectual" left, and Soviet officialdom. His sin was writing what he saw and felt was true, regardless of the conventional wisdom and herd emotion of the moment. For instance, he was one of the few who recognized that the 1932-33 famine in the Ukraine, which killed some seven million people, was Stalin-sponsored. Others, like the New York *Times*'s Walter Duranty, not only could not see, but did not *want* to see and denied what was happening. Today that Ukrainian famine is infamous as perhaps the *only* example of a famine deliberately created to control the people. And the world missed it, except for a few journalists and newspapers who were consequently branded cranks and extremists for reporting it. Ironically, though he fell from grace with the liberal left, Muggeridge found that conservative elements were still reluctant to trust him.

When Muggeridge left Moscow and the *Guardian* and went to work as a free-lance writer in Switzerland, he was strapped for income and abandoned by erstwhile left-wing friends and supporters because of his awakening to ideological reality. In a poignant passage of his autobiography he notes that he had a much harder time making ends meet as a conservative writer than as a socialist or left-winger; there was far more money to be made as a left-wing writer since the left looks after its own and makes sure that ideologically acceptable articles get published. No one ever starved for supporting the left. As he put it: "In the leftist legend of the thirties it is usually assumed that attacking the Soviet regime was made temptingly lucrative, whereas supporting it involved penury and perhaps martyrdom. For the most part, precisely the opposite was the case; most of the best-selling writers about the USSR were strongly favorable . . . whereas antagonistic works were difficult to get published and sure to be knocked or ignored." Even George Orwell had enormous difficulty finding a publisher for *Animal Farm*, one of the few genuine classics of our times that graphically shows the world moving toward collectivism, a world in which the only truth is slogans, the only duty is conformity, the only morality is power.

Things have changed only in degree from those days. One need only to examine bureaucratic media organizations such as the Canadian Broadcasting Corporation (modelled on the BBC, which in turn was the model for Orwell's Ministry of Truth in his other work of genius, *1984*) to see the network of ideologically and politically compatible "friends" helping and protecting one another. In varying degrees, most media outlets reflect the syndrome, even though officially they deny it.

I first encountered the syndrome in a small way when I went to have a look at the war in Vietnam after covering China's brief but successful invasion of India in 1962. I spent a month or so there—enough to get a feel for the place and to reach certain conclusions. But no one paid much attention to Vietnam in those days. In fact, my series in the *Telegram* appeared under the now-ironic logo "The Forgotten War." The Americans were known officially as "advisors," even though there were 10,000 of them in Vietnam and they were virtually running things. The press (Saigon was filled with permanent and transient correspondents even then) was more or less faithfully, lazily, and unquestioningly following the Pentagon line that the war was on the verge of being won, and certainly would be by the following fall.

The two main journalist hotels in Saigon were the Caravelle, the most modern, where everyone who was anyone stayed, and the Continental, which was across the road and cheaper, and where the overflow from the Caravelle went. I was in the Continental, and in some ways it was more satisfying. It had a large colonial verandah, tired fans on the ceiling slowly churning the moist air and a more exotic atmosphere. I felt closer to the street and the sounds of the city.

Even then Saigon was a seething cauldron of corruption and self-interest. I quickly made contact with the Americans and arranged to go to their helicopter base at Soctrang in the Mekong Delta, where the war against the Vietcong was fairly intense—though nothing like it was to become. I was to go on missions and try to get a feeling for a war that was "officially" being won, in spite of the fact that the government forces, the good guys, controlled only 20 percent of the countryside.

Prior to going to Soctrang I was anxious to get a wash-and-wear suit of clothes, which I felt would be ideal for travelling. Saigon was famous for its bargains, especially since the black market exchange rate for foreign currency was such that you could not afford *not* to buy imported goods. Clothes in particular were cheap because the tailoring depended on human labor—the one thing there was an abundance of in Saigon. I negotiated a made-to-measure suit for $25 and arranged to pick it up when I returned from the field. Had I wanted, it could have been made overnight.

The other business I felt some urgency to deal with was changing money on the black market—at two or three times the official rate. I had found that I could generally keep travelling from crisis to crisis as long as I didn't have to ask for more money, which inevitably would result in a recall. I could always justify expenditures later when it came time to mollify accountants with expense accounts. By that time it was a bookkeeping matter and of little importance. I'd take as much as I reasonably could on leaving Toronto and then travel as cheaply as possible, change money on the black market, and stretch out the funds. Canadian newspapers don't have the large circulation necessary to support many permanent foreign correspondents, and the *Tely* in those days was the most ardent practitioner of fire-brigade journalism. Sending someone from home office to cover a particular crisis was cheaper and enabled maximum coverage.

On my last day in Saigon before heading into the wilds of the Mekong Delta and the Vietcong, I strolled casually along Tu Dai Street waiting for the inevitable money-changers to strike. Sure enough, a small, skinny, disreputable man in an overlarge sport shirt that hung down to his knees appeared at my elbow and asked how long I planned to be in Saigon. I saw no point in telling him the truth and said I was leaving the next day—which was partly true. I neglected to say I would be returning. Glancing furtively around—money-changing was illegal—he nervously asked if I wanted to change American dollars. I brushed him off and showed only moderate interest—setting the hook, so to speak, to get a decent rate. The greater my interest, the lower his rate. We haggled a few moments and he mentioned a rate of exchange that was surprisingly high. I said okay, I'd change $100.

He then bristled into action and, mixing business with super-caution, looked hastily in all directions and hustled me up a side street, somewhat against my instincts. Periodically glancing everywhere and muttering about danger and police, he'd leap into a doorway and begin laboriously counting out piastres. Then suddenly taking fright that we might be watched, he'd bundle the money under his shirt, we'd dog-trot to another secluded doorway, and he'd start counting again.

Again he'd stop, look anxiously in all directions, mutter that we had to be careful, and we'd dash off to another doorway. I was growing impatient and scornful of what seemed excessive caution. Still, I, too, was uneasy. Did he know something that I didn't? After all, it *was* his city and he presumably knew what he was doing.

I finally told him: give me the money and we get out of here, or we forget the deal. Reluctantly he agreed and I seized the bundle of Vietnamese bills, shoved it in my pocket, and we beetled off in our respective directions.

I went back to the hotel to count my bundle and, lo, discovered I'd been trapped by the oldest game in the world (well, second oldest). Rather than a good rate of exchange, I'd gotten lower than the official rate. The fat wad of bills had big denominations on the outside, small stuff on the inside that got even smaller as I counted down. I was angry and mortified at being so naïve, but there was nothing I could do about it. It was even humorous, in a way: he had pretended to be so nervous that he made me anxious to be out of there.

Soctrang, the base where I was heading, was the starting point for ambushes and raids and reinforcements all over the delta. Perhaps two-thirds of the country's fourteen million people lived in the delta, which in peaceful times was the ricebowl of Southeast Asia. The most common complaint of the 10,000 American advisors in South Vietnam was that they couldn't order the Vietnamese military to do anything, but had to suggest and advise that they take certain actions. And there was always the oriental problem of "face" to worry about. The Americans felt that if they could order the Vietnamese to do certain things, the war could be won quickly. (They were to get their chance later, and it didn't work either, but that was ten years away.) The prevailing belief was that since American advice was rejected or altered as often as it was accepted, the war would take longer to win.

Still, few doubted eventual victory, especially since the Vietnamese had recently adopted a tactic that had been so successful in fighting the Communist insurgents in Malaya: strategic hamlets. This was the ploy of making isolated villages virtual strongholds, walled and bristling with guns at night and surrounded by a moat with sharpened stakes at the bottom to impale anyone trying to cross in a night attack. The Americans and the Vietnamese were very proud of these strategic hamlets yet the rebels, or insurgents, still controlled 80 percent of the countryside at night and 20 percent by day.

The Americans had another secret or not so secret weapon: the Special Forces, or Green Berets, guerrilla or commando units that went into the countryside and took the war directly to the enemy, organizing locals to defend themselves. The Special Forces were not widely advertised then—John Wayne hadn't yet discovered them, and vice-versa. They were the American version of the British Special Air Services (SAS) and the Chindits of the Burma campaign of World War II. Good, but not as good as they thought, or their publicity and press clippings later pretended.

I did the rounds with the Americans for a couple of weeks. I went on helicopter raids and once found myself put behind a helicopter machine gun and told to cover their assault if they were fired upon—questionable behavior for a journalist, but perhaps understandable when your life may be threatened and those you depend on for safety are few in numbers. One does not get overly righteous in dicey situations. Repeatedly, we flew Vietnamese troops to mount surprise attacks, few of which surprised anyone. Or succeeded.

Our helicopter troops once captured a couple of Vietcong: two

skinny kids with a homemade bomb. We flew them to a Vietnamese unit for imprisonment in a compound, the pair trussed with
telephone wire like chickens for the market. Hands were wired
behind their backs, and the wire at their ankles was looped over
their necks so that they lay on the floor of the helicopter arched
back like gymnasts. If they stretched their legs, they'd throttle
themselves. It was harsh, but not as bad as the sadism, cruelty and
hate that was to come. At the time only 60 Americans had been
killed, yet the South Vietnamese casualties were some 500 a week
killed and 1,500 wounded. Or so it was said. Casualty figures
couldn't be trusted, especially estimates of enemy casualties, which
Americans for some inexplicable reason seemed to gauge by the
number of rounds fired.

One could be impressed and depressed by Vietnam at the same
time. I found, for example, Father Hoa, a Chinese Catholic priest,
an inspiring character. Known as the pistol-packing padre, he had
once commanded a Chinese infantry battalion after the war and
had opposed *both* Mao Tse-tung *and* Chiang Kai-shek. Ideologically, he was neither Communist nor anti-Communist; he merely
wanted to be left alone. When Mao won China, Father Hoa did
not want to remain in that society of ants, nor did he relish living
on Taiwan under Chiang. So he led 1,000 people out of China
into Cambodia. In 1959 he came to Vietnam with 200 devoted
supporters. The fifty-four-year-old priest had an ardent parish of
local villagers and had also built up a personal army of 1,800 men,
women, boys, and girls to fight the Vietcong.

He was a colorful showpiece for the Americans, who helped
him with supplies but otherwise left him alone. South Vietnam
president Ngo Dinh Diem, the Vietnamese nationalist who got his
start by fighting pirates and corruption, but who'd been corrupted
by power himself, called Father Hoa "my fierce sea swallow who
picks Communists out of the rice paddies as the sea swallow picks
bugs off the rice crops."

When I landed by helicopter in Father Hoa's warlike village-
turned-strategic hamlet, he was wearing a helmet and had a revolver belted around his cassock. He spoke in imprecise, exuber-
ant English—everything eminently quotable. "I have run for the
last time," he said as we shook hands and he, incongruously, returned the salutes of civilians and Vietnamese soldiers. "I am
fighting for these people; I am fighting a godless system; I shall
only stop when I am killed." His assistant was a curvaceous young
Vietnamese girl, armed to the teeth with bandoleers, pistols, knives,

and somehow seeming sexier and more feminine in battle garb than she would have been in a *cheongsan*.

Father Hoa's office was a blend of command post and confessional. Battle maps were mixed with crucifixes, Bibles, and ammunition. On a shelf were eight silver trophy cups of various sizes, ranging from egg cup to Stanley Cup. Whenever someone killed a Vietcong or performed with valor, he (or she) had a photograph taken with a cup of the appropriate size for the deed being honored, and then the cup was returned to the shelf for the next winner to be photographed with. The photos were a form of medals and decorations for valor.

Father Hoa's village was mostly under water, a Venice of the Mekong, with little bridges everywhere and raised walkways and boats going from stilted house to stilted house. There was the stockade and the general store amid a mortar site. The stockade walls were made of mud topped with barbed wire and needle-sharp bamboo spikes. Father Hoa's motto was "Shoot first—pray later." He was unusually successful against the Vietcong, who left him alone and concentrated on harassing more vulnerable villages.

Sunday school for the kids was accompanied by rifle practice. The Old Testament's Joshua was Father Hoa's inspiration, and there was no turning the other cheek in his religious interpretation. Yet he was deeply religious and radiated compassion and affection that his flock clearly identified with.

Even in his aggressive parish, Father Hoa estimated that the Vietcong dominated 60 percent of his area of 25,000 peasants— better than the 80 percent elsewhere, but still not very encouraging. He had three compounds of Vietcong prisoners: hard-core Vietcong, women, and the less fanatic who, if they could persuade him of their conversion, would be released, incorporated into the village life, and given plots of land of their own. He had surprising success, even though those Vietcong who joined him became targets for Communist reprisals and atrocities. Exposing the prisoners to village life and prevailing attitudes and letting them see for themselves did more to persuade them to join him than any political indoctrination or intimidation. Undeniably, the followers of Father Hoa were content, proud, and reasonably prosperous.

He called himself a "cheerful pessimist" and insisted, "One should never be afraid to fight for what is right, no matter what the odds." In the light of history, his was a lost cause. "The Vietcong," he said, "are like the tide; they rise and they fall, but they always keep coming. They will win someday, and it will be bad for Vietnam, but I shall keep fighting with God's blessing." With more Father Hoas, Vietnam might not have been lost.

When I returned to the fleshpots of Saigon after being in the field with the army for a couple of weeks, I felt, in a small way, the combat soldier's contempt and disdain for those who are in the rear echelons. Being in the company of fighting men is somehow cleaner, more decent, than being in the company of those who profit from war or who don't share the dangers of those at the front.

When I got back to the Saigon military base, dirty and sweaty, I dropped in to see General Joe Stillwell, son of the late, great Vinegar Joe of China fame. Young Joe commanded U.S. forces in Vietnam. As a lieutenant in Korea I had known him when he was a colonel in command of a neighboring regiment. Before that, he was a frequent visitor to our home in Vancouver when he was U.S. liaison officer to Pacific Command and my father was general officer commanding there immediately after World War II. His father and mine had been mutual admirers, both endowed with salty outspokenness and fierce integrity.

In Saigon the orderly officer took one look at my somewhat disreputable condition and was loath to even take a message to General Joe. The idea that this apparition might be a "friend" of the general taxed credulity. Yet something made him pause. With Young Vinegar Joe, as with Old Vinegar Joe, you just never knew. The spit-polished young officer sent the message in to the general's adjutant while I shuffled uneasily before the disapproving eyes of officers and men, wondering if perhaps I hadn't erred. Almost immediately the door burst open and out rushed Joe Stillwell. Without breaking stride he embraced me and began reminiscing at the top of his voice about Korea and British Columbia, taking the whole orderly room into his conversation.

There was enough ham in Stillwell to enjoy the moment. He invited me to Christmas dinner, volunteered a staff car to take me in to Saigon and put his aide-de-camp at my disposal. He then launched into a eulogy about the war in Korea, how battle-tough the Princess Pats were and how American troops could learn a thing or two from them. I'd been battalion Intelligence Officer the night the neighboring Royal Canadian Regiment had been attacked in the spring of '53, and as soon as dawn broke Joe Stillwell had come over to see how bad things were with us and to breakfast in our trenches. He told his orderly room an exaggerated tale of how he and I had shared a breakfast of bacon and eggs on a sunny Korean morning in Canadian trenches, overlooking the bodies of a smashed Chinese attack "and boy, if you guys think Vietnam is tough, you should have been there with us in Korea, eh P.J.!" It was all rubbish, but nice rubbish. Thereafter I was treated in style.

General Stillwell said he'd be flying back to the United States shortly and asked when I was going. There was the suggestion of getting a lift with him. I said I wasn't going home just yet, but on to Hong Kong.

As it turned out, I went home first. The next I heard of Joe Stillwell was that his plane had vanished over the Pacific, with all on board lost. He was a gallant friend, a fine soldier with a down-to-earth decency that gave the army a good name.

In Saigon I picked up my wash-and-wear suit and was on my way back to the hotel when I saw, wonder of wonders, the little guy who'd bilked me out of my black-market dollars. He was courting another American when I came up behind him, seized him by the neck, and dragged him into the lobby of a hotel that had been taken over by the Canadians who were on the International Control Commission and saddled with the thankless and shabby job of working for peace and documenting violations on both sides. Gripping the man's wrists, I said loudly that I wanted the "police." I scowled furiously at him and began generating righteous anger within myself. A couple of young girls—around ten or twelve—followed us into the empty lobby and started wailing and imploring me to let him go. His children, I supposed. The Fagin of Saigon. I was unyielding and kept tugging as if to go to a policeman.

The man recognized me, expressed some surprise and disappointment that I had not told him the truth about leaving Vietnam, fished in his pocket, pushed a roll of bills at me. One of the girls offered more bills. Piastres galore. I relented and, throwing the guy my dirtiest look, took the bundle of money, whereupon he and the two girls fled. Back at the hotel, I counted the money. It not only more than made up my losses, but left me with a considerable profit. I was mildly embarrassed at the whole escapade, and it was years before I dared admit it to anyone, much less write about being a sucker to an age-old con game.

I clearly recall the moment when in a flash of insight it dawned on me that contrary to all the propaganda and brave words, the

Vietnam War was *not* being won by the Americans and the Saigon government—that it could not be won the way it was going, and that, in fact, the Vietcong/Hanoi side was winning. That sounds self-evident today, but it was a radical and extreme idea in 1962. It was during a so-called helicopter attack: troops jumped out, fired into bushes, and raced for the sanctuary of a strategic hamlet, congratulating themselves on not being ambushed. These were not winners; they were losers.

It colored my outlook and my thinking for the rest of my time in Vietnam. I began to see everything in terms of the eventual over-all outcome. In my series for the *Telegram* I concluded that at best the United States could only delay inevitable Communist triumph. Trying to make some sense of the U.S. involvement and support of the obviously unpopular, corrupt regime of Ngo Dinh Diem (whom the CIA was to help kill in a few months, probably exceeding the wishes of President Kennedy, who merely disapproved of him), I felt that the United States was using South Vietnam as a huge training school in order to give itself a battle-trained guerrilla or counter-insurgency army for future camouflage wars. I speculated that the United States might be planning to use this new army in a guerrilla war against Fidel Castro's Cuba. Despite the benefits of training a combat-tough military at cheap cost, I felt the Americans were the wrong fish in the wrong sea. The dicta of Mao's revolutionary warfare should be learned and understood.

When the series was published in the *Tely* and syndicated in the United States, I got two main reactions: conservative or right-wing elements wrote or phoned to call me another Canadian pinko who was betraying democratic principles of freedom and why didn't I go to Russia? Left-wing and liberal admirers thought it about time someone saw the truth of America's support of fascist regimes.

I felt moved to insist to the anti-Ameriks who contacted me that I was *not* anti-American, that I had unbridled admiration and affection for the United States, which I saw (and still see) as the only hope of the free world. My reporting from Vietnam was simply what I found. I tried to follow where the story led, as all reporters should, and if my superficial findings were radical, unorthodox, unusual, or wrong, they were honestly arrived at and not the product of ideological prejudice or latent anti-Americanism.

This seemed to puzzle the left (and was rejected by the right) and I was quickly dropped. In retrospect I did not understand or appreciate the power of ideology. Had I been wiser, or different, I might have taken the opportunity to use the platform to get other ideas across. As it was, I simply viewed Vietnam as a "story" and, when it was over, looked forward to the next one. I did not see it then as *the* story of a generation.

One of the problems with Western journalism in Vietnam was that the U.S. authorities—the Pentagon, State Department, White House, everyone—were so conditioned to lie, distort, and to think wishfully about Vietnam that by the time it was realized that the whole fabric was nonsense, all mutual trust and confidence was lost. No one believed anything the Pentagon said, even when it was telling the truth. Nor is it believed or trusted today. The media became committed to the other side when, in fact, the other side was *always* worse than the South Vietnamese side. But we of the media refused to see it, or simply couldn't see it, even though it was always relentlessly obvious. Anyone who tried to put Vietnam into perspective was called a puppet of the Pentagon, naïve, or an apologist for American imperialism.

Collectively speaking, the media rarely asked itself the basic question that should have *always* been asked when it was trying to determine right and wrong in Vietnam: why did refugees always head south? Because that is what they did, even when the Saigon government was collapsing and the Hanoi regime had won. Vietnamese refugees always knew something about the Hanoi regime that Western journalists hadn't the wit or courage to see: Hanoi was brutal and oppressive and life under it would be far more cruel than under Saigon. The vast majority of Vietnamese wanted no part of it if they could possibly avoid it.

The most eloquent testimony to this fact was that when "liberation" threatened, thousands of Vietnamese preferred to take their chances swimming and paddling away from the tip of Vietnam into the unknown perils of the South China Sea rather than endure Marxist liberation.

Yet the media preferred—still prefers—to remember My Lai where a platoon of ill-led Americans shot up a defenceless Vietnam village and mercilessly slaughtered women and children. As if that were the norm rather than an aberration. And while remembering that obscenity and extrapolating from it, the media rarely, if ever, recalled the provincial capital of Hué where regular troops of North Vietnam and the local Vietcong methodically rounded up citizens and wreaked vengeance by burying untold numbers alive and shooting others in mass graves. That *was* normal, and every refugee knew it. What happened in Vietnam, and later in Cambodia after liberation, rivals anything Hitler or Stalin did. One we can't forget; the other we won't remember.

We of the media also deliberately and/or unwittingly misinterpreted the outcome of the Tet offensive in 1968 when the Vietcong came into the open to try and seize control from the Americans and the Saigon government in a brave, daring, desperate gamble—and lost. The Vietcong ceased to exist as a military force after Tet: they were destroyed on the ground. Yet few journalists saw this. Political and ideological interpretation dominated military reality, so that what was a considerable military victory for the South turned into a propaganda defeat. The Vietcong didn't have to win the fighting in order to achieve victory. The mere fact that they were able to mount such a wide-ranging attack guaranteed the Communists favorable publicity and the *appearance* of victory. The military saw clearly what had happened, but this time no one was prepared to believe the truth, so the truth became a tissue of lies.

The distinguished Australian journalist Dennis Warner, one of the few who saw reality uncluttered by ideology or preconceived prejudice, has called Vietnam the only war lost in the pages of the New York *Times*.

Seven years later, in the first year of "liberation" in Indochina, Warner was among the few to recognize the genocidal policies unleashed by the Khmer Rouge in Cambodia, where perhaps 50 percent of the population was systematically murdered. Proportionately, Kampuchea (Cambodia) was a far greater holocaust than the one Hitler unleashed on Jews. Yet it was largely unreported. Four times as many Cambodians were killed in the first year of "liberation" as were killed in the previous five years of war—2 million to 500,000. A year later, Amnesty International, which tries (to give it the benefit of the doubt) to be even-handed, reported that the massacres in Cambodia were unsubstantiated, and were probably exaggerated ("seem to be based on belief, rather than evidence"). So much for them. Amnesty is also the body whose annual report in 1975-76 on the state of political prisoners and human rights abuses around the world saw nothing incongruous in giving three pages to outrages against political prisoners in South Korea, but offered no evidence of any abuses by North Korea. In the 1981 Amnesty report there were seven pages on South Korea, one page on North Korea.

When the Vietnam War ended with Hanoi's victory in 1975, after the United States bailed out and reneged on earlier promises to help Saigon with arms, the media lost interest. It wasn't until 1978 that the plight of the Boat People captured media attention—for a while. Meanwhile, the "re-education" camps of Vietnam continue to punish dissenters and suspected opponents of the regime with hardly a murmur of international criticism, and Vietnam's troops have invaded and occupied Kampuchea without foreign witnesses. Silence, if not peace, has descended over Indochina. Or, if one dares call it "peace"—it is the peace of the grave.

The future was all there to be seen twenty years ago if only we could have understood it.

17

Judgment, Texas-style, pounces on an assassin

TORONTO TELEGRAM
NOVEMBER 25, 1963

Most people who were around at the time can remember with almost total recall what they were doing the precise moment they heard the news that President John Kennedy had been shot in Dallas, that Friday noon of November 22, 1963.

What stands out in my mind are the ringing bells of the UPI teletype machines at the Toronto *Telegram* signalling a bulletin. There are bulletins and bulletins, and the greater the urgency, the more demanding the ring. Or so it seems. This time it seemed to ring endlessly and editors and desk men gathered around the machine. I wondered idly what was happening and drifted over.

"There's a report of shots at President Kennedy," said Art Cole, the lugubrious city editor, looking balefully around as if someone in the newsroom had done it. At first it wasn't known if anyone was hit. Then came the news that the president had been shot. How badly hurt, no one knew. The newsroom turned silent. No tap-tap of typewriters, no laughter, only the ringing of ignored telephones. The bulletin bells on all the teletype machines were still clanging.

Cole looked glumly at me. "You'd better get ready to go to Washington," he said.

We flew out that afternoon to make contact with our Washington man, Gordon Donaldson, who was in Dallas with the president and was probably the best crisis writer we had. There were three of us: Dorothy Howarth, first woman to win a National Newspaper Award in Canada, an innovative feature writer and so-so news reporter with an inability to spell (as befits an ex-schoolteacher); Ken McTaggart, the dean of Canadian reporters who was in his sixties but had the enthusiasm of a teen-ager, resembled a natty

Dean Acheson, and was a gentleman to the core; and me, the paper's international fireman, so to speak. We had no time to pack and caught the first plane to Washington. We would be working with Donaldson who, as the *Tely*'s Washington bureau chief, would be in charge. He was flying back with the body of the slain president.

On the flight down we didn't talk much, except to plot what each would do in Washington in order not to overlap. We were all shaken in different ways, for the Kennedy magic had touched us all. It was a difficult time for objective, detached reporting, and yet it wasn't. By reflecting our own thoughts and feelings, we were reflecting everyone's. In the capital of the nation we tried to give readers at home a feeling of what the soul or nerve centre of America was going through. I found that I couldn't think of who had done it or why, but only of the devastating deed itself. Jack Kennedy belonged to everyone, not just his own country. Every story that night became a color story, an emotional outpouring of heartache.

Friday night in the driving rain outside the White House was one of the more mournful times I can recall. People came just to be there; some came with their kids, others to put flowers on the sidewalk. I remember postal worker Ralph Harkin compulsively talking to people—strangers linked by tragedy: "This is a sadder day than Pearl Harbor. An American has done what the Japanese couldn't do in the war: killed our president."

A father stared, unseeing, into the rain in Lafayette Square across from the White House, a toddler on his shoulders. He murmured to the child, gurgling happily in the downpour: "Remember this day, son; it's the day our President died." Strangers conferred and passed opinions, just wanting to talk and relieve the emotional pressure. There was so much to say, yet nothing to say. I've rarely felt such a bonding with people, a strange unity of sadness. It was hard to write about without appearing cheap and tear-jerking.

Saturday, there was more rain and covering angles to the story that every other journalist had thought of. It has all become an emotional blur over the years, yet I can't recall a story where personal feelings were so involved. In those days it struck me as odd (it no longer does) that Kennedy was so much more loved and admired outside his country than inside it. Americans were more inclined to see his flaws, his failings, unaware of the hope and optimism he inspired in the rest of the world. Today, when emotions are less involved and there is a semblance of objectivity, it is acknowledged that in his 1,000 days in office John Kennedy achieved relatively little in terms of legislation.

His great strength, indeed the miracle of Kennedy as president, was his style and grace—another way of saying leadership. We all saw in him what we wanted to see. He had an aura about him; he radiated a confidence, personified the dreams of people. All people, not just Americans. He represented the future, the potential of mankind. He should not be judged on what he achieved or didn't achieve, but on the spiritual and psychological effect he had on his nation and the world. Rarely has a statesman's death touched off such deep, genuine, and spontaneous grief around the world as did Kennedy's. I don't think it is an overstatement to suggest that the world hasn't been the same since, nor has there been an American leader who commanded similar qualities of loyalty, love, hope, and faith. It was ordinary people who were most affected by Kennedy.

And, for those with a conspiratorial bent, the very qualities that made Kennedy so special were the precise reasons his enemies and those who stood against what he stood for might have wanted him eliminated.

After working around the clock, it suddenly occurred to Donaldson, McTaggart, Howarth and me that having all of us chasing leads and stories in Washington was redundant and that we had left Dallas uncovered. The *Tely* had no one there to follow the fate of the alleged assassin, Lee Harvey Oswald, who had shot a policeman and been arrested in a theatre. It is a reflection on the chaos of the situation that none of the editors at the *Tely* had apparently thought beyond the death of the president. We realized with a start that the paper had no one to keep tabs on Oswald and that our great blood rival, the Toronto *Star*, had had the foresight to have a man there from the start: Rae Corelli, an able, experienced, reliable journalist who could handle any type of story.

We debated which of us should catch the midnight milk run flight to Dallas, but there really was no choice. None of us much wanted to go—sleep was our main desire—but I was the logical one. With relatively good grace I volunteered, at which point Dorothy offered to go instead, Donaldson said he'd go but Washington was his beat, and McTaggart was so senior that no one would suggest, even in humor, that he scramble onto a midnight milk run.

After a Saturday evening of letting go with other journalists gathered at Donaldson's house, I managed not to miss the last flight to Dallas, which seemed to stop at every landing field in between. All I recall of the flight is a drunken passenger with a Southern accent who periodically proclaimed that Kennedy had asked for what happened to him, and that it was only a matter of time before someone shot his lousy brother, too. Had the guy not been drunk, I suspect there'd have been an incident. As it was, I was surprised that the deeper south one went, the greater the hostility and resentment toward the Kennedy name.

We landed in Dallas on Sunday morning and I immediately checked in at the Statler Hotel, intending to sleep until afternoon and then file an overnight for the Monday paper. I was exhausted, rumpled, unshaven, and generally disreputable-looking, wearing the same clothes I'd worn almost constantly since Friday, when the story began. The Sunday papers said that Oswald was to be transferred that evening from the police station to the county jail. I was free until then. For reasons I can't explain, I decided that before going to bed I'd learn the layout of the land and reconnoitre the Dallas police station where Oswald was being held so that I wouldn't have to do it later. In the army they like to say that time spent in reconnaissance is never wasted. Like most clichés, this one has the virtue of being right.

I wandered around the Dallas police station unmolested, the few officers around showing no interest in me. I finally stopped someone and asked where I could get some information about Oswald. The officer looked at me suspiciously, undoubtedly wondering about the seedy appearance and slept-in clothes. Without being asked, I explained that I was a Canadian journalist. This seemed to satisfy him and he told me that Oswald was going to be transferred to the county jail.

"In the evening, I understand," said I.

"No. There's been a change."

"Oh. When?"

"Fairly soon. From the underground garage. Take the stairs over there."

"Is it okay to go down?"

"Sure. Why not? Others are."

"Where's the county jail?"

"It's at the foot of Main Street. But we aren't going down Main Street. We'll be sending a decoy van down that way, then take Oswald down Commerce, just to play it safe. So don't pay attention to the first car . . ."

I thanked the officer and went to the basement garage, grateful yet puzzled at such openness and frankness to a stranger who looked as if he belonged in a police line-up. Canadian police would never be so forthcoming. Maybe Texans *were* more trusting and friendly than others. The Dallas police simply accepted my assurances that I was who I said I was, no proof required. They babbled willingly, openly.

Down in the garage there was pandemonium: TV cameras, newsmen, photographers, detectives. The big names of American TV news were all there interviewing one another and various police and officials. I mingled with the mob, chatting with a couple of reporters I'd met the previous summer during a strike of doctors in Saskatchewan. I got chummy with one young detective, Roy Lowry, and we casually speculated on the whys and wherefores of the assassination.

Suddenly there was a commotion and the word was: "He's coming!" Television cameras, photographers, and assorted journalists bunched across from the door while I stood with Lowry and the other police against the wall facing the crowd of journalists. Oswald came out, his hands manacled, his right wrist handcuffed to a policeman. He wore a dark sweater; his mouth was small and tight, his eyes quick and lively, darting in and out of the crowd. A tall, self-important, rather stunned-looking man in a Stetson—Captain J. Will Fritz, head of the Homicide Bureau, as it turned out—gazed neither left nor right. Just straight ahead. I recall Oswald had a bruise on the right side of his forehead and what seemed to be a cut on one cheek.

"Why'd you do it, Lee?" shouted someone—Ike Pappas, a New York radio reporter, I think. As Oswald glanced in the direction of the voice there was another commotion: a squat man in a fedora plunged from the crowd toward the group and suddenly there was the muffled crack of a shot. I felt the shock waves of the discharge hit my abdomen, and afterward Detective Lowry and I compared notes and remarked that we were lucky the guy was a good shot. Oswald doubled over in pain and shock. He gasped "Ohhh, Ohhh, Ohhh" several times while slowly crumpling to the pavement where he lay in a fetal position, conscious but in obvious pain.

Above the instant turmoil there was a yell which came, it was said later, from Detective E. H. Combest, who'd recognized the assailant: "Jack, you son of a bitch . . ." Lowry had thrown himself onto the man and was clinging to his leg. There was soon a pile of bodies struggling with the person who fired the shot. We couldn't make out who it was. Both the victim and his attacker were quickly hustled inside the station. I still thought it was a journalist and remember thinking: "God, he's spoiled it for the rest of us!" Meanwhile the Dallas police, literally, went berserk.

It is a marvel that there wasn't an added tragedy. Pearl-handled Texas revolvers came out, shotguns appeared. I was thrust against the wall with a shotgun under my chin. Someone said there was a mysterious TV crew who might be assassins, and one of the network crews suddenly had arms splayed against the wall and were being searched. All over the underground garage people were being checked, held at gunpoint, forced to show identity. The security precautions that had been so lax—hell, nonexistent— were now suddenly put into effect with a vengeance.

No one knew whether the assassination of the supposed assassin was an individual act or a gang reprisal. Uncertainty reigned. By this time I feared it was the reporter with whom I'd been discussing the Saskatchewan medicare strike. In some panic I tried to remember his name and what we had discussed, knowing I'd have to recall his words for a he-told-me story of my conversation with the assassin of the assassin. But my mind was blank. I could remember nothing.

Outside the garage, streets were lined with people waiting to see Oswald leave. News of the "secret" move had gotten around quickly. Few secrets are kept in Dallas, it seems. As the word spread through the crowd that Oswald had himself been assassinated, a loud cheer rippled down the street.

"He deserves a medal," yelled someone. People began to laugh and nudge one another with some satisfaction. Crude justice had been done, although on reflection most would realize that the shame that was Dallas had been added to, not diminished, by the deed. It always struck me as odd that this rather interesting reaction was never brought up at the trial of the assassin.

Jack Ruby was a seedy strip-joint operator, dog lover, smalltime hanger-on of big-time hoods, a publicity-seeker; a character on the fringes of crime and sleaze. His Carousel Club was a strip joint and a watering place for visiting mobsters, people with names like Needle Nose Labriola, Frank (the Enforcer) Nitti, Murray (the Camel) Humphreys. Ruby was a bachelor who partook of the wares of his girls and often beat them up. One of his strippers, Little Lynn, whom he'd recently beaten up, said: "I don't wanna say anything bad about him; he likes dogs." As well as being an errand boy for hoods, Ruby was also a police informer, eager to curry favor with all factions. There was very little about him that was appealing.

An ambulance arrived to take the wounded Oswald to hospital. Again I was with the police when he was wheeled out on a stretcher. One look at the unconscious man—his half-open glazed eyes and his skin fast becoming the color of dry cement—was enough to know that to all intents he was already dead, though still breathing. Fatally wounded people have a certain look, exude a certain feeling, have a certain color. Oswald had that greenish-grey tinge of those about to die.

As he was being lifted into the ambulance his sweater was lifted and as well as the neat hole under his heart on the left side, there was a small lump on his right side in the kidney area. It was the bullet, which hadn't broken the skin. He'd been shot in the side and the lead slug had churned its way through his vital organs and lost all momentum, so that it did not emerge from his body.

It was 11:30 in the morning. Amid the chaos it suddenly occurred to me that I should let the *Telegram* know I was on the spot and that I'd be filing a story. I thought they'd already have the bulletins, but would be anxious to know my whereabouts. I got to a pay phone and called the city desk which would usually be quiet on a Sunday. But on this Sunday it was full steam ahead.

"Just wanted to let you know that I'm here and have the story in hand," I said, expecting a sigh of relief from the other end that I was on the job.

"Yeah, we know," said the desk. "We've been looking at nothing but you on TV all morning. You need a shave."

I was surprised. It was the first I knew that the cameras were shooting live. I guess if I'd thought about it I would have known, but usually the stories I covered were foreign crises where TV cameras used film or tape for showing later. I was mildly disappointed because I would have liked to have created a bit of suspense at the office since my getting there was such a close thing. I wasn't sure they realized how lucky they were that I hadn't immediately gone to bed as originally intended. TV had ruined my one-upmanship.

"You seen the Toronto *Star* there?" asked the office.

"No. Corelli, isn't it? Is he alone?"

"Yeah. Funny. We've been looking for him on TV but can't see him. All channels have you. Do you suppose he isn't there?"

"That's too much to hope for," I said, "but I haven't seen him either . . ."

As it turned out, they were looking at the same television in the newsroom of the *Star* and asking the same questions. "We see the *Telegram*, but where's our guy?" they said.

Eventually someone phoned Corelli at his hotel in Dallas. "Hi, Rae, what's doing?" the *Star* editor reportedly said.

"Nothing," said Corelli. "F'r God's sake, I haven't had sleep for two days and you call me to ask silly questions. They're moving Oswald around 5 P.M. I'll have the story. Relax."

"Well, Rae, there've been changes," said the editor gently. "They moved Oswald half an hour ago, some guy jumped out and shot him in the Dallas police station—and the goddam *Tely* is there, all over TV, and you aren't. We've been beat, but good, so get your ass moving and you better have a damn good reason why the *Tely* knew and you didn't." Poor Corelli. What happened to him was the nightmare of every working journalist.

The next problem in Dallas after the shooting of Oswald was to write the story. It was almost too big, too dramatic, to capture in words. I remember my lead: "Justice, Texas-style, caught up with Lee Harvey Oswald in a dimly lit Dallas police underground garage yesterday . . ." I went on to establish quickly that I was a few feet away from Oswald as Ruby gunned him down, and then plunged into the color of what it was like to be there when macabre history is made. It was personal journalism intermingled with what few facts we knew and what everybody had seen on TV.

To this day I still puzzle at what persuaded me to make that Sunday morning reconnaissance of the Dallas police station instead of catching up on lost sleep, as common sense dictated, thereby becoming the only Canadian eyewitness to a dramatic bit of history and participating in journalistic legend.

By some curious osmosis or collective psychological process, Jack Ruby, by killing Lee Harvey Oswald, in a symbolic way assumed Oswald's guilt. The initial animal glee at crude justice catching up with Oswald in the Dallas police garage quickly became hostility toward Ruby in the face of the nation's sorrow. Even in those first days there seemed more resentment than sorrow in Dallas, more embarrassment than remorse, that Kennedy had been killed in that city. Emotionally, Ruby became the president's assassin.

Dallas was not a city where Kennedy was loved, but a place where he was generally thought of as a pinko. Dallas, remember, was a city where Chief Justice Earl Warren was regarded as a Communist and newspapers carried full page ads urging his impeachment. A city where Picasso paintings were banned from the art gallery because he was a Communist. A city where UN Ambassador Adlai Stevenson was spat upon because he was considered an intellectual and soft on Commies.

Over the years, friends have tended to assume that because I was there, I have some theories or inside knowledge as to the whys and wherefores of Kennedy's assassination. I don't. Then, as now, there was speculation about who was behind it, whether more than one person fired the shots, whether Oswald was even the right guy. Why, how, who, et cetera. Personally, I have no evidence to support any theory, except that in the immediate aftermath of the tragedy there was no feeling that more than one gunman was involved. That speculation began to emerge later, almost as if people were being steadily conditioned to think of a conspiracy. Of course, there was unseemly impatience to get the matter resolved. But Homicide Captain J. Will Fritz's assurances within hours of Oswald's assassination that he was "satisfied" Oswald had shot the president, that he was acting alone and that the case was closed, were a bit hasty even for Texas where, historically, complex legal disputes had been settled by hanging the survivor.

All that I *do* have is a feeling for the mood at the time, and the thinking of the moment before it was readjusted or altered to suit facts, prejudices, preconceived notions, and wishful thinking. I have no special knowledge on theories that have been expounded to the effect that Oswald was the pawn of big business, big labor unions, the oil barons, organized crime, Lyndon Johnson's ambitions, the CIA, right-wing fanatics, racists, rednecks, and so on. Mentioned, but rarely stressed or thoroughly explored, even at the time, were Oswald's Soviet connections.

The most cursory examination of Oswald's background leads one inexorably to the possibility of KGB involvement, or Soviet vengeance. It seemed too monstrous a thought to cope with then. Today, it seems slightly more feasible, although just as appalling. We now know that the KGB can sponsor Bulgarian assassins with poisoned umbrella tips to eliminate enemies; we know that the man who headed the Soviet system, Yuri Andropov, actually approved, if not initiated, the plot to assassinate the Pope; we know that it's a matter of Soviet policy to periodically put sane citizens who disagree with the system into psychiatric prisons and to treat them with hallucinatory drugs to drive them mad.

While there was no excuse for *not* knowing the nature of the Soviet system then (Kennedy had won a propaganda victory with the Cuban missile crisis, just as he'd lost one the year before with the Bay of Pigs), there was a conspiracy of silence about the Soviet connection with Oswald. Whatever the truth, we didn't want to learn anything that would force a drastic decision and possibly make a head-on confrontation inevitable. It has remained for others to explore Oswald's Soviet links. If I had known then what I know now about the Soviet system, I would have raised more questions in the *Telegram*. But I didn't. Unanswered questions now fill books—perhaps the best of which is Jay Epstein's *Legend, the Secret World of Lee Harvey Oswald*, an example of outstanding journalism.

There are many inexplicable aspects to the Oswald/Soviet story. The only hard, independent information we have about Oswald in the USSR after he defected in 1959 comes from Yuri Nosenko, who defected to the Americans in Switzerland after the Kennedy slaying, claiming to be a KGB lieutenant-colonel who was active in the Oswald case in the USSR. Grilled interminably, Nosenko was caught in so many lies and distortions that he was widely believed to be a KGB plant to divert American suspicions from the Kremlin in the Kennedy slaying. He wasn't even a colonel in the KGB. His claim that the KGB had no interest in Oswald after his defection to the Soviet Union makes no sense. Nevertheless, the Americans were eager to believe Nosenko, even though it defied logic that Oswald, a former U.S. Marine who'd been stationed at U-2 spy plane bases in the Orient, would be of no interest. Gary Powers's U-2 had been shot down over Russia in 1960, scuttling the summit meeting between Eisenhower and Khrushchev, and Oswald would have had enough firsthand information to make the Soviets salivate. Yet, officially, the KGB never debriefed him.

Before changing his mind and redefecting to the United States two and a half years later in the fall of 1962, Oswald married Marina, who claimed she could not remember the name of her father (she was illegitimate)—although she has stated since in interviews that her father was Nikolai Didenko, who was executed on charges of treason. Marina used a couple of surnames, including Medvedeva and Prusakova. Her patronym, Nikolaevna, indicates that her father's first name was Nikolai. Her passport showed that she was born in Severodvinsk, which at the time of her birth in 1941 was known as Molotovsk, after Vyacheslav Molotov, Stalin's friend and a former premier. When he was disgraced in 1957, the city was renamed Severodvinsk. Normally, her papers would show the name of the town as it was when she was born.

Marina's "uncle," Ilya Prusakov, was a colonel in the MVD, the Interior Ministry responsible for internal security in the USSR. With such connections, when Oswald changed his mind about staying in the Soviet Union, it is inconceivable that the Soviets would let Marina go to the United States with him even if they let him leave, which would be unlikely now that he was a Soviet citizen. One only has to glance at a newspaper today to know how difficult it is for anyone who marries a Soviet citizen to get that person out of the Soviet Union. If it is hard today, it was unheard of then—especially for anyone with intelligence connections. Yet Marina and Oswald *did* leave. Why?

Less puzzling, but nonetheless strange, was the fact that the United States accepted Oswald back after he'd offered to give the Soviets classified information gathered while in the Marine Corps! However, we in the "free" West are always behaving without logic when it comes to espionage and treason—giving traitors indexed pensions and spies immunity from prosecution because we don't want embarrassment. And how does one account for his activities, once he was back in the United States? For example, Oswald's visit to Mexico City two weeks before Kennedy's assassination, as reported to the FBI by the CIA? There he called in at the Soviet Embassy and met with one Valeri Vladimirovich Kostikov, who was identified as a KGB officer with the 13th Department, which is responsible for kidnappings, assassinations, sabotage.

It has been made public and even admitted that the FBI destroyed a letter Oswald wrote to the Bureau ten days before Kennedy's assassination, presumably because it was considered unimportant—or because its existence subsequently embarrassed the FBI. Other than that, little is known about the contents. For an agency that has the reputation of never destroying any evidence in any files, the FBI's treatment of the Oswald letter is inexplicable. I suspect it was a panic reaction to get off the hook for negligent behavior. There is also evidence that Oswald's signature changed and that his Marine Corps records show him with "hazel" eyes, yet the Dallas police records taken on his arrest show him with blue eyes. This and other factors persuade some people that the Oswald who defected to the USSR was not the Oswald who came back—that a switch was made. The truth is still not known and possibly never will be. All that can be said for certain is that Lee Harvey Oswald and his wife Marina received extraordinary treatment from Soviet authorities, treatment no other person who is not a Soviet plant or agent has ever got. Perhaps KGB defector Nosenko will some day tell his story and shed a bit more light on a mystery that has deepened over the years and which no one in position of authority wants, or dares, to have resolved.

As someone who has really never stopped wondering about the "truth" of the case, I think one aspect that has never been stressed enough is the age-old method in every police investigation of a mysterious crime: look first for who profits most from it. In the case of President Kennedy, who stood to profit most if he were dead? The same who would profit most, fifteen years later, if Pope John Paul II were killed by a deranged assassin "acting alone": the Soviet Union. It is now virtually irrefutable that the KGB was behind the Bulgarian secret police who contracted the Turkish hit man, Mehmet Ali Agca, to kill a Pope whose involvement with Poland and the Solidarity movement was a thorn in the Kremlin's side. If the Kremlin would risk assassinating the Pope, why not an American president?

In 1963 Kennedy was the elegant symbol of America and the Western Alliance. His opposite number was the buffoon-like Nikita Khrushchev, who'd already been humiliated by Kennedy over missiles in Cuba and whose Soviet system was made to look especially bad when Kennedy went to Berlin, derided the obscenity of the Wall, and established himself as the leader of freedom with his historic rallying cry *"Ich bin ein Berliner."* Kennedy single-handedly was making anti-communism look respectable. With him eliminated, the Kremlin would be rid of a persistent, effective nuisance who was impeding Soviet influence around the world.

This is not to say the Soviets *were* responsible for Kennedy's murder. It is just to say they are the prime suspects, and always were, even when no one dared voice the thought. Today, it is acknowledged that the Kremlin and the KGB are involved in assassinations around the world, including the international terrorists' network, and are supplying arms, training, and support to such diverse groups as the IRA, Red Brigades, PLO, Basques, Sandinistas, SWAPO, and so forth. As well, author Claire Sterling in her investigative books *The Terror Network* and *Time of the Assassins* has documented the Soviet involvement in international murder.

Why is the Soviet connection in the assassination of Kennedy rarely examined? Because the consequences of finding evidence of Soviet complicity are so horrendous that no one dares contemplate them. *If* there had been *conclusive* evidence of Soviet involvement, war probably would have been inevitable. The system, without ever admitting it, has almost instinctively agreed that it must be covered up (as was done by the Warren Commission), downplayed, ignored, forgotten.

What America lost in Kennedy's death, what the free world lost, is a leader of inspirational qualities whose like has not been seen since. None of his successors have been presidents of stature, of dreams, ideals, and goals that inspired. The only one with *some* of the Kennedy mystique is, curiously, Ronald Reagan, who is also beset by enemies in his own country, just as Kennedy was.

As for Kennedy assassination theories, there is only one that meets the test of common sense: Moscow.

18

Let's give him a fair trial—then fry him!

BILL ALEXANDER
ASSISTANT DISTRICT ATTORNEY
DALLAS, TEXAS
FEBRUARY 1964

If Britain is notorious for having the most bizarre murders in the world, America surely is the winner when it comes to bizarre trials that capture the public's imagination. The Manson trial of 1970, the Rosenberg spy trial of 1951, the Lindbergh kidnapping trial of 1935, the Scopes Monkey trial in 1925, Leopold and Loeb in 1924, Sacco and Vanzetti in 1921—all are solidly imbedded in history and are now joined by what, in its way, must be the strangest court case of all: the twenty-four-day trial in 1964 of Jack Ruby who killed Lee Harvey Oswald. It was a trial that had everything—except dignity, decorum, and the law.

For starters, Jack Ruby was an unlikely candidate to be the avenger of Jack Kennedy. He was the antithesis of what Kennedy stood for: grace, style, class, a sense of mission, hope. Born Jake Rubenstein in 1911, the son of an alcoholic Russian immigrant, Ruby had no home life or normal childhood to speak of. His mother was institutionalized as a paranoid after her husband walked out on her and eight kids when Ruby was twelve. He grew up on the fringes of the Chicago underworld, shrewd, vain, touchy, and sensitive about his Jewishness to the extent that all his life he was ready to fight anything he interpreted as an anti-Semitic slur. (He legally changed his name after he moved to Dallas in 1947.) His flash temper earned him the nickname "Sparky."

Though Ruby consorted with prizefighters, hookers, and hoods, he yearned to be taken seriously and to be seen with celebrities. He was drafted into the army in World War II but was never overseas. Despite a record of occasionally slugging noncommissioned officers, he was discharged with a Good Conduct medal. His first nightclub in Dallas, the Silver Spur, folded in 1952, but by the time Kennedy made his ill-fated visit to the city on November 22, 1963, Ruby was the owner of the more successful Carousel Club.

My first sight of Ruby was in the underground garage of the Dallas police station when he plunged out of the crowd of journalists, shot Oswald and was immediately buried under a pile of cops who ignored his plaintive cry: "Hey, you know me, I'm Jack Ruby . . ." My next encounter was three months later in a Dallas courtroom where he looked wan, twitchy, and haunted, but was still vain to the point where he insisted that reporters call him "Mister," not "Jack."

An unusual array of lawyers had competed to defend Ruby almost from the moment of Oswald's assassination. One of the Dallas lawyers bidding to defend him and thus win immortality of sorts was C. A. Droby, to whom I was chatting when he got a phone call from his wife claiming the family's lives had been threatened if he took the case. It didn't deter him from seeking to defend Ruby. Tom Howard, another lawyer hoping to get the case, stated that Ruby deserved the Medal of Honor for what he did. However, it was Melvin Belli, "Ole Doc," one of the more spectacular practitioners of American jurisprudence, who acted in Ruby's defence. Belli was the big name in personal injury suits. He had won more $100,000 settlements for clients in litigation than any lawyer in captivity, and was known for innovative courtroom tactics. Once he had his client strip to the waist to show the jury botched cosmetic breast surgery after failing to find a doctor who would testify as to the incompetence of a colleague. He was assisted by Joe (Bullmoose) Tonahill of Jasper, Texas, a man who at six-foot-four and 260 pounds had all the elegance of a longhorn steer.

At that time the martyred President Kennedy personified decency and hope in America. Not that Kennedy was without warts or flaws, but they weren't seen—and certainly not reported by the media until much, much later when it became safe and even chic to point out what most Washington insiders had known: JFK's womanizing, his affair with Marilyn Monroe, his sharing a girlfriend with a mobster, his questionable election tactics, his father Joe's "buying" of the presidency. There were even rumors of paternity suits, hints of a previous hushed-up divorce. Kennedy may not have been a modern Galahad, but we thought he was.

With the flamboyant Belli as his lawyer, Ruby was presented as being tormented by the vision of lovely Jackie, her pink suit stained with blood from her husband's mortal head wound, to the point where impulse demanded he purge the world of the monster who had committed the vile deed. While trying to paint Ruby in the glowing colors of a misguided patriot and devotee of the Kennedys (with a severe case of puppy love for Jackie), even Belli couldn't camouflage the fact that Ruby cheated on his income tax and had never in his life shown any civic responsibility or political awareness. He would do anything for money, and was known to carry a $1,000 bankroll on one hip and a .38 pistol on the other. Through Ruby, suspicions of a Soviet connection with Oswald were diluted and it was he, I suspect, who gave credence to the view that organized crime might be behind the slaying.

It's fair to say that Dallas was a mixture of anticipation and apprehension over its so-called trial of the century. On my return three months after the Kennedy slaying, I found things had settled down. Like other foreign journalists who descended on Dallas for the trial, I spent a lot of time trying to analyze the city and the curious flavor it exuded. It was a white-collar city of some 1.3 million, modern skyscrapers, and the headquarters of insurance companies and banks. There was little leavening influence of industry or blue-collar workers. It was considered a right-wing, ultra-conservative city where the liberal or left-leaning newspaper, the *Times Herald*, advocated the invasion of North Vietnam and taking the war to the Communists. Dallas had a frontier approach to justice. Its version of having strict gun laws meant that you could only have a pistol in your house, your car, or your office, and you weren't supposed to carry one on the street. But weapons were easy to buy. Special sales offered two pistols for the price of one: $49.95. At the time of the Ruby trial, the *Times Herald* sent a reporter out to see what would happen if he tried to buy a gun for the stated purpose of killing someone.

"I want a big pistol—I want the rat to suffer," the reporter told the pawnshop clerk.

"Take this one," replied the salesman. "It'll flatten an elephant."

Texas had the Paramour Law, which rules that it is justifiable homicide if a man kills someone who is committing adultery with his wife, or if he *believes* he is *about* to commit adultery. It was also justifiable to kill someone who'd threatened you if you said you believed he meant it. A no-nonsense state! Small wonder it was known as murder capital of the United States, holding that title temporarily over Detroit.

Dallas was a city of Protestants, with more churches than any other city its size—1,000 of 'em, mostly Baptist, Methodist, and Church of Christ. It was also known as a "Committee City," run by the Dallas Citizens' Council comprised of some 250 business executives who virtually chose who would run for elected office. A mixed blessing, this benevolent oligarchy was primarily responsible for speeding up racial integration in the economic sense and permitting blacks to use white premises at a time when there was lingering segregation in other parts of the States. It wasn't racial equality that worried Dallas; it was creeping socialism, the blight of mankind to be thwarted at all costs.

Into this atmosphere hove Mel Belli, the big, brash, blustering liberal who thrived on headlines and controversy. His first act on reaching Dallas was to call a press conference, insult the coverage by one of the two Dallas newspapers, and praise the objectivity of the other. The villain was the more conservative *Morning News*; the good, or at least *better*, paper in Belli's view, was the less conservative (in conscience, only a Texas fanatic would call it "liberal") *Times Herald*. (In the weeks to come, I got quite friendly with Belli, and Ray Timson of the Toronto *Star* and I were accorded the honor of carrying his courtroom paraphernalia to and from the courthouse and the Statler Hotel where we all stayed.) Belli explained that his notoriety or fame made it difficult for him to get any sort of fair coverage in a potentially hostile town, so he would pick a fight and boycott one newspaper while complimenting and giving interviews and tidbits of information to the other, thus forcing the natural rivalry of the press to assert itself. This would result in the insulted paper going on a frontal attack, while the other paper would almost by default become Belli's defender. The fuss this raised amused Belli enormously. He had a raucous, pie-in-the-face sense of humor to complement a subtle wit. It contributed to his effectiveness and unpredictability in the courtroom. Opponents could never relax.

But he made one, big, insurmountable error in judgment in his defence of Jack Ruby in Dallas: he argued the law, presenting a legitimate if controversial defence rather than throwing himself on the mercy of the court and appealing to emotion. Dallas was not prepared to consider a defence for Ruby or listen to an outsider from San Francisco. Ruby was a condemned man before the jury was even picked, although no one realized it at the time.

The Ruby trial was pure showbiz. It has always struck me as odd that few of the various books that have been written about it have managed to catch its flavor. While the witnesses and characters who surfaced during the trial were Damon Runyon, the judge and lawyers seemed straight out of Al Capp and Dogpatch. Judge Joe B. Brown was an earthy, goodnatured, folksy character whose legal education before he was elected to the bench consisted of three years of night school thirty-five years earlier. He held the Texas record for having the most judgments reversed on appeal. Even in Dallas he was a bit of a joke and was known as Necessity—"because necessity knows no law." One local lawyer was even more disparaging: "Hell, Brown ain't even got any curiosity about the law!"

Pressure was brought to persuade Judge Brown to forgo his place in the rotation and to turn the case over to a more competent judge—Judge Frank Wilson to be precise, who had the fewest reversals on appeal. But Judge Brown would have no part of it. He claimed that he had four years before re-election and this was going to put him on the map. He enjoyed the TV exposure and the exchanges with the world's press and all the cartoons and photos of him that appeared around the world. On occasion during the trial he'd summon a *Paris Match* journalist to the bench to translate cutlines that appeared under his picture in the magazine. It was disconcerting to the jury and the defence lawyers. However, the district attorney was used to "Jedge Brown" and ignored the by-play.

Judge Brown liked to collect memorabilia about himself. In a celebrated trial against stripper Candy Barr in 1959 on narcotics charges, he had summoned the stripper to his chambers to pose with him for photos—then sentenced her to fifteen years.

Locals shuddered every time he appeared on TV. One day before court convened, the 350 or so assembled journalists failed to notice him enter at the rear. Judge Brown bellowed "Fire!" and thus attracted an impromptu press conference. Prior to the trial the Sam Bloom Advertising Agency was hired to handle press accreditation, and there was vigorous competition for the forty-odd courtroom seats allotted to the media on a one-per-agency basis. Name tags and photo identities were issued and everyone had to be searched before entering the courtroom. Periodically, someone would be found with a gun, but it was okay because there was no malicious intent. The person just forgot.

Curiously, it was the same courtroom where, years earlier, Ray Hamilton had been sentenced to 263 years for being a member of the Bonnie Parker gang (of Bonnie and Clyde fame), which terrorized the Southwest in an orgy of Robin Hood-like robberies and murders until they were gunned down. Overhead in the courtroom, the same nine ceiling fans churned the turgid air, which was blue with smoke. Judge Brown usually permitted smoking in his relaxed courtroom; for the Ruby trial, however, to add a touch of class in deference to the foreigners, he banned the smoking of cigars. He himself preferred chewing tobacco, and rarely missed the green spittoon beside his raised bench which, he said, gave him the best seat in the house to "watch the girls."

Some non-Texans found it symbolic and unwittingly appropriate that the lobby of the courthouse displayed a wall-size mural of Law West of the Pecos: a portrait of Judge Roy Bean standing in front of a barrel, a law book and a six-gun within easy reach. Things hadn't changed much.

Selection of the jury took two weeks and 162 jurors were processed before 12 were found who were acceptable to all. The two main criteria to be a juror were to have not seen the Kennedy assassination on TV and/or to have no views whatever on Ruby's guilt or innocence. On that basis, finding acceptable jurors would mean finding 12 of the stupidest or most deceitful or most naïve people in America. Belli and Tonahill insisted that a change of venue was necessary, but Judge Brown rejected the bid. He said if the 900 prospective jurors were rejected, he personally would go on the street and "corral another 900." No one doubted him. An all-white jury of eight males and four women was finally chosen (Belli was to later complain that one juror had boasted he was going to see that Ruby got the chair).

In the jury selection it was agreed by both sides that the Kennedy slaying would be kept out of it. The agreement lasted as long as it took both sides to violate it. Belli and Tonahill took turns questioning jurors; in some ways, Tonahill was more entertaining. He wore a pistol-shaped tie clip and when it came to the death penalty, he was fond of asking prospective jurors: "Would yuh like to be a member of the first Texas jury to send an ex-G.I. to the 'lectric chair for killin' a dirty Communist?"

· This would cause Judge Brown to interject, "C'mon now, Mr. Tonahill, git on with sumpin' else."

I went to see the district attorney before the trial to do a story on the mood: what was likely to happen, the "official" impression from Murder Capital, U.S.A. The D.A. was Hank (Buck) Wade, a former college football star who kept getting re-elected on the strength of his athletic past. He was silver-haired and handsome with a penchant for chewing unlit cigars, in and out of court.

Wade's assistant district attorney was a lean, mean-looking man named Bill Alexander, shrewd, able, and about as friendly as a meat cleaver. He was known as "The Burner" because of his record of sending some twenty men to the electric chair. It took a bit of getting used to every official in Dallas seeming to have a nickname. More Damon Runyon. After a while we of the foreign press got into the spirit of things and began inventing our own.

When Judge Brown decided in a fit of concern for the feelings of foreign visitors that "thar'll be no smokin' of cigarettes in mah court, nor seegars neither; we're gonna maintain dignity," District Attorney Wade looked pained and contented himself with chewing unlit cigars while listening to testimony. Leonard Parkin, then of the BBC, and I used to time how long it took him to consume a cigar. He'd chew it, masticate it, and roll it around his mouth, the length of the cigar gradually growing shorter. Every so often he'd direct a stream of brown, cigar-flavored spit at one of the spittoons that adorned the court. Eventually the cigar would be reduced to a stub; when about half an inch long it would disappear into his mouth like a caramel, to be tucked in his cheek and savored for almost exactly twelve minutes before the remains emerged in a lumpy, lethal wad, which occasionally hit the green spittoon. The whole journey from adult cigar to masticated blob took about fifty-five minutes. Parkin and I found the process fascinating.

While Wade did not give the impression of being one of the incisive legal minds of our time—or even of Texas—he was smart enough not to talk too much. Alexander, on the other hand, while sharper, just didn't give a damn. He was outspoken to a fault. I once asked what he thought would happen to Ruby. He looked at me coldly, sizing me up before answering, then replied casually: "We're treatin' this as jest another nigger killin'; we'll give him a fair trial—then fry him."

When it was said that Ruby's brain should be examined, Alexander responded: "Stick around and we'll send it to you."

When asked what he thought would happen to Ruby, Alexander replied that he didn't know "but if I was him I'd be careful about sittin' in any chairs." Good taste was not one of Alexander's strong points.

When Belli failed to get a change of venue, he felt he had his grounds for an eventual appeal (he was right: a new trial was ordered in a different city, but Ruby died of cancer first). As a matter of record, during the course of the trial every objection by the prosecution was upheld, every objection by the defence initially overruled. When the trial finally began, Belli brought in a succession of expert witnesses who testified that Ruby had rare brain damage called psychomotor epilepsy, which caused him to lose self-control and develop amnesia during highly emotional situations. Thus he neither was in charge of his body nor had any memory when he pulled the trigger on Oswald. An esoteric point— Belli nonetheless had a plausible case and some high-level names testifying to this effect. Dr. Roy Schafer of Yale University, with long experience in clinical psychology and psychiatry, testified that tests indeed showed Ruby had minor brain damage that might lead to erratic, violent behavior; Dr. Martin Towler, professor of psychiatry at the University of Texas, testified that during a seizure a person might act as if he knew what he was doing when actually he didn't; Dr. Manfred Guttmacher, a distinguished expert on psychiatry as it applies to murders, expressed the belief that epilepsy superimposed on a disturbed personality made Ruby "incapable of distinguishing between right and wrong and the nature and consequences of his act at the time he killed Oswald." Guttmacher was a powerful, unflappable witness whom Buck Wade and especially Burner Alexander couldn't shake, no matter how much contempt, ridicule, and abuse they heaped on him.

In fact, newspaper accounts of their ridicule of "psychomotor epilepsy," which they variously referred to as "motorcycle epilepsy" or "psycho-motor-pool epilepsy," so offended Dr. Frederic Gibbs when he read about it in Chicago that he, the pioneer in using electroencephalograms in diagnosing epilepsy, felt moved to reverse his earlier decision not to appear as an expert witness and asked to be allowed to testify in defence of diagnostic treatment of epilepsy. He made a persuasive case for Ruby's possibly being out of control when he shot Oswald.

In the midst of this, picketers appeared at the trial distributing literature attacking Belli for implying that epileptics were inclined to be murderers and prone to violence. At one point, Belli waved a finger at Maurice Melford of the National Epilepsy League, who was distributing quasi-religious literature about epilepsy, and berated him as "this sandwich man from the convulsive league . . ."

Those of us conditioned to the British traditions of courtroom behavior could never get used to Judge Brown's informality and his irritation with Belli for insisting on standing up to address the court. The judge would shuffle in wearing carpet slippers, read a magazine during complex testimony about epilepsy, and occasionally summon journalists to the bench to chide them about their coverage of him.

"You run an informal court, Judge," said one journalist non-committally during one break.

Judge Brown looked pleased. "Yeah, Son, Ah sure do. Ah'm in favor of informality—ain't everyone?"

Occasionally, when he felt in need of a Dr. Pepper soft drink or when the sticky air of the courtroom got too oppressive, the judge would call an impromptu recess and look at the press and say: "Take a break boys . . . go have a coffee or slug of sumpin'."

In an effort to show his client as a goodhearted soul, Bullmoose Tonahill cross-examined Ruby's strange roommate, one George Senator, about the five dachshunds Ruby owned and which he used to refer to as "my children." In telling an anecdote about Ruby and his "children," Senator managed to confuse Judge Brown—not a difficult achievement. "Ah thought Mr. Ruby wasn't married," said the judge.

"He isn't, Judge," said Senator, a mite puzzled at the interruption of his anecdote.

"You said he had five children in his car."

"They weren't children, they were dawgs."

"Then why'd you call 'em children?"

"Because that's what Jack called 'em."

"But you said he didn't have children. . . ." And so on.

Tonahill used the dogs on a member of the jury: "Do you like dawgs?"

"I guess so," said the juror.

"Jack Ruby luuuuved dawgs," gushed Tonahill.

It was too much for Judge Brown. "Ah like dawgs, too, Mr. Tonahill, always have. Git on with sumpin' else. . . ."

Both Belli and Tonahill detested the assistant district attorney, Bill Alexander. They were kinder to Buck Wade, who was more gentlemanly, although at one point when Wade was less than courteous to a Belli witness, Ole Doc scolded: "This is the most insulting district attorney I've ever heard. He can outshout anyone. This is incompetent, irrelevant, immaterial, dirty, salacious, meretricious, and insulting. . . ."

"And furthermore it's un-Texan," chimed Tonahill from the sidelines.

"Git on with sumpin' else, Mr. Bell-eye," intoned the weary Judge Brown.

It became a status symbol to get into the trial and the elite of

Dallas, such as the Neiman Marcus clan (who seemed too elegant and sophisticated for the steak and barbecue standards of Dallas), held parties and receptions for the foreign press and tried to present a more civilized impression of their city. In return for this hospitality we of the press would lend our press and admission cards to our new friends so that they could spend a half-hour watching history. Occasionally I lent mine to Ham Richardson, the tennis player.

Throughout the trial Belli was working on a movie and a book about the case. He was shooting film that would be fitted into a script later. Judge Brown would even return to court after hours to re-enact the day's proceedings, with Belli making arguments and the judge responding. It was incredible. Belli had planned to go to nearby Huntsville Penitentiary to be filmed sitting in the electric chair but cancelled his plans. "Just as well," cracked his movie producer, Sam Gallu. "After what Mel's been saying about Dallas, he'd be nuts to sit in their electric chair!"

For such a serious case, the atmosphere was almost slapstick. It was Monty Python's Flying Circus a decade ahead of its time. For instance, the day of the jailbreak. Just before 4 P.M., as stripper Little Lynn—who wasn't so little at the time, being nine months and three days pregnant—was waiting to testify, seven prisoners in the connecting county jail grabbed a woman hostage and raced down the corridor to freedom. They'd fashioned a pistol of soap and pencils and shoe polish, persuaded guards that it was real, and made their break, witnessed by some 100 million TV viewers.

Little Lynn, who was waiting in the corridor with Belli's beautiful ash-blonde wife, Joy, immediately fainted, thinking they were gangland hoods out to wreak vengeance on her for testifying. It looked for a moment as if Doc Belli would have to play midwife. Four of the jailbreakers were quickly captured—again on TV, this time in the street in front of the courthouse. The courtroom doors were immediately locked to keep everyone inside in case it was a rescue attempt. When it was realized this was merely a run-of-the-mill Texas jailbreak, court recessed while order was restored. I asked a guard at the courtroom door if he'd seen the escape and he replied nonchalantly: "Yep, Ah saw 'em, but Ah couldn't leave mah post."

Belli was incredulous. "Upstaged," he said. "Now the American Bar Association will accuse me of arranging this. . . ."

Leonard Parkin had been on the pay phone in the corridor to his Washington office, hooked into the BBC news in Britain, when the jailbreak occurred. He picked up the action and gave running commentary as events unfolded. Parkin was having trouble convincing London that his broadcast was genuine. The discourse went something like this:

"As I speak there is a chap running towards me with what appears to be a gun. No, it is three chaps . . . no, seven men and a woman who appears to be a hostage . . . she is screaming . . . the gun seems to be a toy or made out of something . . . goodness, it seems to be a prison break . . . My God, there is a collapsed witness . . . she is pregnant and I think—great heavens, it looks like she is having a baby! . . . Television cameras are following the break. As I speak the event is being broadcast in America . . . What . . . no, my dear chap, I am not kidding . . . no, I have *not* been drinking . . . listen, you bloody fools, this is America, this is Texas . . . Any bloody insane thing is possible here . . . I know it's crazy . . . well, if you don't believe it, don't use it . . . Dammit, why do I stay in this crazy business. . ."

And he hung up and went for a drink.

The next day the New York *Daily News* ran an eloquent black headline "Oh, Dallas!"

For a month the trial went on. Ruby became almost incidental. The quest for truth was lost, the goal of justice forgotten. Little evidence was introduced to show that security at the police station was lax the day Oswald was shot, though repeatedly police witnesses insisted that security precautions were adequate.

There is a Russian proverb to the effect that "he lies like a witness." The Dallas police brought this proverb to mind when Doc Belli grilled Detective Tom McMillon for almost five hours trying to shake his testimony that he heard Ruby yell as he shot Oswald: "You rat son of a bitch, you shot the President." And the detective swore he heard Ruby say as he lay handcuffed on the jail floor: "I hope I killed the son of a bitch." Police also testified that Ruby told them: "I meant to shoot him three times, but you police moved too fast and I got off only one shot."

Police Captain Glenn King testified that when he said, "Of all the low-life scum things, this takes the cake. Why'd you do it?" Ruby replied: "Somebody had to do it . . . you guys couldn't."

Curiously, none of these alleged quotes appeared in any records or notebooks of policemen. And the Dallas police hadn't mentioned them to the FBI. They were being heard for the first (and only?) time at Ruby's trial. Belli was foiled in attempts to have the police witnesses take a lie detector test, just as he had been foiled in his bid to have jurors submit to a Rorschach inkblot test to judge their psychological stability. Belli was nothing if not innovative. Not for nothing were his tactics called "Machiavellian": do anything that helps your client and confuses the opposition. Nor was he successful when he protested that original police documents, reports, and notes should be submitted as evidence, instead of carbon copies and photostats, which he called "as valid as a Chinese laundry ticket."

To this Judge Brown responded: "Overruled, Mr. Bell-eye. Git on with sumpin' else."

During police cross-examination, District Attorney Wade was fondling the murder revolver when a nervous Joe Tonahill asked: "Hold that gun a little higher, Hank, I don't know if it's loaded or not . . ."

"Let's check it to be sure," drawled Wade—and pulled the trigger at Tonahill's chest. As the loud "click" reverberated through the silent courtroom, Belli hit the roof. Screaming and shouting, he had little effect on anyone except the spectators. Wade was grinning and Judge Brown calmly uttered his trademark: "Let's git on with sumpin' else, Mr. Bell-eye."

Strangely, as the trial drew to a close, of three defence lawyers who addressed the jury it was Joe Tonahill who stole the show from Mel Belli. He made his pitch on behalf of Ruby, "a sick man, sufferin' from psychomotor epilepsy . . . this ex-G.I., a good man, a patriotic man, doin' the best he can. . . . Ladies and gentlemen, write a verdict the world will praise you for. . . ."

Tonahill drew upon all his Texan eloquence, as he proclaimed: "And Bill Alexander . . . Bill Alexander would jest love to travel through the rollin' hills, the bluebonnets, the dogwood, and the tall pines of east Texas on his way to Huntsville [penitentiary] to watch another man electrocuted. He'd go—he'd *looove* to go. Can't you see the pleasure in his eyes if you gave him the death sentence? You've seen those eyes, those great tarantula-like eyes . . . nasty, repulsive-lookin' eyes . . ."

On this occasion the judge interrupted, to suggest that Tonahill might be going a mite far and to ask what was his point.

Tonahill wasn't deterred: "Jedge, Ah've been lookin' into them eyes f'r a month now—and they are *reeeepulsive!*" Then Tonahill turned and stared long and hard at the bemused jury. He leaned forward and in a voice so low and confiding it was almost a whisper: "Ah see greeeeeat character in *yore* eyes!"

If the jury wasn't shaken by this oratory, certainly the rest of the courtroom was. District Attorney Wade was brief, succinct, and businesslike by comparison: "Jack Ruby is a glory-seeker who wanted the limelight, who wanted to go down in history. You can bet your last dollar if this man is set free the Communists will be darned happy . . . Turn this man loose and you'll turn civilization back a century, back to lynch law. What will you want history books to say about you? You want them to say that we slapped this man's wrists and gave him a little penitentiary sentence?

"Jack Ruby and his defence ask for mercy and sympathy. I ask you to show him the same sympathy as he showed Lee Harvey Oswald. You want the world and communism to know that we believe in a world of law."

When the jury retired, it was after 1 A.M. They went to bed to reconvene in the morning. Everyone was emotionally and physically exhausted. Few could think straight. Few expressed an opinion. As one who had covered the trial from start to finish and fluctuated between horror and amusement at Dallas justice, it never occurred to me that the end of the trial would be out of character with the rest of it. Like others, I didn't believe Ruby would get the death sentence; there were too many doubts about his sanity. Also, it would be wrong to execute the last living link to a possible connection with the Kennedy slaying. Besides, no one is killed in a Laurel and Hardy movie!

Everyone was surprised when the jury reconvened at 9.15 A.M., reviewed the twenty-four days of testimony from sixty-five witnesses in 140 minutes, and reached a "guilty" verdict. In Texas, juries also set the penalty, and this jury opted for the electric chair. No one had expected the chair, especially when conventional wisdom had it that a quick verdict from complex testimony indicates "not guilty." Pandemonium erupted, with reporters and cameramen clambering all over one another (George Brimmell of Southam was crouched over a table writing up Belli's outburst when a TV cameraman literally ran up his back onto the table for a better shot. Brimmel, with a huge dusty footprint in the middle of his blue jacket, was speechless with indignation.)

Mel Belli is one of those people who becomes even more articulate when angry. The indecently quick "guilty" verdict of the Dallas jury meant that Belli's thoughtful, persuasive defence had no effect whatever. The whole trial and the careful sifting through 162 potential jurors to reach 12 "good people and true" was an exercise in fatuity and futility.

Belli, with heavy irony, thanked the jury for a "victory for bigotry and injustice . . . I hope the people of Dallas are proud of this jury." He went on: "Any second-year law student could have gotten Ruby off with a life sentence by begging for mercy . . . We didn't beg. We had a legal case; I made the mistake of arguing the law in Dallas.

"I shall never return here; it's an evil, bigoted, rotten, stinking town. They wanted Ruby to grovel, to say, 'I'm a Jew and you're the master race and I'm so sorry.'

"I want to go to New York, stand in Times Square, and see some Jews walk by, Puerto Ricans, Dagos, Niggers, white people, and say, 'Thank Christ I'm back in America, they are free men.' "

He predicted that the appeal courts would "chastise this kangaroo-pouch judge who sat on this case—he didn't walk to the bench, he hopped." Afterward, when Judge Brown approached Belli with his hand outstretched, the lawyer refused the gesture: "I can't shake hands with you, judge, you've got blood on them."

Judge Brown looked sad: "I'm sorry you feel that way, Mel . . . come back and see us sometime."

Ruby, for his part, had been growing more and more erratic during the trial and occasionally Joe Tonahill would try flashing photos of Jackie Kennedy at him, apparently hoping he would break down and reinforce the defence argument of emotional instability. After the verdict Ruby asked Belli to burn his clothes, fearful that they'd wind up in a wax museum to be gawked at.

Meanwhile, Dallas revelled in the verdict, pleased that Belli had been put in his place, relieved that Ruby, who also wore Oswald's guilt, would purge them of their extremism by his death.

As it happened, Ruby didn't die in the electric chair at Huntsville penitentiary. He died three years later, almost to the day of the trial, from cancer. But before that, Belli's predictions had come true: the appeal courts had ordered a new trial in a different city. The change of venue that Belli had insisted was necessary was ordered by the appeal courts. The request had been refused by Judge Brown because, more than anything on earth, he wanted to be part of history in the trial of the century. He got his wish, but not the way he intended.

As for Belli, shortly after his outburst, he was fired as Ruby's lawyer by Ruby's sister, Eva Grant, who said she disapproved of the way Belli had conducted the case and expressed horror that he could think and say such unkind things about the city of Dallas. Earlier, he had cracked that Dallas was the sort of town where Santa Claus would get a ticket on Christmas Eve for parking outside an orphanage. Belli realized he'd alienated future chances in Texas with his outburst, and quit anyway, having guaranteed there'd have to be a new trial.

Jack Ruby won a form of immortality and a place in criminal and political legend. Was he part of a plot, or was he not? Was he the predetermined executioner of the executioner, or an accident of fate? The flaw in any conspiracy theory is that Oswald was an ideologue, a semi-literate left-wing extremist, while Ruby wouldn't know what an ideologue was unless it did a strip-tease for him. Ruby was a fringe underworld character with mental stability like quicksilver. So was Oswald. To choose two such perfect foils on which to base a presidential murder plot challenges credulity. The trouble with both the Oswald and the Ruby cases is that there has been so much official deceit, perjury, rationalization, and cover-up that the deeds *seem* more sinister than they may actually have been. We will probably never know the truth.

For me, personally, the trial left a scar. Whatever the Dallas fiasco was, it wasn't "law." Nor was it "justice." Nor was it right. I retreated into some complacency, thinking that at least in Canada our system was better. We don't elect judges or district attorneys, so law and justice have a better chance when administered by those who have no obligation except to truth. The American system of justice can hide as much as it reveals, and one sometimes gets the feeling that if the "truth" is disquieting or dangerous— or deemed in the national interest *not* to be revealed—then it will be camouflaged, altered, or buried.

19

Screw the Chinese—wanna go to Russia?

JOHN BASSETT
PUBLISHER, TORONTO *TELEGRAM*
SEPTEMBER 1964

I had just returned to Toronto from a frustrating summer languishing on the beaches of Hong Kong, waiting in vain for a visa to enter China with an eye to possibly opening a bureau there for the Toronto *Telegram*. I had hoped to be the first journalist allowed into China after the Great Leap Forward had stumbled and fallen on its face and just prior to the Cultural Revolution, which was to contort China and do inestimable harm. The *Tely* was embroiled in a printers' strike, and the editorial staff were defying union picket lines to publish the paper—even though the staff were members of the Newspaper Guild and supposedly should honor another union's picket line. But it was a bad strike, a foolish strike, in which the headquarters of the International Typographers' Union in Colorado Springs had overruled the local union's acceptance of a contract and ordered the walk-out, thus constituting interference in Canadian affairs from abroad.

I had gone to Hong Kong on instructions of publisher John Bassett, who was now running his strikebound newspaper rather as the commanding general ran the siege of Leningrad—or as he would have when he was a company commander of the Seaforth Highlanders in the Italian campaign during World War II. He was having the time of his life. Bassett spotted me as I slunk into the newsroom. Like most reporters who don't succeed in getting the story they were sent after, I felt vaguely to blame for failing to get into China after having virtually been promised a visa.

"Hi, Pete, where've you been?" boomed Bassett, grinning from his six-foot-four matinée-idol height. Bassett didn't talk; he shouted, he bellowed.

"I'm just back from Hong Kong," I said. "Sorry about China."

"What about China?"

"Sorry they wouldn't let me in."

"They wouldn't? Why'd you want to go there anyway?"

"Because you sent me."

"I did? Well, screw the Chinese. Guess we're too tough for them, eh!" And he roared with laughter at the thought that his paper was too blatantly capitalistic for the Commies.

"No, they said because I'd been in the Korean War."

"Screw 'em. Wanna go to Russia?" Bassett roared again.

"What's the story?"

"No story. To live. Open a bureau. Show we're a responsible newspaper. Interested?"

"Of course. When?"

"Whenever you want. You figure it out. Tell JDM. See me before you go."

And Bassett was off to the current battlefront in the composing room, where the forces of unionized socialism were head-on against journalistic free enterprise. "JDM" was Doug MacFarlane, the editor-in-chief who had been a top city and managing editor and was then in fading glory, trying to anticipate the whims of Bassett who had enough of the bully in him to try and dominate free spirits and turn independent thinkers into yes-men if they let him. Those who capitulated to Bassett lost his respect; those who stood up to him won his friendship—or his everlasting enmity. The outcome was a gamble. A lot of newspaper editors are that way too, most of them doomed to mediocrity. The wise ones encourage individuality and welcome initiative because it also makes them look good.

For nearly three months I'd stayed incognito in Hong Kong, every day visiting the New China News Agency (Hsinhua), to see if my promised visa for China had been authorized by Peking. Every day the answer had been no. The positive, friendly assurances of its approval at the beginning of summer—only a technicality delayed it, and please return tomorrow—had altered to increasingly frosty receptions. Peking finally decided I was not acceptable. I demanded to know why I had been led on, and a somewhat sheepish Hsinhua man said that Peking had decided I was an enemy of the People's Republic, *not* because I had fought in the Korean War as an infantry officer with the Canadian army, but because I had flown in spotter planes with the Americans and marked targets for jets to bomb. They felt that this showed excessive zeal and therefore I'd be unwelcome at this time. Sorry, but try again next decade.

So now, on return to Toronto and in the midst of apologies to Bassett, I was suddenly slated to open a bureau in Moscow for the *Tely*, the only Canadian newspaper to be represented in Russia. It was all part of the *Tely*'s international look to build circulation and prove we were a thoughtful, responsible newspaper as well as providing hellbent "*Tely* man on the spot" journalism. It was also typical of Bassett's dealings with me: an apparently impetuous decision that he might forget in twenty-four hours.

However, this time he meant it. My wife Helen, also a journalist, was enthralled at the prospect of living in Moscow. The plan was that I'd go first, arrange an apartment, and in a couple of months she'd follow with our son Casey, who'd been born that May. While I would be the "official" correspondent, she would write a woman's-eye view of Moscow, and we'd give double coverage.

I was a little uneasy because the strain on our marriage, due partly to all my travelling, had not eased. We both hoped that sharing a foreign adventure would somehow cement the marriage. Moscow captured Helen's imagination: for once she was going to participate. We planned with enthusiasm. We sold all our furniture and belongings at a giant newspaper auction. We didn't want to be saddled with material things. It felt as if a chain was being unlocked. I wondered if I'd ever live permanently in Canada again. Living abroad as a correspondent was a dream come true: independence with someone else paying.

Amid all these preparations I got a phone call from my father in Ottawa who, with forced cheerfulness in his voice, announced that medical tests had shown cancer in his bowels. I took it in stride, not wanting my voice to betray real feelings. "What did the doctor say?"

"Oh, they think they've caught it early. The sawbones wants to put me under the knife."

"Well, do it. It's good they caught it early." What do you say when your father, whom you considered indestructible even as he was approaching eighty, announces his death warrant?

"Yep. Well. Just wanted you to know."

I could sense the apprehension in him. He wasn't yet reconciled to the blow. That would come later, when he would delight in shocking people by announcing, say at a party, that he wasn't feeling too well.

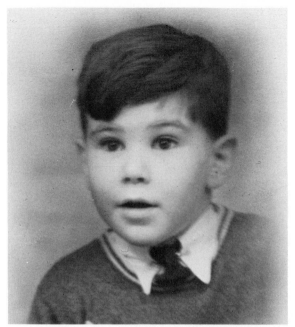

Age 4, at Fort Osborne Barracks, Winnipeg. When the photographer hit father with a newspaper to make us laugh, my sister Robin fled in tears and I looked on in amazement.

Age 17, trying to look battle-worn after a few months in the navy in World War II.

My father in command of Camp Borden in 1945 after being sent home from overseas as too old to take his 4th Armoured Division into action in Normandy.

With my parents at the unveiling of a bust of my father in a tank park named after him, Camp Borden, 1964. He died in 1967 and is buried in the park, surrounded by his beloved tanks.

In the Korean trenches of the Princess Pats with Colonel (later General) Joe Stillwell after a Chinese assault. He was later to command Americans in Vietnam.

With Gamal Abdel Nasser in Egypt, 1959, after delivering a shipload of milk powder for needy Egyptian kids, a Toronto *Telegram* stunt to show what great humanitarians we were.

Dr. Albert Schweitzer with patients at his jungle hospital at Lambaréné, Gabon, in French Equatorial Africa. The place resembled a slum rather than a hospital when I was there.

With Dani tribesmen in central Dutch New Guinea a few years after these prehistoric people had been discovered by the outside world. They had a "war culture" which the Dutch tried to curb.

At the slaying of Lee Harvey Oswald in the underground garage of the Dallas police station. The picture, taken off television, shows me looking puzzled at the sudden turn of events.

The Canadian Embassy hockey team in Moscow in the process of defeating the Czech Embassy team in 1965. At the time, the Canadians were the only undefeated Canadian hockey team in international play!

My Russian translator Olga, who defected from the
USSR, caused concern among the KGB and
Western security, and hastened my departure from-
Moscow.

With Emeka Ojukwu, the Biafran head of state. The African messiah turned out to be just another demagogue.

Taken as Biafran forces captured a road on the outskirts of Owerri
and were awaiting the counterattack by Nigerian forces, 1969.

The birth of the Toronto *Sun*, November 1, 1971, (left to right) Doug Bassett, our printer, *Sun* General Manager Don Hunt, Publisher Doug Creighton, City Editor Ray Biggart and the slightly punchy Editor.

Prime Minister John Diefenbaker was an ardent admirer of the *Sun*'s editorial policy. Here he talks to Danielle Crittenden, my stepdaughter, who is now a reporter.

In 1976 RCMP Security Services raided my office under terms of the Official Secrets Act, in search of a letter from the RCMP about the Prime Minister which was leaked to the *Sun*. It concerned the order not to hold security clearance interviews with government employees who might have Quebec separatist sympathies.

I face the press after being charged under the Official Secrets Act in 1978 for writing about a top secret RCMP document dealing with Soviet espionage activities in Canada.

When the *Sun*, its Editor and Publisher were charged under the Official Secrets Act, protesters gathered at Toronto's Old City Hall in support. Most were from East Europe.

In happier days (1981), Prime Minister Joe Clark visits one of the most cluttered offices in journalism where a photo of a hard-eyed Pierre Trudeau gazes on my work.

After losing the Progressive Conservative nomination in the Broadview-Greenwood by-election in 1982, MP David Crombie urges me to make the choice of Bill Fatsis unanimous.

Running as an independent in the Broadview-Greenwood by-election in 1982 and coming a close second to the NDP.

Finally breaking through and winning the Tory nomination in Broadview-Greenwood in 1984, after two years of struggling. Wife Yvonne also seems pleased.

"Oh dear, you've got that bug that's going around, I expect," someone would say solicitously.

"Nope. Not a bug. Worse than that," Worthy would say.

"Oh. What?" The fly walked into the trap.

"Cancer. Of the bowel. Probably terminal." And the group would reel in horror, not knowing what to say. My mother would get furious: "For shame, Worthy, you *mustn't* do that to people, it isn't fair." And he would guffaw—all of it a defensive reaction to cover the shock of knowing, yet not wanting to admit.

On the other hand, the moment he announced on the phone that he had cancer I knew it was all over. My father, who all his life had overflowed with enthusiasm and energy, was mortal after all. It is a realization that comes to all of us, but is no less painful because of it. I went for a long walk that night and tried to resign myself to the prospect of his death. The operation would be over before I left for Moscow, and I thought that reacting casually and without undue concern would be the most positive thing I could do for him.

There wasn't time to fully prepare for Moscow and learn the Russian language, so I tried at least to learn the alphabet. Misha Allen, one of the leading collectors of underground ballads, songs, and poetry in the USSR and an avid observer of the Soviet press who'd emigrated to Canada years ago, undertook to teach me basic Russian. I planned to get a full-time teacher once I was in Moscow.

After my recent experiences with the Chinese, I was uneasy about the Soviets. But there was no problem. The embassy officials in Ottawa seemed as pleased at my going to their country as the Chinese had been cool. My contact was Mr. Murashev, and we had several lunches comparing notes while he tried to establish rapport. I met several times with Soviet diplomats who expressed hope that the "understanding" of *Telegram* readers would be enhanced by my reports. I could easily agree with that goal without perjuring or committing myself. The Soviet Embassy knew of some of the work I had done, knew my reaction to Vietnam, was aware that I had been briefly jailed and thrown out of Angola and Mozambique and that I had been unwelcome in Rhodesia and unpopular in South Africa for my views on racism. On the surface I must have seemed a likely candidate for fellow travelling.

I was also briefed by External Affairs officials and RCMP security. They seemed concerned that I, a foreigner, might wind up being compromised or trapped in espionage or subversion. I was amused. "I think it most unlikely that I'll become a Soviet spy," I said flippantly.

"We certainly hope not," was the reply. "But be careful."

"What do I have to be careful of if I don't intend to be a spy?"

"Blackmail. You never know."

"How would they be able to blackmail me?"

"Sex. They may seduce you and then blackmail you with photographs."

"Ahh!"

"Yes. We advise you to be especially careful of 'friendships' with beautiful Russian women you may meet. Assume they are all KGB."

"Well, I'm not often besieged by beautiful women," I quipped, thinking it all a bit of a lark.

"Don't be too sure. We can almost guarantee that there will be attempts to seduce you—any foreigner, in fact, who goes to live in the USSR. When it happens, be careful."

I was suddenly intrigued. "Who is likely to do it?"

"One never knows, but the KGB likes to use the Bolshoi ballerinas."

"They do? Well, I'll certainly be on the lookout." I made a mental note to go to the Bolshoi Ballet at the earliest opportunity. I still didn't take this part of the conversation too seriously, but assumed they knew what they were talking about. To end any suspense on the reader's part, not only did I *not* get seduced in Moscow, I don't think I encountered one ballerina, much less got picked up by one. Still, the advice wasn't bad since strange things happen to foreigners in the USSR.

I was to fly to Moscow in January 1965, and Helen and Casey would follow by boat later, going to Odessa on the Black Sea with a couple of steamer trunks loaded with belongings. We wanted to have enough Western goods to last for two years—things that were unavailable in Moscow. After I'd scouted the territory, I would write Helen about what she should take. Helen was to write of her sea trip with our eight-month-old baby, under the logo "To Russia with Casey."

On the way to the USSR, I stopped over in Britain to work out a deal to also represent the London *Sun*, then pre-Rupert Murdoch and mildly left-wing and respectable—that is, before it specialized in full-page photographs of topless girls on page three.

On a crystal-clear, cold January night I flew by Aeroflot into Moscow, where someone from the Canadian Embassy was to meet me. After resisting blandishments by the plump stewardess to buy bottles of vodka (surely she couldn't be a ballerina after bigger game?), I yielded and bought a bulky medallion of cosmonaut Yuri Gagarin, the first human to orbit the earth. Her quota met, she lost interest in me. The first surprise of Moscow was that airport formalities were informal, quick, casual. A ridiculously young soldier collected all passports when the plane landed at Sheremetievo Airport, and I assured a suspicious woman in a uniform that I was carrying neither firearms nor gold—the only items that seemed to interest her. My passport was returned and I was let into the country without a baggage search or any special interest shown. I was met by Bill Warden, second secretary at the Canadian Embassy, who would take me to the Ukraina Hotel. I was still impressed with the speed and ease of passing through customs. "Guess a lot of what we hear about Russia is nonsense," I ventured to Warden. "A lot of right-wing, anti-Communist propaganda perhaps?"

Warden looked at me cautiously and said not to jump to conclusions. "Wait a while before you write how liberal and easy and misunderstood Russia is," he advised. How typical of diplomats to be suspicious and cagey, I thought to myself. Perhaps we'd be better served if we took people and political systems at face value and didn't react on preconceived notions. It was a passing thought that didn't last long enough to blossom into anything permanent or embarrassing.

I was bursting to know about Russia *and* the Soviet Union: Misha Allen had impressed upon me that I should *not* confuse the two. Russia was *not* synonymous with the Soviet Union. At first I thought that a bit petty, since mostly Russians run the USSR, but I soon learned it is offensive and simply wrong to assume that all citizens of the Soviet Union are Russians. It's like saying all citizens of the British Isles are English. Russia is simply one of the fifteen republics that comprise the Soviet Union, although it is the whip hand of the system. Put another way, Russians are as much victims of the Soviet system as are Ukrainians, Estonians, Latvians, Armenians, and so forth, who've been incorporated into the Red empire.

I was interested in seeing the Kremlin and Red Square and in learning the nuts and bolts of life in Moscow. How did one get an apartment, buy a car, get accreditation? What did KGB mean, did the phones work, were you followed, was it true that Bolshoi ballerinas seduced willing foreigners, could one meet Brezhnev or Kosygin or the famous unperson, Nikita Khrushchev? And so on. The questions poured out, while Warden, polite and helpful, was more interested in whether or not I played hockey. There were only five Canadians in Moscow who played hockey of sorts, and they needed a sixth to make a full team. Hopefully, me. Warden's manner warmed considerably when I replied yes, I used to play hockey—not well, but enthusiastically. But that was over twenty years ago. Never mind, said Warden, hockey is like riding a bike, you never completely forget. Would I play? Practice the next night at the British Embassy: they flooded the tennis court and used it.

I'd be delighted to play but warned again that I'd been away from the game for a long time. Besides, I had no skates.

"Never mind the questions," said Warden. "That's for later. We'll get you skates. I'll pick you up at seven o'clock tomorrow. We play the American Embassy Sunday. Be ready!"

Warden actually seemed glad I had arrived. I was to quickly learn that his unenthusiastic, even gloomy manner was endemic in Moscow, not confined to foreigners or anti-Communists, but anyone who lived there, including Soviet citizens. There is something about Sovietism that is cheerless, soulless, heavy, and depressing, no matter how enthusiastic a fellow traveller one might be.

Warden must have felt a bit guilty. "Relax. Everything seems confused now. We've all been through it. I'll introduce you to Jack Best of Canadian Press, he's just got his apartment and can tell you. He's a good guy—hell of a hockey player! And David Levy of CBC, he's in your hotel, too, waiting for an apartment. They'll be a big help. Levy doesn't play hockey, though."

So began my two-year stint in Moscow, during which time our six-man hockey team never lost a game and was the only consistently successful Canadian hockey team in international play.

In 1965 I had already been in journalism for eleven years, nine of them specializing in covering foreign crises, civil wars, revolutions, coups, and so on. Even though most crises involved the USSR in some way, I knew little of ideology or Russian history and, like most journalists (even now), thought the fixation of some on Soviet subversion and espionage mostly a manifestation of right-wing paranoia, even McCarthyism.

The fact that the Soviets had sided with the Allies against Naziism had affected people in the immediate postwar period. I was still impressed at how the Soviets had fought long and hard to defeat

Hitler and recalled the siege of Stalingrad that had won the admiration of people everywhere. Victory made people forget the
earlier Hitler-Stalin pact whereby the two had divvied up Poland.
We rationalized that Stalin had to sign a nonaggression treaty with
Hitler for his own protection and ignored the fact that the "deal"
guaranteed Hitler's invasion of Poland, thus starting World War
II. It would be twenty to thirty years before the shameful secrets
of the war's end emerged: accounts of forced repatriation whereby
the British and the Americans conspired to forcibly send millions
of refugees and emigrés back to Stalin and certain death. Churchill, in his memoirs, never mentioned a word of this infamous
policy—arguably, the most shameful in British history.

Like many Canadians, I felt betrayed by our former ally after
Igor Gouzenko escaped from the Soviet Embassy in Ottawa with
documents that made it impossible to ignore widespread Soviet
espionage. But it didn't mean much in personal terms. Even while
fighting the Chinese Communists in Korea, I had no personal
animosity. Canadian soldiers don't usually have to engender hatred
in order to fight well. They do their job professionally and with
detachment. (A criticism of the American military was that they
tended to "hate" their enemy, while the British dined with them
once they were captured; I was conditioned to think British-style
soldiering was superior to American.) If I still felt neutral about
communism after going to war against it, I suppose it should have
been no surprise that I'd cover the world as a journalist without
having strong feelings. Of course after the uprising ("revolution"
is too grand a description) in Hungary in 1956, I felt communism
was something free men should not passively accept but in those
days I was unsure whether communism or Russia was to blame
for Hungary: was it Stalinism, Sovietism, or Russian chauvinism?
At the time there was debate. We now know that Hungary and
all that has happened since was an inevitable consequence of
Marxism and Leninism.

As the representative of the first Canadian newspaper to open
a bureau in Moscow, I was determined to be fair and avoid politics
and Kremlinology. I would write about daily happenings and try
to give readers an honest impression of Soviet life.

The Ukraina Hotel where I was to stay was built in the mid-
'50s—one of six wedding-cake structures that dot the Moscow
skyline and are ornate, inefficient, grotesque, and somewhat reminiscent of a Walt Disney film gone haywire. Variously described
as Gorky Street or Coney Island Gothic, the 1,800-guest Ukraina

was run mostly by women. It had the slowest elevators in the world, a cavernous, dimly lit lobby filled with stuffed armchairs in which sullen, pudding-faced men in fedoras lounged and were assumed to be KGB waiting to follow someone somewhere. Only one side of a double door was ever opened, winter and summer, making it necessary for people to queue up to get in and queue up to get out. A permanent traffic jam. I though I might have to live in the Ukraina for a month, but it stretched into a year while a new apartment building for foreigners was constructed (again by women laborers) across the street.

Logistical problems were such that I had little time to concentrate on serious journalism, so instead of trying to keep on top of "news," I wrote about my experiences, hoping to convey what it was like to move from an easygoing, consumer-oriented North American free-enterprise society to a controlled, production-planned, Soviet socialistic society. Both David Levy and Jack Best were helpful. Books have been written about what living in Moscow is like, and it really requires a book to give an accurate depiction. Nothing in the Soviet Union is easy. There are enormous suspicions toward anything that isn't difficult. I found the daily battle to get settled rich in material to write about.

For foreigners the most important organization is one known as UPDK, pronounced phonetically "Oopedika," which handles most things involving foreign residents. It has direct links with the KGB. Through UPDK I arranged for a Russian teacher, Natasha, to come for an hour, three days a week, to teach me the language. UPDK also sent me a translator/interpreter who would be a combination secretary, fixer, advisor, and so forth. UPDK would eventually find me an apartment, let me buy a car, get a leaking roof fixed or a stove repaired. The translator is essential, even for those who speak Russian. With a population then of seven million, Moscow had (and still has) no phone book; each citizen collects a personal list of important numbers. Hire a translator and you have access to his (more likely her) contacts. A fixer.

UPDK didn't know how long it would take for me to get an apartment but mentioned a year. I blanched, but even that seemed optimistic. If I was going to live a year in the Ukraina, complete with wife and baby, I was determined to have some comfort, so I got a suite that rented for $15 a day. It had a vestibule that led into a sitting room, which contained a large round dining table, a piano, a couple of glass bookcases, settees along the wall, and a temperamental black-and-white TV set. A door at one end of the sitting room led to a bedroom which also had an entrance to the vestibule. At the other end of the sitting room was an office that, too, led to the vestibule. At both ends there were bathrooms. Because there was no kitchenette in the suite, I bought a hotplate and converted the bathroom next to the office into a kitchen by placing a sheet of plywood over the bathtub to make a table. There was no refrigerator, of course, so milk and perishables were kept on the outside window ledge.

My two top priorities were to get a translator and to buy a car. Being in Moscow without knowing the language was akin to being perpetually lost. Very few people speak English; there are no little stores into which one can pop and ask directions. If lost, one is in trouble. Signs are unreadable, and if you forget the word for "hotel" (*gostinitza*) you have no way to get home. The Russian alphabet is a mixture of Roman and Cyrillic script and hard to fathom at first, especially when familiar letters have unfamiliar pronunciations. *P* sounds like *R*, *C* like *S*, *H* like *N*. *D* is a *D* unless it is in handwriting, then lower-case *g* is *D* and lower-case *m* is *T*. The Russian word *pectopah* is pronounced "restoran." Confusing.

Jack Best and his wife Joan had recently got an apartment, and they were an invaluable source of useful advice, especially with the domestic dilemmas; the CBC's David Levy, who spoke Russian, was staying at the Ukraina and helped me buy my car.

Moscow-based journalists, being special creatures with diplomatic privileges, could buy Mercedes cars through the German Embassy at cost, no taxes, no duty—$2,400. While tempted, I felt I would be more self-sufficient if I had a Russian car. Also, I'd blend into the surroundings better, and getting spare parts should be easier, repairs more convenient. At least that's what I thought. Little did I know that spare parts for Soviet cars are often available only if you import them from Finland or Western Europe. I arranged to buy a Volga—rather like a 1938 Dodge or Plymouth—for $1,500 in U.S. funds, instead of the equivalent of $7,500 in roubles.

The fancy big Russian cars were the Chaika (Seagull), which was the size of a 1950 Mercury, and the ZIL, which was for high-level government officials. It had curtains in the windows, obeyed no traffic regulations, and could run red lights or drive in the centre strip and never fear a whistle from the omnipresent militia. The smallest car was the Moskevich, which was the Russian version of a Volkswagen—only a Volkswagen is reliable. There was also a lousy little car called Zaprozhets, which was like a mini-Morris.

Not only were cars expensive, but for Soviet citizens there was a five- to seven-year waiting list. Anyone with the required money to buy a car was probably involved in the black market, since the average wage for doctors or factory workers was $120 a month.

Despite being somewhat stiff and uncomfortable—a bit like riding in a jeep—the Volga was a solid, reliable car. The first problem in mid-winter was to get anti-freeze. There was none to be had. I was desperate and had no idea what I'd do with the temperature plunging to −20°C and −30°C every night. Levy and I spent a day driving to every machine shop, garage, and supply centre without luck, but finally managed to buy crude alcohol-based anti-freeze on the black market. Joy was shortlived. It evaporated quickly and by the next day was almost gone. I thought I'd have to resort to the Russian method of either putting the car on blocks for the winter or draining the radiator every time the car was not in use for any length of time, and refilling it when the car was needed.

The Volga, which was the size of a modest compact, drove roughly, but it was hardy and started in winter, which was a blessing since there are no electric heaters for engines. On cold mornings, all over Moscow, the few citizens with cars would get out early and build small fires under the engines so the rising heat would make the cars easier to start.

By throwing myself on the mercies of Canadian Ambassador Robert Ford, I got permission for Canadian journalists to use embassy anti-freeze. I should have gone to the Embassy in the first place. The Americans, too, were unstintingly generous with their facilities to all foreigners in need.

Anti-freeze was only the first problem. For some inexplicable reason, windshield wipers are a much-sought-after item in Russia, even today. Car owners always remove their wipers when they aren't being used, and those who fail to do so have them stolen. If stolen, they are impossible to buy in Moscow: it seems that all are sent abroad to service Volgas around the world. I was forever having mine stolen. For a long time I was convinced that the militia officer in front of the Ukraina ran a theft ring. Once I left the wipers on when I went into the hotel and remembered before I got onto the elevator. I rushed out to save them. Too late, they'd already been nicked and, no, the burly militia officer on duty hadn't seen a thing. I wished I was in position to conduct a body search of him.

Windshield wipers were not the only things that disappeared. One midnight I came out of the Ukraina to find the trunk of my

Volga jimmied open and the spare tire stolen. David Levy and I went immediately to the police station to report it. I went through a laborious grilling.

"Can you describe the tire?" said the captain.

"No. Just a tire. Unused. For a Volga."

"Hmmmm. Any distinguishing marks?"

"Don't think so. It was brand new."

"Could you identify it?"

"Of course not."

The captain shook his head and glowered at Levy, who was translating: "A difficult case," he said.

We left somewhat despondent. Three days later I routinely checked back, without much hope. "Ah, yes," said the militia captain. "We have your tire!"

I went around and indeed they had it. New and beautiful. The office filled with militia types who took turns patting the tire and grinning. They were pleased that I was pleased. I shook the captain's hand. "Amazing," I said. "I must tell you that in my country if I had the tire stolen, I would never have gotten it back so quickly. I must compliment you and your men on being marvellous detectives. James Bond could do no better."

I laid it on a bit, for being friends with police is never wasted. The captain looked enormously pleased and the whole office burst into applause. "We do our best," said the captain modestly. I sent around a bottle of whisky. It was one of the more cheerful moments of my two years in Moscow. God knows what happened to the unlucky wretch they caught stealing from a foreigner!

In Moscow a motorist can be fined on the spot if the car is dirty. It is, or was, a city of trucks, and this cost the state dearly since trucks, which are more expensive to run than cars, were used for pleasure by those with access to them. Empty trucks on streets were the symbol of Moscow. Most amazing was that Moscow had only eight public gasoline stations and you had to join long lines for a fill-up. You filled your own and couldn't pay cash—only coupons, which you purchased elsewhere. So you had to buy gas by the precise litre. In the USSR, no one cleans your windshields, puts air in your tires, checks your oil. You do it yourself.

Foreigners have special licence plates, so while the Volga might blend with its surroundings where a Mercedes or Chevy would stand out and attract crowds, the licence plate was a give-away. Militia stations on the highway would phone ahead that such-and-such a licence should be passing in whatever time it took. If your car didn't appear, the militia would come looking for you. Done for security reasons, it was still a comfort if you weren't a spy. It meant that it was impossible for a foreigner to get lost driving in rural Russia. Someone would come and find you if you took too long passing a checkpoint.

I was having no difficulty finding things to write about while I puzzled my way through the system. Even using the restaurant at the Ukrainia produced stories. The service in Soviet restaurants is notoriously bad and it was impossible to get a quick meal. The menus tend to be several pages long, yet only a few items have prices on them or are available. Some foreigners swear that the menus date back to tsarist times of plenty. One day I was sitting at a table in the uncrowded Ukraina restaurant and no one would serve me. I tried to be patient, but finally hailed the maître d' who looked at me with bewilderment when I announced that I was in a hurry: "If you are in a hurry you should not have sat at this table."

"This table is fine. But I'm still in a hurry."

He shrugged and strolled off—he was wearing a tuxedo with an open-neck shirt. Nothing happened. I waved him down again. "Please, I *must* leave soon."

"That is not a good table to be served quickly."

"Why not?"

"Because the waiter who serves it is sick today."

"But why can't someone else serve it?"

"Because the others have their tables."

"Then why wouldn't someone tell me?"

"You didn't ask."

I missed lunch that day.

Every Sunday at an outdoor rink we would play the U.S. Embassy hockey team: athletic ex-football players and military attachés with old West Point sweaters. Great, energetic, natural athletes, but lousy hockey players.

We'd thump the Americans by 10- or 20-goal margins, and rink-rat crowds of Russians would invariably cheer the Yanks on, proving that sportsmanship favoring the underdog overrules ideology. The oddity was that each upper-echelon American diplomat had his KGB watchdog with long-lens camera, who'd snap his target upside down, sliding into the boards, wobbling over the blue line, in every variety of undignified pose.

One memorable moment came when a flying puck hit the American military attaché's KGB sleuth full in the face. With blood streaming down and Canadian and American players clustered solicitously around him, he had to stay on the job until relieved and pretend to be so engrossed in the game that he wouldn't allow himself to be given first aid, or even allow the flow of blood staunched. Eventually, a comrade phoned headquarters, a change of guard arrived, and the wounded watchdog vanished to get medical attention.

Over the two years we played Soviet teams, TASS (the Soviet news agency), the Czech Embassy, and so on. We tied a couple of games but the closest we came to losing was when we played at the Czech Embassy rink. We had built up a handsome 5-1 lead at the end of the first period, but between periods we downed vodka and caviar provided by our hosts—and barely managed to hold on for a 10-9 win. Or was it a 9-9 tie? Memory is blurred. I found the hockey a joyous release from the pressures of Moscow.

Natasha, who came in to teach me Russian three days a week, was pretty, cheerful, and a compliment to the system. She accepted the Soviet Union for what it was, didn't seem to yearn for the unattainable, lived a decent, unimaginative life, and had not the slightest interest in politics. At the time Moscow was preparing for the twentieth anniversary of the Great Patriotic War and across from my hotel window were huge portraits of members of the Politburo. I was trying to learn their identities, and would ask Natasha who was who. Her laughter would tinkle gaily: "I haven't the faintest idea; they are our leaders."

"Yes, but their names?"

"Who knows? They are always changing."

"Yes, but you *must* know some of them."

"Well, let's see—there, that one who is first, I think he is Brezhnev."

"Of course it's Brezhnev. I know what *he* looks like. And Kosygin, the guy next to him."

"That's Kosygin? So that's what he looks like!"

I stopped trying to obtain a political education from Natasha, who was a good teacher with a gentle sense of humor but, like so many Soviet citizens, who knew the way to best survive was to take no interest in things political. I found it very difficult to fully comprehend that many of them have no opinions about the merits of those who rule them, who decide the fate of the nation. "Why should we?" asked one. "The leaders are there until they are gone and then they are replaced by someone else—who is usually worse." The lack of opinion I found comparable to an adult's view of the sky or the grass. We simply accept that one is blue, the other is green, and rarely puzzle why they are those colors and not others. These things may puzzle a child, but an adult never thinks about them. The same with politics in the USSR. They are beyond the control or influence of the majority of people.

My real education in Moscow began about a month after my arrival when Olga, my Russian translator and fixer, came onto the scene. She was provided by the state, was paid by the *Telegram*, and worked for the KGB. Journalists in Moscow, as I learned, are in the ridiculous position of paying the KGB to spy on them; every Soviet citizen hired by foreigners as domestic help, chauffeur, language teacher, or translator reports regularly and independently to the KGB. Periodically the translators (and others) are brought together to dissect and discuss their employers. Anything indiscreet or derogatory about the foreigners is brought out, especially drinking problems, sexual propensities, political idiosyncrasies, money problems. The translators are also assessed and their observations are constantly cross-referenced with the other reports. Any Soviet employee who gets too fond of or close or loyal to the person for whom he or she works is quietly removed from the job and replaced. Therefore friendships have to be concealed. The employer has no rights other than the right to refuse the person the State sends him. The State will keep supplying bodies until the foreigner accepts someone.

Without necessarily taking action against foreigners, the KGB wants to keep track of everyone. All apartments are bugged, as are phones. Mail from abroad is routinely read, therefore little of interest is missed. Rather than having every foreigner under constant surveillance, there are spot checks and surveillance can be intensified whenever it is deemed worthwhile.

Olga was a striking redhead with pale blue eyes and a unique way of looking at things. She was the third candidate to apply for the job. One person's English was so bad I couldn't understand a word; he eventually went to work for a Japanese correspondent, whose English was also unintelligible. Another translator missed the interview—or rather I had to cancel at the last moment and dash off to cover a violent demonstration of Vietnamese students in front of the American Embassy—and she never returned.

Olga was acknowledged by my colleagues as one of the more enigmatic and intriguing translators. She had never worked for a journalist before and had nothing resembling news sense. She was inclined to say that she approached politics like a chicken: "One peck forward, two hops back." When she read *Pravda* she would quickly say that there was nothing in it worth reporting. I recall once that Marshal Malinovsky, the head of the Red Army, made a particularly bellicose speech against America which Olga had ignored.

"How could you miss it—it's all over page one!" I stormed.

"Surely there's nothing newsworthy in a Soviet marshal yelling slogans at America?"

"Any time the head of the Russian army threatens war, it's news."

"He doesn't mean it. It's just hot air for home consumption."

"That's not the point. It's who's saying it that's news."

"But if it's all nonsense, why call it news if you know it isn't?"

"Dammit, Olga, that's my decision, not yours."

"How do you expect people to know what's important if you get them frightened for no reason?"

"You don't understand, do you?"

"I suppose not. No wonder Western civilization has been in a decline since the sixteenth century . . ."

Olga escaped the ugliness of the present by taking refuge in the past. She was well versed in art and architecture. Although myopic, she was reluctant to wear glasses because, as she would say: "Why should one go out of one's way to see ugliness more clearly?" All the time she was working for me she wore glasses that had one of the arms broken. She had to balance them precariously on her nose, head tilted at an angle so that they wouldn't fall off.

"Why don't you get them fixed?" I would ask.

"Because they are Italian glasses and the fools here would either steal them or destroy them," she would reply. End of discussion.

She considered Moscow crude, with its huge beige buildings, its wide streets, and slab architecture, broken only by the wedding-cake architecture that was popular in the last years of Stalin. A dour city. Not like Olga's beloved Leningrad, the only Soviet city capable of bringing tears of longing to her eyes.

I was settling into the routine of Moscow when in the spring of 1965, Helen and Casey arrived in Odessa. It had been a long trip for them, and I was apprehensive about how my wife would like the Moscow hotel and the prospect of a year there. I took the overnight train to Odessa to meet the boat. It was my first exposure to Soviet trains; compartments are turned into four-person sleeping cars at night, men and women mixed indiscriminately. Helen, Casey, and I stayed overnight in Odessa and caught the train back

to Moscow. Our compartment companion was a motherly Ukrainian woman who adored Casey, then ten months old. He returned
her interest by throwing up all over her. She seemed flattered by
the attention and more or less adopted him for the trip. We discovered Soviet trains to be informal and pleasant, with lots of tea
in glasses and not too much bureaucratic interference.

Helen was not too impressed with the Ukraina suite, especially
the bathroom-turned-kitchenette. David Levy had hired a twenty-
three-year-old Finnish girl, Karen Lindqvist, to come to Moscow
and look after his ten-year-old son. That relationship was growing
a little tense because Karen objected to sharing a room with the
boy and Levy wasn't keen on renting another room. Eventually
he fired her, although she felt she had a year's contract. I was
fond of Karen, as was Helen, who wanted help with Casey, and
so we arranged to hire her as a permanent nanny/helper/friend.
She moved into the suite. Karen, Helen, and Casey shared the
bedroom, while I slept on a cot in the office. As I look back, it
was a bizarre arrangement and further testimony to the growing
alienation between Helen and me. Helen, Karen, and I shared
the duties. We'd alternate cooking the meals, take turns washing
Casey's diapers, and when Helen and I had to go out, Karen would
stay home. Otherwise, she would have the evening off. Olga would
arrive in the morning, let herself in to the office, and begin reading
Pravda and the morning papers for newsy bits that might be of
interest to Canada. She never found any.

Casey became the pet of the Ukraina. The motherly women
who ran the hotel would dash out when I took him downstairs
into the lobby, smother him in their bosoms, and bury him in
kisses and tender phrases. I found that if I had copy to cable to
Canada, I could enhance my chances of getting my stuff sent
quickly by taking Casey with me. Russians are terrible busybodies,
and in winter there is no end of advice on what children should
wear. Russian kids don't have snowsuits or synthetic lightweight
winter clothing, and parents tend to swathe youngsters in layers
of woollies so that they look awfully cute but can hardly move.
The women looked with horror at Casey's being taken outside
with what they considered insufficient clothing and would cackle
disapproval until they realized he was a "foreign baby," at which
point they understood that foreign children do not get as cold as
Soviet children!

For Olga, Natasha, and Karen it was awkward being caught in
the middle of domestic turmoil. To add to the situation, at the

end of the summer my parents visited Moscow. My father had recovered from his cancer operation and seemed quite well. He was looking forward to visiting a Soviet armoured division, but that plan fell through largely because the Soviets had switched from trying to woo me with favors to punishing me by refusing everything I requested. They seemed to be coming to the view that the longer I was in Moscow and the more I learned, the more hostile I was becoming to the system. They liked me as an individual, but professionally were increasingly giving me the cold shoulder and isolating me.

I found out the hard way that they don't mind journalists writing about the politics of the system, which will be read abroad by relatively few and not understood anyway; what they dislike most are articles about the imperfections of the system—how you can't buy bathing suits in summer or overshoes in winter; how there are shortages, queues, substandard consumer goods, black markets, bribery, and cheating to survive each day. People can understand these things, and judge the failure of Marxism through them.

A week before my parents were to return to Canada, my marriage reached a crisis and I suggested to Helen that she return with them. It was a difficult moment. We talked vaguely about divorce. Helen's main concern was that if the separation did not work out, we should decide quickly so that she could get on with her life and not be frozen in indecision. I felt badly because of my father, who was fond of Helen, as she was of him. But both parents could see that the tension between us was acute.

When they left, it was as if a huge load had been lifted from my life. The journalism, which was consuming every working minute anyway, suddenly was easier, better, more fun. At least a decision had been made. I had been in Russia for nine months, Helen for about five. I began to burrow deeper into the system, writing perhaps three articles a day and, although I was churning out three times the number the *Tely* would print, I wanted at least to get it down. I was writing for the *Telegram* and the *Sun* and having a wonderful time. Helen never returned to Moscow. I wrote to her that we should get divorced, and three years later we were.

I was soon to expand my reporting from print to radio. Hughes Rudd, the correspondent for CBS, did not enjoy being based in Moscow in the least. Most of his job entailed radio reports: three one-minute spots a day, which would be packaged and sold to affiliated stations all over North America. Rudd was leaving Moscow and asked if I would fill in for him until another correspondent was transferred. I said yes and took over. CBS never sent anyone else, and I found it an invaluable outlet for offbeat commentary. Rudd had a wry, whimsical attitude and regarded the Soviet Union as one huge loony bin in which the inmates had taken over and the sane folk were the victims. I identified with this point of view and found it one way to maintain perspective. It also meant that I had very little social life or spare time—I was writing for the *Telegram* and the London *Sun* and broadcasting for CBS: three different masters, three different styles, three separate contents. Not unusual for the world of journalism.

20

"In our country no expense is too great to advertise something that doesn't exist"

OLGA
MOSCOW, 1965

I was strolling through Moscow's massive year-round Exhibition of Economic Achievement, which has eighty display pavilions on its massive 530-acre site, wondering how even a potentially rich and all-powerful country like the Soviet Union could afford to keep the exhibition going. Some twelve million people a year visited it to look at Sputnik, marvel at the capsule in which Yuri Gagarin orbited the world, and see all the technical advances and new farm machinery that would eventually filter down to the republics.

I was doing a story comparing the permanent exhibition with Toronto's Canadian National Exhibition, which attracts some three million visitors in the three weeks it is open and has a hard time breaking even. How could the Soviets afford to keep this huge park functioning? Olga listened for a while, then said with the sort of sigh that long-suffering nannies use when explaining something to slow-learning youngsters for the hundredth time: "You must remember, Boss, that in our country no expense is too great to advertise something that doesn't exist."

That phrase, better than most, sums up the Soviet Union. When visitors from the far regions of the USSR come to Moscow, they are encouraged to visit the Exhibition of Economic Achievement. Looking at the displays of tractors, harvesters, and machinery, the visitors all assume that these things are in use in other parts of the country, and that eventually it will be their turn to get them. But as was pointed out by the White Queen in *Alice Through the Looking Glass*: "The rule is, jam tomorrow and jam yesterday— but never jam today." The Soviets go one step further than Alice

263

and *pretend* that they have jam today when they have nothing, and half the world believes them. The words become the reality.

It is impossible to avoid the flaws and failings of the system when you live there. It is really two systems—intertwined, yet separate. There is the *system* itself and anything that directly helps or advertises it, be it arts, culture, sports, spies, the ballet, circus, dancers, chess, whatever. And there are the *people*, who do not count. As all visitors notice, the Soviet Union takes great pains to refurbish its museums and historic sites, yet lets accommodation and benefits for the people remain substandard. The Soviet Union has not yet invented frozen food, nor are fresh vegetables available everywhere in winter, nor are ballpoint pens reliable. Those things don't matter. They are for the people. Meanwhile, the chosen of the system buy quality foreign goods at special stores at discount prices and have the right to speed through traffic lights and live on country estates.

Foreigners living in Moscow generally considered it a hardship post. Compared to what most of them left behind, it is. But life is still so much better for them than for Russians and Soviet citizens that there is no comparison. Shortly after I arrived in Moscow, the Soviets established "dollar stores," where only foreign currency could be used. For tourists these were the *beriozhka* (named after the birch tree) for the purchase of souvenirs, while for foreign residents they were mini-supermarkets for food shopping. The dollar store served several purposes. It brought in hard currency. It sold quality food at cheaper prices, and the great convenience and ease of shopping meant that most foreigners would use it rather than compete in Soviet stores and experience the push and heave of the daily grind. It further isolated the foreigner in the most painless, effective way. The dollar store, for instance, sold whisky, gin, and liqueurs for about $1 a bottle when I was there.

Foreigners were further isolated by being housed in "ghettoized" apartment buildings, with a militiaman or cop on constant duty to prevent unauthorized Soviets from visiting. Most foreigners tended to mild paranoia, fearing they might be compromised at the drop of a briefcase. Such was the reputation of the KGB. I knew staff at the Canadian Embassy who had never been on the subway, never risked being alone in a crowd of Russians. The whole Soviet experience was wasted on them.

The day-to-day inefficiency and deliberate inconveniences affected some people to such a degree that their nerves cracked and they had to be evacuated home. Others were unable to cope with the Soviet practice of spying and keeping tabs on everyone—the Big Brother syndrome. The mere *thought* that their apartments were bugged by the KGB, that their phones were tapped and that their mail was opened and read unnerved some of them to the point that they had to be transferred. I don't know anyone who lived in Moscow who wasn't sympathetic to such people and understanding of the problem.

Still, for me it was a gold mine of articles. My car and eventually my apartment were invaluable sources for stories—windows into the workings of the system, so to speak. My theory that owning a Volga car would make servicing easier shattered in the face of Soviet reality: there were no spare parts for citizens; all were used for export. The *Telegram* actually owned the car, so I decided to use the Soviet system for a bit of free-enterprise marketeering. I ordered a Mercedes from Germany for $2,400 and sold the Volga to a Bulgarian diplomat for 5,500 roubles—the equivalent of $6,000 at the official rate of exchange. Considering that I had paid $1,500 in hard currency for the car, it was not a bad profit—which went, sadly, to the *Tely*. I then used *my* money to buy another $1,500 Volga and a month later sold it to another Bulgarian diplomat for $7,000 in roubles. I thought I was onto a good thing until the Soviets changed the law so that foreigners couldn't do this sort of wheeling-dealing any more.

I felt myself changing in Moscow; the more I learned and the more I saw, the more I became appalled at the cynicism, callousness, moral corruption. I didn't dislike the people or even the *aparatchiks* (bureaucrats) who make the system work—after a fashion. But I detested the system itself, which corrupted people, pandered to all the baser instincts, and turned individuals into informers and bullies, forcing them to be acquisitive, petty, fearful, and inferior. I changed in Moscow from someone who could never be a Communist but who was tolerant of and unconcerned about it, to someone who sees Marxism as a curse and a menace to values that civilized people consider important. When I went to the USSR I was hard pressed to define whether I leaned to the left or right (I still am, but for different reasons). I emerged with strong feelings against the *realities* of Soviet communism.

Much of the problem in understanding the Soviet system from the outside lies with the media. We tend to use *their* words and *our* definitions. I remember covering elections to the Supreme Soviet, which the Western press often depicts as "the Soviet version

of our parliament." The Supreme Soviet is no such thing. Our
members of Parliament are elected after bitterly contested election
campaigns and meet in the capital most of the year to debate
policies and bring up issues that interest and concern their constituents. Members of the Supreme Soviet are chosen by the Communist Party and merely endorsed by the voters. They meet in
Moscow for a few days a year and carry the word of the Politburo
and ruling Central Committee back to the boondocks. Quite a
difference!

Soviet "elections" are not elections are all. There is one name
on the ballot and instructions read "cross out the name of the
candidate you do not want." Thus on election day if Ivan doesn't
want to vote for Chernenko, he goes into the closed booth where
the pencil is kept and crosses off Chernenko's name—or the name
of the prize-winning dairy maid or bricklayer whom the party is
honoring by putting in the Supreme Soviet. True, it is a secret
ballot and no one sees him cross out the name. But everyone is
looking at him as he emerges from the booth and wonders what
sort of kook or trouble-maker he is. Otherwise, voters merely fold
their ballots with a flourish and pop them in the box. Those who
go into the booth have their names recorded by functionaries
standing by.

Elections are also a way to protest. The polls open at 6 A.M.,
and remain open until midnight or until everyone has voted. Great
status is given to polling stations that have 100 percent turnout
the earliest. After voting, everyone goes off and gets drunk. If
Ivan has a leaking roof he cannot get repaired or is feuding with
the local commissar, he goes out of his district at mid-morning
and gets drunk across town. He may return to vote at one minute
to midnight, thereby making his point, or he may skip it entirely.
In a few days a minor official comes around and wonders, comrade, why didn't you vote? Ivan tells him about his leaking roof,
and the official may make note of it and actually help get it repaired. In which case the protest has worked. Whatever it is, it
isn't democracy.

In the months after Helen and Casey left, I was preoccupied
with getting an apartment. I watched the women bricklayers and
construction workers putting up the building across Kutuzovsky
Prospekt from the Ukraina Hotel. I made Olga check regularly
with UPDK and say that I was in danger of going mad unless I
got a place of my own. I would periodically visit the head of UPDK,
a lugubrious man called Griaznov who reportedly had a bad heart.

Like all the other foreign petitioners, I'd tell him my woes while he nodded sympathetically. Then he'd relate even more harrowing tales of bureaucracy gone mad. Some women brought their children along to underline their plight, and one diplomat's wife even borrowed a neighbor's children. Nothing worked, simply because UPDK's supply of apartments came nowhere near matching the demand. Still, I got the feeling that Griaznov would help when he could. Housing was, and remains, the single greatest problem for Soviet citizens.

One day Olga brought the glorious news that I could move into my own apartment: I was to have first choice among foreigners in the new building I'd watched go from the ground to twelve stories. Olga advised: "Boss, take either the apartment second from the top or second from the bottom. Your choice. Under no circumstances take the top or the ground floor apartment. That's my advice."

"Why, Olga?"

"The roof invariably leaks and if you take the top apartment, you'll have no end of grief, because our illustrious Soviet workmen will never repair it properly. Another disadvantage with the top apartment is that our heroic Soviet lifts are often broken and it will mean a lot of climbing up stairs. On the other hand, you'll be away from the odors of other apartments. Under no circumstances take the ground floor apartment because it is too easy for our progressive Soviet citizens to break in and rob you of your capitalistic property. I suggest an apartment on the eleventh floor."

"Olga, I think you exaggerate."

"Believe me, Boss, I know my comrades."

I asked for an apartment on the eleventh floor. "A very wise choice," said Griaznov, flashing a glance at Olga who was looking myopically at a portrait of Lenin. The first thing I did with my apartment was to get the floors sanded and varnished. I could have asked UPDK to arrange it, but that would have taken weeks. Instead, at Olga's urging, I approached a couple of workmen and offered to pay them directly if they did it in their spare time. They agreed on condition that I buy Swedish varnish, not the normal Soviet variety, which was inferior. The job was done overnight.

"Well done, Olga," I said.

"It's nothing, Boss. Just remember, the only way to survive in our country is to bribe or blackmail people. Never go through channels. It takes too long and is done too badly."

My apartment was not the greatest. If it were public housing in the West, it would be a scandal. However, by Soviet standards it was luxurious. Four rooms, all for me. If it were for Soviet citizens, it would hold four families. While that seems crowded, it is better than in the past, when there were several families to a room, all subdivided by blankets strung across on wires. Still, one family per room, and a couple of families sharing the kitchen and bathroom facilities, can lead to terrible conflicts. People have been murdered for raiding the wrong shelf of the refrigerator. During my stay there was a scandal when an old woman in a communal dwelling grew so impatient with togetherness that she began putting arsenic into her neighbors' borscht. For a while it worked wonders in getting rid of obnoxious neighbors, but by the time four or five had unexpectedly expired, the authorities became suspicious and she was caught. Rather than resenting her crime, Soviet citizens were inclined to sympathize with the old woman and understood what drove her to commit it. I also heard of divorces that foundered on who would get the apartment. Often the divorced pair would simply divide the room in half with a blanket and go their separate ways, sharing the same quarters. In one case the divorced chap remarried, and brought his new wife into his half of the apartment, while the "old" wife offered critical advice and comments from her side of the room. On occasion the two women—wife and ex-wife—would compare notes and align themselves against the wretched male. For someone brought up in a society where privacy is prized, it is an environment that is impossible to understand. Significantly, the Russian language, in some ways richer and more versatile than English, has no word for "privacy."

My apartment at 7/4 Kutuzovsky Prospekt proved to be a rich source of material. At first I was dismayed that the floors had a distinct slope—I liked to say from west to east, but I wasn't sure. In places the floor rolled like a roller coaster. At most points the wall joined the floor, but in some places there was a gap of an inch. I had a small second toilet next to the kitchen, but the door wouldn't close (or open) if the seat was down. What bothered me most were three hinged windows that wouldn't quite close. The carpenters had not centered the latches with the catches, and the frames didn't quite fit anyway. When I drew this to the attention of the building superintendent, I was told that I had four windows that wouldn't open, therefore the problem somehow balanced out. But having windows that won't close can be fatal in a Moscow winter. The door to the balcony wouldn't open: it was for show, not use.

When I tried to put up curtains and pictures on the walls, I found that I needed a cold chisel and small sledge-hammer to drive two-inch gouges in the concrete walls, into which I stuck branches from trees. In these I drove the nails or supports for the curtain rods.

The workmanship in the apartment was shoddy, but the *pièce de résistance* was a garbage chute in one cupboard. By the third month the aroma emerging from this area was distinct and pungent and got into my clothes. It was also a highway for cockroaches, which quickly infested the place. When I suggested buying some Raid or cockroach spray from Sweden, Olga scoffed: "Forget it, Boss. Your lousy Western cockroach poison is nothing but a cocktail for our robust Soviet cockroaches!"

The apartment building, the entrance of which was next to the offices of United Press International, had a fancy elevator of East German design which we residents fondly called the Steel Coffin. It was fully automated and when you got in (it would hold three, possibly four people, but no more) and pushed the button, there'd be a whirring and clanging of machinery and the coffin part would suddenly drop a fraction of an inch before the gears connected and it took you down or up. It was exciting. For the first year it broke down a lot and was under repair as often as it functioned.

After eight months of climbing up and down stairs, I finally asked a workman how long before the bugs were ironed out. He looked at me slyly, wiped some grease on his nose, and said with one of those expressive shrugs that Russians specialize in: "In our country automation will never replace human labor, because for every man done out of a job by automation, two more have to be hired to keep it working." It was one of those spontaneous quips that makes Russians so endearing.

Olga was terrified of the elevator and would only enter it with a little jump, in case its steel doors slammed unexpectedly. It had an added hazard: some of the children of Arab diplomats used it as a mobile latrine, and you never knew what might await you when you stepped in. Whenever I had a slow day, I would write an update article on my apartment.

After living in the USSR one is impressed with two facets of Sovietism: the difference between Marxist rhetoric and theory, and between Marxist deeds and reality. The theory can be debated endlessly—like the number of angels on the head of a pin. The reality is beyond discussion. Marxism doesn't work.

Marxism is fine for controlling people, rotten at doing things. Just the opposite of American democratic capitalism, which is bad at guiding or managing people, but wonderful at doing things, like moving mountains, taming rivers, alleviating famines, feeding the world.

A study by Cyril Black of Priceton University, which ranks countries socially and economically, has found that the Soviet Union's ranking "has probably not changed significantly" from the beginning of the century. That is, contrary to its propaganda and its five-year plans, since the 1917 revolution the Soviet Union has not passed any country that was ahead of it then, and the nineteen or twenty countries that were ranked ahead of it in 1900 were still ahead of it in 1917—and in the 1980s. The fact that the regime has not moved up is a tremendous indictment of the system, considering the blood of its own people that it has shed, the murder, terror, misery, subversion it has imposed on itself—not to mention the world.

The Soviet Union has made itself into a world power, *not* defensive in nature as its propaganda and its apologists sometimes pretend (look at any map over the years and see how the territory that was originally Russian has expanded), but aggressive and imperialistic. (The very name, Union of Soviet Socialistic Republics, was chosen so that no one country was predominant, and every country on earth could eventually be included.) But what is remarkable, even unique, about the Soviet Union is that it is a one-dimensional superpower. All its influence stems from its armed might. The ideological appeal of the Soviet Union has waned in recent years, thanks to the likes of Khrushchev, Solzhenitsyn, and Sakharov and to events in Czechoslovakia, Angola, Afghanistan, and Poland. It is left with only its military as the root of its power. The essence of a war economy.

In every other area—human rights, freedom, economic welfare, consumer goods, production, medical science, technology, literature, industry, agriculture—the Soviet Union lags badly. No other system performs so ineptly for its people. After seventy years, the largest country on earth, with the most natural resources, an able and energetic people, a government that has absolute power and has to answer to no one, still cannot adequately house, clothe, and feed its own people. It depends on Western progress to survive.

It has always puzzled me at international conferences on, say, world hunger, why attention is invariably riveted on the United States, which is blamed for not doing enough to feed the hungry of the world—this of a system in which a mere half of one percent of the people are engaged in agriculture and yet produce enough food to feed, in one way or another, nearly 25 percent of the world.

If the USSR could be persuaded to abandon centralized control of the economy, it would flourish and produce enough to alleviate much of the hunger that plagues the Third World. But doing that would require the system to relinquish some power and ease its stranglehold on the economy and the population. Those who direct the Soviet system dare not do that. A *little* rope to the people is more dangerous than no rope. Give a little and they will want more. Slaves do not revolt. That, at least, the Soviets understand.

It is not ideology or idealism that makes the Soviet system work, but unprincipled ambition and lust for power and privilege. The USSR is the most rigid, class-conscious, and privileged society in existence, North American society the most egalitarian. Only we don't realize it. Ours hinges on money, which theoretically (and often in fact) is available to any who can earn it or think of an idea to make it. Soviet society hinges on rank, on privilege, which is bestowed or seized and not available to all.

In the fall of 1965 I pulled a muscle in my thigh while playing football with American journalists. A blood clot the size of a tennis ball formed, and my leg, from groin to ankle, was blue-purple with a massive bruise of leaking blood. The leg ached, I was feverish, so I went to see the doctor at the British Embassy. He advised me to go to Helsinki for treatment. Instead, I went to Moscow's Botvinik Hospital. The woman doctor who examined me was concerned that the clot might move to the heart and advised: "If you were my son—or even my husband—I would put you in hospital this very moment!"

I wondered briefly what she had against her husband, but let myself be committed. Botvinik Hospital is Moscow's best; it's where foreigners go. It is far better than other Soviet hospitals, which are overcrowded and have a chronic shortage of beds. Beds and stretchers line the corridors; relatives and friends of patients are expected to bring them food.

I was put into a semi-private room with a Chinese military attaché who had an ulcer and was convinced the Soviets were trying to poison him with their terrible food. He spoke virtually no English, but he and I managed to communicate in a hybrid mixture of pidgin-Russian and English. He immediately ordered that masses of Peking propaganda in English be sent over from his embassy for me to read, and extra Chinese food be sent so that I, too, would not perish from Soviet food poisoning. For my part, I thought the Soviet food palatable, if you like lots of porridge and cabbage, which I do. But Chinese food, even in a Moscow hospital, leaves all food a distant second.

The military attaché warned me not to let the Soviet doctors operate and to be wary of letting them stick needles into me. At that time Chinese-Soviet relations were bitter and mutual paranoia at a peak; the Chinese were especially difficult to approach because of the Cultural Revolution. The Russian woman doctor warned that if the clot didn't dissolve with electrical treatment, they might have to operate. If things got really bad, it was possible the leg might have to be amputated. This information made me somewhat uneasy. Dr. Oliver from the British Embassy came around, strictly as a friend and nonprofessional, and again "suggested" that if he were in my position and anyone wanted to operate, he'd catch the next flight to Helsinki. I agreed. Despite its noted scientific achievements and its hyperactive propaganda mill extolling virtues, real and imagined, of the system, no foreigner in day-to-day Moscow had much faith in Soviet medicine.

On the other hand, Olga was more composed. "In our country," she said, "if the challenge is great enough, treatment may succeed. If you have a brain tumor you might be saved; but the common cold can be fatal."

The clot began to subside and in two weeks I was discharged. The Chinese military attaché and I had a rather emotional parting, proving that one does not need to be able to share a common language in order to communicate and build friendship. I think we genuinely liked each other. He had a lively sense of humor beneath his revolutionary dogma, and we used to argue interminably over whether or not the Americans and the Russians were in cahoots to embarrass and crush China. My fondest memory is his burst of unrestrained laughter when I was shaving at dawn one morning in front of the tiny basin and a 40-watt light bulb and a harried nurse arrived with my penicillin shot. Instead of going through any formalities—such as asking or warning me—she simply pulled back the rear of my pyjamas and plunged the needle into my rump. I almost sliced off an ear, to the considerable amusement of the Chinese and, when she thought about it, the nurse.

The next time I saw the Chinese officer was at Army Day celebrations during which foreign military attachés listened to a speech by Marshal Konstantin Rokossovski, one of the Red Army heroes. He had fought in all the major campaigns, from Moscow to Stalingrad, Kursk to Berlin; because of his Polish origins, he had been Poland's Defence Minister, Commander-in-chief of Polish forces, and Deputy Premier of Poland. So much for Polish sovereignty in those days, too! When the legendary marshal denounced American imperialism in Vietnam, the American military attachés staged a walk-out. At the end of the meeting when Western military attachés were clustered in ideological groups—NATO allies huddled together, Warsaw Pact comrades together, the Chinese keeping to themselves—my former hospital-mate and I simultaneously spotted each other across the room. We automatically and impulsively came together and embraced. I declared that I didn't recognize him with his clothes on and he grinned and said something to the effect that he was surprised the foul Russian food hadn't yet poisoned me.

I looked over his shoulder and saw the astounded looks on the faces of Western officers, none of whom had any links with the Chinese. At that moment I felt my friend stiffen as he looked over my shoulder at *his* comrades, who were also staring with horror at unseemly friendship with a foreign devil. We sprang apart, muttered a few niceties, and hastily parted.

Perhaps it was coincidence, but in the coming weeks I had several dinner invitations from military types who were interested to learn how I had gotten to know the Chinese and wondered if we had talked about anything interesting. I imagine my Chinese friend had to answer similar questions in a far more formal setting. To me it was amusing; for him it might have been alarming.

The next time I saw my hospital friend was at the railroad station when Chinese students at Moscow University were being expelled because of the rift between the two countries. They were all chanting and singing to the glory of the great Helmsman and waving their Little Red Mao Books.

I sidled up to him and said deadpan that expelling the Chinese was all a Soviet-American plot and that imperialist running dogs were all the same. He looked at me with delight and gushed: "Yes, yes, yes . . . it is true, you are right . . . finally you understand . . .

didn't I tell you all along that there was no difference between Americans and Russians—both imperialists . . ."

It was rather sad. I felt that we had understood each other better when we both wore pyjamas and shared his won ton in hospital. I never saw him again.

21

Better a free sparrow than a caged canary

OLGA
MOSCOW
MARCH 1965

It was early afternoon, nearly three months after Olga had started working for me as my translator in Moscow, and we were in the underground passage crossing from Red Square to Gorky Street. Out of the blue, Olga suddenly blurted: "Boss, are you a Communist?"

I was startled. No one had ever asked me that before. "Good God, no," I said. "Whatever makes you ask that?"

"I didn't think so, but wasn't sure. I wondered why they'd let you work here if you weren't a Communist. You sure you're not?"

"I'm sure. Why?"

"Because," said Olga, taking a deep breath and staring guilelessly at me, "I want to escape this prison of nations. Will you help?"

I was taken aback, but not as startled as I might have been. For some time it had seemed to me that Olga was talking in riddles, dropping hints, making provocative comments that could be taken different ways. I hadn't been sure whether it was my imagination or not, but at times she seemed to be inviting questions about leaving. Once when I'd mentioned I planned to take a holiday in Greece and was there anything I could bring her, she replied: "Yes. A file." I had laughed nervously and changed the subject. Another time, when I had remarked on her relatively good life in Moscow, she had responded with the observation that it was "better to be a free sparrow than a caged canary." I had ignored all hints, aware that they might be a trap.

All this poured through my head at Olga's extraordinary remark. I also recalled meeting Leslie James Bennett, the head of RCMP counterespionage, prior to coming to Moscow and he had warned about provocateurs. Alarm bells started ringing like mad when Olga made her request. I tried to ignore it.

"I'm sure you can apply for a trip abroad," I said. "Lots of Soviets are tourists."

"No, I've already lived abroad. I want to escape."

There was no equivocating. "Let's talk about it later," I said. Could Olga be setting a KGB trap? Of course. But was it likely? No, it wasn't. The Soviets do not want trouble with resident journalists. Most of them are docile and play the Moscow game of not going too far in what they write. Moscow-based correspondents who don't look for trouble, who don't probe too deeply, who don't delve into the dissident movement, who don't write about racism or the pernicious influence of the KGB, tend to get favors. They are granted interviews with defectors' wives, or invited to see the space centre, or leaked exclusive information that the Soviets want disseminated. The bribe, or favor, works far more effectively among Western journalists than intimidation or threats. The Soviets well know that a Western journalist will do almost anything for an exclusive story, a beat on his rivals. In this regard, the Fleet Street popular press are the greatest journalistic whores of all. Therefore it was extremely unlikely that Olga would deliberately set me up so that the KGB could embarrass me and force Moscow's foreign press corps to close ranks and support a colleague, as they most certainly would if one were framed.

I began thinking long and hard about Olga's request. A lot of things started to fall into place—especially her nervousness whenever the topic of the KGB came up, and her irreverence, ill-disguised contempt and enigmatic remarks about the merits of the Soviet system. I remember writing my first long article on the transition of the various secret police bodies, through the Cheka, OGPU, GPU, NKVD, MVD, up to the present KGB. While we all know about the Soviet secret police, it came as a shock to me to see how it can paralyze every thought, every action. There is no office, apartment building, sport, cultural, artistic, or social group that does not have its KGB informers and watchdogs. We in the West tend to think of the KGB as an espionage agency, trying to root out the secrets of the West and spread subversion abroad. But in fact it is mostly domestic, more concerned with keeping its own citizens under control, for they are a greater potential threat to the system than foreigners. The Soviet border guards responsible for keeping citizens in the corral, and the minefields, barbed wire, and guard dogs that keep citizens from escaping fall under the authority of the KGB.

After writing the article, I showed it to Olga before I sent it to Toronto. She became most agitated. "Don't send it, Boss. It's big trouble."

"But why? It's true, isn't it?"

"Yes. That's the trouble. Don't print it."

"That's not your decision, Olga. I just want to know if my assessment is right. Am I off base?"

"No. You may be too restrained. But this is trouble for you. Believe me, name the devil and he will appear. Don't write about the K-people." Olga could not bring herself to even mention KGB. Her superstitious nature forced her to use euphemisms, else the topic of apprehension might appear like some evil genie.

I ignored Olga and sent the article, which the *Tely* ran full page, decorated with barbed-wire borders. A selection of photos was run, including Beria, Yagoda, Vyshinsky, Stalin, and Lenin as the architect of the Soviet secret police system. Olga was right. I was in trouble. I was summoned to the foreign ministry for an official reprimand and told that they weren't happy with any of my articles about daily life in Russia. If I insisted on writing lies about the KGB or libel about the USSR, or if I made fun of Lenin, I'd be expelled.

I protested and wanted to know what the errors were.

"Mr. Oorzhington," said a Mr. Simonov with harsh sweetness, "we are not here to debate with you; we are telling you: any more of this and we will take action. Do you understand?"

I understood. Finally. For what it is worth, when Soviet officialdom was cross with me they pronounced my name "Ooor-zhington," like slime; whereas normally they pronounced it "Vortington." The first version sounded so slippery that Olga burst out laughing whenever she heard it.

In retrospect I understand better why the Soviets were upset. For example, the final paragraph of the ill-fated full-page article read: "The Secret Police, whatever its name at the moment, is a man-made monster that thrives on crisis, feeds on emergency, hungers for power and whose appetite seems satisfied only with blood." A bit colorful, but not a bad description of the various mutations and variations of the Soviet secret police since 1917.

I think from the start I knew that I would have to help Olga. My main concern was whether she was serious. But Olga was *always* serious. Without being foolhardy, there was no way I could *not* help her. One day while we were visiting Novodevichi monastery where Stalin's unhappy wife, who committed suicide (or was murdered by Stalin, some believe), is buried, I told Olga I'd be willing to help her.

Once the ice was broken, she relentlessly pursued the topic. How could she escape? The greatest indictment against the Soviet system is that it keeps its citizens prisoner, does not trust them to travel like other civilized peoples. Could I arrange for the Canadian Embassy to smuggle her out in a diplomatic bag? Could our security service send a submarine to pick her up off Leningrad? Could I arrange a foreign trip by car and take her? I remained cautious and vague, listening but never suggesting anything.

My first December in Moscow I was flown back to Toronto by the CBC, which wanted me on its TV game show "Front Page Challenge." While in Canada I went to see Jim Bennett and told him about Olga's desire to defect. Bennett wanted to think about it, and contacted his opposite number in the CIA, the legendary James Angleton, who later made news as a mysterious force guiding CIA policies and who fell victim to a colleague's ambition. A few days later Bennett met me and told me that Olga's husband's name occurred in the book, *The Penkovsky Papers*, and that it was almost certain that I was being set up. For God's sake, be careful, he urged. To him, Olga was almost certainly a double agent.

I returned to Moscow filled with doubts about my translator who, if she was KGB, was the most un-Soviet Russian I had ever met. She wore foreign clothes purchased by friends abroad or at secondhand commission stores. In summer she viewed the sun as an enemy and if parasols had been available in Moscow, she'd have carried one. As a substitute she carried a white umbrella with blue flowers on it. But since everyone knew that blue was an unlucky color, she'd splattered red ink over the blue to bring luck. Kids in the foreign compound stopped playing when Olga wafted by, oblivious to the world. They called her "the lady who carries an umbrella when it isn't raining."

Olga was so un-Soviet-like in character that the more one encountered her idiosyncrasies, the less likely it seemed that she could be an agent or spy on a mission. She wore rings on her thumbs, believed in Greek mythology, and thought that the gods and goddesses actually existed. She felt that Western civilization had reached its zenith by the sixteenth century and had been going downhill ever since and escaped the harsh realities of Sovietism by taking refuge in the past: in history, art, architecture. She believed that wearing red clothes warded off diseases, that crushed strawberries made a healthy cosmetic for the face, that cream of wheat porridge was good for cleaning rugs, that cat fur cured arthritis. She believed that drinking unboiled tap water filled the body with dangerous minerals, that powdered parsley was a digestive cure-all, that iodine on the skin helped the glands, that raw onions and garlic cured any unspecified ailment and soothed the nerves, that holding one's palms over one's eyes improved the vision because of electric nerve ends in the palms. She wore wooden shoes, spoiled the true red of her hair with henna, plastered her face with talcum powder to the point that she sometimes resembled a corpse. And so on.

Olga was an eccentric, but an intriguing one, with an original and individualistic mind—a mixture, perhaps, of Miss Jean Brodie and Charley's Aunt, with a passionate belief in freedom, endless cynicism about man's innate indecency, relentless affection for all animals, especially tigers. I was intrigued, puzzled, amused by her, and found her enormously stimulating and unexpectedly wise. One thing she wasn't was boring, and we became friends as well as employer-employee.

Olga intimidated the most boorish of Soviet *aparatchiks* with her aloof elegance and superiority. She was lithe, had an elegant form, and cut a startling figure walking gingerly past the Soviet militiaman on duty at the foreign apartment buildings. I recall Joan Best, wife of Canadian Press's Moscow man John Best, once watching Olga pick her way through the rubble of the parking lot and sighing: "There she goes, Miss St. Petersburg 1902!"

As I got to know her, I rejected the RCMP/CIA assessment and advice. Gradually I loosened up and came to believe she was on the level. We began to plot how she might escape. She, too, began to open up. Yes, her husband, Vadim, was named in *The Penkovsky Papers*, which she'd borrowed from me and read with great interest. She and Vadim had known Colonel Oleg Penkovsky who, until then, represented the greatest known Western penetration of the Soviet Intelligence apparatus.

Eventually I learned Olga's background. She was a survivor of the Leningrad blockade, the 900 days of siege during which a third of the city's million residents died. Just out of university, she spent the war witnessing cannibalism, starvation, bombings and shelling, death; eating glue rendered from book bindings and furniture joints; searching library books for crumbs that students had dropped while eating sandwiches long ago. Her family had traded jewellery for chocolate, and she'd seen bread rations sprayed with water to make them heavier when distributed by weight, thus enabling those in charge of rationing to get a bit extra.

Olga married Vadim Pharmakovsky, a naval officer seconded to GRU (Military Intelligence). He'd been assigned to the espionage staff of Colonel Penkovsky, who operated under the cover of the Co-ordination Committee dealing with Western businessmen. Unknown to the Soviets, Penkovsky had "turned" and was working for the CIA and British Intelligence, providing invaluable information about Soviet espionage. He was that most perilous of beings, a defector in place. Penkovsky is said to be the one who first warned that the Soviets intended to put missiles in Cuba and, after Kennedy challenged Khrushchev, that the Soviets intended to back down. A greedy, bold, pleasure-seeking man, Penkovsky had a lavish generous streak to go with his crude, foolhardy daring. Because of his seemingly limitless power, he felt immune to danger, invulnerable.

Before working under Penkovsky, Vadim and Olga had been considered for special training as a husband-wife espionage team, to be sent into the United States, through Canada, posing as citizens of Quebec. Instead, Vadim was made resident GRU spymaster in the Soviet Embassy in Stockholm with the rank of lieutenant commander. After Penkovsky was caught turning over an incredible amount of information to British and American intelligence, the Soviets isolated everyone who had had any contact with Penkovsky—the process of cauterization to limit the damage. All who had worked for, knew, or were in any way associated with Penkovsky were recalled, questioned, and removed from the GRU. In the process of eliminating, removing, or imprisoning all who have been exposed to contamination, the innocent suffer along with the guilty—and in Penkovsky's case, this included Olga and Vadim, who were recalled to Moscow from Sweden. Expelled from GRU, Vadim was fortunate that he had been trained as a civil engineer and was needed in Soviet light industry; he thus escaped exile to an eastern region or worse. His English was excellent and he was intelligent, with a quiet sense of humor. I got to know him, but not well, in Moscow.

Olga told me about Penkovsky, who was still fresh enough in her memory to cause alarm. *The Penkovsky Papers* was published while I was in Moscow and there was great speculation about whether the book was actually Penkovsky's memoir (written at night and smuggled out later, as the foreword claimed) or a CIA/

British Intelligence concoction. Expert Western and media opinion leaned toward concoction; Olga and her friends in the KGB
and GRU felt that it was certainly not written by Penkovsky, but
that it was compiled from his notes, debriefings, and gossip. Olga's
KGB friends ruefully said that it was largely accurate. Word was
that Penkovsky had sold material by the page and consequently
filled his reports with gossip which, while not hard intelligence,
was titillating, illuminating and intriguing.

Because of his love of the good life, Penkovsky was eventually
caught in espionage through his own carelessness. Olga learned
from KGB friends that one of Penkovsky's young agents had come
to him and fearfully reported that he had had sexual relations
with a woman in Switzerland who was known to work for British
Intelligence. The agent wanted to confess to someone. Penkovsky
grilled him and came to the conclusion that the agent had revealed
nothing. On a friendly basis Penkovsky had advised him to say
nothing to anyone and forget it. The man did.

A year later while the agent was being routinely questioned by
the KGB, he admitted his indiscretion in Switzerland. When the
KGB demanded to know why he hadn't mentioned this before,
the man said he had told Colonel Penkovsky. A check through
the files revealed no record of Penkovsky's having made a report,
as he certainly should have done as part of normal security precautions. The KGB began to look more closely at the GRU officer
and inevitably discovered his links with the British. A trap was
laid and Penkovsky's British contact, businessman Greville Wynne,
was kidnapped in Budapest and smuggled to East Berlin, where
he and Penkovsky confessed.

Wynne was eventually exchanged for Colonel Konon Molody,
alias Canadian Gordon Lonsdale, whom the British had caught
and sentenced for espionage. Penkovsky, who was reportedly shot
in 1963, was actually executed in 1966. The Soviets kept him
around for a few years after reporting his death in case other
things came up that needed probing. When they were eventually
satisfied there was nothing else he could tell them, they shot him.

In the meantime Olga and Vadim were trying to build new
lives, and Olga was determined that hers would be in the West,
not the USSR. Sweden had given her a taste of freedom, and she
wanted more. Vadim had more trust in the Soviet system than
Olga. While both escaped serious reprisals, both were in disgrace
because of Penkovsky. Vadim was unable to get a job for a year
until the light industry post opened up, and Olga got work trans-

lating for the fur industry. She worked with Intourist, then with
the Foreign Ministry, where she became an interpreter for the
Nepalese Embassy. Finally she came into the employ of the Toronto *Telegram* and me, working for the KGB.

In her second year of working for me Olga got, through KGB
circles, a holiday cruise in the Mediterranean. It was on this trip
that she would make her bid for freedom. I was then having more
family troubles, since I had written Helen that I felt we should
get divorced. Our respective mothers had somehow decided that
I was being brainwashed by the KGB and persuaded my father,
albeit reluctantly, to ask John Bassett to invent a reason to bring
me home. Somewhat sheepishly (if my father was capable of being
sheepish), Worthy asked the publisher if he'd consider recalling
me.

"Done!" said Bassett. "I'll bring him home at once."

He sent me a cable saying he wanted me home to advise on
whether to open a bureau in Poland. I cabled back that I thought
it ridiculous to consider Poland and that I didn't see any need to
come home. Bassett wired again that these were urgent meetings
and to catch the next plane back. I wired back that a bureau was
uneconomic, that no news ever came out of Poland(!), that it was
best to forget it. Bassett's next message was a direct order for me
to get my ass out of Moscow and come home at once. Mystified,
I did so, and found that my parents were worried about my sanity
for wanting a divorce from Helen. I was furious but contained
my anger. My father was not as robust as before; clearly, cancer
was winning the battle. I felt badly that he'd humiliated himself
at the urging of the "women" in the family, and he vowed he
would never interfere again.

The visit provided the opportunity to see Jim Bennett and tell
him the latest events: that I had overruled his previous advice,
that I thought Olga was straight, and that I had advised her to
defect in Greece, which was anti-Communist, if she got her Mediterranean cruise. Bennett apparently gave details to the CIA and
Jim Angleton and then got back to me to the effect that they still
felt she might be a double agent, but that if she was serious about
defecting, to do it in Beirut, which was safer than Athens. Olga
had wanted to defect to the British, but Bennett advised against
it and said the American Embassy would be expecting her.

It was the fall of 1966 and the cruise ship was to leave Odessa,
stop at Istanbul, Beirut, Alexandria, Naples, Athens, and Cyprus
and then return to Odessa. I told Olga that it must be Beirut, and

the Americans not the British. She agreed, somewhat reluctantly. Before leaving she had to go through an amazing set of rituals, including psychological and psychiatric examination. She also had to obtain permission from the Communist party, complete with recommendations from those who would be held responsible if she defected. She gave me an airline flight bag filled with heirlooms and jewellery and personal items dating back to tsarist times and an aristocratic ancestry. I was uneasy about keeping this stuff because, if found, it constituted evidence of complicity on my part and would land me in a labor camp as the instigator of the defection, or at least a conspirator. So I took the bag to the Canadian Embassy and asked if I could leave it there because I wanted to send it back to Canada with my editor, Arnold Agnew, who was coming over on an Air Canada inaugural flight. There was nothing important in it, I told him, just personal items—they could look if they liked. I gambled that no one would be interested. No one was.

A week or so after Olga left on her cruise, Scott Bruns, on duty with UPI, phoned me around 11 P.M. "Where's your translator?" he asked with no advance niceties.

"She sure as hell isn't here at this hour, Scott. Anyway, she's on holiday."

"Where on holidays?"

"Why?" I asked, sensing what was coming.

"What did you say her last name is?"

"I didn't. Why?"

"Is it Pharmakovsky, by any chance?"

"Yeah, that's it. What gives, Scott?"

"Well, you'd better grab yourself a vodka. We've got a report here that she's asked for political asylum in Beirut and her husband is a commander in naval intelligence and mentioned in *The Penkovsky Papers*. Another report out of London says she may be 'a top Soviet intelligence agent . . . a coup for the West in the cold war . . . key figure in recent espionage disclosures.'"

"Jesus!" I was genuinely shocked—not at the news item, but at the detail. How had so much been learned about Olga so quickly? It was exaggeration, of course, but the Penkovsky connection and the information about Vadim were dynamite.

I went over to UPI to read the wires, and by then Dick Longworth, acting bureau chief while Henry Shapiro was holidaying, appeared with a bottle of vodka. They had difficulty reconciling the reports about espionage connections with their knowledge of

Olga, whom they knew as an eccentric. "This is pretty far out," I said, and Longworth agreed. "You don't have to convince us; we aren't writing this stuff."

First news reports said she was employed by the Toronto *Globe and Mail*. I hadn't anticipated publicity and felt it would hurt me. One of the wire stories called her a possible "modern Mata Hari." Longworth told UPI to cool the story, which they did, and eventually AP and Reuters did the same. The next morning I called Canadian Ambassador Ford, perhaps the most experienced and knowledgeable diplomat in Moscow, and arranged to meet him. Two days earlier, at his weekly background meeting with Jack Best and me, he had discussed the Air Canada inaugural flight, an Ontario trade mission that was due, and the visit of External Affairs Minister Paul Martin. The timing was lousy.

"Oh, God," said Ford, when I told him the news about Olga, leaving out all details about my involvement and planning. One of his nightmares had become a reality. "I think you should leave the country," he said. "If they'll let you."

"I've done nothing wrong. I had nothing to do with her defection."

Ford looked at me sideways. "What has innocence got to do with it? You know the Soviets. If they want to make an incident of this, if they want to take a swipe at Canada, what better choice than you? You're not especially popular here—your writing isn't admired by the Soviets. God knows, they complain to me enough about it. This might be seen as a chance to get rid of you and take a crack at Canada."

He offered to try and get me on the Air Canada flight back to Canada. Failing that, I might board Paul Martin's plane.

"No way," I said. "I'm riding it out."

"It's up to you, of course, but think it over. Ask your paper . . ."

"My editor is flying over on the Air Canada flight. Not a bad guy and a personal friend."

"Good. Ask him. And if you can—leave."

This conversation was held in the ambassador's office, and to make it secure from possible bugs, Ford had flicked a switch under his desk and loudspeakers in the top and bottom corners of the room had suddenly blasted forth with the babble and tinkle of a recorded cocktail party. While the sounds of the party echoed around us, the ambassador and I put our heads together and screamed in each other's ear in order to be heard. It felt ridiculous and I started to laugh, while he had the grace to look embarrassed.

When he finally turned the sound off, we found we were still yelling at each other.

The person most shaken by the defection was Natasha, my pretty Russian teacher. When I told her that Olga had asked for asylum, she gasped and clutched my arm. "What will they do to you?" She didn't wait for an answer. "But they can't do anything to you, can they? How awful. Now they will write something in the paper. But what can they write—you haven't done anything. They daren't do it. They mustn't. Oh dear, now they'll do bad things to you."

Poor Natasha, trapped at last by the system, knowing what it can do and how innocence is no protection. After a week or so when nothing happened and the theme was shifting from my culpability to Olga's presumed madness, *Pravda* suddenly ran an article about me—"Bloodhound Worthington"—saying I'd been writing nasty articles about the *Pravda* man in Canada, Vladimir Ozerov who, I suggested, was more KGB than journalist. He had done nine articles in a year and they were so anti-Canadian that I had wondered why he stayed in Canada if he found it so offensive, especially when he'd lobbied among Canadian politicians and gate-crashed embassy parties to make his pitch when he was denied a visa for a couple of years. *Pravda* said that I was a cold warrior, trying to spoil relations, and had spy-mania, while Ozerov was nothing but an honest journalist.

There was no mention of Olga, but Natasha thought that was a sign of worse to come. "That crazy woman did this to you. Why did she have to get you into such trouble?" I pointed out that this was a different issue. Natasha said that didn't matter; that was often how they built up to attack someone.

Officially, of course, no one in his (or her) right mind defects from the Soviet Union. Those who do fall into three general categories: they are in the pay of foreign imperialists; they have been corrupted by unprincipled foreigners or traitors; or they are weak-minded or mentally unstable. Why else would anyone choose to flee this socialist paradise? In Olga's case, since the KGB had approved the trip, there was added embarrassment. If she was an agent of imperialism or if she'd been corrupted by an unprincipled foreigner (that is, by me), why hadn't the KGB known about it? How could they pin blame on anyone and yet themselves stay absolved of responsibility?—presuming, of course, that it wasn't all an elaborate hoax to penetrate an agent into the West.

In my new celebrity status, diplomats I'd met only in passing suddenly invited me to dinner to hear the inside story—which I willingly told, omitting any details of my participation. I was in a deadly earnest struggle to appear innocent, and therefore had to behave as normally as possible. This meant taking umbrage at any Soviet allegations of collusion and preparing to write a rebuttal in case *Pravda* wrote a nasty article or any action was taken.

When Paul Martin arrived, I had a session with him and told him roughly what I had told Ambassador Ford, again mentioning nothing about my dealings with the RCMP security people or that the defection had been well orchestrated. I refused offers to join Martin's entourage: I told him that I was damned if I was going to flee the country like a thief, and that if the Soviets wanted to frame an innocent person, let them take the propaganda consequences. There was some bravado in all this, but I also knew that word would get back to the Soviets and I wanted them to feel my righteous indignation.

The very last thing I wanted was to have a politician know the *real* story of the defection, because, if arrested, I wanted the full weight of an outraged Canadian government fighting for my release. I didn't want its protests tempered with the knowledge that I indeed had helped a person flee the cage. I trusted the RCMP and Jim Bennett not to tell.

What I didn't know then, but was to learn later, is that the Canadian Embassy in Moscow was (is?) considered thoroughly penetrated, top to bottom, by the KGB. Two ambassadors in the post have turned out to be homosexuals and security risks; at least one military noncommissioned officer was blackmailed into treason and bugged the embassy for the KGB. When posted to the Canadian Embassy in Peking, he did the same thing. (He was eventually caught in West Germany.) I suspect that if I had let anyone at the embassy know the truth of Olga's defection, word would quickly have reached the KGB.

Speculation was rife among Moscow's foreign community, a virulent rumor mill at the best of times: was I or wasn't I having an affair with Olga? Soviet sources spread a lurid account of romance and illicit love. She was given as the reason why my wife had quit Moscow and why a divorce was in the works. The diplomatic and journalistic community, a trifle wistfully I felt, came to the conclusion that I probably was innocent because there is no way one could have a fling in Moscow without the KGB knowing about it. And if the KGB had known about an affair, Olga would have been punished, transferred, and *never* allowed to go on a holiday abroad. After her defection, all foreign trips for translators were cancelled.

Vladimir Kostiria of *Novosti Press* who was my KGB "control," so to speak, for whom Olga worked—and who indirectly had tried to persuade me to write more favorable articles—told other correspondents that unless I confessed, I was in for trouble. I knew through Olga that he was a top KGB man; the other journalists weren't sure and considered him a "contact." Kostiria had been of considerable help in trying to arrange for my father to visit Soviet tank soldiers when he came to Russia. And he obtained for me a spectacular set of Soviet war photos to show at the Canadian National Exhibition in Toronto marking the twentieth anniversary of the war. Kostiria questioned other correspondents about my morals and implied that there was a file of compromising photos of me with Olga which would be released unless I soon confessed. It became a bit of a joke among my friends, since the variety and venom of Soviet-sponsored gossip served steadily to confirm my innocence.

Gradually, the thrust of the rumors changed. Olga began to be depicted as a madwoman who did erratic things, such as roaming the streets of Moscow at midnight searching for homeless cats to save. (Olga later explained that this was probably because she'd raised a fuss when she stopped someone in her apartment building from dumping a litter of unwanted live kittens down the incinerator.)

One day Olga's husband, Vadim, called me to have lunch at the Hotel Berlin. Obviously wired for sound, he berated me for "stealing" his wife and urged that I confess all. It was just the truth he wanted, nothing more, and if I'd confess he'd be satisfied. I lashed back: how dare he threaten me, and he knew better. He then said that Olga had been in a mental asylum, and had a history of emotional instability. I responded by being surprised that the KGB used people with a history of mental illness. Ours was a tense luncheon of thrust and parry; I suspect the purpose was primarily to assess my reaction to pressure. A couple of weeks later we had another luncheon, during which he got quite ugly: "I trusted you and you deceived me, Peter," he said—then excused himself to get some cigarettes. When he returned he began again: "I believed you at our last meeting. Now I have proof you lied . . ." Vadim suddenly stopped and felt inside his jacket, then excused himself again and headed for the washroom. I assumed he was having trouble with his tape recorder.

After one more false start he continued: "You see, Peter, you were careless. You were seen kissing her. Do you remember the circumstances? Tell me. Go on, admit it. We have photographs, you know. Shall I tell you where it was? Or will you tell me? I tell you there is no doubting the proof. Just admit it, and I shall understand. After all, these things happen and we are both men . . ."

It was like a Victorian melodrama. I started to laugh, then began to get angry: "Vadim there was no such incident. How could there be? If you are serious, I suggest you doubt your so-called 'friends' who gave you the information, and not Olga or me. The whole world knows how the Soviet Union frames people, and if you want a confession out of me, you are going to have to fabricate one."

Vadim turned ugly again: "I shall ruin you, Peter. Really ruin you. I shall write letters explaining what happened. To your wife, to your publisher. Your mother, your ambassador. Yes, I am out to destroy you, Peter, and I don't care how long it takes. I am not warning you—I am promising you. You are finished as a respectable journalist and I'll make it so that no one will hire you. Ever. There is only one way you can save yourself"—he paused and looked at me through narrowed eyes. Then he added: "As I say, Peter, all I want is Olga back."

It was a difficult lunch, but I felt Vadim was playing a role. The KGB wanted to have a shred of fact or evidence on which to build a case against me. I was just as determined because I knew that there was no real evidence, no photographs, nothing. Still, it was unpleasant.

I was under constant pressure. On one occasion I was at the post office where I did my regular CBS broadcast to London, where it was re-transmitted to New York for use in North America. A person approached me, begging to be taken to any embassy. Failing that, would I deliver this note to my ambassador? I refused to be drawn into what I was sure was a trap. Periodically, others would come up uttering anti-Soviet remarks and trying to get me interested. One man even jumped in my car and demanded to be driven to the Canadian Embassy because he wanted to escape. Another day, my car was hit by a truck near the Bolshoi Theatre, and that evening and the next day I got anonymous calls that there'd be more "incidents" if I wasn't careful. It was all so obvious. I fought back as best I could. I wrote stories and sent them to Toronto to be ready for use if I was arrested.

When Arnold Agnew arrived in the middle of this turmoil, I told him what was happening, but not that I had helped Olga.

Agnew was in a dilemma. His Air Canada colleagues were revelling in how great and friendly the Russian city was, and here Agnew was seeing another face of Sovietism that was threatening his man in Moscow. I urged him to let me handle it and to do nothing and write nothing until I gave the okay.

In deciding to risk sending Olga's bag of treasures out of Russia with Arnold, I was gambling that he'd not be examined by Customs. I told him it was stuff for my father. But I was very worried. *If* the Soviets suspected me, who better to nab as a courier than my editor? At the last minute I had what I thought was a brilliant idea. I took Arnold and Mark Harrison, then with the rival Toronto *Star* (and later editor-in-chief of the Montreal *Gazette*), to the Peking Restaurant for a ghastly farewell Chinese dinner (China's revenge). I asked Harrison if he'd take the flight bag to my father in Canada, since he was flying directly to Toronto. He agreed willingly. I figured they'd *never* suspect him.

I admit to some apprehension at the time plus a twinge of macabre relish at the thought of the rival newspaper smuggling out Olga's goods. Had Harrison been searched and the stuff found, I would have had to confess. Poor Harrison would have undergone several weeks of interrogation, while I would have been sentenced to several years in a labor camp. But no one was searched. A couple of years later I told Harrison what I'd done, but he wasn't as amused as one might think.

Christmas was approaching and I tried to get permission to go to Britain for the season. The Soviets kept refusing me an exit visa. When I was about to lodge an official protest through the Embassy, they allowed me out—giving me an unusually thorough check at the airport, as if to make sure I wasn't taking out anything of importance which might signify that I didn't intend to return. Indeed, it was my intention to return. I flew to London and doubled back to Brussels where Olga was by this time. I had lost her trail, since something had gone wrong in Beirut. I was puzzled about why she was not in the United States by now, as had been the plan. I had followed the case through the news agencies, which filed daily and then periodic stories.

I learned that it was a nightmare for Olga, not the well-oiled process that I had been led to believe it would be and had assured her about. When she left the Soviet cruise ship *Litva* to go ashore for a group walk in Beirut that sunny Sunday in October, she wore two dresses and a leather coat. She dawdled when she walked at the best of times, and the group got impatient with her slowness and went ahead. When they were out of sight, she caught a cab to the St. George's Hotel, where she switched to another cab (thus shaking any tail in the best spy-novel manner), went to the American Embassy and announced to the Marine guard that she wanted asylum. The startled young Marine called a political officer, who turned her over to someone identified only as "Walter," who took her to the apartment of an embassy woman introduced as Rita Schneider. Rita was cultured, kind, and one of the few people Olga encountered in those early days who was sympathetic. "Walter" turned out to be Lou Severe, the embassy CIA man, who gave her a preliminary debriefing. At first the Americans were friendly; they gave Olga a false Mexican passport in the name of Alexandra Ostrovsky, dyed her hair black and gave her a false background to memorize: born in Poland, lived in England during the war, travelled extensively in South America, and finally settled in Mexico. Walter said she would be flown to Munich for further debriefing. Olga, as was her wont, misunderstood and thought she was to be sent to a spy school to be sent back into the USSR to work for the CIA. She became frightened.

Things quickly began to sour. The Americans were sure she'd have inside KGB information and when they found out she didn't, they turned nasty. They were determined to get information from her, not because they thought she might have it, but because she was all they had. It reminded Olga of the Russian proverb of a person searching for a lost coin under a lamp. When someone points out that the coin was lost over there where it's dark, the person says yes, but it's much easier to look here.

A few days after taking her in, the Americans abandoned her, announcing that they were turning her over the UN refugee centre where Arab refugees were kept. "If you do that it means the end of me," said Olga. "The Soviets will find me immediately."

"That's not our concern," said Walter.

"Walter, have some heart," Olga recalls Rita saying.

It seems that word had come through from Jim Angleton at CIA headquarters in Langley, Virginia, that Olga was probably a plant, and to dump her quickly. Meanwhile her application for a visa to the United States was being considered.

Beirut was alive with Soviet activity. The Soviet Embassy and its staff were prowling the city, looking for Olga. Western correspondents based in Beirut got wind of the fuss and began poking around. John Cooley, correspondent for the *Christian Science Mon-*

itor, happened to be reading *The Penkovsky Papers* at the time and came across the name "Pharmakovsky," and wondered if the passenger missing from the Soviet cruise ship was related. Olga Pharmakovsky thus became the "key figure" in agency reports for espionage disclosures.

"Walter was not after truth; he wanted information," said Olga later. "Information I didn't have." Walter was intelligent, with a cruel streak. Even Rita seemed offended by him. He took back the fake Mexican passport, turned her over to a Mr. Bishop, who was counsellor at the Embassy. He took her to the UN Commission for Refugees where a Mr. Goodyear was in charge. Neither of these Americans knew her background and could not understand her agitation at being sent to a refugee camp. Bishop was especially concerned and wondered if she'd like to come to his home and meet his wife and children.

"Not right now, thank you," said Olga.

"Maybe you'd like to play some sports?" said the well-meaning man. Despite her despair Olga, who detests all form of physical exercise, was bemused at the American penchant for thinking that sports and/or kids were the ideal therapy for any emotional problem.

Bishop and Goodyear took Olga to the Pontifical Mission for Palestine, where the executive director, Constantin Vlachapoulos, showed genuine concern for her welfare—"the one person I felt I could trust in Lebanon," said Olga, "a good, compassionate man anxious to help me for my sake; my only friend. . . ."

She was taken to the Franciscan convent on Museum Street which she remembers with horror and anger. She was put in a room and told that no food would be brought to her and that she'd have to make a ten-minute walk down a bustling street to a communal dining hall. Olga feared Soviet reprisals if she went unprotected into the street, but the Franciscan nuns were adamant. No food was allowed to be brought to her. For three days she stayed in the room without food, and then ran away back to Rita's place.

"What have I done wrong—why did you throw me out?" she cried.

Walter was there. "There's no mistake. Every refugee is treated like this."

"My God, I'm not 'every refugee.'"

"Why did you go to the UN then?"

"I didn't go—you sent me there."

"You should have known. I can't help you. You must learn to accept things and not come running to me."

Olga wept. Rita interjected: "Oh, Walter, how can you expect her to understand what's happening?"

Walter seemed suddenly ashamed. "Well, these things take time. Go back and be patient. And don't come back here."

"If you think I'm a spy, put me in jail until you check me out. Or give me a lie-detector test. At least give me protection."

"You don't know what you're talking about. Go away and don't come back."

He gave Olga $60 and put her in a taxi. (Olga wouldn't spend the money and, later, when she was flown in a disguise to Belgium, she gave the $60 back to Bill Anderson, apparently the CIA man who dealt with her at the American Embassy in Brussels.) Constantin Vlachapoulos was alarmed at the undue activity among the Soviets regarding Olga. "It's not safe for you here," he said.

"That's what I've been trying to tell everyone," said Olga.

Commissioner Omar of the Lebanese security police, a soft, fleshy man with a self-important manner, entered the scene and announced that the Russians were putting extreme pressure on the case. Olga would have to be moved to a more secure place.

She was next taken to the Dominican convent on Verdun Street where four security men were assigned to give her twenty-four-hour protection. Olga found the Dominican sisters as gentle and humane as the Franciscan nuns were harsh and unpleasant. "How can two orders of nuns, both professing the same religion, interpret Christ so differently?" she wondered. She recalled Sister Catherine, about seventy, as "an angel . . . I never knew such people could exist . . . she used to read newspapers every day just to find out who needed her prayers." Sister Augustine, in her thirties, did all she could to make Olga's life comfortable—a bright memory during a tortured period.

Before Olga left Moscow I had given her the name of a friend in Beirut to contact in case of emergency: Joe Alex Morris, who had been with the New York *Herald Tribune*, gone to *Newsweek*, and finally wound up with the Los Angeles *Times*. I considered him my best friend in the Middle East. Olga phoned Morris in desperation. He not only brought her hamburgers and tried to help her, he did her the greatest service of all: he didn't write about her when everyone else was scrambling for the story. It was an act of considerable friendship, which put me permanently in his debt.

The Soviets continued putting pressure on the Lebanese while their embassy staff scoured Beirut for Olga. Commissioner Omar went through Olga's story and ordered that she meet with the Soviets. A man introduced to her as the Lebanese Ambassador to Moscow, Salim Haidur, told her she *must* meet the Soviets. Olga was concerned that people in Moscow might suffer because of her deed and wanted to be officially regarded as ill or mentally deranged. Twice she had to meet Soviets, one of whom was the counsellor at the embassy and the resident KGB man, Viktor Stepanovich. He was solicitous at first about her health and jovially suggested she come home to her husband.

"He doesn't love me," said Olga.

"Of course he does, Olga Alexandrovna," said Stepanovich. "He misses you greatly."

"Then why won't he come to see me?" asked Olga.

"He can't, but he's worried and wants you home," said the KGB man.

"If he loved me, he'd come to me. Why doesn't Vadim come?"

The Soviets got increasingly agitated at this line because they'd never let Vadim out. Afterward the Lebanese diplomat scolded Olga. "Why did you insist on your husband coming here? You know they'd never allow that!"

"Do you consider it strange that a woman in trouble would want to see her husband?"

"No, but you know the Soviets . . ."

"Mr. Ambassador, why don't you pass judgment by Western standards, not Soviet standards?"

The ambassador's face turned red and he walked out.

Olga was ordered to undergo a mental examination, after which the Armenian psychiatrist said: "I think you are very sane . . . and very brave."

At a second meeting with the Soviets, Olga finally declared she would not meet them again. Omar said she would see whomever the Lebanese wanted her to see. By now Olga knew that she had some rights and that she could not be forced to meet the Soviets. She declared that this was the last meeting. Salim Haidur looked uncomfortable and Stepanovich leaned forward, his voice hushed with controlled menace: "We know what you are doing, Olga Alexandrovna . . . we shall never let you forget, never let you alone . . . we shall get you. . . ."

Olga was taken to court and fined $17 for illegal entry into Lebanon. The next day, disguised in a wig, she was flown by

Swissair to Brussels via Geneva under the strange name Lotti d'Lotzi, while the press followed her trail as best they could. In Brussels she was met by Tamara Miller of the Tolstoy Foundation, which looks after refugees from Iron Curtain countries. Mrs. Miller was a White Russian who'd escaped in 1925, married a Belgian, and worked closely with Belgian security. Olga became the personal responsibility of two Belgian security officers she was to dub the "donuts"—Henri Vincent and his superior, Mr. Andre. NATO had just decided to move its headquarters to Belgium and that would mean a lot of Soviet intelligence activity. From the beginning Henri told Olga: "We shall be very happy if you are a spy."

"Why?"

"Because you could tell us things."

"Well, I'm not a spy."

"We shall see. . . ."

When it became clear that Olga had little to tell them, the Belgians increased the pressure. She was moved to a different "safe" house, was forced to undergo interrogation at strange hours, day and night, to make her break. Vincent and Andre claimed that she was holding out, pretended to phone me in Moscow. Once Olga told them that I had helped her get out, they used this as a blackmail device to persuade her to talk. She was a virtual prisoner, with the "donuts," as she called them in derision, determined to get a confession and thereby look good. They, too, wanted her to see Soviet officials and also to take a mental examination. She refused both. "You are being difficult," Vincent told her. "You must remember Belgium is a small country and Russia a large one and you are not making things easy for us."

At one point Mrs. Miller accused the "donuts" of being too soft. "Behave like security men—get tough!" she scolded.

Olga was moved to another house, owned by a former British colonel who'd won an MC in World War I. Increasingly, she was getting what could best be described as the Gestapo treatment when I arrived on the scene.

I never got through passport control at Brussels airport, but was intercepted, taken into custody, and driven straight to security headquarters, where I met Andre and Vincent. They asked if I would help get a confession from Olga, whom they considered a KGB plant. Her application to go to the United States was still pending, and she'd complained to Anderson about the hostile, inconsiderate treatment, thus managing to get dental care and more consideration. It didn't take me long to realize that security was so bad and Olga such a nervous wreck it would be foolhardy for me to return to Moscow. I felt I would inevitably be compromised and the Soviets would learn of my involvement. Besides, someone had to protect Olga from the determination of the Belgians to prove her to be a spy.

I contacted Jim Bennett at RCMP headquarters in Ottawa, the key figure in the defection, and tried to enlist his help. He was sympathetic but noncommittal. John Bassett, publisher of the *Tely*, was most understanding. I said I'd take leave of absence in Brussels until the Olga business was settled, but Bassett insisted I do it on *Tely* time and salary. I stayed in Brussels, routinely being interrogated by Belgian security and fighting with them.

One day the American consul phoned Olga. She and I went to the embassy and the consul, a Mrs. Fowler, said Olga's application to go to the United States had been rejected. The consul was upset and puzzled, but could do nothing. "I don't know what to suggest," she said. "I've never had anything like this happen since I've been on the job." Her greatest act of generosity and compassion was to tell us the verdict before telling the Belgians. I asked for thirty minutes' grace before telling the Belgians, called a taxi, and raced to the Canadian Embassy, where I saw the chargé d'affaires, Pat Black, and made application for Olga to come to Canada on the grounds that I was going to marry her. The fact that I was already married, technically, didn't seem to concern anyone.

When the Belgians learned of her rejection by the United States, they were prepared to take off the gloves and interrogate her more zealously. They were furious to find that her application to go to Canada was now pending, thus making them wait even longer before having a free hand.

In their annoyance they bluntly accused me of being a Soviet agent. To them it was inconceivable that the KGB could be fooled twice by amateurs. Once was unlikely; twice was impossible. "We think perhaps you are being blackmailed, or may not even know you are being used, to get this woman infiltrated into the West," said Andre. He said the only way to clear my name was to confess and help persuade Olga to confess. I was furious and made an official complaint to the Canadian chargé d'affaires. I wrote a letter spelling out the accusations of Belgian security, and demanded that Canada react. Pat Black was unhappy with the sequence of events and reluctant to accept my letter. He reasonably pointed out that it could cause trouble and embarrassment; but worse, it would almost certainly make things more difficult for

Olga. There seemed little concern on his part that a Canadian citizen had been accused of being a spy. I wondered where the righteous indignation of the Canadian government was.

He had a good point, however, so instead of formally complaining through the embassy, I wrote a letter of complaint to the Belgian Foreign Minister. I showed it to Andre and Vincent, warning that if they did anything else I'd deliver it. Thereafter they tended to leave us alone.

Initially I had tried to cooperate with the Belgians, who were caught in a dilemma not of their making, but increasingly I began to get angry and disgusted at the whole security foul-up. The defection was supposed to have been "arranged" to go without a hitch, and I had told Olga exactly what to do and had insisted that all would be okay. Over her more suspicious instincts, she had complied—and was in the borscht. I felt betrayed by our security.

I was also angry that they had reduced Olga to a bundle of jangled nerves with Gestapo-like questioning, threats, bluffs, and general lack of compassion. Their problems—and the problem of all Western security—was (and I presume still is) that they create such an awesome, all-powerful spectre out of the KGB that they think everything is a plot, all is a conspiracy, that nothing happens by accident. In fact the KGB bungles all the time, and is riddled with incompetence and staffed with potential defectors. It is the only way we know what it is up to.

I blew my top at Andre and Vincent and they were somewhat startled. I contacted Bennett in Ottawa, told him what I'd done, and gave him an ultimatum which was meant for the Americans. I said if there were any grounds for believing Olga was a plant, tell me what and I'd accept it. But if they were merely suspicious and playing it safe, I would not accept it and would write the story about the defection, my role in it, Canada's role, and the American role of providing a phony Mexican passport. I would make what trouble I could. I alerted Fleet Street and my news agent contacts, as well as American journalists to the story of betrayal and how a stage-managed defection had gone sour.

I pointed out that I was not only the *Telegram*'s correspondent in Moscow, I was also the London *Sun*'s and the CBS man in Moscow, and had access to a fair amount of potential publicity if necessary.

Finally British security undertook to question Olga in Brussels and me in London. They'd match stories and see if key areas differed. The interviews worked out and we were both cleared, so to speak, and a somewhat reluctant British security gave Olga the benefit of the doubt. Canada agreed to let her enter on a Minister's Permit.

By that time circumstances had forced us together, and in Toronto we lived together for a couple of years until we went our separate ways—still friends, ever tied by a bond of being through the fire together and linked by mutual experience. Olga went to the University of Toronto, got an M.A., and studied for a Ph.D. Far from being considered a security risk, she became regarded as a security coup, an example of Canadian security showing independence and initiative and overruling CIA knee-jerk prejudices. No mention of blackmail or pressure.

At the time, my association with Olga blacklisted me from working as a correspondent in Washington (thanks to Jim Angleton, I suspect) which is where I was slated to go after Moscow. In one way it bothered me; in another, it didn't. I wasn't sure that I was cut out to report the diplomatic circuit, and instead preferred the cut-and-thrust of civil wars and revolutions. But I was not going to abandon Olga simply to go to Washington for another stage in my career. Besides, in the Olga escapade I had acquired a ringside education in the vagaries of Soviet life, and especially the machinations of both the KGB and Western security agencies.

It also made me more aware of the fallibilities of Western security. The system is designed to work for the *guilty*, those with useful information, who want to leave the USSR. It doesn't work for the *innocent*, or those with no secret knowledge. Olga was more realistic about their foibles and failings than I, and generally contemptuous of their intellect and ethics.

As I see it now, the *real* reason the defection was so successful, and why we both got away with it, was because I trusted no one, told no one anything. The ambassador didn't know, no friends knew, no politicians were told. None could be trusted, for the simplest hint that there was collaboration or conspiracy would have inevitably reached Soviet ears. Fortunately, in the light of what I now know of Soviet penetration into Western institutions, we instinctively did the right thing. Nothing much has changed today. Olga was one of the few occasions when the Soviet system was beaten, and the canary escaped and became the sparrow.

22

"Holy War" more mindful of
Peter Sellers than Genghis Khan

LONDON SUN
JUNE 5, 1967

For some reason people are always interested in how dangerous a certain situation is. The reporter who's been covering an international crisis, civil war, revolution, whatever, is often asked: "Were you ever in any danger?"

It's a hard question to answer. Even if there was some danger, you can't very well say with a straight face: "Yes, I was in extreme peril most of the time, but my steady nerves and unusual courage saved me." On the other hand, to pooh-pooh any suggestion of risk is also phony and seems a reverse way of saying that there was considerable danger. Of course, one could always find ways of getting a message of valor across, like the apocryphal lieutenant who recommended his batman for a Victoria Cross "because he followed me everywhere I went."

Most journalists, quite sincerely I think, are reasonably quick to deny that they are ever in danger, even if they secretly think they may have been. All know that the stories that appear in print are usually more dramatic and exciting in the telling than they are in the happening. The eye of the hurricane is usually calmer than the edges. Besides, when you are in the middle of a story your blood is up and you think about little except what is going on. Almost invariably, it is the unexpected that ambushes journalists, who really do have a god that protects or looks after them, like drunks and children. Even if they don't, they find comfort in believing they do!

I don't recall ever feeling in much danger but, as I look back, I suspect the most volatile situation I was ever in personally—or the time I was foolish and could have become a victim or a statistic—was being caught in a mob in Cairo during the 1967 Six Day

298

War between Israel and Egypt. It was a curious crisis, for just when it seemed to be all over, it blew up and Israel attacked Egypt.

I was sent to Cairo before the war started, shortly after returning to Canada from Belgium, where I had rescued Olga from the Western security agencies which were anxious to believe she was a KGB plant. There was considerable curiosity among journalists in Toronto at the sequence of events; Olga was widely assumed to be the reason my marriage with Helen had foundered, and everyone relished the idea that I had fallen in love with the wife of a Soviet spy and was cloak-and-daggering through the shadowy world of international espionage. Publisher John Bassett was himself providing grist for the gossip mills by leaving his wife of nearly thirty years to elope with the pretty education reporter, Isabel Gordon, winner of a media beauty contest and wife of Crawford Gordon, son of a well-known Canadian industrialist. To an outsider, life at the Toronto *Telegram* must have seemed reminiscent of the declining days of the Roman Empire.

I didn't know about Bassett and Isabel when I got back to Toronto and heard only that Isabel was off in Jamaica, apparently recuperating from the breakup of her marriage. Isabel and I had always been friends, so I sent her a silly letter telling her to cheer up saying, "all is forgiven and I know how it feels to have a marriage shatter."

I was summoned to Bassett's office soon after this and he bellowed: "Just saw a friend of yours. She sends you best wishes."

I was puzzled. "What friend?"

"Isabel Gordon. She got your letter in Jamaica."

"Oh, yes, Isabel. Tough about her marriage. How come you saw her?"

"How come? Jesus Christ, she and I are going to be married!"

I was flabbergasted. "Good Lord, that makes Olga and me seem like small fry."

"Whaddaya mean?" Bassett seemed genuinely puzzled.

"I mean, what does anyone care about my escapades when they've got you to gossip about?"

"Aw, I don't think anyone is interested."

"Are you kidding? Not interested in Casanova Bassett's love life?"

"Well, I gotta admit there was some trouble with the boys at first." (His sons John and Douglas were Isabel's age.) "But I fixed that. I told 'em they didn't have to call her Mommy."

I closed my eyes and shook my head. Bassett was incorrigible.

He sent me packing to Cairo to "write about that goddam Nasser if he's dumb enough to attack Israel." All that spring Cairo had been filled with journalists on a sort of deathwatch, waiting for the war that seemed inevitable after Egypt's President Nasser had impetuously given the United Nations Emergency Force forty-eight hours to leave Egyptian territory. He had announced a blockade of the Gulf of Aqaba at the Straits of Tiran, thus blocking Israel's back door. Somewhat to Nasser's surprise, UN Secretary-General U Thant agreed without murmur to withdraw UNEF. Canada, the mainstay of UNEF since its formation in 1956, was distressed at the decision and denounced the blockade. Nasser promptly singled out Canada for special criticism, calling it "neo-colonialist . . . totally biased in favor of Israel . . . a co-plotter with American imperialism." There were hints that the Canadian Embassy, for the first time anywhere, might be the target for "organized, spontaneous anti-imperialist demonstrations."

Off the record, Canadian diplomats in Cairo said they felt that Nasser was not bluffing this time and that he could well attack Israel. Despite influential voices like Nasser's mouthpiece newspaper *Al Ahram* predicting "war is now inevitable . . . there is no escape from it," various civil defence precautions, and bellicose speeches by politicians and the Egyptian press, one got the feeling in Cairo that it was all an act. The people didn't expect war, didn't want war; Egypt would not attack. The regime and its supporters were simply indulging in the rhetoric of super-patriotism.

While Canadian diplomats fretted about their unusual role of being a target instead of a trusted conciliator and committed neutral, Nasser finally invoked his reprisal against Canada for not siding with him: he cancelled Egypt's plans to issue a special stamp in honor of Expo, the world's fair being held that year in Montreal. That would show us!

As the spring of posturing, breast-beating, and sword-clanging dragged on, it seemed less and less likely that Egypt would ever attack. Increasingly it was realized, Canadian diplomats notwithstanding, that although Egypt had recovered from the debacle of the 1956 Suez War in everything except pride, it was in no position to invade anyone. Instead, it seemed that Nasser's international bluff had worked. The world was prepared to swallow anything in the interest of preserving peace, any sort of peace. Except Israel, of course, although few realized it at the time. Journalists, those locusts of crises and harbingers of misery, were already beginning to leave Cairo when, on the morning of June 5, Israel attacked.

I was in my room at Cairo's Nile Hilton Hotel at about 9 A.M. trying to make a phone call before legitimately adjourning to the swimming pool for suntanning and socializing with those of the press corps who went in for that sort of thing. I heard planes overhead and the distinctive "crump-crump" of bombs somewhere in the distance. I didn't pay much attention until a hysterical maid burst into my room screaming, "It's started, it's started . . . bombs, bombs, bombs!" She gestured that everyone should go to the air raid shelter in the basement—which, to the best of my knowledge, no one did. She babbled something about Israelis and war and death, then, in full cry, raced on to the next room. From the balcony I could see smoke rising in the direction of the airport and planes diving in the sky. Pandemonium broke loose.

It turned out that the Israeli air force had simultaneously attacked all of Egypt's military airfields, including Cairo's, and had caught most of the Egyptian aircraft on the ground. In the space of a few minutes, Egypt's air force and retaliatory capabilities were literally annihilated.

At the time, however, we didn't know what was happening. Loudspeakers, which dot Cairo, had switched to patriotic martial music, and life went on more or less as usual. Like other journalists I rushed to the hotel lobby carrying my typewriter and prepared to write an on-the-spot story for the *Tely*, which was now close to deadline. Details were impossible, so I concentrated on mood and color and impressions. Curiously, there was no censorship in Egypt for foreigners—although there was in Israel. It seemed paradoxical to have no peacetime censorship in a dictatorship, yet to have it in a democracy. Censorship would soon be imposed, however, and all twenty-two American correspondents in Cairo would be expelled in reprisal for Israel's attack.

The loudspeakers periodically interrupted the martial music with news bulletins. The first announcement was to the effect that 27 Israeli planes had been shot down. I put that in my story. "By tomorrow Israel will have no air force," gloated one citizen. Another responded: "By next week we'll be giving guided tours of Tel Aviv."

Half an hour later, the figure was revised to 42 Israeli planes destroyed. Cheers in the street. As I raced toward the cable office another broadcast boomed that 75 Israeli planes had been shot down. I stopped, changed the figure, and continued on. By noon the loudspeakers were proclaiming a massive victory, with 127 Israeli planes shot down. By then, most people began to suspect that Israel's surprise attack might have been even more devastating than originally suspected. Egyptians, used to their own propaganda and excessive hyperbole, became increasingly depressed as each new triumph was trumpeted.

At the Nile Hilton I spoke to one of those oracles of political wisdom, a cab driver, and he wryly noted that 9 Israeli planes had attacked the airport and 13 had been shot down. As it turned out, the war was a shambles. Egypt was humiliated again. The embarrassing scandals that emerged later resulted in a massive shake-up of the military. Nasser's friend, vice-president, and assistant chief of staff, General Abdul Hakim Amer, who was never much good (a product of patronage), was due to face treason charges. Tanks defending Egypt had all apparently been dug in to turret depth in a line facing Israel. They were wiped out by aircraft and Israeli tanks that simply went behind them instead of head-on. Cairo streets grew ugly with an undercurrent of hostility toward foreigners in general and Americans in particular. When the American journalists were expelled, Hughes Rudd of CBS, who had turned over his broadcasting job to me when he had left Moscow, asked if I'd broadcast for CBS in Cairo. I did so until the Egyptians realized they were being circumvented. They confronted me with an ultimatum: decide whether I was American or Canadian—and if I made the wrong choice I'd be expelled. End of CBS for me.

Those of us left in Cairo could get very little information about the war, but lots of impressions. From an Egyptian viewpoint it was going badly. We struggled to write different angles. I had interviewed Egypt's leading belly dancer, Nahed Sabry, on her political assessment of the crisis, and had gotten an unusual story that was as relevant as anything else being disseminated at the time. She thought war was just plain silly in that it kept the tourists away and was bad for business. Of more immediate concern to her was whether she might one day have the honor of being Egypt's first legitimate topless dancer. She railed against stupid laws that forbade her to reveal a bare tummy (a filmy veil covered it). Censors also ruled against excessive rotation of tummy muscles, which she somehow attributed to Israeli perfidy. I wrote the story for the London *Sun*, which had not yet been rescued by newspaper magnate Rupert Murdoch's topless page-three girls and was more socialist and staid.

The *Sun* gave the belly dancer story bigger play than it gave the war, while the *Telegram* ignored it entirely, as befits lacklustre

Canadian papers. Writing for both a British paper and a Canadian one was turning out to be an exercise in schizophrenia: invariably the British were more professional and more likely to recognize a lively story, whereas the Canadian paper was more stodgy. The British are more competitive and produce more imaginative journalists; Canadians are uneasy if they differ too much from their competition.

One charming, bizarre memory of the Six Day War was the sandbag wall outside the press centre, down from the Hilton Hotel along the Nile. With great fervor Egyptians were building this wall to protect the press centre in case of future bombings. It was more symbolic than real. The press and TV photographed and filmed the men at work and the Egyptians, a mixture of soldiers and civilians in *djellabahs*, were very proud and pleased to be the centre of such attention.

It was not difficult to see that they had never used sandbags before, nor built a wall. They were filling the bags from an enormous pile of sand that trucks brought in, chanting and singing and praising Nasser. As the baffle wall went higher, all semblance of order or design to it disintegrated. Instead of sandbags interlocking, they were piled in any direction. It was apparent that the wall would soon collapse. More TV cameras arrived, and every foreign journalist in the area gathered for the show. The Egyptians, misreading the interest, grinned more broadly and worked even harder. The wall grew taller—perhaps fifteen feet high and fifty feet long. It looked hilarious, sandbags pointing every whichway. Suddenly, with a mighty shudder, the wall slowly leaned over and collapsed. There were sandbags and clutter everywhere.

It was funny but sad. One felt sorry for the Egyptians and tried not to laugh at them. But it seemed to symbolize their performance in war, at least in those days. The workers glumly went back to work rebuilding the wall while officers, who hitherto had been preening and strutting in front of cameras with studied lack of interest, began berating the workers, defaming their ancestry, and accusing them of treason. There was no more singing, no chanting, no slogans. Cameras packed up and left, and the wall was eventually built properly. I quipped in the London *Sun* at the time that Egypt's "holy war" was more mindful of Peter Sellers than Genghis Khan. Unkind perhaps, but true.

The Six Day War was in its third day, I think, when in late afternoon the rumor spread among the press corps that Israeli prisoners were arriving at the main Cairo railway station. The word on the street was that 3,500 Israeli prisoners were due in—a ludicrous figure now, but reasonable then, considering that every day Egyptian headlines and propaganda stressed defeats for the marauding Israelis and anticipated Nasser's triumphant entry into Tel Aviv. There was a mood of excitement throughout the city. Taxi drivers swore that the rumor was true. All had a pipeline into Nasser's command post. Don McGillvray of Southam News, Gunnar Nielsen of Stockholm's *Expressen*, and I grabbed a cab and headed for the station. The driver, exuding confidence and enthusiasm, had intended to go there anyway. All the way he rattled off information about the devastation being wreaked on the Israelis, chortling and slapping his thigh as he drove.

As we got near the station, the traffic intensified. We couldn't get within blocks of it because of the masses of people pouring in, the poor, the halt, the lame—all to see firsthand the Israeli prisoners. There was a holiday atmosphere because none had ever seen a real-live Israeli, much less one who was a prisoner, and it was a chance to see if they had horns.

The station has a tall iron fence around it, and people were pressed against it shouting slogans against Israel and demanding to see the prisoners. While the mob had a festive air, there was also a restlessness that I, for one, didn't like. Nor did Nielsen, with whom I'd shared that horrendous thirty-two-hour taxi ride across the desert from Damascus to Baghdad in 1958, to be the first journalists into Iraq after the revolution against young King Faisal. Nielsen and I also knew each other from the Congo and Algiers, and, though not close friends, we felt comfortable working together. For journalists as well as soldiers, it is important to know what to expect of someone with whom you may be sharing an anxious moment.

Our taxi driver, insisting there was no problem, left his cab at the fringe of the howling mob and began working his way through the crowd, beckoning for us to follow. Reluctantly, we did. Since we were approaching from behind, no one paid us too much attention. A curious stare, a question or two, and our driver was suddenly a very important person ushering us forward. It was soon too late to change one's mind. The closer we got to the main gate, the thicker became the crowd. And uglier. There were increasing shouts of "Bring out the Jews!"

When we finally got to the main gate the soldiers quickly let us through into the station area. A young police colonel, immaculately dressed in white, was not happy to see us but was courteous.

Sweating and agitated, he insisted there were no prisoners. "It is a mistake," he said. "A rumor. You know Cairo. If there are prisoners, they've been taken another route. Look at this crowd—can you imagine what would happen to Jews here?" He urged that we leave, the sooner the better for our sakes. An army officer and a couple of soldiers escorted us back to the main gate, which was packed with even more people.

As far as one could see, there were flag-waving, fist-raised, cheering, jeering Egyptians from the poor districts of Cairo—the Nasser-loving, Israeli-hating mobs.

"Can you give us an army escort to our cab?" I asked.

The young officer, who spoke passable English, shook his head "No. My soldiers are needed here. Besides, if soldiers go with you, they'll think you are prisoners and there might be trouble. Better that you go alone."

"Maybe we should stay here?"

"You can't stay here. You'd attract attention. No one invited you here. You came on your own—leave on your own. I should hurry if I were you."

The officer had a point.

It was also clear that the three "foreigners" in sport shirts and nervous smiles were becoming the focus of attention. Delay was simply further fuelling the mob's agitation. McGillvray plunged first into the crowd, followed by Nielsen. They disappeared in a swirl. I hung back for a moment. It seemed the height of foolishness to go into that maelstrom, yet even more foolish to be separated from my companions. I plunged after them and was immediately encircled by bodies screaming, spitting, waving. They were denouncing Israel and imperialists and yelling in our ears. While those near us knew we were not Israeli prisoners, the crowd behind didn't. As the pressure from the back increased, the chant was taken up that we were the Israeli prisoners.

I could see Nielsen's red head bobbing in front as I caught up to McGillvray. I began to get punched in the back and on the arms. Then suddenly someone stepped in front of me and drove his fist into my stomach. Fortunately, I had time to tense and I tried to show no sign of concern. I felt that if I showed pain, or doubled up, it would incite the crowd and they'd tear us apart. I saw McGillvray punched in the face, his glasses smashed. It was getting quite nasty.

Suddenly a young Egyptian attached himself to McGillvray and me. Speaking in English, he told us for God's sake to keep moving.

He yelled at the crowd that we were journalists, not Jews, and not to make a mistake. He was punched. An older man emerged, put himself at the head of our triumvirate, and also began taking the abuse of the mob in order to protect us. All the time we were moving ahead. Our defenders had given the demonstrators pause, but tension was building again and there were shouts of "traitor" and "Jew-lover."

Eventually we neared the fringe of the crowd and saw, unexpected but welcome, a taxi. The driver was sleeping. We pushed in and demanded to go quickly to the Hotel Hilton. The driver looked sleepily at us, not the least perturbed. The crowd closed in around the cab and began rocking it, pummelling the roof, standing on the bumper. Someone spat at me through the window; another punched. I tried to thank our benefactors, but they were now fearful for their own safety and wanted only that we leave. Theirs was an act of considerable courage and generosity, for no apparent reward. There was no reason for them to intervene on behalf of strangers. On the contrary, there was good reason *not* to! Had these two anonymous Egyptians not materialized, I'm not sure the three of us would have escaped so lightly.

Our taxi driver leisurely got out of the cab, struggled to the left front fender—and activated the meter before moving. It was such an incongruous act that one couldn't help laughing. Like turning out the lights to save electricity when your house is on fire. Our driver didn't like us and drove us immediately to a police station where he turned us in as possible Israeli spies. We quickly established our identities and returned to the hotel.

Other journalists had heard the rumor about Israeli prisoners, but none had been able to verify it. As it turned out, McGillvray, Nielsen, and I and our near-miss became the overnight story. The British press especially gave play to the item about the three journalists who had a close call with the Cairo mob. I wrote what I thought was a lively story for the *Telegram*, which wasn't much interested and trimmed it down for modest play. Editors at the *Tely* had periodically received my stories about getting charged by mounted Belgian police, the Congolese army, Algerian terrorists, the Arab Legion, Baghdad mobs, French riot police, Lebanese rebels, Rhodesian police, the secret police in Angola, and so on around the world. Each one read more dramatically than was actually the case, but it seemed a useful way to get readers involved quickly, and hopefully to entertain and interest as well as inform. Still, that day in Cairo was special, and I think the three of us were just an incident away from becoming statistics of the Six Day War.

It was a time when foreigners stayed off the streets in Cairo, not wanting to risk an incident because Egyptian pride and self-respect were once again in shreds. The day the war ended, a CBC crew arrived in Cairo after a tortured journey by the Russian cruise ship *Bashkiria* from Cyprus via Latakia, Syria, to Beirut then Alexandria, where they hired a car to Cairo. Their adventures getting to the war were more exciting than mine inside the target area. I wrote what I thought was a cheerful piece about "an inspiring little tale of ingenuity and determination which has won for the [CBC] the unrecognized honor of being the first news organization to reach Cairo after hostilities ceased." Gordon Donaldson, the commentator, and producer Don Cameron were old friends, and the Cairo newsmen had sport praising the CBC for being last in war, first in peace. Still, they had shown initiative and resourcefulness in even getting to Egypt, which had been closed since the war started.

Prior to coming home, the ever-present Joe Morris and I searched out the Cairo home of Said Ahmed el Shukairy, the fifty-eight-year-old, Cambridge-educated head of the Palestine Liberation Organization and commander-in-chief of the so-called Palestine Refugee Army of commandos, drawn from the *fedayeen*, or peasantry. He was the forerunner of Yasser Arafat, and even then was considered a hawk among hawks. Shukairy didn't look like a warrior, any more than Arafat did. Where Arafat looked perpetually unshaven, scruffy, self-indulgent, and unwholesomely sensuous, Shukairy was fat and clean-shaven, with a neat grey moustache, and looked as if he should be in a Beirut boardroom making financial deals.

His modest stucco bungalow in the suburbs of Cairo was guarded by two Palestinian soldiers in red berets carrying automatic weapons. Beside a shiny black Mercedes were tethered two goats. The odor of raw sewage permeated the area. Shukairy wore starched and pressed bush clothing as if they were diplomat's striped clothes— which figured, because for fifteen years he had worked in the United Nations and variously had represented Saudi Arabia and Syria, occasional foes of Nasser and of one another. Loyalties are flexible in the Arab world.

Shukairy's views were significant because, although we didn't know it then, he was a bellwether of the future. He warned that

Palestinian patience was exhausted and that guerrilla raids and acts of violence were now seen as the only way to fight Israel. "The people of Palestine must liberate themselves by their own war and depend on no one else to fight for them," he said in a variety of ways. "For every Arab everywhere and for always, Israel is a Holy War, a *jihad* which must be fought until it is won. That is our future, our legacy. It will never change." Shukairy's major innovation was an agreement among Arab countries that a so-called "liberation tax" would be imposed on all Palestinian businessmen in Arab countries, from Kuwait to Morocco, to support the upcoming war of liberation. Meeting Shukairy provided a glimpse forward into the 1970s and PLO terrorism.

Joe Morris was one of the few who took the PLO and Shukairy seriously. He and I had a memorable meeting with the PLO who, even then, were starting to raid Israel and trying to set up training bases in Egypt, a move that Nasser was preventing. (The PLO then opened bases in Jordan and King Hussein eventually had to turf them out, using the Arab Legion in a brief, ugly showdown. Next they moved to Beirut and literally tried to take over Lebanon. The Syrians stormed in, as Russia had marched on eastern Poland when the Nazis invaded in 1939, and prevented total domination of the country by the PLO. The Palestinians became a cancer, destroying from within the countries that gave them sanctuary.) Although I really didn't take Shukairy too seriously (the *Tely* story was facetiously headlined: "This Arab hawk heads his own private army"), our seeing him exemplified Morris's dictum: "The first law of journalism is that when you've nothing to do—do something. No interview is ever wasted. Who knows, maybe Shukairy will be useful someday."

Morris was the best foreign correspondent I knew and we had been friends since the Lebanese civil war of 1958. We met only at crises and usually teamed up—me tagging along after him. Among other things, we had flown with King Hussein for a memorable Bedouin feast at Aqaba, chased around Cyprus trying to find George Grivas's EOKA terrorists who were trying to take over in 1958, and later we were at it again when Turkey invaded the island. I had never forgotten his kindness to Olga during her escape from the Soviet Union.

Joe Morris was to die in Teheran while he was covering Ayatollah Khomeini's revolution against the Shah, hit by a stray bullet in the heart. The Los Angeles *Times* and the craft of journalism lost a great reporter and I lost a special friend, colleague and teacher.

There were reports coming out about the dreadful plight of Palestinian refugees in Jordan and I suggested to the *Telegram's* managing editor, Andy MacFarlane, that I go cover the refugee story. MacFarlane, a dynamic and imaginative journalist who usually complied with such suggestions, uncharacteristically said no, to come home. I telexed him (we at the *Tely* didn't go in much for long-distance phoning) that since I was in the area and Arab refugees were the hottest story of the moment, we should cover it and unless I heard otherwise I intended to do that. I got an instant response that for once I should obey orders and come home forthwith—a very unusual message for MacFarlane. I thought perhaps the paper was not happy with my Cairo story. In any case, on returning to Toronto, I found that all was well except for the fact that I couldn't get a satisfactory reason for his not wanting me to cover the Arab refugee story, which anyone could see was going to be the insoluble problem of the Middle East.

On return to Toronto I had dinner with publisher John Bassett, an uncritical fan of Israel. He never tired of hearing—or talking—about how good the Israeli military was and how inept the Arabs were. He delighted in hearing the antics of Cairo at war. I agreed that Israel's handling of the war was awesome, and also agreed that its surprise attack was justified, made against the wishes and exhortations of the rest of the world. A country—any country—is not only entitled to do what it thinks it must to survive, but has a duty to do what it feels is in its best interests. Israel was vindicated in putting the posturing, strutting, bellicose Egyptians in their place.

But on purely moral grounds, I was more pro-Arab than pro-Israeli. The only *right* of the state of Israel to be created in the first place was the right of *might*—American strength, Zionist determination and, unpleasant as the thought may be to some, the use of terror and murder. However, the reality of Israel cannot be changed—unless it is someday defeated. *Blitzkrieg* was and is Israel's main weapon. I told Bassett that I thought we had missed a super story by not covering the plight of Arab refugees after the war. Bassett looked at me, grinned and said: "Bugger the goddam Arab refugees." I suddenly had the reason my story suggestion was killed.

I found the *Tely's* uncritical pro-Zionist sympathies overdone, sometimes embarrassing, and often wrong. I occasionally felt that my views were tolerated as a token gesture of impartiality. It didn't bother me—although it seemed to me unnecessarily provocative of the *Tely* to have a rabbi as the paper's main writer on Israeli affairs, a rabbi who on appropriate occasions had his reports from Israel run with a picture of himself wearing a helmet. Ironically, after the *Tely* died, Rabbi Reuben Slonim began showing more sympathy for the Palestinian cause (in a loyal pro-Israel sense, of course!) while I shifted more toward an Israeli viewpoint as Palestinian terrorism increased and Yasser Arafat became the paramount bully and blackmailer of the Middle East.

Most journalists covering the Middle East could see both the Israeli and the Arab point of view, though the Israeli side got the bulk of sympathetic treatment. Not fully appreciated was that Israel's was a war of survival, and not simply the topic of debate that it became in so many North American living rooms and newsrooms, where freedom and security are unearned and unsought and are considered irrevocable. Nor is the fervor of Palestinians fully appreciated today. They yearn just as desperately as Israelis did for a return of their homeland—a homeland that in their minds is the garden of plenty that Israeli determination and American money have made it.

After the Six Day War I felt very strongly that *if* Israel genuinely wanted peace in the Middle East, it had to make the initial gesture. I felt its triumph had been so dramatic that it could afford to be magnanimous and, in return for recognition of its borders, return the Sinai and the conquered lands—certainly to Egypt and Jordan, if not to Syria, which was an ideological rogue regime anyway. Israel's great error would be to confuse the military incompetence of Egyptians and Arabs with cowardice, lack of intelligence, or potential. Arab ineptness was temporary, and every war became more difficult, more precarious, for Israel. Now was the time for Israel to make a gesture—not at some future date when its bargaining position might not be so favorable.

Near the end of the Six Day War, Egyptian hostility was centred on the USSR, which had failed to honor its pledges to support Egypt. The world was treated to the unusual spectacle of the Soviet Embassy in Cairo being picketed by "spontaneous" demonstrations of people protesting betrayal. The Libyan Embassy (pre-Colonel Khadafy) was also being harassed because it was believed that American air force bases in Libya were being used to fly cover for Israeli jets attacking Egypt. It was scapegoat time in the Arab world.

When the surrender (that's virtually what it was) was announced, Nasser pulled off one of his great political coups. One might argue that he saved Egypt from violence and internal turmoil brought on by shame and defeat. He went on television one evening and, in a surprise announcement, took full responsibility for the defeat "at the hands of Anglo-British imperialist forces supporting Israel," and promptly resigned. He said he'd make his *formal* resignation to the National Assembly the following day. Immediately—and I mean within minutes—the streets of Cairo erupted with people, carrying torches and banners and chanting that Nasser, their god who walked like a man (or vice-versa?), should not abandon them. For the moment, fear of losing Nasser overshadowed their shame at another humiliating military defeat by Israel.

The next morning Nasser withdrew his resignation and announced through the Speaker of the National Assembly, Anwar Sadat (the future president who promoted peace with Israel and was assassinated), that street demonstrations urging him to stay in office were so persuasive he would carry on "until all traces of aggression are eliminated." Nasser would, in the words of Sadat, "comply with the will of the people." Meanwhile, countries like Algeria, Jordan, Yemen, Syria, and Saudi Arabia urged Nasser to stay on. Nasser declared that he would, after all, remain as President.

Cairo again burst forth in joyous celebrations, with innumerable bands of people marching everywhere, chanting and cheering. All signs of defeat and bitterness evaporated in the widespread euphoria of having their precious Nasser back. It was victory for the people. How orchestrated it was is open to debate, but without it there could have been real ugliness. It was one of the few occasions upon which total defeat was instantly transformed into the appearance of victory by having the humiliated leader agree not to depart! Usually it is the other way around but, as is so often pointed out, the Middle East is not like anyplace else.

Egyptians are particularly adept (they've had enough practice) at depicting defeat as victory, and while it may be tempting to make jest of the practice, *all* losers do it if they can; the Egyptians are just more skilled at it than some others. (One recalls President Nixon's "peace with honor" rationale for losing the Vietnam War and abandoning his Vietnamese allies as a classic example of trying to portray defeat as triumph.) The great contribution of Nasser to his country and to Arabs was that he gave them a pride that had been lost or dormant since the pharaohs. Under Nasser, Egyptians ceased being "Wogs" and became a nation. It was his crowning achievement. He died in 1970—some say of a heart attack. More likely it was a broken heart.

23

Whose side is your embassy on?

ANDY BOROWIEC
WASHINGTON STAR
PRAGUE, CZECHOSLOVAKIA
AUGUST 1968

Journalists who specialize in covering international crises—the
"firemen" of the craft—rarely find right and wrong clearly defined. Often in international disputes, one side is not the personification of virtue, the other, the epitome of evil. Good and bad
can exist on both sides.

Despite this rather obvious truism, international disputes are
often distorted in the media. Journalistic shorthand tends to ignore shadings and qualifications and come to absolute conclusions.
The media in North America for example, when reporting the
Vietnam War, favored the view that America was wrong to be in
South Vietnam, therefore, it was the bad guy; *ergo* Hanoi must
be the good guy—that sort of false logic. Since the media is usually
the *only* source of information for the general public, and since
it can inadvertently take sides when it doesn't intend to, it means
that people get a distorted impression of reality.

The media tends to reflect a conventional collective prejudice
or pack wisdom that is acceptable to the audience it writes and
performs for. Quickly foreign correspondents become cynical or
"realistic" and stop trying to change what cannot be changed. This
isn't to suggest that they lack conviction or moral courage, or that
they docilely reflect their employers' biases. It is just that the individual on the scene usually sees both sides, and this may put
him on collision course with home office if compromises are not
made or certain themes are not avoided. Thus, necessary adjust-
ments are made, taboos and sacred cows respected, unpopular or
unfashionable causes ignored. Rarely mentioned in the media, for
example, is the idea that South Africans are *not* Europeans, but
a *white* African tribe; that what we call black majority rule in Africa

313

is usually black minority dictatorship; that "liberation" wars are often wars of subjugation.

The most dramatic example of biased coverage in recent years has been of Israel, which in its first twenty years was for the most part in sympathetic terms, as if it was more sinned against than sinning. In the last fifteen years or so, the tone of the coverage has been reversed and now the Palestinians get the sympathy, while Israel tends to be regarded as bellicose and intransigent.

In some twenty-five years and forty to fifty crises, I recall only one major story I covered in which right and wrong were clearly defined and letting one's emotions run rampant was an accurate reflection of reality. That story was Czechoslovakia, August 1968, when Soviet tanks rolled in to crush Alexander Dubček's gallant, futile attempt to give communism a human face.

For the six months preceding the "invasion," speculation raged as to whether or not the Soviets *would* invade. When Dubček succeeded the crude Anton Novotny as party leader and began to relax repressive communism, the relief that swept the country was like a narcotic. Despite the mantle of democratic humanist and martyr that Dubček now wears, it can be argued that he never *intended* to liberalize the country to the extent he did. He was still a Communist, committed to Communist ways, a party man who reached the top. But once he started to relax the iron grip with which the party held the country, he couldn't easily reclench the fist. Having started something he couldn't stop, he became the captive of his own liberalization policies. Dubček, in fact, experienced something no Communist leader experienced before or since: popularity verging on adoration of the masses. He personified the people's hopes and desires for freedom.

The general feeling among "experts"—those Sovietologists, Kremlinologists, and Soviet Affairs specialists in Western chancelleries and government offices and in the media, including journalists based in Moscow—was that the Soviet Union would *not* invade. It was felt that the Soviet Union of 1968 was not the Soviet Union of 1956 when Khrushchev sent tanks into Hungary to crush the rebellion. The Kremlin was believed to be more liberal, more tolerant of dissent, more sensitive to adverse public opinion in 1968.

This view was held by Pierre Berton, perhaps Canada's best-known author, pop historian and TV personality, who took issue with the opinions of Lubor Zink, political columnist for the *Telegram*, on the question of Czechoslovakia and communism in general. Zink had been critical of Berton's impressions of Czechoslovakia while he was there to do TV programs.

Zink was a student activist in Prague who was put on a death list when the Nazis took over his country in 1938. He escaped to serve in the British Eighth Army during World War II. He got a commission, won three medals for valor, including the Military Cross, and returned to Czechoslovakia after the war to work in the Foreign Ministry under Jan Masaryk. When the Communists took over in 1948, Zink was on their blacklist. Again he escaped, this time crossing the mountains into West Germany after depositing his British-born son at the British Embassy in Prague. He worked for a time with the BBC in Britain and came to Canada where he entered journalism, won a National Newspaper Award, and became, in a sense, the conscience and uneasy prophet of Canadian journalism.

Zink disagreed that Soviet communism was softening. He criticized Berton's optimism about the liberalization trend under way in Czechoslovakia, even when the Stalinist leader Anton Novotny was still in charge. Berton responded to what he called Zink's "archaic" views. Mocking his "International Communist Conspiracy" mentality, he said Zink "cannot seem to get it through his head that the world is going through an historic re-alignment— that Stalin is actually in his grave, that the satellites are proceeding in their own individualistic and nationalistic courses, that countries such as Hungary, Poland, Yugoslavia and Czechoslovakia are leaning significantly toward the West, and that the seeds of a new liberalism, still admittedly sickly, have taken roots in part of Eastern Europe."

On August 21, 1968, the Kremlin proved Zink's case.

The *Telegram*'s man in Moscow, Aaron Einfrank, who had succeeded me and who by comparison made me seem a bleeding-heart liberal, categorically predicted that the Soviets would *not* invade. A month before the invasion, Einfrank appeared on the front page of the *Telegram* predicting that "the best the Russians may be able to get is a face-saving compromise, in which Prague gives lip-service to Moscow while continuing on its liberal way." He added: "The Kremlin would lose too much prestige now to use force. Anything they do will have to be done more subtly." This from a hard-line anti-Communist!

To someone like myself who does not pretend to be an expert on Marxist theory but who has a fair understanding of Communist and Soviet reality, not only *could* the Kremlin invade, but it *must* invade and/or crush the beginnings of freedom and independence in Czechoslovakia. Two days after Einfrank's views appeared, I wrote " . . . the Soviet Union will never permit a neighboring Communist country to become anything but a Communist country. Even at the price of sending tanks into Prague, they would not permit such liberalization that might result in a bloc country becoming non-Communist. Those who say the Soviets will not, cannot, use force today, reveal an unawareness of the Soviet philosophy."

The survival of the Soviet system demands total subservience and absolute control. Freedom of choice is the *one* thing the Soviet system cannot tolerate because once it is accepted, the whole empire will start to crumble. There are examples of Marxist or Communist governments being freely elected to power, but no major example of their democratically relinquishing power—of allowing themselves to be voted *out* of office. In fact, there is no example of a free and democratic election in any Marxist-ruled state. (Thus, the Solidarity movement in Poland was doomed from the start and, while Soviet tanks weren't required to crush Solidarity, they *would* nonetheless have been used if the jackboots of General Jaruzelski had proved inadequate.)

When the news of Soviet tanks rolling into Czechoslovakia hit the news wires, I was dispatched to try and reach Prague. Getting somewhere *after* the fact is always tough. How was I to travel to Prague when the border would undoubtedly be sealed as soon as the Soviets could manage it? I flew to Vienna, registered at the International Hotel where journalists from all over the world had gathered. We were all trying to find a way into Czechoslovakia. I immediately used the hotel Telex to send a story of what it was like on the fringes of the crisis, and outlined the confusion and problems involved—a phony story, mainly for the dateline to show the *Tely* cared and was trying. It could have been written from Orangeville or Brazil for all the fresh information it contained. Perhaps I was also putting an excuse on the record in case I failed to get in.

At the hotel I ran into an old friend, Andy Borowiec, formerly with AP and now with the Washington *Star*, whom I knew from such stamping grounds as Algiers, Cyprus, Beirut, the Congo. He was brash and competent with an irrational temper, considerable impatience, and a quick sense of humor. Borowiec was of Polish origin and comfortable with Slavic languages. Up to then Andy and I hadn't been close friends, as Joe Morris and I were. But because we knew each other from various crises, we automatically tended to trust one another. It was a Friday night and Andy had heard of a border station that was allegedly open. We hired a taxi for 6 A.M. Saturday and began driving along the Viennese side of the Czechoslovakian border, hoping to find a crossing point that had not yet been occupied by the Red Army.

We found one early in the afternoon. The Czech border guards were tightlipped and bitter at the Soviets. They were delighted to see Western journalists trying to get into their country, and they bent rules to let us in. The more foreign press in Prague, the better. It was their way of protesting. "You are all we've got left," was a refrain heard repeatedly. "Tell the truth. Make the outside world understand. No one else will . . . "

My passport had been issued the previous year by the Canadian Embassy in Moscow. This incited a buxom Czech woman immigration official to scold: "This is a Canadian passport. It is a good passport, a respectable passport. Why do you desecrate your honorable passport by getting it issued in Moscow, a name which will forever taint the decency of your respectable passport?" She spat. Again it was a reaction I was to encounter repeatedly in Czechoslovakia.

On our drive to Prague, all road signs were either taken down or reversed in order to confuse the Soviets if they came along. We'd ask the way to Prague and get imprecise, evasive answers until we explained we were foreign journalists. Then we were given detailed directions, maybe a bit of food, and suggestions for places to buy gasoline, which already was in short supply. It seemed odd to be in a Communist country where the foreign press was seen as a savior instead of being regarded with suspicion as a potential enemy. It is at times like this that one realizes how important and precious a free press is, and how much people in bondage depend on it.

There was little travel on the highways, and no sign of Russians—until the outskirts of Prague. There we saw a sight that chilled me then and still chills me to remember it. It was a field filled with Soviet tanks. Not just the odd tank scattered discreetly under trees or camouflaged, but row upon row upon row of tanks. So many tanks that it felt like a punch in the stomach. I thought that if I were a Czechoslovakian and intended to fight back, perhaps to even Molotov-cocktail a tank, the massive strength and numbers would drain all enthusiasm and resolve. Undoubtedly that was the intended effect and it worked. A feeling of utter hopelessness, resignation, and despair pervaded Prague. I recall one wistful Czech noting: "Last week Wenceslas Square was filled with young people singing, 'We Shall Overcome.' Instead, it is Soviet tanks which have overcome us."

Physically and architecturally, Prague is one of the beautiful cities of Europe—the world, in fact. On this occasion, cobbled streets, ancient buildings, endless spires and monuments to a re-vered past, instead of being colorful and capturing the past, seemed threadbare and forlorn. There were none of the usual noises of a vibrant city. No laughter, no jostling, none of the normal activ-ities. Just dourness, silence, resentment.

We checked into the Alcron Hotel in the centre of Prague—an island of anarchy and freedom amid a sea of apprehension. Our taxi fare was $150, and for his return drive the driver picked up a load of Czechs anxious to escape. The flight of citizens was to become a flood.

The Alcron was occupied only by journalists—not many, but enough to tell the story. I seemed to be the only Canadian jour-nalist in Prague, and I felt a great sense of obligation to tell what was happening, give my impressions, relay what the people them-selves said and felt. It would be difficult because the Soviets had control of the telegraph offices and post office, and were limiting communications. There was no link to North America. It is the nightmare of every journalist: having a dramatic story but no way to tell it to readers.

There were line-ups at the hotel Telex, but it was a haphazard situation. In those days the *Telegram* refused to use Telex, and never really understood it. The editors weren't even interested in learning about it; so, as one who travelled a lot, I had set up my own communications network. I had long ago established relations with Radiopress Paris, which specialized in journalistic commu-nications. (It is now out of business, thanks perhaps to computers and portable video display terminals that give direct communi-cation to home offices.) Wherever I was, I'd link with Radiopress and they would transmit to Toronto. The *Telegram* simply paid the bills and had no idea how stories reached them.

Though contact between Prague and the outside world was tenuous and erratic, the Czech operators, where possible, would try to assist. Even the Czech secret police tried to help. And mem-bers of the Czechoslovakian Communist Party would help for-eigners thwart the Soviets, as would members of the Central Committee. The nation was united as never before. It was as if people had suddenly had a bellyful of repression, of persecuting one another, of informing on friends and neighbors, of spying, of bullying, of clawing to survive the imposed system. They wanted no more. In the previous six months Czechoslovakia had gone from being the most Stalinist and repressive of Soviet satellites to arguably the freest, happiest, most democratic country on earth. It was perhaps the last chance for a Communist state to prove that it could embody the abstracts of freedom. Dubček had tried— and lost.

He had been flown to Russia as a prisoner and was being held in custody somewhere. Unknown to any of us, he was being humiliated, broken. Dubček was forced to foul his own clothes, was not allowed to wash or change, and for a few days lived worse than any animal. Then, in this condition, he was forced to negotiate with the Soviets. Small wonder he never recovered. A man will break more from being degraded than from torture. The treatment he endured was reminiscent of the Stalinist purges of the military in the '30s when, as Robert Conquest relates in his definitive work, *The Great Terror,* one officer who withstood all the physical tortures and deprivation had his spirit broken and signed a false confession when the GPU (forerunners of the NKVD and KGB) pushed his head into a bucket of human spit. Once he signed, he was shot.

As for Dubček, he was probably saved by the old soldier, Ludvik Svoboda, the president of Czechoslovakia, who had once been imprisoned by Stalin for no particular reason. He was the epitome of courage, a figure of unquestioned prestige. He refused to negotiate with the Soviets unless Dubček was included, ridiculing Soviet threats to his life. He reportedly told the Soviets that if he were to die, he'd prefer it to be now, when he was standing up for freedom, than to be tortured later in a cell. Within a week Dubček was back in Prague, insisting that all was well and that his power was restored, but there was not a smidgin of truth to it. Dubček was finished.

Amid this atmosphere the 14th Congress of the Czechoslovakian Communist Party was due to be held September 9. But the party contacted delegates and held a secret meeting at the end of August. Knowing that word would reach the KGB, a decoy meeting was arranged while the *real* meeting was held in a factory with the 1,100 delegates attending in overalls and disguised as workers. The Congress re-elected Dubček as head of the party, a decision

that was overturned as soon as the Soviets learned of it. The pliable
Gustav Husak was appointed in his place.

Meanwhile in Prague, with events breaking around the clock,
we journalists were frantic to relay news to the waiting world. I
periodically made contact with Radiopress Paris, and the agency
that had saved me in so many places around the world rescued
me again whenever the erratic Czech communications system would
allow contact.

Most correspondents were using the Telex facilities at their
embassies. Unusual circumstances necessitated unusual methods:
embassies, which usually shun the press (and vice-versa), apparently in response to the critical situation, cooperated with their
own journalists. Even the Swiss Embassy heeded its nationals—
unusual, because the Swiss have a reputation of being smug and
uncooperative. Only one Western embassy refused to cooperate
with its journalists in getting news out of Czechoslovakia: the
Canadian Embassy. I would daily, sometimes hourly, plead with,
berate, implore my embassy to help. The fact that *all* other Western embassies were cooperating with their press had no effect.
The embassy was adamant. It contacted Mitchell Sharp, Minister
of External Affairs, who supported the bureaucratic decision and
refused to violate international codes by letting its Telex facilities
be used by a journalist. I lodged a formal complaint, as did publisher John Bassett. To no avail. Sharp responded to the effect
that to help a journalist might jeopardize the embassy's position
with the Communist government. Besides, the embassy's communications facilities "were severely overtaxed . . . some 2,500
message groups behind in processing." Tough luck, *Tely*.

No country was subsequently punished for its decision to let its
embassy help get the news out. Because it was cowardly and misguided—possibly even sympathetic to the Soviet position—the
Canadian government, through its embassy, betrayed freedom
and truth in Czechoslovakia. It has been, of course, a Canadian
characteristic, almost a tradition, to abandon its nationals in trouble. This attitude increased under the Trudeau government, perhaps because Trudeau himself feels some affinity for left-wing or
Communist regimes, no matter how brutal. (Mitchell Sharp's first
official reaction to the Soviet invasion of Czechoslovakia was that
it was "unfortunate"—an extraordinary understatement).

I failed so consistently at the Canadian Embassy that it got to
be a joke among the other correspondents. Andy Borowiec had
difficulty accepting what I was telling him and found it amusing—

until he, too, checked. In the context of the times the Canadian Embassy seemed almost pro-Soviet and anti-Czech. Borowiec finally remarked: "Tell me, old boy, whose side is your embassy on?" I couldn't answer.

My main communication problems were solved by the American Embassy. I threw myself on their mercies, reminding them that the previous year I had been the CBS man in Moscow, and when I ran into an information official who used to hear my broadcasts, I was given access to their Telexes. Thinking back, I recall very few occasions when I needed help overseas that I ever got it from a Canadian Embassy. External Affairs is imbued with a "don't-make-waves" ethic.

It wasn't until three days later that I discovered another Canadian in Prague—Terry Hammond of the Vancouver *Sun*. He was not experienced in foreign assignments and had few contacts or a way of getting his stories out. Another victim of our embassy, he had been unable to file all week and was going mad with frustration. I put him in touch with Radiopress Paris, and eventually he made contact. I have never forgiven External Affairs, and suspect its attitude has hardened, not softened, over the years.

Prague was an emotional story from beginning to end. There was no official source of information, and members of the Central Committee of the Czech Communist party would look up journalists in the Alcron Hotel, feed them tips, and keep them informed. It was fascinating and very moving to walk along the street and see a crowd gathered in front of a Soviet tank crew or in front of a couple of young Red Army conscripts on guard duty, demanding to know why they were there. The Soviet soldiers were under the impression that they were protecting the Czech people from West German revisionists, that they'd been invited by the Czechs to help protect them from enemies of the people. In fact, as Czech citizens would tearfully proclaim, their only enemies were the Red Army soldiers.

"Look at us!" one girl screamed, pounding her chest. "*We* are the people—are *we* the enemy you are protecting us from?"

"You are victims of propaganda," a young Red Army officer replied nervously.

"Propaganda? You know our country. You know your country. The only propaganda is the propaganda of the state."

"Agitators. There are foreign agitators stirring up trouble, telling lies."

"Look around you. Look at us. Look at me. Are we 'foreign agitators'? Why would we agitate in our own country? No. It is you, the soldiers of the Kremlin, who are the 'foreign agitators.' "

And so it would go. Occasionally I found myself sympathizing with the plight of a young Soviet soldier being outargued and outclassed by the Czechs. I saw one youthful tank officer's eyes fill with tears, and watched him walk dejectedly down an alley when confronted with the overwhelming evidence that *he* was the invader, the enemy. There were reports of idealistic young soldiers committing suicide when faced with irrefutable evidence of their perfidy.

Word was passed that at certain hours all who were opposed to the Soviet invasion should drive their cars and honk horns. At the appointed hours, Prague would erupt in a cacophony of car horns: eloquent testimony to the widespread unpopularity of the Soviet presence.

At various times the hero of Czechoslovakia, the great distance runner Emil Zatopek, winner of four Olympic gold medals and an army officer, would appear at a main corner in central Wenceslas Square and make an impassioned impromptu speech before a fast-gathering crowd, berating the Soviets for their aggression. He would urge that the USSR be barred from the upcoming Olympic Games in Mexico City. He'd talk for five minutes or so, then lope off, in that distinctive crouched way he had of running, to another site to make the speech again. Then he'd broadcast over Radio Free Prague, which had a mobile transmitter that moved from one building to another before the Soviets could track it down. For his stand Zatopek was expelled from the Czechoslovakian Olympic Committee, kicked out of the army, fired as track coach of the national team; his army pension was cut and he was expelled from the Communist party. But in the eyes of the people he never looked greater than when jogging the streets of Prague, making stirring speeches, and fighting for liberty.

Radio Free Prague tried to keep the people informed, giving instructions for opposing the Soviets as well as details of what was happening elsewhere in the country and what the outside world reaction was. It wasn't much, but it was something. Yet even RFP was victim of Soviet disinformation, and at one point broadcast that all power had been restored to Dubček. Wishful thinking blinded their common sense, as it sometimes does to people of good will.

What was happening in Prague—throughout Czechoslovakia—

was *not* "passive" resistance, but "nonviolent" resistance. Such resistance was in character for the people, and historically the way they have survived—against the Nazis in 1938, the Communists in 1948, and the Soviets in 1968. Czechs are Slavic survivors and a calculating people, rarely headstrong and impetuous, or given to gallant but futile gestures. Perhaps it was the most sensible form of protest the people could employ. Still, it was not the sort of resistance that would satisfy some nationalities. It did not invoke great admiration.

I found myself wondering what other people would do if faced with a similar situation. I suspect that Hungarians or Poles would be unlikely to react in the Czechoslovakian way. Hungarians would probably have reacted violently, would have fought and suffered great casualties and reprisals. As would the Poles, I suspect, if Soviet tanks were to fill Warsaw's streets. I hoped, but was not sure, that Canadians would fight back if their country was occupied. I wonder, even now, if survival at all costs is so important. Personally, I think that *how* you live can be more important than *if* you live. Sometimes it is more important to fight back, even if it means destruction, than it is to survive.

The one battle the Czech people won was the war of the posters. All over Prague, faster than they could be torn down, posters were put up with the universal theme of equating the hammer and sickle with the swastika. This symbolism especially affected the young Red Army soldiers, conditioned as they were to the Soviet triumph over Naziism in the Great Patriotic War, which is as fresh in memories today in the USSR as it was twenty-five years ago.

At the height of the "occupation," Novosti News Agency, the Soviet propaganda outlet and journalistic cover for KGB agents, had Comrade Makhotin, one of its senior men touring Canada, visit Andy MacFarlane to see if the *Telegram* would publish photographs of happy Czechoslovakian peasants greeting smiling Red Army soldiers, and the streets lined with happy people waving at Soviet tanks. At the same time I was writing from Prague about Soviet photographers travelling in armoured personnel carriers taking pictures while Soviet soldiers stood in the background and threatened to shoot people unless they threw flowers, smiled, and showed joy. *Chutzpah*, thy name is Novosti! MacFarlane filed the Novosti photos in the waste basket.

President Svoboda became the symbol of oppressed Czechoslovakia. At one point he vowed before an adoring, desperate, self-deluded crowd of thousands that Czechoslovakia would not give up the liberalization policies established under Dubček's enlightened Marxism. "Not one inch will we retreat," he declared to a delirious throng. Sadly, Czechoslovakia was, in fact, retreating far into the past—to 1948, when the tyranny of Soviet communism was first imposed and democracy died. In 1984, sixteen years after Svoboda's stirring speech, there is still not a glimmer of light or hope in the long, dark tunnel. It is interesting to note that today Czechoslovakia is firmly under the Communist boot while an impulsive people like the Hungarians have managed to turn their bloody revolution into a victory of sorts, and now have freedoms that the more docile slaves don't have.

I grew increasingly uneasy in Czechoslovakia, as only the year before I had left Moscow suddenly after Olga had defected. There were undoubtedly those in KGB circles who would have relished a chat, or worse, with me about the circumstances of the defection. And here I was for the picking in Prague. I figured that the KGB knew I was there and, if they wished, could reach me. But I also felt that I probably had fairly low priority and that it would be some time before they'd get around to such a relatively minor matter.

When Prague began to settle down, the *Telegram* began to get nervous about my being there also. Andy MacFarlane cabled that I should come home soonest. I knew that cables were being monitored and that if the KGB were interested in me, they'd make a move if they thought I was about to leave the country, so I created a smoke screen. I replied that I had no intention of leaving and that I would come home in a few weeks' time. MacFarlane impatiently cabled back that he was ordering me out by the weekend. I responded, sorry, but I wouldn't abandon the story until later. The next day at dawn I hired a taxi and headed for Vienna.

Czechoslovakia remains one of the few places I've covered where there was no civilized justification for the Soviet invasion. And yet the indignation of the West was short-lived. The 1968 Olympics went on without concern, with only Norway threatening to boycott the Mexico City Games on principle if the Soviets attended. When no other country followed its lead, Norway abandoned its gesture and went to the Games along with every other "free" country.

I wrote that Canada should boycott the Olympics, end the student exchanges, suspend trade and cultural connections. It had no effect. Canada continued to sell bumper crops of wheat to the USSR, and within three years Prime Minister Trudeau was paying a visit and signing a "friendship" protocol with Premier Kosygin—

similar to agreements that Finland, Afghanistan, and Nazi Germany once had with the Kremlin. The prestigious Ottawa Press Club, in a classic gesture of impropriety, turned over its premises to *Pravda* to throw a reception for the new *Pravda* (and KGB) representative, Konstantin Geyvandov, who was expelled six years later for espionage-related activities.

The whole Czechoslovakian interlude was intensely emotional. I felt a constant mixture of anger, sorrow, outrage, admiration and bitterness. It is a terrible thing to see a people robbed of liberty and hope, and it is even more heartrending to see a people who had lost their freedom, unexpectedly regain it, and then have it taken from them again—this time with even less hope of salvation. It is even more frustrating to see the rest of the world shrug, and not only ignore the outrage, but rationalize it, misinterpret it, and deliberately ignore it.

How quickly we forget. How quickly we rationalize that the rattlesnake is benign, that the leopard can change its spots. Czechoslovakia was one story where self-indulgent writing and reporting from the heart was a completely accurate and objective reflection of reality.

24

Two million dead and not
a twinge of church conscience

TORONTO *TELEGRAM*
JANUARY 1970

George Orwell recalled in 1944 his discovery early on that whatever newspapers reported, they usually got wrong. That's not only
a reasonably accurate observation, but also a fairly healthy attitude
to take toward the press—disquieting as it may be for those who
practise the trade and care about it. The miracle is that sometimes
newspapers get it right. (One could include television, which is
worse, but since no one can ever recall precisely what is said on
TV, it doesn't much matter.)

The Biafran War—or Nigerian civil war—between 1967 and
1970 was classic for a variety of reasons. It illustrated a lot of
uneasy realities about today's world and, depending on one's viewpoint, it also illustrated Orwell's gloomy assessment of journalism.
Few recognized what was going on at the time or, what is even
more disturbing, understand it now. Biafra already seems something in the remote past.

Three times the size of South Africa in area, the equivalent to
the combined area of France, Italy, Belgium, and the Netherlands,
Nigeria was Africa's largest, potentially richest, and most popu-
lated country. Some 46 million Nigerians were subdivided into
some 200 tribal and linguistic groups living in four regions. Half
the population fell into three major groups: the 24 million Fulani-
Hausa people of the feudalistic, ill-educated Moslem North; the
9 million of the Yoruba West and mid-West; and the 13 million
of the Ibo East (Biafra).

Until 1966 Nigeria basked in the myth that it was the most
stable, sensible, and cooperative of the African states. Its police
and military were in the British tradition, it practised democracy,
had (and still has) the freest press in black Africa. It produced

able politicians, academics, writers, artists and, in general, provided hope and inspiration for the rest of Africa. But, as in many parts of Africa, the mythology bore little resemblance to reality. Beneath the surface tribalism flourished—the curse of black Africa that prevents it from being truly liberated, democratic, progressive. In Nigeria every group tended to be suspicious of the others, but of them all, the Ibo were most resented and envied because they seemed, the most prosperous, clever, successful, ambitious. Ibos comprised the heart of commercial activities; they were the core of the officer class in the army and the most Christianized. Not for nothing are the Ibos known as the Jews of Africa.

Nigeria's myth of democratic tranquillity and harmony was shattered forever in January 1966 as a result of a coup that took place simultaneously in the major capitals of the different regions. While there had been rumors of the impending coup, none had been taken very seriously. After all, the whole of Africa is a huge rumor mill. And wasn't Nigeria the most peaceful country in black Africa? In fact, tension had long been brewing and violence erupting in the country, but the warnings had been downplayed. The *New Nigerian*, for example, had reported the headline "Only 153 people killed in the West" following rigged elections that had resulted in thousands being killed. On the night of January 14, 1966, a group of Ibo officers—five majors and a captain—motivated by a desire to rid the country of corruption and dishonesty, staged the bloodiest, most brutal coup black Africa had known. It is important to examine this coup at length, for everything that has happened since had its origins here.

In the Nigerian capital of Lagos, using the codename "Operation Damisa" (leopard), Sandhurst-trained Major Emmanuel Ikeajuna (who had been Nigeria's champion high-jumper and the first Commonwealth athlete to clear six-foot-nine at the British Empire Games at Vancouver's Empire Stadium in 1954) led his troops who were mostly Northerners to the federal prime minister's residence. Bursting into his room at 2 A.M., he took Sir Abubakar Tafawa Balewa away in his car and shot him. Senior military officers were rousted from their beds and killed. They missed Major-General John Aguiyi-Ironsi, also an Ibo and commander of the Nigerian army, who heard of the coup while returning home late from a party. He rallied the police to oppose the mutiny and armed only with a revolver confronted rebel troops at the radio station, persuading them to change their minds. As resistance to the coup grew in the army, Ikeajuna fled to neighboring Dahomey, where he was regarded as something of a hero. The mutiny was short-lived in Lagos.

Meanwhile in the Western capital of Ibadan, a truckload of mutineers under the command of Artillery Captain Nwobosi made a detour to take a pregnant woman to the hospital as they headed for the premier's residence. Then they attacked the home of the premier, Chief Samuel Akintola, the high priest of the rigged vote. After a short gun battle the premier threw down his submachine gun and surrendered—and was shot on the spot along with those loyal to him.

In the northern capital of Kaduna, Major Chuckwuma Nzeoguwu, also Sandhurst-trained and the popular senior instructor at the Northern Military Training College, staged night maneuvers with live ammunition and attacked the residence of Sir Ahmadu Bello, the Sardauna of Sokoto and premier of the Northern region, who cringed against the wall of his bedroom while his senior wife and bodyguard tried to shield him with their bodies— and died with him.

In the Eastern capital of Enugu the coup failed, mainly because Archbishop Makarios, president of Cyprus, happened to be visiting and the rebelling officers were reluctant to do anything that might injure him. At the same time in the northern garrison town of Kanu, Lieutenant-Colonel Emeka Odumegwu Ojukwu, millionaire son of a knighted Nigerian businessman, prevented a mutiny and kept troops under control.

By Saturday morning, January 15, thanks to General Ironsi, the coup was already a failure. Yet the federal prime minister and two premiers were dead, along with senior politicians and upper ranks of the army—and the politics of Nigeria were changed permanently. At first there was rejoicing in the army, and General Ironsi was considered a hero. He took power, suspended political activity, and tried to restore order. But he made horrendous errors. He sought to centralize power in Lagos and earned the suspicions of the regions. Though he had no prejudices about tribalism himself he failed to realize the emotional pull it had on others. He tended to live luxuriously, and didn't recognize the growing enmity of Northern soldiers towards Southern soldiers (Ibo). While a brave and intelligent soldier, he lacked subtlety and guile. Contrary to suspicions at the time, Ironsi seems not to have been involved in the attempted coup; he had been in command of UN forces in the Congo and as a blunt, honest soldier, didn't believe in mixing soldiering with politics unless it was to rescue the country from chaos.

During his seven months in power, adulation steadily turned to anger and Ironsi became regarded as part of an "Ibo plot" to take over Nigeria. Within the army, troops from the West and North refused to be commanded by Ibo officers. The failure of the mutiny in the East was further evidence of the Ibos' involvement. Colonel Ojukwu was named military governor of the East and, as far as anyone can tell, tried to do his duty. Yet tension mounted.

There were increasing incidents of reprisals against Ibos, who were periodically slaughtered by the hundreds although "official" casualties were much lower. Ironsi tried the army cure of discipline. It failed, partly because he forgot a basic truism: one unpunished mutiny inevitably leads to another. By neglecting to sentence the Ibo officers involved in the coup, he fed the belief that he, too, was in on the plot to seize Nigeria. At the end of July 1966, while on a tour of Nigeria to calm the country down, he became the victim of an anti-Ibo coup, and his own soldiers killed him at Ibadan. A splurge of fresh killing erupted throughout Nigeria.

His successor as head of state was Sandhurst-trained Lieutenant-Colonel Yakubu (Jack) Gowon, then in his late twenties, a member of a minority tribe and a Christian evangelist who didn't drink or smoke or hold grudges. He seemed an ideal compromise and, indeed, turned out to be one of Africa's more decent and moderate leaders. The only problem was that Colonel Ojukwu resented an officer junior to him, with nowhere near his intellect, being vaulted over him. Ojukwu disputed the decision, and increasingly opposed the centralizing of powers to the detriment of the regions.

As violence against Ibos increased in the West and North, more and more Ibo refugees began streaming to their Eastern homeland and non-Ibos were expelled or were slaughtered, though not on a scale to match atrocities against Ibos. On one occasion a British commercial aircraft was prevented from taking off at Kano and all Ibo passengers were removed and summarily shot. Ojukwu began exaggerating atrocities to solidify his political power. He steadily escalated the estimated 7,000 Ibos massacred during October, to 50,000. Conferences were held between Gowon and Ojukwu, ostensibly to negotiate a compromise and settle differences. All these were lost by Gowon, who was too direct, too naïve, and too nice to match Ojukwu.

In February 1967, Ojukwu issued an ultimatum: if the Nigerian government did not implement terms of an agreement reached at Aburi, Ghana, he would declare secession of the Eastern region. Ojukwu wanted a "confederation," a loose alliance of autonomous regions, while the Lagos government wanted a "federation"— more centralized control of all regions. The clause that Ojukwu could not accept in the compromise talks was the right of the Supreme Military Council to declare a state of emergency with the agreement of any *three of the four* regions—a prospect that clearly made Iboland vulnerable. Ojukwu, a superb manipulator, told his Eastern Assembly that the choice was theirs—continue to accept domination by Gowon and the North, which was essentially a stalemate, or assert their own self-determination and thus ensure survival. The way it was presented, the latter was the only choice.

On an international level, the public was intrigued by Ojukwu and the image of a gallant, gutsy Biafra fighting for principle and survival. Despite hectic activity by outside nonaligned mediators and negotiators, Ojukwu declared independence: "Biafra" was no longer a part of Nigeria.

The irony is that threats of secession had traditionally been a Northern ploy to gain concessions. Until Ojukwu proclaimed independence, Eastern politicians had expressed disgust at Northerners for using secession to blackmail concessions from the Lagos government. In a way the North was like Quebec and the rest of Canada: do this else we quit. In early July 1967, fighting started, laboriously, reluctantly, sporadically. At first the Biafrans enjoyed military success because of their officers. But due to greater reserves, wealth, and strength, the Nigerians began pushing the Biafrans back. Relatively early, it was apparent that from a military standpoint Biafra had no chance—unless, of course, international opinion and aid could be mobilized against Nigeria.

Throughout 1968 the Nigerians steadily isolated Biafra in a shrinking, landlocked enclave, with only Tanzania, Zambia, the Ivory Coast, and Gabon affording full diplomatic recognition to the beleaguered state. Increasingly, Biafra's lifeline was the airstrip at Uli—a mile of highway turned into a runway where flights loaded with supplies arrived from the Portuguese island of São Tomé and the former Spanish island colony of Fernando Po, now taken over by Guinea. The islands were located in the Bight of Biafra (known irreverently to journalists as the Armpit of Africa), and the influx of free-lance and mercenary pilots and planes was a boon to the islands' economies. Nigerian artillery and mortars fired on incoming flights at Uli, despite pleadings and efforts by the church and humanitarians to allow these planes of mercy to land. Charges of genocide were made, along with accusations of torture and a policy of mass starvation. Meanwhile, the USSR supplied Nigeria with MiG fighters, and Britain provided armoured cars in the form of Scorpions, Ferrets, Saladins—weapons whose greatest value was that they demoralized the enemy more than they damaged him with firepower.

When Colonel Ojukwu claimed self-determination for Biafra as endorsed by the UN (when it is a black versus white issue), he opened a Pandora's box. It not only raised the spectre of tribalism gone mad and threatened the whole concept of unity in Africa, it also tested the principle of the right of self-determination and self-rule. One would have thought the issue a natural for the UN to deal with, since that Tower of Babble has rarely been reluctant to cite the principle of self-determination when it means forcing European or developed countries to relinquish colonial holdings. But persuading or pressuring Marxist or Third World imperialists to grant self-choice to those they dominate is another matter and one the UN prefers to avoid.

Nigeria could not contemplate the idea of an independent Biafra, especially when its vast oil reserves were mostly in Biafran territory. Nor did the great powers relish the prospect. With the co-operation and approval of most Western governments, the USSR and most Third World countries (which could envisage themselves in a similar plight and split by rampant tribalism, which is a primitive form of nationalism) set out to crush Biafra by force of arms and starvation.

Biafra's valiant fight against overwhelming odds captured the world's imagination. The Christian churches and relief agencies in free countries supported its attempts to secede for various reasons. There were Inter-Church Aid, Caritas (Catholic), Canairelief, the World Council of Churches, and every country with its own agency. The churches and their followers in the West accepted uncritically the theme that the predominantly Catholic Ibos faced genocide at the hand of the Nigerian government forces, and actively participated in raising money and sending aid to Biafra. The do-gooders of the world united, and a Swiss-based public relations firm—Mark Press of Geneva—waged an imaginative and effective public relations campaign around the world on Biafra's behalf. For a time, money was no obstacle. The church pretended that it contributed only humanitarian aid, not aid for killing—a theme it was to adopt for aiding terrorists (freedom fighters) in Mozambique, Angola, Rhodesia—but it overlooked the fact that such aid enabled the recipients to use other money to buy arms. The French and Scandinavian governments also supported Biafra; France, especially, was a continuing source of clandestine arms and ammunition.

Some purists, caught up in the principle of self-determination, had difficulty seeing why the UN would *not* support Biafra when it adamantly supported self-determination for Angola, Rhodesia, South Africa. Could it be that the UN had one standard when it came to blacks oppressing blacks and another when it was a white-versus-black situation? Even at the height of the Biafran war, the world was more offended at Rhodesia, where no one was dying, for not turning power over to blacks, than it ever was with Nigeria for killing its own people by the hundreds of thousands in order to prevent their independence.

I was approached in Toronto by Ted Johnson, later moderator of the Presbyterian Church and the one mainly responsible for Canairelief. He invited me to visit Biafra as their guest to see for myself what was happening, with no commitments either way, and to write my findings in the *Telegram*. Dr. Johnson explained that only through church/Biafran auspices was it possible for journalists to get into the country; they would have to take the nightly food (and ammunition) flights from São Tomé. Unmentioned, but implied, was the fact that *mostly* select, hand-picked (and therefore reliably sympathetic) journalists were allowed into Biafra. Since I subscribed in theory to the validity of Biafra's right to self-determination (and Katanga's, for that matter), I was deemed to be potentially useful in the propaganda war.

The Canadian church groups had purchased a Super-Constellation aircraft and hired a crew, mostly from Nordair, to make the nightly run from São Tomé. The plane was leaving from Montreal with a load of supplies. They were willing to take me along. I agreed to go on condition that the *Telegram* pay my costs in Biafra, though the free flight was acceptable. Dr. Johnson seemed a trifle reluctant, but accepted the principle that by my having the *appearance* of independence, anything I wrote would have more credibility. He had no doubt that I'd share his view of the situation. Johnson sincerely believed Ojukwu to be the "messiah" of Africa.

"I consider him one of the great men of our times, and perhaps the most outstanding leader in Africa," he said. "He may be the Moses of his people. A devout Christian, a true leader." As history was to reveal, Ojukwu was little more than another demagogue on a power kick, whose interests were more selfish than altruistic. But that came later—two million deaths later.

From the start, the most encouraging thing about that flight was the crew: a group of professionals under Captain J. S. (Pat) Patterson of Montreal, a longtime Nordair pilot of the Canadian North who'd been a World War II bomber pilot. He was taciturn, tough, funny, unflappable. A stickler for preventive maintenance, he believed in crew discipline. The Super-Connie was a complex electronic nightmare and not ideal for bush or seat-of-the-pants flying. The aircraft was crammed with a Land Rover and every manner of equipment and food. There were a couple of rows of removable seats at the back for the few passengers on the flight. One of them was cartoonist Ben Wicks, who at the time was participating in sit-ins and hunger fasts on behalf of Biafra and wanted to see it for himself. I insisted that he was going along to draw the humorous side of starvation, or the comic aspects of genocide. But I was glad of the company.

Also along was Denny Braun, a young fellow representing the national office of the New Democratic Party. He and the NDP were interested in Biafra, especially since Trudeau was on record as callously asking, "Where's Biafra?" External Affairs Minister Mitchell Sharp echoed his master and would not let Canada raise the issue of Biafra at the UN—*not* because Canada didn't believe in the cause, but because it couldn't win in a vote. Thus, principle was again sacrificed to expediency. At the time there were some who thought that the Canadian government's lack of sympathy for Biafra was motivated by the Quebec situation: if we supported Biafran independence, how could we refuse Quebec's? The answer was, of course, that we couldn't, if the majority of Quebeckers wanted independence.

It was a long flight by way of the Azores, Ghana, and São Tomé. The church almost did us in because those who loaded the plane and prepared the manifest in Montreal had lied about the weight we were carrying. Apparently they thought that weight limits were a bureaucratic imposition and not determined by fuel and distance. Therefore, they added extra goods and falsified the manifest to make it seem that we were carrying less weight than we were. We made it to the Azores with no problems; but on the flight to Liberia the next day, we ran short of fuel off the west coast of North Africa and virtually glided onto the Portuguese island of Sel, a hush-hush staging base for sending troops to fight rebels in Angola. Sel, a barren dot of real estate 1,000 miles off the coast of Senegal, saved us from ditching. I was playing chess with Wicks when we were told to prepare for an emergency landing, possibly on the water in case we couldn't make it to the Sel airstrip. I remember castling my king to protect it in case we crashed. We landed safely, and I won the game. Patterson was furious at what he considered duplicity with the manifests, but I argued that the intentions were good and the incident should be viewed as an example of how do-gooders inadvertently cause trouble when they twist rules to try to help.

São Tomé was something out of an Errol Flynn movie. Every manner of adventurer-flyer and arms dealer had gathered there to make money on the hazardous night flights of arms and supplies. Some pilots were getting $1,000 a flight. They all had to find the mile-long strip of highway at Uli in the dark and, as they made a final approach by guess and by God, runway lights would be flashed on for a few seconds to enable the incoming aircraft to make final corrections. That was also the signal for the Nigerian artillery to cut loose with barrages. Usually they missed. In daylight it was more nerve-wracking because the makeshift landing strip was necklaced with crashed and wrecked aircraft, which were invisible in the dark. Just as well. All but emergency flights were done at night.

To add excitement to hazard, there was a Nigerian aircraft known as the Intruder, which would bomb the runway as planes were landing. The Intruder had a British pilot (mercenary?) who would talk by radio to the incoming cargo planes, and would identify himself as "Genocide." Pat Patterson used to remark wryly that the only thing Nigerians didn't hit with their bombs was the runway. He would defy Genocide on the radio to "come and get us!"

If landing on a highway in the total darkness of the Biafran jungle seemed unreal, it was positively Alice-in-Wonderland once one arrived. As bureaucrats, the Biafrans were as insufferable and autocratic as East Indians. They insisted on full immigration and customs control, including updated health certificates. The latter seemed bizarre in a state dying of starvation and every manner of disease. In the darkness, people tried to steal what they could. Others sold Biafran stamps and coins, all of which were useless except as souvenirs and curiosities. (I actually managed to mail some letters in Biafra, and have often wondered if the cancelled Nigerian stamps overprinted with "Biafra" have any value. I've never been able to find out.)

Our young socialist companion, Denny, had brought in a suit-case filled with tampons and sanitary napkins, which someone at NDP headquarters in Ottawa had told him were more precious than gold in Biafra. Socialists will try anything! He intended to barter his way with them or hand them out as gifts to select people. Wicks and I were amused, but faintly disgusted. As far as I know, the napkins were useless, although he slipped a couple to the young lady at the airport who helped us. I wondered how on earth you'd give someone a Tampax as a house gift: "Thank you for the delicious dinner, Mrs. Ojukwu. By the way, I hope you'll accept this sanitary napkin as a token of my appreciation."

In the Biafran capital of Umuahia, life went on as usual. Elaborate arrangements were made to accommodate journalists, visiting politicians, and bigwigs who were potential propagandists for Biafra. They were given guides and driven to refugee camps, hospitals, clinics, and so forth, where the poverty was extreme and the starvation obvious and disturbing. The average journalist or visitor stayed three days; he made a set tour, was suitably impressed at the grit of Biafrans and appalled at the conditions; he photographed any number of bellies of children distended from protein deficiency and topped the tour with an "audience" with Ojukwu. Then the visitor(s) would fly back to São Tomé on the nightly run from Uli for the first decent meal in three days, filled with anecdotes and admiration for the courageous Biafrans.

Canadian parliamentarians Andrew Brewin of the NDP and David MacDonald of the Conservatives spent the daylight hours of one day in Biafra and returned to Canada to become Parliament's resident experts and apologists for the breakaway state and critics of the government's callous indifference and skepticism. They even used their experiences as the basis for a book, *Canada and the Biafran Tragedy*.

Journalists stayed at a guest house—a term used loosely—formerly named the Doris Casino. The main hazard was pretty Ibo girls who sought to seduce (often successfully) foreigners, whom they rewarded with venereal diseases too frightful to contemplate. There was no electricity and the bedding was rarely washed ("This is war—we have no luxuries," was the answer when one asked for fresh sheets). As it was, our sheets were covered with spots of blood—not because they came from the military hospital, but because previous occupants had scratched all night, thanks to a combination of bedbugs and mosquitoes.

A ration card got one into the messhall (Progress Hotel), which served fried bananas, garri (like bland Cream of Wheat porridge) and a cube of goat meat with the skin and hair intact to prove, it was said, that the flesh was not human. The food was terrible though there was no shortage of pineapples, oranges, coconuts, which were mostly ignored by the locals. To outsiders, fresh fruit seemed an unexpected bounty. Of course, they weren't suffering from protein deficiency. Since one could bring in only a limited amount of canned goods, even those who intended to stay more than the usual three days found themselves forced by hunger to leave sooner than planned. Yet three days was not sufficient to begin to understand Biafra.

Wicks left after the mandatory number of days while I, having a cast-iron stomach, stayed on. I was eager to get to the "front," see the makeshift Biafran army in action, and size up the war. Indicative of both the genocide propaganda and its effect was the reaction when a lone Nigerian plane flew over Umuahia and dropped bombs. It caused wide-scale panic and people raced around screaming "genocide"—including missionaries and doctors, who should have known better.

"You see with your own eyes, it is genocide!" shouted our guide, Elizer Chuku, a nice young man given to hysteria.

"It's more terror bombing," I said. "One plane hardly seems like genocide."

"That's because you haven't been bombed every day or seen your family and friends become victims," said the Biafran scathingly.

While "genocide" was a catchy term to rally the Ibo people, malnutrition and starvation were greater threats. The amount of church aid in the form of foodstuffs that was flown in was insufficient to feed the entire population. The dilemma facing the aid people was whom to feed. It struck me that, if they truly felt the Ibo race was in jeopardy, then they should have concentrated on saving the race, not on trying to feed everyone a little and thereby saving no one. That would have meant deciding who among the Biafrans were the ones most likely to survive and repropagate the race. It would have meant giving the most food to the young adults, the people in the productive (and reproductive) age group. Clearly, that would have been difficult to do and it would have seemed inhumane to bypass the elderly and the very young to feed the most healthy. Instead, children got preferred treatment, and the food was shared more or less equally. This may have been the easiest, least controversial course, but it was also one that would have had the least effect in preserving the race *if* genocide had been the aim of the Nigerians—which it wasn't.

I always felt that the church took the cowardly way out by not being more selective with its meagre food rationing. No one likes to play God and decide who shall eat and live, who shall not get food and die. The preservation of the race is a fundamental issue, and the church, which had involved itself in the first place and taken sides, had a moral obligation to make such hard decisions. It's all academic now, but it was pertinent then. Had there really been a policy of genocide, the church would have even more on its conscience today than merely encouraging a war to be prolonged at the unnecessary cost of several million lives.

On Ben Wicks's last day in Biafra we attended a press conference, or audience, thrown by Ojukwu. It was an unusual affair. Often the more threadbare and insecure a leader is, the more pompous and pretentious he is in order to give the impression of power and importance. That was certainly Ojukwu's style. The few members of the press in Umuahia at the time were seated in armchairs at his headquarters when Ojukwu came in through French doors leading to an especially pretty garden. Several soldiers shouted for everyone to stand up. Ojukwu, looking disquietingly sleek and well fed for the leader of a starving state, took his place at a desk in front of us and broke open a new pack of State Express 333 cigarettes. He made a short, well-rehearsed speech about the iniquities of Nigerian genocide and how Nigeria's head of state, General Gowon, was a mirror image of Hitler. (In fact Gowon at the time was probably the most gentle and Christian leader in Africa, as well as the most boyish and handsome. He was deposed after the war by a military coup—Africa's answer to free elections.) Ojukwu radiated great optimism and confidence that was hard to justify. During the speech Wicks, who was lounging at the back, was suddenly roughly grabbed by a soldier and ordered to "take those hands out of your pockets while His Excellency is speaking." Wicks was simultaneously amused and indignant, but discretion dictated that he not argue. He spent the next few years reminding me of the incident, which, more than any other, I suspect, persuaded Wicks that Ojukwu might not be the humanitarian he once thought.

For my part, I was mesmerized by Ojukwu's brand-new shoes, with the soles still unscuffed, the tailored Mao costume, and his imported cigarettes. Each correspondent was allowed a few minutes' exclusive interview with Ojukwu, who sat at a table while a photographer snapped pictures or TV cameras whirred. The interviewer occupied the chair in front of the messiah, and from a certain angle it would appear to be a private talk. In fact, it was an assembly line of interviews, which no one at home would realize unless the reporter in question chose to reveal the slightly undignified treatment. Wicks took a photo of me during my interview, and I took one of Wicks. In the garden afterward, I asked Ojukwu if I could go to the front and visit his troops. He agreed and gave orders on the spot that I be outfitted with a uniform and sent to where Colonel Joseph Achuzie, the divisional commander, looked to be on the verge of recapturing the town of Owerri.

As it turned out, I went to Achuzie's S (Strike) Division, ostensibly for an overnight visit, and stayed two weeks, daily going out on attack with his "army," hoping to capture Owerri and publicize the triumph to the outside world—a propaganda shot in the arm that Biafra badly needed. Every night I wrote stories and sent them by courier to Umuahia for transmission to Toronto via Mark Press. Mine was mostly color stuff: what it was like, the heroics of the young army (comprised of an alarming and pathetic number of thirteen-year-olds). But steadily doubts and disillusionment about the Biafran cause took root in me. Those doing the fighting were virtually abandoned by those back in the relative luxury of Umuahia, where rhetoric was more ferocious. Even in Biafra there was profiteering and wheeling-dealing. Idealists were offset by opportunists.

I had a relatively free run of the division. Colonel Achuzie claimed to have been an infantry platoon commander attached to Australian forces in the Korean War, and later with the Kent Fusiliers in the 1956 Suez War. I half-thought he might be romanticizing. Still, he was by far the most colorful and daring commander on the Biafran side and forever apologizing for the lack of training and discipline among his troops.

"You'll not find this like Korea," he said. "These soldiers are no good. Children. Remnants. They're all we can get. Can't call them soldiers at all. Well, we do what we can . . . " He was unnecessarily apologetic, but his candor was refreshing. I found myself defending his troops, suggesting they were not too bad.

Achuzie would then look contemptuously at me and spit. "They are terrible; Australians are better." With that I couldn't disagree.

Achuzie was a remarkable leader—something of a legend on both sides. He was fascinatingly ugly, with a pug face, straggly goatee, bandy legs, and exceptional courage. He went regularly into battle at the head of his troops, unarmed except for a large walking stick, as did the British senior officers in Korea. I wondered, occasionally, what the divisional commander was doing leading the attack and who was controlling the rest of the troops. But I soon realized that being there was the only way Achuzie could guarantee that his troops would attack.

"These are not *real* soldiers," he'd say endlessly, as if obsessed with the theme. "They are children. With *real* soldiers I'd be past Owerri by now and heading for Port Harcourt. These people I have to bully, to chase, to frighten into battle. I have to make them more frightened of me than they are of the enemy." He exuded contempt which, I felt, was partly for my benefit and partly to justify the fact that his side was losing. Repeatedly I saw him pull a revolver and threaten to shoot whoever it was, officer or private, for hesitating, or for some alleged misdeed.

Because of his elderly, wizened appearance, Achuzie simply did not look like a soldier. One day he dressed in rags and, with a long walking stick, hobbled across the savannah country, through Nigerian lines, into the town of Owerri to see for himself the disposition of enemy troops. He then returned to his own lines, changed into his uniform, and launched an attack.

Another time Achuzie took me and a couple of aides on a reconnaissance far ahead of his own lines, to the outskirts of Owerri, where we stumbled on a Nigerian Saladin armoured car, the most formidable weapon in the Nigerian arsenal, and one that terrified the Biafrans. Achuzie grabbed a rocket launcher and beckoned me to follow him. We crawled to within fifty yards of the scout car and he prepared to blast it. I wondered briefly about the neutrality of journalists, then shrugged it off, knowing full well that if I were caught with Biafran forces I'd be deemed a mercenary and dealt with accordingly. The usual method was to cut off the testicles and stuff them in the mercenary's mouth, then kill him, or shoot him through the knees and leave him to die slowly. Not an appealing prospect.

It turned out that the wrong ammunition had been brought and could not be used in the rocket launcher. Achuzie was livid with rage and pistol-whipped the wretched person who had made the mistake, vowing to have him shot. I was relieved because it spared us from enduring a counterattack.

On another occasion, I got the scoop of the war as far as I was concerned. I was with Biafran troops of Tiger Battalion when they reoccupied the grass hut village of Naze on the southern fringe of their front. Naze had been captured by the Nigerians some weeks before, and when we entered the village we found bodies—actually little more than skeletons covered with dried, tanned skin—of Ibos whose hands had been tied with telephone wire behind their backs and whose knees had been snapped at the joint. They'd been left to die; their crawl marks were still visible on the arid ground. I took colored slides, which I felt provided conclusive proof of atrocities. The Biafran side always claimed that atrocities were being committed, while the Nigerian side adamantly denied them. International observers from Canada, Britain, Sweden, and Poland were sent to assess the allegations, but they were with the Nigerian forces, not the Biafran. They failed to find a single atrocity during the course of the war.

After I'd been with the Biafran army for ten days or so, messages began coming from headquarters in Umuahia to Achuzie wondering why I was staying so long. Orders were that I return immediately. Colonel Achuzie ignored the signals; therefore I did, too. We both wanted an eyewitness version of the fall of Owerri to reach the outside world, so he decided to launch a massive final assault before direct orders came from Umuahia to get me out of there. The big push started in the pre-dawn hours, like so many other attacks, amid hesitancy and confusion.

Achuzie's green child-soldiers were frightened and bewildered. We filed along jungle trails toward the assembly zone for attack. There were 500 troops, 90 of them without weapons; they had to wait until someone became a casualty, then pick up the fallen soldier's gun. Some 200 had been in the army less than two weeks and were without training. Achuzie never pretended that his was an elite fighting force. He simply took what he was given and did as well as he could. Ojukwu, of course, never went near the front to see for himself what conditions were like.

As we walked cautiously, half-crouched through the shrub bush country, there'd be an occasional burst of gunfire, and like as not we'd find that some of S Division had shot others of S Division. As we got closer to the Nigerian positions, Achuzie's assault force was shooting itself up at an alarming rate. Time and again a trigger-happy youth would blast at a noise in the bush, only to find he'd shot another child in ragged, makeshift uniform, or a terrified sentry. And both the wounded and wounder would dissolve in tears. Anything but a superficial flesh wound usually meant death.

As it turned out, on this particular day our frenzied, screaming, disorganized dash at the main highway outside Owerri drove the Nigerian forces back. We established a toehold on the outskirts of town and straddled the highway to the south—enough for me to legitimately claim that we were back in the town, at least temporarily. It was impossible to know what was happening; corrugated iron shacks were being blasted by Nigerian scout cars and there was confusion and shooting everywhere. The ground was littered with casualties, with no one paying much attention to them. Moans and sounds of weeping filled the air.

Instead of consolidating their newly won ground, the Biafran troops immediately raided a store looking for beer or palm wine, and began celebrating. I was alarmed, feeling that at any moment there'd be the inevitable counterattack, which would be very dangerous indeed unless we were ready. Achuzie was unable to motivate his troops to take defensive precautions: their blood was up and they were intent on celebrating what they considered a great victory. As a matter of survival, I asked if he wanted me to help, and he said yes. I called on my memories of the Princess Pats and Korea and began bullying noncommissioned officers into moving their troops into defensive positions, digging shallow trenches, establishing fields of fire, and putting out scouts and sentries. The Biafrans were used to my presence by then, and the habit of obeying whites, regardless of their position, was strong enough to make them respond to my orders. Despite this, I had little confidence in them and personally felt increasingly vulnerable. A white face, albeit stubbled and dirty, is hard to conceal in a mass of black and might incite Nigerians to extra effort if they saw me.

I left the position before the inevitable counterattack recaptured the position and I quickly wrote a story about our great, if brief, victory. The next day an armed escort came from Umuahia to take me back. Achuzie said bitterly that there were questions at higher command about my loyalty and he ridiculed the speculation that I might even be a spy for the Nigerians. "It means we are closer to losing than even I thought," he said. "It means we are beginning to make excuses and search for scapegoats. Well, I don't expect to survive. I don't like the parasites in the rear who send me soldiers who are children who should be in school. Too many behind the lines have the soft jobs, the good food, while we at the front have no ammunition and only the responsibility of saving the parasites. Well, we are losing. And it is their fault, not mine . . . "

Colonel Achuzie was echoing sentiments that generations of fighting soldiers before him have uttered in one form or another. Somehow I felt cowardly at leaving him. I even said I'd stay on if he wanted to risk it. He laughed and poured a half-glass of whisky for a final drink. "Go, but don't be too harsh on us." He seemed infinitely sad and lonely. As it turned out, our attack had resulted in 200 casualties among the attacking force, a staggering forty percent casualty rate. Achuzie eventually did win all of Owerri, only to lose it six months later when Nigeria won the war. The sacrifice was for nothing. Before that, however, he was replaced as commander—not because he was unsuccessful, but because he was *too* successful, *too* independent, and *too* critical of the way the war was being fought.

I returned to Umuahia and flew out the next day to the (relative) fleshpots of São Tomé, where the Canadian air crew were now the undisputed superstars of the airlift, never missing a mission, always completing their assignment, never losing their way, their plane always in top shape. They were the acknowledged aces of the Biafran airlift. At that time they were flying forty tons of supplies a night to Uli—three round trips.

The São Tomé mercenary flyers liked to wear cowboy boots, Stetsons, and bandoleers of ammunition, with an assortment of side guns and rakish outfits. At first they had tended to mock the Canadians as fuss-budgets for worrying about such things as air-craft maintenance. Now all were subservient to them. Pat Patterson's team was unflappable, unstoppable, the ultimate professionals and I felt a vicarious pride in them.

Patterson's Super-Connie was hit a while later, killing some of the crew. I looked for their graves when the war was over and I returned to Biafra with the first journalists after the surrender. Among the twenty-nine graves of pilots and air crew were those of the four Canadians, among them Vince Wakling of Montreal, the engineer on our Super-Connie who had taken his holidays to come to the aid of Biafra. His grave was marked "Vince Williams": whoever buried him didn't even know who he was.

Then again, no one was sure of who anyone was at the Uli strip. Most of the air crew were never seen in daylight, only in darkness.

Somehow the mistaken name seemed appropriate and emphasized the futility of it all. Still, these men were testimony to the skill of Canadian airmen — a tradition begun in World War I when half of the top twenty Allied aces were Canadian: Bishop, Brown, Barker, Collishaw, McEvoy, Maclaren, *et al.* In World War II the reputation was enhanced.

Hoping for a chance to visit the Owerri battle from the Nigerian side, I hitched a ride on a transport going to Ghana, from where I caught another ride to Lagos. The Nigerian capital has always been a steambath slum, a cesspool noted for corruption, inefficiency, and impossible poverty, a human time bomb with a soggy fuse. While Biafra was the centre of international controversy and was impoverished, Lagos was in the throes of a certain wartime affluence, although no one realized it then. The port was filled with ships delivering supplies necessary to win the war—a victory that the big powers wanted in order to preserve the flow of oil. The American Embassy economists compiled gloomy reports about the corruption, noting that the average turn-around time for a cargo ship in Lagos was two weeks to a month, and that Nigerian longshoremen accomplished in ten hours what their counterparts in other countries achieved in two. Bribery and the black market flourished.

Representatives of the world press were gathered in Lagos, mostly staying at the Federal Palace Hotel, where the international observers also stayed and where every week one had to pay a $20 bribe to the hotel clerk in order to keep a room. The international observers made a mockery of impartiality and fair play. Had it not been for the participation of Canadians and Swedes who tried to maintain some semblance of integrity and honesty, the observers would have been a blatant propaganda instrument for Nigerian interests.

I told the Canadian representative, Brigadier-General Charles Hamilton, about the bound skeletons with snapped knee joints I had found and photographed in Biafra. It was hard to tell whether he felt more curiosity or embarrassment at the disclosures. Interestingly, he didn't question their authenticity. When pinned down, the observers acknowledged the duplicity of their mission and the impossibility and unfairness of the mandate they were trying to operate under. It seemed wicked of our government to force honorable men to participate in such a charade.

The fact that I had just come from the Biafran front was of

some curiosity to the observers and the Nigerians. The latter seemed to harbor vague suspicions that I might be a spy, or at least committed to the Biafran viewpoint, as so many of the media were.

Hamilton was an honest, sensible man trying to do a good job. He agreed to take me on one of their periodic trips to Port Harcourt in Iboland, "liberated" from Biafra by Nigeria's most exotic troops, the Third Marine Commando Division. Its commander was the remarkable twenty-nine-year-old Colonel Benjamin Adekunle, who had served with UN forces in the Congo and was known throughout Nigeria as the Black Scorpion. He was a folk hero among Nigerians and a popular song about him topped the Lagos hit parade. His unprecedented string of battle successes was in danger of going to his head.

It was a feature of the Nigerian civil war that the various divisional commanders became like ancient Chinese warlords, each with total authority in his area, answerable to virtually no one, beyond the control of even Lagos. The personality of the units varied according to the commanders, and none was as flamboyant and daring as Adekunle; no unit had the arrogance and panache of the Third Marine Commandos. He reminded me of Biafra's Colonel Achuzie who opposed him at Owerri.

"We can only take you to Port Harcourt. We can't guarantee Adekunle will let you stay," said General Hamilton. "He is an exceptional man, but not the most predictable of human beings. In fact, some think he is unstable. There's no telling what he may do—witness Norman Depoe."

Depoe, who was to die in 1980 at age sixty-two, was a top CBC newsman and pundit in his time and exuded a certain arrogance to go with undeniable competence. Norman had a bigger reputation in Canada than elsewhere, but saw no reason to change his style to blend with surroundings. However, what was acceptable or tolerated in Canada was not always appreciated in other countries, where neither his colleagues nor his interviewees were aware of his star status.

Apparently Depoe went to Port Harcourt and got into a shouting match with Colonel Adekunle over whether or not he should be allowed to travel. The Black Scorpion did a bit of stinging of his own by forcing Depoe to stand on the tarmac of the airport for most of one day, unprotected from the scorching sun, without water or refreshment. Then he packed him on the evening flight back to Lagos. By that time Norman was dehydrated, deflated, and disconcerted. As one who liked Norman and who had been exposed to his sometimes haughty manner, I was more intrigued by than indignant at the episode, and felt that anyone who could do this to him couldn't be all bad.

At Port Harcourt, the observer group was escorted under guard to Adekunle's headquarters for a brief meeting. I was kept in a room to be interviewed by the commander later. After half an hour the observers nervously came out and said they were being confined to the hotel while a decision was being made about whether they'd be allowed to travel. General Hamilton, bless him, was a bit worried about me and said he had mentioned me to Adekunle, who was interested that I had been on the Biafran side and said that he would deal with me separately. Hamilton warned me not to get Adekunle excited or he might do something "even worse than he did to Depoe." If they didn't hear from me later, well, he'd decide then what should be done.

Adekunle was a slender, wiry man with a squashed-in mahogany-colored face. Cocky, and belligerent, he also had a sense of humour and was a born leader. He asked me point-blank if I was a spy. A trifle nonplussed, I said no. He asked me what I thought of the Biafran army and I told him more or less what I had written: that the Biafrans were fighting as best they could with what little they had and that they believed in their cause. But I said that they were down to the dregs and to children and were not much good, though Colonel Achuzie was terrific—too good for the troops he commanded. Adekunle was amused that Achuzie's nickname was "Air Raid"—because when he's around everyone takes cover. Adekunle said that though he didn't know Achuzie personally, he respected him as a good commander who was causing the Nigerians a lot of problems at Owerri. He approved of the fact that I had once been a soldier, and we chatted for perhaps two hours. He made a point of refusing to question me about the Biafrans, saying that it would not be ethical or proper. If I wanted to tell him, fine, but he wouldn't ask.

Adekunle's moods would vary wildly as you talked to him. He often raged and threatened to shoot anyone who interrupted him. His staff were terrified of him to the point of paralysis. Even the international observers grovelled before him and were nervous in his presence, although they cautiously ridiculed him when he wasn't around. They were convinced that he was psychotic. After all, a couple of months earlier he'd threatened to horse-whip a Swedish general and had cast aspersions on the military credentials of Canada's Lieutenant-Colonel Bert Pinnington, who was one of the better officers of the observer group. Adekunle would curtly refuse to let the observers into his area and then "summon" them to see some prisoners. He was out of control.

During our interview, Adekunle told me his version of capturing Port Harcourt with small loss of life against seemingly big odds. Instead of invading from land and running into ambushes, mines, tank traps, and bulldozers converted into tanks, he had made rafts and lashed armoured cars on top of them, then towed them into the harbor and used them as floating monitors or impromptu warships. The floating scout cars shooting and invading from the sea had utterly confused the more orthodox Biafran military and Adekunle's troops landed and drove the Biafrans into full-fledged retreat. The legend of the Black Scorpion's invincibility was born.

Adekunle finally slapped the desktop with his swagger stick. "Decided!" he yelled, apropos nothing. "I've made up my mind. You go back to the hotel with your friends the observers. I am going to expel them. Officially, I cannot guarantee their safety. Tomorrow they go back to Lagos. No one gives the Black Scorpion orders in Port Harcourt, especially not foreigners. And not these foreigners. You . . . you can stay. Tomorrow I'll give you a uniform, transport, and you can go up to the front to see for yourself—even to Owerri, which we will hold. We will destroy your precious Colonel Achuzie."

And so it was. I returned to the hotel and gave a censored version of our talk to General Hamilton, who again murmured something about Adekunle's being unstable and dangerously erratic. I didn't tell him that he and the others were to be ejected from the area. Let Adekunle do that. Besides, he might change his mercurial mind.

That night we dined on the open air balcony of Port Harcourt's Presidential Hotel, a virtual mausoleum. It was a clear, hot night and war and politics seemed a long way off. My companions were a Canadian general, a Polish civilian, a Swedish major, an Ethiopian captain, and an Algerian commander, the latter two representing the Organization of African Unity. Also joining us was the head of the British observers, Brigadier Sir Bernard Ferguson, former Governor-General of New Zealand and a Chindit in the Burma campaign of World War II. The observers had been told they would have to leave and everyone was rather glum and irritated at the way events had unfolded—or hadn't unfolded.

We'd just finished *hors d'oeuvres* and were about to order wine

when a very agitated Nigerian lieutenant came in and said something unintelligible. Nervousness clouded his speech, sweat streamed
down his face. He mentioned something about the commander
wanting to see the Canadian. General Hamilton beamed, "Well,"
he said, puffing up slightly, "in that case I'd better go. Perhaps
we'll now get some action. Knew Adekunle would come to his
senses." He rose, nodded his farewells, and said he'd see us later.
The young Nigerian officer got more agitated. "No, no. The commander wants the journalist. Only the journalist. I mustn't bring
anyone except the journalist . . . Please, God, *only* the journalist!"

Everyone looked at me. Hamilton moved back to his seat mum-
bling. I got up and said something to the effect that I'd try to put
in a good word for the group and that I hoped to see them all
back in Lagos if it turned out that Adekunle was immune to my
pleadings on their behalf. No one said a word but all threw me
dirty looks.

When I arrived at Adekunle's residence, a party was well under
way. The host was in a sport shirt drinking with his officers as a
gaggle of voluptuous women fluttered around them. Whisky mixed
with orange soda pop was the favorite drink, and everyone was
pretty well smashed. Adekunle was in high spirits and his every
remark was greeted with guffaws and nervous laughter. He recalled his two years at Sandhurst and claimed with some pride to
have been spat at full in the face by a drill sergeant of the British
Guards. His dearest dream was that his son grow up to be a soldier,
too.

He detested Biafra as much for its religious fervor as for its
political and nationalistic drive. "Religion is nothing but propaganda and the Ibos are using it to exploit Europeans," he ranted.
"My parents were pagans, they worshipped idols, and the Ibos
use religion, use the Pope, to gain a foothold in Europe, to gain
acceptance. The Ibo man is the Ibo's worst enemy. The Ibo has
no history, no culture, nothing but avarice. What they are saying
to Nigeria is: 'If you want unity, give us the goods jobs.' The
moment I get the word, I can be in Umuahia, then we'll end this
'Biafra' foolishness." An angry young man.

Suddenly Adekunle called for a hypodermic and without further ado gave himself an injection by plunging the needle through
his trousers into his thigh. I was startled but he explained that he
had diabetes. Then a movie was shown, a dreadful film, *Of Love
and Desire*, starring Merle Oberon and Steve Cochran. Throughout it, Adekunle screamed advice, raged at the heroine, and rushed

the screen making passes at the actors. It was an unbelievable display by the top commander of the Nigerian military. It made one wonder about his sanity.

I was returned to the hotel after midnight with the assurance that in the morning a vehicle would be at my disposal to take me to the front under Adekunle's personal orders. And true to his promise, the observers were taken under guard to the first plane back to Lagos. We parted company after breakfast, all aware that this was another example of the vagaries of Africa.

I travelled across the Southern Biafran front under Adekunle's command. The Hausa were closing in from the North, and the Biafrans were being hard pressed. The difference between the two forces was extreme. The Nigerians had so much equipment, manpower, beer, and resources that one wondered how the Biafrans held out at all. At any time of day the Nigerian soldiers seemed deep in beer. Their commitment to the war appeared to be minimal, for they showed little interest in fighting. Man for man, the Biafrans had more fervor and less matériel, and I found it more depressing to be with the Nigerians than with the Biafrans. Most units were wary of me and clearly intended to show me nothing, just endure me and then pass me on to the next unit. None could understand why I was there, only that the Black Scorpion wanted it, and woe betide any who questioned his wishes. When I returned to Port Harcourt, I was careful with Adekunle but told him there was no comparison in equipment and I had no doubt about who would win. Adekunle was pleased and promised to contact me prior to the final assault so that I could fly out and have breakfast with him in Umuahia when he captured it. Sure enough, a few months later when I was back in Toronto, I got a letter from Adekunle warning me to get ready for our breakfast. But he was relieved of his command before his goal was achieved and given a training job in Lagos that would keep him out of the headlines and keep his growing political power under control. He was eventually given the task of relieving the congestion and corruption of the Lagos docks and harbor, where his blunt, ruthless ways were startlingly effective.

In Lagos I also came across information about a massacre at Christmas 1969 in the Eastern region around Afikpo which was being covered up. I went to missionaries, relief workers, and British Save the Children people who'd been in the area. They knew what I was after but were reluctant to talk. I was met with equivocation. Finally, I went to the International Observer team and patched together a fairly logical account that stood up, eventually writing it for the *Tely*. I told how troops of the Third Marine Commandos massacred several Ibo villages as thoroughly and ruthlessly as ever the Americans did at My Lai, or the North Vietnamese at Hué. The massacres were reportedly in retaliation for a grenade explosion in an army compound. On Christmas Day in the village of Ndukwe, for example, women and children were herded into a cinder block house, which was then blown up. Any survivors were shot; 106 people died. In another village, Anofia, villagers were shot and their neck muscles were severed with machete blows, the victims living for some days with their heads dangling uselessly on their shoulders.

As for the international observers investigating atrocities, they made halfhearted inquiries, got confirmation, but never followed up. If was as if they were afraid of what they would find. My reports, which were the first ones on the subject, did not cause a ripple. The world was tiring of the subject. Biafra was now an old war, a fading war, and as public interest dwindled, so did media concern. So what if black tribes murdered one another? If the media aren't interested in an event, it might as well have not happened. If the media are interested, the event can be blown into world significance. Even the *Tely* treated the Nigerian massacres with a yawn and token coverage.

While I disagreed with the Biafrans' claim that they were victims of genocide, I also felt it wrong to let the international observers see only one side of the war. When I eventually returned to Canada, the *Telegram* at first refused to publish my atrocity photos on the grounds that they were too gruesome. Because I felt strongly that their news value warranted big play, I bypassed the editors and went straight to publisher John Bassett, who was in hospital with a broken leg. I made my pitch that atrocities were a major issue in the Biafran story and that my findings and photos constituted an important news story. Bassett, who was always journalist first, businessman second, agreed and ordered the editor in question, Arnold Agnew, to publish them. It didn't make me popular with the editors, whom I also thought of as friends.

Then I learned that they planned to run a picture in the back of the paper, near the comics. Again I went to Bassett and complained that this was bad judgment. Again Bassett got on the phone to Agnew and ordered that the photo run on page one. My popularity in the newsroom plummeted.

The photo eventually did run on page one: a small two-column

cut at the bottom of the page with an apology for possibly offending readers with an unpleasant picture. It should have run
across the top of page one with an outraged demand for answers
from the Canadian government and other countries participating
in the international observer charade. My modest experiences
trying to get proper play for a dramatic news picture proved, once
again, that a reluctant bureaucracy has the power to thwart its
bosses without actually challenging or defying precise orders. Only
the "spirit" of the instructions was violated or ignored. It is ever
thus, be it in newspapers, business, government. Even in the Soviet
Union the bureaucracy, the *aparatchiks*, can bypass and hobble the
power of the Politburo or Central Committee.

In this case, my atrocity photos begged the question: how is it
possible that a lone journalist can discover atrocities that professional military observers insist cannot be found and do not exist?

At the time I had difficulty understanding the reluctance of the
Telegram to run with what could have been a good, exclusive story.
It was only later I realized that what most newspapers want is to
be *second* with big stories. Being first with a controversial story is
lonely, puts you out on a limb, makes you vulnerable. Being second
with the story is safe, and you reap the rewards of appearing to
be gutsy and investigative.

A few years later there was an example of the reverse: a nonexistent massacre elevated into a major story. In the summer of
1974 while Portugal's African empire was in its death throes, the
exalted London *Times* (the organization that gave the world the
fake Mussolini diaries in the mid 1960s, then fifteen years later
bought the fake Hitler diaries) announced the discovery of an
African My Lai: the massacre by the Portuguese military of all
400 residents of the Mozambique village of Wiriyamu. A British
missionary, Father Adrian Hastings, was quoted in the *Times* recalling Spanish missionaries telling him of Portuguese soldiers
playing football with the decapitated heads of children, slicing
open pregnant women with bayonets to show the mutilated mothers the sex of their unborn children, and committing other atrocities. It was a ghastly tale.

The only problem was that Wiriyamu was shown on no map;
no one had ever heard of it, much less knew where it was. Father
Hastings at first said it was in western Mozambique, then in eastern
Mozambique, and then he wasn't sure. *Time* magazine and *Newsweek* sent people to find it, but couldn't. Meanwhile the angry
denials of the Portuguese were ignored: cover-up, it was said. The

British *Spectator* finally called the *Times*'s action "a stupendous act of journalistic irresponsibility" and added that: "The *Times* has not only been guilty of gullibility and possibly of complicity in a propaganda plot . . . " Meanwhile the phony story reverberated around the world and was used in church-involved demonstrations against Portugal and its Prime Minister, Marcello Caetano. Truth is in the eye of the beholder, it seems. We see what we want to see.

As far as Biafra was concerned, thanks in large part to the encouragement of the Christian church, the war dragged on for two years instead of six months and up to two million people died instead of a couple of hundred thousand. And when it was over, Ojukwu, the leader that the church had decided was a messiah, packed up and fled Biafra for Gabon and then the Ivory Coast to collect the wealth he'd stashed away in Switzerland (his merchant father was already a millionaire).

Ojukwu abandoned his people just as the Protestant missionaries abandoned their parishioners and fled to save their own skins—as I've already pointed out, something Protestant missionaries are prone to do. To their credit, the Holy Ghost Fathers of Ireland stuck it out in Iboland and shared the unknown future with their followers, prepared to endure whatever the Ibos endured. But then Catholic missionaries are made of sterner or more faithful stuff than their Protestant counterparts, which may explain why they have more success than orthodox Protestant faiths.

When Biafra collapsed, the Christian church, with not a blush of shame or self-doubt about its role in encouraging so many to die so futilely, moved on to make an issue of Rhodesia and Portuguese Angola and Mozambique and lent material and moral support to terrorism and revolt there—violence that led to black dictatorships replacing white authoritarian rule. In the case of Rhodesia-cum-Zimbabwe, one-party repression replaced partial democracy. In every case, the church crusade created more misery than it alleviated. Again, not a twinge of conscience or self-analysis. And no recriminations from anyone.

In their final report of the war, the international observers made modest mention of the allegations and employed euphemisms like "flushed with success" and "in high spirits" to explain the orgy of pillage and rape that the Nigerian forces indulged in when Biafra surrendered. I was among the first journalists to enter conquered Biafra in 1970 and after being exposed to some horrendous examples of cruelty and negligence, happened to encounter the observers on the road. We had an impromptu press confrontation.

Brigadier-General John Drewry had replaced General Hamilton as the top Canadian, and poor Drewry gave an epic display of ineptness in dealing with the media. Replying to observations that there was no food, Drewry suggested Ibos were "stupid" to leave their homes to search for food and commented that many were "fat as pigs." He said he'd seen Indians in Canada in worse shape than the Ibos. The British press pounced on Drewry, especially Nick Carroll of the *Sunday Times* of London, who noted that "as a piece of studied indifference to suffering and a total failure to grasp a public relations opportunity, his [Drewry's] performance would be hard to beat."

In response to his reported statement "I do not consider it serious until 10 women are raped at the same time in the same place," General Drewry claimed that the *Daily Telegraph* had misquoted him. "I didn't say until 10 women were raped . . . I said 20 women. . . ." On this note the international observer team, which during the war was unable to find one atrocity, ended its sixteen-month obscenity. Only the final report after the war gave any hint of butchery and atrocity. Until that report, the Nigerian civil war was officially the most humane in history.

I probably spent more time with both sides in the Biafran war than most journalists and, as usual, found that neither side had a monopoly on all virtue or all wickedness. Although it was sometimes difficult to sort out right from wrong, I wrote a series that tried to be fair to both sides and to put things in perspective. The Nigerians, unused to relatively fair coverage from a Biafra-biased media, were pleased with the reports, while the Biafrans for the most part accepted that it was fair reporting. The church seemed to reject my coverage as distorted and a betrayal of hospitality. As it happened, I got a National Newspaper Award for the series.

25

Don't worry, we've won . . .
Bassett will settle

BOB RUPERT
NEWSPAPER GUILD NEGOTIATOR
TORONTO, SEPTEMBER 17, 1971

In some ways, the death of a newspaper is as traumatic as any human death. For those directly involved, death is a painful experience, no matter how expected it may be. When it finally happens, it comes as a shock and there is an indescribable emptiness in the lives of those nearest and dearest.

Most of us have experienced it with the death of loved ones—and those who haven't yet, will. I grappled with it when my father died of cancer in 1967, the year of Canada's 100th birthday, an otherwise joyous year in the nation as it lived and celebrated as one. It was perhaps the last time the country was genuinely unified and in harmony with all its parts—with the possible exception of a few brief weeks in the fall of 1970 when the FLQ (*Front de Libération du Québec*) kidnapped British Trade Commissioner James Cross and kidnapped and murdered Quebec Labor Minister Pierre Laporte. Prime Minister Trudeau, answering the call of the country to do something, imposed the War Measures Act that put the army into the streets and incensed the country's intellectual left wing. For most citizens this was an immensely popular gesture and showed the country that someone was in charge. It restored order and confidence in Canada—particularly in Quebec where the majority were pro-Canada—and it was possibly the last time Pierre Trudeau was in tune with the country he tried to rule like a democratic dictator.

When he died, my father was approaching eighty. He had been operated on for cancer of the bowel three years earlier so we all knew his time remaining was limited. While shattered inside, my mother remained serene on the surface. Our family guards its emotions, and lets no inkling of deep personal feelings reach

353

public view—or even one another. To keep herself from brooding morbidly on Worthy's illness, my mother buried herself in writing a book about the military history of the Royal Canadian Dragoons, *Spur and Sprocket*, which she was upset with when published because of shaky proofreading and printing errors. Later she could barely remember writing it, so deep was her emotional turmoil at the time.

Books were my mother's safety valve. At age sixty she had decided to write a biography of my father, who was happy to see her occupied until her book was accepted for publication by Macmillan. Then he became alarmed that all his tall stories might boomerang. But my mother was meticulous in her research and the book, *Worthy*, got good reviews. For a long time my father refused to read it—might even have been a little jealous—but then when people showed interest in him, he blossomed. And my mother pouted because, after all, she was the author and deserving of more attention! She wrote a Canadian history of World War I, *Amid the Guns Below*, which was really quite good and unearthed a lot of hitherto-unknown details about Canada's involvement in that war. She documented how the British determinedly downplayed the Canadian participation because Canada insisted that its troops fight as a corps and not as units to be scattered piecemeal through the British forces, the way the Australians were.

I'm not sure Worthy accepted that he was dying. Intellectually he knew it, of course, but he was so bursting with life, enthusiasm, and vigor that it seemed inconceivable he could die. All his adult life he'd seemed indestructible. We didn't talk much at home about the future. He still talked as if tomorrow would never come, and lived life to the hilt. When he went into the military hospital in Ottawa in August 1967, the malignancy again out of control, he dreaded another bout on the operating table more than he did the inevitable consequence. The cancer was so advanced that we didn't want him to suffer, ordered treatment suspended, and let nature take its course. His doctors gave him twenty-four to forty-eight hours to live unless he got treatment or was operated on. Then, they said, death might be briefly delayed, but not without great pain and discomfort. My mother, sister, and I didn't talk about it, but we hoped he would die quietly without realizing this was the end. However, he didn't die. He went on and on and on, filled with drugs to kill the pain, until just before Christmas. It even seemed for a while that he was getting better—a final remission, which is a sure sign to the layman exposed to cancer that the end is near. The candle really does burn brightest just before it goes out. In one of his moments of lucidity and reason when the pain was low and the drugs unnecessary, he apologized to me for lasting so long. "I'm sorry," he said. "It's just that I don't know how to die." It was the most painful thing I'd ever heard. Even today I can't think of that calm, wistful statement with complete composure.

And yet it wasn't all morbid. In the early days I had given instructions to the nurses *not* to encourage the chaplains to visit him. This would only make him suspicious. We were still hoping he'd die quietly in his sleep. I arrived at the hospital one evening and the whole floor was in turmoil. An agitated nurse grabbed me and began apologizing, saying that someone else had "let them in." I didn't know what she was talking about. When I entered my father's room, I understood. He was propped in bed where he'd been interrupted while writing what he hoped would be a children's story and three army chaplains were grouped around him, Roman Catholic, Protestant, and Jewish.

My father eyed them suspiciously. "Now I know I must really be near the end if you three sky pilots are in to see me!" They laughed nervously. My father was not a religious man in the conventional sense, but he had sensitivity toward all religions and in the army made maximum use of chaplains, always demanding "down-to-earth, blood-and-guts padres" in his division. He had very little use for the New Testament but relished the Old Testament, which he read periodically all his life, especially the book of Joshua. While he was dying he even wrote an article on Joshua as an innovative, unconventional soldier whom he considered one of the great commanders of history. It was published in the *Jewish Times* in Toronto.

My father looked at the three chaplains and asked each in turn what he thought of Joshua. They looked at one another and gave conventional answers. Worthy rejected them all. "Wrong," he said. "None of you understands a damn thing about Joshua. Study him. He's essential reading for a soldier." He stopped, glared at each one owlishly over his spectacles, and said: "I'll make a deal with you ghouls. The one who comes back with the most satisfactory explanation of what Joshua was all about can have my soul. Now off with you and do your homework."

The three trooped out, grinning and shaking their heads, and wondering out loud what the old warhorse would think of next!

My father roared with laughter while I had to fight back tears.

When the end was clearly imminent, a colonel approached me in the corridor and asked for a moment of my time. He didn't want to bother my mother for obvious reasons, "but in the unlikely event that the general doesn't pull through, could we discuss arrangements that should be made?"

I looked at him coldly. "Unlikely event that he doesn't pull through!" I mimicked, emotions brittle by this time and nerves frayed. "For Christ's sake he's dying. If he pulls through it'll be a bloody miracle. What do you mean, 'unlikely event'?"

The colonel was understanding. "About the funeral. It'll be a military funeral from the cathedral, of course. Now the usual format is to have a horse with stirrups reversed . . . "

I interrupted with some indignation. "Horse! For God's sake, *don't* have a horse at my father's funeral. All his life he fought the 'horse' mentality when trying to get tanks into the army. Whatever you do, don't give a *horse* the final triumph."

The solemn look on the face of the colonel, who was Armoured Corps, changed into a beatific smile: "We were hoping you'd say that . . . we were thinking that an armoured car, a scout car, carrying his casket would be more appropriate. What do you think?"

"Perfect. So long as it isn't a horse. Hell, if the Old Man felt a horse would have the last laugh, he wouldn't go."

And so it was. After the funeral in Ottawa, the body was flown to Camp Borden where he was buried on a hill in the park across from the museum bearing his name and surrounded by tanks of various armies dating back to World War 1. My father had so enjoyed thinking about his funeral in Camp Borden that one sometimes felt he was impatient to get the show on the road.

The feeling of loss when his long-expected death finally happened was brought to mind when the *Telegram* died four years later. The feeling was not so personal, of course, but poignant and devastating in its own right. Under the leadership of its publisher, John Bassett, the *Tely* was more than just another newspaper. Not a great newspaper, as Bassett and nostalgic fans like to think, but a *good* paper and far more lively, broad-minded, and open than its rival, the *Star*, which finally defeated it.

It's not only the employees of a newspaper who feel the loss when it goes out of business, but the whole community. Any form of journalistic expression that taps a responsive chord in the community is important. The more opinions available in print, the greater the choice and the better chance for knowledge and understanding among people. No paper gave a wider range of opinion than the *Tely*, which was branded arch-conservative largely because of Bassett's flamboyant Tory partisanship and his unabashed eagerness to use his editorial pages to support his Conservative prejudices. The paper was viewed as being out of touch with the times. It had, in reality, become wishywashy; in trying to please too many factions, it wound up believing nothing—or at least giving that impression.

If Bassett was arguably the best publisher in the business to work for, he also could be the most frustrating and infuriating. He was a buccaneer who, at times, chased the ladies (and vice-versa), chased stories, chased success, chased life. His father had been publisher of the Montreal *Gazette*, a Horatio Alger type of Northern Irish immigrant who came to Canada and worked his way into becoming a journalistic presence in the halls of federal Conservative power.

In his education, young John had mixed academic achievement with sports and a zestful social life. He was a golden youth. He toured Europe, playing hockey and breaking hearts, and then became a reporter for the Toronto *Globe and Mail* just prior to World War II. In the war he joined the Canadian army, not as a public relations officer, as so many journalists were wanting to do, but as an infantry officer—a fighting soldier. He served in Italy with the Seaforth Highlanders, having what is known in the military as "a good war."

Bassett returned home a major, impossibly handsome and rakishly charming, and ran for federal Parliament as a Tory in Sherbrooke, Quebec, where he lost handily. The people then, as ever, were not quite ready for a Bassett to represent the common touch.

He ran again in the Toronto riding of Spadina in the early 1960s, this time as a publisher and with every conceivable element going for him—losing even more handily as he fell to the charisma of a Liberal nobody named Perry Ryan. Bassett was not running to be an MP or even a cabinet minister. He was running to be prime minister and had he been elected, he likely would have achieved his goal. In the night of the long knives against Prime Minister John Diefenbaker, Bassett would not have turned soft and mushy as did his Tory compatriots and co-conspirators, who had difficulty plunging the knife (figuratively) into their chief when the moment came. Bassett was made of sterner political stuff. Whether he'd have been a good Prime Minister will never be known, yet the voters saw something they weren't happy with in Big John and rejected him. Had he been elected, it is arguable that Pierre Trudeau might never have emerged to dazzle the nation and the world. An interesting thought!

After the war, Bassett joined the *Tely* as general manager and became a friend of, advisor to, conspirator with the publisher George McCullagh. The paper was running down and when McCullagh died, Bassett bought it with the financial backing of his friend, John David Eaton, of the Eaton's department store empire. From 1952 to 1971 John Bassett treated the *Telegram* as his personal fiefdom and practised an intimate style of scrappy journalism that made Toronto perhaps the most competitive, combative newspaper city in North America.

Bassett gave free rein to Doug MacFarlane, who'd come to the paper from the *Globe and Mail* as city editor. MacFarlane set journalism in Toronto on its ear. He seemed a genius of energy, imagination, and innovation, and was probably the most demanding and decisive editor in captivity at the time. He quickly became managing editor and rose steadily in the *Tely's* hierarchy until inevitably he became a casualty—but until then he and Bassett made the *Telegram* into a dynamic force. Never profound or philosophical men, both thrived on challenge and drama: sponsoring swims of Lake Ontario or the English Channel, covering mine disasters (Springhill), bringing retired Scotland Yard detectives over to solve local murders, hunting for missing persons and chasing heiresses, fighting to get the inside word on love affairs of movie actresses visiting Toronto (Elizabeth Taylor and Richard Burton), offering rewards for the first one to provide a photograph of the Queen (or Princess Margaret) in a bathing suit.

I recall being sent to Montreal to walk the 250 miles to Toronto (I quit at the halfway mark) with a well-known marathon walker of the time, Dr. Barbara Moore, and being packed off to cover the Congo before the blisters healed. The following year I completed the same walk with a couple of professionals who were doing it for the Toronto Police Games. As a stunt, my wife Helen and I were sent to live in a 150-year-old pioneer village under conditions of the time, while hordes visited us to see our progress. We were sent to pan for gold in the Klondike as part of the *Tely's* publicity binge. Reporter Gordon Donaldson, later a TV newsman, lived for a week in a bomb shelter erected at city hall and filed dispatches about the growing claustrophobia he and his family were experiencing. The *Star* depicted it as a hoax, while we sent a reporter to the shelter at midnight to pour sugar down the air vent because Donaldson had forgotten it among his supplies. I remember chasing the *Star* for the story of an eloping teen-age heiress running away with the hired hand, and relieving reporter Frank Drea on a stake-out. Drea was supposedly getting the *Star* photographer drunk when I relieved him, but had imbibed too much himself. When we found that the *Star* had eluded us, I was sent into their hotel room through the window to let Drea in. He promptly stole the elopers' luggage and took it to the *Tely*. The night police reporter, Bert Petlock, returned it to the hotel and made peace with the police. Meanwhile, Drea has passed out in the washroom and I, junior to him, had to write a story under his byline about the romantic happenings. Drea went into provincial politics after the *Tely* folded and became a cabinet minister. He also went on the wagon.

The *Tely* at one time had more foreign correspondents (using the word loosely) than any Canadian paper. It gave its readers a ringside seat at all the big international stories for a time, coupling the reporter's adventures with hard facts, thereby entertaining readers while informing them. It forced the *Star* to do likewise. But the *Tely*, once the city's leading newspaper, could never quite catch the *Star*. It came close, but always fell short.

In the latter half of the '60s, after Bassett divorced his wife and remarried, he seemed to develop interests that took priority over the newspaper. The *Tely* began to slip. It is easier to see the demise in retrospect than it was at the time, yet the symptoms were always visible. Now everyone claims to have seen the writing on the wall although few said so then. And certainly no one told Bassett, who wouldn't have listened anyway.

The *Star* was Canada's largest, richest, and perhaps nastiest newspaper. The *Tely* was less business-like, less efficient, less profit-oriented. It traditionally paid its staff less than the *Star* but treated its employees (and the public) better. It had more heart. Still, by most barometers, the *Star* was a better product, partly because it *was* so large and rich, partly because it tended to steal ideas the *Tely* had pioneered, refine them, and do them better. The *Star* had money, bundles of it; the *Tely* had *esprit*, lots of it—or used to have until its final years when lethargy, bitterness, and cover-your-ass journalism took over.

Though no one realized it at the time, in the summer of 1971 when the *Star* settled its union negotiations with something like a $40 pay hike over two years, it meant the death of its archrival. The *Tely* union, whose contract had expired six months earlier, wanted a similar raise for its members. But the *Tely* had a $1 million *loss* in 1970 compared to the *Star*'s $3 million profit. It was impossible for Bassett to match the *Star* unless he was prepared to divert profits from his other interests—and that was unrealistic to expect. Negotiations were waged like a chess match until both sides, or at least the union, lost sight of reality and began to think of the whole affair as a game to be won or lost with no thought of who would pay the bill.

When Bassett offered a $10 weekly raise and opened his books to union auditors, the negotiators thought he was capitulating. Certain that victory was near, they scoffed at the offer, reminded Bassett that he owned a TV station, a football team, a hockey team, and interests in other cities, and insisted that they would accept nothing but a settlement similar to the *Star*'s.

But it was not to be. Bassett wasn't going to pour good money after bad. In round terms, the *Tely* had revenues of $29 million a year and expenditures of $30 million. The difference between breaking even and losing money, of surviving or perishing, was $1 million, or about 3 percent. No matter how many economy drives or cutbacks the *Tely* attempted, losses still mounted. There just wasn't enough discipline or restraint within the paper to economize or trim. And the least disciplined of all, when it came to stories or lifestyle, was John Bassett himself.

One of the reasons for the *Telegram*'s editorial failure was alarmingly simple: like many newspapers, the *Tely* had an unwitting policy of no bad bosses, only bad employees. Instead of replacing mediocre or redundant middle management with brighter and more efficient and innovative people, the *Tely* shuffled them into different jobs and fired reporters. It was like trying to deal a royal flush by constantly reshuffling a deck of management cards that contained no aces and few face cards. Only jokers. No matter how many times you shuffled and dealt—or how often you switched jobs—with few face cards it's hard to draw a winning hand.

Everyone expected Bassett to do something. Just what, no one was sure, but something dramatic. That was the man's style, as when he had singlehandedly provided the leadership to break the printers' strike seven years earlier. Then he'd stood on the loading platform of the *Tely* and rallied the unionized staff to defy the arrogant printers who were trying to be a tail wagging the newspaper dog. Bassett had provided the drive and inspiration that enabled all three Toronto papers, *Globe*, *Star* and *Tely*, to break the printers forever. The *Tely* staff had believed his emotional pledge that *he* would never sell the *Telegram* and that his sons who would follow him would never sell it. It was here to stay. Forever. John Bassett said so. They might joke about his blarney, but they had essentially believed their publisher, and had followed him. That was in 1964. This was 1971. Time and events had eroded his credibility.

It was the age of Vietnam and peace marchers, of flower children and permissiveness. Of cynicism and denigration of the work ethic. Old values and traditions were held up to ridicule. Bassett was out of touch. Among his staff there was a core still loyal to him, to the paper. There was some faith that in moments of crisis (or strike) he'd think of something. He still liked to stand on the loading dock off the mailroom and address the staff with colorful, emotional eloquence. But now, instead of rousing the troops, his eloquence incurred catcalls—*sotto voce* catcalls, but catcalls nonetheless.

There were signs all that summer that the *Tely* was in worse shape than anyone had realized. Management was gearing up to publish during a strike, if necessary, and the staff was uneasy. I was especially apprehensive, because in conscience I felt I could not honor the picket lines of a strike; yet I could not support a management that I thought was incompetent and wrong. I knew, too, that if it came to a strike and I *did* cross the picket lines and the paper failed, it would be the end of my journalistic career in a unionized newspaper industry. And I wanted to remain a journalist. I also knew that loyalty to Bassett would prevent me from joining a picket line. My only option would be to quit if a strike was called, thereby sacrificing all benefits. It was a difficult time.

Amid all the warning signs, the union called a special meeting of members on September 16 in the ballroom of the King Edward Hotel to get a mandate to call a walkout. It was an explosive situation, with the over-all thrust of the meeting for a strike. Under terms of the membership, part-time, transitory workers in circulation and production who came and went to jobs on whim and circumstance had equal vote with reporters and business office employees whose careers and lives were often wrapped up in the *Telegram*. The motives and aspirations of the two groups were totally different, often totally opposed. The first group wanted quick money and immediate gratification. It had little loyalty. The second group was more concerned with security and the survival of the paper.

The union, clearly wanting a strike, set the scene by outlining the negotiators' one-sided view of events. Bassett was depicted as a robber baron trying to profit from the pockets of his employees, and luckily for the workers, they had a vigilant union! I especially remember Freddie Jones, former labor reporter at the *Tely* and now a full-time union executive, recalling that he'd negotiated with Bassett for twenty years and had never seen him behave as he was doing now. Jones said he was disillusioned—but the only alternative was to fight for what they felt was right and vote for a strike.

The parade of speeches from the floor added fuel to the fire, indulging in anti-management rhetoric to the point that it became difficult and even frightening to dissent. Five people spoke against the strike. I got up and directed remarks at Freddie Jones, saying that if this was a different Bassett than he'd been used to, perhaps the reason was that Bassett was telling the truth when he said the cupboard was bare. If, as they all claimed to think, Bassett was a robber baron intent on trapping the staff into calling a strike so that he could close the paper, for God's sake, they shouldn't fall into that trap and make it easier for him. I said I knew Bassett at least as well as Jones and in my view he might gamble, but he didn't bluff or lie. If he warned that he might have to close the paper if wage demands were too high, it meant he was prepared to do so. Ignore the warnings at your peril, I said.

I was hooted down as a management fink, as were others: Bob Pennington in sports, Helen Gagen in Women's and, most eloquent of all, TV columnist Dennis Braithwaite, who had recently been hired away from the *Star* and who had been one of the prime movers for the Newspaper Guild when it was introduced in Toronto in the early 1950s. He held Guild card No. 1. Now he was being yelled down by the hoppers and yahoos as a management lackey. Rarely was there better evidence of the blood lust of the mob when they turned on the man who'd been through the fire for the union in the early days and had even been branded Communist and subversive. It was typical of the left, and in a small way resembled what happened to the old Bolsheviks in Russia when the party ate its children. There was hate for Braithwaite, who had been one of them, while there was mere ridicule for me, who had always been an outsider.

There was humor, too. Kesley Merry, a mountain of a man who was a police reporter and not someone to take very seriously, leapt to his feet and was greeted with boos when he argued against a strike. Later in the meeting he again took the floor and was greeted with cheers when he declared he'd been wrong, was now in favor of a strike, and urged union solidarity. After the vote, when fellow reporters berated him for his waffling, he sheepishly said that he'd voted *against* a strike anyway!

John Marshall, a white-haired reporter, swing-shift editor, and ideologue, made a short speech that delighted the pro-strikers. He said that old as he was (maybe forty-five), he'd go out and shovel snow rather than debase himself and accept a wage settlement below that of the *Star*; his dignity wouldn't permit him to so demean himself.

The next morning at the *Tely*, Margaret Kmiciewicz (whose name was unpronounceable for most staff, so she was called simply Mrs. K.), the head switchboard operator and a ferocious Bassett loyalist and anti-striker, marched over to Marshall's desk and slapped down $2. "It's for your snow shovel, Mr. Marshall," she said in her broad Scottish accent. "And frankly, I don't think you're man enough to use it."

When the vote was called that night it was a foregone conclusion: 298 for a strike, 111 against. The die was cast. One of the unforgivable aspects of that traumatic and ritualistic meeting was that the union leadership neglected to tell the membership their auditors *had* examined the *Tely* books. The auditors' report indicated that if Bassett had indeed offered a $10 raise, to take it because it could not be justified by the books they'd seen. That surely was indication of whether or not Bassett was bluffing.

The day after the vote, September 17, I ran into Bob Rupert in the newsroom. He was the international representative of the Newspaper Guild and masterminding the negotiations with the *Tely*. He was not a bad guy, though somewhat ineffectual and not of a calibre to make Bassett quake. We had a brief, intense chat during which he said he "knew" Bassett would capitulate, and all would be well. Settlement was in the offing. He implied that he had special or inside knowledge that the staff couldn't possibly be aware of. "Don't worry," he said. "We've won. Bassett will settle!" He was describing a John Bassett I didn't recognize. But then I only worked for him.

That night Bassett came into the paper at midnight, phoned Doug Creighton, the managing editor, and dictated a front page editorial for Saturday, September 18, announcing that he was closing the newspaper. The *Tely* was dead for all practical purposes, even though the death throes would last until Saturday, October 30, the date of the final edition. Bassett had sold the *Tely*'s subscription list (so-called) to the Toronto *Star* for some $12 million. After ninety-six years of publishing, the Toronto *Telegram* was now worth more dead than alive.

Despite frantic attempts by groups and individuals to reverse history and save the *Tely*, it was not to be. There was no raising the *Titanic* once it hit the union iceberg and started sinking. As it turned out, the *Star* was moving to a new building and would have enormous problems with its new presses for a year. Had Bassett realized this and held on for that time, the *Tely* would almost certainly have profited greatly from the *Star's* problems and regained vital lost circulation. It is a measure of the mediocrity with which he had surrounded himself that Bassett wasn't told this and none of his minions apparently realized it.

There was six weeks' notice for the *Tely's* 1,350 staff to scramble for new jobs. I phoned Dick Doyle, editor of the *Globe and Mail*, wondering if he was interested in me. While pleasant, he clearly wasn't. I got a call from Marty Goodman, managing editor (and later president) of the *Star*, who said come on over and talk. He and Ray Gardiner, editor of the Insight section, which passed for investigative reporting, offered me a job at more money than the *Tely* was paying. Their main concern was that as I had been such a free spirit and unguided missile at the *Tely* I might not respond to the greater discipline of the *Star*.

I replied that if I came to the *Star* I didn't anticipate trouble in that way, that discipline was no problem. Nor was loyalty—if I accepted their money. I also suggested that when assessing *Tely* people to hire, they might remember Genghis Khan who, when his Golden Horde was vanquishing the world, would incorporate into his armies those enemies who had fought him the hardest. He'd put to the sword defeated enemies who surrendered passively, the theory being that those who fought the hardest *against* him would be more likely to fight hardest *for* him once they pledged their loyalty.

I went away to consider Goodman's job offer, not comfortable with the idea of joining the enemy, but knowing that I had little alternative since the *Globe and Mail* wasn't interested. One consolation: I thought I was a better second baseman than the one who usually played for the *Star* softball team in the press league, and maybe I could win that position. I was already thinking ahead.

The most eloquent reaction to the *Tely's* demise was that of Ted Reeve, the legendary Moaner of Canadian sports and sports writing. Tales of his courage and stamina when playing football and lacrosse in the 1920s and 1930s have grown with the years: playing with a broken shoulder to joining the army though wracked with arthritis. He'd been writing a sports column for the *Tely* for forty-three years—since 1928 when he was already a sports legend. When asked his reaction to the closing, Reeve quipped: "They told me when I came here that this would be a steady job." He was an oasis of wit amid an otherwise mournful scene.

Toronto, for a moment in its history, wept for its lost paper, even those who disliked its politics.

At the time of the *Tely*'s closing I was in a state of restlessness. My divorce had come through three years earlier. Helen was working for the Toronto *Star* and I had given her what money I'd saved—some $15,000. Olga and I by now had gone our separate ways, but kept in contact. Since helping her to defect there was a bond that no one else could share or fully understand. I was reminded of the Chinese proverb to the effect that having saved someone's life, the rescuer is obliged forever to look after the one saved. Not a perfect analogy for Olga and me, but close.

When the news editor of the *Telegram* had walked out on his Australian reporter wife one day and moved in with one of the women copy editors, I felt very sympathetic toward the abandoned one and made it a point to be friendly. At the time I had no idea that a couple of years later I'd marry her. But that's what happened, and in 1970 Yvonne Crittenden and I got married in one of those antiseptic ceremonies at City Hall in front of a bored judge (with whom I had fought in court some years earlier when I'd been fined for a traffic offence). Yvonne's friend Mary Lawson, now Mary Wood, was a witness and *Tely* photographer Dick Loek was the best man. After the noontime ceremony we all went back to work. It remains one of the romantic highlights of Yvonne's life. She had two children from her first marriage, Guy, eight, and Danielle, six, and I had Casey, five. Fortunately, the youngsters blended together to make a fairly harmonious family, and the second marriage has outlasted both of our first attempts.

It so happened that Yvonne and I had had warning of the *Tely*'s demise. Earlier that September, Bassett had invited us to go with him to New York to see the U.S. tennis championships at Forest Hills. With us was Bassett's longtime friend and Conservative powerhouse, lawyer Eddie Goodman, a congenitally cheerful bundle of nervous energy who had been badly wounded in the tank corps during the war and who had run and been defeated for provincial

Parliament just after the war. Goodman was deeply concerned about the *Telegram* and its fate. The union negotiations had all but collapsed and a strike was more a probability than a possibility. So was closing the paper. No one was sure. It was something we didn't discuss, although Bassett was curious to know what the newsroom was thinking. I told him that people were worried, frightened, weren't sure what to think. I then added a personal note and said that I hoped that *if*—God forbid, but *if*—the paper had to close, that it would be done without a strike. It was clear that *if* Bassett sought a reason to close it, the smart way would be to let a strike occur and then close down and avoid severance pay to the staff. I was more concerned that employees would not be confronted with the choice of crossing the picket line, and that if the paper were to close, that it not be accompanied by the acrimony, hostility, and bad blood that is inevitable in a strike.

"The *Tely* has always been something special in journalism, and my main hope is that if it is to close, it be done so honorably and that we all go down together with good memories and not divided and fighting each other." I said. "We are all friends, and I'd not want to see anything damage that spirit."

Bassett said something noncommittal about saving money if the paper closed after a strike was called. I replied that I didn't believe John Bassett would take the cheap route and that he'd do whatever was honorable and right. Bassett grunted.

The next night, while at the theatre in New York, Bassett suddenly whispered to Yvonne: "If you or Peter have any chance to get another job, I suggest you take it." That was it. Yvonne felt a chill. At that minute we suspected all was finished with the *Tely*. In his way, Bassett was giving us warning to start looking for new jobs ahead of the herd of 1,350 staff who'd soon be unemployed.

During that soggy weekend of rained-out tennis, Goodman and I strolled through Central Park, visited the Museum of Natural History, saw and appreciated the movie *Hellstrom Chronicles* with its message of survival of the species, of all things, and discussed our philosophy and ideas on newspapers—what they should be, how we would run them, why the *Tely* was failing, how the problems could be corrected, and so forth. Eddie Goodman has about as open and lively a mind as anyone I know and brims with energy and enthusiasm. He was a mixture of frustration and eagerness that weekend. The conversation was to have fateful consequences.

It was in the *Tely's* death-month of October that a group of us decided to start a new paper, a tabloid, with no home delivery, only street sales (thus cutting down on circulation costs). The idea of a tabloid had come up at the *Tely* a few years before, and a mock-up had even been done. The publisher's eldest son, Johnny F., had favored changing the *Tely* to tabloid, but was overruled as a young Turk who didn't understand the business like his elders. The idea of starting a tabloid in staid Toronto was so radical that it couldn't be resisted. For me it was a way to stay in newspaper work, yet to escape the *Star*.

While the Newspaper Guild bears little responsibility for the problems of the *Tely*—the slipshod, apathetic middle management—it bears maximum responsibility for killing the *Telegram* in the fall of 1971. The union made it easy for Bassett to dump the paper, and it was only by luck that he was not ruthless and didn't encourage a strike in order to avoid paying severance pay or compensation. For me it served as confirmation that the leaders of unions tend to ignore the interests of their members and increasingly become more like the employers and fat cats they were originally designed to fight.

The depressing thing is that the union leadership, to this day, refuses to acknowledge *any* responsibility for the death of the paper. And diehard unionists insist on no culpability. The syndrome partly explains why workers are increasingly suspicious and jaundiced when it comes to the motives and methods of unions these days. I suspect, in this age of minimum wage laws, arbitration boards, human rights legislation, and relatively enlightened and reasonable employers that if a union moves into a hitherto non-unionized company, it is management's fault. Few sensible workers *want* unions, which can be as degrading as unscrupulous management.

Just as a way to "encourage" governments to fight inflation would be to implement laws whereby politicians and civil servants would take a percentage decrease in their pay for every increase in the inflation rate above a certain percentage, so union leaders who call a strike should by law be required to forgo their regular salaries and live on the same allowances they give to striking workers. It would encourage far more responsible behavior.

Speaking personally, I have to admit that had the *Globe and Mail* wanted to hire me, I would have probably resisted the lure of helping to start a tabloid, which eventually materialized as the

Toronto *Sun*. As it turned out, the *Sun* became, in its way, the most innovative, radical, and important newspaper in contemporary journalism anywhere. And arguably the most successful new paper to start in North America in over fifty years. I shall ever be grateful to the *Globe and Mail* for not wanting me.

26

This son of a bitch cost me $6 million!

JOHN BASSETT
TORONTO
NOVEMBER 1971 TO 1984

The idea of starting a tabloid in Toronto to replace the fallen *Telegram* was Doug Creighton's. Creighton had gone through the ranks of the paper from the police desk to sports editor to city editor and finally to managing editor when the last edition was published that Saturday, October 30, 1971. For most of his journalistic career he had been senior police reporter and *bon vivant* at the *Tely*. His remarkably ageless, prosperous appearance was somewhat reminiscent of an affluent Billy Bunter. He knew everyone worth knowing, was likable, smart, easygoing, generous. He was a firm believer in helping friends, and loyal to those who were loyal to him. Creighton took life as it came, not much interested in abstract concepts or philosophical questions. The greater issues of whither freedom and whither Western democracy didn't overly concern him. He was not one to seek confrontations, but was inclined to the view that most thorny problems solve themselves if left alone. He was right most of the time.

Without anyone's actually saying so, Creighton was automatically publisher-designate of the proposed paper. The second member of the triumvirate was Don Hunt, the *Tely*'s syndicate manager and the closest thing we had to business brains—and therefore automatic choice for general manager. He had previously dabbled in public relations, but most of *his* journalistic life had been in sports. A huge man, he was known affectionately around the paper in later years as Dr. No, while Creighton made a career of being Dr. Maybe, or Probably, or Why Not—except when he forgot. For all his blunt, sometimes insensitive exterior, Hunt was kind, scrupulously honest, and competent. He was also

369

somewhat secretive and, to quote Creighton, "wouldn't hurt a fly"—though some at the paper might argue that.

As a reporter with the strongest views in the triumvirate on what the world *should* be like, I was interested in what the editorial approach would be and had a clear idea of how I thought the paper should respond to reality. I felt editorials in most papers tended to be wishywashy, on-this-hand-on-that-hand, and overly cautious about taking what were seen as unpopular stands. In my opinion, the job of editorials was to present a strong point of view, to offer a solution to issues being discussed, to clearly illustrate a problem, and/or to stimulate readers into thinking for themselves. Whether or not people agree with the editorial line is not important. They should be believed by those who write them, or else they lose conviction and the paper loses credibility. To be avoided at all costs is the "spring-is-here" editorial, which rejoices in the seasons as they arrive and calls for good will and nice thoughts at Christmas and Easter. Ho-hum. Naturally, I grabbed the job of editor on the new paper—from reporter to editor in one scuttled newspaper.

While the *Tely* was in its last month of operation and other groups tried to find a way to keep it alive, Creighton, Hunt, and I began trying to raise money for the new venture. Other key people—Ed Monteith (managing editor), Andy Donato (art director and cartoonist), Bruce Tuttle (advertising), George Gross (sports editor), Jim Brown (finance and business office), John Lemay (circulation), Art Holland (administration), Margaret K. (switchboard)—began trying to put together a staff on the quiet. We scattered over the city looking for angels interested in investing in a new paper that would fill the gap left by the *Tely*. Mostly we were greeted with sympathy and skepticism, but no money.

The first person I approached as a possible investor was Steve Roman, pugnacious head of Denison Mines and a ferocious anti-Communist and Slovakian patriot. Roman is a perfect example of an immigrant making good in the New World and out-WASPing WASP society at its own game. He carries big grudges and is not known as a bleeding heart—unless it is his enemy's. He is dedicated to the concept of Western freedom. Without having the faintest idea of how much it cost to start a newspaper, I suggested to him that $6 million might be reasonable. Roman didn't blink, but adamantly disagreed with the concept of a morning tabloid. He wanted an afternoon paper to compete with the Toronto *Star*, which he professed to hate at that moment. I got the feeling that the main reason Roman *might* be interested in a newspaper would be to get even with someone. It quickly became apparent that while certain of our prejudices and biases coincided, Steve Roman was not the type to be an angel of mercy to a bunch of unemployed journalists seeking to become entrepreneurs.

We floundered among friends, acquaintances, and contacts through the first half of October trying to find a source of investment money. At that time most of the serious money interests were still concerned with buying the *Telegram* or saving it—including Roman, who'd made an offer on the *Tely* that involved a wage freeze, a 20 percent cut in staff, keeping all advertisers, and a guaranteed money-back guarantee, all of which which provoked John Bassett to quip: "If that's how you do business, Steve, no wonder you're a millionaire!" Bassett rejected the offer, insisting that he couldn't make agreements involving others. Broadcasters/authors Pierre Berton and Charles Templeton, the unions, Lord Thomson of Fleet himself, and others were mentioned at various times as being ready to save the *Tely*. But for various reasons all lost nerve or interest and backed off.

Increasingly, it appeared that the *Tely* was beyond resuscitation, despite all the activity of would-be saviors. Only Johnny F. Bassett, the publisher's eldest son and future publisher apparent, voted not to sell the paper. He was anxious to have another go at trying to make it profitable. Young John was pro-tabloid, but was outvoted when he suggested changing the *Tely*. Big John had done the decent thing and closed the paper voluntarily. His gimlet-eyed accountants had urged him to let a strike occur—even to encourage it because it would save him millions. Bassett, the nineteenth-century romantic who was the first publisher in Canada to give women equal pay with men in the newsroom resisted blandishments that he be "sensible" and save money.

In later years he liked to blame me for his "honorable" decision to close the paper voluntarily, and with any encouragement would announce at dinner parties or social occasions that "this son of a bitch" (and he'd glare in mock anger at me) "cost me $6 million to close the *Tely*—for all the thanks I got!" I would reply—and still believe—that I was simply Bassett's conscience and that he would have done the right thing with or without me. Anyway, he *didn't* get much thanks for his gesture, either then or since, but it *was* the right thing to do and it enabled him to maintain self-respect in a business that historically has had its share of robber barons.

Our plans for a tabloid seemed to be going nowhere fast until mid-October. Conventional wisdom was that Toronto could not sustain three healthy newspapers and that John Bassett had performed a minor miracle by keeping the *Telegram* alive for nineteen years. Creighton, Hunt, and I—and all who came with us—didn't disagree with the general view that newspapers were increasingly vulnerable in North America, but disagreed vehemently with this assessment of Toronto. Our intent was to have a morning tabloid with street sales only and to compete with the *Globe and Mail*, Canada's most prestigious and stuffy newspaper. If not the best, the *Globe* was certainly the most overrated newspaper in the country. It radiated then, as it does now, smugness and pious self-satisfaction. It is also not very accurate. It sold barely 100,000 copies in Toronto itself, and we felt generally that if we had to invent competition, we'd invent a paper like the *Globe and Mail*. Although it was unquestionably the most influential paper in the country and the one to whose editorial pronouncements politicians and "intellectuals" (real and ersatz) tended to pay attention, the *Globe* had little of the common touch and ordinary people ignored it.

On Thursday before Canadian Thanksgiving weekend, we would-be publishers met in the offices of lawyer Eddie Hyde, who was a prospective backer. Andy MacFarlane had been on the periphery of discussions for a new paper and he was the editor at the *Tely* with whom I had the greatest rapport as a journalist. He suddenly announced that he was backing out of the plan and going to work for the provincial government instead. With MacFarlane gone, I said I would also back out and probably accept an offer to join the Toronto *Star*. That was it. We all quit. We shook hands and left Hyde's office to go our separate ways. A new newspaper seemed a noble idea, but was simply not in the cards. Creighton and Hunt went to relax at a cottage in Muskoka for the long weekend. Creighton was planning to accept a senior public relations job with Air Canada, and Hunt was talking of heading for California to work for a U.S. feature syndicate service.

I came home that night feeling mildly depressed and guilty at having been one of the ones to sink the ship before it had even been launched. Though I had never thought of myself as a tabloid writer and had always been a loner, relishing challenges on my own and avoiding responsibility for others, I had the uneasy feeling that perhaps I had made a mistake. Yvonne had similar feelings; she had taken a new job doing public relations for the United Way, so as not to put all our economic eggs in one basket again.

"Do as you think best," said Yvonne. "But if you try a tabloid and fail, you're no worse off than you are now; I've got a job and we can make out. So do what you want."

"What the hell," I thought, "If there's *any* chance to start our own paper, it's worth one last try. There'll never be a better chance than now." And I started to hunt for money in earnest. I phoned Eddie Goodman and told him what we had in mind, recalling our lengthy conversations in New York at the tennis matches. We were on the same wavelength, and knew the kind of paper we both favored.

"How much are you looking for?" asked Eddie.

"We figure we need a minimum $1 million." (Our price had come down somewhat from the one quoted to Steve Roman.)

"Okay. Give me a day. I'll get back to you." That was Eddie. No wasting time.

I phoned Paul Hellyer, the former defence minister in Lester Pearson's Liberal government who had unified and integrated Canada's armed forces over pathological opposition of some senior officers. He had once been a contender for the leadership of the Liberal Party and had been deputy Prime Minister when he quit the cabinet in opposition to Trudeau's policies and joined the Conservative Party. Hellyer was a self-made millionaire, an intense and determined patriot who could be relentlessly stubborn and singleminded when a matter of principle was involved. He was also someone I respected and liked. I told him the situation. He was interested for the right reasons and saw the importance of having another journalistic voice in the community. I suggested he get in touch with Eddie Goodman.

On Sunday I got a call from Goodman. "Okay, we've got the money," he said with customary gusto and disregard for details.

"You got $1 million?"

"Close enough. Nearly $700,000 pledged. The rest is easy. It's altruistic money—people wanting a tax write-off. The next move is yours."

I phoned Creighton in Muskoka and caught him at the local bakery. I explained that the money was apparently available and all systems were go provided that we were still interested and could re-activate everyone.

Creighton laughed. "Jesus, we do it the hard way, don't we? Phone Gross and see what he thinks . . . "

George Gross, the sports editor who may have the best contacts in Canada (and whose escape from Czechoslovakia and communism in 1948 by paddling a canoe down the Danube River into Austria has become part of his legend) was doubtful.

"I don't know," he said. "It all sounds so fragile . . . "

"What's the matter with you, George!" stormed his Hungarian-born wife Elizabeth. "If you'd hesitated like this, you'd have never gotten out of Czechoslovakia. You took a chance then—take one now. Try it, for heaven's sake . . ."

Gross laughed. "You heard her—okay, I'm in."

And so it went. With a few exceptions, most of the original members of the team were on side again.

As it turned out, most of the backers Goodman had contacted were linked to developers. None seriously believed the venture would succeed, but all thought there was need for a conservative philosophy in journalism. Besides, it could be written off as a tax loss and it might be exciting. No one investor had more than 10 percent of the shares, and for our professional contribution to the new paper Creighton, Hunt, and I split 20 percent equally among us, with another 15 percent or so going to key staff. From the start, the three of us insisted that there should be a profit-sharing scheme for employees when and if there was a profit, and we agreed that all the original *Sun* staff should get free shares when and if we went public. The idea was to motivate the staff, make them part of the operation, reward them. Instead of having a newspaper filled with vaguely disgruntled socialists, we'd create a staff of modest capitalists.

I think all those involved knew that the *Sun* would succeed, but none of us expected the scale of success we achieved almost from the beginning. From a standing start on Monday, November 1, 1971, after working on the final edition of the *Telegram* of Saturday, October 30, a group of sixty-five unemployed newspaper people produced their first tabloid. The first month's circulation was around 50,000 to 60,000; the paper was printed in a plant thirty miles from the newspaper offices. Barely a year later the paper was being printed at three separate plants, the page negatives being made at the *Sun* offices and shipped in three different directions to different plants, each paper a slightly different size.

It was always clear sailing at the *Sun*, which, from the start, was a paper unlike any other. Apart from being different from its competitors, the *Globe and Mail* and the *Star* which were traditional broadsheets, the *Sun* broke new trails in journalism that I don't think are yet fully realized.

The likes of Lord Thomson of Fleet predicted its demise ("a hopeless proposition, quite hopeless") as did virtually every expert in the field, including John Bassett, who while he wished his erst-while staff well, was convinced the venture would fail. He none-theless helped us immeasurably by selling us the *Telegrams*'s record room—the invaluable memory of any newspaper—for $1 and en-abling us to get the *Telegram* street sales boxes, which we changed overnight to *Sun* boxes. The *Sun* managed to keep contact with its readers in a variety of ways that other papers *could* emulate, but rarely do. The three original principals, Creighton, Hunt, and I, could hardly be more different. We didn't start with a set policy or philosophy, but improvised as we went, argued and disagreed. Often the compromise that emerged took a different form from what anyone expected.

In the first month there were three signs that boded well for our future: the prime minister's office sent us a nasty letter, Pierre Berton and Charles Templeton delivered a writ to sue over the *Sun* questioning their sincerity on a radio program, and the paper had a bomb scare. Not bad. The PMO sent several letters before giving up on us, B. and T. didn't sue, and the bomb didn't go off. But it was a spendid start for a young paper.

The *Sun* was really two papers—the frivolous, superficial *Sun* of the provocative *Sun*shine girls, axe murders, three-alarm fires, rapes, car crashes, and animals in distress, and the *Sun* of deep and genuine concern for democracy and freedom, for Western values and the plight of mankind. We deliberately sought col-umnists who were outspoken, knowledgeable, passionate; edito-rially, we were relentlessly suspicious of the Soviet Union, concerned about defence, and angry at human rights groups, which we be-lieved actually create racism by their intemperance; we saw the United States the best hope for the free world, worried about Eastern Europe, believed in free enterprise, and fought govern-ment bureaucracy and tyranny whenever we could. All with a sense of humor where possible, and a streak of mischief and ir-reverence.

Oddly, it was mostly through its editorial page and columnists that the *Sun* got its reputation for being gutsy. This attitude was not reflected in the news pages, where it was more conventional.

Often it seemed that the editorial pages and the news pages were on different courses. Gradually, the two came closer together, but at first the *Sun* depended on "scalping" the *Globe and Mail* for hard news. There was some validity to the wry observation of Clark Davey, then managing editor of the *Globe* (and later publisher of the Vancouver *Sun* and Montreal *Gazette*), who excused himself from a social function with the following words to managing editor, Ed Monteith: "I've got to go back and put out the *Globe* so you guys will be able to print a paper tomorrow."

In the early days the Toronto *Sun* had only one investigative reporter who churned out original, exclusive stories, and that was Bob MacDonald, who'd been on the *Tely*. A maverick Nova Scotia Tory who over the years had developed good political connections, he repeatedly unearthed stories embarrassing to the government and the Ottawa press gallery, whom he despised as fellow travellers. He also had good judgment and a strong news sense. Without MacDonald, the *Sun* would have been stripped of any originality in news stories.

The *Sun's* obvious sincerity enabled it to be accepted where other papers expressing a similar view might be regarded as cynical. Editorially, the paper was not subtle and rarely used a stiletto where a broadsword would do. It once immortalized the leader of the Ontario Liberals by dubbing him a "dink" (we did not, despite the legend, label Joe Clark a "wimp," although it would have been in character).

From the start the paper encouraged its writers to have opinions about what they were covering, feeling that a reporter displaying his assessments openly was more honest and less hypocritical than disguising views with such tricks as the "feeling among observers is . . . " or "sources say . . . " or using selected quotes to reinforce a viewpoint. We preferred what I term the sports writer syndrome: commenting on the event that everyone was seeing on TV and standing or falling on one's impressions and interpretations.

We also decided to give one-line responses to letters to the editor—something that makes journalistic purists shudder. The traditional view is that the reader has a right to respond, without any comeback from the newspaper. Why not give a response that gets a dialogue going? Others can join in, and the editor may even be persuaded that perhaps he was wrong or too hasty. The one-line put-down or boost-up is a hazard of writing to the *Sun* and has proved popular with readers. The *Sun* was involved with people and would send makeshift teams to play sports events at half-time, judge cake-making contests, have prize crossword contests, and even turn elections into contests by having readers guess the results and giving a prize of a huge, ugly trophy and/or a phony front page of the person as the world champion political pundit.

When the *Sun* began in a rented, seedy downtown office called the Eclipse Whitewear Building, sharing space with a bankrupt firm, columnists even documented the antics at the paper—notably one Paul Rimstead who won a considerable following by discussing the publisher's penchant for martinis and for investing in unsuccessful restaurants and taking free trips all over. Rimstead would also comment on the general manager's tight-fisted honesty and the editor's determination to halt the Communist menace and to play second base with awesome enthusiasm and questionable competence on the paper's softball team. Never before has a newspaper made such fun of its executives, and in few papers has there been such journalistic freedom of expression. Many found it incongruous that a paper of such profound "conservative" beliefs could be so liberal in its treatment of staff—not realizing that this was the essence of consistency for a paper that believes in and trusts individuality.

What was unusual about the *Sun* was that it took issues seriously, but never itself. Publisher Creighton, in speeches, would tell the story of the differences in the three Toronto papers. In covering, say, the sinking of the *Titanic*, the *Globe and Mail* would note the loss in shipping tonnage and predict the effect on Cunard Line stock. The *Star* would concentrate on a Toronto survivor who was in the third lifeboat and who had given up smoking and found God. The *Sun* would run a headline about sex-crazed crew assaulting female passengers and announce a contest to guess the number of victims and win a ticket to the football game.

The *Sun*, in fact, had more journalistic coups than its intellectual detractors realized or would admit. It was the first paper to conclude editorially that the KGB was involved in the assassination attempt on the Pope; it broke stories about ministers of the government improperly using government aircraft and about improper phone calls from politicians to judges sitting on cases; it got a confession of spying for the USSR from Laval University Professor Hugh Hambleton, who was later convicted in Britain of espionage; it rallied the greatest mass protest in Canada against forced metrication; it was almost the only newspaper to react against the Trudeau government's secret Emergency Planning

Order authorizing the establishment of internment camps for civilians and imposing censorship and taking control of all media outlets in the event of a national emergency of the government's definition. In its first twelve years the *Sun* won ten Firefighter Awards, thirty Police Awards, eleven National Newspaper Awards and Citations—a creditable record for a spunky, irreverent but rarely irrelevant upstart.

The *Sun* is *not* a good newspaper in over-all terms, and certainly not as aggressive and determined as it should or could be. But in its way it is arguably the most interesting newspaper in the country. Its very existence in a time of monopolies and one-newspaper towns (only Toronto and New York have three, healthy, competing English-language newspapers) makes it unique. It proves that if you come up with something different, you can create a new newspaper relatively cheaply and make a profit quickly. If a group of unemployed journalists with no special knowledge can do it once, it can be done again. The secret is doing it inexpensively and producing a product that is different. Most competing newspapers in North America are indistinguishable from one another.

Interestingly, Canadian royal commissions and various bodies looking into the press and media and problems of freedom and control tend to overlook or dismiss the *Sun*. I think they should study it more carefully. Most of those who write about newspapers don't like the *Sun*, and therefore ignore it. So much for their commitment to a free and viable press!

Not all of the competitiveness of the *Sun* was wasted on the opposition. Some of it overflowed into the paper itself—a hazard of bringing together a lot of bloody-minded types who are encouraged to think for themselves and be prima donnas. I began to delve into domestic politics and write editorials on all the subjects I felt strongly about. I unleashed a rage against Trudeau which I'd never been able to do on the *Telegram*, urging a common-sense foreign policy, and presented the world in what I felt were realistic terms that too seldom got exposure. In our in-paper polls the editorials had over 90 percent "always" and "sometimes" readership—the best-read items in the paper. It was like finding a golden key to readers, something few papers had been able to achieve with editorials.

The first time I resigned as editor was when we sold the centre spread—originally designed to be sacrosanct as a daily feature and photo layout—to Eaton's for an ad. We had already sold the back page—originally intended to be the first sports page—to Simpsons on a yearly contract. Journalistic purity burned hot in those days and I objected to such categorical compromises. We even lost a Loblaw's ad when we ran a picture of a half grasshopper someone found in a can of corn, complete with the label of the can showing. A couple of days later we ran another picture of a grasshopper found in another can in another supermarket. Creighton rather plaintively urged that the newsroom try not to be quite so vigilant in finding grasshoppers in our advertisers' cans of corn.

My second resignation occurred when Creighton, Hunt, city affairs columist John Downing, cartoonist Donato, and I met to decide whom we'd be backing in the 1972 mayoralty race—Tony O'Donohue, David Rotenberg, or David Crombie. O'Donohue was the favourite, Rotenberg the choice of big business (and developers and Conservatives), Crombie a populist outsider. We all favored O'Donohue, with Crombie second. Only Creighton and our board liked Rotenberg. At the last moment I urged that we switch to Crombie—that he was making a hell of a run for it and might conceivably pull it off. Regardless, he was a little guy in an uphill fight, he was down-to-earth, cheerful, cheeky and our kind of guy. Win or lose, we should support him.

I even wrote an editorial giving the virtues of all three, then concluding why we were going with Crombie. Creighton invoked publisher's prerogative, rejected Crombie, and, feeling that Rotenberg was by far the best ("not the most popular, but the best") ruled that the *Sun* was supporting him. I feared that our board of directors was speaking through Creighton, and said I wouldn't write the supporting editorial. Creighton then took the editorial in which I came out for Crombie, and changed it to support for Rotenberg. Wounded, I submitted my resignation, only to pull it back when John Webb, our rough diamond composing room foreman and later production manager, urged me not to do anything that might undermine the paper.

Sports editor Gross was another great one for periodically resigning, but he was such a vital cog in the operation that it was unthinkable for him to leave. Some felt his sports pages made the paper. Feelings were intense at the *Sun* because it was so much a part of all our lives. The fact that opinion had been almost universal that we'd fail cemented the bond that tied us together.

As it turned out, where the *Telegram* allegedly failed because it was too Big "C" conservative, the *Sun* seemed to succeed because it was even *more* conservative, albeit sometimes anti-establishment conservative. It had the appearance of being for the little guy, and its columnists and editorials were perpetually in the throes of apoplexy over issues of the day.

Since we were concentrating on columists to provide depth and different viewpoints, we tried to get mavericks or independent thinkers of various political persuasions. What we didn't want were partisan hacks. Among those with socialist, or New Democratic Party leanings we had the wild-card, all-purpose Dr. Morton Shulman, to whom nothing was sacred and who at the time was a socialist member of the provincial legislature—and one of the best natural journalists around. And we had Doug Fisher, former socialist MP and a voice of sanity and common sense. We eventually had Tories like Dalton Camp, Lubor Zink, William Buckley, David Crombie when he was an opposition MP, even Roy McMurtry before he ran for the legislature and became Ontario's attorney-general.

The greatest problem was finding independent-minded Liberal spokesmen, not counting Paul Hellyer. We briefly tried Senator Keith Davey, the Liberal election honcho and resident rain-maker. Davey had headed a celebrated Royal Commission inquiry into the media, and seemed a possible columnist. But we found his *Sun* columns appearing in other publications under the bylines of different Liberal cabinet ministers. It seems they were being sent out for others to use as policy stands. I was indignant, consulted Creighton, and we fired Davey—with some relish. After his dismissal Davey wrote a letter to Creighton that is a classic. He explained that everything that had appeared under his name he had "written, participated in writing, or caused to be written." That gives fair latitude, especially for an expert on journalism!

A priceless asset on the newspaper was cartoonist Andy Donato who had struggled for years inside the *Telegram*'s art department and, while appreciated, was not generally recognized as something of a cartooning genius. With the *Sun* his talents blossomed and he devised advertising schemes, promotion stunts, and layouts and drew what his fans consider the best, most provocative editorial cartoons in the country. He also played catcher for the *Sun* softball team—his only area of incompetence. Too untemperamental to be really appreciated, he and I had possibly the most harmonious editor-cartoonist relationship in journalism, and his cartoons were the most popular item in every survey the paper ever conducted. I claimed credit for inspiring his best cartoons, he took blame for ones that aroused controversy. His cartoon of the American Dream at the time of American hostages in Iran—U.S. Marines raising

the Stars and Stripes in the rear end of Ayatollah Khomeini—
won prizes at international competitions as the best political cartoon in the world in 1979. It was ignored by judges of newspaper
awards in Canada, who have difficulty recognizing anything of
merit in the *Sun*, of which they generally disapproved.

The *Sun* was a success. The start-up costs of the paper were
roughly $250,000 of the original $700,000, and in the first year
the *Sun* showed a $50,000 profit. We called on investors to ante
up more, and ten years after the *Sun* first rose from the ashes of
the *Tely* it had built its own plant in mid-Toronto; had a circulation
of 250,000 on weekdays, 450,000 on Sundays; had grown from
a 40-page paper to a sometimes 200-page paper; was turning a
profit of $1 million a month; had started new *Suns* in Edmonton
and Calgary; was the principal proprietor of United Press Canada;
had a syndicate service, a business wire, a feature photo service;
was employing some 1,300 people in three cities; and had gone
on the stock market at $11, had split three for one when it hit
$35, and was one of the few hot properties on an otherwise slug-
gish market in a stagnant economy. In 1983, it also bought the
Houston *Post*, the seventeenth largest newspaper in the United
States, for $100 million.

The failure of the *Telegram* was the best thing that happened
for most of the employees of the *Sun*, which really did seem to
profit from the mistakes committed by the *Tely*. The problem
would be to remember our origins, not lose sight of our audience,
and to remain straightforward, indignant, and irreverent in the
face of all temptations to be complacent.

27

The KGB is an enemy of this country . . . I don't consider the Soviet Union an enemy

PRIME MINISTER PIERRE TRUDEAU
OTTAWA
MARCH 2, 1978

In his book *Officially Secret*, British journalist/Tory MP Jonathan Aitken, a victim of the Official Secrets Act, tells the story of Charles Marvin who, in 1878, started a sequence of events that led to the creation of the Act so that Britain could protect itself from spies and traitors. Marvin was a vain, ambitious, poorly educated clerk with a gift for languages and a photographic memory who worked in the treaty department of the British Foreign Office. He also moonlighted as correspondent for the London *Globe*. Britain and Russia (Foreign Secretary Lord Salisbury and Russian Ambassador Count Shouvaloff) had signed a secret treaty on the eve of the 1878 Berlin Congress that Marvin had to copy. He paraphrased the points and leaked them to the *Globe*, to the consternation of Queen Victoria, Benjamin Disraeli, the Foreign Office, and London *Times*.

When questioned about the *Globe* story in the House of Commons, Lord Salisbury denounced the newspaper report as "wholly unauthentic." The *Globe*'s reputation for accuracy plummeted accordingly. Marvin, angry and humiliated, called upon his prodigious memory, recalled the precise wording of the treaty, and wrote the exact wording of the text for the front page of the *Globe*. It showed clearly that the Congress was a charade and that Britain and Russia had signed a treaty in advance. It did no damage, but embarrassed the government.

Marvin was charged under the Larceny Act with theft of a document, but he was acquitted on grounds that he had stolen nothing. Whereupon the *Globe* slammed the government for its "ill-advised" prosecution: ". . . the petty revenge of exposure was zealously striven for not in the interests of truth but to appease the ire of sensitive officialdom."

Anxious that there be no repeat of Marvin's disclosures, Lord Salisbury pushed for a law. Eleven years later, in 1889, the Official Secrets Act was passed, with total emphasis on espionage and treason. The Act was amended in 1911 and again in 1920—this time, with emphasis to protect government information and preserve civil service secrecy more than to combat spies and traitors.

In 1939, on the eve of war with Germany, Canada borrowed almost word for word from the British Official Secrets Act and, after a few minutes of discussion of the bill in Parliament, passed it into law. Since then the Act has been invoked four times to combat espionage—only once partially successfully.

There is some irony that the Official Secrets Act was born as a result of a newspaper report that embarrassed the government but did not threaten the nation. Exactly 100 years after Charles Marvin's extraordinary feat of memorizing the secret treaty between Russia and Britain, the Toronto *Sun* became the first Canadian newspaper ever to be charged under the Official Secrets Act after I had written a column revealing details of Soviet espionage activities in Canada. It was the culmination of a long-standing feud between the *Sun* and Prime Minister Pierre Trudeau, who was the source of all chicanery as far as the *Sun* was concerned. The London *Globe*'s observations about the government of its day could well have been written in reference to the Trudeau government and the *Sun*.

In Britain, the Official Secrets Act has long been used to attack the press when it embarrasses government. There is an average of almost one case a year whereby the Act is used to persecute or punish journalists—something the London *Times* anticipated in 1920 when it observed editorially: "If we are to have legislation on the Press, let it not be mixed up with penal provisions aimed at spies and revolutionaries." Under the broad, vague terms of the Act, virtually *anything* can be regarded as an "official" secret including, as has been pointed out, the number of cups of tea consumed in a ministry per day and the color of the minister's new rug.

Jonathan Aitken was charged under the Official Secrets Act in 1972 when as a journalist covering the Biafran War, he quoted extracts from a diplomat's report on that war which embarrassed the British government. He noted in his subsequent book: "Indeed the Civil Service's obsession with secrecy has grown to such an extent that the legitimate operations of journalists are today more hindered by the Official Secrets Act than are the illegal machinations of spies."

Canada's charges against me had their origin in events long ago. Ever since Moscow in 1965 and Olga's defection to the West, I had contacts inside the RCMP Security Service, especially with the head of the Soviet desk, Jim Bennett. He was an enigmatic figure, even to members of the Security Service. He had originally worked with British Intelligence (and Kim Philby) and had come to Canada where he worked himself over a period of eighteen years into a virtually indispensable and unassailable position within RCMP Security as the mastermind of Canadian counterintelligence activities and an expert on Soviet espionage.

When the Americans—notably Jim Angleton, head of CIA counterespionage—rejected Olga's application to enter the United States and branded her as a probable KGB plant to penetrate the West, I disagreed. Bennett sided with me, and after she and I underwent detailed and separate interrogations by British Security acting for the RCMP, she was allowed into Canada, where she has proved a reliable citizen ever since. I was blacklisted from working in Washington as long as I was associated with Olga.

Bennett's sudden retirement from RCMP Security in 1972, ostensibly for health reasons, touched off a spate of rumors about *his* reliability. The Security Service was suddenly alive with allegations. Everyone, it seems, was suspicious, and security types love to gossip. I was aware of the RCMP concerns and was re-examined by the Security Service about Olga's defection. Although I had been through all this before with both Belgian Security and British Security, Canadian Security wanted to see if the testimony had been tampered with or fabricated. It was Bennett they were checking on this time, not Olga or me. There were those in RCMP Security who believed that Bennett might have been trying to infiltrate a KGB agent in the form of a defector by using me, the unwitting dupe. However, the trail petered out when our stories jibed. Bennett had, in fact, initiated nothing in the Olga case, but had merely been the channel through which various security services were alerted to her defection; and through him I received instructions as to how to orchestrate it. In fact, Bennett had repeatedly warned me that she was suspected of being a KGB plant and urged me not to get involved. It was Bennett's advice I'd overruled, no one else's.

After taking early retirement, Bennett moved to South Africa, where the climate was healthier for his asthma. Tom Hazlitt, a tough investigative reporter for the Toronto *Star* whose body was already wracked with terminal cancer, had good RCMP contacts and had heard about the suspicions of Bennett. He went to South Africa and tracked him down. When confronted with accusations of espionage, Bennett wrote a statement for Hazlitt declaring that he, Bennett, had never been an agent for the KGB. The *Star* published the story and there was considerable interest, discussion, and public speculation about Bennett's loyalty.

I phoned Bennett in South Africa. He told me his version of the story and was interested in writing a piece for the Toronto *Sun*. In the article he specifically denied that "my abrupt departure from the RCMP was because I was the Canadian Philby," thereby making the hitherto-taboo comparison with the traitor Philby usable in his own words. He had made the reference, so the media could now quote him safely.

He added in his article: "I felt that such ridiculous and libelous rumors should be buried for the sake of Canada, my family and myself. This is why I prepared the statement: 'This is to certify that I have never been at any time during my life either a witting or unwitting supporter of the Communist cause and as such, never a member of the Soviet bloc Intelligence services.' " Bennett said his record was that of a "dedicated anti-Communist."

I was flabbergasted that Bennett would write such an affidavit for a journalist. If I were a former security official and some journalist asked me to write a statement declaring I'd never been a traitor, I'd throw him out. Bennett apparently complied for reasons I don't understand.

His ideological enemies worried the subject for years, and the taint of suspicion followed Bennett wherever he went. Such details as the fact that he had been interrogated by the CIA before being retired from the RCMP were viewed by some as evidence of guilt when, in fact, all it showed was that others were concerned about his reliability or were following up perhaps-unsubstantiated allegations.

Included in the suspicions was the report that a KGB defector to the United States, Yuri Nosenko—himself suspected of being a KGB plant to divert and confuse CIA investigations—had identified Bennett as a KGB mole. Nosenko claimed to have been in charge of Lee Harvey Oswald's case in the USSR, and his defection was believed by Angleton to be a KGB assignment to clear the

Kremlin of any involvement with Oswald in the assassination of President Kennedy. Nosenko, to this day, remains one of the twilight mysteries and question marks in the long murky history of spy and counterspy—the shadowy realm of Psst and Shhh.

Bennett then moved to Australia to be closer to his teen-age daughters, who lived with their mother after their parents' marriage broke up. When I went to Australia for a visit in 1974 with my Australian-born wife and our kids, I hoped to see Bennett. The RCMP Security Service asked if I'd brief them on our conversation after my return. I asked if there were suspicions of him and was told categorically that he was considered innocent of all allegations and was presumed to have been totally loyal and dedicated. Why, then, would they want me to interview him on their behalf? I refused to act as an informer on an innocent man.

In the late 1970s Bennett again stormed into headlines and political controversy. Left-wing Canadian journalist and author Ian Adams wrote a "novel," supposedly based on fact, called *S, Portrait of a Spy*, which contended that a Bennett-like character in RCMP Security had been, in effect, a *triple* agent, working initially as a KGB mole inside the RCMP and later turned by the CIA. The book depicted me as "Hazelton," a corpulent editor for a sleazy "Tits and Bums" newspaper who was trying to get his Russian translator into the United States on behalf of the KGB, and who was so disillusioned at being used that he turned into a mindless anti-Communist fanatic.

While working on the book, Adams had wanted to interview me about Bennett, but I had refused. He later asked if I would give him Bennett's address because he was going to Australia and planned to interview him. He said his book was about Bennett. I contacted Bennett and asked if he wanted to meet Adams. He didn't, so I respected his privacy. When the book was published, security matters were in the news and a daily item of debate in Parliament. About Adams's book an unidentified Mountie said in the Toronto *Star*: "There's no doubt, it's 90% based on fact, 10% on fiction." I read it, contacted Bennett about its contents, and said I considered it libelous. I sent him a copy of the book and recommended a friend, Julian Porter, as a libel lawyer if he so desired. I would have acted similarly with any friend about to be pilloried.

Bennett sued Adams for libel and eventually won a modest settlement that more or less cleared his name. From the start, Adams blamed me for masterminding the libel case because I had publicly identified the fictional character "S" as Bennett, and because I had alerted Bennett to what Adams was doing.

I suppose the jury will always be out on Bennett because as he says himself in security matters there is no way to ever know for sure. Once the allegation is made it lingers forever. Canadian writer John Sawatsky wrote a provocative book about the Bennett case, *For Services Rendered*, in which he concluded that Bennett was *probably* not a spy, but that the Security Service was certainly incompetent. I'm not sure which Bennett would consider the most offensive: the idea that he was a traitor or the suggestion that he was a bumbler!

It seems the height of journalistic irresponsibility, not to say cowardice, to malign someone without proof or even usable evidence, as Ian Adams did, simply on the grounds of suspicion. Yet, the lib-left *literati* establishment rose in outrage to hold fundraising benefits in defence of Adams's right to use fiction to destroy the reputation of a former RCMP Security Service officer. Siding with Adams without knowing the details of the case or, apparently, caring, were groups such as the Periodical Writers Association of Canada, the Association of Canadian Publishers, ACTRA, Writers Union, Guild of Canadian Playwrights, League of Canadian Poets, and the like. They and others rallied to Adams's side, raised money on his behalf, and, supported his right to malign the name and reputation of a former security official. Labelling something "fiction" was, to them, sufficient justification to destroy the reputation of anyone they viewed as too right wing, or involved in preventing espionage. The sword of literary freedom cuts mostly one way—from left to right. *S, Portrait of a Spy*, was a poor book, difficult to follow, and has since vanished into well-deserved oblivion.

Olga's defection plus my exposure to the Soviet system and the omnipresent machinations of the Soviet secret police network made me exceedingly sympathetic to the need for Western intelligence and security. In fact, the more one examines the question of security, the more one realizes that Western intelligence defences are woefully inadequate. Canada, in particular, is an essential cog in the Soviet espionage apparatus, and Canadian governments have almost traditionally ignored or downplayed Soviet espionage activities here. Canada's record of catching and prosecuting Soviet spies is the worst in the Western world: none since the Gouzenko revelations during World War II.

When I returned to journalism in Canada after Moscow and went back to globe-hopping and crisis-covering, I was more conscious of the ideological war, which I had previously only vaguely been aware of. I began to specialize in security matters and periodically would contact Bennett to check out rumors of spies in Canada. Bennett—always wary, who liked to answer questions with other questions, or respond in riddles—would point me in the right direction, avoid comment, or categorically deny the rumor in question. To my knowledge he never lied to or tried to deceive me. He might not answer, but he never misled. I trusted him implicitly. He was what is known in journalism as a "source" or "contact" and exceedingly useful. To the Adamses of the world who view Western security as something malignant to be opposed (and who tend to regard Soviet espionage as a benign entity to be ignored, if not physically helped), I was the next thing to an agent for the RCMP, and sometimes the CIA—whenever I came up with a story concerning KGB espionage. Since I wasn't, this never bothered me. So long as the stories checked out and were true, I would accept help from whomever would give it—Canadian, American, or British security. It seemed to me then, as it seems to me now, that Western security services are on our side. And while one may not approve of all the things done in the name of security, the motives or aims are important to consider. It is essential to take into account the alternatives. I suppose it hinges on one's upbringing but to some, treason is the most heinous crime and espionage is something to be prevented where possible and punished when caught.

When the *Sun* emerged from the wreckage of the failed Toronto *Telegram* in 1971 and my role changed overnight from reporter to editor-in-chief, I still wrote a twice-a-week column, kept up security contacts, and wrote the occasional news story as I came across it. Gradually my security contacts lapsed. The longer Pierre Trudeau lasted as prime minister, the more wary I became of my security contacts, who at first were distraught over the prospects of Trudeau as PM but steadily became more complacent and relaxed about him. They also became increasingly wary of me, the more adamantly and publicly I disagreed with Trudeau's policies and opposed his attitudes and actions. I saw erstwhile friends inside the Canadian Security Service steadily shift from being almost paranoid about Trudeau and convinced he was dangerous to becoming resigned to his regime and, in some cases, supporting him for pragmatic reasons of pension and promotions. I felt that many were co-opted into joining what they could no longer fight.

Vigorously, security-conscious elements were eased out of the

Security Service into early retirement. Few dared speak out, for to do so would violate terms of the Official Secrets Act and might result in loss of pensions and benefits at best, or in imprisonment at worst. Under Trudeau, security in Canada went from being flabby to irrelevant. Coupled with various investigations and Royal Commissions into the RCMP, even public confidence which had once backed the Mounties over the politicians, eroded into disillusion, disappointment, and cynicism.

In the mid-70s, much to the puzzlement of those who believed (erroneously) that I had a special relationship with RCMP Security, I began to get into hot water. First when Konstantin Geyvandov, the *Pravda* correspondent in Ottawa, was expelled for "activities not related to journalism" there were legitimate questions in the House of Commons about what he had been doing. The government refused to say. Some felt it was the people's right to know, broadly, what the so-called Soviet journalist had been up to that so threatened Canada's security. No dice. For years I had decried Geyvandov as a KGB officer whose predecessor in Ottawa, Vladimir Ozerov, had also been KGB. Geyvandov was more outgoing than Ozerov, and people who should have known better—such as the *Sun*'s respected columnist Doug Fisher—seemed to think Geyvandov was unlikely to be a Soviet spy, either because he was a nice guy or because he gave the impression of being too dumb ("big, silly, amiable and dumb," to quote Fisher). As it turned out, with the exception of being big, he was none of those things.

I got a tip that Geyvandov was expelled because he had approached a Canadian Broadcasting Corporation journalist to do work for *Pravda*, ostensibly on a free-lance basis, writing profiles and assessments of MPs, journalists, and bureaucrats in Ottawa. The CBC person supposedly got $100 per article. The Soviets would ultimately have wanted "profiles" that would reveal who liked to sleep around, who drank too much, who spent too much money, who was in debt, who liked the good life, who was likely to be sympathetic to Soviet causes, who might be susceptible to bribes or blackmail. And so on. Although there is no evidence the CBC knew it, what the Soviets wanted is another matter. There is little doubt that this, among other things, was the Soviet intent.

Besides, being on the KGB payroll, even disguised as a *Pravda* contributor, was the first hook to snag someone into KGB service. A civil servant who accepts money from a Soviet official for a roadmap that can be obtained free from a government office has *not* broken the law but *has* taken the first step toward being corrupted and co-opted into espionage. It is not *what* is being purchased that matters, but the *taking* of money. The first hook is painless, but when you try to remove it later, it is too late.

There was considerable speculation in Parliament and the press as to the identity of the CBC journalist. I drew parallels with the case in Australia in 1953 when Vladimir Petrov, the resident KGB man (Australia's Igor Gouzenko), defected and told all. The Soviets tried to abduct his wife back to the USSR, and were thwarted at Darwin airport when burly Australian police staged a dramatic rescue from the plane. In the subsequent Royal Commission it was revealed that a hitherto-respected Australian journalist, Rupert Lockwood, had been working for the Soviets, writing character assessments of MPs and political journalists that could be used later by the KGB in exploiting weakness to gain informers and agents of influence through bribes and blackmail.

Lockwood had been so indiscreet as to prepare his assessments using a Soviet Embassy typewriter, feeling that would protect him from prosecution as technically he was not on Australian soil. Petrov turned over the evidence to Australian authorities. The uproar over Lockwood's betrayal of his colleagues was so great that he had to leave Australia and honest journalism. He ended up in Moscow writing for the Australian Communist newspaper, the *Tribune*. I knew him quite well in Moscow, where he was among the best-informed, most critical, and amusing journalists. I liked Lockwood, detested his values, and felt a reluctant sympathy for him as a lost, abandoned, and compromised soul. A journalistic pariah.

The Canadian case over twenty years later bore a remarkable similarity to the Petrov case, and it would have been useful to know more than the scraps one could scrounge and piece together.

One day my phone rang and a mysterious voice suggested that the CBC person with whom Geyvandov was dealing was Mark Starowicz, executive producer of the popular CBC radio interview show "As It Happens." I checked with RCMP sources who said, yes, he was the one. But not for attribution. Presumably, other journalists got the same message, including the Liberal Party executive-turned-Conservative MP Tom Cossitt, who raised Starowicz's name in the privileged confines of the House of Commons. Why were the RCMP—presuming it was they—so forthcoming?

I was told that an article was being prepared for a national magazine, supposedly *Saturday Night*, to the effect that Starowicz had been working with Geyvandov to get "As It Happens" to visit Moscow and do interviews about life there. The article would say that paranoia inside the Security Service was such that this sort of journalism was deemed subversive, therefore Geyvandov was expelled. In fact, the "As It Happens" plans to visit Moscow had nothing to do with the expulsion. The possible recruitment of a Soviet agent did—or rather the attempts of the KGB/journalist to recruit a Canadian citizen were unacceptable. It was clearly in the interests of the RCMP to get the truth out before any magazine version was published—which it never was. I passed the information to the *Sun* news desk and checks were made.

When Starowicz's name was mentioned in the Commons there was a hullabaloo in his defence. By then he was being promoted from executive producer of "As It Happens" to a prestigious new Sunday morning radio news show, and then went to run the CBC's television nightly flagship news show "The Journal." CBC president Laurent Picard defended Starowicz. I wrote in the *Sun* that Picard "condemned what he called 'McCarthyism and witch-hunting' because Starowicz's CBC radio show "As It Happens" had won many international awards." A classic non sequitur that was to be endlessly repeated.

Roy McMurtry, the Attorney General of Ontario, raised the Geyvandov/Starowicz issue and clearly there were concerns in High Places. The matter faded, periodically to rise again. Starowicz acknowledged that he was the one linked with Geyvandov, admitted that he'd been paid for pieces he wrote between 1970 and 1973, insisted they were political and not personal in nature, and apparently never wondered why his free-lance pieces never appeared in print. This aspect was never raised in Parliament, nor was it ever explained. Occasionally, Starowicz would sue, or threaten to sue, when he felt a journalist went too far in speculations—notably Lubor Zink of the *Sun*, a vigorous and knowledgeable anti-Communist. Of course, those who feel Soviet espionage is a myth or unimportant were offended at Zink and others who fret about KGB subversion. Some felt that I was again revealing myself as an RCMP lackey.

In the summer of 1976 I received anonymously in the mail a copy of a letter from the head of RCMP Security, General Mike Dare, to Robin Bourne, a former artillery colonel who was Chairman of the Security Advisory Committee, an intermediary between the RCMP and cabinet ministers with the job of selecting and evaluating security information.

Dubbed the "Sooper Snoopers," Bourne's group had the job of taking raw intelligence from the RCMP, analyzing and assessing it, and passing on some, filing some and, presumably, discarding some. No one was sure. As it turned out, the Sooper Snoopers were as much an impediment as an aid to security, and served mostly to isolate concerned ministers from direct contact with the RCMP. It was another bureaucratic intrusion at best, a potential instrument for concealing truth or distorting reality at worst. It was an agency that encouraged more secrecy than security, that covered up more than it revealed.

General Dare was a World War II tank soldier with no previous experience in intelligence work before being appointed to head RCMP Security. His letter to Bourne complained about a recent order by Prime Minister Trudeau not to investigate the loyalty of the Parti Québécois and its members. He complained that it was impossible to carry out adequate security screenings or determine the loyalty to Canada of civil servants and federal job applicants if no questions could be asked pertaining to a person's beliefs or loyalties concerning Quebec separatism. Feeling that the order made a mockery of the security screening process, General Dare asked for the matter to be placed on the agenda of the Advisory Committee. After all, the most critical internal issue facing the nation was one of loyalty to the concept of Canada versus loyalty to the concept of an independent Quebec.

I gave the letter to Bob MacDonald, the *Sun*'s investigative reporter. He hated routine, preferring to make his own path and develop his own stories, using his wide network of sources. Editors tended to complain that he used the same sources over and over, but virtually all of MacDonald's stories stood up and his independence made him both respected and resented as a rival. MacDonald verified the authenticity of the letter and a story was published. The Opposition in Parliament took up cudgels against the government. A friend in the RCMP contacted me and asked for the letter. I said sorry. He said they were under pressure to find the leak and would I slip it to them quietly. I was embarrassed for them, but refused.

The next day three Mounties arrived at my office. What bothered them, inexplicably at first, was that my office had glass walls. "I thought your office was closed in," said one officer, disappointment in his voice.

I was puzzled but uncomprehending and replied: "No, my office has always had glass walls. Why?"

"Oh, nothing. Just wondered." I was soon to find out why the glass bothered them.

We talked briefly about the need for security, how rotten left-wing academics were, and I sympathized with them for having to fight a reluctant government as well as the KGB. They looked approving and said if I felt so strongly about the need for security, please, wouldn't I give them the letter? No, I wouldn't. Surely, they could understand that I was sympathetic, but in conscience I couldn't help.

A search warrant was produced and, under terms of the Official Secrets Act, I was read my right to remain silent but that anything I said might be used as evidence. I was both amused and appalled. It wasn't their decision, they said, but Ottawa's—the implications being that the Prime Minister's Office was determined to plug the leak and find the culprit.

"Now that you see we're serious, can't you give the letter to us?" said one Mountie. I grinned and he shrugged. They proceeded to get ready to search my office. "Can you at least give us a hint where it is?" said one. "Point us in the right direction?"

"Sorry, fellas, you're on your own on this one."

By this time someone had phoned other news media and the *Sun* newsroom was filling with TV cameras and press. Very self-conscious, the RCMP continued their search, throwing furtive glances through the glass walls at the filming of the whole thing. Mounties don't like lights on them.

I suspect I had the most cluttered office in journalism. I had more files than filing cabinets, and papers, books, and documents were everywhere. On one wall were framed letters from important people telling me what a swine I was to write such-and-such, or from people like lawyer Eddie Goodman asking that we print a letter from him saying how "full of crap" he thought I was on a particular issue. With no more room in my office to file things, I was steadily being submerged in clutter.

Bob Johnston of the CBC looked at the mess through the glass wall and murmured: "Jesus, I don't know if they'll find a letter in that mess, but they may lose a Mountie!"

I found it interesting that the Mounties started their search by feeling under the tables to see if the letter was stuck under the table top. Then they began to look behind pictures: was it stuck there? Then they began to flip the pages of every book in the bookcase: was it there? Then under the edges of the rug and behind the curtains. Next, they went through the filing cabinets and file folders. Meanwhile, phone calls were coming in from media across the nation: was it true the RCMP were raiding the *Sun*? Yes it was—I could see them through the glass wall; they were up to the "M" in my files. It was the first time any Canadian newspaper had been hit with the Official Secrets Act and the press were understandably curious.

Some four to five hours later they opened the top drawer of my desk and there, on top, was the envelope containing the infamous letter. They took it, signed a receipt for me, and marched out in triumph. I said something about next time I'd make it really tough for them and leave it on top of the desk.

That was the last I heard officially about the case of the purloined letter, although RCMP friends said later that they had indeed traced the source and the person, who had been motivated by concern for the country, had been fired, though not prosecuted. Apparently, he'd been caught because either the duplicating machines had been coded or certain clues are included in documents that enable easy identification of their source.

I always felt badly about this unknown person. His actions may have been wrong, but his motives were honorable and his concerns valid. He became a victim because neither of us had expected a "raid." I vowed never to be taken by surprise again. Canada clearly was into a different era.

As for the contents and charges of the letter, the PM denied them and said that General Dare was "confused" and mistaken, although both Bourne and Dare had earlier confirmed the policy. After a brief fuss in Parliament, the issue died down and today, officially, it never happened. Except that it did. One can look at Ottawa and legitimately wonder what percentage of civil servants is loyal to the concept of Canada and what percentage is loyal primarily to Quebec. Does anyone in Ottawa have any idea of who falls into which category? Certainly not the Security Service after the Dare letter . . .

When questions were raised in the House of Commons, in a burst of pique Prime Minister Trudeau branded the *Sun* as "scurrilous, inaccurate . . . venomous" and thereby assured that we'd get more publicity than usual on that day's news. It was only the latest incident in a continuing feud.

As it turned out another collision with the Official Secrets Act was to follow two years later. In 1978 Conservative MP Tom Cossitt was involved in a running security battle in Parliament. A gadfly who was unpopular within his own party because of his unrepentant hostility toward Trudeau and also Soviet subversion, he had been an executive in the Liberal riding association of Leeds, Ontario, when Trudeau was first elected. He was so offended and alarmed by Trudeau (he had read his writings) that he switched to the Conservative Party. He was elected to Parliament and until he died of a heart attack in 1982, maintained a constant barrage against Trudeau that drove the Sole Leader crazy. He was an endearing activist who, unfortunately, tended to confuse an issue because he'd start shooting before he had all the ammunition. Sometimes he made it difficult for others to join the fray without being labelled extremist and half-cocked.

For several days Trudeau fended off repeated questions from Cossitt in the House of Commons about security. Finally Cossitt asked if the Prime Minister was aware of a particular RCMP document labelled top secret, "For Canadian Eyes Only," entitled *Canadian-Related Activities of the Russian Intelligence Service*? There were warnings that Cossitt himself was risking being charged under the Official Secrets Act if he revealed such vital information, whatever it was. Many suspected it was all hot air and bluff.

At his weekly press conference in early March 1978, Trudeau stated that while the KGB might be "an enemy of Canada," the Soviet Union as a whole was a friend. He said that just as the CIA did things that the U.S. Administration might not be aware of, so might the KGB do things the Kremlin was unaware of. I then wrote a column saying that the PM was wrong to divorce the activities of the KGB from Soviet policy, and insisted that he knew it was wrong because the preamble of the document noted that under detente the Soviets were indulging in more espionage than ever before and that the KGB was an arm of Soviet policy and the greatest known threat to our security. I asked in print: "Does he [Trudeau] truly think the Soviet government can be viewed separately from its intelligence and espionage forces?"

The document in question had such wide circulation that it could hardly be regarded as "secret." Besides, I felt that neither the RCMP nor any responsible security service would include *active* or *live* cases. All would be case histories of closed files. Or so I believed. I paraphrased from this document, a copy of which had come into my possession, giving the general details of *sixteen* of the cases of Soviet espionage involving Canada and Canadians.

One case was that of a research professor who had travelled to the USSR in 1971 as a visiting scientist and been seduced by his

Intourist guide, Galina Nousinova, wife of a KGB officer. He was persuaded to smuggle a highly classified laser from the National Research Council in Ottawa to the USSR. When caught he explained he did it for love and to show good will toward the USSR. He was neither charged nor fired from his job.

Another case was that of an Armed Forces noncommissioned officer, Frank Sales, stationed at our embassy in Moscow, who was co-opted by the KGB to plant bugs in the Canadian Embassy and suggest likely recruits within the embassy. Sales was never charged but given an honorable discharge with an indexed pension—at the time of the charges against me, he was selling real estate in Victoria. He was rewarded for treason.

There was also the example of the Carleton University professor who routinely provided Captain Yevgeny Andreyevich Smirnov of Soviet Military Intelligence (GRU) with copies of all scholarly papers he received in connection with international conferences, some of them classified.

The Geyvandov affair involving the CBC's Mark Starowicz was also mentioned—and I quote in full from the RCMP document: "Active in the development of channels of influence are Soviet press representatives who frequent the House of Commons and National Press Gallery. A *Pravda* representative, Konstantin Yervandovich Geyvandov, managed to persuade a Canadian journalist to act on behalf of Soviet interests when reporting Canadian political events. In addition, Geyvandov, in a surreptitious, clandestine and intelligence-oriented way, regularly obtained from the journalist an assessment of certain events which were likely to have an impact on future Canadian policy. As a result of these activities, Geyvandov was denied a visa in 1974 to re-enter Canada following a holiday in the USSR."

And so it went: case after case of Canadians being coerced, bribed, persuaded, seduced, or trapped into working for the Soviets—information that Trudeau not only denied, but wanted withheld from the Canadian public. `

Creighton was furious that we had run the column since he felt it put the paper in jeopardy under the Official Secrets Act. As editor-in-chief I took full responsibility, believing that it was one of those situations in which the national interest demanded that we do something. We had caught the Prime Minister misleading the country in a way that endangered national security and we had an obligation to print the truth.

Within a week after the offending article and a follow-up column appeared, the *Sun*, Creighton, and I were charged under the Official Secrets Act. We ran a front-page editorial insisting that we had acted out of conscience and would continue to do so. Thus began a year of unsought publicity and preliminary hearing court appearances.

As a result of being charged, Creighton and the board of directors imposed a stringent set of rules that, in effect, gave lawyers the final decision on editorial matters. (The condition became worse after we lost a libel action brought by John Munro, Minister of Indian Affairs. A reporter who was a liar conned the *Sun* into publishing a story about alleged stock deals by Munro which turned out to be untrue. Consequently, the *Sun* became even more wary— although, in fact, it was never as aggressive or bold as its street reputation suggested.) A case can be made that newspapers are not basically interested in breaking stories that run the risk of libel. Lawyers increasingly make editorial decisions. But any paper that plays it safe and lets lawyers determine its editorial policy is no newspaper at all, and has increasingly less impact and self-respect.

With charges laid against us in an apparent head-on confrontation with the RCMP, which we usually supported editorially and philosophically, the left wing and those who viscerally oppose security were in some confusion. Could the despised *Sun* be all bad if the RCMP was prosecuting it? To some, the charges were a staged cover-up, while to others it was an indication that perhaps we really *were* our own masters. The paper made inroads into academic and intellectual areas that had hitherto been denied us; circulation jumped some 15,000 a day and stayed there.

A battery of prominent lawyers was handling the preliminary hearing: Eddie Goodman, a longtime Tory and political activist, represented the *Sun* as a corporation. J. J. Robinette, perhaps the most distinguished lawyer of his time, represented Creighton. Julian Porter, handsome, with flair and occasional flamboyance, specialized in libel but on this occasion represented me. Julian is a good friend who has no record of avoiding publicity, and I felt comfortable with his being responsible for my future. If the worst occurred, I saw myself playing second base for the Millhaven Penitentiary Angels and perhaps writing a book, fourteen years hence, on penal reform.

The lawyer who worked behind the scenes and pulled everything together was David Stockwood of the Goodman & Goodman firm, who was soon to leave and open his own office. Stockwood had been the libel lawyer for CFTO, and it was a while before he and I were used to each other. I felt that he had the wrong idea about newspapers and the law. It seemed to me that as a TV lawyer he was more concerned with keeping the station *out* of trouble, while his job with a newspaper was to help us get *into* trouble as safely as possible. In other words, not to avoid trouble, but to survive it, to reduce the odds a bit on our behalf. After some initial difficulties, Stockwood and I got on well and, from my viewpoint, he became a splendid, resourceful libel lawyer for a newspaper.

Creighton wrote me a memo saying that he considered my offending column "an act of bad faith, besides being stupid" and the height of irresponsibility and "very disappointing." I replied that I had first quoted from the document in question nearly six months earlier, with no reaction. I pointed out that very few libel cases had originated from me and that I thought the real danger was not in taking controversial stands but in letting lawyers make our editorial decisions. Although Creighton and I basically disagreed on the case and relations were strained for a while, we remained friends. Passions burned even more strongly after I went on William Buckley's TV show, "Firing Line," to discuss the case. Doug felt that this risked contempt of court. I told Buckley that while I supported the need for an Official Secrets Act, I opposed its use by governments to silence or intimidate critics. I felt the Act was designed to fight spies and traitors, not to punish dissent or silence criticism.

Creighton noted in another distressed memo that he'd watched the program "with more amazement than interest"and felt I was jeopardizing the future of the *Sun* and himself: "I can see no set of circumstances under which you could appear on the show and say the things you did without first discussing them with me . . . I am not prepared to sit still while you commit what — in my view — is contempt of court and, in the process, possibly jeopardize myself and the company." Throughout the case he was uneasy because I seemed incapable of *not* sounding off whenever a microphone was shoved in my face. He had a point. The RCMP, in the meantime, seized tapes of interviews I'd given on radio and TV.

It was the first time a Canadian newspaper had been charged under the Official Secrets Act; in fact, it was only the fourth time in Canada that the act had been used in a prosecution. A case was under way at the time against Peter Treu, an electronics wizard who'd worked on electronic defence systems for NATO. He was charged and subjected to the first all-secret trial in Canadian history, after taking documents home—with official permission. Treu was eventually freed on appeal, and his case today constitutes perhaps the greatest abuse of power a democratic government could bring against a defenceless—and innocent—citizen. The *Sun* had been the first and most ardent editorial defender of Treu against a callous, authoritarian government.

After he was cleared, Treu was broke and in debt. Five years of having to defend himself had resulted in a shattered marriage, poor health, disillusionment, loss of self-respect, no job opportunities. The government refused him any compensation. Broken and bitter, he left Canada and vowed never to return. Today he is history, seldom recalled or considered by anyone.

The two earlier cases involving the Official Secrets Act focused on espionage: the Gouzenko spy case and the case of a Pole, Tomasz Biernacki, who was sent by Polish Intelligence to Canada in 1960 and who less than a year later was caught by the RCMP, confessed, and was charged. However, the prosecution was botched and thrown out at the preliminary hearing: Biernacki had confessed to Security officers, not to the criminal investigation police. He was freed on a technicality and returned to Poland. The only Official Secrets Act convictions resulted from the Gouzenko spy disclosures.

I wasn't overly concerned about our case because I couldn't imagine a jury convicting someone who revealed the presence of espionage while the perpetrators of treason went free and were even honored by a derelict government. I thought I could prove "public interest" because the Prime Minister himself had been caught in lies and distortions about the nature of the KGB and the USSR. I looked forward to the challenge, despite the high stakes involved. Neither my co-defendant nor our lawyers were as optimistic or enthusiastic about the case as I. I had clear opinions about security and more experience with the topic than most and felt we could make a strong case before a jury.

Two weeks after I was charged, I was scheduled to have open heart surgery—a triple bypass—and there was some concern among doctors that the strain of a suit might affect the operation. My cardiologist offered to phone Justice Minister Ron Basford to

delay the court case, or perhaps delay the operation. I was appalled at the suggestion and felt the charges were more likely to
be an incentive to recover faster.

Throughout the year of off-and-on preliminary hearings, the
reaction of the rest of the media was mixed. For the most part,
the *Sun* was supported, albeit reluctantly, by those who not only
don't much like it, but actively detest it. The most ardent defender
was Pat O'Callaghan, the rambunctious publisher of the Edmonton *Journal*, who opined in print that the *Sun* was a "scapegoat"
and damned the government for vindictiveness and "its obvious
haste to silence a persistent and probably cruel critic of the Liberal
party—a newspaper that has always been a thorn in the side of
the prime minister in particular." The Toronto *Star*, closest thing
in journalism to a Liberal Party echo and virtually the last paper
to comment, came out with an editorial headlined "Toronto *Sun*
should have a fair trial"—which was reassuring, if noncommittal.
The rival *Globe and Mail* attacked the Official Secrets Act as "atro-
cious" in being "so broad, so vague, so capable of abuse . . . that
it cannot serve the public interest."

Although various East European and anti-Communist bodies
protested and demonstrated, and most newspapers editorially disapproved of what the government was doing, not once, to my
knowledge, did that bastion of freedom and human rights, the
Canadian Civil Liberties Union, ever utter a word of public protest
on behalf of the *Sun*. I once raised the question with Alan Borovoy,
general counsel for the CCLU, and he noted enigmatically that
it was a terrible thing and that he was all for us and that one of
these days the Civil Liberties Union would take a stand. But it
never did. I suspect it was because the *Sun* was anathema to the
values human rights activists espouse.

The Crown was basing its case on four examples I had written
about which allegedly jeopardized Canadian security because they
were "active" cases. The main witness for the Crown at the preliminary hearing was Chief Superintendent Mike Spooner, whom
I had not met before. But we knew *of* each other. Imagination or
not, it struck me that whenever he said anything in court that was
questionable, he'd glance in my direction—as if I should know
the truth. I finally figured that he was fudging if he looked my
way.

Eventually, Judge Carl Waisberg threw the case out, ruling that
the "top secret" document in question had been circulated to sixty-
seven bodies two years before in the United States, Britain, Aus-

tralia, and others. How could it continue to be regarded as "se-cret"? It was, to all intents, now a public document. The judge ruled that the designation "secret cannot be determined to be 'secret' by the mere stamp itself. Secrecy must lie in the very nature of the document itself . . ."

He added: "Since the Official Secrets Act is a *restricting* statute, and seeks to curb basic freedoms, such as freedoms of speech and the press, it should be given strict interpretation. The statute must, in clear and unambiguous language, articulate the restriction it intends to impose upon a citizen." The fact that the document had been so widely distributed meant it was "now 'shopworn' " and "no sufficient case is made out to put the accused on trial," Waisberg ruled.

The judge also implied that there was a certain vindictiveness or political motivation in the government's suit. In short, it was a devastating repudiation of those who'd ordered the RCMP to lay charges in the first place: the PM or the Attorney General of Canada, since only they can authorize charges to be laid under the Official Secrets Act.

There was no mention of security aspects that interested me, and I regretted that we'd never be able to explore how a security agency could dare put "live" or active security or espionage cases into what had been described by the Crown as a "teaching" doc-ument. That alone would have constituted a far greater security breach than anything I had done.

In talking to the press and TV cameras after the verdict, Creigh-ton, who had long since regained his sense of humor, noted that while he was pleased at the verdict, his co-defendant wanted to appeal. Untrue, but funny at the time.

If the case had gone to trial and *if* I had testified—and despite the wishes of the lawyers I would have had to take the stand in order to make certain points about security—I would have had to explain how I'd obtained the original top secret document in the first place. The fact was that I had received *three* copies prior to being charged—the first one the previous fall, the next two separately but in the proverbial plain brown envelope. It struck me that the number of copies I had received indicated the casual and widespread circulation of this document. At the conclusion of the case, every important media outlet in Canada mysteriously received a copy of the original document in the mail.

Why did Trudeau prosecute? My feeling is that there was great concern about a pipeline developing from the Security Service into the *Sun*. If there was substance to various allegations about Trudeau himself, the RCMP would be the most likely source for confirmation. Already there were allegations about the availability of the notorious Featherbed File, which the government has confirmed existed. It dealt with Soviet espionage inside the Canadian establishment dating back to Gouzenko days. There have long been rumors about Mr. Trudeau's personal life and ideological beliefs, which with proof the *Sun* would be the most likely to publish. And as everyone knows, the truth is not always provable, and a rumor is far less damaging than a printed fact. Therefore, anything smacking of a liaison between the Security Service and the *Sun* had to be crushed immediately and dramatically—not to punish the *Sun* so much as to warn those inside the Security Service. They had already trapped the person who had sent the purloined letter of General Dare, and by charging the *Sun* for revealing old espionage cases, would make anyone tempted to send more brown envelopes from RCMP headquarters reconsider. Whatever the reason, it worked. While I made certain that no one who gave us information would ever be identified, our sources dried up. Personally, I still wait with hope . . .

After my case was dismissed, there was considerable agitation to get the Official Secrets Act updated or scrapped altogether. Indeed, it has not proved much use in Canada in its first forty-five years of existence, and has not deterred either espionage or treason. The British Act has been used to punish critics as much as it has to curtail subversion, and judging from the plethora of espionage disclosures in Britain, another form of deterrence seems needed. It is an ill-considered act that denies an accused the right to an open trial, denies the defence access to the prosecution's evidence (if national security is involved), confers the decision to prosecute *not* to police but to politicians, and is easy to abuse.

A new or revised Official Secrets Act should change the wording "safety and interests of the state" to "safety or defence of the state." That alone, as British MP Jonathan Aitken has pointed out, is sufficient "to ensure the conviction of all spies and traitors." And prosecution *must* be removed from political contamination. Elected or partisan politicans like the Attorney General or Prime Minister should not be the ones to decide whether or not to prosecute. Their immediate political interests are not necessarily national interests.

Section 4 of the Act is iniquitous in that it makes it an offence to communicate *any* official information to *anyone* regardless of its importance or purpose. We get back to the cups of tea and color of carpets. That aspect is simply redundant in this day of presumed open government and freedom of information. Even the terminology of the Act reeks of the old-fashioned and the obsolete—repeated use of "munitions, code word, pass word, sketches, dockyards, models, plans, apparatus for wireless telegraphy, fortifications, counterfeit die, seal or stamp, mines, minefield, telegraph, telephone wireless or signal stations," and so on. Nothing about such things as computers, silicon chips, microdots. The act remains archaically lethal.

The *Globe and Mail* put it succinctly when it noted that under the Official Secrets Act "a man may be pursued, charged, tried and convicted and sentenced (to a maximum of 14 years imprisonment) and eventually released with barely a single public syllable uttered. And it doesn't stop there. A victim of the Official Secrets Act may be ordered never to discuss any matter relating to his case—on pain of prosecution—because to do so would breach an official secret." The *Globe* further noted that "an official secret is whatever the government decides it does not want the people to know." Even the Toronto *Star* eventually got around to commenting and compared the Official Secrets Act to "a poisonous snake coiled in a cupboard . . . an intolerably bad law."

Members of Parliament from all parties, Cabinet Ministers included, vowed that at the earliest opportunity the Official Secrets Act would be scrapped, changed, updated, or improved. In fact, nothing has happened. On the contrary, in 1981 by Order-in-Council—which means without debate in Parliament and, unless someone looks it up, secret legislation—Prime Minister Trudeau passed the Emergency Planning Order, which enables the government to take over *every* aspect of Canadian life in case of a national emergency of the government's definition. Why such legislation is needed now has never been explained. It virtually enables a democratic government to do what the Polish government did when it clamped down on Solidarity and the Polish people. Compared to the Emergency Planning Order, which was not necessary in the three wars Canada has participated in during this century, the Official Secrets Act is wishywashy, do-good legislation.

The day after the case against Creighton, the *Sun*, and me was dismissed, I got another brown envelope with still another copy of the not-so-top-secret document. Following the orders of the crown attorney about what one should do in such a case, I went into the street, waved down a passing police cruiser, and turned over the document to a slightly startled officer who was at first reluctant to accept it but realized something strange was up when he saw cameras taking pictures. He gave me a receipt and drove off with the offending document.

I felt by this gesture that the *Sun* and I had had the last word— until next time. Prime Minister Trudeau had been caught misleading the Canadian people, his attempts at revenge had been foiled by the courts, the *Sun*'s status had risen, and we were utterly unrepentant. One could recall Mr. Justice Caulfield's words in the 1971 British Secrets Act case over embarrassing disclosures in the Biafran War: "It may well be that prosecutions under this Act can serve as a convenient and reasonable substitute for a political trial . . . the opinion-forming and informing media like the press must not be muzzled. If the press is the watchdog of freedom, and the fangs of the watchdog are drawn, all that will ensue is a whimper, possibly a whine, but no bite. And the Press so muzzled becomes no more than the tenement of the political poor."

Small wonder, perhaps, that Pierre Trudeau was so unforgiving of the Toronto *Sun*.

28

I allow you one crazy adventure a year

DR. GARY WEBB
TORONTO
FEBRUARY 1982

In the spring of 1982 I finally got the chance to do what the Chinese had prevented me from doing in 1964: visit their country. This time it was not as a journalist per se but as a member and co-sponsor of a Canadian mountain-climbing expedition to the Chinese Himalayas near the Tibetan border, which had been closed to foreigners since the beginning of World War II. It was an unusual opportunity to be among the first foreigners to see first-hand the effect, not only of Chinese communism on an area that was ethnically Tibetan but also of the cultural and post-cultural revolutions.

There was nothing clandestine or surreptitious about my going; the Chinese were aware that I was a journalist and didn't object. In fact, the post-Mao Chinese have done such an about-face from the past that in some ways one cannot recognize China as a Communist country. The new regime has adapted to capitalistic, free enterprise ways and is skimming what foreign exchange profits it can from foreigners who are willing to pay up to $25,000 for the privilege of climbing mountains. Our mountain was Mount Gongga, which prior to the Communist revolution was called Minya Konka. Nearly 26,000 feet high, it was largely unknown as late as 1930.

It had been scaled once—in 1932 by a team of four young Americans—but no one had proof of climbing it since. The Chinese claimed to have done so in 1957, but all four of the climbers perished in an avalanche and Chinese propaganda ridiculed the earlier American triumph as a fraud (they've since acknowledged that it was real). The region had been opened to climbers only in 1981, and an American expedition had failed when it was wiped out in an avalanche that caused one death and a variety of smashed

405

bones. The following fall a Japanese expedition failed, with nine deaths. Ours was the third, and the first Canadian expedition into China. For me, the whole sequence of participating in the climb (I intended to stay mostly at base camp and not attempt the hand-over-hand stuff) had an unreal quality.

It began in the fall of 1981 when the Conservative Party pragmatist, patron of the arts, race-horse owner, tennis buff, and Himalayan trekker Eddie Goodman phoned to say that he had a wonderful idea for the *Sun* and me and that we must get together and talk publisher Creighton into it.

"What have you got in mind, Eddie?" I asked.

"Mountain climbing," he said. "I think it would be very exciting if the *Sun* were to help sponsor the first Canadian team to tackle a major Himalayan mountain in China. Great for Canadian morale . . . "

"What mountain?"

"Dunno. Tom Kierans has got one. Some climbers in B.C. want to be the first to climb it. Be wonderful publicity for Canada. Labatt's would help, too. You could go along. Be a great experience. Great story too. Really sell papers." These little bursts were typical of how Goodman talks, especially when he's enthusiastic, which is most of the time. Not much fact, but plenty of emotion.

I told Eddie I'd love to go to the Chinese Himalayas, but it was hard to see how sponsoring a mountain-climbing expedition would benefit the *Sun*. "You know, our circulation isn't as big in that area of China as you might think," I said. But Goodman missed the irony.

"I'll give you a call Monday and we'll take Creighton to lunch. After a couple of martinis he'll think it's his idea. Okay?"

"Okay, Eddie, but I have my doubts."

That was the beginning. We never had that lunch, but Goodman and Tom Kierans, who was president of McLeod, Young, Weir, a stockbrokerage firm, when he wasn't off peregrinating to Nepal with Goodman, got to Creighton and persuaded him that it would be patriotic of the *Sun* to sponsor the expedition, with me along to immortalize the triumph.

There was never any doubt on anyone's part that the mountain would be climbed. Ignorance spawns overconfidence. Mount Gongga is one of the most remote and unexplored mountains in the world, as well as one of the most lethal. Local Tibetans believe it is the home of Buddha, whom they call *Darjalutra*. Teddy and Kermit Roosevelt had written about it in 1929 (*Trailing the Giant*

Panda) and included a rough survey and map. They speculated that it might be 32,000 feet, higher than Mount Everest. That account fired the imagination of a twenty-two-year-old Harvard University student, Terris Moore, who was also a climber. It was at the worst of the Depression, jobs were scarce, opportunities few, so he and three others—Jack Young, Dick Burdsall, and Art Emmons—decided to take a year out of their lives and have a go at climbing this mysterious Chinese mountain on the fringe of Tibet. If stories of Minya Konka proved false, their intention was to head straight for Mount Everest. They never did.

The instability of China, what with the Japanese invaders, the warlords, Communists, and the central government all competing for power, didn't deter them and starting from Shanghai. They set off up the Yangtze River through warlord country toward Tibet and Minya Konka, which few had heard of and even fewer had ever seen. Although its exact location was unknown, the four reached the mountain and established good relations with lamas at a nearby lamasery to whom they paid a bag full of silver coins for the right to climb the mountain in order to burn juniper and pay homage to Buddha. After months of exploring and abortive attempts, two of the group, Moore and Burdsall, reached the top, took 360-degree photographs, and came down. Burdsall got frostbite and had to have toes amputated. Fifteen months after they set out, the four returned to America to modest acclaim. They had made the highest ascent of any American up to then.

In later years Terris Moore became president of the University of Alaska and president of the Boston Museum of Science. A former bush pilot, celebrated climber, author, lecturer, and academician, he is now retired and lives in Cambridge, Massachusetts. In his home, a large painting of Minya Konka dominates the living room. Art Emmons became a diplomat and died of cancer in 1962. Dick Burdsall, while becoming the second American to scale 23,000-foot Mount Aconcagua in the Andes in 1953, joined a rescue attempt of an Argentinian party and died of exhaustion and exposure.

In 1982 the Chinese had opened the hitherto-closed Himalayan regions to Western climbers because the need for foreign currency had become acute. For the privilege of "renting" Gongga for six weeks or so, we agreed to pay the Chinese Mountain Association (CMA) $15,000. The Chinese rented us pack horses and Tibetan carriers for something like $12 and $15 a day respectively (of which the Tibetans themselves might get a "hero" badge or food credit coupons, rather than cash, for their efforts). Mao's successors are well aware of free enterprise and the profit motive, though they still call it communism. This fact alone makes them smarter and more pragmatic than their Soviet counterparts. What the Chinese call Communist economics today bears as much resemblance to Marx or Lenin as voodooism does to the Church of England.

The leader and originator of the Canadian attempt on Gongga was Roger Griffiths, a recreation director in Vancouver, British Columbia, with some twenty years' experience in the Canadian Rockies and elsewhere. He had obtained permission from the Chinese to mount an expedition to climb Gongga, provided that he could come up with the $150,000 to $200,000 the attempt would cost. He had a team of about eleven, which eventually bloated to seventeen, including hangers-on like TV people and me. None of the climbers had been much higher than 15,000 feet. At a meeting of sponsors and principals at Toronto's Albany Club, watering place of Conservative Party diehards and nearly-deads (politically speaking), it was decided that all systems were go. Labatt breweries was the principal sponsor, possibly because Goodman was its lawyer and Labatt's president, Peter Widdrington, was also a Himalayan trekker (Nepal) with Eddie and infected by his enthusiasm. Canadian Pacific Airlines was also a sponsor, contributing free air passage for the team and nearly five tons of equipment. CP Air had agreed to participate because Air Canada was sponsoring a million dollar assault on Mount Everest in the fall and this would be a worthwhile gamble to upstage a competitor relatively cheaply.

Up to the last minute I questioned the value of the enterprise to the *Sun*, which sparked an indignant outburst from Goodman: "For Chrissake, Worthington, you made a career of going to strange places for the *Telegram* and now you hesitate about going to China for the *Sun*. Whattsa matter with you anyway?"

"Going for the *Tely* was John Bassett's money; I just don't see $50,000 worth of value for the *Sun* in what I'd write."

"God," said Creighton, "Worthington's suddenly gotten financially responsible!"

Mine being the only skeptical voice, the expedition was on. A press conference was held, and Terris Moore was brought in from Boston. I wondered half-facetiously if I was being sent to Tibet because I'd been the lone vote on the *Sun* board of directors opposing the sale of 50 percent of the paper to Maclean Hunter for $54 million, thereby exchanging our independence for financial security. Not everyone realized I was kidding. I told no one that I had already tendered my resignation as editor.

We took along a photographer, Mike Peake, who appeared in subsequent articles as my "trusty photographer" and turned out to be a gem. He'd have made a splendid infantry soldier. A four-man television crew from Extra Modern Productions also joined the expedition and their equipment accounted for nearly one-third of the luggage. One of the Goodman firm's lawyers, Kathy Robinson, tagged along until we reached base camp; she was to be a courier and bring stories and film out. I was initially grumpy about a woman passenger in what was fast becoming a battalion of bodies, but she pulled her weight and proved good company. All of us were sorry when she went home, carrying enough of my stories to con readers that these were dispatches hot off the mountain.

My one concern was my heart. After having had a triple bypass four years earlier, I was unsure whether I was being foolish. My cardiologist and friend, Dr. Gary Webb, was frank and said he didn't know what effect high altitudes had on people like me. Not much research had been done on the subject.

"Well, should I go?" I asked.

"Do you want to go?" Webb replied.

"Yes, but I also want to come back. Is it safe?"

"I don't know. The thing is, do you want me to say you can go?" Webb is a splendid doctor if you are not the nervous type.

"I guess so—but not if I'm going to fly apart or anything at 16,000 feet."

"No, I doubt you'll fly apart any more than usual. Let's see, have you done any crazy thing this year?"

"No. I went to the Galapagos a couple of years ago and rafted down the Grand Canyon before that and then went hang-gliding. But they hardly count."

"Okay. I allow you one crazy adventure a year. The mountain is this year's quota. Have a good time. If you come back, tell me about it."

Yvonne wasn't as reassured by Webb's attitude as she might have been. Nor was my surgeon, Dr. David. Yvonne phoned Webb a couple of months later to say that we were off the mountain and on our way home. "I tell you he sounded *very* relieved!" she said.

We flew to Hong Kong, then to Canton and finally Chengdu, the capital of Szechuan province, where the Chinese Mountain Association people fêted and lectured us. "Don't get too friendly with the Tibetans," they warned. "Don't buy souvenirs from them, don't give them money, don't give presents. Don't buy or trade for their silver knives, their jewellery, their distinctive fur hats. Don't do anything that might interfere with the culture. They are simple folk, unused to the ways of the world, and we must protect their culture as best we can. Understood?"

Yes, understood. Although no one said anything, it did seem ironic that the Chinese were worried about the fate of the Tibetan culture: after they'd spent the last thirty years trying to annihilate it, now they wanted to preserve it. Hypocrisy is the monopoly of no nation or culture. I suspect what the Chinese did not want was excessive contact between Tibetans and foreigners, lest the Tibetans get uppity ideas. As it turned out, the Tibetans far preferred the company of foreigners to the presence of our Chinese guides and guardians.

There was the inevitable pre-trip banquet with innumerable toasts. Our Chinese hosts repeatedly invoked the name of Dr. Norman Bethune and talked of friendship, peace, harmony. One thing the Communist Chinese have learned in dealing with Canadians is that we go all soppy at the mention of Bethune. Never mind that until the Chinese immortalized him as one of their heroes, only a select few Canadians had ever heard of him.

Bethune was a remarkable man—but in the cause of Marxism and communism, not democracy or Canada. His achievements with blood transfusions on the battlefields of the Spanish Civil War were innovative and exceptional. But Bethune was unlike George Orwell, who also fought in Spain and saw the Communists for what they were and realized, irrevocably, that they were as bad as, if not worse than, the enemy. In China Bethune helped Mao's army, not the Chinese people. He saved Communist soldiers, not innocent civilians. He was a warrior surgeon, an angry ideologue. Canadians confuse his achievements with do-goodism.

Bethune is not one of my heroes, so listening to the adulation, I wondered how to respond in a toast without prostituting myself, committing intellectual perjury, or insulting our hosts. After several glasses of powerful burning liqueur, which we dubbed Drano, I responded to a toast by saying that we in Canada had our own Great Helmsman who, like the late Great Helmsman of China, was trying to take us in a direction he thought best and who undoubtedly admired Norman Bethune as much as anyone in China. God willing, our Great Helmsman would be as successful in his ambitions as I hoped their Great Helmsman would be in his. It wasn't very clever, but it was the best I could manage at the time. Having no feeling for ideology or history, our mountain climbers wondered what this "Great Helmsman" stuff was, and automatically assumed I was drunk. Kathy Robinson understood and seemed more amused than chagrined, despite being a great supporter of Pierre Trudeau, then Canada's elected Great Helmsman who, by my terms, was wrecking the country.

For three days, we took a couple of mini-buses along the Great Tea Route toward Tibet, passing truckloads of soldiers on hairpin turns, spending nights at resthouses, and gorging on Chinese banquets, until we reached the Tibetan village of Luba at the end of the road. There we picked up our porters and horses and travelled for another three days through Himalayan passes to the Gongga lamasery, where the porters left us.

En route we had a taste of how quickly modern civilization can corrupt. The American climbing team that had preceded us and quit after losing a man had given porters sunglasses to shield their eyes from the snow. Now our porters wanted sunglasses, despite the fact that they'd been climbing these hills forever without them. The third morning out, they staged a sit-down strike until we loaned them sunglasses which, while exotic, were not functional. Mr. Liu and Mr. Wu, the two young Chinese with us, ranted and ordered to no avail. The Tibetans gazed at them impassively— and ignored them. One got a mild feeling of what it must have been like when the Chinese military tried to tame Tibet with whips and boots. The Tibetans took it all—including the killing—and quietly resisted, their religion and their stoicism sustaining them. In our case the Chinese guides, angry and humiliated at what they considered a loss of face, forced the Tibetans to continue wearing the sunglasses long after they tired of them and wanted to take them off. They were hardly worth going on strike for—but it was the principle of the thing rather than the usefulness or the need of the glasses.

The tragedy for the Tibetans was that corruption had begun on only their second exposure to foreigners. They were on their way to becoming greedy, acquisitive, dishonest. While the Chinese with their oppression and their policy of cultural genocide had been ineffectual against the Tibetans, we benign Westerners, perhaps because of our decent intentions, friendliness, and good will, were harming and changing the Tibetan culture far more than their enemies and oppressors had, or could. And we didn't even realize it. Nor, sadly, did they.

All of our group suffered varying degrees of altitude sickness. It takes a month or so at high altitudes before the blood develops sufficient red blood cells to adequately distribute oxygen through the body. The reduction in white blood cells impairs healing of cuts and scrapes, and throughout my time there, my fingertips had cuts and gouges that wouldn't heal. For anyone who hasn't experienced living and functioning at 14,000 to 18,000 feet (the highest we got on the 26,000-foot mountain), it is hard to describe the constant effort required to do the most simple tasks. There is simply no strength in the legs and they perpetually feel leaden. You move in slow motion, every step deliberate; you stop to rest, yet no relief comes. You gasp for breath without being fulfilled. Great sucking globs of air don't satisfy; rests don't improve the resiliency. In fact, it is best to keep moving slowly rather than stop. Of course the body adjusts, but if you press too hard too soon, altitude sickness can occur: your lungs fill with fluid and unless you immediately descend to lower altitudes, you literally drown.

Unfortunately, to come down from our 14,500-foot base camp, we'd have to descend to 12,000 feet, then go over a 15,000-foot pass in order to get down to 9,000 feet. And that would take four days. It meant that anyone who got seriously ill at Gongga would likely be buried there. (I'm sure that thought gave great comfort to Doctors Webb and David in Toronto.)

The second strike of Tibetan porters was potentially more serious than the first one and could have threatened the expedition. We were camped at the lamasery that Terry Moore wrote so affectionately about. Perched on a shelf at around 12,000 feet in a valley that winds upward toward Mount Gongga in the distance, the lamasery was in ruins, thanks to the Red Guards of the Cultural Revolution. The porters were to carry our supplies to the alpine plain at the base of Gongga where we planned to set up base camp. It was an unpleasant hike: down a thousand feet, then along a rocky creek bed up to 14,500 feet—a journey of a few hours with a load. The first porters went about halfway, then dumped their loads and came back to the lamasery, refusing to do any more carrying. There was no particular reason for the strike, but I suspect it was against the Chinese more than against us. Mr. Liu and Mr. Wu were mortified and at a loss. They again ordered, threatened, and pleaded, but the Tibetans remained impassive. Finally Brent Ash, the deputy leader, solved the situation by declaring that every day, the porters who made the fastest trip with the loads would be rewarded with a small pin of a Canadian flag, a package of gum, or a chocolate bar, and would have his photograph taken. The impasse was broken and from then on Tibetans were up at dawn racing the difficult terrain to be first and win a Canada pin. The profit motive had been re-invented.

The Chinese were extremely impressed with Ash's shrewd wisdom. And enormously grateful, because if the expedition failed as a result of a strike, they would be the ones to suffer when we complained. From then on, all the rules about not trading or dealing with Tibetans were forgotten, and we established full authority over the expedition. The Chinese now worked for us; instead of being suspicious watchdogs, they became enthusiastic colleagues.

As it turned out, we didn't climb the mountain. In fact, Gongga was never in much danger of being subdued by our team. For one thing, the weather turned foul after a mild, snowless winter. During a twenty-day period at base camp in the shadow of Gongga's magnificent peak on the plain we shared with a herd of yaks, we had eighteen days of intermittent blizzard and thaws. The thunderous sound of avalanches filled the days and nights and made serious climbing impossible.

We had also not allotted ourselves enough time to get adequately acclimatized to high altitudes. In a way we may have been fortunate in having bad weather, for it prevented our climbers from going too high too fast, thus incurring altitude sickness. Our planning was not all it could have been, and even though they all knew one another, our members had never climbed together as a team. But most damaging to our morale was the food. We brought in mostly space-age stuff—freeze-dried, dehydrated dinners of noodles and beef jerky, which could never be properly cooked at the high altitude and were barely edible. We had none of the fresh food that was available in the area and we had no flour, no frying pan, no kettle, no big spoons or knives.

Each team member was issued a plastic cup and bowl and a spoon. That was it. "Travel light" had been our creed, although inexplicably we did have a couple of cases of beer and a few cartons of chocolate bars, which became as coveted as gold. Our two Chinese guides and guardians and the Tibetan porters and horse-handlers, who had fresh eggs, potatoes, and green onions, lived in fear of being asked to dine with us. Food is all you basically think of when you are isolated, as we were, and meals are the only thing to look forward to. But not dried jerky and raw noodles. (Roger Griffiths disagrees vehemently with my negative assessment of the food and its effect, but as one who survived quite adequately on the starvation rations of Biafra and thought army cooking *haute cuisine*, I have considerable faith in my judgment.)

Mount Gongga simply intimidated most of our mountaineers. Some later admitted that as soon as they saw it from a distance, their confidence disappeared like spilled water on a desert. The closer we got to it, the more our faith in ourselves diminished. It was my first prolonged exposure to mountain climbers, and I hadn't realized before how fragile their egos can be, how important is the ritual of telling one another anecdotes of close calls and near-disasters. There is a comradeship, a sensual, esthetic, and psychological attraction to mountain climbing that is difficult for the outsider to identify with. There is a slightly spurious play-acting mystique to it—a sense of performance, ritual, tradition. I felt, being close to them, that one could tell, without knowing their abilities, who were the good ones, who were mediocre; who were genuine, who were sham.

But no one died and no foolish risks were taken. And given that it was arguably the world's most deadly and unforgiving mountain—fifteen deaths in five expeditions—that alone might be considered a triumph in responsible leadership. More than anything, our attempt underscored the incredible feat of Terry Moore and his Sikong expedition of 1932, which went largely unnoticed and unacclaimed except among mountain-climbing purists.

By far the most useful aspect of the expedition was that it afforded a unique opportunity to visit that part of China and observe the lives of those isolated Tibetans and their relationship with their conquerors. They have nothing but a subsistence economy, yet they seem a serene people. Despite being dominated by the Chinese, they are not in the least subservient. Without any doubt the kindest thing one could do for them would be to leave them alone. The most appreciated foreign aid would be nothing—neither Western nor Chinese. They still plow their fields with yaks or young girls harnessed to wooden plows, and whole villages (or "production units," as the Chinese now call villages) gather to do the work in an atmosphere of conviviality and gossip. The people shun the

modern Chinese clothing of blue or olive or grey sameness and
opt for traditional dress of black robes with six-foot sleeves (for
carrying things) that wrap around their bodies. They wear dashing
fur hats at rakish angles, with tufts of color and splashes of silver.
Every man carries a silver dagger, every woman wears turquoise
and silver jewellery. Despite all they've been through, their spirit
isn't quenched, and there is more animation and exhilaration in
their manner than is in the drab cloned effect of the Chinese
whose clothing, short hair, and expressionless official faces mask
every thought and emotion.

The Cultural Revolution was particularly hard on the Tibetans;
indeed since 1948 the Chinese have tried in varying ways and with
varying intensity to eliminate the Tibetan culture, desecrating their
lamaseries, destroying the prayer flags that adorn the hills—with
each flap of a flag another prayer is released into the world—and
wrecking their *mani* piles of stones with prayers laboriously carved
on them (custom dictates that you must pass on the left side, never
the right, else incur the wrath of the god *Darjalutra*).

The lamasery that so impressed Terry Moore and his three
companions in 1932 when it was a flourishing outpost of religious
fervor impressed us in 1982 as a monument to the obscenity of
the Cultural Revolution. That the violence and violation could
extend this far into the outer regions of China made us realize
how widespread and relentless it must have been. Though the
buildings were in ruins, frescoes of dragons and Buddhas on the
walls were bright and seemingly immune to weather. The Tibetan
porters would not burn wood from rafters, but instead chose to
scramble miles in the hills for twisted branches and what scraps
of dead shrubbery they could scrounge for fuel. They viewed
anything connected with the lamasery as holy, and we quickly
adopted their ethic and respected the ruins. At first our Chinese
guides casually used the wood of the ruins for fires; then they,
too, almost by osmosis, ceased and began scrambling the hillsides
for wood to burn.

There are now hopes of rebuilding the lamasery, and while no
one can live in the rubble, a Tibetan monk and his family live in
a black tent nearby and daily conduct prayers and make offers to
Darjalutra, who presumably looks down from his home atop the
peak of Mount Gongga, ten miles off. Since Mao's death, the
velvet-glove policy with Tibet has resulted in much more cor-
diality. If they don't welcome the Chinese presence, the Tibetans
at least tolerate it. The Chinese patiently send roving schoolteach-

ers from village to village (or production unit to production unit), seemingly prepared to invest a few centuries in bringing Tibetans into the fold of the ant-like society of modern China.

Now, with Peking's present pragmatism and cautious tolerance of Tibetan culture, the prayer flags have reappeared, this time higher on hillsides and less accessible. The *mani* piles have also reappeared, larger and more defiant than before. The ravaged lamaseries are being rebuilt. The Tibetans still smile, are still serene, as resilient as time itself, and are still quietly hostile to the Chinese interlopers whom, for the moment, they have defeated by merely surviving.

I found the close-up look at Chinese communism both reassuring and distressing. Reassuring in that, while I see very little that is redeeming in any form of communism, the Chinese version is utterly different in personality from the Soviet version. I am not sure they were ever as similar as they were different, even when Stalin was a folk tyrant in both countries and before Khrushchev shattered the myth. Foreign admirers—or detractors—of both systems tend to see what they want. It is characteristic for the visitor to Communist countries to go overboard in "admiration" if people or officialdom are pleasant and helpful. Visitors can also be unforgiving if restaurant service is poor or clothes are drab. Perhaps a reason that Western academics are so prone to identify with Soviet Marxism has been because the Soviet system pays homage to them, treats them as elite. And look at how many Western clergy saw hope and inspiration worthy of emulation by Christians everywhere in the example of China during the height of the Cultural Revolution. Many did not even see what was going on when it was happening before their eyes.

I think Chinese communism would be intolerable to live under. With a billion people, China is reduced to a society of ants— everyone busily and mindlessly striving for the group, not the individual. This may be necessary in an overpopulated country. However, while it is a harsh, totalitarian system that has methodically killed millions of its own people, China does not pose the world-wide threat that the Soviet Union does. Its agents are not tirelessly working for the destruction of other systems.

The evidence of more than sixty years of Sovietism is that the USSR intends to someday rule the world; no country has *ever* maintained such a long-lasting campaign of subversion, deceit, and aggression against every other nation. Power is both the means and the end. It may also be the only hope of the system to survive.

The Soviet Union uses external enemies—for the most part imagined—to justify the hardships and deprivation it imposes on its own people. And when it has conquered the world (not by force of arms but by intimidation, fear, and blackmail) its citizens will have no outside example to aspire to or envy and will be easier to control. The regime need answer to no one. Ironically, China more than any other country recognizes the global threat of the USSR. China has always looked inward rather than outward, and a case can be made that with such a huge population and limited food resources, there has to be a form of dictatorship—preferably benign, but not necessarily so.

The irony is that by seeing "people" as China's greatest resource and weapon and encouraging a population explosion, Mao Tsetung (or Maozedong as Pinyin style now insists) built China into a modern force, but also made it impossible for that country to cope with itself. With its population beyond control, it must either expand its territory or eliminate a large proportion of its people. Right now it makes a fetish of family planning: fines for more than one child and penalties increasing for additional children. This has already resulted in the revival of infanticide of the bad old days. Those internal problems are not a threat to the west . . . yet.

Even so, being in China as a visiting foreigner is not as oppressive as being in the USSR. The relentless gloom of the Soviet Union—the soulless system of cheating, corruption, and meanness—is not reflected in China. Despite the assembly-line similarity of every Chinese—even all the bicycles tend to be painted black—there is more animation, cheerfulness, humor. You do not see the omnipresent police and army. Controls may indeed be even more rigid, but the *appearance* of police-state totalitarianism is missing.

I suppose a major difference between Soviet communism and Chinese communism is their response to change. The Soviets change direction with agony, reprisals, purges, and blame. When the Chinese change direction, they do so without the bombast and justification. They pretend they haven't. Although Mao's latter years were a disaster for China and he has become irrelevant, his statues still stand, his name is still respected. Stalin is also still honored in China—but ignored. An example of the transitory effect of the Cultural Revolution—where playing Beethoven or Mozart could be a capital offence—is that today in the villages, the loudspeakers play, in that distinctive tinkle-tinkle style, "Ave Maria" and "Red River Valley." No one bats an eye. Of course, reversals can occur quickly in totalitarian countries, and there is no guarantee that conditions won't become harsh again. But right now China is practising a form of totalitarian capitalism and abandoning the perversions of Marxist economics. The farmers or peasants are doing what they've done for centuries, and it is hard to see how Chinese agriculture could be made more efficient than it now is.

On our last day in the Tibetan region before taking mini-buses back to Chengdu and civilization, some of us wound up in one of the massive stone houses chatting in sign language with several generations of one family and eating potatoes baked in the open fire. Underneath the second-storey living space the yaks were kept, their body heat rising to help warm the room and the communal beds of the Tibetans. I watched an old man meticulously working on a scroll with paintbrushes and peering squint-eyed through an ancient pair of round steel-rimmed spectacles, the glass part the size of twenty-five-cent pieces. I asked to see them, and they barely magnified. On impulse I gave him my $6.95 Woolworth glasses that were straight magnification. He tried them on and his face lit up. It was like a miracle as suddenly the old fellow saw a world that had long since grown dim. He had twice been to Lhasa on pilgrimage and was much respected for his holiness and his artistry. I felt good knowing that for perhaps the next century my Woolworth glasses might enable a family in the remote Himalayas to see better and continue their fine painting and scrollwork. For a short time I knew how missionaries must feel: it is a very selfish if satisfying emotion.

Upon my return to Canada I wrote a series for the *Sun* which, while critical was, I felt, fair. Nonetheless it incurred the displeasure of the expedition, which somehow felt betrayed. I had tried to warn them that trusty photographer Mike Peake and I were wearing two hats, one as team members emotionally involved in the project, the other as journalists on a story. I felt that in the unlikely event another sponsor could be found, they'd do better next time.

Tom Kierans, who had encouraged the climb and who likes winners, was scathing in his condemnation of the expedition, unfairly calling it a disaster, a con job, and so on. But it wasn't all failure. The subsequent film, with broadcaster Patrick Watson narrating, salvaged something and painted defeat in heroic terms. Otherwise it bore little resemblance to the real thing. I was gratified at having finally made it to China, richer in knowledge and experience, but still not sure it was worth the $50,000-plus that it cost the *Sun* to expose me to Tibetans, and vice-versa.

As for Eddie Goodman who made the original phone call, he couldn't recall trying to persuade me or the *Sun* to participate.

29

The final triumph of Igor Gouzenko
over the Soviet system

TORONTO SUN
JULY 2, 1982

In one version of his perpetually recycled memoirs, Malcolm Muggeridge recalls his wartime days as a member of Britain's Secret Intelligence Service when he was being instructed in the way to send secret messages in an emergency. The chap told him that pigeon droppings, dissolved in water, made an ink that when dried was invisible until heated with the flame of a match, at which point the writing became visible. Muggeridge was shown how the resourceful agent could accidentally drop his handkerchief on some pigeon droppings and scoop them up unnoticed for use later in making invisible ink, when apparently casually strolling through the streets (presumably of the country being spied upon).

Muggeridge wrote that at that moment he realized British Intelligence didn't yet trust him, was testing him, and that someday they'd end the charade and let him in on the inner workings instead of the make-believe stuff. Only later did he realize that indeed what he was going through was the real thing. That realization made him wonder even more how we won the war. Finally, he realized that whatever inanities were being practised by our side, the enemy was being just as bizarre, if not more so.

I thought of Muggeridge at the funeral of Igor Gouzenko in 1982 which was a mixture of Evelyn Waugh and Monty Python.

Present at the funeral home were Gouzenko's family of ten grown children and their respective spouses and children. The only outsiders were myself, the lawyer and the minister, a veteran of World War II who wore his campaign ribbons. We all knew whose funeral it was, yet the minister maintained the fiction of Gouzenko to the end, referring to him as "Mr. Brown," the public cover-name he had used for most of thirty-eight years. The minister eulogized him as "a man from Czechoslovakia" who found peace and happiness in Canada. Try as I would, I could not understand the need for such secrecy when everyone there knew who he was. But old habits die hard. He was buried in a cemetery a few miles from his home and as the funeral procession raced along the Queen Elizabeth Way at sixty miles an hour, most of the funeral flags blew off. Instead of being inconspicuous, the procession was a Keystone Cops skit, racing at breakneck speed to the cemetery, causing heads to turn and everyone to wonder who was being buried in such a hurry. Gouzenko was buried posthaste, and everyone departed as if at any moment the KGB or the press might materialize.

As it was, the press almost found out. That morning, unaware of Gouzenko's death, I had been on the phone to the Toronto *Sun*'s associate editor (later my successor as editor) Barbara Amiel, who was on her way to do a free-lance radio commentary. My assistant, Christina Blizzard, handed me a note in some agitation and whispered, "Peter Brown has just died." I blinked uncomprehendingly, at which point Chris's voice dropped a notch: "Peter Brown, you know . . . *Igor Gouzenko*," and her eyes darted nervously around. "His wife wants you to call."

I broke off my conversation with Amiel by telling her that Gouzenko had just died. The news apparently so shattered Amiel, who appreciated his true value, that she promptly scrapped her prepared script and went on radio with a tribute to him and the enormous contribution he had made to Western security. At first, the radio station didn't realize the significance of Gouzenko and tried to talk her out of using the item. But Amiel insisted. Within minutes, other radio stations picked up the news and were calling the station. Amiel, flustered at the stir, immediately gave me as the source of information. The media and news agencies began calling me—as did the RCMP, which also knew nothing of the death. The trust company in charge of Gouzenko's affairs had not been informed either and was soon on the phone. I was in a quandary and somewhat irritated at being upstaged. I answered all queries by telling everyone to ask Amiel, since she was making these announcements. But the news was out. Amiel had managed to scoop her own newspaper. From that moment the reporters and copy editors at the *Sun* began calling her "Scoop." It was my fault for speaking in the first place, and after I cooled down it *did* seem ironic that fifteen years of friendship with Gouzenko had resulted in everyone recording his death before the one paper that had consistently taken him seriously and championed his cause.

In 1943, Igor Gouzenko, a lieutenant in the GRU (Soviet Military Intelligence), was assigned to the Soviet Embassy in Ottawa as a cipher clerk responsible for encoding and decoding espionage messages between Moscow headquarters and one of several Soviet spy rings operating in Canada at that time through the embassy. Two years later Gouzenko selected over 100 documents from embassy files that detailed the workings of a spy ring headed by the military attaché, Colonel Nikolai Zabotin (later recalled by Stalin and executed), turned them over to the Canadians, and asked for asylum. The story of Gouzenko's difficulties in obtaining sanctuary and being taken seriously are legendary. When he tried to give the documents to the Ottawa *Journal*, the night editor viewed him as a crank and advised him to go to the local police, who in turn suggested the RCMP. Justice Minister (later Prime Minister) Louis St. Laurent refused to see him. When Prime Minister Mackenzie King learned of the defection, his first reaction was one of horror and a desire to give Gouzenko and the papers back to the Soviets.

It was only when the staff (NKVD and GRU) of the Soviet Embassy broke into Gouzenko's apartment and Gouzenko with his wife and baby were given refuge by a neighbor who was in the Royal Canadian Air Force that Canadian authorities realized something unusual was happening and acted. William Stephenson, who had headed Britain's Intelligence liaison in North America during the war, happened to be near Ottawa, intervened on Gouzenko's behalf and stiffened the government's sagging spine. Intrepid hid the Gouzenkos at mysterious Camp X, near Oshawa, Ontario, the hush-hush camp for agents training to be parachuted into occupied Europe.

Mackenzie King's diaries (selective and heavily edited, but still devastating reading) reveal that he wanted Gouzenko followed and was even hoping that the defector might commit suicide. If he did, his papers could be seized, copied, and returned to the Soviet Embassy. King and his advisors—notably Norman Robertson, then deputy minister of External Affairs, and later the powerful Clerk of the Privy Council—felt that Gouzenko's defection would make the Soviets angry at Canada and could lead to war. In reporting the defection to the prime minister, Robertson called it "a most terrible thing . . . " King felt strongly that Stalin would never knowingly permit espionage to be carried out by his embassy in a friendly country like Canada. ("I don't believe his [Gouzenko's] story about their [the Soviet Union] having avowed treachery," King told his diary.)

When the subsequent Royal Commission Inquiry into the Gouzenko evidence was completed, Norman Robertson wanted to give the report to the Soviet Embassy immediately. This intention "amazed" Prime Minister King, who told his diary that "It shows how tired he [Robertson] is, or he could never have thought of letting a document of the kind get into the hands of the enemy before it was even presented to Parliament." For his part, Gouzenko went to the grave suspecting that Norman Robertson was part of the Soviet conspiracy: a fellow traveller at best, a Soviet agent at worst. "He never liked me and I could feel that he was uncomfortable and afraid when near me," Gouzenko told me dozens of times. King's diaries repeatedly reveal that Robertson was reluctant to believe ill of the USSR and had difficulty accepting that Colonel Zabotin headed an espionage ring. "This man had been one of the pleasantest that he, Robertson, had had to deal with," King wrote. At first King planned to go to Moscow to explain personally to Stalin what naughty things were going on in the Ottawa embassy. It seems criminally naïve in retrospect, but the depth of ignorance, wishful thinking, and lack of understanding about espionage, security, and the Kremlin has since been reflected in a succession of Canadian governments. Attitudes are similar today; only the manifestations are slightly more sophisticated and subtle.

Mackenzie King, a dedicated spiritualist who regularly consulted his dead mother (which the press of those days *never* reported, though it was well known), came almost to deify Gouzenko as a messenger from God to warn the free world about the evils of Soviet communism. And King eventually saw himself in heroic terms. "It can honestly be said that few more courageous acts have ever been performed by leaders of the government than my own in the Russian intrigue against the Christian world and the manner in which I have fearlessly taken up and begun to expose the whole of it," he confided to his diary. He even began referring to the USSR as "the enemy."

Curiously only one volume of some fifty diaries that Mackenzie King wrote has vanished: it is the one dealing extensively with Gouzenko's defection and the reactions of senior people in Ottawa. It is now known that many in the civil service of that day were excessively sympathetic to Marxism and the left and would go to great lengths to have the USSR presented in a positive light. Those with suspicious natures wonder if the missing King diary might not have contained damaging or embarrassing observations that some in power today would not like disseminated or discussed before the public. There are those who think the diary in question was not lost but stolen or destroyed.

Despite his high-level support after a shaky start in his new country, Gouzenko had a rough time throughout his thirty-eight years in Canada. He was never fully appreciated. Instead, he was regularly maligned or sniped at by the media, by "intellectuals," even from within the RCMP Security Service itself. At various times he was depicted as opportunistic, venal, grasping, paranoid, erratic, unstable, unwholesome, and so on. When he died of a heart attack in his home on the outskirts of Toronto in the spring of 1982—blind from diabetes and in the middle of conducting a mock symphony he was listening to on radio—his family was, as usual, secretive.

Gouzenko is still largely unrecognized for his contributions. He not only revealed the activities of one of several spy rings operating in Canada (and supplied information that tied in with such people as Alger Hiss, formerly of the U.S. State Department, Harry Dexter White in Treasury, the Rosenbergs, the Philby network, and Klaus Fuchs and the atomic spies), but his presence revealed much about Canada that could have been investigated. As a result of his revelations in 1945, some twenty Canadians went on trial for espionage-related offences, half of whom were convicted, including Sam Carr and Fred Rose, MP, the only professional, Soviet-trained spies caught and prosecuted in Canada since World War II. At least five Soviet agents identified in the Royal Commission report at the time only by their cover names were never prosecuted but went on to enjoy successful careers in espionage for the Soviet Union. Undeniably, Gouzenko provided the most significant post-war espionage breakthrough; his disclosures resulted in the West's attitude toward Soviet benevolence being changed forever. The wartime Grand Alliance of the USSR and the West was finally dead and buried by Gouzenko's revelations of perfidy.

In the light of such information, it is ironic that no country in the free (or partly free) world has a record as dismal as Canada's for failing to catch and prosecute Soviet spies. And no country is as regularly used by the Kremlin as an espionage centre or as a cover for its spies. Most of the big Soviet spy cases since 1920 have in some way involved Canada, and the Canadian passport is notorious as an essential part of espionage equipment. The Sorge ring in Japan (which tipped off Stalin about Hitler's plans to invade) carried Canadian passports; Colonel Abel entered the United States using Canadian cover; Leon Trotsky's assassin carried a Canadian passport (acquired from a Canadian killed in the Spanish Civil War), as did Gordon Lonsdale (Colonel Konon Molody), the Kruger couple, and Tito when he was with the pre-war Comintern; the Lucy ring, which fed Stalin the battle plans of the *Wehrmacht* throughout World War II, was financed through Canada. And so on, through the seemingly endless examples of Soviet subversion of friends, neutrals, and foes alike. Apart from occasionally expelling Soviet diplomats and charging a handful of homespun traitors, Canada has traditionally been reluctant to bring Soviet spies to account.

Canada's failure to catch and prosecute Soviet spies operating illegally reveals one of three possibilities:
- There are no Soviet spies here—which is clearly ludicrous;
- Canadian Security simply can't catch them;
- Security can catch them, but the government won't prosecute them—which is the case.

Canada doesn't want to catch spies or traitors, either because it thinks that doing so might be seen as an unfriendly act and annoy the Kremlin to the point where it might refuse to purchase our wheat—or because our system is thoroughly infiltrated with secret Soviet sympathizers.

This reality constantly bothered Gouzenko and people like me who knew something of Soviet reality and were deeply offended at espionage and treason. To Gouzenko it was a clear indication that Canadian government and security organs were deeply and thoroughly penetrated by the Soviet agents. He rarely shirked saying so, and this, combined with everything else, brought him only ridicule. As a consequence, Gouzenko was often suing people to clear his name. The myth took root that Gouzenko's income was largely gained by suing; this was grossly untrue but so often repeated, along with other canards, that he felt forced to sue again to clear his name. At the time of his death at age sixty-three he had four suits pending, all of them winnable. His concern was that if he didn't protect his name, no one else would. ("My name is all I have and if I don't defend it, no one else will," he'd say. "By clearing my name I am also damaging Soviet subversion.")

His cause was complicated by the fact that some of those who spread falsehoods about him were inside the RCMP Security Service itself, unquotable sources who'd tell reporters on the sly that Gouzenko was an alcoholic (he didn't drink), that he was a spendthrift (he had little money), that he'd blown millions he'd gotten from his books and from the government (the government gave him nothing until he'd been in Canada almost fifteen years and was on the brink of poverty). For instance, John Sawatsky, in his otherwise competent book *Men in the Shadows*, quotes unnamed RCMP personnel as saying he was a drunk and disreputable; David Martin's *Wilderness of Mirrors* repeats similar untruths. Of considerable interest would be the sources of these allegations, whom the authors quote anonymously.

Gouzenko got settlements, but none of them was large. His award-winning novel in 1954, *Fall of a Titan*, earned him some $74,000, but nothing from movie rights, which were never picked up. His first ghost-written book, *This Was My Choice*, was translated into a dozen languages and became a Hollywood movie, *The Iron Curtain*, starring Dana Andrews and Gene Tierney, now the property of the midnight TV movie set. He wrote a sequel to *Fall of a Titan* called *Ocean of Time*, but it was never published. He once sought to get a Canada Council grant to pay for the translation from Russian to English, but was rejected. At that time I was with the Toronto *Telegram* and fumed in print that he was the only winner of Canada's highest literary honor, the Governor-General's award for fiction (and also a nominee for a Nobel Prize in Literature) to be rejected out of hand as not having sufficient talent! Gouzenko was turned down in 1961-62 with a form letter over the signature of Canada Council director A. W. Trueman. I tried to persuade him to reapply in 1969, but he'd been so humiliated in the past that he wasn't interested. I was thinking primarily of the potential story of his being rejected again, which I was sure he would be, in a year in which a former member of the Central Committee of the Canadian Communist Party (Stanley Ryerson) got a grant to write a "Marxist interpretation" of Canadian history, and Marxist student activists were getting grants. When he died, Gouzenko had completed some eighty volumes of memoirs in Braille, plus thousands of pages of diaries and novels and observations of an ever-wary lifetime in Canada.

Ironically, at the time of his death, Gouzenko was emerging from the shadows into renewed prominence, thanks in large part to the explosion of espionage and treason revelations in Britain, as if in echo to his forlorn cry in the postwar years.

I first met Gouzenko in 1967 after I returned to Toronto from my two-year stint in Moscow. One day he appeared at the *Telegram* unannounced. For security reasons, he'd never give warning of coming, and this made luncheon appointments a haphazard, impromptu affair. Someone on the news desk said, "Pete, Mr. Brown is here to see you."

I was writing something and didn't want to be distracted. "Jeez, get someone else to see him, will you?"

"You don't understand: Mr. Brown, *Peter* Brown, you know . . . *Peter Brown* . . . "

"No I don't know. Who's Peter Brown?"

"Peter Brown, you ass"—and the voice dropped conspiratorially—"Gouzenko. Igor Gouzenko. Peter Brown . . . "

"Oh. *That* Peter Brown. Why didn't you say so?"

Every newspaper person of a certain generation knew Gouzenko by sight, knew that he called himself Peter Brown, knew that they had to pretend not to know him. He himself never realized that everyone in the newsroom recognized him. To the end he played out the Peter Brown myth, but I'd always forget and have to be reminded until finally, at the *Sun*, Margaret K. on the switchboard would call and say, "You-Know-Who is here to see you." Somehow, You-Know-Who was easier to remember than Mr. Brown.

In 1967 Gouzenko arrived at the *Tely* to talk about Moscow. He expressed surprise that I could write from there as freely as I had and be as critical of the system as I was. He had watched my metamorphosis from vague neutrality to hostility and repugnance for the Soviet system, though not for the Soviet people.

Gouzenko had several things on his mind when I first met him: a vastly inadequate pension from the government, granted by John Diefenbaker, which he felt should be increased; and the conviction that the RCMP Security had been penetrated by the Soviets and even the upper levels, reaching into the commissioner's office, were not secure from modernday Philbys. He was convinced that Prime Minister Pearson hated him and was possibly a Soviet agent. Superimposed on this was his continuing theme of a five-point plan to get other Soviets with useful information to defect to the West. Rather than dismiss Gouzenko's allegations out of hand, I used to listen to his reasoning and examine his theses. Often, if one examined his material with an open mind, one was forced to some very unsettling conclusions. It was more comfortable, but not necessarily accurate, to dismiss him as a crank.

For instance, Gouzenko wrote a memo in 1952 at the request of British Intelligence based on what he had heard from the chit-chat of other cipher clerks at Moscow "Centre" in Ottawa, which clearly indicated the presence of a high-level Soviet spy inside British Intelligence. In hindsight, it seemed that Gouzenko had provided an uncanny lead to Philby. But Philby was MI6 (Intelligence) while Gouzenko always insisted *his* spy was MI5 (Security); MI6 was offensive—information-gathering, espionage, while MI5 was defensive—counterespionage, stopping spies. A distinct difference. Regardless, the memorandum was a classic bit of astute analysis by a first-class brain. Reading it reinforced the shame that the RCMP had never used Gouzenko's talents, but let them lie fallow and vegetate for the whole of his life in Canada.

I published the memo in the *Telegram* and it was later picked up by the London *Times*, which began to wonder about a fourth and fifth man now that Philby had been identified as the third man who had tipped off Soviet spies Guy Burgess and Donald Maclean that their days were numbered and they had better do a bunk to Moscow. I speculated that there were unknown traitors in Britain who had possibly been knighted and retired with honors who might have been caught, had Gouzenko's warnings been heeded. It was a decade later that Sir Anthony Blunt, the Queen's art advisor and former intelligence officer confessed to treason— and was granted immunity from prosecution.

As for Lester Pearson, in 1953 he had shown inexplicable hostility toward Gouzenko when the U.S. Senate Internal Security Subcommittee, headed by Senator William Jenner, sent a formal note to the Canadian government asking to interview Gouzenko. This request followed on the heels of an interview in which Gouzenko told Eugene Griffin of the Chicago *Tribune* that he had information he'd like to give the Americans.

Pearson, then Canada's Minister for External Affairs, refused the American request saying that Gouzenko had been misquoted by the Chicago paper, that he had nothing new to offer, and that was that. It was at the height of McCarthyism in the United States and Canadians generally didn't like what was going on there. Besides, Pearson had recently defended Canada's ambassador to Japan, Herbert Norman, who had been named a member of a Communist study group and was even suspect as a Soviet agent. Pearson supported his friend Norman in and out of the privileged confines of Parliament, insisting that there was no evidence to justify suspecting him as a security risk and that "exhaustive" security screenings had cleared him. As it turned out, there had been vitually *no* security checks on Norman, and what there had been had turned up abundant evidence to warrant concern about his security reliability. Even those in the U.S. hearings who had identified Norman as a member of Communist cells—not vindictively, but in passing—were never questioned by RCMP Security.

In the middle of the controversy, Gouzenko approached the Toronto *Telegram* and wrote a bylined article to the effect that Griffin had quoted him accurately in the Chicago *Tribune*, that he *did* want to testify to the Americans. While it was true that he had no new information, he did have "advice," ideas, and suggestions that the Americans might find useful. It was not the Americans who were telling untruths, it was Mr. Pearson, said Gouzenko.

The Americans sent another note requesting an interview. Pearson responded by saying that, of course, Gouzenko was free to speak with whomever he wished, but if he testified to the Americans he might forgo all the security and protection that Canada was providing. Gouzenko responded (in another article) saying that faced with the alternatives of his continued security and safety or not testifying, he chose safety for the sake of his family. It was a pity, he said, because he felt his testimony might assist Western security.

It was finally agreed that the subcommittee could talk to Gouzenko if he was interviewed in Canada and if a Canadian official attended the meeting to make sure that Gouzenko named only Americans. If any individuals other than American citizens were named, the referee would forbid reference to them. Gouzenko later expressed the opinion that he thought Pearson and others were frightened that he would inadvertently, or unwittingly, identify traitors in Canada that even he, Gouzenko, didn't realize he knew.

The transcript of Gouzenko's testimony to the Americans contains such intriguing tidbits as the following statement: "When I was in Moscow in general headquarters, I mentioned one agent from whom a telegram would come, was in (name of organization deleted); it talked of a man in (name of organization deleted) which is (name of organization deleted)." It now seems that the organization being referred to was Britain's MI5, and the man Anthony Blunt or someone as yet unknown or unidentified.

Gouzenko always felt that a motor accident was to have occurred en route to his rendezvous with the U.S. Security subcommittee. He took along a friend as witness to whatever might happen.

Paranoiac, perhaps, yet Gouzenko managed to live a long time and died peacefully, which is more than many defectors from Soviet espionage manage to do.

Gouzenko never forgave Pearson (and vice-versa?). Even John Diefenbaker came to believe that Pearson was behaving suspiciously in the Norman/Gouzenko affair. In his book, *Special Counsel*, former lawyer for the U.S. Senate Security subcommittee, William Rusher (later publisher of William F. Buckley's *National Review*), identifies Pearson, though he doesn't name him, as a suspected Soviet sympathizer. He also scrutinizes Herbert Norman's astonishing behavior as a possible Soviet spy. Elizabeth Bentley, a courier for the Soviets, identified Pearson as one of the Soviet contacts in the Canadian Embassy in Washington (Norman was another). And so the mystery remains.

Norman's Communist connections were to come up again in 1956-57 when he was ambassador to Egypt. As he had done in 1953, Pearson vehemently denied that there was any substance to Communist allegations ("rumors, suspicions and slander which we reject as unfounded").

Conventional wisdom is that Norman, a decent, sensitive man, was hounded to suicide by McCarthyism and Communist witch-hunters in the United States. If one looks at the evidence available since the day in 1957 when as Canada's ambassador to Egypt he jumped from the roof of a Cairo building to his death, one comes to a different conclusion. For years I assumed that he was guilty of dabbling in espionage for the Soviets. And indeed he may have been. But that wasn't what drove him to suicide. In fact I think he was committing his version of *hara-kiri*, doing the honorable thing to save his friends and defenders from embarrassment as befits a scholar of Japanese history and culture. In my opinion he was driven to suicide by his great friend, Lester Pearson, who made it impossible for him to continue living.

Pearson's lies to the public defending Norman and in fact denying what many already knew, put Norman in an intolerable position. If he supported Pearson, he'd have to lie, too, and everyone he cared about would know it; if he admitted his Marxism, he'd be betraying Pearson. His only escape with honor was to commit suicide. In other words, he was Pearson's victim, not McCarthy's. He should *never* have been put into such security-sensitive jobs as Pearson put him in. And then Pearson lied to save his own skin—something he did with some regularity, if one examines his record and the accounts of people like Judy La-

Marsh, a cabinet minister under Pearson. It was only *after* Norman committed suicide in 1957 that Pearson acknowledged the association.

It's possible that Pearson was trying to defend the reputation of his friend Norman and other idealists who had been temporarily mixed up with Marxism and communism. Years later it was acknowledged that Norman *had* been a Communist Party member at Cambridge at the time of Blunt, Burgess, Maclean, Straight, James Klugman, John Cornford (the only Cambridge Communist killed in the Spanish Civil War) among others. Other Canadians who subsequently rose to senior heights in the civil service were in the same group at Cambridge. None of this means that they were all Soviet agents, just Soviet sympathizers.

Twenty years after his death, the truth finally began to emerge. In his book *Six Journeys* author-lecturer Charles Taylor described Norman's Marxist links when he was at Cambridge in the 1930s and joined the Communist party. He was still attending Marxist study groups when he went to Harvard and wrote "the study of American Capitalism from a Marxist point of view." In a letter to his brother in 1937 he wrote: " . . . the real standard bearer for humanity, for liberty and man's right to develop freely—is communism."

In his 1983 book, *Reading from Left to Right*, H. S. Ferns, professor emeritus at Britain's University of Birmingham and a former Canadian civil servant, recalls how Norman was well known in External Affairs and among friends as a Marxist. ("Herbert had been a Communist in his youth, which everyone concerned with the matter including Herbert himself admitted . . . ") In fact, it turns out that *everyone* in a position to know was aware he was a Marxist. Professor Ferns expressed the view that "a change in the political climate in the United States may very well produce a spate of right-wing charges that Herbert Norman was not only a Communist, but a Soviet spy." However, the basic issue was that Norman was a security *risk*, not a security breach.

Curiously, Pearson bore lifelong resentment toward Sir William Stephenson, who probably saved Gouzenko from being returned to the Soviets when he defected. Pearson seemed determined that Sir William should *not* receive the Order of Canada, which he himself instigated to honor citizens who have performed outstanding service to the country. It wasn't until the nine-month government of Conservative Joe Clark in 1979 that Sir William received his long-overdue Order of Canada, making his own country the last of the wartime Allies to honor its secret warrior. Needless to say, Gouzenko never received the award, despite being repeatedly nominated for it and being credited by Mr. Justices Robert Taschereau and R. L. Kellock who headed the Royal Commission on Security with having "rendered great service to the people of this country and thereby placed Canada in his debt."

For a while I was inclined to dismiss Gouzenko's wariness of Pearson as overreaction or personal dislike. However, facts kept intruding. I found Pearson's three volumes of memoirs astonishing in what they omitted. (The third volume, published after his death, was ghost-written by his son Geoffrey and others and therefore not *real* memoirs.) To me, memoirs are recollections of important events in one's life; yet Pearson omitted any mention of his feud with Gouzenko; he didn't record Norman's suicide and his feelings at the time; and there was no mention whatever of Soviet espionage courier Elizabeth Bentley. Why would Pearson omit any mention of such significant events—if not world-shaking, then certainly personally memorable? If one wants to block out such memories, one shouldn't write memoirs. To me these omissions are inexplicable.

When Gouzenko sought to testify at the Royal Commission on Security, which published a report in abbreviated form in 1969, his request was refused. The commissioners did not want to hear what he had to say and did not think he had anything relevant to offer, even though they were in a position at the time to know that the KGB had recently attempted to assassinate him and the British were gearing up to re-interview him about their espionage concerns. Perhaps it was because there was no interest in hearing Gouzenko's views on the new Prime Minister of Canada, Pierre Elliott Trudeau, which were unfashionable in the surge of Trudeaumania engulfing the country.

When Trudeau was campaigning in the spring of 1968 to be Pearson's successor (and, as Pearson later acknowledged, his personal choice to be leader), Gouzenko published a document that he personally distributed at the 1968 Liberal leadership convention outlining why he considered Trudeau to be a Canadian Castro. The Toronto *Star* editorially called Gouzenko one of the main purveyors of hate literature in Canada, and dismissed his charges. But in the light of events, it was a remarkable document based on an analysis of public reports; it is even more interesting today than it was then, though there are errors of fact and interpretation. Still, believing what he did about Trudeau, Gouzenko was risking severe reprisals to publish it.

In the spring of 1973 when I was editor of the Toronto *Sun*, Gouzenko came to me and said that British Intelligence wanted to interview him again about his 1952 memo concerning spies in the British security system. Gouzenko was uneasy that it might be a setup to assassinate him, and he wanted me to go with him to the session in the Royal York Hotel. I, too, wondered why they wanted to question him again after twenty-five to thirty years, but said I was sure to be as welcome as a skunk at a picnic. In case something happened to him, Gouzenko said, he wanted me to know that he had no intention of committing suicide—for example by jumping from the hotel window, a favorite Soviet "suicide" technique to get rid of defectors. Before his interview he told the British security people that he'd informed me of the meeting.

All went well, and Gouzenko returned with what seemed an astonishing tale. The British security people had shown him the interview he'd allegedly given to them right after his 1945 defection in Ottawa: several pages of information that Gouzenko said were utter nonsense and fabrication.

"It was a fake interview," he said. "All invention, all rubbish. Why, the interview even had me saying that we, the Soviets, knew the British had spies inside the Kremlin and inside Soviet intelligence. This is foolish. The British had *no* spies there. It is impossible. Anyone reading this interview, who knows the truth, would simply dismiss it as mad ravings. I told the security people that whoever did that interview has to be a Soviet agent. Look no further. Or, rather, look at who sent the interviewer, because he, too, might be an agent. Besides, I remember the interview, if not the person who made it. It took two minutes—very quick, as if the person wanted to end it quickly. The whole interview is invented. Why would they wait until now to let me see it?"

At the time it made little sense to me, except that British Intelligence was still probing. Later it turned out that Sir Roger Hollis, head of British Intelligence, was now suspected of being a Soviet spy, though the media were not yet aware of it. And who was it who had come to Canada to interview Gouzenko nearly thirty years earlier? None other than Roger Hollis, who worked in conjunction with British Intelligence's Washington man, Peter Dwyer, later the head of the Canada Council and over whom a cloud of suspicion has always lingered.

In his disinformation book about his espionage activities after his escape to Moscow, Kim Philby heaped praise on Dwyer for his "brilliant analysis," which led to revealing Klaus Fuchs as a Soviet spy. What it was that was so "brilliant" about his "analysis" remains a mystery, as do Philby's motives for gratuitously praising Dwyer. Was it to help him or hurt him or just to cause mischief? There is no proof either way, just suspicions, although it seems irrefutable that whoever compiled the phony Gouzenko interview was trying to discredit him and was working for the Soviets. For his part, Gouzenko ridiculed Philby's assessment of Dwyer's brilliance. "If he was so 'brilliant' why didn't he 'analyze' that Philby was also a Soviet spy? It all smells fishy to me." But then everything smelled fishy to Igor.

Gouzenko's passion for his five-point plan encouraging agents with valuable information to defect burned strongly to the day he died. Every year on the anniversary of his defection, the Royal Commission, his birthday, whatever excuse, Gouzenko would ask that I or someone whom he felt understood, such as *Sun* reporter Bob MacDonald, write about his plan to remind people that there *was* a way to woo defectors. I never met a knowledgeable security person who did not have praise for the program, for its simplicity and common sense. But no Western country adopted it.

Gouzenko's proposals:

- Give defectors with important information immediate citizenship.
- Provide *friendly* (note the stress) protection.
- Give some financial support in the form of a grant or pension.
- Provide employment according to the person's ability and profession.
- Give a document confirming the person's service to the state.

According to Gouzenko, that program would guarantee a flow of important defectors who still comprise the surest way of finding out what the Soviet Union is up to.

In the late 1960s a Soviet agent who'd been sent to Canada to take deep cover in Alberta some four years earlier was activated to come east and assassinate Gouzenko. But Anton Sabotka (his cover name) had been corrupted by the good life in Canada and confessed all to the RCMP. Why kill Gouzenko after such a long time? There are two main theories. Killing Gouzenko after so many years would be an eloquent reminder that the KGB never forgives, never forgets, and that no one is ever safe from reprisal. It would be an effective, dramatic way to discourage would-be defectors. But more likely it was because Moscow did not relish

Gouzenko's astonishing memory being retapped about British spies as yet uncovered—information the value of which not even Gouzenko might realize. One thinks immediately of the allegations about spies and traitors still in high places inside British Intelligence and Security.

At Gouzenko's strange funeral I found myself wondering about what sort of a life he had had in "freedom" and whether he'd ever regretted the decision he'd made so long ago with his wife Anna to stay in Canada. Whenever he'd been asked the question, he'd get indignant and insist that, no matter how frustrating life in the West was, it was infinitely preferable to life in a slave colony. And he would point to his children born in freedom as conclusive evidence. Still, one sometimes wondered if he was making virtue of necessity. In a way it was tempting to think that his life was a failure. Here he was, alone at death, no friends, no mourners, only family. Even his neighbors supposedly did not know his true identity. And Canadian officialdom had been less than understanding, cooperative, sympathetic. In fact, it sometimes seemed as if the government and its security organs resented and even hated him.

Gouzenko was a lonely, difficult man. He could be irritating, stubborn, single-minded. But he was a committed patriot who, despite unsympathetic treatment in Canada, was dedicated to democracy and the West. To me his life was not a tragedy, but a triumph. He took on the malevolent Soviet state for all the right reasons of decency and justice, and exposed it for what it is. The world was not the same after his disclosures, the Kremlin never fully recovered. Looking at his large family, university-educated, all endowed with a passion for democracy and ethics, all of whom worshipped their father, all Canadian citizens born in freedom with full and satisfying lives before them, there is no way that such a life can be deemed a failure.

The simple feat of dying of natural causes amid the peace and comfort of his family in a free country represented a triumph over evil and, in its way, was Igor Gouzenko's greatest victory over the Soviet system he abhorred. He was, in his perverse way, a great man, a considerable Canadian; he was better than we perhaps deserved. I, for one, was proud to have been able to call him a friend. And I would feel better about my country had we ever seen fit to recognize or honor the man who did so much to alert us to the enemy seeking to destroy us.

30

Worthington subverting the democratic process

JOE CLARK
FEDERAL PC LEADER,
SEPTEMBER 26, 1982

For over twenty-five years in journalism I avoided as much as possible getting involved in political reporting, either at the local municipal level or the provincial and federal levels. I preferred the international scene, where one could avoid the picayune, paint with a broad brush, comment on world events. Reporting from Jordan, for example, I could have the king tottering on his throne, but from city hall I couldn't comment on why an alderman was scowling. Besides, international affairs were more stimulating and challenging: what to do about China (cooperate), how to negotiate with the USSR (toughly), should we give aid to Tanzania (no), what to do about Albania (nothing), and so on.

Occasional assignments to cover Parliament in Ottawa I found consistently boring, and diligently sought to avoid getting trapped there. Nor did I care much for the types who went into politics— generally those who, in the words of British social commentator Auberon Waugh, wanted to boss people around.

As well, I found the relationship between the media and the politicians disquieting and unwise—from the journalist's viewpoint, not the politician's. The practice of government "raiding" or recruiting information officers and executive assistants from among political reporters is, I contend, an unhealthy reflection on, even an indictment of, journalism in general. In a democracy, government and the press should be loyal antagonists, not bedmates. Otherwise the people get shortchanged.

Political reporting at the federal level in Canada is possibly the worst and most subservient in the Western world. Canadians like to say that Watergate couldn't happen here. They are right for the wrong reasons. Watergate couldn't happen because our press would never expose it. And if, perchance, a reporter did uncover a national scandal, it is unlikely that his employers would have the nerve to print the story.

When Pierre Trudeau was first running for the job of prime minister in 1968 there was confusion about whether he was forty-seven or forty-nine years old. The press was unable to discover the truth until after he was PM (forty-nine). To this day the press has been unable to discover the identity of the twenty anonymous businessmen who allegedly contributed to building a $200,000 swimming pool for Trudeau. Nor have the media ever been unduly concerned about $20 million in kickbacks of CANDU nuclear reactor sales to South Korea and Argentina. The $20 million supposedly went as fees to an agent in Israel who had an unlisted phone number and no fixed address! The press accepted secret legislation by Order-in-Council to set up a uranium cartel involving Canada, France, South Africa, Australia, and the Rothschilds of Britain, to undercut American uranium sales—and to impose a penalty of a year in jail for anyone who even discussed the cartel. And in 1981 the Emergency Planning Order, cited earlier, was implemented by semi-secret Order-in-Council at Trudeau's request, with barely a peep from the media, with the exception of the Toronto *Sun*, which was labelled hysterical for reacting strongly. There is no shortage of examples to illustrate both the chicanery of government and the laziness, mediocrity, and lack of curiosity and concern of the media.

Even before I had my triple bypass operation in 1978—which revived my failing prowess as a Walter Mitty tennis and baseball player—I was growing restless in the job as editor-in-chief of the Toronto *Sun*. I had written virtually all the editorials that had appeared since the paper began in 1971, plus a couple of columns a week, and my assistant, Chris (a perfectionist who is English-trained and therefore knows grammar and spelling) and I organized and edited the op-ed page columnists. In a way it was like a squirrel cage, with the pair of us working at breakneck speed to get through each day. When I looked at the future and saw only more of the same as the ten years that I had completed, I felt it was time to start looking for something different. I didn't want to stay in a rut, no matter how comfortable that rut might be.

There were aspects of the *Sun* that were gratifying and commendable. But increasingly, as it became a commercial success, the *Sun* broke fewer and fewer stories and became less innovative, more staid. It sometimes seemed more interested in matching stories the other papers carried than developing its own. What I had criticized in other papers was also true of us. And my disappointment reflected on me as much as the paper. Considering all the fuss the *Sun* raised in its editorials against a slothful, mischievous government, it was amazing how seldom it was ever able to develop exclusive news stories about the government's abuse of power and its corruption. The only reporter who broke political stories or exposés was Bob MacDonald, and even he became beaten down. Cartoonist Andy Donato kept attacking in his own cheerful, funny, biting way, and George Gross kept the sports pages the brightest in the city, but they were virtually laws unto themselves.

Perhaps I spread myself too thin, was too concerned with writing, with policy, with over-all direction, and was not demanding enough. "Too much democracy," as MacDonald occasionally put it. My partners, Doug Creighton and Don Hunt, didn't share my concerns, and the balance book certainly favored them. In any event, I felt it time for a change.

Prior to leaving I had to find an associate editor who could take over from me—someone who shared a similar philosophy, who would understand the curious mixture of irreverence and concern, the blending of the superficial and inconsequential with the profound and serious (for instance, opposing the USSR and making fun of our own anti-communism).

I first offered the job to Bob Nielsen of the Toronto *Star*'s editorial page, but he opted to go into semi-retirement and cut wood in New Brunswick or some remote place. Then I offered it to Gary Lautens, a humor columnist, later executive managing editor of the Toronto *Star*, and after that something called editor emeritus. He was interested but said no. I understood, and soldiered on. Then I sounded out Norman Webster of the *Globe and Mail*, a correspondent in London and later editor-in-chief of that paper. Although the idea seemed to pique his sense of humor, he declined. Then it was the turn of John Fraser, the *Globe*'s correspondent in Peking, to turn down the possibility of being editor of the *Sun*. In between I suggested to Lisa Hobbs that she might like my job. She was one of the better journalists in the business and had covered the Vietnam War for the American papers, had worked for the *Globe and Mail*, the Vancouver *Sun*, and was now working for the National Parole Board. Though intrigued at the possibilities, she felt obligated to the parole board.

Finally I felt lucky when Barbara Amiel, high-profile columnist for *Maclean's* magazine, was available. She seemed best of all and I took her on the understanding that when I left she'd be considered for my job. I found Amiel terrific in that we saw East-West issues in roughly the same way and had a similar outlook on politics. I was enthralled with her quick, if somewhat malicious, sense of humor and felt she would be a daring choice to replace me.

In early 1982 the Maclean Hunter publishing empire offered to buy 49 percent of the *Sun* (and its Western papers) for $54 million. A couple of years earlier, Maclean Hunter had tried to buy in, and at first I had been favorably inclined. However, after a board meeting in Calgary when Elio Agostini and Hartley Steward, publishers of the Edmonton and Calgary *Suns*, respectively, vigorously opposed the sale on the grounds of morale in the West, I agreed with them. The board did, too, and terminated negotiations.

The surprise 1982 offer was debated at a board meeting, and the mood was different. I opposed the sale on grounds that we would be exchanging our independence for financial security. I felt that independence was the most precious quality we had and was reluctant to sell it if we didn't have to. I said I felt so strongly that if we sold, I'd have to resign. This threat so alarmed the board that they immediately voted to sell—the economy was tight and the money would ensure that we'd be immune to a downturn in the economy. I submitted my resignation to Creighton, who accepted it—to take effect at some unspecified future date if I didn't change my mind.

Soon after the deal was announced I departed to immortalize the Mount Gongga expedition in the Chinese Himalayas. It is not true, as Barbara Amiel was to write somewhat facetiously that "Peter Worthington went up the mountain as editor-in-chief of the *Sun* and came down planning to be a politician," as if some mystical change of life had occurred. In fact, she knew my future at the *Sun* had already been decided.

When I returned, Laura Sabia, former head of the Status of Women Council in Ontario, one of the country's leading feminists and a *Sun* columnist, suggested that I consider running as a Conservative Party candidate in a federal by-election for the vacant seat of Broadview-Greenwood, which had been a stronghold of the New Democratic Party for most of twenty years. Sabia caught me at a time when I was increasingly frustrated at how impotent the Opposition was in dealing with Trudeau who, I felt, was undermining our traditions and was bent on remaking Canada into a socialist Utopia of his own design. Politics had been suggested to me before, and always I'd dismissed the suggestion, sometimes rather rudely. This time my response was different.

"Laura, I'm no politician," I said. "I wouldn't fit in."

"Nonsense. You persuaded me to run last year. Now it's time you put up, if you care about this country."

She had a point. The year before, Trudeau had elevated Peter Stollery, a mundane MP from the safe Toronto Liberal riding of Spadina, to the Senate, so that his ex-advisor, Jim Coutts, could win a seat in Parliament, become a cabinet minister and, possibly, his successor. Despite her wishes to the contrary, I had urged the high-profile, outspoken Sabia to run as a Tory simply to provide opposition to Coutts. She had agreed and it was a tough by-election which a radical Marxist-oriented Anglican minister-turned-city-alderman, Dan Heap, won for the NDP. Sabia's strong showing among Italians and Portuguese took votes from Coutts and contributed to his defeat. Hers was a triple victory: the Liberals were humiliated, the federal NDP were saddled with a maverick, and she didn't have to go to Ottawa, yet was instrumental in beating Coutts.

I agreed to meet with the person heading the search committee for the Broadview-Greenwood Tory riding association, an aggressive, somewhat grating, but competent accountant named Dave Simmons, who persuaded me to meet the riding executive of which he was a member. I eventually agreed to contest the nomination against six other contenders, two of them Greek. The riding executive was nervous that the Greek contenders (10 percent of the population of the riding was Greek) might mobilize and steal the nomination by packing the association with its members.

Usually the Tory membership hovered around the 120 mark. With 7 candidates recruiting frantically at $3 a membership, eventually some 13,500 names were submitted, with perhaps 10,000 of them real. Dead people, former residents from past electoral lists, phony names, fraudulent residents—all were among the new "members." One candidate inadvertently submitted names of the NDP executive as new Tories, causing joy to the NDP, gnashing of teeth among Tories, amusement in the media, and ridicule from the public. The riding executive was reluctant to deal with improprieties and tried to ignore them. I kept squawking, the media reacted, and the party resented the questionable publicity more than it did the improper practices.

When it looked as if the Greek candidates were too strong, the riding executive decided to postpone the nomination convention for six weeks, to September 9. I objected that it wasn't fair to extend the length of the game until your team won, and felt that since it was clear what was happening, it was up to Tories to beat the Greeks at the recruiting game within the time-frame. I threatened to drop out and go public saying the tactics were unethical and against an ethnic minority. A compromise was reached and the nomination convention was delayed three weeks instead of six.

In the light of what happened at the convention, my concern about fair play seems ironic. Dirty tricks were the order of the day, and I had a running battle with rival candidates and the Tory executive over the antics while, in my innocence, I tried to run a straight and clean campaign.

I recruited over 4,000 new members to the association and, as a political neophyte, was amazed at how many party people flocked to my cause and worked tirelessly. Naïvely, I had at first intended to continue playing baseball with the press league as well as tennis. Physical exercise was as important to me as being elected. However, when people turned out in droves to help, a guilty conscience wouldn't let me take time off. Also a deterrent was the horror expressed by my political advisors when they caught me about to sneak off to play sports. As a consequence I played little ball, and the only tennis I got in was when I played hooky one day and was caught by the CBC—to whom I explained I had an important meeting with bankers and my tennis outfit was just coincidental. The silly asses took the explanation seriously.

It took a while for me to realize that many of those committed Tories who came from all over to help were not captive of my charisma or my ideas; in fact, some of them had neither read a word I'd ever written nor had a clue about what I stood for. Many were political groupies joining the only game in town. They worked hard, but it was the contest, not the candidate, that turned them on. For a long time I neither understood nor was comfortable with their enthusiasm.

In some ways my campaign to woo members was too successful. I knew the Greeks were strong, but the two contenders—right-wing George Vlahos and left-wing Bill Fatsis—stayed within the Greek community and were not seen at other doors. My workers were seen everywhere, and the general reaction of people was: "Oh, we'll vote for you in the by-election, but you're such a sure thing for the nomination that there's no need for us to go."

"No, no, no," I'd say. "Remember Dewey and Truman. You gotta come out if you want me to win."

"G'wan Peter, you know you got it sewed up."

"Believe me, nothing is sewed up."

"You're just saying that. Relax. You're a cinch."

Had my workers been a little less enthusiastic, it might have seemed a closer contest in the community, and those who wanted me to win might have turned out in bigger numbers.

Curiously, people in Broadview-Greenwood who at first expressed concern that I would become "just like them in Ottawa" if elected—dislike and disappointment in *all* politicians was rampant—increasingly seemed to accept that I might *not* change. They seemed to like the idea.

Everywhere I found tremendous and justified cynicism toward politicians, political parties, the system in general. People believed that politicans lacked real conviction, were greedy, had little regard for propriety, and were dominated by self-interest. There was almost a feeling that they viewed their mandate from the voters as a right to pillage the public till. Frustration with government and bureaucracy was manifested in apparent apathy. But it was *not* apathy. It was resignation, disappointment, disgust. None of the three major parties was highly thought of.

I found the question "What will you do for us if elected?" somewhat disquieting, as if the promise of favors was more important than what the person stood for. At first I tried answering with a quip: "I think what the people most want is for MPs to get a pay raise." That would occasionally invoke outrage and rarely produced a chuckle: too close to the truth. So I changed the response: "First I am going to arm the Latvians," I would joke. This sometimes amused people until I met one serious lady at the door who responded: "How about us Estonians? Aren't you going to arm us, too?"

"Of course," I replied, and then realized she *wasn't* kidding. I dropped that approach, too, and finally resorted to saying I didn't intend to do a damn thing for them, but would work to take bureaucratic obstacles from their path to enable them to do something for themselves. Most people not only accepted this but welcomed it.

The Tory nomination meeting for Broadview-Greenwood was

more like a leadership convention or an American primary. It bore little resemblance to past Tory nomination meetings in the riding, when a bare dozen people had chosen the candidate. This interest was partly because of hostility to the Trudeau government and the possibility of a Conservative winning a traditionally socialist riding; and partly because I had a fairly high profile and was an unlikely candidate who attracted attention and controversy.

The Coliseum at the Canadian National Exhibition was packed with about 5,000 people, some 2,400 of them voting members. Most were for me or Bill Fatsis. And the mood was ugly. The Fatsis supporters were almost exclusively Greeks, many of whom could not speak English. Many did not have adequate identification, were suspected of not living in the riding, and therefore not eligible to vote. Protests went for naught. By the time of the convention the federal Tory party had lost its earlier enthusiasm for me. Some seemed to suspect that although I could probably win the riding for the party, I might also be difficult to tame to the party line. They were not eager for a maverick. Though I had cleared my running with party leader Joe Clark, who at first seemed enthusiastic, this enthusiasm waned as the campaign dragged on. I had been critical of Clark's leadership in numerous editorials and although careful when questioned by citizens, I couldn't pretend he was Margaret Thatcher.

One of the contenders for the nomination was self-made millionaire Michael Hordo, who travelled in a gold Rolls Royce in the predominantly ethnic and working-class area. He had withdrawn from the race and thrown support to me the week before the nomination. He claimed to have 1,000 Chinese supporters who would come to me. I was skeptical. Any candidate who could attract 1,000 Chinese Tories in Broadview-Greenwood was not only likely to win, but would risk creating hysteria among others by an invasion of the Golden Horde. As it turned out, all I got from Hordo was eighteen cases of soft drinks for my workers— no Chinese voters to speak of.

At the convention, speeches from the six candidates were in alphabetical order, so I was the last one before the vote. Speeches were routine except by Bill Fatsis, who had been asked earlier to be the Liberal candidate in the same by-election and had recently worked for Liberals. Prior to that he had been an NDP supporter. He was widely known as a "Papandreou Greek" (*i.e.*, an admirer and supporter of Andreas Papandreou, the left-wing prime minister of Greece). Philosophically, Fatsis seemed more socialist than conservative.

In his speech Fatsis took direct aim at me and accused me of racism largely because of a column I had written against the government's multicultural policies, stating that the government had no business spending vast sums to promote cultures other than Canadian and, in a sense, paying ethnics to be different and to resist integration into the Canadian scene. I supported unhyphenated Canadianism, as advocated by the late John Diefenbaker, opposed the idea of "founding races" (French and English) and "others" (ethnic) for Canada, and felt *all* Canadians should be first class with equal status. Fatsis and a Greek-language newspaper he helped found interpreted (or distorted) my theme as anti-Greek and therefore racist. He poured oil on the fire by delivering part of his speech in Greek and broadened his "racist" attack on me to include former Toronto mayor and Tory cabinet minister David Crombie, who was nominating me. It was a nasty scene and alien to the Canadian tradition.

I felt badly at being a source of embarrassment to Crombie, who was more used to accolades and huzzahs in Toronto than catcalls and obscenities. However, he weathered it well, even with humor, though his speech was drowned out by the jeers and insults of the Fatsis mob. I felt even worse on behalf of all those who supported me: white, black, brown, oriental, British, Estonian, Latvian, Portuguese, Italian, and, yes, Greek. Fatsis had insulted them, too, and mocked democracy.

I was unable to deliver my speech, thanks to the screaming Greeks who crowded around the stage shaking fists, making gestures, and screaming abuse in a mixture of Greek and English. Throughout the fifteen minutes allowed for speeches, barely a word could be heard. Directly behind the raging Fatsis supporters sat Joe Clark and Tory dignitaries and guests—shocked but helpless. Though no one realized that the evening would erupt in such unpleasantness, it had been predictable that it would be intense. It seemed unnecessarily provocative and foolish for the leader of the party to attend such a display. Yet he stayed. The results of the first ballot showed me ahead with 1,125 votes, Fatsis with 915, Vlahos with 351, and the other three with 145, 26, and 13 votes.

I had missed a simple majority by 145 votes and knew I was dead. The Greeks would combine to beat me on the next ballot. Many of my supporters thought I had won, or would win, and so they went home. The Tory "professionals" helping me saw the writing on the wall, too, but were too stunned to do anything. No one had made preparations to keep my supporters in the Coliseum, to discourage them from leaving. There was a fifteen-minute hiatus before enthusiasm was regenerated and by that time it was too late. I spoke to the Vlahos people, and while philosophically they agreed with my conservatism, they felt obliged to support Fatsis. "We have to live tomorrow in the Greek community," said Paul Vlahos, George's cousin and campaign manager. "We have no option, we have to support Fatsis. Sorry."

Later resentment and disillusion crept into the Vlahos camp when they realized that half the 700-plus people that his buses brought to the convention voted for Fatsis and were, in effect, a fifth column infiltrated into his camp, getting a free ride from the man they were sabotaging. Weeks later Vlahos joined me and we became friends.

The other three candidates joined Fatsis. There was resentment toward me because I was not blindly partisan and had been openly critical—even contemptuous, perhaps unnecessarily so—of some of their tactics and antics. Besides, I suspect they saw me as robbing them of potential support. On the second and final ballot, Fatsis got 1097 votes to my 1028—sixty-nine votes spelling the difference between success and also-ran. If those who voted for me in the first round had not gone home, I'd have won. But I didn't. To this day it puzzles me as to why the Tories running my campaign had not made plans to keep delegates around for a possible second ballot; it seems like a basic contingency plan, even to a relative neophyte.

Instead, the main regret of some of my Tory brain trust was that they had played it straight and honest. One key person said he had wanted to bring 200 phony identities to infiltrate the convention on my behalf, but that he hadn't because he knew I wouldn't tolerate it. "I was awake half the night over it," he said. "Should I or shouldn't I? My wife finally said, 'Forget it; do it Peter's way,' Unfortunately, I listened to her." He claimed to have two shopping bags filled with fake identities for use specifically at Tory nomination meetings. Again, it is a sad reflection on the political system when a longtime senior Tory's main regret is *not* doing something dirty and unethical in order to win. It may be another reason why the public is so disgusted with the way party politics are practised in Canada.

(In some ways the Broadview-Greenwood shenanigans foreshadowed the future Conservative leadership campaign in which winos, children, "Kung Fu Koreans"—as contender John Crosbie called them—and others were hustled from riding to riding to stack the membership for either Joe Clark or his main challenger, Brian Mulroney. The slightly facetious analogy favored by another contender, David Crombie, was that Broadview-Greenwood was to the Tory leadership campaign what the Spanish Civil War was to World War II: a testing ground for tactics and dirty tricks to come.)

When I lost the nomination I tried to be gracious, but was mildly puzzled at Joe Clark's enthusiastic endorsement of Fatsis as "my kind of Tory" (it was an apt analogy, judging from Fatsis's later practice of stacking other ridings with Greeks on Clark's behalf). On losing, I moved to make the vote unanimous—a meaningless ritual—and announced that this was my first and last venture into the world of politics.

That vow lasted ten days. The by-election was three weeks hence and there was considerable pressure for me to run as an "Independent" candidate—something legal but just not done by the party faithful. Lynne Lake, one of the residents of the riding who had been the recipient of a phony Tory membership and was very angry about it, had come to my headquarters to complain to anyone who would listen, and had stayed to work for me. After the nomination she urged I go independent. I said no, and wrote a column saying so.

Undaunted, Lake then organized a petition and in a week had 1,500 names of people urging me to go as an independent; otherwise, they felt disenfranchised with no one to vote for. I checked the authenticity of the names, phoned a few of them, poked around the riding, and found Tories bitter over the tactics at the nominating convention and vowing that they intended to vote NDP in protest. In fact, there was *no* philosophically conservative candidate, and NDP signs were already up on some Tory lawns. I felt Fatsis had no chance to win.

So I called a press conference and announced that I was running as an independent. If necessary, I was prepared to sell some *Sun* shares to pay for my campaign. The media reacted with skepticism and curiosity. I rerented the same old house across from the Broadview subway station to be our headquarters, and the campaign was on. Some of the Tories who helped during the nomination phase joined me, others went to help Fatsis, a lot simply dropped out in disgust. For the most part it was people from the street with little or no previous political experience who came out for me: amateurs often ridiculed by the party pros and groupies. The atmosphere quickly became electric, enthusiastic, fun.

I had never been comfortable as an "official" Tory, having to defend leader Joe Clark, who was hard to respect, and to assure voters I'd try to be my own man yet not defy the party or challenge its dogma. As an independent, the workers were for me as a person, as a symbol to express their disillusionment with conventional politics. It was soon apparent that there was considerable nonpartisan support for me in Broadview-Greenwood. Excluding Leonard Jones in New Brunswick, who won as an independent on the French language issue only, I was the first independent in memory in Canadian politics who had a chance to win a by-election. We in the campaign saw this before the media did, and our only hope of winning hinged on their seeing the reality and reporting it. For their part, the media couldn't or wouldn't see what was happening at first. Independents have an abysmal record in Canada and invariably lose their deposits (less than 5 percent of the popular vote), and conventional wisdom was that I had no hope.

Toronto's CITY-TV reporter/commentator/personality, Colin Vaughan, a former alderman and political warhorse, was the first to recognize that something unusual was happening in the riding. With only two weeks of serious campaigning possible before the vote, it was essential that I get people thinking positively and the media were the only vehicle to get the idea of an upset across. The Toronto *Star* questioned the validity of a straw poll conducted by its reporter in Broadview-Greenwood that showed me with strong support, and wouldn't publish the results. Not even my own paper, the *Sun*, seemed aware of the story. Everyone was caught up in the orthodoxy that independents have no chance. How to get momentum going?

Bill Marshall, a political guru who had the reputation (the image is the reality) of never backing a loser, joined me because it was the only challenge in town. He composed an open letter to Joe Clark publicizing our personal, impromptu door-to-door polls that up to then the media had ignored. I read the letter at a press conference, and it was reported that I was finding a response that showed the NDP winning the seat by 42 percent, me next at 38 percent, Fatsis of the Tories at 15 percent, the Liberals out of it at 4 percent, and candidate David O'Connor losing his deposit.

The open letter and the press conference gave me more respectability, and the media began taking my campaign more seriously. But it was the home stretch, and five days later than we would have preferred. Joe Clark didn't read the signs, didn't believe the reports—more evidence of his bad judgment and foolishness. Five times he came into the riding and attacked me on each occasion, thus giving me unexpected credibility among the voters, who for the most part viewed him as a wimp. I even had to deny that I was paying him to come into Broadview-Greenwood! Clark called my independent campaign undemocratic. In fact, it was the essence of democracy, going to the highest jury of the land, the people themselves. What I was doing was unconventional and unorthodox, but it was legal and certainly democratic. Clark declared that Fatsis would annihilate me. He insisted on jogging through the area, knocking on doors where, unfortunately for him, he kept encountering Worthington supporters. Television recorded these sorties, and people began wondering why Joe was so obsessed with Worthington and the riding, unless both were giving him big trouble. (In retrospect, I think I gained most when Joe Clark went jogging. There can be few sillier sights than the uncoordinated Clark jogging in a three-piece suit through the largely working-class streets of Broadview-Greenwood.)

Then it was discovered that the official Tory literature being disseminated over Fatsis's signature as PC policy was a direct lift from my earlier writings. It provoked questions as to why the Tory candidate would steal the precise words of the abhorred independent. By the final week most of the media were focusing on me as the dark horse. Despite protestations of the three major parties, I was now seen as the main threat to beat the NDP candidate, Lynn McDonald.

Looking back, I far preferred the enthusiasm of the independent campaign to the orthodox Tory phase. There were those who stayed steadfast throughout, people like Janus Raudkivi, a huge Estonian who had the unusual political credential of having played the feature role in the Grade-B movie *Bigfoot* and who was an unguided missile wreaking alarm and havoc throughout the riding. We had no official campaign manager, and everyone worked in a loose alliance of ideals, interests, and goals, though John Gunning was our most experienced hand and very steady under fire. Broadview-Greenwood became a riding of independent-minded scrappers who wanted a better country, a better political system, a government that left people alone and didn't loot the till. They were "street Tories," the kind any party would welcome, but which the drawing rooms of the Albany Club feel uncom-

fortable with and don't quite understand. Though I was grateful
for all that the other, more conventional Tories had tried to do
for me earlier and felt pangs of wistfulness when some of those
who'd been with me joined Fatsis, I felt they were the ultimate
losers. Even David Crombie, almost as if atoning to the party for
earlier supporting me, came out to be photographed with Fatsis.
Under pressure, he sent a masterfully lukewarm letter supporting
the official candidate to all Broadview-Greenwood residents of the
constituency. The letter disappointed some of Crombie's fans in
Broadview-Greenwood. Other longtime Tories, recognizing that
the official Tory candidate did not reflect their philosophical outlook or politics, came to me and defied the party. Dr. Morton
Shulman sent a letter to all residents saying that he was supporting
me, and he urged others to do likewise.

Fatsis, as the official Conservative candidate, was campaigning
on behalf of Joe Clark, while I campaigned on a platform of
electing a Conservative government, which I saw as the only solution to the inept and corrupt Trudeau government that was
destroying the confidence of Canadians. I insisted that if I were
elected as an independent, I'd champion the people's complaints
against *all* politicians for a while, but eventually would join the
Tories in order to participate in government and hopefully influence the party and the country.

In reaction to my impertinence, Clark would froth that I would
not be welcome in his caucus. I would cheerfully remind him that
it wasn't *his* caucus, that his was only one voice in it. If I won, I
doubted that the party would reject the choice of the people of
Broadview-Greenwood. However, my heresy put a lot of my Tories on the spot; they liked me and didn't think much of Clark.
(Interestingly, some of the Tories who were helping me in my
nomination campaign and bad-mouthing Joe later tried unsuc-
cessfully to help him retain the leadership of the party. It was the
hypocrisy, the sudden conversion to the magnetism of Clark that
I had difficulty understanding. But it was vintage party politics.)
I pointedly didn't ask anyone to come and help, especially Tory
friends who were embarrassed by my acts.

A case in point was Julian Porter, my lawyer in the Official
Secrets Act case, a lifelong Tory whose father had been Chief
Justice of Ontario, and whom I considered a loyal friend. He
didn't dare be seen with me, much less solicit votes on my behalf.
But on election day he couldn't resist and offered to discreetly

drive people to polling stations. I was touched, and we drove through the riding together, chatting. On my return to my headquarters, I found Colin Vaughan from CITY-TV waiting with cameras. In some panic, Porter raced upstairs to hide in the closet until Vaughan was gone, understandably loath to answer questions about why he was in my campaign offices. Julian was not the only one and I have teased him ever since.

As it happened, I lost the by-election, but so did Joe Clark. The NDP got almost 10,957 votes, I got 9,004, the Tories had 4,999, the Liberal candidate, with 2,728, suffered the indignity of losing his deposit. There was some surprise that an independent could do so well, especially in a by-election when the full influence of the major parties is directed at voters on behalf of their candidates. It was unprecedented to have a ragtag independent humiliating the two major parties and scaring the pants off the third: I won twenty-five traditionally NDP polls and all the traditionally Conservative polls. The NDP won most of the Greek polls, with Fatsis barely splitting what was left. Later, "conservative" Greeks came out for me. But it was then too late.

When the costs and tax benefits of the by-election were assessed, I became the first candidate in Canadian history to show a profit in that the government pays a portion of expenses to all candidates who get over 15 percent of the vote. I had to return some $5,000 to the government, over and above my expenses, whereas if I had been representing a party, it would have got the extra. Most of the contributions, to the tune of some $10,000, had come in unsolicited small amounts from ordinary people.

Ethnically, Broadview-Greenwood is a microcosm of Canada, containing every race and nationality—ostensibly a mosaic, but in fact a melting pot. The residents want primarily one thing: to be left alone by government and allowed to make their living without bureaucratic obstacles or disincentives to save, work, and show initiative or enterprise.

I think that rather than being support for me personally, the strength of my showing indicated a deep resentment on the part of working people and small business-folk toward the political process. The vote for me was a message to all political parties that the people want them to clean up their act and be more responsive to the interests of the people. Interestingly, *all* the parties disapproved of what I was doing, which showed irrefutably that something was wrong with them in the eyes of voters. At the time I felt that defeat in Broadview-Greenwood spelled finish, or at least a pause, in my political aspirations, such as they were.

31

It's a rigged nomination . . . there is no chance to win

PETER WORTHINGTON
BROADVIEW-GREENWOOD, TORONTO
JANUARY 25, 1984

On the heels of losing the Broadview-Greenwood by-election and while trying to reassess my life, I was contacted by Tommy Finan. There was a chance to ransom six young men who'd been kidnapped four months earlier by anti-government dissidents while touring in Zimbabwe's Matabeleland, the dissident area in the southern half of what was once Rhodesia. Finan, a retired commanding officer of the Royal Canadian Dragoons, was a professional soldier all his adult life. Instead of disappearing into obscurity or a mundane civilian job, he got into the international arms business and won notoriety of sorts when in 1978 the London *Sunday Times* carried a sensational exposé of an attempted coup in the African country of Togo. A group of former British Special Air Services (SAS) mercenaries under the command of a mysterious "Colonel Tom" had narrowly missed killing Gnassingbe Eyadema, president of that unpleasant little dictatorship, where civil liberties and political rights are one degree worse than in the Soviet Union, China, or Chile.

Colonel Tom turned out to be Finan, and his sudden publicity rippled through the military and caused astonishment and disbelief among friends and former comrades who all insisted that he was quiet, competent, and an unlikely candidate for such an exotic occupation. Among some, Finan's name became instantly unmentionable, tainted with the twin epithets, mercenary and arms dealer.

As far as I am concerned, he is an interesting character who is very tough, very realistic, and true to his own principles. He *was* in the arms business—one of the more successful independent dealers who actually knew how to use and deploy the weapons he sold—but never, so far as I can tell, did he ever do anything to

451

subvert or betray Western interests. On occasion, he actually trained the troops (Somalia) of those who purchased his product. He was alleged to have a $500,000 bounty put on his head by Libya's Colonel Khadafy. In all my dealings I found him honorable.

Finan told me he had reason to believe that the rebels in Zimbabwe *might* be willing to trade their six captives for a token ransom. He claimed to have access to up to half a million dollars if necessary. His problem was to find someone he could trust to investigate and perhaps negotiate a deal. I was interested, both as a "chance" to rescue the six—two British, two Australians, two Americans—and as a potential story. I went to Zimbabwe in the fall of '82 with free-lance journalist and adventurer, Bill Howe, who had spent time in Vietnam and Southeast Asia and had good contacts among Zimbabweans. For five or six weeks in Zimbabwe we dealt alternately with Prime Minister Robert Mugabe's Minister of State (Intelligence), Emmerson Munangagwa, and with anti-government elements loyal to Joshua Nkomo, who was widely suspect of being involved with the kidnapping, or at least of knowing who did it. There had been no word of the fate of the six, and the feeling was they could not survive much longer, if indeed they were still alive. Word was that one, possibly two, were already dead.

We drove a rented car along makeshift roads in the bush area near Bulawayo, hoping to be "kidnapped" so that we could negotiate a rescue of the hostages, who were believed to be in that region. Our prearranged rendezvous never materialized. Just as well, perhaps. Finan's original plan involved getting the hostages and racing cross-country to the Botswana border, where elements of the South African military would be waiting with helicopters to fly us out. All very dramatic. My reward of a world-class story was not to be; yet the gamble was worthwhile. A couple of months later, unconfirmed word came through that the six were dead, either from disease or killed by their captors when the Mugabe government refused to exchange political prisoners for their release.

While I was in Zimbabwe, the members of my independent political campaign in Broadview-Greenwood, all of whom were still in the Conservative Party, attended a meeting to choose delegates for a leadership review convention scheduled for Winnipeg in January 1983. My supporters outnumbered the rest and, much to the consternation of Joe Clark and his team, I was one of five delegates chosen. (The sixth was Fatsis—an automatic choice). It was a hectic meeting that involved strong-arm tactics, hurled insults, and such flamboyant gestures as Lynne Lake wrapping her arms around the ballot box and refusing to let it go when it looked as if Worthington supporters would be denied their ballots. The media relished the rhubarb, and my supporters were euphoric at finally winning a battle. However, the credentials committee of the federal party later ruled that we were ineligible to be delegates.

I returned from Africa in the middle of the uproar to find TV cameras and a mob of supporters at Toronto airport waving "I Want Worthington" placards (left over from the independent campaign) to the bewilderment of myself and other passengers arriving. I told interviewers that I thought the wishes of the Tories of Broadview-Greenwood should not be disregarded so casually, and that I would fight back. On the advice of Barbara Amiel, I contacted Eddie Greenspan, perhaps Canada's top criminal lawyer, to represent me. He brought in his colleague, Phil Epstein, who is as meticulous and reserved as Greenspan is flamboyant and impetuous. They make a superb team. We held a press conference, filed a notice to sue Tory leader Joe Clark for conspiracy, and sought an injunction against the party for trying to prevent the due selection of delegates.

After the credentials committee tried and failed to disqualify the five of us as delegates, the steering committee of the federal party's executive ruled that we were "deemed not to be members of the Progressive Conservative Party" and again, we were barred from attending Winnipeg as delegates. I was appalled at the flouting of the democratic rights of the Conservative voters of Broadview-Greenwood and even more upset at the party's blacklisting people merely because they supported me. One, John Gunning, had been a sacrificial Tory candidate in the 1972 election in the Liberal stronghold of Windsor and had labored diligently for the party before and since. The same was true of Dave Simmons, Sue Robinson, and Chris Steer. I felt *someone* in the party hierarchy should have been asking what drove these dedicated Tories away from the riding association and the official candidate and into the camp of an independent who was more "conservative" than the official candidate. Had headquarters done that, they'd have seen rot in the riding association. But blind party obedience and orthodoxy overrode all other considerations.

Increasingly, people were disgusted or amused, or both, at the antics that made headlines and also made the party and Joe Clark look inept. The popular refrain went something like this: "If Clark has so much trouble dealing with one small riding in Toronto, what'll he do if he ever gets a serious problem like China?" And: "If he can't handle Worthington, how will he deal with Andropov?" On the other hand, there were those who felt that I was being disloyal to the party, both by my actions and by exposing Joe's weaknesses. I tried, with mixed success, to say that I was not trying to pick a fight with the leader, but doing what I felt was right; the leader was picking a fight with me.

Thanks to Greenspan, the five of us won the right to plead our cases directly to the party executive. The outcome of an ersatz inquisition at headquarters in Ottawa was that my four supporters were resurrected or rehabilitated and allowed to go as delegates to Winnipeg. I was rejected, primarily because I had committed the folly of saying on TV earlier that I thought former Liberal Finance Minister John Turner (and perennial leadership contender) was philosophically more conservative than Clark. With characteristic indiscretion and overstatement, I said that I could even support the Liberals if Turner were leader. The TV interviewer, Tom Clark, and his station CFTO reported that I said I would "join" the Liberal Party if Turner were leader (thus reinforcing my view of the general incompetence of TV journalists), and this was broadcast as a news item prior to the interview being aired. The party executive picked it up and punished me. My sin was *not* so much fighting with the party or feuding with the leader but of saying about Turner what every Tory thought and feared. The greater the truth, the greater the offence. Eddie Greenspan was bemused at Tory antics and remarked sadly that he had managed, once, to get a woman off who had stabbed her husband eight times in the back. Yet he could not clear me before the Tory hierarchy. He remarked wistfully as TV cameras followed us through Toronto airport: "You know, you're almost the first client I've had whom my mother isn't ashamed of." Most of Greenspan's clients do more heinous things than try to run for Tory politics.

Prior to the 1983 Tory leadership convention in Ottawa that June, I had interviewed the various candidates and come to the view that John Crosbie, finance minister in the brief Clark government, was the best choice. However, I was primarily ABC— Anyone But Clark. I interviewed the eventual winner, Brian Mulroney, in Montreal and we talked briefly about Broadview-Greenwood. He had once participated in a fund-raising dinner there and knew the riding. He was frankly puzzled at how the situation had gotten out of hand. He seemed unconvinced when I tried to explain that it was an unusual riding, and he implied that had *he* been leader, it would not have deteriorated to the degree it did. I was noncommittal and said that as far as I was concerned, what was allowed to happen in the riding showed the fatal flaw of Clark as a leader: bad judgment.

I dropped my suits when my supporters were cleared and I went to the Winnipeg convention as a journalist and as an "undelegate" and the symbolic head of the Broadview-Greenwood delegation. At Winnipeg most delegates were cautious and tense. The Broadview-Greenwood gang, as individuals and collectively, and I were among the few willing to babble about what we considered Clark's bad judgment and the need to replace him. I even felt that if he stayed as leader, a splinter faction might break off and form a conservative wing, or rival conservative party. When Joe failed to get more support than he had two years earlier—67 percent—he announced that he was calling a leadership convention and that he would be a candidate. It was a victory for the pro-review faction. This was a loose coalition of elements that really were not operating as a cohesive unit and which Red Tory Dalton Camp disparagingly described as a "cashew coalition," implying that those against Joe were mostly rednecks, bigots, right-wing nuts. To them Joe was the "moderate." To others he was a Red Tory.

In their independent ways the anti-Clarkites were very effective. There were several active groups: one a group from Newfoundland; supporters of Brian Mulroney from Quebec; a Western group centred in Calgary; some MPs whose symbols were MPs Otto Jelinek and John Gamble; Elmer MacKay and Robert Coates; a group fronted by John Morrison, who was persistent in organizing for a review; young university Tories; and finally the Broadview-Greenwood group, which stood as a monument to Joe's ineptness. Had any one of the factions stumbled, Joe would have gotten the minimum 70 percent he felt he needed to stay on as leader. As it was, many felt that 51 percent was all he needed to hold on, which would have meant that he'd have been like a general trying to fight a war when 49 percent of his army wanted to mutiny. Had Joe hung on, I think he'd have destroyed the party. As it was, he was eloquent and graceful in defeat and won respect if not converts.

After the vote I was being interviewed on TV about Clark when a voice in the crowd said he disagreed with me entirely. The man who spoke up was John MacDougall, who had won the Timiskaming seat in the 1982 by-election. He announced that Joe had come into his riding and helped him greatly. I couldn't resist adding that I had had the same experience as Mr. MacDougall— that when Joe had come into my riding this had helped me tremendously, too!

Bitterness reigned for a while after Clark's defeat, and I was one of those blamed by some for having torpedoed him and "handed the Liberals victory on a platter." On CBC-TV Barbara Frum noted that longtime Liberal Lorna Marsden (now a senator) deplored what had happened to the PCs. I replied that any time Lorna Marsden was bemoaning the fate of Tories, it was a great day for Tories. Flora MacDonald, External Affairs Minister under Joe Clark, announced with some petulance that she was not going to run for Parliament again, which, if true, didn't displease me since I felt she was wrong in that portfolio. Although supporters gloomily opined that "Liberals must be cheering to see Tories crucify their leader once again," opinion polls instantly showed a surge in Tory popularity. The Tory roof wasn't collapsing after all, and Canadians were enthusiastic about the prospects of a new leader.

Shortly after Winnipeg the pro-Worthington faction in Broadview-Greenwood challenged the local PC riding association at the annual meeting and tried to form the executive. But again Bill Fatsis, the defeated candidate, rallied his Greek supporters from all over Metro Toronto to come out and soundly trounce the pro-Worthington slate, which was pushing John Gunning for riding president. My political aspirations went into hibernation once more.

Meanwhile in Broadview-Greenwood, the remnants of my independent campaign started a group they called the Broadview-Greenwood Political Action Committee—Bugpac, for short—and tried to keep alive the issue of my eventually contesting the nomination again. I neither encouraged nor discouraged them, but kept options open and plodded away at the book and columns.

In covering the subsequent leadership convention in Ottawa as a journalist I found a mixture of emotions, attitudes, and ideologies among delegates. There was great empathy among the Mulroney and Crosbie supporters for what the Broadview-Greenwood delegates and I were deemed to stand for, but with Clark supporters there was animosity and bitterness that made the convention seem at times like two separate parties. One side was open, optimistic, friendly; the other side narrow, dour, hostile. I had not supported Mulroney in his 1976 leadership bid because I had show what was happening would be to force them to turn out and been offended that someone would try for the leadership without ever having been elected to anything and, what's more, without even trying to be elected. It struck me that someone who only wants to be a general without serving in the ranks was not someone you want in charge. In a way that held true for 1983, but apart from Crosbie he seemed the best hope for the party. Besides, he had Maritimer Elmer MacKay, incorruptible as an MP, supporting him; if MacKay backed Mulroney, that was good enough for me.

Roughly one-third of the 3,000 delegates were for Clark on the first ballot, and essentially stuck with him for the next two. Mulroney was second, Crosbie third, and though Crosbie gained the greatest percentage each ballot, time ran out and he had to drop off, and his support went to Mulroney.

Apart from some Clark people, there was general satisfaction at the results. For me the biggest surprise was how solidly the Clark people hung in—and was another reason why he had to go. As for the country, it was elated and Mulroney's popularity soared to an unprecedented 62 percent in opinion polls.

With Mulroney in and Clark gone, I felt that the circumstances were favorable for my returning to the fold and perhaps contesting Broadview-Greenwood again as a Tory. Despite nibbles from other ridings, I made it clear I was only interested in that constituency and hoped the new leader would express an interest in having me run, to show that past battles and differences were now only footnotes to memories. However, while it was generally acknowledged that I had the best chance to knock off the NDP, there was no laying on of hands, or manipulating, as the Liberals are reputed to do. Mulroney declared a freeze on the selection of candidates until after the New Year.

After Christmas, Bugpac slipped into gear and began organizing. They had a meeting with John Graves, whom Fatsis had put in as president of the riding association. Graves assured my supporters that there were no plans for a surprise or sudden nomination meeting. Then Bugpac met David Crombie, who was in charge of candidate selections in Metro Toronto and considered to be my friend. While he expressed sympathy and support for me, he said there was nothing he could do except assure them that they would have ample time to recruit new members before the next nomination meeting. Bugpac prepared letters urging people to start renewing past memberships—especially the 4,000

In early January 1984 John Graves announced that the nomination meeting would be on February 9. Membership was immediately frozen, no new members could join, and old members from 1982 could not vote. Graves had been campaign manager for another candidate in the 1982 nomination, but had dumped him to join me in the final week and had seconded my nomination. He'd since joined Fatsis. He'd also alternately supported Clark, Crosbie, Mulroney. Fatsis declared that he would not be a candidate this time, and said he was supporting Nancy Elgie, wife of Ontario's Minister of Consumer and Commercial Relations, Bob Elgie, for whom Fatsis had been a special assistant. It had a vaguely incestuous or family compact feeling.

My supporters were livid. I received advance warning of the move from Ottawa with the implication that if I contested the nomination, Mulroney would not be unhappy. What the party did not want was another rhubarb replete with dirty tactics that would make the Tories look bad in the eyes of the public.

After some prodding, Graves gave me a list of the members eligible to vote. As I suspected, of the 1,200 or so names, nearly 800 were Fatsis Greeks. The nomination was, in effect, rigged— logically no one but Mrs. Elgie had a chance. It was to be a coronation, not a contest. Names of some of my supporters as well as Greeks who were known to be conservative had been dropped from the lists (although we were able to get some names back on). There were false addresses, people shown twice with first and second names reversed, the usual stuff for Broadview-Greenwood. The hope in Toronto party headquarters seemed to be that I would recognize the inevitable and back off.

I consulted my supporters and spelled out the apparent hopelessness of the task. At first, I planned to hold a press conference, announce what I saw was happening, and explain that was why I was not running. I didn't want to put my supporters through the ordeal of having sand kicked in their faces again. We all agreed, reluctantly, that this was the sensible course, but I brooded about the decision overnight. The next morning Yvonne phoned me at work to say she had been thinking the matter over.

"So have I," I said. "Let me tell you first."

I felt that accusing the riding association of rigging the nomination sounded like sour grapes and that if no one contested it, none of the Fatsis cabal would appear; a handful of riding members would rubber-stamp the riding association's choice and grassroots democracy would be sidetracked . . . again. The only way to

or more who had supported me for the first nomination.
make them fight. And the only way to do that was to run. Besides,
this was one of those occasions when it was more important to
fight for a principle and lose than it was to win. I couldn't walk
away from a fight simply because it would be lost.

"That's exactly what I was thinking!" said Yvonne.

I told Bugpac my thinking. They, being fighters by nature, were
delighted. We called an emergency meeting of riding association
members we knew, and I put the issue to about 100 of them at
Withrow Public School: "I can't do it alone, but if you are willing
to turn out and be kicked again, I'm willing to self-destruct to
prove a point. We can't win—but we can fight back. How do you
feel?" I asked them.

Everyone said to go for it.

The next day I held a press conference at which I said that the
nomination was rigged by the riding association controlled by a
Fatsis junta, and that while I had no chance of winning, I was
running anyway. I showed them the riding lists and the overwhelming preponderance of Greek names. Colin Vaughan glee-
fully announced that the Broadview-Greenwood "road show" was
back on track, while Larry Zolf, CBC radio's peripatetic political
commentator, called it a "Kamikaze" attack by me on the riding
association. Eddie Goodman regretted that I was self-destructing
when I could probably run in a different and easier riding. Ste-
phen Lewis, former Ontario New Democratic Party leader, went
on TV to chortle that I was committing political suicide and that
Nancy Elgie was a fine candidate. Laura Sabia, who had originally
urged me to run, was now publicly endorsing Mrs. Elgie. Herb
Solway, friend and board member of the *Sun*, was the only close
friend openly approving of what I was trying to do. Even the
managing editor of the paper, Ed Monteith, thought it was a
forlorn and quixotic gesture, and he and publisher Creighton
decreed that no one on the paper should be allowed to write about
my candidacy.

With two weeks to go to the nomination, my forlorn cause began
to look a little more encouraging. Nancy Elgie, apparently unaware of the intense feelings in the area, knocked on non-Greek
doors and was greeted with tirades about how awful the last nomination had been and how much they wished I had been elected.
Some of the reaction verged on the abusive, or at least was rude,
and it can't have been very pleasant for her. When I went door-
to-door I found that most people were reluctantly willing to sub-

ject themselves to one more try. In the process, I began to feel we *might* have a chance since there was not the enthusiastic Greek support for Elgie that she might have expected. Fatsis was not as well liked among the Greek community as he was in party head-quarters, where he had persuaded the bureaucracy that he was the key to bring the Greek community into the Tory fold. In fact, the Greek community is too divided and too individualistic to be controlled or manipulated by one person. My message was simple: "We have a chance if we all come out; no chance if we don't. The other side is overconfident, there's not much enthusiasm, we *can* do it if we work."

There was skepticism, but most people I approached were will-ing. Estonians, Latvians, and East Europeans in the riding were the most determined. "Of course we will be there," said one Lat-vian woman at the door, who was typical of many; she was amazed that I would stress the necessity. "After all, *we* are your people!"

Gretchen Van Riesen, who was with me at the time, was bowled over by the staunchness of the East Europeans. The innumerable articles I'd written on behalf of the captive nations of East Europe were paying off. Former Fatsis supporters were now coming to me and saying they had been misled last time into thinking my reservations about multiculturalism were an anti-Greek bias. Some joked how they had voted six times at the annual meeting. If colored ballots were distributed for successive votes, they claimed they could have replicas printed within twenty minutes down the street! Many people came from other areas and pretended they lived in Broadview-Greenwood, assuming false identities. More than anything, these "confessions" reflected disillusionment with their erstwhile leaders.

We hired off-duty police to attend the nomination meeting in the hope that their presence would discourage any intended il-legalities. Party headquarters moved in to run the meeting and to ensure that things were reasonably straight. The media were poised for improprieties. A day before the nomination the To-ronto *Star*'s top Ottawa reporter, Val Sears, wrote that I was Mul-roney's "personal standard-bearer" in Toronto against the remnants of the Clark forces, and we reprinted and distributed this with considerable effect among those who wondered if I was still in party disfavor. As well, Greek press, radio, and TV began giving me friendly exposure. Animosity of the past was missing.

On nomination night the Danforth Technical School audito-rium was filled, and from the signs it was hard to tell who was ahead since not everyone could vote. Elgie balloons and signs decorated the hall. Nancy Elgie was nominated by someone who spoke mostly in Greek to the mostly Greek supporters, and she gave a routine speech that the bulk of her supporters could not understand since they didn't speak English. Julian Porter nominated me with a crisp, effective introduction. Then I went into my speech. Neither candidate's words changed any minds, but at least gave supporters something to cheer about.

The most dramatic speaker was George Vlahos who, after a few polite words in English, launched into Greek and a scathing attack on Fatsis. He accused him of near-racism and betrayal, recalling that at the first nomination meeting in 1982 Fatsis had called on Greeks to support a Greek, and that he, Vlahos, against his conservative persuasion, had supported Fatsis. And now Fatsis was not supporting him but was urging Greeks to support a non-Greek, Mrs. Elgie. I couldn't understand the words, but looking at the faces one could see that his words were having some effect, and Greeks were embarrassed.

After the first ballot I was being interviewed on TV with Nancy Elgie when a sign was flashed at Colin Vaughan stating that she was ahead 200 to 140 out of nearly 450 ballots cast. My heart sank when I read the numbers, and I felt it was all over. She looked pleased. However, the final totals for the first ballot turned out to be 216 for Elgie, 210 for me, 11 for Vlahos, and 1 for Wayne Shillinglaw, who had also run (and voted for me, as did his wife Willi; only his mother had voted for him, which everyone found kind of sweet!). There was pandemonium as the closeness showed I was doing better than expected. Nancy Elgie was 4 votes short of an absolute majority. The second ballot would be the last one.

I felt that this would now be the test of whether we had learned anything from the vote in 1982, when nearly 100 of my supporters had gone home before the second ballot and I was hung out to dry. My people manned the doors and urged my supporters not to leave. They almost physically kept people in. Between votes I tried to encourage and rally people. I suggested to one lady, Blanche Levesque, that her husband looked tired.

"No wonder, he just came out of hospital today!"

"Good heavens, take him home! It's not worth it."

"Nonsense. He feels fine. Don't you, dear. Dear? Clifford, answer Mr. Worthington. You feel fine, *don't you!*"

He looked at me with glazed eyes, and dabbed at a trickle of saliva coming from his mouth. He didn't look fine. I muttered something about not staying if it endangered his health and hustled on, hoping that *if*, perchance, he *did* expire, it would be *after* he voted and not *before*.

The second ballot was 210 for Worthington, 183 for Elgie—all my people had held firm, and I was finally the official Tory candidate, after nearly two years of trying. I was pleased, mostly on behalf of those who had worked so hard. My supporters went berserk. It was a happy moment for them. Nancy Elgie and Bill Fatsis were both gracious in defeat.

So the Kamikaze campaign on principle worked. I would now be meeting the NDP in the coming election and, if successful, would be going to Parliament in Ottawa. The next morning news headlines announced that Yuri Andropov, president of the USSR and head of the KGB for fifteen years, had died. I wondered how the news from Broadview-Greenwood had travelled so fast to Moscow! A few weeks later Pierre Trudeau announced that he was stepping down, and the Liberal leadership race was on. I pondered about these events being an omen—my path to Parliament opens up, Andropov dies, and Trudeau quits! While Andropov is replaceable, Trudeau is unique; it seemed odd that *if* I went to Ottawa, he would be leaving.

A lot of people seemed to think I would be a problem for the Tory leader. Allan Fotheringham in *Maclean's* magazine opined that I was "a loose cannon on deck"; one Tory was quoted as saying that "compared to Worthington Jack Horner is a team player." Although they weren't true, such observations wouldn't hurt me in Broadview-Greenwood even if they raised eyebrows in the party structure.

As for myself, I still didn't feel a part of the process. It takes time. I found it difficult to adjust to saying "we" and "us" when referring to the Tory party rather than "you" and "they." The journalist still struggled within.

Like many, I have been disgusted at MPs and politicians in general. Too often they seem intent on either looting the till or crowding in at the trough. They give themselves exorbitant pay raises and indexed pensions, and ignore the people's concerns about such things as capital punishment, immigration, language, metrication, foreign aid, defence. Canadian political parties have developed what I call the Nuremberg syndrome—loyalty to the party overrides loyalty to conscience, constituents, country. Republicans and Democrats in the United States can vote against the party on matters of principle without being branded disloyal, and in Britain Tory and Labour MPs can vote against their party on occasion and not be deemed traitors. It may be foolhardy at this point to say that I cannot imagine myself voting against something I believe strongly in merely because party loyalty demands it, but that is how I feel. Compromise is important, even essential; but so are certain principles. I feel that the adversarial role of political parties and uncritical partisanship is sometimes unfortunate. It strikes me that if the government party introduces good legislation, the opposition parties can enhance their credibility by acknowledging it and voting for it. Opposing merely for the sake of opposing is old-fashioned and contrary to the wishes of most citizens today who don't care a fig about party allegiance and simply want what is best for the country.

For the most part it is MPs' abuse of powers and privileges that is offensive, and this perception by the public has contributed to the near-contempt people feel for politics. I would like to see some elected person using the House of Commons to spell out the dismay and disgust that the people feel toward the political process. We *must* improve the impression that politicians create. We *must* restore the concept that leadership implies loyalty from the top down, instead of the reverse. Otherwise cynicism will increase and the decline will continue.

The creed that the politician's first duty is to get elected, his second duty to get re-elected, has to change if the country is to progress and improve. The people recognize this, but do the politicians and bureaucrats who control the system? Only politicians can rescue themselves from the quagmire of their own making.

It will be interesting to see if someone who feels this way, as I do, *can* be elected and, if elected, *can* do anything about it.

Index